AMERICAN CONVERSATIONS

FROM COLONIZATION THROUGH RECONSTRUCTION

AMERICAN CONVERSATIONS

FROM COLONIZATION THROUGH RECONSTRUCTION

Volume 1

Volume 1 edited by *James H. Merrell*
Volume 2 edited by *Jerald Podair and Andrew Kersten*

James H. Merrell
Vassar College

Jerald Podair
Lawrence University

Andrew Kersten
University of Wisconsin—Green Bay

PEARSON

Boston   Columbus   Indianapolis   New York   San Francisco   Upper Saddle River
Amsterdam   Cape Town   Dubai   London   Madrid   Milan   Munich   Paris   Montréal   Toronto
Delhi   Mexico City   São Paulo   Sydney   Hong Kong   Seoul   Singapore   Taipei   Tokyo

Editorial Director: Craig Campanella
Editor in Chief: Dickson Musslewhite
Publisher: Charlyce Jones Owen
Editorial Assistant: Maureen Diana
Director of Marketing: Brandy Dawson
Senior Marketing Manager: Maureen Prado Roberts
Marketing Assistant: Christine Riva
Production Manager: Fran Russello
Art Director: Jayne Conte
Cover Designer: Suzanne Duda

Cover Art: Library of Congress Prints and Photographs Division
Media Director: Brian Hyland
Media Editor: Andrea Messineo
Supplements Editor: Emsal Hasan
Full-Service Project Management: George Jacob/ Integra
Printer/Binder: Edwards Brothers Malloy
Cover Printer: Lehigh Phoenix
Text Font: 10/12, Palatino

Credits and acknowledgments borrowed from other sources and reproduced, with permission, in this textbook appear on the appropriate page within text.

Library of Congress Cataloging-in-Publication Data
American conversations/edited by James H. Merrell, Jerald Podair, Andrew Kersten.
   p. cm.
   ISBN-13: 978-0-13-244683-9
   ISBN-10: 0-13-244683-9
   1. United States—History—Sources. 2. United States—Civilization—Sources. I. Merrell, James Hart, 1953- II. Podair, Jerald E., 1953- III. Kersten, Andrew Edmund, 1969-
   E173.A7235 2012
   973—dc23

2012020977

10 9 8 7 6 5 4 3 2 1

ISBN 10:   0-13-244683-9
ISBN 13: 978-0-13-244683-9

CONTENTS

PREFACE

American Conversations is a two-volume anthology of original sources treating U.S. history from early colonization through the turn of the millennium. Drawing upon our many decades of teaching and writing about American history, these books assemble on one stage a remarkable, colorful cast of characters that will captivate students of America's past. As the title suggests, our aim is to strike up a number of different conversations: between our readers and us, between the past and the present, and between the authors, painters, and photographers whose works fill these pages.

FEATURES

American Conversations includes a number of features that make it stand out from the many U.S. history readers on the shelf today:

1. **Primary sources.** Decades of teaching both original sources and scholarly works confirm our belief that history is most vividly and powerfully brought to life through texts composed in times past. Even the finest historical scholarship imposes a screen, a filter, between the reader and that past. Students respond well when brought face-to-face, as it were, with men and women who lived in bygone days.

2. **Longer excerpts.** Most primary-source anthologies contain many texts by many authors. It is common to have five or even ten brief excerpts in a single chapter, clamoring for the reader's attention. Whatever this approach gains by way of inclusion, the cacophony of voices breeds confusion rather than clarity. Instead, *American Conversations* offers lengthy excerpts of greater richness and substance. This enables readers to become more thoroughly acquainted with one person, one text, or one topic, to acquire a better sense of the flavor and feel of the American past. We are confident that the sources in *American Conversations* will become part of students' lifelong historical sensibility, challenging them to integrate the American history they learn into the America they experience.

3. **Texts by both famous and obscure Americans.** *American Conversations* reflects a commitment to bring forgotten people—Native Americans and African Americans, women and workers—out of the backwaters and into the historical mainstream where they belong. At the same time, however, we believe that all students of American history should be acquainted with certain leading figures and core texts. Accordingly, we juxtapose the forgotten and the famous. Volume 1 includes a West African creation story and Benjamin Franklin, a Revolutionary war soldier named Joseph Plumb Martin and Thomas Jefferson, the Pequot Indian William Apess and the abolitionist Frederick Douglass. Similarly, Volume 2 offers the Railroad Strike of 1877 and Andrew Carnegie, Japanese American war internee Charles Kikuchi and Norman Rockwell, and *Life* magazine's "American Women" of the 1950s and Elvis Presley. This combination offers a more robust understanding not only of hitherto unknown texts but also of documents and images that Americans think they already know well.

4. **Images.** On billboards and buses, on television and the Internet, Americans nowadays are bombarded with images, so much so that we tend to take them for granted and do not really "see" them as texts worthy of study. But examined with the same critical acumen devoted to written texts, images can be indispensable tools for illuminating the past. To sharpen the reader's eye, both volumes include

chapters devoted to visual texts. Volume 1 invites consideration of pictures of Native Americans in the 1580s, of nature and nationalism in nineteenth-century landscape art, and of depictions of the Battle of Gettysburg. Volume 2 includes examples of the Great Depression photography of Dorothea Lange and Walker Evans, Norman Rockwell's "Four Freedoms" illustrations, and the Pop Art of Andy Warhol.

5. **Substantive head notes.** Accompanying the longer passages of primary sources are longer head notes introducing each chapter. These aspire to accomplish several things: capture the reader's interest and attention; tell the story of the text's author and its audience; shed light on the times that produced both author and audience; pose questions about the broader implications of the document; and ignite a conversation between the author and others in the book.

6. **Questions for Consideration and Conversation.** At the end of each head note are questions aimed at shaping the reader's experience without confining it to particular issues or particular answers. We have found over the years that students welcome having a few things in mind as they tackle a source—a few, but not too many. They can and will come up with other questions (and other answers) on their own.

7. **Genuine "conversation."** *American Conversations* is no mere catchy title: It conveys the volume's central purpose and carries several different meanings. The most obvious is the dialogue between reader and text, between now and then, today and yesterday. Then there is a running conversation between editors and reader as questions are raised to provoke thought and discussion. That discussion—with other readers and other students of history—is yet another form of conversation. Finally, there is the conversation across chapters, which the head notes promote. Rather than finishing one chapter, forgetting about it, and moving on to the next, students of American history will be able to give thought to time's cumulative power, to the ways different people in different eras speak to one another about common areas of interest and concern. The head notes invite these conversations between history's actors, between (for example) the aristocrat Dr. Hamilton and the democrat Thomas Paine, between the Puritan woman Mary Rowlandson in the 1670s and the Quaker women Angelina and Sarah Grimké in the 1830s, between railroad baron Thomas Scott in the 1870s and chronicler of the rural poor James Agee in the 1930s, and between the integrationist W. E. B. Du Bois in the 1900s and the separatist Malcolm X in the 1960s. This cross-fertilization profoundly enriches these volumes by helping to forge connections across chapters and centuries in important, illuminating ways. It makes for volumes that view the past not as static and divorced from the present but as the scene of dynamic and spirited conversations among Americans across generations, centuries, and eras.

American Conversations is, then, a guided tour through some fascinating precincts of this country's past. It aspires to tap into the very real, very powerful curiosity about American history that is evident in everything from the History Channel and Hollywood films to the streets of Williamsburg and the fields of Gettysburg. Channeling that curiosity, that energy, down a path we have marked out, it hopes to get readers to appreciate both the "pastness" of the past and its abiding hold on the present—and on the future.

ACKNOWLEDGMENTS

American Conversations is itself the product of many conversations over many years with friends, colleagues, students, and editors. Chats with Steve Forman, David Glassberg, Scott Moyers, and especially Clyde Griffen helped in the formative stages. Andrew Wylie and his staff at the Wylie Agency shepherded the project through many twists and turns on the way to publication. The Department of History and the Wilson Library at the University of Minnesota generously provided me space to work on the book during the many summers I spent in my home state. One August day on one of those Midwestern sojourns the university's Colonial History Workshop gathered to offer advice on my plans. John Howe and Jeani O'Brien, who arranged that session, went above and beyond the obligations of friendship to listen, each and every summer I spent in the Twin Cities, as I described the work's progress (or lack thereof).

Here at Vassar College I have benefited from generous funding and sabbatical leaves for scholarly pursuits such as this one. Generations of student research assistants—Matt Ambrose, Meghan Carey, Kate Collins, Carrie Maylor, Tawny Paul, Andrew Thibedeau, and Mariah Vitali—aided with various tasks. Even more generations of Vassar students—with others at the College of William & Mary (1982–84) and Northwestern University (1998–99)—helped by reading and discussing the texts in Volume 1. These chapters have been, as it were, "road tested" in classrooms across three decades: I have assigned nearly all of them in my courses, most of them many times.

Vassar colleagues, too, have been extraordinarily magnanimous with their time and knowledge. The Vassar History Department's administrative assistants, Norma Torney and Michelle Whalen, have helped in ways large and small. Bob Brigham, Miriam Cohen, Rebecca Edwards, Quincy Mills, and Nikki Taylor offered their expertise in U.S. history and in teaching the American past. Ismail Rashid guided my thinking about West African history for Chapter 1. Leslie Offutt, hoping I would take a hint, presented me with not one or two but three different editions of Cabeza de Vaca's account of his adventures and misadventures (Chapter 2). Tony Wohl bestowed much-needed encouragement and good cheer early on in this work's life, and throughout the long gestation period Bob DeMaria's friendship and scholarship have sustained me.

When I embarked on this long journey, my son Dave was in sixth grade and his brother Will was in nursery school. Both are now grown men. Over the years neither has supplied so much as a word, a source, or an idea to this volume; nonetheless, their contribution has been as profound as it is immeasurable. And the boys' contribution is nothing compared to that of their mother, my wife Linda Keiko-Yamane Merrell. Our conversations across almost forty years have been the most important and most deeply cherished of them all.

James H. Merrell
Poughkeepsie, New York

It has been a pleasure to work on this project with my coeditors, who are also my friends. Thanks to James Merrell for asking me to collaborate with him. His invitation gave me the opportunity to think about American history in novel and exciting ways. I'm grateful to Andrew Kersten for joining me on Volume 2, as well as for his support and loyalty over the years. I hope these volumes will justify the confidence Andrew Wylie and his staff have shown in us. Special thanks to Ekin Oklap in the Wylie Agency's London office for helping me out in a pinch.

Lawrence University is a model among liberal arts colleges in its encouragement of faculty scholarship. Thanks to Provost and Dean of the Faculty David Burrows for setting the institutional tone in this regard. Lawrence's Robert S. French Chair in American Studies has made it possible for me to live the life of the mind. Lawrence's generous faculty leave policies gave me the time and intellectual space to chart this volume's course. My experiences in London as Lawrence's London Centre Visiting Professor challenged many of my assumptions about American history and made me a better student of my own country's past. Wonderful student research assistants—Alyson Richey, Caitlin Gallogly, Hayley Vatch, and Jennifer Sdunzik—helped me translate my thoughts and ideas about this book to the printed page. Lori Rose, Valerie Carlow, and Maggie Marmor came through with their usual calm efficiency when I needed them most. My students in Lawrence's senior research seminar, "The Practice of History," inspire me year after year with their knowledge, ability, and enthusiasm for the best subject of all. Finally, I am proud to be a member of one of the finest liberal arts college history departments in the country at Lawrence University.

I am grateful to many fellow historians who have served as intellectual guides and role models, including James McPherson, Alan Brinkley, Gary Gerstle, Vernon Burton, and Daniel Rodgers. I became a historian because many years ago I fell under the spell of master storytellers like Walter Lord, William Manchester, Bruce Catton, and Jim Bishop, who took me to places I never forgot and made me want to tell great stories of my own.

My great friend Jerry Seaman has heard about this book for more years than he can count over lunches and dinners at our favorite Appleton diner; thanks for listening and for helping me settle the world's problems. Thanks also to Dr. Robert Klein, my old college roommate with whom I've laughed so often at life's inanities.

I owe most to my family. My late father, Simon Podair, taught me from an early age that books hold the world's riches, and of course, he was right. My late mother, Selma Podair, may not have loved history, but she certainly loved me. My daughter, Julie Podair, is a brilliant and courageous young woman, and I'm lucky to be her father. Speaking of luck, meeting Caren Benzer was, to borrow from Thomas Wolfe, "that dark miracle of chance which makes new magic in a dusty world." My world is a joyous place thanks to her.

Jerald E. Podair
Appleton, Wisconsin

I would like to thank James Merrell and Jerald Podair for inviting me to contribute to this project. I appreciate their generosity, patience, and creativity. Writing my chapters in the second volume of *American Conversations* reminds me of the tremendous diversity in the American experience. Despite the great investment of time and space in these chapters, I feel that we have only scratched the surface of the "conversations." And, yet, that is the genius of these books; these pages will foster more debate and discussions about the nature of the American past.

I would also like to thank my family, namely the three women with whom I live: Vickie, Bethany, and Emily, who were quite encouraging as I changed my sabbatical plans so that I could contribute to Volume 2. They were quite patient and attentive as I related all that I was learning about Elvis, the invention of the television, and various critical topics in modern U.S. history.

Andrew E. Kersten
Green Bay, Wisconsin

We wish to thank the following reviewers of *American Conversations* for their insightful comments in preparation for this first edition:

Stephen R. Boyd,
University of Texas, San Antonio;

James A. Hijiya,
University of Massachusetts, Dartmouth;

Rebecca Hill,
Borough of Manhattan Community College;

Michael Hucles,
Old Dominion University;

Carol Sue Humphrey,
Oklahoma Baptist University;

Kevin Kern,
University of Akron;

Robert O'Brien,
Lone Star College—CyFair;

Linda K. Salvucci,
Trinity University;

Jeffrey G. Strickland,
Montclair State University; and

Ericka Kim Verba,
Santa Monica College.

ABOUT THE AUTHORS

James Merrell, editor of Volume 1 of *American Conversations*, is the Lucy Maynard Salmon Professor of History at Vassar College. He has been studying history for forty years, writing and publishing it for thirty, and teaching it for more than twenty-five—mostly at Vassar, with brief stints at Northwestern University and the College of William and Mary. Though he has taught everything from Machiavelli and Luther to McCarthy and LBJ, his main area of interest is American history from the opening of European colonization to the close of Reconstruction some three centuries later. Born and raised in Minnesota, Professor Merrell earned bachelor's degrees at Lawrence University and Oxford University before receiving his M.A. and Ph.D. from the Johns Hopkins University. Prior to arriving at Vassar in 1984, he was a Fellow at the Newberry Library Center for the History of the American Indian (now the D'Arcy McNickle Center for American Indian and Indigenous Studies) at the Newberry Library in Chicago, and at the Institute of Early American History and Culture (now the Omohundro Institute of Early American History and Culture) in Williamsburg, Virginia. He has also received fellowships from the American Council of Learned Societies, the John Simon Guggenheim Memorial Foundation, and the National Endowment for the Humanities. Professor Merrell's research interests are in early American history in general and relations between Natives and newcomers in particular. Co-editor of three volumes (two anthologies by Routledge and one by Syracuse University Press) and author of numerous articles, his first book, *The Indians' New World: Catawbas and Their Neighbors from European Contact through the Era of Removal* (University of North Carolina Press, 1989; twentieth-anniversary edition, 2009), won the Frederick Jackson Turner Award and the Merle Curti Award from the Organization of American Historians as well as the Bancroft Prize. His second book, *Into the American Woods: Negotiators on the Pennsylvania Frontier* (W.W. Norton, 1999), was a finalist for the Pulitzer Prize and won Professor Merrell his second Bancroft Prize, making him one among the handful of historians ever to win that prestigious award twice.

Jerald Podair, coeditor of Volume 2 of *American Conversations*, is Professor of History and the Robert S. French Professor of American Studies at Lawrence University, in Appleton, Wisconsin. A native of New York City and a former practicing attorney, he received his B.A. from New York University, a J.D. degree from Columbia University Law School, and a Ph.D. in American history from Princeton University. His research interests lie in the areas of American urban history and racial and ethnic relations. He is the author of *The Strike That Changed New York: Blacks, Whites, and the Ocean Hill-Brownsville Crisis*, published by Yale University Press, which was a finalist for the Organization of American Historians' Liberty Legacy Foundation Award for the best book on the struggle for civil rights in the United States, and an honorable mention for the Urban History Association's Book Award in North American urban history. *Bayard Rustin: American Dreamer*, his biography of the civil rights and labor leader, was published in 2009 by Rowman & Littlefield. His most recent book is a coedited volume entitled *The Struggle for Equality: Essays on Sectional Conflict, the Civil War, and the Long Reconstruction*, published in 2011 by the University of Virginia Press. His articles and reviews have appeared in *The American Historical Review*, *The Journal of American History*, *The Journal of Urban History*, *Reviews in American History*, *Radical History Review*, *Labor History*, and *American Studies*. He contributed an essay, " 'One City, One Standard': The Struggle for Equality in Rudolph Giuliani's New York," to *Civil Rights in New York City: From World War II to the Giuliani Era*, edited by Clarence Taylor, published by Fordham

University Press in 2011. At Lawrence University, he teaches courses on a variety of topics in nineteenth- and twentieth-century American history, including the Civil War and Reconstruction, the Great Depression and New Deal, the 1960s, and the Civil Rights Movement. He also teaches Lawrence's first course in American Studies, which he introduced in 2007. He is the recipient of the Allan Nevins Prize, awarded by the Society of American Historians for "literary distinction in the writing of history," and a Fellow of the New York Academy of History. He was appointed by Wisconsin governor Jim Doyle to the state's Abraham Lincoln Bicentennial Commission, on which he served from 2008 to 2009. In 2010, he was honored by Lawrence University with its Award for Excellence in Scholarship, and in 2012 with its Faculty Convocation Award.

Andrew Kersten, coeditor of Volume 2 of *American Conversations*, is Frankenthal Professor of History in the Department of Democracy and Justice Studies at the University of Wisconsin–Green Bay. He teaches courses in U.S. history—the U.S. history survey, U.S. immigration history, and U.S. labor history—and interdisciplinary courses relating to his department. He researches and writes about American history since Reconstruction. His books include *Race, Jobs, and the War: The FEPC in the Midwest, 1941–46* (University of Illinois Press, 2000), which is an investigation of President Franklin D. Roosevelt's Fair Employment Practice Committee; *Labor's Home Front: The AFL during World War II* (New York University Press, 2006), which is a history of the American Federation of Labor during the war; *A. Philip Randolph: A Life in the Vanguard* (Rowman and Littlefield, 2006); and *Clarence Darrow: American Iconoclast* (Farrar, Straus, and Giroux, 2011). Currently, he is working on an online digital database of A. Philip Randolph's writings, as well as an anthology of new historical interpretations about Randolph's life and legacy. He has two other professional passions. Kersten frequently collaborates with public historians and museums such as the National Railroad Museum and the Experimental Aircraft Association's Museum. He also enjoys working with K–12 history teachers. From 2003 to 2006, he led a Teaching American History Grant Program of his own design that offered intensive professional development for history teachers, and he continues to collaborate on curricular design and other educational issues.

Introduction

The past is a foreign country: they do things differently there.

—L. P. HARTLEY

The past is never dead. It's not even past.

—WILLIAM FAULKNER

Americans have never gotten along very well with their past. For at least two centuries, people have noticed that history here is woefully neglected. In 1809, former president John Adams bemoaned the "very extraordinary and unaccountable Inattention in our Countrymen to the History of our own Country." A generation later, the French visitor Alexis de Tocqueville, whom you will meet in Chapter 13, found that in America "the track of past generations [is] lost. Those who have gone before are easily forgotten." More recent observers agree that "[w]e have no collective memory, none," and that Americans' "short attention span" means that they "like history as long as it's over fast enough."[1]

Symptoms of the nation's amnesia abound. The nineteenth century saw neglect of the country's historic sites: In 1812, Philadelphians demolished Benjamin Franklin's house, while farther south George Washington's Mount Vernon, like Thomas Jefferson's Monticello, sat for decades in "desolation and ruin." Historical documents often suffered a similar fate. "When the occupants of the Georgia State Capitol warmed themselves by burning discarded state records...," writes W. Fitzhugh Brundage, "they felt satisfied that they had found a new use for seemingly worthless artifacts." "In North Carolina," Brundage goes on, "colonial and Revolutionary War records were stored in an abandoned outhouse near the state capitol," and in Tennessee's statehouse a "janitor...won praise from state employees when he gathered up several cartloads of old records that 'lay piled in masses on stone floors' and burned them. They, after all, were 'wet and nasty and smelled bad.'" Meanwhile the Library of Congress, which might have housed America's records, was homeless before the 1890s and no National Archives even existed until the 1930s.[2]

Indifference has bred ignorance. As the bicentennial of the Declaration of Independence neared in 1976, pollsters learned that 28% of Americans did not know "what pivotal event had occurred in 1776" and that a "great majority...are unwilling to sign [the] Declaration if it is presented to them without its identifying label." During the Constitution's bicentennial in 1987, surveys discovered that half of Americans believed that the nation's charter contained the line "From each according to his abilities, to each according to his needs," a phrase coined not by Franklin, Washington, or Jefferson but by Karl Marx. Most agree that "historical illiteracy" in "The United States of Amnesia" still runs rampant today.[3]

On the other hand, however, there is evidence that the memory loss is less severe than some claim. In 1809, the very year John Adams condemned the country's "Inattention" to history, Mason Locke Weems published the ninth edition of his runaway best-seller, *The Life of Washington* (Chapter 10). In 1831, during his American tour, Tocqueville spent July 4 in an upstate New York town: First came a parade featuring a bust of Benjamin Franklin, then a reading of the Declaration of Independence that sent through the crowd "an electric current [that] made the hearts vibrate." These Americans seem neither inattentive nor forgetful.[4]

In our own day, too, people venture into the past down many different paths. Turn on the television and you find shows about the Civil War and the American Revolution or about slavery and immigration. Go to the movies (or on the Internet) and you can watch Mel Gibson kill redcoats in *The Patriot* or Daniel Day-Lewis slay Irishmen in *The Gangs of New York*. Farther afield you can join throngs filling the streets of Williamsburg and the fields of Gettysburg. There and elsewhere, actors and re-enactors dress up as Thomas Jefferson or George Washington, as slaves or Indians, as Rebels or Yankees in an effort to bring the past to life.

How to explain what historian Michael Kammen calls "the anomaly of historical ignorance on the part of a people that appear to share a widespread enthusiasm for the past"? The secret, Kammen believes, lies in the fact that Americans prefer "highly selective, sentimental, and sanitized versions of American history," a sort of "sugar-coated history." This is nothing new: Weems's popular biography, as you will see, sugar-coated George Washington; nor would those New Yorkers celebrating July 4, 1831, have welcomed the likes of Joseph Plumb Martin (a Revolutionary War veteran you will meet in Chapter 9), who in 1830 published a book about the war that was anything but celebratory.[5]

And today? Some argue that Colonial Williamsburg remains too clean, too white, and too male to accurately recreate early American life. Others wonder why the nation still lacks a national museum devoted to African American history and culture (one is due to open in 2015). Still others point out that all the attention to Civil War battles and soldiers' equipment overlooks what that conflict was about, and what it cost. Perhaps re-enactors personify prevailing notions of American history: lots of fanfare, noise, and smoke, but no blood, no screams of the dying, and no dead; at the end of the day everyone goes home for dinner.

Inattention? Enthusiasm? Amnesia? Sugar-coated history? Whatever the syndrome is called, the nation's very enchantment with its past suggests that whatever ails us is curable. It testifies to a curiosity about bygone days, which can be directed in ways that add the key variables of complexity and ambiguity, of depth and darkness to the American equation. As the novelist Ralph Ellison wrote, "we possess two basic versions of American history: one which is written and as neatly stylized as ancient myth, and the other unwritten and as chaotic and full of contradictions, changes of pace, and surprises as life itself."[6]

American Conversations: From Colonization through Reconstruction aspires to haul some of that hidden history out of the shadows and into the light, to make the past more complex (and more interesting) by adding elements of chaos, contradiction, and surprise. It is grounded in a belief that America's uneasy relationship with its past can be made easier, stronger, by more (and more direct) encounters with that past.

That there is a need for knowledge about American history is clear every time you open a newspaper or log onto the Internet, for there you find countless stories about people debating what power the past ought to have over the present—and the future. Should African Americans be paid reparations for slavery? Do Native Americans' historical treaty rights include the right to construct a casino? Should the Confederate flag fly at college football games or atop state capitols? Is it fair to call colonial American rebels "terrorists"? Should the nation's schools have a set of history standards? If so, what should those standards be? These and a host of other issues binding today and yesterday attest to the truth of what the writer James Baldwin noted in 1965: "History…does not refer merely to the past….[H]istory is literally *present* in all that we do."[7]

American Conversations, as its title implies, aims to strike up a lively dialogue between you and the past. But the notion of *conversations* means more than that. It also stands for a running discussion between you and me; hence my direct, informal way of addressing you, the reader. Then there are the conversations that will, I hope, go on with your fellow American historians (for we are all historians, whether we have been studying history for three decades or three weeks) about the individuals and ideas inhabiting these pages. Last and by no means least, *conversations* should go on among the chapters—between, for example, the Puritan woman Mary Rowlandson in the 1670s and the Quaker women Angelina and Sarah Grimké in the 1830s, between the proslavery gadfly George Fitzhugh and the former slave Frederick Douglass. This cross-fertilization profoundly enriches the volume by forging connections across chapters and centuries in illuminating ways.

Choosing Rowlandson, Douglass, and the rest was no easy task; plenty of others were clamoring for a chance to be heard. Several principles guided me as I searched for likely candidates to bring to your attention. First, they had to be primary sources, documents produced at the time (Franklin's autobiography) rather than scholarly treatments (a biography of Franklin). As the notes throughout and the "Further Reading" at the end attest, there is a library's worth of fine scholarship on American history available; as the notes and "Further Reading" also attest, in developing this volume I found these works indispensable. But I wanted you to come as close as possible to the past rather than encounter it at one remove, set apart by a screen—however well-made—of scholarly interpretation.

As I then browsed among the vast trove of original sources, I kept several other principles in mind. One was to mix texts (and authors) who were familiar with others long forgotten: Hence Ben Franklin sits beside a Scottish physician you have never heard of while Abraham Lincoln is not far from the Pequot Indian William Apess. This blend reflects my conviction that even famous Americans and renowned documents—Franklin and Lincoln, the Declaration of Independence and the Gettysburg Address—are *known* more than they are *studied*; their renown makes them crucial to the American conversation, yet that conversation will be much enhanced if they are not merely revered but scrutinized. Including them here makes that possible; juxtaposing them with unfamiliar documents also enables you to read them in a new light.

A similar penchant for unusual combinations led me to include works that were best-sellers in their own day as well as others that drew little or no notice at the time. Mary Rowlandson's Indian captivity narrative, Thomas Paine's *Common Sense*, Weems's *Life of Washington*, Thomas Cole's landscape paintings—these and other documents were enormously popular when they appeared. In that popularity—as in the neglect of works by Joseph Plumb Martin and William Apess—lie clues to American values and preoccupations.

Cole's paintings bring me to another feature of this American conversation: images. In three chapters, pictures are the main course. Too few historians treat a painting or photograph as a vital text that, as one scholar puts it, "brings us 'face-to-face with history.' " To end "the invisibility of the visual," to aid the "visually illiterate," *American Conversations* invites you to study how Europeans depicted Native Americans in the 1580s, how painters two hundred and fifty years later pictured the new nation, and how photographers and other artists treated the Battle of Gettysburg during the Civil War.[8]

Last but by no means least, in selecting sources I went against the grain of most anthologies and included *fewer* texts so that you would have *more* of each. It has been my experience in the classroom that including snippets from three, five, or even eight primary sources in a single chapter can be a formula for difficulty if not disaster. Each author must be introduced, each document's context set forth; a brief excerpt rarely does justice to the original; it leaves readers with a confusing medley to make sense of; and students come into class with a cacophony in their heads, while the instructor must try, in a short span of time, to give each voice, each text, its due.

Obviously I believe—and I hope I will convince you!—in the benefits of longer passages (or more pictures). But there is a cost as well: Abandoning the smorgasbord approach that gives just a taste of many dishes does sacrifice "coverage" of the American experience. Of course, even a book with twice as many selections (or ten times as many) would be committing sins of omission. But I am the first to admit that this book might commit more than most of its kindred on the shelf. A glance at the Table of Contents reveals gaps—geographical, chronological, topical—in the itinerary of this voyage through America's past, but in my view the added depth of treatment compensates for the loss of breadth.

Accompanying the longer selections you will also find longer headnotes than most anthologies supply. These introductions aspire to accomplish several things: Tell you a little about the text's author and audience; sketch the context of the times in which author and audience lived; pose some questions about the document itself, questions both embedded in the headnote and extracted (and sometimes supplemented) at the end for easy reference; and suggest ways of starting conversations between a particular chapter and its fellows. I have found that these texts are proven conversation-starters; they strike a chord in readers, provoking thought and argument, admiration and anger. Connecting them in this fashion, having them engage with one another, only enhances their power to spark conversations.

Informed by my own teaching experience and my reading of the scholarly litera-ture, these chapter headnotes (and this Introduction) are one of the benefits of the price of admission to this volume. Some of the written and visual pieces of the past in *American Conversations* are available on the World Wide Web. For all its wonders, however, what the Internet cannot provide is the underlying philosophy I have just spelled out and the links I forge across the chapters and the generations. You are embarking on a *guided* tour (or, rather, a *self-guided tour* along a route I have mapped and marked), and that is far different from aimlessly surfing the Web or (to use another marine metaphor) fishing the Internet's vast, uncharted seas.

Throughout my years teaching history and my years crafting *American Conversations*, the star I steered by, my "true north," has been the imperative to sow what I tell my students is *creative* or *constructive confusion.* By that I mean something akin to Ralph Ellison's "contradictions, changes of pace, and surprises": a history that shakes up settled ideas, that musses up tidy notions, that calls into question rote celebrations of American triumphs and American "progress," that undermines easy assumptions about the way things were and the way they "had to be." For example, you will learn in the pages to follow that few Americans in 1750 thought "All Men are Created Equal," in 1775 that independence from Great Britain was a good idea, or in 1860 that the abolition of slavery was possible, much less desirable. You will also see how proper, pious women could be reviled for speaking to "promiscuous" audiences (men and women together!) and how the camera *does* lie.

Most constructively confusing of all, perhaps, is accepting that both of the statements opening this Introduction are true. At first glance, that seems impossible: How can the past be "a foreign country" where people "do things differently" *and* be "not even past"? As I mentioned, the truth of William Faulkner's assertion can be found in your daily newspaper or your favorite Internet site. L. P. Hartley's insight is harder to grasp, but it is, perhaps, even more important. Students of history, especially visitors to more remote eras, need to keep in mind that the people we meet on those forays are different in ways we can only begin to fathom. They are not akin to the actors at living history sites like Colonial Williamsburg or Plimoth Plantation, quaint folk who dress oddly but are, in their hearts and minds, just like us. The way those folks long ago lived, the way they thought about all manner of things—life and death, day and night, work and play, men and women, childhood and old age, kin and country, this world and the next—was profoundly alien to our way of thinking. We do them (and ourselves) a disservice if we impose our values on ancient America.[9]

It is also a mistake to think of those centuries as nothing more than a prelude to "modern" times, mere way stations on a path from past to present, a path so clearly marked that all could see what lay ahead. No colonists arriving in 1600 or 1700 or 1750 thought of themselves as founding a new nation; no Native American watching those newcomers disembark imagined that by the end of this period a continent that, since time out of mind, had been Indian Country would be Indian Country no more; and so on.

None of them would understand the categories into which we parcel out history—*the colonial period; the pre-revolutionary era; antebellum* [pre-Civil War] *America*—any more than you or I could label our own era as "pre-"anything.

What is needed, then, is some way of keeping *both* Faulkner and Hartley in mind at the same time. The poet T. S. Eliot caught something of this trick when he wrote of how "the historical sense involves a perception, not only of the pastness of the past, but of its presence." We must try, in other words, to explore the past with an eye toward understanding it on its own terms as well as pondering what it bequeathed to us.[10]

It might make it easier to achieve this balance if we realize how much we view our own lives in this fashion. If you are, say, eighteen, think for a moment about when you were eight or twelve. Looked at one way, you probably feel that you are an entirely different person than your younger, smaller self: You have changed and grown immeasurably in that span. And yet looked at another way, the connection between that "other" person and who you are now is clear: Who you *were* is very much alive in who you *are* and in who you *will be*. (If you are, like me, somewhat older than eighteen, both the distance from and the connection with your younger selves are, I assure you, even more keenly felt!)

In attempting to sow constructive and creative confusion, *American Conversations* aspires to greater clarity, to a better appreciation for the complexities and ambiguities, for the famous and the forgotten, for the triumphs and tragedies in American history. It has an approach, a guiding philosophy. Does it have an overarching theme? History painted on this large a canvas resists a simple, tidy plot. The great nineteenth-century poet Walt Whitman, who knew America better than most, knew well how messy a place and a people it was. "Do I contradict myself?" Whitman asked in *Leaves of Grass* (1855). "Very well then....I contradict myself; I am large....I contain multitudes."[11]

American Conversations also contains multitudes, but those multitudes do engage a cluster of themes. Relations between the sexes and the races, between individual and community; the role that God (of whatever sort) played in American life; the contest between hierarchy and equality; what people remembered and what they chose to forget; an author's biases and blind spots, distortions and silences; the balance between change and continuity over time—these are a few of the topics that recur across the chapters and across the generations. As you go on this journey, you doubtless will find still others that were—and are—part of America's conversations.

Endnotes

1. Michael Kammen, *Mystic Chords of Memory: The Transformation of Tradition in American Culture* (New York, 1991), 9 ("collective memory"), 49 (Adams); Kammen, *A Season of Youth: The American Revolution and the Historical Imaginative* (New York, 1978), 4 (Tocqueville); Kammen, *In the Past Lane: Historical Perspectives on American Culture* (New York, 1997), 164 ("short attention span"); Anna Quindlen, "American Forgetting," *Newsweek*, September 17, 2007, 86 ("over fast").

2. Kammen, *Mystic Chords*, 53–56, 77; W. Fitzhugh Brundage, *The Southern Past: A Clash of Race and Memory* (Cambridge, MA, 2005), 107.

3. Kammen, *Mystic Chords*, 664–65; Michael Zuckerman, "The Irrelevant Revolution: 1776 and Since," *American Quarterly*, 30 (1978), 241 (Declaration); *Poughkeepsie Journal*, April 30, 1987, 16A (Constitution); Gore Vidal, *Imperial America: Reflections on the United States of Amnesia* (New York, 2004).

4. George Wilson Pierson, *Tocqueville in America* (Baltimore, 1996 [originally published 1938]), 179–84.

5. Kammen, *Past Lane*, 214, 219.

6. Ibid., 164.

7. David W. Blight, *Race and Reunion: The Civil War in American Memory* (Cambridge, MA, 2001), 1.

8. Peter Burke, *Eyewitnessing: The Uses of Images as Historical Evidence* (Ithaca, NY, 2001), 9–10, 13.

9. L. P. Hartley, *The Go-Between* (London, 1953), 9; W. Faulkner, *Requiem for a Nun* (New York, 1951), Act 1, Scene III, 92.

10. Kammen, *Mystic Chords*, 5.

11. W. Whitman, *Leaves of Grass: Facsimile Edition of the 1855 Text* (Portland, Maine, 1919), 55.

Africans, Americans, and Europeans Imagine Their Origins

"In the beginning"

One of the first tasks facing every student of history is also one of the hardest: trying to see the world as people in times past saw it. Finding ways to get into the heads of those people, to look through their eyes, and to walk in their shoes is not only the most challenging but also one of the most exciting and rewarding things about being a historian. Central to that imaginative leap is trying to forget how things turned out. It is impossible, of course, to simply erase from memory the American Revolution or the Civil War, the rise of racial slavery or the demise of Native America. But it is necessary to attempt this if we are to glimpse life in the past.

Nowhere is the need to cultivate this skill greater than in considering the confluence of peoples—from Europe, Africa, and America—that occurred after 1492 in the lands we now call *the United States*. Knowing that Europeans ended up conquering Native Americans and herding them onto reservations while enslaving Africans and dragging them to these shores, it is easy to assume that conquest and enslavement were the only possible paths toward the present.

Europeans at the time—and many white Americans since—explained their successes by saying that God was on their side, by insisting that they were *civilized*, Americans and Africans *savage*. Such views are, happily, outmoded nowadays. Nonetheless, we have not altogether shed the old assumptions of European superiority. The very words still used reveal the powerful hold of a "Euro-centric" mind-set. *Old World* and *New World*, for example, take a European frame of reference: Europe's "new world," after all, was very old indeed to the Iroquois and native peoples who had lived here for millennia. Similarly skewed is talk of how *settlers tamed* a *wilderness*: Native pioneers had already occupied and ordered the land long before the first European colonists arrived; it was no wilderness to those earlier Indian settlers.

Just as the habit of calling America a *virgin land* suggests that the continent was untouched by human hands, so common terms for Africa—*darkest Africa, dark continent*—hinted that those regions, too, awaited European *settlement, enlightenment*. And so the winners' refrain goes: Europeans had *kings* ruling *nations*, Americans and Africans *chiefs* of *tribes*; Europeans had *religion*, the others *superstition*; Europeans had *law*, those they encountered *custom*; and European cultures were *sophisticated* and *complex*, the others *primitive* and *simple*. Such a vocabulary gives Europeans every advantage and makes the story of their ultimate triumph a straightforward one.

It did not look that way at the time. For all their talk of superiority, for all their ambitions, Europeans were slow to conquer. Most of North America remained Indian Country until at least 1800, some three centuries after Europeans first set foot on its shores. Africans, meanwhile, confined these strangers to the coastal fringes of that continent for an even longer span of time; not until the late nineteenth century did European nations gain something like command of that continent. What looks today quick, easy, and inevitable was anything but that to people—American, African, *and* European—living then.

Nor was European superiority or sophistication so evident—to anyone but Europeans! Natives in eastern North America could not believe that the bedraggled English folk at Jamestown or Plymouth starved in what locals considered a land of plenty. West Africans, meanwhile, were shocked by everything from the newcomer's pallid color to his weird clothes and customs.

But it is true, as people say, that "winners write history." It is also true that Europeans kept most of the records of this history. In order to escape the clutches of European sources and the European mind-set, to better compare the three neighborhoods of the Atlantic world—western Europe, western Africa, eastern North America—that came together, imagine that an outsider from some other corner of the globe traveled through these domains around 1400; on the eve of encounter, that sojourner would have been hard pressed to say which of these three worlds was "superior" or more "sophisticated."[1]

Consider their economies, for example. While we tend to think of Europeans as settled farmers, Americans as nomadic hunter-gatherers, and Africans as wandering herders, in fact farm towns dotted all three landscapes. West Africans had been growing rice, yams, and other crops for thousands of years. Domesticated plants had come to eastern North America more recently than that, but centuries before Columbus, the "three sisters" (corn, beans, and squash) mentioned in the Iroquois creation myth below were the stuff of life. Peoples then ate less meat than modern Americans do, and crops originally developed by native farmers make up much of the nation's current agricultural production. Remember that it was Squanto, friend of the Pilgrims, who taught the struggling newcomers how to grow crops in the colonists' new land.

The idea that Europeans were shrewd and experienced traders who duped their naive African and American counterparts must also be set aside. From villages in all three worlds, traders set out to swap goods with others near and far. West Africans carried on long-distance trade (some of it all the way across the Sahara Desert) in such goods as gold, salt, ivory, ironware, cloth, and slaves. Long-distance as well as local exchange was also common in eastern North America. Pipestone from the Great Plains, obsidian from the Rocky Mountains, copper from the Great Lakes—these and other prized items found their way to natives near the Atlantic coast, swapped from town to town and people to people.

In politics, too, our imaginary voyager through the Atlantic world would have found fewer differences than we might expect between Europeans on the one hand and Africans or Americans on the other. European societies then were far from consolidated, confident, powerful nation-states: Localism contended with nationalism, kinship with kingship, as the wide variations in housing, dress, and dialect—within "England," say, or "France"—would attest.

Those variations could also be found in eastern North America, of course. But so could impressive chiefdoms (especially in the Southeast and the Mississippi Valley), chiefdoms ruling over hundreds of miles and thousands of people. At the head of these governments stood a ruler said to be descended from the gods. To mark that divine status, this leader was set off from the populace in a capital city that might (as at Cahokia on the Mississippi River around 1150) number 25,000 or more. Dressed in ornate finery, carried about on a canopied litter, he often lived atop a high mound surrounded by retainers, the only people permitted in his presence. Such headmen had powers of taxation and trade, and they commanded large armies as well as navies that might boast two hundred large canoes, each filled with scores of warriors.

African kings had, if anything, even more imposing armies (numbering 100,000 men or more), along with navies that cruised coastal waters and major rivers. Leaders of such West African kingdoms as Mali (which was at its height from about 1250 to 1400) and Songhay (1450–1600) also commanded extensive bureaucracies that included departments of fisheries, forests, agriculture, and finance. Sitting on a golden throne, dressed in fabulous robes and a cap made out of spun gold, the king's arms and royal crest beside him, such a ruler was an imposing sight, made even more imposing by the custom (as at Mali in 1532) that all those approaching him had to put on ragged, dirty clothes while advancing "on all fours, sprinkling dirt on their head and shoulders" in a "position of humility."[2]

The same holds true for the religious beliefs and customs of these three regions on the eve of their encounter. Looking up at Europe's towering cathedral spires, entering those vast sacred spaces, it is tempting to conclude that Europeans had a powerful, organized religion, but Americans and Africans had mere superstition. Here again, however, a closer look places the three on more equal footing.

For one thing, calling Europe "Christian" cannot do justice to the spiritual complexity and ambiguity there. Alongside Christianity—sometimes interwoven into the fabric of that faith, sometimes at odds with it—stood ancient lore and custom that many then labeled "pagan" and many now would consider "superstition." It was a "world of wonders" filled with signs and portents, divining rods and love potions, magical rocks and trees, "cunning folk" and fortune tellers, not to mention wizards and witches.[3]

For another, faiths in America and Africa were more complex than European intruders knew. True, peoples there tended to be polytheistic, believing in many gods. But they, too, usually considered one of those gods supreme. (Chastised by Christians for worshipping so many deities, Americans and Africans pointed out the resemblance between their own "lesser" gods and the roster of Catholic saints, not to mention the Virgin Mary and Jesus Christ.) Moreover, just as Christianity coexisted with so-called pagan beliefs, so, too, Islam for centuries had attracted followers in West Africa, followers who did not always shed the older spirituality of their people.

One way to bring African, European, and American worlds into comparative focus is to peer beneath economics and politics, beneath even religious beliefs and customs, in order to consider the creation stories that told of the very foundation of these societies. It might seem odd to devote the first chapter of an American history book to stories that tell of a woman falling from the sky onto a turtle's back, of a serpent and an apple, and of leaves turning into elephants and sardines. In fact, however, such tales reveal much. Just as the famous myth of George Washington and the cherry tree can be studied for clues to abiding American values (Chapter 10), so lore about the world's beginnings can be read for the insights it provides into a people's thinking, their deepest fears and highest hopes. If not *factual*, they are in a deeper, more important sense *truthful*; as Ulli Beier, who collected the African story you will read, points out, "truth and fact are not necessarily the same."[4]

To approach these three texts, we also need to set aside the idea that one—the Book of Genesis—is revealed Truth, the Word of God, the other two mere myth. But whether or not one is Christian, it might appear that Genesis *is* different from the tale told among the Iroquois in what is now upstate New York and from the Fang story heard in the West African nation of Gabon. The Christian version below, from the

King James Bible, was published in 1611 as a translation of documents written down more than a thousand years earlier; we can be sure, then, that this version was one that English colonists would have known.

We cannot say the same of the African or American genesis. These two texts were collected and published only in the twentieth century, from oral traditions that might well have changed dramatically, even completely, since earlier times. Scholars have recorded more than forty different versions of the Iroquois creation story, and hundreds of African origin tales have the first humans emerging out of everything from a reed to a tree, from the earth to the sky. It might seem, then, that there is a single Christian "origin myth," but many American and African ones.

Examined more closely, however, once again the gap between Europeans on the one hand and Americans or Africans on the other narrows. Genesis, too, was "mere" oral tradition, passed from one generation of storytellers to the next before finally being written down in Hebrew some three thousand years ago. Nor did writing the story down settle matters: Different manuscript versions traveled down the centuries, as did varying translations. Scholars and believers have been arguing about the Bible ever since it first found its way to the page, and they will continue to do so because both its language and its meaning are open to interpretation.

Take, for example, the famous phrase from Ecclesiastes (11:1), "Cast thy bread upon the waters," which one translation rendered, "Lay thy bread upon wet faces."[5] Or think of a later part of the Bible's Old Testament than Genesis, the prophecy about the coming of a new messiah (the Book of Isaiah, 7:14): "Behold, a virgin shall conceive." As historian Benson Bobrick notes, the original Hebrew word for the messiah's mother was *almah*, meaning "young woman," not "virgin" (which was, in Hebrew, *bethulah*). When writing in the New Testament about the life and death of Jesus, however, Matthew (1:23) quoted Isaiah's prophecy not from the original Hebrew but from a Greek translation of it; that translator had used the word *parthenos*, which can indeed mean "virgin." Is, then, the Christian concept of a *virgin* birth true to the original?[6]

Given the enormous challenges of translation, no wonder there were so many different English versions of the Bible in 1604, when King James I, at the beginning of his reign (1603–1625), authorized yet another one. In order to settle religious unrest—which could spill over into political strife, even civil war—"His Highnesses wished, that some especiall pains should be taken…for one uniforme translation" that would "bee ratified by his Royall authority" and "read in the whole Church [throughout the realm], and no other [version]." Small wonder, too, it took a team of some fifty "best learned" scholars seven years of painstaking work (and, sometimes, bitter arguments) to produce that new Bible—and even then, they did not get it entirely right! (The Hebrew and Greek texts "the Translators" consulted were not the oldest or the best, and their knowledge of the particular form of Greek was limited.) As if that were not enough, the royal printer was so inept that, Adam Nicolson reports, "no copy of the 1611 Bible is like any other," and each copy is "riddled with mistakes." To be sure, no error was as great as that in an edition two decades later that, omitting a single word, told believers "Thou shalt commit adultery." Nonetheless, the first edition had "she" instead of "he" and (worse) "Judas" instead of "Jesus." "The curious fact," Nicolson concludes, "is that no one such thing as 'The King James Bible'—agreed, consistent and whole—has ever existed."[7]

Just as the Christian account is less fixed and more various than it might at first appear, so the Fang and Iroquois stories are *more* fixed and *less* various than they seem. In "oral tradition," anthropologist Dean Snow observes, "the essential things remain but are subject to variation and elaboration."[8] In fact, the more than forty recorded Iroquois versions, stretching back all the way to 1623, bear a remarkable resemblance to one another in their outline, structure, and message. (One new wrinkle, on race, is included here. What are the implications of that revision?)

While the West African tale here lacks that time depth—no one jotted it down in the 1620s—scholars generally agree that a creation story written down in recent times "still incorporates elements of different ages." Particularly with a tale about such fundamentals as the world's beginnings, the creation of man, and the reasons for death and sorrow, writes historian Jan Vansina, "the readjustment of ultimate values and cultural identity is usually a slow process." While certainly reflecting modern concerns and modern ways of thinking, such "traditions of origins and Genesis" are also clearly a "message from the past." Moreover, although there is considerable variation across space as well as over time, folklorists have found elements of the Iroquois story not only among nearby native nations but throughout North America. In Africa, too, scholars like John Mbiti report, origin stories are "remarkably similar across the continent."[9]

You are now prepared to approach these three tales with something like the same outsider's eye as our imaginary traveler on the eve of the American encounter. As you read, think about where the stories agree, and where they differ. Do all of them try to answer the same questions? Are you struck more by the similarities among the three, or the differences? (Do not presume that any similarities you find represent European influence, even though Iroquois and Fang stories were collected long after Christian missionaries visited Africa and America. That trees feature in all three, for example, is more likely independent invention than borrowing of Christian elements. Embedded deep in the earth yet reaching high into the sky, trees bridge this world and the next, the visible and the invisible realms, and have long been objects of fascination in Europe, Africa, and America alike.)

As you compare these three stories, remember that the peoples telling them centuries ago did not know their future—and *our* past: They did not imagine European colonization, American Indian defeat, and African enslavement. Without that foreknowledge, would they, if they heard the creation myths of the other two, have found a powerful resemblance? Or would the stories have fostered notions of difference, of "otherness," that would help turn American natives into subjects and African natives into slaves?

Questions for Consideration and Conversation

1. Do all three stories treat the same themes, answer the same questions?
2. Are you more struck by the similarities among the three, or the differences?
3. Consider the role that women play in the three stories. What can be said about gender relations from these tales?
4. What role does violence have in each story?
5. What role does nature have in these stories? Are the views of nature expressed here complementary or contradictory?
6. I have placed these in no particular order. Does it matter in what sequence they're read? You might try reading them out of "order" here and compare your reaction to that of others who read them in the arrangement below.
7. I argue in the head note for a more evenhanded consideration of western Europe, west Africa, and eastern North America on the eve of contact. Are you convinced? What might an argument countering that assertion look like?

Endnotes

1. The idea of an imaginary traveler or "outside observer" comes from Mary Beth Norton et al., *A People and a Nation: A History of the United States*, Volume I: To 1877 (Boston, 1982), 11. For a work that does the opposite— that identifies the central differences among these societies to explain how Europeans ultimately came to dominate—see Jared Diamond, *Guns, Germs, and Steel: The Fates of Human Societies* (New York, 1997).

2. G. T. Stride and Caroline Ifeka, *Peoples and Empires of West Africa: West Africa in History, 1000–1800* (New York, 1971), 56.

3. David D. Hall, *Worlds of Wonder, Days of Judgment: Popular Religious Belief in Early New England* (New York, 1989).

4. Ulli Beier, ed., *The Origin of Life and Death: African Creation Myths* (London, 1966), x.

5. Adam Nicolson, *God's Secretaries: The Making of the King James Bible* (New York, 2003), 73.
6. Benson Bobrick, *Wide as the Waters: The Story of the English Bible and the Revolution It Inspired* (New York, 2001), 262.
7. Nicolson, *God's Secretaries*, 59, 224–26.
8. Dean Snow, *The Iroquois* (Cambridge, MA, 1994), 4.
9. Vansina, "Comment: Traditions of Genesis," *Journal of African History*, 15 (1974), 320 ("slow"); Vansina, *Oral Tradition as History* (Madison, WI, 1985), xii, 21; John S. Mbiti, *Introduction to African Religion*, 2nd ed. (London, 1991), 82.

THE WORLD ON THE TURTLE'S BACK (IROQUOIS STORY)

Source: Hazel W. Hertzberg, *The Great Tree and the Longhouse: The Culture of the Iroquois*. New York: McGraw Hill, 1966, pp. 12–22.

In the beginning there was no world, no land, no creatures of the kind that are around us now, and there were no men. But there was a great ocean which occupied space as far as anyone could see. Above the ocean was a great void of air. And in the air there lived the birds of the sea; in the ocean lived the fish and the creatures of the deep. Far above this unpeopled world, there was a Sky-World. Here lived gods who were like people—like Iroquois.

In the Sky-World there was a man who had a wife, and the wife was expecting a child. The woman became hungry for all kinds of strange delicacies, as women do when they are with child. She kept her husband busy almost to distraction finding delicious things for her to eat.

In the middle of the Sky-World there grew a Great Tree which was not like any of the trees that we know. It was tremendous; it had grown there forever. It had enormous roots that spread out from the floor of the Sky-World. And on its branches there were many different kinds of leaves and different kinds of fruits and flowers. The tree was not supposed to be marked or mutilated by any of the beings who dwelt in the Sky-World. It was a sacred tree that stood at the center of the universe.

The woman decided that she wanted some bark from one of the roots of the Great Tree—perhaps as a food or as a medicine, we don't know. She told her husband this. He didn't like the idea. He knew it was wrong. But she insisted, and he gave in. So he dug a hole among the roots of this great sky tree, and he bared some of its roots. But the floor of the Sky-World wasn't very thick, and he broke a hole through it. He was terrified, for he had never expected to find empty space underneath the world.

But his wife was filled with curiosity. He wouldn't get any of the roots for her, so she set out to do it herself. She bent over and she looked down, and she saw the ocean far below. She leaned down and stuck her head through the hole and looked all around. No one knows just what happened next. Some say she slipped. Some say that her husband, fed up with all the demands she had made on him, pushed her.

So she fell through the hole. As she fell, she frantically grabbed at its edges, but her hands slipped. However, between her fingers there clung bits of things that were growing on the floor of the Sky-World and bits of the root tips of the Great Tree. And so she began to fall toward the great ocean far below.

The birds of the sea saw the woman falling, and they immediately consulted with each other as to what they could do to help her. Flying wingtip to wingtip they made a great feathery raft in the sky to support her, and thus they broke her fall. But of course it was not possible for them to carry the woman very long. Some of the other birds of the sky flew down to the surface of the ocean and called up the ocean creatures to see what they could do to help. The great sea turtle came and agreed to receive her on his back. The birds placed her gently on the shell of the turtle, and now the turtle floated about on the huge ocean with the woman safely on his back.

The beings up in the Sky-World paid no attention to this. They knew what was happening, but they chose to ignore it.

When the woman recovered from her shock and terror, she looked around her. All that she could see were the birds and the sea creatures and the sky and the ocean.

And the woman said to herself that she would die. But the creatures of the sea came to her and said that they would try to help her and asked her what they could do. She told them that if they could find some soil, she could plant the roots stuck between her fingers, and from them plants would grow. The sea animals said perhaps there was dirt at the bottom of the ocean, but no one had ever been down there so they could not be sure.

If there was dirt at the bottom of the ocean, it was far, far below the surface in the cold deeps. But the animals said they would try to get some. One by one the diving birds and animals tried and failed. They went to the limits of their endurance, but they could not get to the bottom of the ocean. Finally, the muskrat said he would try. He dived and disappeared.

All the creatures waited, holding their breath, but he did not return. After a long time, his little body floated up to the surface of the ocean, a tiny crumb of earth clutched in his paw. He seemed to be dead. They pulled him up on the turtle's back and they sang and prayed over him and breathed air into his mouth, and finally, he stirred. Thus it was the muskrat, the Earth-Diver, who brought from the bottom of the ocean the soil from which the earth was to grow.

The woman took the tiny clod of dirt and placed it on the middle of the great sea turtle's back. Then the woman began to walk in a circle around it, moving in the direction that the sun goes. The earth began to grow. When the earth was big enough, she planted the roots she had clutched between her fingers when she fell from the Sky-World. Thus the plants grew on the earth.

To keep the earth growing, the woman walked as the sun goes, moving in the direction that the people still move in the dance rituals. She gathered roots and plants to eat and built herself a little hut. After a while, the woman's time came, and she was delivered of a daughter. The woman and her daughter kept walking in a circle around the earth, so that the earth and plants would continue to grow. They lived on the plants and roots they gathered. The girl grew up with her mother, cut off forever from the Sky-World above, knowing only the birds and the creatures of the sea, seeing no other beings like herself.

One day, when the girl had grown to womanhood, a man appeared. No one knows for sure who this man was. He had something to do with the gods above. Perhaps he was the West Wind. As the girl looked at him, she was filled with terror, and amazement, and warmth, and she fainted dead away. As she lay on the ground, the man reached into his quiver, and he took out two arrows, one sharp and one blunt, and he laid them across the body of the girl, and quietly went away.

When the girl awoke from her faint, she and her mother continued to walk around the earth. After a while, they knew that the girl was to bear a child. They did not know it, but the girl was to bear twins.

Within the girl's body, the twins began to argue and quarrel with one another. There could be no peace between them. As the time approached for them to be born, the twins fought about their birth. The right-handed twin wanted to be born in the normal way, as all children are born. But the left-handed twin said no. He said he saw light in another direction, and said he would be born that way. The right-handed twin beseeched him not to, saying that he would kill their mother. But the left-handed twin was stubborn. He went in the direction where he saw light. But he could not be born through his mother's mouth or her nose. He was born through her left armpit, and killed her. And meanwhile, the right-handed twin was born in the normal way, as all children are born.

The twins met in the world outside, and the right-handed twin accused his brother of murdering their mother. But the grandmother told them to stop their quarreling. They buried their mother. And from her grave grew the plants which the people still use. From her head grew the corn, the beans, and the squash—"our supporters, the three sisters." And from her heart grew the sacred tobacco, which the people still use in the ceremonies and by whose upward-floating smoke they send thanks. The women call her "our mother," and they dance and sing in the rituals so that the corn, the beans, and the squash may grow to feed the people.

But the conflict of the twins did not end at the grave of their mother. And, strangely enough, the grandmother favored the left-handed twin.

The right-handed twin was angry, and he grew more angry as he thought how his brother had killed their mother. The right-handed twin was the one who did everything just as he should. He said what he meant, and he meant what he said. He always told the truth, and he always tried to accomplish what seemed to be right and reasonable. The left-handed twin never said what he meant or meant what he said. He always lied, and he always did things backward. You could never tell what he was trying to do because he always made it look as if he were doing the opposite. He was the devious one.

These two brothers, as they grew up, represented two ways of the world which are in all people. The Indians did not call these the right and the wrong. They called them the straight mind and the crooked mind, the upright man and the devious man, the right and the left.

The twins had creative powers. They took clay and modeled it into animals, and they gave these animals life. And in this they contended with one another. The right-handed twin made the deer, and the left-handed twin made the mountain lion which kills the deer. But the right-handed twin knew there would always be more deer than mountain lions. And he made another animal. He made the ground squirrel. The left-handed twin saw that the mountain lion could not get to the ground squirrel, who digs a hole, so he made the weasel. And although the weasel can go into the ground squirrel's hole and kill him, there are lots of ground squirrels and not so many weasels. Next the right-handed twin decided he would make an animal that the weasel could not kill, so he made the porcupine. But the left-handed twin made the bear, who flips the porcupine over on his back and tears out his belly.

And the right-handed twin made berries and fruits of other kinds for his creatures to live on. The left-handed twin made briars and poison ivy, and the poisonous plants like the baneberry and the dogberry, and the suicide root with which people kill themselves when they go out of their minds. And the left-handed twin made medicines, for good and for evil, for doctoring and for witchcraft.

And finally, the right-handed twin made man. The people do not know just how much the left-handed twin had to do with making man. Man was made of clay, like pottery, and baked in the fire. [At a later time the idea was added that some men were baked too little: these were white men. Some men were baked too much: these were Negroes. But some were baked just right: these were Indians. Those who were baked too little or too much were thrown away, but the Indians were settled upon the land.]

The world the twins made was a balanced and orderly world, and this was good. The plant-eating animals created by the right-handed twin would eat up all the vegetation if their number was not kept down by the meat-eating animals which the left-handed twin created. But if these carnivorous animals ate too many other animals, then they would starve, for they would run out of meat. So the right- and the left-handed twins built balance into the world.

As the twins became men full grown, they still contested with one another. No one had won, and no one had lost. And they knew that the conflict was becoming sharper and sharper and one of them would have to vanquish the other.

And so they came to the duel. They started with gambling. They took a wooden bowl, and in it they put wild plum pits. One side of the pits was burned black, and by tossing the pits in the bowl, and betting on how these would fall, they gambled against one another, as the people still do in the New Year's rites. All through the morning they gambled at this game, and all through the afternoon, and the sun went down. And when the sun went down, the game was done, and neither one had won.

So they went on to battle one another at the lacrosse game. And they contested all day, and the sun went down, and the game was done. And neither had won.

And now they battled with clubs, and they fought all day, and the sun went down, and the fight was done. But neither had won.

And they went from one duel to another to see which one would succumb. Each one knew in his deepest mind that there was something, somewhere, that would vanquish the other. But what was it? Where to find it?

Each knew somewhere in his mind what it was that was his own weak point. They talked about this as they contested in these duels, day after day, and somehow the deep mind of each entered into the other. And the deep mind of the right-handed twin lied to his brother, and the deep mind of the left-handed twin told the truth.

On the last day of the duel, as they stood, they at last knew how the right-handed twin was to kill his brother. Each selected his weapon. The left-handed twin chose a mere stick that would do him no good. But the right-handed twin picked out the deer antler, and with one touch he destroyed his brother. And the left-handed twin died, but he died and he didn't die. The right-handed twin picked up the body and cast it off the edge of the earth. And some place below the world, the left-handed twin still lives and reigns.

When the sun rises from the east and travels in a huge arc along the sky dome, which rests like a great upside-down cup on the saucer of the earth, the people are in the daylight realm of the right-handed twin. But when the sun slips down in the west at nightfall and the dome lifts to let it escape at the western rim, the people are again in the domain of the left-handed twin—the fearful realm of night.

Having killed his brother, the right-handed twin returned home to his grandmother. And she met him in anger. She threw the food out of the cabin onto the ground, and said that he was a murderer, for he had killed his brother. He grew angry and told her she had always helped his brother, who had killed their mother. In his anger, he grabbed her by the throat and cut her head off. Her body he threw into the ocean, and her head, into the sky. There "Our Grandmother, the Moon," still keeps watch at night over the realm of her favorite grandson.

The right-handed twin has many names. One of them is Sapling. It means smooth, young, green and fresh and innocent, straightforward, straight-growing, soft and pliable, teachable and trainable. These are the old ways of describing him. But since he has gone away, he has other names. He is called "He Holds Up the Skies," "Master of Life," and "Great Creator."

The left-handed twin also has many names. One of them is Flint. He is called the devious one, the one covered with boils, Old Warty. He is stubborn. He is thought of as being dark in color.

These two beings rule the world and keep an eye on the affairs of men. The right-handed twin, the Master of Life, lives in the Sky-World. He is content with the world he helped to create and with his favorite creatures, the humans. The scent of sacred tobacco rising from the earth comes gloriously to his nostrils.

In the world below lives the left-handed twin. He knows the world of men, and he finds contentment in it. He hears the sounds of warfare and torture, and he finds them good.

In the daytime, the people have rituals which honor the right-handed twin. Through the daytime rituals they thank the Master of Life. In the nighttime, the people dance and sing for the left-handed twin.

The First Book of Moses, called Genesis (1611)

Source: The English Bible. Translated out of the Original Tongues by the Commandment of King James the First. Anno 1611.

Chapter I

In the beginning God created the Heaven, and the Earth. And the earth was without forme, and voyd, and darkenesse was upon the face of the deepe: and the Spirit of God mooved upon the face of the waters. And God said, Let there be light: and there was light. And God saw the light, that it was good: and God divided the light from the darkenesse. And God called the light, Day, and the darkenesse he called Night: and the evening and the morning were the first day.

And God said, Let there be a firmament in the midst of the waters: And let it divide the waters from the waters. And God made the firmament; and divided the waters, which were under the firmament, from the waters, which were above the firmament: and it was so. And God called the firmament, Heaven: and the evening and the morning were the second day.

And God said, Let the waters under the heaven be gathered together unto one place, and let the dry land appeare: and it was so. And God called the drie land, Earth, and the gathering together of the waters called hee, Seas: and God saw that it was good. And God said, Let the Earth bring foorth grasse, the herb yeelding seed, and the fruit tree, yeelding fruit after his kinde, whose seed is in it selfe, upon the earth: and it was so. And the earth brought grasse, and herbe yeelding seed after his kinde, and the tree yeelding

fruit, whose seed was in it selfe, after his kinde: and God saw that it was good. And the evening and the morning were the third day.

And God said, Let there bee lights in the firmament of the heaven, to divide the day from the night: and let them be for signes and for seasons, and for dayes and yeeres. And let them be for lights in the firmament of the heaven, to give light upon the earth: and it was so. And God made two great lights: the greater light to rule the day, and the lesser light to rule the night: he made the starres also. And God set them in the firmament of the heaven, to give light upon the earth: and to rule over the day, and over the night, and to divide the light from the darknesse: and God saw that it was good. And the evening and the morning were the fourth day.

And God said, Let the waters bring foorth aboundantly the moving creature that hath life, and foule that may flie above the earth in the open firmament of heaven. And God created great whales, and every living creature that moveth, which the waters brought forth aboundantly after their kinde, and every winged foule after his kinde: and God saw that it was good. And God blessed them, saying, Be fruitfull, and multiply, and fill the waters in the Seas, and let foule multiply in the earth. And the evening and the morning were the fift[h] day.

And God said, Let the earth bring forth the living creature after his kinde, cattell, and creeping thing, and beast of the earth after his kinde: and it was so. And God made the beast of the earth after his kinde, and cattell after their kinde, and every thing that creepeth upon the earth, after his kinde: and God saw that it was good.

And God said, Let us make man in our Image, after our likenesse: and let them have dominion over the fish of the sea, and over the foule of the aire, and over the cattell, and over all the earth, and over every creeping thing that creepeth upon the earth. So God created man his owne Image, in the Image of God created hee him; male and female created hee them. And God blessed them, and God said unto them, Be fruitfull, and multiply, and replenish the earth, and subdue it, and have dominion over the fish of the sea, and over the foule of the aire, and over every living thing that mooveth upon the earth.

And God said, Behold I have given you every herbe bearing seede, which is upon the face of all the earth, and every tree, in the which is the fruit of a tree yeelding seed, to you it shall be for meat: and to every beast of the earth, and to every foule of the aire, and to every thing that creepeth upon the earth, wherein there is life, I have given every greene herbe for meat: and it was so. And God saw every thing that hee had made: and behold, it was very good. And the evening and the morning were the sixth day.

Chapter II

Thus the heavens and the earth were finished, and all the hoste of them. And on the seventh day God rested from the worke, which hee had made. And God blessed the seventh day, and sanctified it: because that in it he had rested from all his worke, which God created and made.

These are the generations of the heavens, and of the earth, when they were created; in the day that the Lord God made the earth, and the heavens, and every plant of the field, before it was in the earth, and every herbe of the field, before it grew: for the Lord God had not caused it to raine upon the earth, and there was not a man to till the ground. But there went up a mist from the earth, and watered the whole face of the ground. And the Lord God formed man of the dust of the ground, and breathed into his nostrils the breath of life; and man became a living soule.

And the Lord God planted a garden Eastward in Eden; and there he put the man whom he had formed. And out of the ground made the Lord God to grow every tree that is pleasant to the sight, and good for food: the tree of life also in the midst of the garden, and the tree of knowledge of good and evill. And a river went out of Eden to water the garden, and from thence it was parted, and became into foure heads. The name of the first is Pison: that is it which compasseth the whole land of Havilah, where there is gold. And the gold of that land is good: There is Bdellium and the Onix stone. And the name of the second river is Gihon: the same is it that compasseth the whole land of Ethiopia. And the name of the third river is Hiddekel; that is it which goeth toward the East of Assyria: and the fourth river is Euphrates. And the Lord God tooke the man, and put him into the garden of Eden, to dresse it, and to keepe it. And the Lord God commanded the man, saying, Of every tree of the garden thou mayest freely eat. But the tree of the knowledge of good and evill, thou shalt not eate of it: for in the day that thou eatest thereof, thou shalt surely die.

And the Lord God said, It is not good that the man should be alone: I will make him an helpe meet for him. And out of the ground the Lord God formed every beast of the field, and every foule of the aire, and brought them unto Adam to see what he would call them: and whatsoever Adam called every living creature, that was the name thereof. And Adam gave names to all cattell and to the foule of the aire, and to every beast of the fielde: but for Adam there was not found an helpe meete for him. And the Lord God caused a deepe sleepe to fall upon Adam, and hee slept: and he tooke one of his ribs, and closed up the flesh in stead thereof. And the rib which the Lord God had taken from man, made hee a woman, and brought her unto the man. And Adam said, This is now bone of my bone, and flesh of my flesh: she shalbe called woman, because shee was taken out of man. Therefore shall a man leave his father and his mother, and shall cleave unto his wife: and they shalbe one flesh. And they were both naked, the man and his wife, and were not ashamed.

Chapter III

Now the serpent was more subtill then any beast of the field, which the Lord God had made, and he said unto the woman, Yea, hath God said, Ye shall not eat of every tree of the garden? And the woman said unto the serpent, Wee may eate of the fruit of the trees of the garden but of the fruit of the tree, which is in the midst of the garden, God hath said, Ye shal not eate of it, neither shall ye touch it, lest ye die. And the Serpent said unto the woman, Ye shall not surely die. For God doeth know, that in the day ye eate thereof, then your eyes shalbee opened:

and yee shall bee as Gods, knowing good and evill. And when the woman saw, that the tree was good for food, and that it was pleasant to the eyes, and a tree to be desired to make one wise, she tooke of the fruit thereof, did eate, and gave also unto her husband with her, and hee did eate. And the eyes of them both were opened, and they knew that they were naked, and they sewed figge leaves together, and made themselves aprons. And they heard the voyce of the Lord God, walking in the garden in the coole of the day: and Adam and his wife hid themselves from the presence of the Lord God, amongst the trees of the garden. And the Lord God called unto Adam, and said unto him, Where art thou? And he said, I heard thy voice in the garden: and I was afraid because I was naked, and I hid my selfe. And he said, Who told thee, that thou wast naked? Hast thou eaten of the tree, whereof I commanded thee, that thou shouldest not eate? And the man said, The woman whom thou gavest to be with mee, shee gave me of the tree, and I did eate. And the Lord God said unto the woman, What is this that thou hast done? And the woman said, The Serpent beguiled me, and I did eate. And the Lord God said unto the Serpent, Because thou hast done this, thou art cursed above all cattel, and above every beast of the field: upon thy belly shalt thou goe, and dust shalt thou eate, all the dayes of thy life. And I will put enmitie betweene thee and the woman, and betweene thy seed and her seed: it shal bruise thy head, and thou shall bruise his heele. Unto the woman he said, I will greatly multiply thy sorowe and thy conception. In sorowe thou shalt bring forth children: and thy desire shall be to thy husband, and hee shall rule over thee. And unto Adam he said, Because thou hast hearkened unto the voyce of thy wife, and hast eaten of the tree, of which I commaunded thee, saying, Thou shalt not eate of it: cursed is the ground for thy sake: in sorow shalt thou eate of it all the dayes of thy life. Thornes also and thistles shall it bring forth to thee: and thou shalt eate the herbe of the field. In the sweate of thy face shall thou eate bread, till thou returne unto the ground: for out of it wast thou taken, for dust thou art, and unto dust shalt thou returne. And Adam called his wives name Eve, because she was the mother of all living. Unto Adam also, and to his wife, did the Lord God make coates of skinnes and cloathed them.

And the Lord God said, Behold, the man is become as one of us, to know good and evill. And now lest hee put foorth his hand, and take also of the tree of life, and eate and live for ever: therefore the Lord God sent him foorth from the garden of Eden, to till the ground, from whence he was taken. So he drove out the man: and he placed at the East of the garden of Eden, Cherubims, and a flaming sword, which turned every way, to keepe the way of the tree of life.

THE REVOLT AGAINST GOD

A Fang Story (Gabon, West Africa)

Source: Ulli Beier, ed. *The Origin of Life and Death: African Creation Myths.* London: Heinemann, 1966, pp. 18–22.

At the beginning of Things, when there was nothing, neither man, nor animals, nor plants, nor heaven, nor earth, nothing, nothing, God was and he was called Nzame. The three who are Nzame, we call them Nzame, Mebere, and Nkwa. At the beginning Nzame made the heaven and the earth and he reserved the heaven for himself. Then he blew onto the earth and earth and water were created, each on its side.

Nzame made everything: heaven, earth, sun, moon, stars, animals, plants; everything. When he had finished everything that we see today, he called Mebere and Nkwa and showed them his work.

"This is my work. Is it good?"

They replied, "Yes, you have done well."

"Does anything remain to be done?"

Mebere and Nkwa answered him, "We see many animals, but we do not see their chief; we see many plants, but we do not see their master."

As masters for all these things, they appointed the elephant, because he had wisdom; the leopard, because he had power and cunning; and the monkey, because he had malice and suppleness.

But Nzame wanted to do even better; and between them he, Mebere, and Nkwa created a being almost like themselves. One gave him force, the second sway, and the third beauty. Then the three of them said:

"Take the earth. You are henceforth the master of all that exists. Like us you have life, all things belong to you, you are the master."

Nzame, Mebere, and Nkwa returned to the heights to their dwelling place, and the new creature remained below alone, and everything obeyed him. But among all the animals the elephant remained the first, the leopard the second, and the monkey the third, because it was they whom Mebere and Nkwa had first chosen.

Nzame, Mebere, and Nkwa called the first man *Fam*—which means power.

Proud of his sway, his power, and his beauty, because he surpassed in these three qualities the elephant, the leopard, and the monkey, proud of being able to defeat all the animals, this first man grew wicked; he became arrogant, and did not want to worship Nzame again; and he scorned him:

Yeye, o, layeye,
God on high, man on the earth,
Yeye, o, layeye,
God is God,
Man is man,
Everyone in his house, everyone for himself!

God heard the song. "Who sings?" he asked.
"Look for him," cried Fam.
"Who sings?"
"Yeye, o, lay-eye!"
"Who sings?"
"Eh! it is me!" cried Fam.

Furious, God called Nzalan the thunder. "Nzalan come!" Nzalan came running with great noise: *boom, boom, boom!* The fire of heaven fell on the forest. The plantations burnt like vast torches. *Foo, foo, foo!*—everything in flames. The earth was then, as today, covered with forests. The trees burnt; the plants, the bananas, the cassava, even the pistachio nuts, everything dried up; animals, birds, fishes, all were destroyed, everything was dead. But when God had created the first man, he had told him, "You will never die." And what God gives he does not take away. The first man was burnt, but none knows what became of him. He is alive, yes, but where?

But God looked at the earth, all black, without anything, and idle; he felt ashamed and wanted to do better. Nzame, Mebere, and Nkwa took counsel and they did as follows: over the black earth covered with coal they put a new layer of earth; a tree grew, grew bigger and bigger and when one of its seeds fell

down a new tree was born, when a leaf severed itself it grew and grew and began to walk. It was an animal, an elephant, a leopard, an antelope, a tortoise—all of them. When a leaf fell into the water it swam, it was a fish, a sardine, a crab, an oyster—all of them. The earth became again what it had been, and what it still is today. The proof that this is the truth is this: when one digs up the earth in certain places, one finds a hard black stone which breaks; throw it in the fire and it burns.

But Nzame, Mebere, and Nkwa took counsel again; they needed a chief to command all the animals. "We shall make a man like Fam," said Nzame, "the same legs and arms, but we shall turn his head and he shall see death."

This was the second man and the father of all. Nzame called him *Sekume*, but did not want to leave him alone, and said, "Make yourself a woman from a tree."

Sekume made himself a woman and she walked and he called her *Mbongwe*.

When Nzame made Sekume and Mbongwe he made them in two parts, an outer part called Gnoul the body, and the other which lives in the body, called Nsissim.

Nsissim is that which produces the shadow, Nsissim is the shadow—it is the same thing. It is Nsissim who makes Gnoul live. Nsissim goes away when man dies, but Nsissim does not die. Do you know where he lives? He lives in the eye. The little shining point you see in the middle, that is Nsissim.

Stars above
Fire below
Coal in the hearth
The soul in the eye
Cloud smoke and death.

Sekume and Mbongwe lived happily on earth and had many children. But Fam, the first man, was imprisoned by God under the earth. With a large stone he blocked the entrance. But the malicious Fam tunnelled at the earth for a long time, and one day, at last, he was outside! Who had taken his place? The new man. Fam was furious with him. Now he hides in the forest to kill them, under the water to capsize their boats.

Remain silent,
Fam is listening,
To bring misfortune;
Remain silent.

CHAPTER 2

Cabeza de Vaca Survives America

"I walked lost and naked through many and very strange lands"

Everyone knows that 1492 was a watershed in history: In that year, Spain completed the *reconquista* (reconquest) of the Iberian Peninsula, driving out the last Moorish rulers and ending a struggle that had been going on since Muslims came over from North Africa in 711. It was also in 1492 that an Italian mariner named Christopher Columbus, sailing under the Spanish flag, returned from lands beyond the western horizon—lands he thought were part of Asia—with six natives, a flock of parrots, an iguana, and "a pile of gold."[1] At the time, the voyage seemed less momentous than the *reconquista*. One was a wished-for and fought-for crusade of liberation from rule by foreigners of a different faith, a dream that had taken almost eight centuries to come true; the other was one more in a series of journeys that for decades had taken Spanish, Portuguese, and other Europeans out into the Atlantic Ocean (where they found the Canary Islands and the Azores) and down the west coast of Africa.

Placing Columbus below reconquest on the scale of importance helps upset common assumptions about historical significance and sows some of the "constructive confusion" mentioned in this volume's Introduction. To be sure, the Columbian expedition set in motion a long chain of events that ultimately led, among other things, to the creation of the United States of America almost three hundred years later. But for nearly all of those three centuries, founding a new nation in North America was far from anyone's mind. Indeed, North America itself sat on the margins—not at the center—of a wider field of enterprise that included all of the African, American, and European peoples living along Atlantic shores. It could even be argued that Columbus's Spanish successors found North America a disappointment: Seeking gold, they were more likely to find mosquitoes; seeking souls for Christ, they often found indifferent, even hostile natives; seeking a passage to the wealth and wonders of the Far East, they found forbidding forests, trackless deserts, and endless mountains. It is no coincidence that, when the English set out to imitate the Spanish overseas enterprise and began looking westward, they planted colonies at Roanoke, Jamestown, and Plymouth, territory Spaniards had little use for, calling it "the frozen north" and concluding *no hay all de oro* ("there is no gold there").[2]

The Spanish ventures that yielded these conclusions about climate and resources serve to undermine common assumptions in another way by calling into question the conventional wisdom about when "American history" begins. Accustomed to considering Jamestown's 1607 founding "the Birth of America," it is easy to forget that in the 1520s Spanish navigators were sailing along the coast as far north as modern Maine (and up the Pacific coast, too), in the 1530s and 1540s Spanish explorers swept through the Southeast and Southwest, in 1565 Spanish settlers founded San Agustín (Saint Augustine) in Florida, and in 1570 Spanish missionaries ventured to Bahía de Santa Maria (Chesapeake Bay) to establish a short-lived outpost in the very neighborhood where Captain John Smith and the rest came ashore a generation later.[3] Early English colonists, so central to America's story, were not in fact the founders of a new nation, not even lead actors in the opening of the American pageant; latecomers to the Europeans' "New World," they were bit players tucked away in what most considered a remote corner of the Atlantic World.

No volume devoted to U.S. history can even begin to do justice to the Spanish enterprise in the Americas (or to the Spanish influence on North American history and culture). Hernán Cortés conquering the Aztecs of Mexico in 1521 and Francisco Pizarro toppling the Incan Empire in Peru a decade later are only the most famous (and infamous) episodes in a saga full of high ideals and low cunning, courage and cowardice, cruelty and kindness, greed and self-sacrifice. But the *Relación* (Account) by one Spaniard from that era, Álvar Núñez Cabeza de Vaca (1485–92 to 1559[?]), can at least offer a sense of the Spanish experience in North America more than fifty years before the English first tried their luck there by planting the ill-fated Roanoke colony in 1585 (Chapter 3). Called "a document of inestimable value" that "is one of the most remarkable in the history of the New World," Cabeza de Vaca's chronicle of his American adventures and misadventures, first published in 1542, is at once engaging and illuminating, intersecting as it does with themes that recur throughout *American Conversations*.[4]

At the beginning of his book, Cabeza de Vaca fretted that what he had to say about his ten-year American odyssey might be "very difficult for some to believe," and no wonder, for it is an incredible tale. The story began in June 1527 when several hundred men, armed with a royal charter and led by the veteran *conquistador* Pánfilo de Narváez, left Spain bound for America. Their mission: officially, to "discover and conquer and settle" *La Florida*, then defined as all of the land north of New Spain (Mexico) stretching from the Atlantic to the Pacific; unofficially, to track down rumors of "fresh Mexicos" to the north where they could find fame and fortune as Cortés had done.[5] Spending the winter in the Spanish colonies of Española (Haiti and the Dominican Republic today) and Cuba, the would-be *conquistadores* finally landed on the west coast of Florida, probably near modern Tampa Bay, in April 1528.

Things soon went wrong. Food was scarce. The natives, veterans of unhappy run-ins with Spanish explorers and slave raiders, were usually unfriendly. Narváez— called "cruel and stupid" by someone at the time and "the most incompetent of all who sailed for Spain" by scholars since—left his ships and the shore to march inland up the peninsula in search of gold and silver.[6] Finding none, he and his men returned to the coast and built rafts (the fleet had left), hoping to reach New Spain, lying somewhere across the gulf. After drifting along the shore for weeks, a handful of them—including Cabeza de Vaca, a royal official—washed up on the Texas coast near modern Galveston Bay.

Their troubles were just beginning. Over the next seven years—most of them on his own among various native groups—Cabeza de Vaca fought hunger, thirst, and hostility in a harsh, unforgiving world. Sometimes a captive, sometimes a merchant, his most spectacular (and, to some readers, his least credible) occupation was as a medicine man. At last, having met up with three other survivors of the Narváez disaster—including a slave named Estevanico, a Christian "Arabic-speaking black man" from Azamor, a city on the northwest coast of Africa—in the summer of 1535 Cabeza de Vaca headed west, accompanied (and guided) by natives, a journey that ended the following spring when they crossed paths with Spanish soldiers on New Spain's northwestern frontier.[7] Seeing him approach, his countrymen could not believe their eyes: "They remained looking at me a long time," he wrote, "so astonished that they neither spoke to me nor managed to ask me anything."

These were only the first of many who would be astonished by the man and his story. Arriving in Mexico City that summer, Cabeza de Vaca and his companions caused "a sensation"; their tantalizing information about the lands and peoples to the north helped inspire the 1540–1542 *entrada* (entry) into what is now the American Southwest by Francisco Vázquez de Coronado.[8] Back in Spain by late 1537 (the other three stayed in New Spain), the survivor's appearance at the royal court again created a stir, firing men's imaginations about *La Florida*. Hernando de Soto's own journey through southeastern North America (1539–1543) was at that very time and place in the planning stages, and Cabeza de Vaca's startling account meant that eager fortune-seekers had to be turned away because the expedition's ships simply could not carry them all.[9]

Though he had an extraordinary experience from 1527 to 1537, Álvar Núñez Cabeza de Vaca was until then in many respects an ordinary man—or at least an ordinary nobleman (*hidalgo* or *caballero*) of middling rank. His values and outlook were forged in a crucible of military prowess, deep piety, advancing the family fortunes through land, trade, and tribute, and honoring the family name. We might consider his last name (*Cow's Head*) comical, but he was proud to be descended from what an early historian called a "noble and ancient house," so proud indeed that on a 1540 journey to South America he carried with him a copy of his family tree to bolster his credentials.[10] Growing up in the southern Spanish town of Jerez de la Frontera (Jerez of the Frontier), he would have known firsthand of the powerful Muslim presence there and of the *reconquista*, for his father and his grandfather had fought in the ongoing battle against Moors in both Spain and North Africa.[11] Once he came of age, Cabeza de Vaca followed in their footsteps, fighting for Spain in Italy and helping to crush a rebellion at home. Married around 1520, as he entered his thirties he found himself, like many others of his station, "rich in historical reputation but relatively poor in material means."[12] Perhaps the lands across the Atlantic, source of so many glittering tales of glory and gold, would add luster to the family name and riches to the family coffers.

In shifting his sights from the Mediterranean to the Atlantic, from Moors to Native Americans, Cabeza de Vaca had plenty of company. Having fought for centuries in their god's name against "infidels" close to home, it was easy enough for the Spanish to think of America as a new front in a long crusade to spread the Christian gospel and establish, as the Bible commanded, "dominion...over all the earth" (Chapter 1). The very fact that 1492 saw *both* the expulsion of the Muslims from Iberia *and* Columbus's return with news of a whole new world made America seem literally heaven-sent; apparently God intended that Spaniards carry on the glorious campaign against darkness. As if this were not divine sanction enough, in 1493 Pope Alexander VI (a Spaniard), "by the authority of the Almighty God," proclaimed that he "gave" these new lands to the Spanish crown.[13] Cabeza de Vaca's own grandfather had conquered and governed one of the Canary Islands, a stepping-stone to America, in the 1480s. Thus, the grandson was not likely to question—at least not at the start of his journey—prevailing theological, cultural, and territorial imperatives. He would have agreed wholeheartedly with another *conquistador* who wrote: "Spaniards had left Europe 'to serve God and his Majesty, to give light to those who were in the darkness and to grow rich as all men desire to do.' "[14]

Such, at least, was the dream. What Cabeza de Vaca found instead was a nightmare. A decade later he "came away naked," with nothing tangible to show for his ordeal: not gold, not land, not glory. What he did have, though, was a good story, and after returning to Spain he wrote that story down. His audience in this version, as he stated at the outset, was one man: the "Holy, Imperial, Catholic Majesty," Charles V. His purpose, less explicit, was also specific: to convince Charles that he deserved another chance, in the form of a commission to command his own expedition to the New World. In a sense, then, when he sat down to write this *Relación*, Cabeza de Vaca was like a job applicant compelled to explain why his last assignment had been a disaster while also attesting to his ability to handle the responsibilities of command and conversion. As you read the excerpt below, consider how this audience and this agenda might have shaped the *Relación*.

In 1540, Cabeza de Vaca got his wish: A Crown commission as governor of Rio de la Plata in South America (modern Paraguay). Though this second American adventure was different from the first, it was no less disastrous: In 1544, he was arrested and sent back to Spain in irons to stand trial on charges of theft, abuse of office, mistreatment of natives, and replacing the royal coat of arms with his own while proclaiming, "I am the prince and master of this land!"[15] Cabeza de Vaca spent the next decade in trials and appeals; in 1555, he published *Relación y comentarios* on both of his American expeditions in order to reach a wide audience and to give his side of the story. While there are hints of defeat and despair—in 1546, he said that he "was poor and lost and bankrupt," and a year later one who met him found him "impoverished and prematurely aged"—there is also evidence that the old adventurer died around 1559 with his honor intact and his fascination with "the wondrous world of the Indies" undiminished, that he was "spared of bitterness and immune to defeat."[16]

If Cabeza de Vaca never found fame or fortune in his New World, he returned with something perhaps even more valuable: the *Relación*. Largely forgotten for centuries, recently this remarkable saga has become popular, appearing in many editions (and many different English translations) as well as inspiring films and radio dramas, poems and novels in Spain, Latin America, and the United States. Some of the appeal can be traced to the account's sheer novelty: He was the first European to cross the continent and live to tell about it, the first to report on bison, armadillos, and possums, one of the first to write of American natives with insight and sympathy. But some, too, lies in the author's talent for "drama" and "suspense," along with his "vivid descriptions, personal tone[,] and down-to-earth style."[17] In an age fascinated by such experiences (think of the Tom Hanks film *Castaway* or the television show *Lost*), Cabeza de Vaca's account strikes a powerful chord.

Readers of *American Conversations* will find, and forge, still other connections with the *Relación*. The account of Native Americans here can be compared with images of them drawn at Roanoke (Chapter 3) and with Mary Rowlandson's recollections of her time as a captive (Chapter 4). More generally, Cabeza de Vaca's efforts to find his way through strange lands and negotiate with strange peoples, his attempt to make sense of an alien world by way of "cultural translation"—putting the foreign into familiar categories and terms—would be common through the centuries (and the chapters) ahead. Perhaps most important, his "personal testimony," which can be set alongside that of many others in this volume, is, to the scholars Rolena Adorno and Michael Pautz, "most 'American' of all": "the firsthand account that attests to traversing the unknown and forging the new—the 'self-making' of new homelands, new identities, and new futures—is," they write, "the quintessence of the American experience."[18] Certainly it is a central theme of *American Conversations*.

But perhaps the greatest source of fascination is the text's enduring mystery. Despite all of the attention, the tale remains open to considerable debate. What route did he take? What native peoples did he encounter? What were their views of him? Was he really a slave? How can we explain the miraculous cures he performed? How far did he depart from other *conquistadores* in his views of Indians? Last and not least, is it true? The search for answers brings people back again and again to Cabeza de Vaca and to his astonishing story.

Questions for Consideration and Conversation

1. Some readers have found Cabeza de Vaca's account quite literally incredible, as in *not* believable. Do you agree? Are there parts of it that ring true, and parts that do not?

2. Consider carefully the views of natives expressed here. How well did the author understand native culture? How much did he respect native culture?

3. Is it fair to say that Cabeza de Vaca truly "went native," that he shed his Spanish heritage, point of view, and aspirations?

4. Some scholars believe that accounts such as this one are so biased by European preconceptions and misconceptions that they can tell us little or nothing about native

cultures and customs. Others disagree, insisting that, read with care and an effort to filter out biases and blind spots, such texts can indeed reveal much about the Indians' world. Which side of this argument gets more support from Cabeza de Vaca?

5. What might a particular native group's account of Cabeza de Vaca and his companions have been like, if one had survived?

6. Scholars observe that Cabeza de Vaca's experiences inspired two major expeditions in the years following his return: Francisco de Coronado's through the Southwest and Hernando De Soto's through the Southeast. Why would anyone, having read or heard about Cabeza de Vaca's experiences, want to follow in his footsteps?

Endnotes

1. Lynn V. Foster, *A Brief History of Mexico*, revised ed. (New York, 2004), 48.
2. David J. Weber, *The Spanish Frontier in North America* (New Haven, 1992), 38.
3. For Spanish activities, see ibid., 6, 36–37, 60–64, 71–72.
4. Martin A. Favata and José B. Fernández, ed. and trans., *The Account: Álvar Núñez Cabeza De Vaca's* Relación: *An Annotated Translation* (Houston, 1993), 11.
5. Rolena Adorno and Patrick Charles Pautz, trans. and ed., *The Narrative of Cabeza de Vaca* (Lincoln, NE, 2003), 7 ("discover"); David Beers Quinn, *North America from Earliest Discovery to First Settlements: The Norse Voyages to 1612* (New York, 1977), 138 ("fresh Mexicos").
6. Jerald T. Milanich and Susan Milbrath, eds., *First Encounters: Spanish Explorations in the Caribbean and the United States, 1492–1570*, Ripley P. Bullen Monographs in Anthropology and History, Number 9 (Gainesville, FL, 1989), 16 ("cruel"); Samuel Eliot Morison, quoted in Rochelle A. Marrinan, John F. Scarry, and Rhonda L. Majors, "The Prelude to De Soto: The Expedition of Pánfilo de Narváez," in David Hurst Thomas, ed., *Columbian Consequences*, Vol. II, *Archaeological and Historical Perspectives on the Spanish Borderlands East* (Washington, DC, 1990), 71 ("incompetent").
7. The translation of Cabeza de Vaca's description of Estevanico is from Adorno and Pautz, trans. and ed., *Álvar Núñez Cabeza de Vaca: His Account, His Life, and the Expedition of Pánfilo de Narváez*, 3 vols. (Lincoln, NE, 1999), I, 416.
8. Carl Ortwin Sauer, *Sixteenth Century North America: The Land and the People as Seen by the Europeans* (Berkeley, 1971), 125.
9. Adorno and Pautz, trans. and ed., *Cabeza de Vaca*, III, 118.
10. Ibid., I, 296, 323–24 (Vera family tree), 321 ("noble and ancient").
11. Ibid., 330, 340–42.
12. Ibid., 342. All of the biographical information is taken from this volume, 293–413.
13. Weber, *Spanish Frontier*, 19, 21.
14. Ibid., 23.
15. Adorno and Pautz, trans. and ed., *Cabeza de Vaca*, I, 396.
16. Enrique Pupo-Walker, "Introduction," in Pupo-Walker, ed., *Castaways: The Narrative of Alvar Núñez Cabeza de Vaca*, trans. Frances M. López-Morillas (Berkeley, 1993), xxiv ("poor," "aged"); Adorno and Pautz, trans. and ed., *Cabeza de Vaca*, I, 406 ("Indies," "immune").
17. Favata and Fernández, ed. and trans., *The Account*, 16.
18. Adorno and Pautz, trans. and ed., *Narrative of Cabeza de Vaca*, 21, 35.

ÁLVAR NÚÑEZ CABEZA DE VACA, *THE NARRATIVE OF CABEZA DE VACA* (1542)

Source: Álvar Núñez Cabeza de Vaca, *The Narrative of Cabeza de Vaca*, ed. and trans. Rolena Adorno and Patrick Charles Pautz. Lincoln: University of Nebraska Press, 2003.

Holy, Imperial, Catholic Majesty,

Among as many princes as we know there have been in the world, I think none could be found whom men have tried to serve with truer will or greater diligence and desire than we see men honoring Your Majesty today. It is quite evident that this is not without great cause and reason....But even when the desire and will of all makes them equal in this matter [of honoring you]..., there is a very great disparity not caused by the shortcoming of any one of them, but only by fortune, or more certainly through no fault of one's own, but only by the will and judgment of God, where it happens that one may come away with more notable services than he expected, while to another everything occurs so to the contrary that he cannot demonstrate any greater witness to his intention than his diligence, and even this is sometimes so obscured that it cannot make itself evident. For myself I can say that on the expedition that by command of Your Majesty I made to the [North American] mainland, well I thought that my deeds and services would be as illustrious and self-evident as those of my ancestors, and that I would not have any need to speak in order to be counted among those who with complete fidelity and great solicitude administer and carry out the mandates of Your Majesty, and whom you favor. But since neither my counsel nor diligence prevailed in order that the endeavor upon which we were embarked be completed as service to Your Majesty, and since no expedition of as many as have gone to those lands ever saw itself in such grave dangers or had such a wretched and disastrous end as that which God permitted us to suffer on account of our sins, I had no opportunity to perform greater service than this, which is to bring to Your Majesty an account of all that I was able to observe and learn in the nine years that I walked lost and naked through many and very strange lands, as much regarding the locations of the lands and provinces and the distances among them, as with respect to the foodstuffs and animals that are produced in them, and the diverse customs of many and very barbarous peoples with whom I conversed and lived, plus all the other particularities that I could come to know and understand, so that in some manner Your Majesty may be served. Because although the hope that I had of coming out from among them was always very little, my care and effort to remember everything in detail was always very great. This I did so that if at some time our Lord God should wish to bring me to the place where I am now, I would be able to bear witness to my will and serve Your Majesty, inasmuch as the account of it all is, in my opinion, information not trivial for those who in your name might go to conquer those lands and at the same time bring them to knowledge of the true faith and the true Lord and service to Your Majesty. I wrote all this with such sure knowledge that although some very novel things may be read in it, very difficult for some to believe, they can absolutely give them credence and be assured that I am in everything brief rather than lengthy, and it will suffice for this purpose to have offered it to Your Majesty as such, for which I ask that it be received in the name of service, because this alone is what a man who came away naked could carry out with him.…

On the seventeenth day of the month of June 1527, Governor Pánfilo de Narváez, with the authority and mandate of Your Majesty, departed…to conquer and govern the provinces that are found from the Río de las Palmas [the northernmost outpost of New Spain at the time, on the Mexican coast south of the Rio Grande River] to the cape of *Florida*, which are on the mainland. And the fleet that he led was composed of five ships, in which there went about six hundred men.…

[Having wintered on Española and Cuba,] we passed over to the coast of *Florida*, and came to land on Tuesday, the twelfth of April [1528].…And on Maundy Thursday we anchored on the same coast at the mouth of a bay, at the back of which we saw certain houses and habitations of Indians.

On this same day the comptroller [a financial officer] Alonso Enríquez went onto an island in the same bay. And he called to the Indians, who came and were with him a considerable amount of time, and by means of exchange they gave him fish and some pieces of venison. The following day, which was Good Friday, the governor disembarked with as many people as he could get into rowboats that the ships carried. And when we arrived at the Indians' *buhíos*, or houses, that we had seen, we found them abandoned and empty because the people had gone away that night in their canoes. One of those *buhíos* was so big that more than three hundred people could fit in it. The others were smaller, and we found a rattle of gold there among the nets. The next day the governor raised the standard on Your Majesty's behalf and took possession of the land in Your royal name and presented his orders and was obeyed just as Your Majesty commanded.…The next day the Indians from the village came to us. And although they spoke to us, since we did not have an interpreter we did not understand them. But they made many signs and threatening gestures to us and it seemed to us that they were telling us to leave the land, and with this they parted from us without producing any confrontation.…

[W]e followed along the coast of the bay…and, having gone four leagues [about twelve miles], we took four Indians. And we showed them maize [corn] to see if they recognized it, because up to that point we had not seen any sign of it. They told us that they would take us to where it could be found. And thus they took us to their village, which is at the back of the bay near there and in which they showed us a little maize that was not yet ready to harvest. There we found many crates belonging to Castilian merchants, and in each one of them was the body of a dead man, and the bodies were covered with deer hides. This seems to the [expedition's] commissary to be a type of idolatry, and he burned the crates with the bodies in them. We also found pieces of linen cloth and plumes that seemed to be from New Spain. In addition, we found samples of gold. By means of signs we asked the Indians where those things had come from. They indicated to us by gestures that very far away from there there was a province called Apalachen, in which there was much gold, and they made signs to indicate that there were very great quantities of everything we held in esteem....And taking those Indians as guides we departed from there....

Upon arriving within sight of Apalachen, the governor ordered that I take nine horsemen and fifty foot soldiers and enter the village. And thus the inspector and I attacked it. And having entered it, we found only women and children, since at that time the men were not in the village. But a little while later, as we walked through it, they rushed in and began to attack, shooting us with arrows. And they killed the inspector's horse, but in the end they fled and left us alone. There we found a great quantity of maize that was ready to be harvested, as well as much that they had dried and stored. We found many deer hides and among them some small woven mantles of poor quality with which the women partially cover their bodies. They had many vessels for grinding maize. In the village there were forty small houses, built low to the ground and in protected places, out of fear of the great tempests that commonly occur with great frequency in that land. The construction is of grass....

For the most part, the land from where we disembarked up to this village and province of Apalachen is flat, the ground being composed of hard, firm sand. Throughout the entire land there are very large trees and open woods where there are walnut trees, and laurels..., [and] palmettos of the type commonly found in Castile....There are many fields of maize in this province. And the houses are scattered about the countryside in the same manner as those of the Gelves [a Mediterranean island]. The animals that we saw in it are deer of three types, rabbits and hares, bears and lions, and other wild beasts, among which we saw an animal that carries its young in a pouch in its belly, and all the while the offspring are small, they carry them there until they know how to forage for food, and if by chance they are searching for food and human beings come upon them, the mother does not flee until she has gathered them up in her pouch. In that region it is very cold. There are many good pastures for grazing cattle....

Two days after we arrived in Apalachen, the Indians who had fled from there came to see us in peace, asking us for their women and children. And we gave them to them, except that the governor kept with him a cacique [chief] of theirs, which was the cause of their being greatly offended. And later, the next day, they returned to make war. And they attacked us with so much skill and swiftness that they successfully set fire to the houses in which we were lodged. But as we came out, they fled and took to the lagoons that were nearby. And because of this and the great fields of maize in the area, we could not do them any harm except to the one whom we killed....

[The expedition marches back to the coast, but their ships are nowhere to be found.] Having...seen the little prospect there was for going forward [overland], because there was no way that would allow us to proceed, and even if there had been, the men could [not] have gone on because most of them were ill and in such a state that there were few by whom any progress could have been made. I refrain here from telling this at greater length because each one can imagine for himself what could happen in a land so strange and so poor and so lacking in every single thing that it seemed impossible either to be in it or to escape from it....And having considered these and many other obstacles, and having tried many solutions, we decided upon one [plan] very difficult to put into effect, which was to build ships in which we could leave. To everyone it seemed impossible, because we did not know how to make them nor were there tools, nor iron, nor a forge, nor...ropes, nor finally any single thing of all those that are necessary, nor was there anyone who knew anything about carrying this out, and above all there was nothing to eat while they were being constructed, nor were there adequate men to perform the tasks we had mentioned. And considering all this, we agreed to think about it for a little longer, and the conversation ceased for that day, and each one went off, entrusting himself to our Lord God to direct him where he might be best served. The next day God ordained that a member of the company came, saying that he would make some tubes of wood, and with some deerskins some bellows would be made. And since we were in such straits that anything that had some semblance of a solution seemed to us a good thing, we said that he should set to the task. And we agreed to make the nails and saws and axes and other tools...from the stirrups and spurs and crossbows and other iron objects that we had. And we determined that, in order to provide means of sustenance during the period in which this was to be carried out, four incursions would be made into Aute [a nearby native village] with all the horses and people well enough to take part, and that every third day a horse would be killed to be distributed among those who were working on building the ships and those who were sick. The forays were made..., and in them up to four hundred *fanegas* of maize [about 640 bushels] were seized, although not without fights and skirmishes with the Indians. We had many palmettos gathered in order to make use of their fibers and coverings, twisting and preparing them to use...for the rafts, the construction of which was begun by the only carpenter in the company....[A]fter loading the provisions and clothing, the rafts rode so low that only a *xeme* [a few inches] of their sides showed above water, and in addition to this, we were so crowded that we could not even move. And so greatly can necessity prevail that it made us risk going in this manner and placing ourselves in a sea so treacherous, and without any one of us who went having any knowledge of the art of navigation....

[Boarding these vessels on September 22, the men continue their] journey along the coast in the direction of the Río de Palmas, each day our hunger and thirst increasing, because the provisions were very few and nearly exhausted and our water was gone because the vessels that we had made from the legs of the horses later rotted and were of no use whatsoever....

[Vaca's oarsmen have trouble keeping up with Narváez, for] the governor carried [on his raft] the healthiest and most robust men among us....I asked him if he would allow me to attach my raft to his so that I might be able to keep up with him....He answered me that...each one should do whatever seemed best to him in order to save his own life, [and] that he intended to do it. And saying this he veered away with his raft [and was never seen or heard from again]....

[On November 6, having reached the vicinity of modern Galveston, Texas, the men on Vaca's raft, seeing] themselves near land,...began to leave the raft half walking, half crawling....Those of us who escaped [were] naked as the day we were born and [we had] lost everything we carried with us....And since it was November and the cold very great, we, so thin that with little difficulty our bones could be counted, appeared like the figure of death itself....God granted that while looking for firebrands from the fire that we had built there, we discovered a flame with which we made great bonfires. And thus we were beseeching our Lord for mercy and the pardon of our sins, shedding many tears....The Indians, on seeing the disaster that had befallen us and the disaster that was upon us with so much misfortune and misery, sat down among us. And with the great grief and pity they felt on seeing us in such a state, they all began to weep loudly and so sincerely that

they could be heard a great distance away. And this lasted more than half an hour, and truly, to see that these men, so lacking in reason and so crude in the manner of brutes, grieved so much for us, increased in me and in others of our company even more the magnitude of our suffering and the estimation of our misfortune. When this weeping was somewhat calmed, I asked the Christians and said that, if it seemed acceptable to them, I would ask those Indians to take us to their houses. And some of them [the Spaniards] who had been in New Spain replied that we should not speak of it, because if they took us to their houses, they would sacrifice us to their idols. But realizing that there was no other solution, and that by any other course death was closer and more certain, I did not heed their words, but rather beseeched the Indians to take us to their houses....[C]arrying us by clutching us tightly and making great haste, we went to their houses. And because of the great cold, and fearing that on the road some one of us might fall unconscious and die, they made provision for four or five very great bonfires placed at intervals, and at each one they warmed us; and when they saw that we had regained some strength and warmth, they carried us to the next one, so rapidly that they almost did not let our feet touch the ground. And in this manner we went to their houses, where we found that they had prepared a house for us and many fires in it. And an hour after we arrived, they began to dance and make a great celebration that lasted all night long, although for us there was neither rejoicing nor sleep, as we were awaiting the moment when they would sacrifice us. And in the morning they again gave us fish and roots and treated us so well that we were somewhat reassured, and we lost some of our fear of being sacrificed....

[F]ive men [other survivors] who were in Xamho on the coast came to such dire need that they ate one another until only one remained, who because he was alone, had no one to eat him....The Indians became very upset because of this and it produced such a great scandal among them....To this island we gave the name Malhado ["Isle of Ill Fate"]. The people we found there are large and well proportioned. They have no weapons other than bows and arrows, which they employ with great skill. The men have one pierced nipple and some have both pierced. And through the hole they make, they wear a reed up to two and a half spans long and as thick as two fingers. They also have their lower lip pierced and a piece of reed as thin as half a finger placed in it. The women are given to hard work. They inhabit this island from

October to the end of February. They sustain themselves on…roots…, which they dig out from under water.…These people love their children more and treat them better than any other people in the world. And when it happens that one of their children dies, the parents and the relatives and all the rest of the people weep. And the weeping lasts a whole year, that is, each day in the morning before sunrise, first the parents begin to weep, and after this the entire community also weeps. And they do this at noon, and at daybreak. And after a year of mourning has passed, they perform the honors of the dead and wash and cleanse themselves of the ashes they wear. They mourn all the dead in this manner, except for the elderly, to whom they pay no attention, because they say they have lived past their time, and from them no gain is to be had, rather, they occupy land and deprive the children of their share of the food. Their custom is to bury their dead, except those among them who are physicians, whose remains they burn. And while the fire burns, they all dance and make a great celebration. And afterward they pulverize the bones. And a year later, upon paying homage to them, they all lacerate themselves, and to the relatives they give the powdered bones so that they may drink them in water.…

On that island…, they tried to make us physicians without examining us or asking us for our titles, because they cure illnesses by blowing on the sick person, and with that breath of air and their hands they expel the disease from him. And they demanded that we do the same and make ourselves useful. We laughed about this, saying that it was a mockery and that we did not know how to cure. And because of this, they took away our food until we did as they told us. And seeing our resistance, an Indian told me that I didn't know what I was saying when I said that what he knew how to do would do no good, because the stones and other things that the fields produce have powers, and that he, by placing a hot stone on the abdomen, restored health and removed pain, and that it was certain that we, because we were men, had greater virtue and capacity. In short, we found ourselves in such need that we had to do it.…The manner in which they perform cures is as follows: on becoming sick, they call a physician and after being cured they not only give him everything they possess, but they also seek things to give him from among their relatives. What the physician does is to make some incisions where the sick person has pain, and then sucks all around them. They perform cauterizations with fire, which is a thing among them considered

to be very effective, and I have tried it and it turned out well for me. And after this, they blow upon the area that hurts, and with this they believe that they have removed the malady. The manner in which we performed cures was by making the sign of the cross over them and blowing on them, and praying a Pater Noster ["Our Father," the Lord's Prayer] and an Ave Maria ["Hail Mary"], and as best we could, beseeching our Lord God that he grant them health and move them to treat us well. Our Lord God in his mercy willed that all those on whose behalf we made supplication, after we had made the sign of the cross over them, said to the others that they were restored and healthy, and on account of this they treated us well, and refrained from eating in order to give their food to us, and they gave us skins and other things.…

All the people of this land go about naked. Only the women cover part of their bodies with a type of fiber that grows on trees. The young women cover themselves with deerskins. They are people who freely share what they have with one another. There is no lord among them. All who are of a single lineage band together. On the island live people of two different languages: some are called of Capoques, and the others, of Han. They have a custom that, when they know one another and meet from time to time, before they speak they weep for half an hour, and when this is done, the one who receives the visit rises first and gives the other everything he possesses, and the other receives it. And a little while later he goes away with it, and it even happens sometimes that after receiving the goods, they part without speaking a single word.…

[After more than a year with these natives, Vaca—tired of hard work and "bad treatment"—leaves them for a group on the mainland, where he spends six years as a merchant, traveling about. To Vaca and another Spaniard he met comes word that] farther ahead there were three men like us, and they told us their names. And asking them about the rest of them [the other survivors of the expedition], they replied to us that they had all died of cold and hunger, and that those Indians ahead had, for their own amusement, killed [three other Spaniards], merely because they had passed from one house to another, and that the neighboring Indians, with whom Captain [Andrés] Dorantes now was, because of a dream they had dreamed, had killed [Hernando de] Esquivel and Méndez. We asked them about the condition of the ones who were alive. They told us they were very ill treated, because the boys and other Indians, who are among them very idle and cruel, kicked and slapped and cudgeled them, and that this was the life they had among them....We gave many thanks to God upon finding ourselves reunited, and this day was one of the days of greatest pleasure that we have had in our lives. And arriving to where [Captain Alonso del] Castillo [Maldonado] was, they asked me what my intentions were. I told him that my purpose was to go to the land of Christians and that on this path and pursuit I was embarked....[T]hey advised me that by no means was I to tell the Indians nor give them reason to suspect that I wanted to go on ahead, because then they would kill me, and that for this purpose it was necessary that I remain with them for six months, which was the time in which those Indians would go to another land to eat prickly pears..., because at the time that they harvested them, other Indians from farther on would come to them, bringing bows to trade and exchange with them, and that when they returned, we would flee from our Indians and return with them. With this plan I remained there, and they gave me as a slave to an Indian with whom Dorantes was staying....

And the other Christians remained with those Indians, who intimidated them in order to more easily make them their slaves, although being in their service they were treated worse than slaves or men of any fate had ever been, because of the six of them, not content to slap them and strike them and pull out their beards for their amusement, for the mere reason of going from one house to another they killed three....All these people are archers and well built....Their sustenance is chiefly roots....[T]heir hunger [is] so great that they eat spiders and ant eggs and worms and lizards and salamanders and snakes and vipers that kill men when they strike, and they eat earth and wood and everything that they can find and deer excrement and other things that I refrain from mentioning; and I believe assuredly that if in that land there were stones they would eat them. They keep the bones of the fish they eat and of the snakes and other things in order to grind up everything afterward and eat the powder it produces....They are a very happy people; in spite of the great hunger they have, they do not on that account fail to dance or to make their celebrations and *areitos* [ritual song and dance]....Many times when we were with these people, we went three or four days without eating, because nothing was available. To cheer us up, they told us that we should not be sad, because soon there would be prickly pears, and we would eat many and drink of their juice, and our bellies would be very big, and we would be very content and happy and without any hunger whatsoever. And from the time that they told us this until the prickly pears were ready to eat, was five or six months....We

found throughout the land a very great quantity of mosquitoes of three types that are very bad and vexacious, and all the rest of the summer they exhausted us. And in order to defend ourselves from them, we made around the edge of the group great bonfires of rotted and wet wood that would not burn but rather make smoke. And this defense gave us yet another hardship, because all night long we did nothing but weep from the smoke that got in our eyes, and beyond this the many fires caused us to be very hot, and we would go to sleep on the shore. And if on occasion we were able to sleep, they would remind us with blows to return to light the fires....Cows [bison] sometimes range as far as here, and three times I have seen and eaten of them. And it seems to me that they are about the size of those in Spain. They have small horns like Moorish cows, and their fur is very long. Some are brown and others black, and in my opinion they have better meat and more of it than those from here [Spain]. From [the skins] of the young ones the Indians make robes to cover themselves, and from [the hides of] the mature animals they make shoes and shields. These cows come from the north forward through the land to the coast of *Florida* and they extend over the land for more than four hundred leagues....

[Their plan to flee is delayed a year when the natives unexpectedly separated them, but at last Vaca and the others make their escape.] Throughout the land there are many and very beautiful grazing lands and good pastures for cattle, and it seems to me that it would be very productive land if it were worked and inhabited by men of reason....

Pursuing our course...with great fear that the Indians would follow us, we saw some spires of smoke. And going toward them,...we saw an Indian who, as he saw that we were coming toward him, fled....We sent the black man after him. And since he saw that he was coming alone, he waited for him. The black man told him that we were going to look for those people who were making those spires of smoke. He responded that the houses were near there, and that he would guide us there....And he ran on ahead to give notice that we were coming. And at sunset we saw the houses....And they lodged Dorantes and the black man in the house of a physician, and Castillo and me in that of others....And although they are of another nation and language, they understand the language of the ones we were with previously....[T]hey already had news of us and about how we were curing and about the wonders that our Lord was working through us, which...were truly great, opening roads for us through a land so deserted, bringing us people where many times there were none, and liberating us from so many dangers and not permitting us to be killed, and sustaining us through so much hunger, and inspiring these people to treat us well....

[The party stayed with these natives from October 1534 to August 1535.] [S]ince throughout the land nothing was talked about except the mysteries that God our Lord worked through us, people came from many places to seek us out so that we could cure them....[When another group asked,] the Indians told me that I should go to cure them because they held me in esteem, and they remembered that I had cured them at the nut-gathering grounds, and because of that, they had given us nuts and hides, and this had happened when I came to join the Christians. And thus I had to go with them, and Dorantes and Estevanico went with me. And when I arrived near their huts, I saw the sick man whom we were going to cure, who was dead, because there were many people around him weeping and his house was undone, which is the sign that the owner is dead. And thus when I arrived, I found the Indian, his eyes rolled back in his head, and without any pulse, and with all the signs of death; so it seemed to me, and Dorantes said the same. I removed a mat that he had on top of him, with which he was covered. And as best I could, I beseeched our Lord to be served by giving health to that man and to all the others among them who were in need. And after having made the sign of the cross and blown on him many times, they brought me his bow and they gave it to me along with a basket of crushed prickly pears. And they took me to cure many others who had sleeping sickness, and they gave me two other baskets of prickly pears, which I gave to our Indians who had come with us. And having done this, we returned to our lodgings. And our Indians, to whom I had given the prickly pears, remained there, and at nighttime they returned to their houses and said that that one who had been dead and whom I had cured in their presence had arisen revived and walked about and eaten and spoken with them, and that as many as I had cured had become well and were without fever and very happy. This caused very great wonder and fear, and in all the land they spoke of nothing else. All those to whom this report arrived came looking for us so that we could cure them and make the sign of the cross over their children....And they said that truly we were children of the sun. Until then Dorantes and the black man had not performed any cures, but on account of the great demands made on us, [the Indians] coming from many places to look for us, we all became physicians, although in boldness and daring to perform

any cure I was the most notable among them. And we never cured anyone who did not say that he was better, and they had so much confidence that they would be cured if we performed the cures, that they believed that as long as we were there, none of them would die....

I have already said how, throughout this entire land, we went about naked, and since we were not accustomed to it, like serpents we changed our skins twice a year. And with the sun and wind, there appeared on our chests and backs some very great ulcerations, which caused us very great distress on account of the large loads we carried, which were very heavy and caused the ropes to cut into the flesh of our arms. And the land is so rugged and impassable that many times when we gathered firewood in the dense thickets, when we finished taking it out we were bleeding in many places from the thorns and brambles that we encountered, for wherever they ensnared us they broke our skin....I did not have, when I saw myself in these difficulties, any other remedy or consolation but to think about the Passion of our Redeemer Jesus Christ and the blood he shed for me, and to consider how much greater had been the torment that he suffered from the thorns, than that which I had to endure at that time....

From the island of Malhado to this land all the Indians whom we saw have as a custom, from the day their wives know they are pregnant, not to sleep with them until after two years of nurturing their children, who suckle until they are twelve years old, at which time they are of an age that by themselves they know how to search for food. We asked them why they raised them in this manner, and they said that because of the great hunger in the land it happened many times, as we had seen, that they went two or three days without eating, and sometimes four; and for this reason, they let their children suckle so that in times of hunger they would not die, since even if some should survive [without it], they would end up sickly and of little strength....All these men are accustomed to leaving their wives when there is disagreement between them, and they marry again whomever they please; this occurs among the childless men, but those who have children remain with their wives and do not leave them....They are all warlike people, and they have much cunning to protect themselves from their enemies as they would have if they had been raised in Italy and in continuous war....

The Indians are more likely to make fun of crossbows and harquebuses [guns] because these weapons are ineffective against them in the flat, open areas where they roam free. They are good for enclosed areas and wetlands; but in other areas, horses are what must be used to defeat them, and are what the Indians universally fear. Whoever might have to fight against them should be advised to prevent them from perceiving weakness or greed for what they have. And as long as war lasts, they must treat them very badly, because if they know that their enemy has fear or some sort of greed, they are the people who know how to recognize the times in which to take vengeance and they take advantage of the fear of their enemies.... They see and hear more and they have sharper senses than any other men that I think there are in the world. They are great sufferers of hunger and thirst and cold, as they are more accustomed and hardened to it than others. This I have wanted to tell because, beyond the fact that all men desire to know the customs and practices of others, the ones who sometime might come to confront them should be informed about their customs and stratagems, which tend to be of no small advantage in such cases....

In the entire land they intoxicate themselves with something they smoke and they give everything they have for it. They also drink another thing, which they extract from the leaves of trees like those of an oak, and they toast it in certain vessels over the fire, and after they have it toasted, they fill the vessel with water, and thus they keep it over the fire, and when it has boiled twice, they pour it into a different vessel and they cool it with half a gourd. And when it has a great deal of foam, they drink it as hot as they can tolerate it. And from the time they take it out of the vessel until they drink it, they shout, saying, "Who wants to drink?" And when the women hear these shouts, they immediately stop without daring to move, and although they may be carrying heavy loads, they do not dare to do another thing. And if by chance one of them moves, they dishonor her and beat her with sticks and with very great rage they pour out the water that they have [prepared] for drinking. And what they have drunk they disgorge, which they do very easily and without any trouble. They give a reason for this custom: and they say that if, when they desire to drink that water, the women move from where they are when they hear the voice, through that water something bad enters their bodies, and that a little while later it makes them die. And all the while the water cooks, the vessel must remain covered. And if by chance it is uncovered and some woman passes by, they pour it out and drink no more of that water. It is yellow, and they drink it for three days without eating. And each day each one of them drinks one and a half *arrobas* [several gallons] of it. And when

the women are menstruating they do not search for food except for themselves, because no other person will eat what she brings. In the time that thus I was among these people, I saw a wicked behavior, and it is that I saw one man married to another, and these are effeminate, impotent men. And they go about covered like women, and they perform the tasks of women, and they do not use a bow, and they carry very great loads. And among these we saw many of them, thus unmanly as I say, and they are more muscular than other men and taller....

[Moving on, the party crosses the Rio Grande River,] and at sunset we arrived at a hundred houses of Indians, and before we arrived, all the people who were in them came out to receive us with so much shouting that it was a fright and vigorously slapping their thighs. They carried pierced gourds with stones inside, which is the item of highest celebration, and they do not take them out except to dance or to cure, nor does anyone but they dare to use them. And they say that those gourds have virtue and that they come from the sky, because throughout that land there are none nor do they know where they might be, but only that the rivers bring them when they flood. So great was the fear and agitation that these people experienced that with some trying to arrive more quickly than others to touch us, they crowded us so much that they nearly could have killed us. And without letting our feet touch the ground, they carried us to their houses. And they fell so much upon us and pressed us in such a manner that we went into the houses they had prepared for us. And we did not consent in any way to their making more celebrations with us that night. They spent that entire night dancing and performing *areitos* among themselves. And the next morning they brought us all the people of that village for us to touch and make the sign of the cross over them.... And after this was done, they gave many arrows to the women of the other village who had come with theirs. The next day we left there, and all the people of the village went with us. And when we arrived at other Indians we were very well received as we had been by the previous ones.... And among these people we saw a new custom, and it is that the ones who were with us took from those who came to be cured their bows and arrows and shoes and beads if they brought them. And after having taken them, they placed those people before us, so that we might cure them.... Departing from these people, we went to many other houses, and at this point another new custom commenced, and it is that receiving us very well, those who came with us began to treat the others very badly, taking their possessions and sacking their houses without leaving them a single thing. About this we were much distressed to see the bad treatment that was given to those who thus received us, and also because we feared that that practice would be or would cause some altercation and scandal among them. But since we were powerless to remedy it or to dare to punish those who did it, for the time being we had to endure it until we had more authority among them. And also the same Indians who lost their households, on seeing our sadness, consoled us by saying that we should not be grieved by that, because they were so content to have seen us that they considered that their possessions had been well employed, and that farther ahead they would be compensated by others who were very rich.... And when we arrived near the houses, all the people came out to receive us with great pleasure and festivity, and among other things, two of their physicians gave us two gourds. And from this point forward we began to carry gourds with us, and we added to our authority this ceremony, which to them is very great.... [At another town,] they gave Andrés Dorantes a large, thick, copper bell, and on it was outlined a face, and they showed that they valued it greatly. And they told them that they had obtained it from other people who lived nearby. And asking them where those people had obtained them, they told them that they had brought it from toward the north, and that there was a great deal more of it there, and it was held in great esteem. And we understood that from wherever it had come, there was metalworking and that they worked it by casting.... [A]t night we arrived at many houses that were set up along the bank of a very beautiful river. And the owners of them came halfway to meet us with their children on their backs, and they gave us many little bags of silver and others of powdered antimony [a silvery metallic element]; with this they smear their faces. And they gave us many beads and many hides of cows, and they loaded all those who came with us with some of everything they had.... And those who received us there, as soon as they had touched us, turned running toward their houses. And then they returned to us, and they did not cease running back and forth. In this way they brought us many things for our journey.... We showed them that bell that we were carrying, and they told us that in the place from which it had come, there were many deposits of that material in the ground, and that it was a thing they valued highly, and that there were permanent houses....

To these Indians we said that we wanted to go to where the sun set. And they replied to us that in that direction the people were far away. And we ordered them to send people to inform them that we were going there, and from this they excused themselves as best they could, because they were their enemies and they did not want us to go to them, but they did not dare to do anything else. And thus they sent two women, one of their own and another who was a captive of theirs. And they sent them out because women can mediate even when there is war. And we followed them and stopped in a place where it was agreed that we would wait for them, but it took them five days to return. And the Indians said that they must not have found any people. We told them to lead us toward the north. They responded in the same manner, saying that in that direction there were only people very far away, and that there was nothing to eat nor was water to be found. And despite all this, we insisted and said that we wanted to go there. And they still declined in the best way they could. And because of this we became angry. And I went one night to sleep in the country-side, apart from them, but later they went to where I was. And they were there the entire night without sleeping and with very great fear and speaking to me and telling me how terrified they were, begging us not to be angry anymore, and that even though they knew they would die on the road, they would take us wherever we wanted to go. And as we still pretended to be angry, and because their fear did not subside, a strange thing occurred, and it was that this same day many of them fell ill. And the following day eight men died. Throughout the entire land where this was known there was so much fear of us that it seemed that in seeing us they would die of fear. They begged us not to be angry nor to will that any more of them die. And they held it for certain that we were killing them by simply desiring it. And in truth this produced in us so much anxiety that it could not have been greater, because beyond seeing those who died, we feared that all of them would die or that they would abandon us out of fear, and that all the other peoples from there onward would do the same, seeing what had happened to these people. We beseeched God our Lord to remedy it. And thus all those who had been sick began to regain their health.... This was the most obedient people we found throughout this land and of the best nature. And they are generally very well disposed. When the ill had recovered, and we had already been there for three days, the women whom we had sent out arrived, saying that they had found very few people and that all had gone to the cows, since it was that season. And we ordered the ones who had been sick to remain and those who were well to go with us, and that two days' journey from there those same two women would go with two of ours to bring out people and lead them to the road to receive us. And with this, the next morning all those who were the most hardy departed with us. And after a three-day journey we stopped. And the following day Alonso del Castillo departed with the black man Estevanico, taking as guides the two women. And the one of them who was captive led them to a river that flowed between some mountains where there was a village in which her father lived. And these were the first dwellings we saw that had the semblance and appearance of houses.... And after having spoken with the Indians, at the end of three days Castillo came to where he had left us, and brought along five or six of those Indians. And he told how he had found houses of people and permanent settlement, and that those people ate frijoles [beans] and squash, and that he had seen maize. This was the thing that gladdened us more than anything else in the world, and for this we gave infinite thanks to our Lord. And he said that the black man would come with all the people of the houses to wait for us on the road near there. And for this reason we departed, and having gone a league and a half, we came upon the black man and the people who were coming to receive us, and they gave us frijoles and many squash to eat and for carrying water and robes of bison hide and other things. And because these people and those who came with us were enemies and did not get along, we took leave of the first ones, giving them what they had given us.... And from there onward, there was another new custom, that is, those who knew about our arrival did not come out to receive us on the roads like the others did, but rather we found them in their houses, and they had others made for us. And they were all seated and all had their faces turned toward the wall with their heads lowered and their hair pulled over their eyes and their possessions placed in a pile in the middle of the house....

And from here we passed through more than one hundred leagues of land, and we always found permanent houses and many stores of maize and frijoles. And they gave us many deer and robes of cotton, better than those of New Spain. They also gave us many beads and some coral that is found in the South Sea [and] many very fine turquoises that they acquire from toward the north. And finally they gave here everything they had, and to Dorantes emeralds made into arrowheads, and with these arrows they make their *areitos* and dances. And seeming to me that they were very fine, I asked them where they had obtained them. And they said they had brought

them from some very high mountains that are toward the north and they bought them in exchange for plumes and parrot feathers. And they said that there were villages of many people and very large houses there.... And among all these peoples, it was taken for certain that we came from the sky, because all the things that they do not have or do not know the origin of, they say come from the sky.... We had a great deal of authority and influence over them. And in order to conserve this we spoke to them but few times. The black man always spoke to them and informed himself about the roads we wished to travel and the villages that there were and about other things that we wanted to know. We passed through a great number and diversity of languages. With all of them God our Lord favored us, because they always understood us and we understood them. And thus we asked and they responded by signs as if they spoke our language and we theirs, because although we knew six languages, we could not make use of them in all areas because we found more than a thousand differences. Throughout all these lands those who were at war with one another later made friends in order to come to receive us and bring us everything they had. And in this manner we left the entire land and we told them by signs, because they understood us, that in heaven there was a man whom we called God, who had created the heaven and the earth, and that we adored him and served him as Lord, and that we did whatever he commanded us, and that from his hand came all good things, and if thus they were to do it, it would go very well for them. And we found such great readiness in them, that if we had had an interpreter through whom we could have understood each other perfectly, we would have left all of them Christians. This we gave them to understand as best we could. And henceforth when the sun rose, with very great shouting they opened their joined hands to the sky and afterward passed them over their entire bodies. And they did the same when the sun set. They are a people of good disposition and diligent [and] well equipped to follow any course....

[Having seen "clear signs of Christians" who were on New Spain's northwestern frontier hunting for natives to enslave,] I took with me the black man and eleven Indians, and following the trail of the Christians I found, I passed through three places where they had slept.... And the next morning I reached four Christians on horseback who experienced great shock upon seeing me so strangely dressed and in the company of Indians. They remained looking at me a long time, so astonished that they neither spoke to me nor managed to ask me anything. I told them to take me to their captain. And thus we went half a league from there, where their captain, Diego de Alcaraz, was. And after I had spoken to him, he said that he was very lost there because it had been many days since he had been able to take any Indians and that there was no way to go because among them there began to be great need and hunger. I told him how Dorantes and Castillo remained behind at a place ten leagues from there with many people who had brought us. And he then sent out three horsemen and fifty Indians of those they were bringing. And the black man returned with them to guide them. And I remained there and I asked that they certify for me the year and the month and the day that I had arrived there, and the manner in which I had come, and thus they did it.…

And after this we suffered many annoyances and great disputes with them, because they wanted to enslave the Indians we brought with us.…We had great difficulty convincing the Indians to return to their homes and secure themselves and sow their maize. They did not want but to go with us until leaving us with other Indians, as they were accustomed to doing, because if they returned without doing this, they feared they would die, and going with us, they feared neither the Christians nor their lances. The Christians were disturbed by this, and they made their interpreter tell them that we were of the same people as they, and that we had been lost for a long time, and that we were people of ill fortune and no worth, and that they were the lords of the land whom the Indians were to serve and obey. But of all this the Indians were only superficially or not at all convinced of what they told them. Rather, some talked with others among themselves, saying that the Christians were lying, because we came from where the sun rose, and they from where it set; and that we cured the sick, and they killed those who were well; and that we came naked and barefoot, and they went about dressed and on horses and with lances; and that we did not covet anything but rather, everything they gave us we later returned and remained with nothing, and that the others had no other objective but to steal everything they found and did not give anything to anyone. And in this manner, they conveyed everything about us and held it in high esteem to the detriment of the others.…Finally, it was not possible to convince the Indians that we were the same as the other Christians, and with much effort and insistence we made them return to their homes, and we ordered them to secure themselves and settle their villages, and to sow and

work the land, because of being abandoned, it was now very overgrown with vegetation, for that land is without doubt the best of any to be found in these Indies and the most fertile and abundant in foodstuffs. And they sow three times a year. They have many fruits and many beautiful rivers and many other very good waterways. There are great indications and signs of mines of gold and silver. The people are of very good inclinations. Those who are friends of the Christians serve them very willingly. They are very well disposed, much more so than those of Mexico. And, finally, it is a land that lacks nothing in order to be very good. When we dispatched the Indians, they told us that they would do what we commanded and would settle their villages if the Christians would let them. And thus I declare and affirm as true that if they should not do it, the Christians will be to blame. And after we had sent them away the Christians sent us off under the guard of an *alcalde* [a local official, a combination of judge and mayor] and three other Christians with him, from which it is evident how much men's thoughts deceive them, for we went to them seeking liberty and when we thought we had it, it turned out to be so much to the contrary. And in order to remove us from conversations with the Indians, they led us through areas depopulated and overgrown so that we would not see what they were doing nor their conduct, because they had conspired to go and attack the Indians whom we had sent away reassured and in peace.…They led us through those dense thickets for two days without water, lost and without a path. And we all thought that we would perish from thirst, and seven men died from it.… [W]e arrived at a village of peaceful Indians. And the *alcalde* who was leading us left us there, and he went on ahead another three leagues to a settlement called Culiacán where Melchior Díaz, *alcalde mayor* and captain of that province, was. Upon learning of our escape and arrival, he departed later that night and came to where we were, and he wept a great deal with us, praising God our Lord for having shown so much mercy to us.…

And having arrived in Compostela, the governor received us very well and from the provisions he had gave us some clothes, which I was unable to wear for many days, nor were we able to sleep but on the ground. And after ten or twelve days had passed, we left for Mexico. And along the entire road we were well treated by the Christians. And many came out to see us along the roads and gave thanks to God our Lord for having delivered us from so many dangers.…

CHAPTER 3

John White and Theodor de Bry Eye the Indians

"The True Pictures of those People"

We live in a world flooded with pictures. Books and magazines, billboards and bus ads, television and film, snapshots and videos, Web sites and computer games—pictures crowd our field of vision at home and school, on city streets and in shopping malls. So common, so much a part of the everyday scene is this ocean of imagery that we tend to pay little attention to it. If asked, we would probably agree that most of what we see is not "real": Films are computer enhanced (if not altogether computer generated); advertisements are designed and distorted to get people to buy a product; photographs can be "doctored" in a host of ways; even so-called reality TV shows are carefully scripted and edited. Rarely, however, do we pause to analyze pictures as texts akin to written sources.

The images in this chapter, like the landscape paintings in Chapter 12 and the Civil War photographs in Chapter 19, are designed to focus a critical eye on visual sources. They remind you that a picture is a historical document, a text that is painted rather than penned, engraved rather than printed. Like *Common Sense* and the Declaration of Independence, for example (Chapter 7), a painting, engraving, or photograph is composed by an author with a particular agenda, and a particular audience, very much in mind.

Saturated as our age is with images produced by all sorts of technologies, it is hard to imagine—to "picture"—a time when this was not so. But the "age of encounter," those centuries when Europe and America discovered one another, was just such a time. By 1492, Europeans had the know-how to build ships that could navigate uncharted seas, skills that opened up what was, to them, a "new world" (see the discussion of the loaded terms "New World" and "Old World" in Chapter 1). But they lacked the means to capture and convey images of what they found there to a wide audience back home. For a century after Christopher Columbus, seeking passage to Asia and "the Indies," first stumbled upon lands that Europeans labeled *America*, the only published pictures of that land and its peoples were crude woodcuts.

This began to change in 1590 with the publication of the first volume in a series called *Historia Americae*, by the Flemish artist Theodor de Bry (1528–1598). Using a new technique called copperplate engraving that allowed sharper detail than woodcuts, between 1590 and 1634 de Bry and his sons published book after book that introduced America to Europe. That first volume, a lavishly illustrated edition of the English scientist and explorer Thomas Harriot's work *A Brief and True Report of the New Found Land of Virginia* (1588), "brought to the European public," writes historian Michael Alexander, "the first realistic visualization of the exotic world opened up across the Atlantic." "I and my sonnes haven taken ernest paynes in graving the pictures therof in Copper," de Bry proudly told "the gentle Reader" in a preface, "seeing yt is a matter of noe small importance."[1]

Seeking as many "gentle Readers" as possible, de Bry published the book simultaneously in four different languages (German, Latin, French, and English). The engravings were the perfect sales pitch. "It was…a common practice at the time to display frontispieces in the streets for publicity purposes," the scholar Bernadette Bucher observes; hence "[t]he pictures that enriched [de Bry's books] could not fail to have attracted a wide range of customers." At last, Europeans curious about those lands beyond the sunset had images to satisfy that curiosity.[2]

De Bry's sensational first volume made famous a struggling English adventure on a sandy stretch of what is now the North Carolina coast. Then called "Virginia" in honor of England's "Virgin Queen," Elizabeth (who ruled from 1558 to 1603), the colony has since entered American legend as "Roanoke, the Lost Colony." Roanoke's story began in the spring of 1584 when Sir Walter Raleigh received royal permission to found a colony in North America. He and his country had a lot of catching up to do: A second- or even third-rate nation compared to Spain and France, the "superpowers" of the day, England had fallen way behind in the race for the riches and resources of Europe's New World.[3] (That Spain and France were Catholic and England Protestant only made the contest more urgent; like the arms race during the Cold War, a desperate contest was on to save American souls as well as mine American gold.)

Raleigh wasted no time: Scarcely a month after getting his Crown license, he dispatched Philip Amadas and Arthur Barlowe to reconnoiter the area in order to find a likely spot to plant a colony. In the fall, this expedition returned to announce that the place was a veritable Garden of Eden. "The earth bringeth foorth all things in aboundance," Barlowe exclaimed, "as in the first creation, without toile or labour." (Perhaps that is why the first engraving in de Bry's 1590 volume showed Adam, Eve, a snake, and an apple tree!) Not only that, the natives seemed friendly. To prove this point, the expedition brought back two Indians, Wanchese and Manteo, who promptly set about learning English and teaching their new companions the local Algonquian language.[4]

The next spring an excited Raleigh sent a much larger force—more than one hundred men, most of them soldiers—to start a settlement and build a fort. The outpost and the troops betrayed the colony's purpose: It was to be a military base, a site from which English men fanned out to hunt for gold while English ships preyed on the Spanish treasure fleet that annually hauled enormous riches from American mines to the King of Spain's coffers. Unfortunately for the newcomers, the spot proved less fruitful and the natives less friendly than Amadas and Barlowe had predicted. When supply vessels failed to show up and conflict with Indians (on whom the English depended for food) began, the colonists abandoned Roanoke scarcely a year after they had arrived.

Undaunted, in 1587 yet another band of English folk left their homeland, bound for Roanoke. This company was different: Under the leadership of a gentleman named John White (1540s?–1606?), who had been with the failed colony the year before, eighty-four men, seventeen women, and eleven children were to establish a cluster of family farms, not a military outpost. Though this venture's aims were different, it had no greater success. Trouble with Indians continued; colonists squabbled among themselves; supplies remained scarce. To hurry along relief ships from England, in the late summer of 1587 John White left the colonists—including his daughter and his newborn granddaughter Virginia—and sailed home.

Once there, however, he ran into one obstacle after another, including orders that all English vessels had to stay close to home to repel an enormous invasion fleet Spain launched in 1588. Not until 1590 did White manage to return to Roanoke. Too late: He found nothing but abandoned houses and cryptic signs indicating that the colonists had moved in with nearby Indians. Though scholars speculate that survivors might have lived among natives for some years, Roanoke's fate remains the stuff of legend.

White could rescue neither his family nor his colony. In the end, however, he did manage to save Roanoke for posterity through his art. Though we know little about White's life before Roanoke, it is clear that he had some artistic training. Clear, too, is that Sir Walter Raleigh, knowing White's gifts, sent him to Roanoke in 1585, probably with orders to "drawe to lief [sic] one of each kinde of thing that is strange to us in England...all strange birdes beastes fishes plantes hearbes Trees and fruictes...also the figures & shapes of men and woemen in their apparell as also their manner of wepons." It is sad indeed that so many of White's hundreds of sketches were lost—some into the sea as colonists hastily abandoned Roanoke in 1586, the rest to the passage of time. But what remains, experts agree, represents the finest images of North American natives "before the days of photography."[5]

White's companion, as he traveled about Roanoke and vicinity sketching, was one of Sir Walter Raleigh's favorites, Thomas Harriot (1560–1621). Young Harriot was indispensable to that 1585 expedition. A brilliant mathematician, an experienced geographer and navigator, he had also learned Algonquian from Wanchese and Manteo. Harriot and White would cross paths again in 1588, when Theodor de Bry visited London looking for material to launch his great publishing venture. White was there, trying to line up backers for Roanoke's resupply; Harriot had just completed *A Briefe and True Report of the New Found Land of Virginia*. Admiring White's watercolors, reading Harriot's glowing account of Virginia's prospects, the visitor from Frankfurt in Germany (he had relocated there from Antwerp to escape religious persecution) decided to pair the two: He would combine *A Briefe and True Report* with engravings based on White's drawings. In 1590, the very year Governor White found only emptiness and silence at Roanoke, his drawings, in de Bry's "translation," entranced Europe.[6]

Because de Bry wanted captions to accompany his engravings (probably written in haste by Harriot and badly translated by de Bry), I include a modernized sample here.[7] But the main attraction, then as now, is the pictures. Study them closely. What messages do they broadcast about this strange new world and its inhabitants? Is the landscape forbidding? Inviting? And the natives: Were they friendly or frightening? Noble savages or merely savages? Europeans were unsure what to make of them. True, Arthur Barlowe in 1584 had pronounced those he met "gentle, loving, and faithfull," "very handsome, and goodly people, and in their behaviour as mannerly and civill, as any of Europe." But others—including other Englishmen who visited Roanoke—considered them inferior beings closer to beasts than to humans. What did White and de Bry think?

Having familiarized yourself with the pictures, compare de Bry's images with White's. (De Bry probably worked from copies White made, long since lost.)[8] Modern scholars differ on how close the resemblance is. Some say that the "quite accurate" engravings "faithfully reproduced their models"; any variations "are rather trivial departures from White's." Others assert that "[r]eaders dependent on de Bry's famous engravings for their image of the American Indian could be forgiven for assuming that the forests of America were peopled by heroic nudes, whose perfectly proportioned bodies made them first cousins of the ancient Greeks and Romans." And still others scrutinizing "de Bry's...translation of John White's drawing into engravings" conclude that "hardly any engraving can be considered as a faithful reproduction." Which view do you favor? Why?[9]

Whether or not scholars think that de Bry was true to White's originals, all agree that he made *some* changes. One place to begin cataloging those "departures" is with the depictions of "Their sitting at meate" (Figures 3-11 and 3-12). Study these figures from head to toe, from posture to facial features and expression; compile a list of the differences. What patterns and tendencies reveal themselves? Having done this with that pair of pictures, you can then go on to the others with an eye trained for the telling detail, the turn of head or shift of perspective.

It is easier to note these differences than to explain them. Were they deliberate? One artist worked amid natives in the chaos of a struggling colony, the other at secondhand amid the comforts of his shop. One wielded a brush on paper, the other an engraver's tool on copper. One had instructions to "drawe to lief" what he saw, the other was out to sell books. Some have wondered if John White, less well trained, was "able to free himself from the artistic conventions of his time" in a way that de Bry could not. Others suggest that, even so, White was keen to promote English colonization in general and to raise funds for Roanoke in particular, which colored what he painted and how he painted it. How might such differences have shaped what you see here?[10]

Just as hard to explain is how de Bry's differences might have affected viewers at the time. (Unlike you, Europeans for centuries only saw de Bry's work; White's was not published until 1964.) How, for example, should we interpret the fact that the woman in White's "Theire sitting at meate" is gazing at her food, smiling in anticipation of a meal, while in de Bry's, wearing the same smile, she looks straight at us? Here and elsewhere, some scholars see profound "ideological implications" in such seemingly minor contrasts. It pays not only to note the variations and ponder their source but also to try coming up with their historical implications.[11]

Whatever you conclude about White's depictions and de Bry's "departures," do not be too hard on them. For one thing, they had plenty of company; many Europeans had trouble drawing an alien world that lay far beyond their experience. Another artist of that era, after living among Brazilian natives for a year, admitted that "[a]lthough I diligently perused...those barbarian people..., yet I say, by reason of their diverse gestures and behaviours, utterly different from ours, it is a very difficult matter to express their true proportion."[12]

For another thing, one might ask whether we do any better. Consider one possible equivalent today of these images, beings who can be considered to us what Native Americans were to Europeans: space aliens. Our versions of these creatures from another world (so far, only fictional and fanciful) vary widely, but, as with Europeans depicting Indians three centuries ago, there tend to be two stereotypes: ferocious (Ridley Scott's *Alien* and its descendants) or friendly (*E. T., the Extra-terrestrial* and *Close Encounters of the Third Kind*). Gentle, wise, childlike, the friendlies seem not at all threatening—and not so different from us. However far our world is from John White's and Theodor de Bry's, we share an impulse to render the foreign familiar.

Questions for Consideration and Conversation

1. Which side do you take in the debate over how well Theodor de Bry managed to accurately engrave John White's watercolors?
2. Whichever side you are on, how do you explain the differences between the engravings and the watercolors?
3. What information did these images seek to convey about America and its peoples? Why?
4. What sorts of images—of the American land and its inhabitants, of early Roanoke—are *not* included in these drawings? Why?
5. Consider the landscape here, and the natives' relationship to the landscape. What message is being sent here about America's present condition and future possibilities? Would it surprise you to know that the area was suffering from a drought in the 1580s, and that food was scarce?

Endnotes

1. Michael Alexander, ed., *Discovering the New World: Based on the Works of Theodor de Bry* (New York, 1976), 7; Thomas Harriot, *A Briefe and True Report of the New Found Land of Virginia* (New York, 1972 [originally published 1590]), 41.

2. Bernadette Bucher, *Icon and Conquest: A Structural Analysis of the Illustrations of de Bry's* Great Voyages, trans. Basia Miller Gulati (Chicago, 1981), 11.

3. Karen Kupperman, *Roanoke: The Abandoned Colony* (Totowa, NJ, 1984), 3.

4. David Beers Quinn, ed., *New American World: A Documentary History of North America to 1612*, vol. III (New York, 1979), 280.

5. Paul Hulton, *America 1585: The Complete Drawings of John White* (Chapel Hill, NC, 1984), 9, 27.

6. Ute Kuhlemann, "Between Reproduction, Invention and Propaganda: Theodor de Bry's Engravings after John White's Water Colours," in Kim Sloan, ed., *A New World: England's First View of America* (Chapel Hill, NC, 2007), 86.

7. David Beers Quinn, "Thomas Harriot and the New World," in John W. Shirley, ed., *Thomas Harriot, Renaissance Scientist* (Oxford, 1974), 47.

8. Kuhlemann, "Between Reproduction, Invention and Propaganda," 81, 87.

9. William C. Sturtevant, "First Visual Images of Native America," in Fredi Chiappelli, ed., *First Images of America: The Impact of the New World on the Old* (Berkeley, 1976), I, 444 ("accurate"); Hulton, *America 1585*, 18 ("faithfully," "trivial"); J. H. Elliott, *The Old World and the New, 1492–1650* (Cambridge, England, 1970), 23 ("Greeks and Romans"); Kuhlemann, "Between Reproduction, Invention and Propaganda," 86 ("translation," "faithful").

10. Kupperman, *Roanoke*, 41; Joyce E. Chaplin, "Roanoke 'Counterfeited According to the Truth,' " in Sloan, ed., *A New World*, 51–63.

11. Frances Pohl, *Framing America: A Social History of American Art* (New York, 2002), 56.

12. Alexander, ed., *Discovering the New World*, 7–8.

THE WATERCOLORS OF JOHN WHITE (1588?) AND ENGRAVINGS OF THEODOR DE BRY (1590)

FIGURE 3-1 Secoton, by John White. *Source:* Library of Congress.

FIGURE 3-2 "The Towne of Secota," by Theodor de Bry. *Source:* Library of Congress.

Their towns that are not enclosed with poles are commonly more pleasant than such as are enclosed, as appears in this figure, which shows well the town of Secotam. For the houses are scattered here and there, and they have gardens (Letter E) where tobacco grows, which the inhabitants call *Uppowoc*. They also have groves where they take deer and fields where they sow their corn. In their cornfields they build a sort of scaffold in which they place a cottage like a round chair (Letter F) and put someone there to keep watch over the field. For there are so many fowls and beasts, that unless they keep close watch, these animals would soon devour all their corn. That is why the watchman makes continual cries and noise. They sow their corn with a certain distance between seeds (noted by H); otherwise one stalk would choke the growth of another and the corn would not become ripe (G). For the leaves of the plant are large, like the leaves of great reeds. They have also several broad plots where they meet with their neighbors to celebrate their main solemn feasts as picture 18 [Figure 3-4] shows, and a place (D) where, after they have ended their feast, they make merry together. Across from this place they have a round plot (B) where they assemble themselves to make their solemn prayers. Not far from that place there is a large building (A) where are the tombs of their kings and princes....They also have a garden noted by the letter I, which they use to sow pumpkins. Also a place marked with K where they make a fire at their solemn feasts, and hard without the town is a river (L), from which they fetch their water. This people therefore, void of all covetousness, live cheerfully and at their heart's ease. But they solemnify their feasts in the night, and therefore they keep very great fires to avoid darkness and to express their joy.

FIGURE 3-3 "Indians dancing," by John White. *Source:* Library of Congress.

FIGURE 3-4 "Their danses which they vse att their hyghe feastes," by Theodor de Bry.   *Source:* Library of Congress.

FIGURE 3-5 "A ritual (with rattles) around a fire," by John White.   *Source:* Library of Congress.

FIGURE 3-6 "Their manner of prainge with Rattles abowt t[h]e fyer," by Theodor de Bry.   *Source:* Library of Congress.

FIGURE 3-7 "The manner of their attire and painting them selves when they goe to their generall huntings, or at theire Solemne feasts," by John White.   *Source:* Library of Congress.

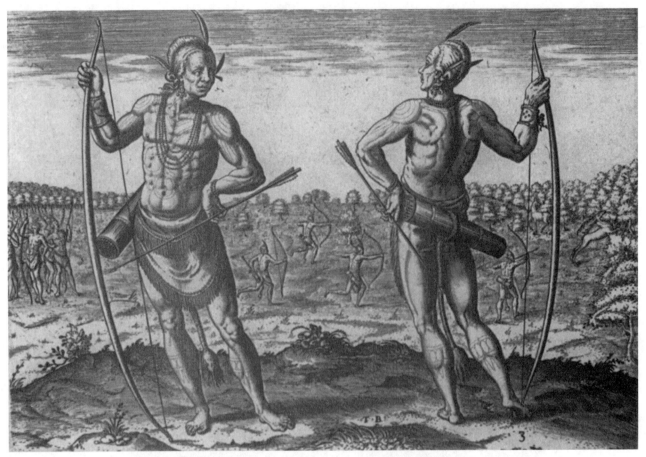

FIGURE 3-8 "A weroan or great Lorde of Virginia," by Theodor de Bry.   *Source:* Library of Congress.

FIGURE 3-9 "A cheife Herowans wyfe of Pomeoc and her daughter of the age of 8 or 10 yeares," by John White.   *Source:* Library of Congress.

FIGURE 3-10 "A cheiff Ladye of Pomeiooc," by Theodor de Bry.   *Source:* Library of Congress.

FIGURE 3-11 "Theire sitting at meate," by John White.   *Source:* Library of Congress.

FIGURE 3-12 "Their sitting at meate," by Theodor de Bry.   *Source:* Documenting the American South, University of North Carolina, Chapel Hill, http://docsouth.unc.edu/permission/copyright.html

Mrs. Rowlandson Endures Travels and Travails

"Come, go along with us"

Sometime between the spring of 1677 and the fall of 1678, a middle-aged Englishwoman named Mary Rowlandson sat down at a desk in her New England home, picked up a quill pen, and began to write. Perhaps she worked by candlelight while her husband and two children slumbered nearby; we know that she was having trouble sleeping. Day or night, it was unusual, in that time and place, for a woman to be writing at all. While most men in early New England could read and write, less than half of the women knew how, and in any case women, like children, were supposed to be seen, not heard. Men kept diaries, sent letters, filed government reports, and handled business accounts; no woman's diary, and precious few letters, survive from those days.

But Mary Rowlandson was no ordinary woman. Born Mary White in England some forty years before, in 1639 she had come to New England with her family. In the 1650s the Whites moved to the frontier village of Lancaster, Massachusetts, forty miles west of Boston. Mary's father became the town's biggest landowner, and in 1656 she confirmed her family's high status by marrying the local minister, Joseph Rowlandson. But what raised Mary Rowlandson from ordinary (though elite) to extraordinary was that in 1676 she had suffered every colonist's worst nightmare—captivity by Indians—and had lived to tell the tale. That tale would become what historian Jill Lepore calls "America's first best-seller."[1]

Mary Rowlandson's America was very different from the one John White and other Roanoke colonists had known almost a century earlier (Chapter 3). In that span of time the English, undaunted by Roanoke and other failed ventures, had planted a string of colonies along the coast reaching from below Charleston to above Boston, including Massachusetts Bay, Plymouth, Rhode Island, and Connecticut, the provinces collectively known as New England. Though these colonies differed somewhat in their religious beliefs (and squabbled loudly over those differences!), all were founded and led by people called *Puritans*, reformers who wanted to "purify" the Church of England, then (as now) the official church of the realm.

Called "the hotter sort of Protestants," these men and women cheered England's break with what many deemed a corrupt and ungodly Roman Catholic Church in the 1530s. In their view, however, the nation's new religious regime did not go far enough in abandoning Catholic forms and restoring the "true Church" they believed had been founded by Jesus Christ and His disciples. To these dissenters, the Church of England (also called the *Anglican* or *Episcopal* church) still looked and sounded too Catholic: It had bishops and archbishops; its clergy were often impious and incompetent men with political connections, not religious devotion; its services were too much like the old ones. "Puritans"—agreeing with Martin Luther in Germany, John Calvin in Geneva, and other Protestant leaders across Europe—wanted simple, not fancy; the Bible's words, not the bishop's; and piety, not politics. Perhaps most of all, they rejected the prevalent idea that "good works"—obeying Biblical teachings, going to church, leading an honest, upright life—would earn entry to heaven. In place of "works," to the Puritan way of thinking, was "grace": They believed that eternal bliss came only from God's free gift, bestowed upon a few "Elect" or "Saints" whom He had chosen.

Had these reformers kept their mouths shut and their pens still, they might have been able to stay in England. It was an age when religious wars between Protestants and Catholics were tearing countries like France apart; Queen Elizabeth (1558–1603), keen to avoid this fate, was inclined to leave dissidents well enough alone. But Puritans were not the quiet type: They thought it their sacred duty to insist upon reforms, whatever trouble they caused England (or England caused them).

Eventually Elizabeth's successors James I (1603–1625) and Charles I (1625–1649), themselves more inclined to favor Rome and the pope than Geneva and John Calvin, had had enough. Facing a government crackdown, dissidents began to think of leaving England in order to save it: God's chosen people, they would found a "godly common-wealth" in America to serve as a model for England and the world, a beacon of saving light that a globe plunged in darkness might emulate. During the 1630s, some twenty thousand English folk, most of them Puritans, sailed for New England to erect that beacon. "[W]ee are entered into Covenant with him [God] for this worke," proclaimed John Winthrop, the first governor of Massachusetts Bay, in 1630. "[W]ee shall be as a Citty upon a Hill, the eies of all people are uppon us." If we succeed, "men shall say of succeeding plantacions: the lord make it like that of New England." But if we fail, "wee shall be made a story and a by-word through the world."[2]

The arrival of so many "boat people" from beyond the seas—not only Puritans bound for New England but thousands of other English emigrants headed for New York, New Jersey, and Pennsylvania, for Virginia, Maryland, and Carolina—shifted the balance of power between native and newcomer in eastern North America. Though the continent would remain largely Indian country as late as 1800, European migrants and the diseases they brought seriously weakened many native nations. In New England alone, the Indian population fell from more than 100,000 in 1600 to perhaps 18,000 by 1675; meanwhile the number of colonists there grew from 0 to 60,000. "When the English first came," the Wampanoag leader Metacom ("King Philip") reminded colonists that same year, remembering when Pilgrims had met his father Massasoit in 1620, my "father was as a great man and the English as a little child." Things looked very different now.[3]

Metacom's speech in June 1675 was part of a last desperate effort to avoid all-out war. It failed: Within a week, Wampanoags attacked colonial farms, thus beginning a conflict (since known as "King Philip's War") that one of its foremost students, Neal Salisbury, calls "the bloodiest and most destructive war in American history." As a percentage of the total population, its losses exceed even those of the Civil War or World War II. In little more than a year, English colonists lost about 5% of their population the Indians around 40% of theirs. (Were the United States to lose equivalent numbers today, that figure would be a horrific 15 million—5%—or, if 40%, an unimaginable 120 million.) To these grim figures, Salisbury goes on, must be added those "on both sides...left seriously wounded, homeless, impoverished, orphaned, widowed, and in the case of the natives, exiled as slaves and refugees."[4]

Charting the descent into darkness from the last chapter to this, from the friendly natives sketched by John White and Theodor de Bry to "wolves," "hell-hounds," and "barbarous heathens" in Mary Rowlandson's account, it is tempting to assume that the bright possibilities, the pleasant scenes you visited in Chapter 3, inevitably gave way to the horrors chronicled below. In fact, however, it would be a mistake to think anything in the past is "inevitable" or to posit some unavoidable clash between "advanced" and "primitive," "civilized" and "savage."

Certainly many New England colonists hoped for harmony. That legends surround "the first thanksgiving," when Pilgrims (a branch of Puritanism) feasted with Massasoit's people, cannot hide the fact that there was indeed a peaceful three-day gathering of natives and newcomers. Later in the 1620s the Massachusetts Bay colony adopted as its official symbol a picture of an Indian saying "Come Over and Help Us"— help us, that is, become civilized Christians like the English. It sounded like Roanoke all over again.

However fictitious this plea—natives wanted no such help; the seal was cast to attract pious investors—some colonists did act upon it. By 1675, Massachusetts Bay missionaries had founded fourteen villages where one or two thousand "Praying Indians" wore English clothes, lived in English houses, and read the Christian Bible (either in English or in an Algonquian translation).

Even natives who refused to live in Praying Towns were profoundly affected by decades of contact with colonists. They pledged allegiance to England's king, signed land agreements, swapped deer hides and beaver pelts for cloth and muskets, kept herds of hogs, took neighbors to court, and in many other ways learned to get along by going along. "Metacom's War," Salisbury concludes, "was not a war between strangers but rather one between neighbors." Some scholars even argue that the conflict was not an "Indian war" at all (natives fought on both sides) but a "civil war" in which a single New England society, stitched together from Algonquian and English communities, came apart at the seams.[5] Would Mary Rowlandson agree?

For all that colonists and natives shared, for all their efforts to avoid combat, nonetheless—as Abraham Lincoln said about another civil war in a speech you will read in Chapter 18—"the war came." Puritans busy repelling the Indian onslaught nonetheless found time to ponder its causes. Mary Rowlandson's work was only one of many that drew on the Bible and on their view of this world and the next to fashion a powerful explanation. As you read about her travels and travails, be on the alert for that explanation.

Scholars since then who seek to understand the war's origins have scouted not heaven but earth, not the Bible but the records of what people then said and did. Their findings suggest that conflict came for several reasons. Depleted deer and beaver populations due to intense hunting brought about a decline in the fur trade that had been one mutually beneficial link across the frontier. Meanwhile, a rapidly growing colonial population demanded ever more Indian territory, a demand sometimes met by shady deals that cheated natives of their land.

Further, as Salisbury points out, there were limits to colonists' idea of harmony, to the hope that natives would become English. Some New England colonists clung to Theodor de Bry's belief that the Indian could be converted and "civilized"; but would even those natives be equal to an Englishman? Would they marry his daughter, vote for (or against) him, sit next to him in church or in court? The fact was, as Metacom and his followers no doubt noticed, "it was the Indians who had done most of the adjusting." Many natives learned English; few colonists bothered to master Algonquian. Many Indians worked for colonial masters; no native master ordered a colonist about. Many Indians became Christian; few if any colonists worshipped *manitous* (gods). (It is worth wondering what Mary Rowlandson and her readers would have thought of the Native American creation story you read in Chapter 1.) Even Praying Indians found themselves segregated, and scorned, by their English brethren. By 1675—their trade collapsing, their lands disappearing, their culture under siege by missionaries and magistrates alike—natives were ready to listen to Metacom, who had long been warning that colonists were bent on conquest, not concord.[6]

In February 1676, Metacom's War came to Lancaster, and to Mary Rowlandson. While her husband was in Boston, an army of four hundred Narragansetts, Wampanoags, and Nipmucks struck the village, killing many townsfolk and taking Mary, her three children, and nineteen others captive. Thus began a three-month ordeal during which Rowlandson, hauled from place to place in what is now central and western Massachusetts, endured gnawing hunger and bitter cold while watching her daughter Sarah die and losing track of her children Joseph and Mary. In the spring her journey came to an end when native foes of the colonies—their food running out, their war going badly—joined Massachusetts officials, Praying Indians, and Mary Rowlandson herself to negotiate the captives' release.

By summer's end the war had come to a grisly close: Rowlandson's Indian "master," Quinnapin, was captured and hanged; her "mistress," the powerful leader Weetamoo, drowned trying to get away from colonial soldiers and had her body "decapitated and displayed" in a New England town; Metacom himself was tracked down and slain, his corpse mutilated, his head stuck on a pike in Plymouth, where it remained for decades; meanwhile his wife and son were sold into slavery, along with untold numbers of other native men, women, and children.[7]

Well before the war was over, Puritans were trying to make sense of the calamity that had befallen them. Between the outbreak of fighting in 1675 and the publication of Rowlandson's book seven years later, Lepore writes, colonists published more than twenty treatments of the conflict. Of these, Mary Rowlandson's *The Sovereignty and Goodness of God* is by far the most famous and the most widely read, both then and ever since. An overnight sensation, in its very first year the work went through four editions (three in Massachusetts, one in London); over the next several decades, it outsold every book but the Bible. It was, modern experts agree, "fantastically," "immensely, even phenomenally popular."[8]

As I mentioned in the Introduction, a text's popularity is an ongoing theme of *American Conversations. The Sovereignty and Goodness of God* is only the first of many best sellers you will encounter in these pages. As you read Rowlandson's account—and as you come, later, to such works as *Common Sense* and *Narrative of the Life of Frederick Douglass*— you should think about why a text attracted so much attention, why it meant so much to so many, and what that popularity can reveal about American hopes and fears, prejudices and preferences.

Upon first following Rowlandson into captivity, it might be hard to imagine why anyone would find her tale compelling. The language might strike you as strange; all those Biblical references might seem annoying; the Preface, by an unnamed "friend" (probably Increase Mather, a leading Puritan minister), might sound sexist and racist. It is, at first, possible to see why the critic Leslie Fiedler dismissed the book as "insufferably dull and pious."[9]

If, however, you can get past these impediments, you might well find yourself drawn into Rowlandson's tale. Her opening scene, which depicts the Indian raid, hits with the force of a blunt instrument; the close, with the former captive wide awake in the quiet of "the night season," "[w]hen all are fast [asleep] about me," is at once poignant and vivid. In between, most modern critics agree, lies a "powerful and deeply moving piece of writing," "a great work of narrative nonfiction, eloquent and dramatic in its timeless appeal."[10]

Part of that abiding popularity, too, is that the saga of an uprooted person travel-ing through a dangerous and forbidding landscape has a deep, almost universal human appeal; certainly it strikes a powerful chord in European and Christian traditions, as the attraction of J. R. R. Tolkien's *Lord of the Rings* (both books and movies) can attest.

In America alone, *The Sovereignty and Goodness of God* spawned an entire literary genre called "the Indian captivity narrative." So hungry for these stories were Americans that over the next two centuries no less than 2,000 such tales would be published, not including countless fictional treatments such as James Fenimore Cooper's *The Last of the Mohicans* (1826) and romance novels today. The popularity of the 1992 Daniel Day-Lewis film based on Cooper's novel suggests that other media, too, find Indian captivity fascinating. Like Daniel Day-Lewis in *Mohicans*, John Wayne in *The Searchers* (1956), Dustin Hoffman in *Little Big Man* (1970), and Kevin Costner in *Dances with Wolves* (1990) are all Mary Rowlandson's heirs. So, too, perhaps, are contestants on the television show *Survivor* and stars of horror movies (usually women) who are left alone to contend with a diabolical killer. Some observers have gone further still, arguing that the September 11, 2001, terrorist attacks have given Mary Rowlandson and captivity narratives a deeper resonance for Americans. "Sept. 11…exactly duplicated the terms of the early Indian wars…," writes Susan Faludi, conflicts that were "[o]ur original 'war on terrorism.' " "On a deep cultural and psychological level," she continues, "our reactions as a nation to 9/11 had as much to do with Mary Rowlandson as with [terrorist] Mohammed Atta."[11]

If it seems hard to link Lancaster in 1676 with the World Trade Center in 2001 or to explain why people nowadays buy those romance novels, why moviegoers flock to these films, why viewers tune in to *Survivor*, it is even harder to figure out why readers in 1682 snapped up Mary Rowlandson's book. Certainly some colonists read it for the thrills, spills, and chills (with even a hint of sex to spice it up), sensations that were then unavailable in most books because Puritan leaders who controlled the presses frowned upon plays and other sorts of fiction. The text was more than mere escape, however. Since most New England readers in the 1680s had lived through the war, many would have known kin, friends, or neighbors who had been taken killed, captured, or orphaned. Absorbed in Rowlandson's story, they would have been thinking, "there but for the grace of God, go I."

Beyond that, it is more difficult to know for certain what attracted people to *The Sovereignty and Goodness of God* so powerfully that only a few ragged pages of the first edition survive because "it was literally read to pieces." Scholars have come up with two different interpretations of the text; as you study it yourself, be on the lookout for evidence that could support (or refute) these interpretations.[12]

On the one hand, it can be argued that for readers—and, no less important, for the clergyman who penned the Preface and the Puritan censors who let it be published—Rowlandson's tale offered the comfort of the familiar. The work blended literary types common at the time, including the spiritual autobiography, the conversion narrative, and the sermon. It also had important but standard lessons to teach pious folk—and, no less important, *im*pious folk—about how a proper Christian should behave.

Equally familiar to readers at the time, this line of argument goes on, and equally comforting and conventional are the racial and gender attitudes on display here. There is evidence aplenty that the work was vital to the "demonization" of American Indians, that its "deeply and pervasively racist" treatment of natives helped spread an epidemic of Indian hating. At the same time, perhaps *The Sovereignty and Goodness of God* won widespread attention because it affirmed gender norms about pious, passive women. Some New England women taken captive resisted or ran away; others killed their captors before fleeing; still others "went native." What course did Rowlandson follow, and why?[13]

Thus it is fair to say that this account won a huge audience because it was as conventional and reassuring in its form as in its spiritual, political, racial, and social messages. On the other hand, however, some scholars suggest that a different story lies just below the surface, that this "is a far more complex document than is generally realized" because "many Mary Rowlandsons" lurk in these pages.[14] She is submissive but also subversive, passive but also aggressive, deferential but also defiant. Devoted to her God, she is not necessarily very devoted to God's leading servants here on earth. Despising Indians as "inhumane creatures" full of "devilish cruelty," she mentions other moments that suggest a more complicated take on them. Considering those other moments, some historians conclude that "her treatment as a prisoner was not particularly harsh."[15]

As with Álvar Núñez Cabeza de Vaca's tale (Chapter 2), Rowlandson's discussion of native peoples offers an opportunity to read between the lines in search of deeper meaning of another sort, not about Europeans but about Indians. For most of this period, few natives could write; hence in order to understand their experiences, the scholar must combine folklore, artifacts, and archeology with documents written by colonists like Rowlandson. Studying her account with care, can you begin to see cultural method behind what seemed to her savage madness? What can we learn from her about gender relations and social status, about war and peace, even if she did not understand it enough to explain it herself? Why did natives taunt her, and about what? Why did they sometimes get mad at her, and how did they express that anger? Why did warriors take her prisoner in the first place, and why, later on, did they not just kill her? Scholars such as Laura Arnold suggest that the harsh words and hard blows Indians gave Rowlandson stemmed from her failure—through ignorance, or stubbornness, or both—to abide by native values.[16] If by some miracle you stumbled across an account by Metacom or Weetamoo that talked about Mary Rowlandson, what do you think it would say?

This line of questioning is vital not just for this text, and not just for Native Americans. *Most* Americans before 1880—slaves and immigrants, women and the poor—left precious few accounts of themselves for us to read. Merely to glimpse their unexplored world, it is imperative to use the likes of Mary Rowlandson—and Dr. Alexander Hamilton, whom you will meet in the next chapter—in an aggressively imaginative fashion that can yield clues deeply embedded in the text, obscured by an author's prejudices and blind spots.

Rowlandson has much to tell us about Puritans and Indians, but her text also intersects with, "speaks to," works you have already read, and many more that you will encounter in the chapters to come. Compare her images of natives with those produced by de Bry and White, for example, or by Cabeza de Vaca. Compare, too, her depictions of the American landscape, both with the Roanoke documents and with scenes made by Thomas Cole and other American artists some one hundred and fifty years later. In the 1830s, too, we will revisit New England natives in general and King Philip in particular, courtesy of Reverend William Apess, a Pequot Indian who shared Mary Rowlandson's devout Christianity but not her point of view.

But those are conversations for another time. Rowlandson was not writing with either Roanoke or Rev. Apess in mind. The Preface tells us why "Per Amicum" ("By a Friend") *thought* she wrote this, but would she agree? We cannot be sure. We do know, however, that well before her narrative went to press, Mary Rowlandson disappeared from history. Only recently have scholars discovered that, after her husband died in November 1678, she married another prominent colonist and moved to Connecticut, where she passed away in 1711. As far as we know, she never wrote anything again. Perhaps this narrative was enough. Maybe it was therapy for her, a means of working through the guilt over her survival and the grief over her daughter. Maybe she slept better afterward. It is also possible, however, that Mary Rowlandson felt forever haunted, that—especially "in the night season"—she could never shed the memory of being "in the midst of a thousand enemies, & nothing but death before me."

Questions for Consideration and Conversation

1. Why did Rowlandson write this? For whom did she write: Herself? Her family? Her community? Posterity?
2. Does Rowlandson's text support the notion that colonists and Indians were indeed part of a single society by the 1670s, with considerable common ground and overlapping cultures?
3. Compare Rowlandson's experience with that of Cabeza de Vaca (Chapter 2). What similarities do you see? What differences? How can you account for the similarities and differences?
4. How do you account for the popularity of Rowlandson's work, both at the time and in the centuries since?
5. Where do you stand in the debate over her treatment by natives? Was she relatively well treated or much abused?
6. If a native person among those she lived and traveled with had left an account of her captivity, what might that have looked like?

Endnotes

1. Jill Lepore, *The Name of War: King Philip's War and the Origins of American Identity* (New York, 1998), 125.
2. Stewart Mitchell, ed., *Winthrop Papers*, II (Boston, 1931), 294–95.
3. Quoted in Neal Salisbury, ed., *The Sovereignty and Goodness of God . . . . Being a Narrative of the Captivity and Restoration of Mrs. Mary Rowlandson . . .* (Boston, 1997), 117.
4. Ibid., 1. James D. Drake puts the percentage of Indian losses even higher, at 60–80% of the "rebel Indians" and about half of the "Praying Indians." Drake, *King Philip's War: Civil War in New England, 1675–1676* (Amherst, MA, 1999), 169.
5. Salisbury, ed., *Sovereignty and Goodness*, 2; Drake, *King Philip's War*.
6. Salisbury, ed., *Sovereignty and Goodness*, 3.
7. Ibid., 37.
8. Lepore, *Name of War*, 51, 126; Kathryn Zabelle Derounian-Stodola and James Arthur Levernier, *The Indian Captivity Narrative, 1550–1900* (New York, 1993), 14.
9. Leslie A. Fiedler, *The Return of the Vanishing American* (New York, 1968), 51.
10. Laurel Thatcher Ulrich, *Good Wives: Image and Reality in the Lives of Women in Northern New England,* *1650–1750* (New York, 1982), 227; Derounian-Stodola and Levernier, *Indian Captivity Narrative*, 94.
11. Susan Faludi, "America's Guardian Myths," *New York Times*, September 7, 2007. See also Faludi, *The Terror Dream: Fear and Fantasy in Post-9/11 America* (New York, 2007).
12. Lepore, *Name of War*, 149.
13. Gary L. Ebersole, *Captured by Texts: Puritan to Postmodern Images of Indian Captivity* (Charlottesville, VA, 1995), 25–26; Ulrich, *Good Wives*, 229.
14. Richard Slotkin and James K. Folsom, eds., *So Dreadfull a Judgment: Puritan Responses to King Philip's War, 1676–1677* (Hanover, NH, 1978), 303; Steven Neuwirth, "Her Master's Voice: Gender, Speech, and Gendered Speech in the Narrative of the Captivity of Mary White Rowlandson," in Merril D. Smith, ed., *Sex and Sexuality in Early America* (New York, 1998), 57.
15. Slotkin and Folsom, eds., *So Dreadfull a Judgment*, 306.
16. Laura Arnold, " 'Now...Didn't Our People Laugh?': Female Misbehavior and Algonquian Culture in Mary Rowlandson's *Captivity and Restauration*," *American Indian Culture and Research Journal*, 21 (1997), 1–28.

MARY ROWLANDSON, *A NARRATIVE OF THE CAPTIVITY AND RESTORATION OF MRS. MARY ROWLANDSON* (1682)

Source: [Mary Rowlandson,] The *Soveraignty & Goodness* of GOD, Together, With the Faithfulness of His Promises Displayed; Being a NARRATIVE Of the *Captivity* and *Restauration* of Mrs. Mary Rowlandson. Commended by her, to all that desires to know the Lords doings to, and dealings with Her. *Especially to her dear Children and Relations,*...Written by Her own Hand for Her private Use, and now made Publick at the earnest Desire of some Friends, and for the benefit of the Afflicted. (Edition: "The second addition [*sic*] Corrected and amended." Cambridge [MA]: Printed by Samuel Green, 1682.)

The Preface to the Reader

...[O]n *Thurseday, Feb.* 10, they [the Indians] fell with mighty force and fury upon *Lancaster....* The most solemn and remarkable part of this Trajedy, may that justly be reputed, which fell upon the Family of that reverend Servant of God, Mr. *Joseph Rolandson,* the faithfull Pastor of Christ in that place, who being gone down to the Council of the *Massachusets* to seek aid for the defence of the place, at his return found the Town in flames, or smoke, his own house being set on fire by the Enemy..., and all in it consumed: his precious yokefellow, and dear Children, wounded and captivated...by these cruel and barbarous Salvages. A sad Catestrophe!...It is no new thing for Gods precious ones to drink as deep as others, of the Cup of common Calamity....But it is not my business to dilate on these things, but only in few words introductively to preface to the following script, which is a Narrative of the wonderfully awfull, wise, holy, powerfull, and gracious providence of God, towards that worthy and precious Gentlewoman, the dear Consort of the said Reverend Mr. *Rowlandson,* and her Children with her, as in casting of her into such a waterless pit, so in preserving, supporting, and carrying thorow [through] so many such extream hazards, unspeakable difficulties and disconsolateness, and at last delivering her out of them all, and her surviving Children also. It was a strange and amazing dispensation, that the Lord should so afflict his precious Servant, and Hand maid: It was as strange, if not more, that he should so bear up the spirits of his Servant under such bereavements and of his handmaid under such captivity, travels and hardships (much too hard for flesh and blood) as he did, and at length deliver and restore....

This Narrative was penned by the Gentlewoman her self, to be to her a memorandum of Gods dealing with her, that she might never forget, but remember the same...all the dayes of her life....Some friends having obtained a sight of it, could not but be so much affected with the many passages of working providence discovered therein, as to judge it worthy of publick view....And therefore though this Gentlewomans modesty would not thrust it into the Press, yet her gratitude unto God made her...let it pass, that God might have his due glory, and others benefit by it as well as her self. I hope...none will cast any reflection upon this Gentlewoman, on the score of this publication of her affliction and deliverance....[T]his was a dispensation of publick note, and of universall concernment, and so much the more, by how much the nearer this Gentlewoman stood related to that faithfull Servant of God, whose capacity and employment was publick in the house of God, and his name on that account of a very sweet savour in the Churches of Christ....

[N]one can imagine what it is to be captivated, and enslaved to such atheisticall, proud, wild, cruel, barbarous, bruitish (in one word) diabolicall creatures as these, the worst of the heathen; nor what difficulties, hardships, hazards, sorrows, anxieties and perplexities do unavoidably wait upon such a condition, but those that have tried it. No serious spirit then (especially knowing any thing of this Gentlewomans piety) can imagine but that the vows of God are upon her. Excuse her then if she come thus into publick, to pay those vows. Come and hear what she hath to say....

Here *Reader,* you may see an instance of the Soveraignty of God....Here you may see an instance of the faith and patience of the Saints, under the most heart-sinking tryals....That God is indeed the supream Lord of the world, ruling the most unruly, weakening the most cruel and salvage, granting his People mercy in the sight of the unmercifull, curbing the lusts of the most filthy..., delivering the prey from the mighty, *and gathering together the out casts of* Israel....

Reader, if thou gettest no good by such a Declaration as this, the fault must needs be thine own.

Read therefore, Peruse, Ponder, and from hence lay up something from the experience of another, against [the time when] thine own turn comes, that so thou also through patience and consolation of the Scripture mayest have hope.

PER AMICAM [BY A FRIEND]

On the tenth of *February* 1675 [1676]. Came the *Indians* with great numbers upon *Lancaster*: Their first coming was about Sun-rising; hearing the noise of some Guns, we looked out; several Houses were burning, and the Smoke ascending to Heaven. There were five persons taken in one house, the Father, and the Mother and a sucking Child, they knockt on the head; the other two they took and carried away alive. Their [There] were two others, who being out of their Garison upon some occasion were set upon; one was knockt on the head, the other escaped: Another their [there] was who running along was shot and wounded, and fell down; he begged of them his life, promising them Money (as they told me) but they would not hearken to him but knockt him in head, and stript him naked, and split open his Bowels....

At length they came and beset our own house, and quickly it was the dolefullest day that ever mine eyes saw. The House stood upon the edg of a hill; some of the *Indians* got behind the hill, others into the Barn, and others behind any thing that could shelter them; from all which places they shot against the House, so that the Bullets seemed to fly like hail; and quickly they wounded one man among us, then another, and then a third, About two hours (according to my observation, in that amazing time) they had been about the house before they prevailed to fire it [set it on fire].... Now is that dreadfull hour come, that I have often heard of (in time of War, as it was the case of others) but now mine eyes see it. Some in our house were fighting for their lives, others wallowing in their blood, the House on fire over our heads, and the bloody Heathen ready to knock us on the head, if we stirred out: Now might we hear Mothers & Children crying out for themselves, and one another, *Lord, What shall we do?* Then I took my Children (and one of my sisters, hers) to go forth and leave the house: but as soon as we came to the dore and appeared, the *Indians* shot so thick that the bulletts rattled against the House, as if one had taken an handfull of stones and threw them, so that we were fain [glad] to give back.... But out we must go, the fire increasing, and coming along behind us, roaring, and the *Indians* gaping before us with their Guns, Spears and Hatchets to devour us. No sooner were we out

of the House, but my Brother in Law (being before wounded, in defending the house, in or near the throat) fell down dead, wherat the *Indians* scornfully shouted, and hallowed, and were presently upon him, stripping off his cloaths, the bulletts flying thick, one went through my side, and the same (as would seem) through the bowels and hand of my dear Child in my arms. One of my elder Sisters children, named *William*, had then his Leg broken, which the *Indians* perceiving, they knockt him on [his] head. Thus were we butchered by those merciless Heathen, standing amazed, with the blood running down to our heels. My eldest Sister being yet in the House, and seeing those wofull sights, the Infidels ha[u]ling Mothers one way, and Children another, and some wallowing in their blood: and her elder Son telling her that her Son *William* was dead, and my self was wounded, she said, And, *Lord, let me dye with them*; which was no sooner said, but she was struck with a Bullet, and fell down dead over the threshold. I hope she is reaping the fruit of her good labours, being faithful to the service of God in her place.... [T]he *Indians* laid hold of us, pulling me on[e] way, and the Children another, and said, *Come go along with us*; I told them they would kill me: they answered, *If I were willing to go along with them, they would not hurt me.*

Oh the dolefull sight that now was to behold at this House! *Come, behold the works of the Lord, what dissolations he has made in the Earth.* Of thirty seven persons who were in this one House, none escaped either present death, or a bitter captivity, save only one, who might say as he, *Job* 1.15 *And I only am escaped alone to tell the News.* There were twelve killed, some shot, some stab'd with their Spears, some knock'd down with their Hatchets. When we are in prosperity, Oh the little that we think of such dreadfull sights, and to see our dear Friends, and Relations ly bleeding out their heart-blood upon the ground. There was one who was chopt into the head with a Hatchet, and stript naked, and yet was crawling up and down. It is a solemn sight to see so many Christians lying in their blood, some here, and some there, like a company of Sheep torn by Wolves. All of them stript naked by a company of hell-hounds, roaring, singing, ranting and insulting, as if they would have torn our very hearts out; yet the Lord by his Almighty power preserved a number of us from death, for there were twenty-four of us taken alive and carried Captive.

I had often before this said, that if the Indians *should come, I should chuse rather to be killed by them then taken alive* but when it came to the tryal my mind changed;

their glittering weapons so daunted my spirit, that I chose rather to go along with those (as I may say) ravenous Bea[s]ts, then that moment to end my dayes; and that I may the better declare what happened to me during that grievous Captivity I shall particularly speak of the severall Removes we had up and down the Wilderness.

The first Remove

Now away we must go with those Barbarous Creatures, with our bodies wounded and bleeding, and our hearts no less than our bodies. About a mile we went that night, up upon a hill within sight of the Town where they intended to lodge. There was hard by a vacant house (deserted by the English before, for fear of the *Indians*). I asked them whither I might not lodge in the house that night? to which they answered what, will you love *English men* still? this was the dolefullest night that ever my eyes saw. Oh the roaring, and singing and dancing, and yelling of those black creatures in the night, which made the place a lively resemblance of hell. And as miserable was the wast[e] that was there made, of Horses, Cattle, Sheep, Swine, Calves, Lambs, Roasting Pigs, and Fowls (which they had plundered in the Town) some roasting, some lying and burning, and some boyling to feed our merciless Enemies; who were joyfull enough though we were disconsolate. To add to the dolefulness of the former day, and the dismalness of the present night: my thoughts ran upon my losses and sad bereaved condition. All was gone, my Husband gone (at least separated from me, he being in the [Massachusetts] Bay; and to add to my grief, the *Indians* told me they would kill him as he came homeward) my Children gone, my Relations and Friends gone, our House and home and all our comforts within door, and without, all was gone, (except my life) and I knew not but the next moment that might go too. There remained nothing to me but one poor wounded Babe, and it seemed at present worse than death that it was in such a pitiful condition, bespeaking, Compassion, and I had no refreshing for it, nor suitable things to revive it....

The second Remove

But now, the next morning, I must turn my back upon the Town, and travel with them into the vast and desolate Wilderness, I knew not whither. It is not my tongue, or pen can express the sorrows of my heart, and bitterness of my spirit, that I had at this departure: but God was with me, in a wonderfull man[n]er, carrying me along, and bearing up my spirit, that it did not quite fail. One of the *Indians* carried my poor wounded Babe upon a horse, it went moaning all along, I shall dy, I shall dy. I went on foot after it, with sorrow that cannot be expressed. At length I took it off the horse, and carried it in my armes till my strength failed, and I fell down with it: Then they set me upon a horse with my wounded Child in my lap, and there being no furniture upon the horse back; as we were going down a steep hill we both fell over the horses head, at which they like inhumane creatures laught, and rejoyced to see it, though I thought we should there have ended our dayes, as overcome with so many difficulties. But the Lord renewed my strength still, and carried me along, that I might see more of his Power; yea, so much that I could never have thought of, had I not experienced it....

The third Remove

The morning being come, they prepared to go on their way: One of the Indians *got up upon a horse, and they set me up behind him, with my poor sick Babe in my lap.* A very wearisome and tedious day I had of it; what with my own wound, and my Childs being so exceeding sick, and in a lamentable condition with her wound. It may be easily judged what a poor feeble condition we were in, there being not the least crumb of refreshing that came within either of our mouths, from *Wednesday* night to *Saturday* night, except only a little cold water. This day in the afternoon, about an hour by Sun, we came to the place where they intended, *viz.* an *Indian* town, called *Wenimesset*.... When we were come, Oh the number of Pagans (now merciless enemies) that there came about me, that I may say as *David*, Psal. 27 13, *I had fainted, unless I had believed, &c.* The next day was the Sabbath: I then rememb[e]red how careless I had been of Gods holy time: how many Sabbaths I had lost and mis-[s]pent, and how evily I had walked in Gods sight; which lay so close unto my spirit, that it was easie for me to see how righteous it was with God to cut off the thread of my life, and cast me out of his presence for ever. Yet the Lord still shewed mercy to me, and upheld me; and as he wounded me with one hand, so he healed me with the other....I sat much alone with a poor wounded Child in my lap, which moaned night and day, having nothing to revive the body, or cheer the spirits of her, but in stead of that, sometimes one *Indian* would come and tell me one hour, that your Master will knock your Child in the head, and then a second, and then a third, your Master will quickly knock your Child in the head.

…Thus nine dayes I sat upon my knees, with my Babe in my lap, till my flesh was raw again; my Child being even ready to depart this sorrowfull world, they bade me carry it out to another Wigwam (I suppose because they would not be troubled with such spectacles) Whither I went with a very heavy heart, and down I sat with the picture of death in my lap. About two houres in the night, my sweet Babe, like a Lambe departed this life on *Feb. 18. 1675* [1676]. It being about *six years*, and *five months* old. It was *nine dayes* from the first wounding, in this miserable condition, without any refreshing of one nature or other, except a little cold water. I cannot but take notice, how at another time I could not bear to be in the room where any dead person was, but now the case is changed; I must and could ly down by my dead Babe, side by side all the night after. I have thought since of the wonderfull goodness of God to me, in preserving me in the use of my reason and senses, in that distressed time, that I did not use wicked and violent means to end my own miserable life. In the morning, when they understood that my child was dead they sent for me home to my Masters Wigwam: (by my Master in this writing, must be understood *Quanopin*, who was a *Saggamore*, and married King *Phillips* wives Sister; not that he first took me, but I was sold to him by another *Narrhaganset Indian*, who took me when first I came out of the Garison). I went to take up my dead child in my arms to carry it with me, but they bid me let it alone: there was no resisting, but goe I must and leave it. When I had been at my masters *wigwam*, I took the first opportunity I could get, to go look after my dead child: when I came I askt them what they had done with it? then they told me it was upon the hill: then they went and shewed me where it was, where I saw the ground was newly digged, and there they told me they had buried it: *There I left that Child in the Wilderness, and must commit it, and my self also in this wilderness-condition, to him who is above all.* God having taken away this dear Child, I went to see my daughter *Mary*, who was at this same *Indian Town*, at a *Wigwam* not very far off, though we had little liberty or opportunity to see one another: she was about ten years old, & taken from the door at first by a *Praying Ind* & afterward sold for a gun. When I came in sight, she would fall a weeping; at which they were provoked, and would not let me come near her, but bade me be gone; which was a heart-cutting word to me. I had one Child dead, another in the Wilderness, I knew not where, the third they would not let me come near to….

The next day,…the *Indians* returned from [a raid on Medfield, another colonial town]….But before they came to us, Oh! the outragious roaring and hooping that there was: They began their din about a mile before they came to us. By their noise and hooping they signified how many they had destroyed (which was at that time twenty three). Those that were with us at home, were gathered together as soon as they heard the hooping, and every time that the other went over their number, these at home gave a shout, that the very Earth rung again: And thus they continued till those that had been upon the expedition were come up to the *Sagamores Wigwam*; and then, Oh, the hideous insulting and triumphing that there was over some *Englishmens* Scalps that they had taken (as their manner is) and brought with them. I cannot but take notice of the wonderfull mercy of God to me in those afflictions, in sending me a Bible[.] One of the *Indians* that came from *Medfield* fight, had brought some plunder, came to me, and asked me, if I wou'd have a Bible he had got one in his Basket, I was glad of it, and asked him, whether he thought the *Indians* would let me read? He answered, yes: So I took the Bible, and in that melancholy time, it came into my mind to read first the 28. *Chap.* of *Deut*[eronomy] which I did, and when I had read it, my dark heart wrought on this manner, *That there was no mercy for me, that the blessings were gone, and the curses came in their room, and that I had lost my opportunity.* But the Lord helped me still to go one [*sic*] reading till I came to *Chap.* 30 the seven first verses, where I found, *There was mercy promised again, if we would return to him by repentance; and though we were scattered from one end of the Earth to the other, yet the Lord would gather us together, and turn all those curses upon our Enemies.* I do not desire to live to forget this Scripture, and what comfort it was to me.

Now the Ind. *began to talk of removing from this place, some one way, and some another.* There were now besides my self nine, *English* Captives in this place (all of them Children, except one Woman)….The Woman *viz.* Goodwife *Joslin* told me, she shou'd never see me again, and that she could find in her heart to run away; I wisht her not to run away by any means, for we were nearly *thirty miles* from any *English Town*, and she very big with Child, and had but one week to reckon; and another Child in her Arms, two years old, and bad Rivers there were to go over, & we were feeble, with our poor & coarse entertainment. I had my Bible with me, I pulled it out, and asked her whether she would read; we opened the Bible and lighted on *Psal.* 27, in which Psalm we esp[e]cially took notice of that, *ver. alt, Wait no* [on] *the Lord, Be of good courage, and he shall strengthen thine Heart, wait I say on the Lord.*

The fourth Remove

And now I must part with that little Company I had. Here I parted from my Daughter *Mary,* (whom I never saw again till I saw her in *Dorcester,* returned from Captivity[)], and from four little Cousins and Neighbours, some of which I never saw afterward: the Lord only knows the end of them. Amongst them also was that poor Woman before mentioned, who came to a sad end, as some of the company told me in my travel: She having much grief upon her Spirit, about her miserable condition, being so near her time, she would be often asking the *Indians* to let her go home; they not being willing to that, and yet vexed with her importunity, gathered a great company together about her, and stript her naked, and set her in the midst of them; and when they had sung and danced about her (in their hellish manner) as long as they pleased, they knockt her on head, and the child in her arms with her: when they had done that, they made a fire and put them both into it, and told the other Children that were with them, that if they attempted to go home, they would serve them in like manner. The Children said, she did not shed one tear, but prayed all the while....

The fifth Remove

The occasion (as I thought) of their moving at this time, was, the English *Army it being near and following them:* For they went, as if they had gone for their lives, for some considerable way, and then they made a stop, and chose some of their stoutest men, and sent them back to hold the *English* Army in play whilst the rest escaped: And then, *like* Jehu, *they marched on furiously, with their old, and with their young: some carried their old decrepit mothers, some carried one, and some another* ... till they came to *Bacquaug* River.... In this travel, because of my wound, I was somewhat favoured in my load; I carried only my knitting work and two quarts of parched meal: Being very faint I asked my mistriss to give me one spoonfull of the meal, but she would not give me a taste. They quickly fell to cutting dry trees, to make Rafts to carry them over the river: and soon my turn came to go over: By the advantage of some brush which they had laid upon the Raft to sit upon, I did not wet my foot (which many of themselves at the other end were mid-leg deep) which cannot but be acknowledged as a favour of God to my weakned body, it being a very cold time....

The first week of my being among them, I hardly ate any thing; the second week, I found my stomach grow very faint for want of something; and yet it was very hard to get down their filthy trash: but the third week, though I could think how formerly my stomach would turn against this or that, and I could starve and dy before I could eat such things, yet they were sweet and savoury to my taste. I was at this time knitting a pair of white cotton stockins for my mistriss: and had not yet wrought upon a Sabbath day; when the Sabbath came they bade me go to work; I told them it was the Sabbath-day, and desired them to let me rest, and told them I would do as much more to morrow; to which they answered me, they would break my face. And here I cannot but take notice of the strange providence of God in preserving the heathen: They were many hundreds, old and young, some sick, and some lame[,] many had *Papooses* at their backs, the greatest number at this time with us, were *Squaws,* and they traveled with all they had, bag and baggage, and yet they got over this River aforesaid....On that very day came the *English* Army after them [to] this River..., and yet this River put a stop to them. God did not give them courage or activity to go over after us; we were not ready for so great a mercy as victory and deliverance; if we had been, God would have found out a way for the *English* to have passed this River, as well as for the *Indians* with their *Squaws* and *Children,* and all their *Luggage: Oh that my People had hearkened to me, and* Israel *had walked in my ways, I should soon have subdued their Enemies, and turned my hand against their Adversaries,* Psal. 81- 13.14....

The eight[h] Remove

...We travelled on till night; and in the morning, we must go over the [Connecticut] River to *Philip's* Crew....When I came ashore, they gathered all about me, I sitting alone in the midst: I observed they asked one another questions, and laughed, and rejoyced over their Gains and Victories. Then my heart began to fail: and I fell a weeping, which was the first time to my remembrance, that I wept before them.... [O]ne of them asked me, why I wept, I could hardly tell what to say: yet I answered, they would kill me: No, said he, none will hurt you. Then came one of them and gave me two spoon-fulls of Meal to comfort me, and another gave me half a pint of Pease; which was more worth than many Bushels at another time. Then I went to see King *Philip,* he bade me come in and sit down, and asked me whether I would smoke it (a usual Complement now adayes amongst Saints and Sinners)....

During my abode in this place, Philip *spake to me to make a shirt for his boy, which I did, for which he gave me a shilling: I offered the mony to my master, but he bade me keep it: and with it I bought a piece of Horse flesh.* Afterwards he asked me to make a Cap for his boy, for which he invited me to Dinner. I went, and he gave me a Pancake, about as big as two fingers; it was made of parched wheat, beaten, and fryed in Bears grease, but I thought I never tasted pleasanter meat in my life. There was a *Squaw* who spake to me to make a shirt for her *Sannup*, for which she gave me a piece of Bear. Another asked me to knit a pair of Stockins, for which she gave me a quart of Pease: I boyled my Pease and Bear together, and invited my master and mistriss to dinner, but the proud Gossip, because I served them both in one Dish, would eat nothing, except on[e] bit that he gave her upon the point of his knife....

The ninth Remove

...One bitter cold day, I could find no room to sit down before the fire: I went out, and could not tell what to do, but I went in to another Wigwam, *where they were also sitting round the fire, but the* Squaw *laid a skin for me, and bid me sit down, and gave me some Ground-nuts, and bade me come again: and told me they would buy me, if they were able, and yet these were strangers to me that I never saw before.*

The tenth Remove

...[B]eing hungry I went again back to the place we were before at, to get something to eat: being encouraged by the *Squaws* kindness, who bade me come again; when I was there, there came an *Indian* to look after me, who when he had found me, kickt me all along: I went home and found Venison roasting that night, but they would not give me one bit of it. Sometimes I met with favour, and sometimes with nothing but frowns....

The twelfth Remove

It was upon a Sabbath-day-morning, that they prepared for their Travel. This morning I asked my master whither he would sell me to my Husband; he answered me *Nux*, which did much rejoyce my spirit. My mistriss, before we went, was gone to the burial of a *Papoos*, and returning, she found me sitting and reading in my Bible; she snatched it hastily out of my hand, and threw it out of doors; I ran out and catcht it up, and put it into my pocket, and never let her see it afterward. Then they pack'd up their things to be gone, and gave me my load: I complained it was too heavy, whereupon she gave me a slap in the face and bade me go; I lifted up my heart to God, hoping that Redemption was not far off: and the rather because their insolency grew worse and worse....

[In camp] [d]own I sat, with my heart as full as it could hold, and yet so hungry that I could not sit neither: but going out to see what I could find, and walking among the Trees, I found six *Acrons* [sic], and two *Ches-nuts*, which were some refreshment to me. Towards Night I gathered me some sticks for my own comfort, that I might not ly a-cold: but when we came to ly down they bade me go out, and ly some-where-else, for they had company (they said) come in more than their own: I told them, I could not tell where to go, they bade me go look; I told them, if I went to another *Wigwam* they would be angry, and send me home again. Then one of the Company drew his sword, and told me he would run me thorough [sic] if I did not go presently. Then was I fain to stoop to this rude fellow, and to go out in the night, I knew not whither. *Mine eyes have seen that fellow afterwards walking up and down* Boston, *under the appearance of a* Friend-Indian, *and severall others of the like Cut.* I went to one *Wigwam*, and they told me they had no room. Then I went to another, and they said the same; at last an old *Indian* bade me come to him, and his *Squaw* gave me some Ground-nuts; she gave me also something to lay under my head, and a good fire we had: and through the good providence of God, I had a comfortable lodging that night....

The thirteenth Remove

Instead of going toward the Bay, *which was that I desired, I must go with them five or six miles down the River into a mighty Thicket of Brush: where we abode almost a fortnight....* In this place, on a cold night, as I lay by the fire, I removed a stick that kept the heat from me, a *Squaw* moved it down again, at which I lookt up, and she threw a handfull of ashes in mine eyes; I thought I should have been quite blinded, and have never seen more: but lying down, the water run out of my eyes, and carried the dirt with it, that by the morning, I recovered my sight again. Yet upon this, and the like occasions, I hope it is not too much to say with *Job, Have pitty upon me, have pitty upon me O ye my Friends, for the Hand of the Lord has touched me....*

I asked him [Thomas Read, a new captive] about the wel-fare of my Husband, he told me he...was well, but very melancholly. By which I certainly understood (*though I suspected it before*) that whatsoever the *Indians* told me respecting him was vanity and lies. Some of them told me, he was dead, and they had killed him: some said he was Married again, and that the Governour wished him to Marry; and told him he should have his choice, and that all perswaded I was dead....

As I was sitting once in the *Wigwam* here, *Phillps* [sic] Maid came in with the Child in her arms, and asked me to give her a piece of my Apron, to make a flap for it, I told her I would not: then my Mistriss bad me give it, but still I said no: the maid told me if I would not give her a piece, she would tear a piece off it: I told her I would tear her Coat then with that my Mistriss rises up, and takes up a stick big enough to have killed me, and struck at me with it, but I stept out, and she struck the stick into the Mat of the Wigwam. But while she was pulling of it out, I ran to the Maid and gave her all my Apron, and so that storm went over....

That night they bade me go out of the *Wigwam* again: my Mistrisses Papoos was sick, and it died that night, and there was one benefit in it, that there was more room. I went to a *Wigwam*, and they bade me come in, and gave me a skin to ly upon, and a mess of Ven[i]son and Ground-nuts, which was a choice Dish among them. On the morrow they burried the *Papoos*, and afterward, both morning and evening, there came a company to mourn and howle with her: though I confess, I could not much condole with them....

The sixteenth Remove

We began this Remove with wading over Baquag *River: the water was up to the knees, and the stream very swift, and so cold that I thought it would have cut me in sunder.* I was so weak and feeble, that I reeled as I went along, and thought there I must end my dayes at last, after my bearing and getting thorough so many difficulties; the *Indians* stood laughing to see me staggering along: but in my distress the Lord gave me experience of the truth, and goodness of that promise, *Isai.* 43.2. *When thou passest thorough the Waters, I will be with thee, and through the Rivers, they shall not overflow thee.* Then I sat down to put on my stockins and shoos, with the teares running down mine eyes, and many sorrowfull thoughts in my heart, but I gat up to go along with them. Quickly there came up to us an *Indian*, who informed them, that I must go to *Wachuset* to my master, for there was a Letter come from the Council to the *Saggamores*, about redeeming the Captives, and that there would be another in fourteen dayes, and that I must be there ready.... [En route,] came a company of *Indians* to us, near thirty, all on horseback. My heart skipt within me, thinking they had been *English men* at the first sibht [sight] of them, for they were dressed in *English* Apparel, with Hats, white Neckcloths, and Sashes about their wa[i]sts, and Ribbonds upon their shoulders: but when they came near, their [sic] was a vast difference between the lovely faces of Christians, and the foul looks of those Heathens, which much damped my spirit again.

The eighteenth Remove

...[W]e came to another *Indian Town*, where we stayed all night. In this Town there were four *English Children*, Captives; and one of them my own Sisters. I went to see how she did, and she was well, considering her Captive-condition....Then I went to another *Wigwam*, where there were two of the *English Children*; the *Squaw* was boyling *Horses feet*, then she cut me off a little piece, and gave one of the *English Children* a piece also. Being very hungry I had quickly eat up mine, but the Child could not bite it, it was so tough and sinewy, but lay sucking, gnawing, chewing and slabbering of it in the mouth and hand, then I took it of the Child, and eat it my self, and savoury it was to my taste. Then I may say as *Job Chap. 6.7. The things that my soul refused to touch, are as my sorrowfull meat.* Thus the Lord made that pleasant refreshing, which another time would have been an abomination. Then I went home to my mistresses *Wigwam*; and they told me I disgraced my master with begging, and if I did so any more, they would knock me in head: I told them, they had as good knock me in head as starve me to death.

The nineteenth Remove

...At last, after many weary steps, I saw *Wachuset* hills, but many miles off....Going along, having indeed my life, but little spirit, *Philip*, who was in the Company, came up and took me by the hand, and said, *Two weeks more and you shal be Mistress again.* I asked him, if he spake true? he answered, Yes, *and quickly you shal come to your master again;* who had been gone from us three weeks. After many weary steps we came to *Wachuset*, where he [her master] was: and glad I was to see him. He asked me, *When I washt me?* I told him not this month, then he fetcht me some water himself, and bid me wash, and gave me the Glass to see how I lookt; and bid his *Squaw* give me something to eat: so she gave me a mess of Beans and meat, and a little Ground-nut Cake. I was wonderfully revived with this favour shewed me, *Psal.* 106.46 *He made them also to be pittied, of all those that carried them Captives.*

My master had three Squaws, *living sometimes with one, and sometimes with another one, this old Squaw, at whose Wigwan [sic] I was, and with whom my Master had been those three weeks.* Another was *Wettimore*, with whom I had lived and served all this while: A severe and proud Dame she was, bestowing every day in dressing her self near as much time as any of the Gentry of the land: powdering her hair, and painting her face, going with Neck-laces, with Jewels in her ears, and Bracelets upon her hands: When she had dressed her self, her work was to make Girdles of *Wampom* and *Beads*. The third *Squaw* was a younger one, by whom he had two *Papooses*. By that time I was refresht by the old *Squaw*, with whom my master was, *Wettimores* Maid came to call me home, at which I fell a weeping. Then the old *Squaw* told me, to encourage me, that if I wanted victuals, I should come to her, and that I should ly there in her *Wigwam*. Then I went with the maid, and quickly came again and lodged there. The *Squaw* laid a Mat under me, and a good Rugg over me; the first time I had any such kindness shewed me. I understood that *Wettimore* thought, that if she should let me go and serve with the old *Squaw*, she would be in danger to loose, not only my service, but the redemption-pay also. And I was not a little glad to hear this; being by it raised in my hopes, that in Gods due time there would be an end of this sorrowfull hour. Then came an *Indian*, and asked me to knit him three pair of Stockins, for which I had a Hat, and a silk Handkerchief. Then another asked me to make her a shift, for which she gave me an Apron.

Then came Tom *and* Peter, *with the second Letter from the Council, about the Captives.* Though they were *Indians*, I gat them by the hand, and burst out into tears; my heart was so full that I could not speak to them; but recovering my self, I asked them how my husband did, & all my friends and acquaintance? they said, *They are all very well but melancohly* [sic].... When the Letter was come, the *Saggamores* met to consult about the Captives, and called me to them to enquire how much my husband would give to redeem me, when I came I sate down among them, as I was wont to do, as their manner is: *Then they bade me stand up,* and said, *they were the General Court. They bid me speak what I thought he would give,* Now knowing that all we had was destroyed by the *Indians*, I was in a great strait: I thought if I should speak of but a little, it would be slighted, and hinder the matter; if of a great sum, I knew not where it would be procured: yet at a venture, I said *Twenty pounds*, yet desired them to take less; but they would not hear of that, but sent that message to *Boston*, that for *Twenty pounds* I should be redeemed. It was a Praying-*Indian* that wrote their Letter for them.... There was another Praying *Indian*, so wicked and cruel, as to wear a string about his neck, strung with *Christians* fingers. Another Praying-*Indian*, when they went to *Sudbury fight*, went with

them, and his *Squaw* also with him, with her *Papoos* at her back: Before they went to that fight, they got a company together to *Powaw*; the manner was as followeth. There was one that kneeled upon a *Deer-skin*, with the company round him in a ring who kneeled, and striking upon the ground with their hands, and with sticks; and muttering or humming with their mouths, besides him who kneeled in the ring, there also stood one with a Gun in his hand: Then he one [sic] the *Deer-skin* made a speech, and all manifested assent to it: and so they did many times together. Then they bade him with the Gun go out of the ring, which he did, but when he was out, they called him in again; but he seemed to make a stand, then they called the more earnestly, till he returned again: Then they all sang. Then they gave him two Guns, in either hand one: And so he on the *Deer-skin* began again; and at the end of every sentence in his speaking, they all assented, humming or muttering with their mouthes, and striking upon the ground with their hands. Then they bade him with the two Guns go out of the ring again; which he did, a little way. Then they called him in again, but he made a stand; so they called him with greater earnestness; but he stood reeling and wavering as if he knew not whither he should stand or fall, or which way to go. Then they called him with exceeding great vehemency, all of them, one and another: after a little while he turned in, staggering as he went, with his Armes stretched out, in either hand a Gun. As soon as he came in, they all sang and rejoyced exceedingly a while. And then he opened [upon?] the *Deer-skin*, made another speech unto which they all assented in a rejoicing manner: and so they ended their business, and forthwith went to *Sudbury fight*. To my thinking they went without any scruple, but that they should prosper, and gain the victory: And they went out not so rejoycing, but they came home with as great a Victory. For they said they had killed two Captains, and almost an hundred men.... Yet they came home without that rejoycing and triumphing over their victory, which they were wont to shew at other times: but rather like Dogs (as they say) which have lost their ears. Yet I could not perceive that it was for their own loss of men: They said, they had not lost above five or six: and I missed none, excep[t] in one *Wigwam*. When they went, they acted as if the Devil had told them that they should gain the victory: and now they acted, as if the Devil had told them they should have a fall. Whither it were so or no, I cannot tell, but so it proved, for quickly they began to fall, and so held on that Summer, till they came to utter ruine. They came home on a Sabbath day, and the

Powaw that kneeled upon the *Deer-skin* came home (I may say, without abuse) as black as the Devil. When my master came home, he came to me and bid me make a shirt for his *Papoos*. About that time there came an *Indian* to me and bid me come to his *Wigwam*, at night, and he would give me some Pork & Ground nuts. Which I did, and as I was eating, another *Indian* said to me, he seems to be your good Friend, but he killed two *Englishmen* at *Sudbury*, and there ly their Cloaths behind you: I looked behind me, and there I saw bloody Cloaths, with Bullet-holes in them; yet the Lord suffered not this wretch to do me any hurt; Yea, instead of that, . . . five or six times did he and his *Squaw* refresh my feeble carcass. . . . [Y]et they were strangers that I never saw before. . . .

The twentieth Remove

. . . On a Sabbath day . . . came Mr. John Hoar *(the Council permitting him, and his own foreward spirit inclining him) together with the two forementioned* Indians, Tom *and* Peter *with their third Letter from the Council. . . .* [T]hey [her captors] presently called me in, and bade me sit down and not stir. Then they catched up their Guns, and away they ran, as if an Enemy had been at hand; and the Guns went off apace[.] I manifested some great trouble, and they asked me what was the matter? I told them, *I thought they had killed the* English-man (for they had in the mean time informed me than an *English-man* was come) they said, *No;* They shot over his Horse and under, and before his Horse; and they pusht him this way and that way, at their pleasure: shewing what they could do: Then they let them come to their *Wigwams.* . . . [I]n the morning, Mr *Hoar* invited the *Saggamores* to Dinner; but when we went to get it ready, we found that they had stollen the greatest part of the Provision Mr. *Hoar* had brought, out of his Bags, in the night: *And we may see the wonderfull power of God,* . . . *in that when there was such a great number of the* Indians *together, and so greedy of a little good food; and no* English *there, but Mr. Hoar and my self: that there they did not knock us in the head, and take what we had.* . . . *But instead of doing us any mischief, they seemed to be ashamed of the fact, and said, it were some* Matchit [Bad] Indian *that did it.* . . . God shewed his Power over the Heathen in this, *as he did over the hungry Lyons when* Daniel *was cast into the Den.* Mr. *Hoar* called them betime to Dinner, but they ate very little, they being so busie in dressing themselves, and getting ready for their Dance: which was carried one [*sic*] by eight of them; four *Men* and four *Squaws:* My master and mistriss being two. He was dressed in his Holland shirt, with great Laces sewed at the tail of it, he had his silver Buttons, his white Stockins, his Garters were hung round with Shillings, and he had Girdles of *Wampom upon his head and shoulders.* She had a Kersey Coat, and covered with Girdles of *Wampom* from the Loins upward: her armes from her elbows to her hands were covered with Bracelets; there were handfulls of Neck-laces about her neck, and severall sorts of Jewels in her ears. She had fine red Stokins, and white Shoos, her hair powdered and face painted Red, that was always before Black. And all the Dancers were after the same manner. There were two other singing and knocking on a Kettle for their musick. They keept hopping up and down one after another, with a Kettle of water in the midst, standing warm upon some Embers, to drink of when they were dry. They held on till it was almost night, throwing out *Wampom* to the standers by. At night I asked them again, if I should go home? They all as one said No, except my Husband would come for me. When we were lain down, my Master went out of the *Wigwam*, and by and by sent in an *Indian* called *James* the *Printer*, who told Mr. *Hoar*, that my Master would let me go home to morrow, if he would let him have one pint of Liquors. Then Mr. *Hoar* called his own *Indians*, *Tom* and *Peter*, and bid them go and see whither he would promise it before them three: and if he would, he should have it; which he did, and he had it. Then *Philip* sme[l]ling the business cal'd me to him, and asked me what I would give him, to tell me some good news, and speak a good word for me, I told him, *I could not tell what to give him, I would any thing I had, and asked him what he would have?* He said, two Coats and twenty shillings in Mony, and half a bushel of seed Corn, and some Tobacco. I thanked him for his love: but I knew the good news as well as the crafty *Fox*. My Master after he had had his drink, quickly came ranting into the *Wigwam* again, and called for Mr. *Hoar*, drinking to him, and saying, *He was a good man:* and then again he would say, *Hang him Rogue:* Being almost drunk, he would drink to him, and yet presently say he should be hanged. Then he called for me, I trembled to hear him, yet I was fain to go to him, and he drank to me, shewing no incivility. He was the first *Indian* I saw drunk all the while that I was amongst them. At last his *Squaw* ran out, and he after her, round the *Wigwam*, with his mony jingling at his knees: But she escaped him: But having an old *Squaw* he ran to her: and so through the Lords mercy, we were no more troubled that night. . . .

On *Tuesday morning* they called their *General* Court (as they call it) to consult and determine, whether I should go home or no: And they all as one man did seemingly consent to it, that I should go home; except *Philip*, who would not come among them.

But before I go any further, I would take leave to mention a few remarkable passages of providence, which I took special notice of in my afflicted time....

It was thought, if their Corn were cut down, they would starve and dy with hunger: and all their Corn that could be found, was destroyed, and they driven from that little they had in store, into the Woods in the midst of Winter; and yet how to admiration did the Lord preserve them for his holy ends, and the destruction of many still amongst the *English*! strangely did the Lord provide for them; that I did not see (all the time I was among them) one Man, Woman, or Child, die with hunger....

[O]ur perverse and evil carriages in the sight of the Lord, have so offended him, that instead of turning his hand against them, the Lord feeds & nourishes them up to be a scourge to the whole Land....

Another thing that I would observe is, the strange providence of God in turning things about when the Indians *was at the highest, and the* English *at the lowest.* I was with the Enemy eleven weeks and five dayes, and not one Week passed without the fury of the Enemy, and some desolation by fire and sword upon one place or other. They mourned (with their black faces) for their own losses: yet triumphed and rejoyced in their inhumane, and many times devilish cruelty to the *English.* They would boast much of their Victories...and then scoffe, and say, *They had done them a good turn, to send them to Heaven so soon.* Again, they would say, *This Summer that they would knock all the Rogues in the head, or drive them into the Sea, or make them flee the Countrey....* Now the Heathen begins to think all is their own, & the poor Christians hopes to fail (as to man) and now their eyes are more to God, and their hearts sigh heaven-ward: and to say in good earnest, *Help Lord, or we perish*: When the Lord had brought his people to this, that they saw no help in any thing but himself; then he takes the quarrel into his own hand: and though they had made a pit, in their own imaginations, as deep as hell for the Christians that Summer, yet the Lord hurll'd them selves into it....

But to return again to my going home, where we may see a remarkable change of Providence: At first they were all against it, except [unless] my Husband would come for me; but afterwards they assented to it, and seemed much to rejoyce in it; some askt me to send them some Bread, others some Tobacco, others shaking me by the hand, offering me a Hood and Scarfe to ride in; not one moving hand or tongue against it. Thus hath the Lord answered my poor desire, and the many earnest requests of others put up unto God for me. In my travels an *Indian* came to me, and told me, if I were willing, he and his *Squaw* would run away, and go home along with me: I told him *No*: I was not willing to run away, but desired to wait Gods time, that I might go home quietly, and without fear. And now God hath granted me my desire. O the wonderfull power of God that I have seen, and the experience that I have had: *I have been in the midst of those roaring Lyons, and Salvage Bears, that feared neither God, nor Man, nor the Devil, by night and day, alone and in company: sleeping all sorts together, and yet not one of them ever offered me the least abuse of unchastity to me, in word or action.* Though some are ready to say, I speak it for my own credit; *But I speak it in the presence of God, and to his Glory....*

[Hoar, Rowlandson, Tom, and Peter head for Boston by way of Lancaster,] and a solemn sight it was to me. There had I lived many comfortable years amongst my Relations and Neighbours, and now not one *Christian* to be seen, nor one house left standing.... [The next day] we came to *Concord.* Now was I full of joy...to see such a lovely sight, so many *Christians* together, and some of them my Neighbours....Yet I w[a]s not without sorrow, to think how many were looking and longing, and my own Children amongst the rest, to enjoy that deliverance that I had now received: and I did not know whither ever I should see them again. Being recruited [refreshed] with food and raiment, we went to *Boston*..., where I met with my dear Husband, but the thoughts of our dear Children, one being dead, and the other we could not tell where, abated our comfort each to other. I was not before so much hem'd in with the merciless and cruel Heathen, but now as much with pittiful, tenderhearted, and compassionate Christians. In that poor, and destressed, and beggerly condition I was received in, I was kindly entertained in severall Houses....We were now in the midst of love, yet not without much and frequent heaviness of heart for our poor Children, and other Relations, who were still in affliction....

About this time the Council had ordered a day of publick *Thanks-giving*: though I thought I had still cause of mourning, and being unsettled in our minds, we thought we would ride toward the *Eastward*, to see if we could hear any thing concerning our Children.... [After some delays, the Rowlandson children are returned.] Thus hath the Lord brought me and mine out of that horrible pit, and hath set us in the midst of tenderhearted and compassionate Christians....

I can remember the time, when I used to sleep quietly without workings in my thoughts, whole nights together, but now it is otherwayes with me. When all are fast about me, and no eye open, but his who ever waketh, my thoughts are upon things past, upon the awfull dispensation of the Lord towards us; upon his wonderfull power and might, in carrying us through so many difficulties, in returning us in safety, and suffering none to hurt us. I remember in the night season, how the other day I was in the midst of thousands of enemies, & nothing but death before me: It [was?] then hard work to perswade my self, that ever I should be satisfied with bread again.… The thoughts of these things in the particulars of them, and of the love and goodness of God towards us, make it true of me, what *David* said of himself, *Psal. 6.6. I watered my Couch with my tears.* Oh! the wonderfull power of God that mine eyes have seen, affording matter enough for my thoughts to run in, that when others are sleeping mine eyes are weeping.

I have seen the extrem vanity of this World: One hour I have been in health, and wealth, wanting nothing: But the next hour in sickness and wounds, and death, having nothing but sorrow and affliction.

Before I knew what affliction meant, I was ready sometimes to wish for it. When I lived in prosperity; having the comforts of the World about me, my relations by me, my Heart chearfull: and taking little care for any thing; and yet seeing many, whom I preferred before my self, under many tryals and afflictions, in sickness, weakness, poverty, losses, crosses, and cares of the World, I should be sometimes jealous least I should have my portion in this life, and that Scripture would come to my mind, *Heb.* 12.6. *For whom the Lord loveth he chasteneth, and scourgeth every Son whom he receiveth.* But now I see the Lord had his time to scourge and chasten me.…Affliction I wanted, and affliction I had, full measure (I thought) pressed down and running over: yet I see, when God calls a Person to any thing, and through never so many difficulties, yet he is fully able to carry them through and make them see, and say they have been gainers thereby. And I hope I can say in some measure, As *David* did, *It is good for me that I have been afflicted.* The Lord hath shewed me the vanity of these outward things. That they are the *Vanity of vanities, and vexation of spirit*; that they are but a shadow, a blast, a bubble, and things of no continuance. That we must rely on God himself, and our whole dependance must be upon him. If trouble from smallar [*sic*] matters begin to arise in me, I have something at hand to check my self with, and say, why am I troubled? It was but the other day that if I had had the world, I would have given it for my freedom, or to have been a Servant to a Christian. I have learned to look beyond present and smaller troubles, and to be quieted under them, as *Moses* said, *Exod.* 14.13. *Stand still and see the salvation of the Lord.*

CHAPTER 5

Dr. Hamilton Reports on His Summer Vacation

"These infant countrys of America"

A generation before a brilliant, ambitious young man named Alexander Hamilton burst on the American scene—going from General George Washington's aide to President George Washington's cabinet to a fatal duel with Aaron Burr and ending up on the $10 bill—another Alexander Hamilton (1712–1756) arrived on American shores. No relation to the famous founder, this Alexander Hamilton was a Scotsman of good family and even better education, having trained as a physician at the University of Edinburgh, then one of the finest institutions of higher learning in Europe. Graduated in 1737, Hamilton, discovering that Scotland had enough doctors, followed a brother to America and set up a medical practice in Annapolis, Maryland.

Soon, however, Hamilton's own health began to suffer from "consumption" (tuberculosis). To escape Maryland's oppressive summer heat—and, he hoped, cure an "[i]ncessant cough" and "Bloody Spitting" so bad that he "discharged at times above half a pint in Large mouthfulls"—in May 1744 he headed northeast with his slave Dromo, more or less following the route to Boston and beyond that Interstate 95 takes today, with a side trip up the Hudson River past Albany. Like many travelers before and since, Hamilton decided to keep a diary of his journey.[1]

Historian Carl Bridenbaugh has judged that travel journal "one of the most illuminating documents of the colonial period." It is, agrees J. A. Leo Lemay, "the best single portrait of men and manners, of rural and urban life, of the wide range of society and scenery in colonial America."[2] On first getting acquainted with Dr. Hamilton, however, you might well disagree; the man is hard for modern readers to like. Though sometimes hilarious, he seems a pompous, arrogant snob. His views of women, African Americans, and Indians are now (to put it nicely) out of fashion, and his attitude toward most colonial men was not much better. "[U]npolished people" less adept at "agreeable conversation" than at "Swearing and drinking punch & drams [small drinks], horse-racing, bullying, and coz[e]ning [cheating]," these bumpkins prompted Hamilton to buy "a very talkative" parrot for company.[3] Traveling through the colonies during the religious revival known as the Great Awakening, Hamilton, who favored reason and moderation in matters of faith, dismissed the movement's leaders (the Englishman George Whitefield and his American colleagues Gilbert Tennent and James Davenport) as frauds and fanatics; their "New Light" disciples, "clowns" in the clutches of a "strange madness," were even worse. The Scot's contempt for those with less money, less education, less polish, and more faith than he had seems downright un-American!

In fact, however, Dr. Hamilton helps us appreciate that few in his day believed "All Men are Created Equal." On the contrary: Most people then assumed that, by natural law and divine decree, the social order was hierarchical, shaped like a pyramid, with the king (under God) at its apex and everyone else carefully arranged in descending order below. "God hath in great wisdom," declared Hamilton's friend, the clergyman Thomas Cradock, "given variety of abilities to men, suitable to the several stations in life, for which he hath design'd them, that everyone keeping his station, and employing his respective abilities in doing his own work, all might receive advantage."[4] True, an exceptionally talented fellow like Benjamin Franklin (Chapter 6) could leave his low "station" and—with drive, skill, and luck—climb up that social ladder. Nonetheless, what Hamilton termed the "difference of degrees" among "the better sort" (gentlemen like him), "the middling sort" (farmers and craftsmen), and "the meaner sort" (sailors and dock workers, tenant farmers and day laborers, Irish servants and African slaves) remained abundantly clear.

And this was clear, "self-evident," to virtually everyone. Note in the next chapter how Franklin (who was in Philadelphia when the itinerant doctor passed through town that summer of 1744) negotiated the "difference of degrees." Or consider how, a few years after Hamilton returned to Annapolis, a teenager on a plantation just forty miles away painstakingly copied out by hand—from an English etiquette book entitled *Youths Behavior, or Decency in Conversation amongst Men*—advice like how low to bow when greeting "persons of distinction," how to speak to those "of greater quality than yourself," and how to behave around "one that is your equal, or not much inferior." The diligent, earnest, self-conscious boy's name? George Washington.[5]

In the 1740s, Washington and Franklin could tell at a glance "quality" and "vulgar." So could Hamilton: That is why this report on his summer vacation is so valuable that, as biographer Elaine Breslaw writes, "no history of colonial life can fail to ignore it."[6] Living today in an era that celebrates "the common man," a time when presidential candidates play up (or, if necessary, make up) humble roots to win votes, it is hard for us to crack the code of everyday life 250 years ago. Here is where the Scottish physician's survey of the social landscape comes to the rescue; here is why dismissing him as a distasteful prig is a mistake. To find our way through early America—which operated by a different set of rules—we need a guide like Dr. Hamilton.

As you read him, then, pay close attention to how *he* read the people he met. What distinguished what he called "the finer parts" of society from "the Coarser parts"?[7] What sorts of people did he respect, and why? What sorts of people did he despise (this, you will see, is a longer list!)—and why? As you follow him, jot down a list of good and bad qualities while also picking a vivid incident or two that illustrates how the social code worked.

Even as you read what Hamilton said about this colonial cast of characters, undertake the same exercise I invited you to try in the last chapter, Mary Rowlandson's own travel account: Read between the lines to see how those he crossed paths with read *him*. Were they awed? Fascinated? Frightened? Indifferent? What do their reactions to and interactions with this tourist tell us about the historically voiceless in America's past?

Once you get your bearings, be alert for how Hamilton joins the American conversation already under way. Does his America—its peoples, its landscape— bear any resemblance to the one Álvar Nuñez Cabeza de Vaca, John White, or Mary Rowlandson knew? At the same time, Hamilton's account speaks to texts still to come. How, for example, would Franklin and Hamilton get along? (We know they met, by the way, if not in Philadelphia in 1744, then ten years later when Franklin, visiting Annapolis, spent an evening at Hamilton's club.)[8] More important, how in the world did the American colonists, little more than three decades after Hamilton wrote, declare not only that "All Men are Created Equal" but also that they were founding a new American nation?

Scholars trying to explain this sudden turn of events have scoured Hamilton's account for clues. Some say that buried in his encounters with "the vulgar" are traces of an egalitarian strain of thinking that would burst forth by 1776. Do you detect such hints? Others argue that the beginnings of an identity as Americans lurk in these pages, that despite Hamilton's talk about differences among "these infant countrys of America" there are signs of an underlying unity. What do you think? Was there an *America* in 1744? Or is that reading too much into Hamilton's journal, keen to find the sources of later nationalism rather than understanding the colonies on their own terms?

Certainly no one Hamilton met, indeed no one at the time, was imagining independence and nationhood, much less yearning for it (see Chapter 7). Colonists proudly thought of themselves as British. Many of them also felt vastly inferior—in their culture, their politics, their architecture, their daily lives—to the realm they called "the mother country." Thinking of America today as a world power, it is hard to conceive of it as most people—including most Americans!—did then: "a Barbarous and desolate corner of the world" (Hamilton's words) inhabited by crude colonials and surly slaves with, as neighbors, "savage" Indians and frightening French Catholics in Canada and Louisiana who seemed a constant threat (as Hamilton found in many anxious conversations that summer about the onset of another "dreaded French war").[9] It was this American sense of vulnerability, this inferiority complex, that Thomas Paine would try to counter in *Common Sense* (Chapter 7).

But that is getting ahead of the story. Dr. Hamilton never would have dreamed of *Common Sense* or the Declaration of Independence (and if he had, they would have been a nightmare), just as he would have been shocked to learn that his 1754 guest, Ben Franklin, had a hand in editing both those texts. Back in 1744, summer was drawing to a close and he was again passing through Philadelphia, homeward bound, finally getting to Annapolis on September 27. There he resumed his medical practice, married into a prominent family, and pursued a gentleman's pastimes of politics, social clubs, music, and horseracing until his death in 1756. His obituary, which called him a "valuable and worthy *gentleman*" who had "gained…the respect and esteem of *all ranks* of men," captured the notions of social hierarchy he personified, as well as his place atop that structure.[10]

By then Hamilton's travel account was gathering dust in Europe. He had spent the fall of 1744 revising the notes he had jotted down over the summer. As he worked on the manuscript, he had in mind not only the many European travel accounts from ancient times to his own day that he had read, but also "a literary form devised by English travelers in more exotic locales." Believing that the best thing for readers unable to visit these faraway lands was "accurate description of [by] a discerning and Judicious traveler," Hamilton was careful to jot down "every thing that passed in Conversation" and to tell stories revealing "the General Characters of men of note in all ranks and Employments, in every place where he had been." If the tales were "well Seasoned with mirth and Laughter," so much the better; if they were a bit bawdy, better still.[11]

At last, satisfied with the result, in November he gave the manuscript to an acquaintance, another immigrant to Maryland named Onorio Razolini. (It was a common practice at the time for gentlemen to circulate their writings among friends.)[12] Razolini took it with him back to his native Italy upon his return home in 1749. There it sat, forgotten, until a century ago, when scholars rediscovered it. Its fate, then, was closer to the obscurity of works like William Apess's (Chapter 13) than to such best sellers as Mary Rowlandson's. Why do you suppose Hamilton never tried to publish it? Why have so few read it since?

Questions for Consideration and Conversation

1. Why did Hamilton write this account? For whom did he write it?
2. Hamilton offers us a series of encounters that illuminate the social contours of colonial society. Map those contours: How could you tell "common folk" from the "better sort"? What impressed Hamilton? What distressed him?
3. Just as Hamilton was "reading" the people he met and placing them in categories, so were they reading him, too, though we lack any account of their "read." Can you gather something of their reactions to him from what he wrote?
4. Some scholars see in Hamilton's writing abundant evidence for a lack of equality in early America; others argue that hints of a growing egalitarian ethos are scattered through his travel journal. Where do you stand in this debate?

5. Some scholars see in Hamilton's account evidence that there was no *America* in 1744, that the colonies were deeply divided and profoundly different; others find in the same text clear indications of unities that neither Hamilton nor the people he met were necessarily aware of but that were nonetheless evident. Which side has the better argument?
6. Consider Hamilton's views on religion. Why did those who disagreed with his views bother him so much?
7. Hamilton divided the men he met into status categories. Did he do the same with women, or was their gender more important to him than their status?
8. Does the "America" Hamilton traversed bear any resemblance to the place depicted in previous chapters of this book?

Endnotes

1. Carl Bridenbaugh, ed., *Gentleman's Progress: The Itinerarium of Dr. Alexander Hamilton, 1744* (Chapel Hill, NC, 1948), xiii–xiv ("cough"); Elaine G. Breslaw, *Dr. Alexander Hamilton and Provincial America: Expanding the Orbit of Scottish Culture* (Baton Rouge, LA, 2008), 104 ("Spitting," "Mouthfulls").
2. Bridenbaugh, ed., *Gentleman's Progress*, xxvi; Lemay quoted in Robert Micklus, *The Comic Genius of Dr. Alexander Hamilton* (Knoxville, TN, 1990), 75.
3. Breslaw, *Hamilton*, 147.
4. Gordon Wood, *The Radicalism of the American Revolution* (New York, 1992), 20. For Hamilton's agreement with Cradock, see Breslaw, *Hamilton*, 295–96.
5. Richard Brookhiser, ed., *Rules of Civility: The 110 Precepts That Guided Our First President in War and Peace* (Charlottesville, VA, 2003), 4, 42, 45, 46.
6. Breslaw, *Hamilton*, 331.
7. Ibid., 295.

8. Robert R. Hare, "Electro Vitrifrico in Annapolis: Mr. Franklin Visits the Tuesday Club," *Maryland Historical Magazine*, 58 (1963), 62–66; Breslaw, *Hamilton*, 168.
9. Breslaw, *Hamilton*, 1 ("desolate"), 79–81.
10. Bridenbaugh, ed., *Gentleman's Progress*, xxii (emphasis added).
11. Breslaw, *Hamilton*, 115–17 (literary roots), 166–68 (humor).
12. Klaus H. Schmidt, "A Scotsman in British America; or, Up Against Provincialism: The Construction of Individual and Collective Identities in Dr. Alexander Hamilton's *Itinerarium*," in Klaus H. Schmidt and Fritz Fleischmann, eds., *Early America Re-explored: New Readings in Colonial, Early National, and Antebellum Culture*, Early American Literature & Culture Through the American Renaissance, vol. 5 (New York, 2000), 151–81.

The *Itinerarium* of Dr. Alexander Hamilton (1744)

Source: Carl Bridenbaugh, ed., *Gentleman's Progress: The* Itinerarium *of Dr. Alexander Hamilton, 1744.* Chapel Hill, NC: University of North Carolina Press, 1948.

Amico suo honorando, divinitissimo Domino Onorio Razolini, manuscriptum hocce Itinerarium, observantiae et amoris sui qualcumque symbolium, dat consecratique.

—*Alexander Hamilton*

[To his honorable friend, the most excellent Signor Onorio Razolini, Alexander Hamilton gives and dedicates this manuscript the Itinerarium as a token of his esteem and affection.]

Itinerarium…

Annapolis, Wednesday, May 30th. I set out…att eleven a'clock in the morning.…[A]s the journey was intended only for health and recreation, I was indifferent whether I took the nearest or the farthest route.…I travelled but 26 miles this day.…Some miles from town I met Mr. H[ar]t going to Annapolis. He returned with me to his own house where I was well entertained.…

Mr. H[ar]t and I, after dinner, drank some punch and conversed like a couple of virtuosos. His wife had no share in the conversation; he is blessed indeed with a silent woman, but her muteness is owing to a defect in her hearing, that, without bawling out to her, she cannot understand what is spoke, and therefor not knowing how to make pertinent replys, she chuses to hold her tongue. It is well I have thus accounted for it; else such a character in the sex would appear quite out of nature.…

Thursday, May 31.…

Just as I dismounted att Tradaway's ["about 10 miles from Joppa"], I found a drunken club dismissing. Most of them had got upon their horses and were seated in an oblique situation, deviating much from a perpendicular to the horizontal plan[e], a posture quite necessary for keeping the center of gravity within its propper base for the support of the super-structure.… Their discourse was as oblique as their position; the only thing intelligible in it was oaths and God dammes; the rest was an inarticulate sound like [François] Rabelais' frozen words a thawing, inter-laced with hickupings and belchings. I was uneasy till they were gone, and my landlord, seeing me stare,

made that trite apology—that indeed he did not care to have such disorderly fellows come about his house; he was always noted far and near for keeping a quiet house and entertaining only gentlemen or such like, but these were country people, his neigh-bours, and it was not prudent to dissoblige them upon slight occasions. "Alas, sir!" added he, "we that entertain travellers must strive to oblige every body, for it is our dayly bread." While he spoke thus, our Bacchanalians [drunken revelers], finding no more rum in play, rid off helter skelter as if the devil had possessed them, every man sitting his horse in a see-saw manner like a bunch of rags tyed upon the saddle.

I found nothing particular or worth notice in my landlord's character or conversation, only as to his bodily make. He was a fat pursy man and had large bubbies like a woman. I supped upon fry'd chickens and bacon, and after supper the conversa-tion turned upon politicks, news, and the dreaded French war; but it was so very lumpish and heavy that it disposed me mightily to sleep. This learned company consisted of the landlord, his overseer and miller, and another greasy thumb'd fellow who, as I understood, professed physick [medicine] and par-ticularly surgery. In the drawing of teeth, he prac-ticed upon the house maid, a dirty piece of lumber [a useless object that takes up space], who made such screaming and squalling as made me imagine there was murder going forwards in the house. However, the artist got the tooth out att last with a great clumsy pair of black-smith's forceps; and indeed it seemed to require such an instrument, for when he showed it to us, it resembled a horsenail more than a tooth.…After having had my fill of this elegant company, I went to bed att 10 o'clock.

Friday, June 1st.… *Susquehanna Ferry.…*

The lower ferry of Susquehanna…is kept by a little old man whom I found att vittles [food] with his wife and family upon a homely dish of fish without any kind of sauce. They desired me to eat, but I told them I had no stomach. They had no cloth upon the table, and their mess was in a dirty, deep, wooden dish which they evacuated with their hands, cramming down skins, scales, and all. They used neither knife, fork, spoon, plate, or napkin because, I suppose, they had none to use. I looked upon this as a picture of that primitive simplicity practiced by our forefathers long before the mechanic arts had supplyed them with instruments for the luxury and elegance of life. I drank some of their syder, which was very good, and crossed the ferry in company with a certain Scots-Irishman by name Thomas Quiet....

This fellow, I observed, had a particular down hanging look which made me suspect he was one of our New Light biggots. I guessed right, for he introduced a discourse concerning [Reverend George] Whitfield and inlarged pritty much and with some warmth upon the doctrines of that apostle, speaking much in his praise. I took upon me, in a ludicrous manner, to impugn some of his doctrines, which, by degrees, put Mr. Quiet in a passion. He told me flatly that I was damnd without redemption. I replyed that I thought his name and behaviour were very incongruous and desired him to change it with all speed, for it was very improper that such an angry, turbulent mortall as he should be called by the name of Thomas Quiet....

I crossed Bohemia Ferry and lodged att the ferry house. The landlord's name I cannot remember, but he seemed to be a man of tollerable parts for one in his station. Our conversation run chiefly upon religion. He gave me a short account of the spirit of enthusiasm that had lately possessed the inhabitants of the forrests there and informed me that it had been a common practise for companys of 20 or 30 hair brained fanaticks to ride thro' the woods singing of psalms. I went to bed att 9 att night; my landlord, his wife, daughters, and I lay all in one room....

Pensylvania—Newcastle

Tuesday, June 5th. I took horse a little after 5 in the morning, and after a solitary ride thro stonny, unequall road, where the country people stared att me like sheep when I enquired of them the way....

I met company going to Philadelphia and was pleased att it, being my self an utter stranger to the roads. This company consisted of three men: Thomas Howard, Timothy Smith, and William Morison. I treated them with some lemmon punch and desired the favour of their company. They readily granted my request and stayed some time for me till I had eat breakfast....

Morison...was a very rough spun, forward, clownish blade, much addicted to swearing, att the same time desirous to pass for a gentleman; notwithstanding which ambition, the conscientiousness of his naturall boorishness obliged him frequently to frame ill tim'd apologys for his misbehaviour, which he termed frankness and freeness. It was often, "Damn me, gentlemen, excuse me; I am a plain, honest fellow; all is right down plain dealing, by God." He was much affronted with the landlady...who, seeing him in a greasy jacket and breeches and a dirty worsted cap, and withall a heavy, forward, clownish air and behaviour, I suppose took him for some ploughman or carman [one who transports goods] and so presented him with some scraps of cold veal for breakfast, he having declared that he could not drink "your damnd washy [weak] tea." As soon as he saw his mess he swore, "Damn him, if it wa'n't out of respect to the gentleman in company," (meaning me) he would throw her cold scraps out at the window and break her table all to pieces should it cost him 100 pounds for dammages. Then taking off his worsted [yarn] night cap, he pulled a linnen one out of his pocket and clapping it upon his head, "Now," says he, "I'm upon the borders of Pensylvania and must look like a gentleman; 'tother was good enough for Maryland, and damn my blood if ever I come into that rascally province again if I don't procure a leather jacket that I may be in a trim [prepared] to box the saucy jacks [fellows] there and not run the hazard of tearing my coat." This showed, by the bye, that he payed more regard to his coat than his person, a remarkable instance of modesty and self denyall....

[H]e told us that tho he seemed to be but a plain, homely fellow, yet he would have us know that he was able to afford better than many that went finer: he had good linnen in his bags, a pair of silver buckles, silver clasps, and gold sleeve buttons, two Holland shirts, and some neat night caps; and that his little woman att home drank tea twice a day; and he himself lived very well and expected to live better....

Cristin Ferry—Willmington—Brandywine....

After dinner [at an inn] we fell upon politicks, and the expected French war naturally came in, whence arose a learned dispute in company which was about settling the meaning of the two words, declaration and proclamation....They grew very loud upon it as they put about the bowl, and I retired into a corner of the room to laugh a little, handkerchef fashion, pretending to be busied in blowing my nose; so I slurd a laugh with nose blowing as people sometimes do a fart with coughing....

This dispute ended, we took our horses and rid moderately, it being excessive hot. I observed the common stile of salutation upon the road here was How d'ye? and How is't?....

Wednesday, June 6th.... *Philadelphia*

The country round the city of Philadelphia is level and pleasant, having a prospect of the large river of Delaware and the province of East Jersey upon the other side. You have an agreeable view of this river for most of the way betwixt Philadelphia and Newcastle....

Att my entering the city, I observed the regularity of the streets, but att the same time the majority of the houses mean and low and much decayed, the streets in generall not paved, very dirty, and obstructed with rubbish and lumber, but their frequent building excuses that. The State House, Assembly House, the great church in Second Street, and Whitefield's church are good buildings.

I observed severall comicall, grotesque phizzes [faces] in the inn wher[e] I put up.... They talked there upon all subjects—politicks, religion, and trade—some tollerably well, but most of them ignorantly. I discovered two or three chaps very inquisitive, asking my boy who I was, whence come, and whether bound....

I delivered my letters [of introduction]....In the afternoon I went to the coffee house where I was introduced by Dr. Thomas Bond to severall gentlemen of the place, where the ceremony of shaking of hands, an old custom peculiar to the English, was performed with great gravity and the usuall compliments....

Friday, June 8....I dined att a taveren with a very mixed company of different nations and religions. There were Scots, English, Dutch, Germans, and Irish; there were Roman Catholicks, Church men, Presbyterians, Quakers, Newlightmen, Methodists, Seventh day men, Moravians, Anabaptists, and one Jew. The whole company consisted of 25 planted round an oblong table in a great hall well stoked with flys. The company divided into comittees in conversation; the prevailing topick was politicks and conjectures of a French war.... The[y] touched a little upon religion, and high words arose among some of the sectaries, but their blood was not hot enough to quarrell....

After staying there [at a coffee house] an hour or two, I was introduced by Dr. Phineas Bond into the Governour's Club, a society of gentlemen that met at a taveren every night and converse on various subjects. The Governour gives them his presence once a week, which is generally upon Wednesday, so that I did not

see him there. Our conversation was entertaining; the subject was the English poets and some of the foreign writers, particularly [Miguel de] Cervantes, author of Don Quixot, whom we loaded with elogiums due to his character....

Saturday, June 9th....The Quakers here have two large meetings, the Church of England one great church in Second Street, and another built for Whitfield in which one [Gilbert] Tennent, a fanatick, now preaches, the Romans one chapell, the Anabaptists one or two meetings, and the Presbyterians two.

The Quakers are the richest and the people of greatest interest [influence] in this government; of them their House of Assembly is chiefly composed. They have the character of an obstinate, stiff necked generation and a perpetuall plague to their governors....However, the standing or falling of the Quakers in the House of Assembly depends upon their making sure the interest of the Palatines [Germans] in this province, who of late have turned so numerous that they can sway the votes which way they please.

Here is no publick magazine of arms nor any method of defence, either for city or province, in case of the invasion of an enimy. This is owing to the obstinacy of the Quakers in maintaining their principle of non-resistance. It were a pity but [if] they were put to a sharp triall to see whether they would act as they profess.

I never was in a place so populous where the gout [relish] for public gay diversions prevailed so little. There is no such thing as assemblys of the gentry among them, either for dancing or musick; these they have had an utter aversion to ever since Whitefield preached among them. Their chief employ, indeed, is traffick and mercantile business which turns their thoughts from these levitys....Strange influence of religious enthusiasm upon human nature to excite an aversion at these innocent amusements, for the most part so agreeable and entertaining to the young and gay, and indeed, in the opinion of moderate people, so conducive to the improvement of politeness, good manners, and humanity....

Tuesday, June 12....I must make a few remarks before I leave this place. The people in generall are inquisitive concerning strangers. If they find one comes there upon the account of trade or traffic, they are fond of dealing with him and cheating him if they can. If he comes for pleasure or curiosity, they take little or no notice of him unless he be a person of more than ordinary rank; then they know as well as others how to fawn and cringe....

They have in generall a bad notion of their neighbouring province, Maryland, esteeming the people a sett of cunning sharpers; but my notion of the affair is that the Pensylvanians are not a whit inferior to them in the science of chicane, only their method of tricking is different. A Pensylvanian will tell a lye with a sanctified, solemn face; a Marylander, perhaps, will convey his fib in a volley of oaths; but the effect and point in view is the same tho' the manner of operating be different....

There is polite conversation here among the better sort, among whom there is no scarcity of men of learning and good sense. The ladies, for the most part, keep att home and seldom appear in the streets, never in publick assemblies except att the churches or meetings; therefor I cannot with certainty enlarge upon their charms, having had little or no opportunity to see them either congregated or separate, but to be sure the Philadelphian dames are as handsome as their neighbours....

Wednesday, June 13.... *Trenton....*

I was treated att my entry into the town with a dish of staring and gaping from the shop doors and windows, and I observed two or three people laying hold of Dromo's stirrups, enquiring, I suppose, who I was and whence I came.

I put up att one Eliah Bond's att the Sign of the Wheat Sheaf. Two gentlemen of the town came there and invited me into their company. One was named Cadwaller, a doctor in the place and, as I understood, a fallen of[f] Quaker. We supped upon cold gammon [ham or bacon] and a sallet. Our discourse was mixed and rambling....

Thus passing from one subject to another in discourse, Cadwaller inveighed bitterly against the idle ceremonies that had been foisted into religious worship by almost all sects and perswasions—not that there was any thing materiall in these ceremonies to cavill att [quibble about] providing the true design of them was understood and they were esteemed only as decent decorations and ornaments to divine service in the temples and churches, but upon account that the vulgar in all ages had been misled and imposed upon by wicked, politick, and designing priests and perswaded that the strength and sinews of religion lay in such fopperies, and that there was no such thing as being a good man or attaining salvation without all this trumpery....

To this I replied that priests of all sorts and sects whatsoever made a kind of trade of religion, contriving how to make it turn out to their own gain and profit; yet notwithstanding, many were of opinion that to inculcate religion into vulgar minds we must use other methods than only preaching up fine sense and morality to them. Their understanding and comprehension are too gross and thick to receive it in that shape. Men of sense of every perswasion whatsoever are sensible of the emptiness and nonsense of the mere cermonial part of religion but, att the same time, allow it to be in some degree necessary and usefull, because the ignorant vulgar are to be dealt with in this point as we manage children by showing them toys in order to perswade them to do that which all the good reasoning of the world never would. The mobile [rabble], that many headed beast, cannot be reasoned into religious and pious duties. Men are not all philosophers. The tools by which we must work upon the gross senses and rough cast minds of the vulgar are such as form and lay before their eyes, rewards and punishments whereby the passions of hope and fear are excited; and withall our doctrines must be interlaced with something amazing and misterious in order to command their attention, strengthen their belief, and raise their admiration, for was one to make religion appear to them in her genuine, simple, and plain dress, she would gain no credit and would never be so regarded....

Thursday, June 14.... I passed thro' Princetown, a small village, at eight in the morning and was saluted with *How' s't ni tap* by an Indian traveller....

Friday, June 15.... *Long Island....*

Att the entry of this bay is a little craggy island about one or two miles long called Coney Island. Before I came to New York Ferry, I rid a bye way where, in seven miles' riding, I had 24 gates to open. Dromo, being about 20 paces before me, stoped att a house where, when I came up, I found him discoursing a negroe girl who spoke Dutch to him. "Dis de way to York?" says Dromo. "Yaw, dat is Yarikee," said the wench, pointing to the steeples. "What devil you say?" replys Dromo. "Yaw, mynheer," said the wench. "Damme you, what you say?" said Dromo again. "Yaw, yaw," said the girl. "You a damn black bitch," said Dromo and so rid on....

New York

This city makes a very fine appearance for above a mile all along river, and here lyes a great deal of shipping. I put my horses up att one Waghorn's att the Sign of the Cart and Horse. There I fell in with a company of toapers [heavy drinkers]. Among the rest was an old Scotsman, by name Jameson, sheriff of the city, and two aldermen whose names I know not. The Scotsman seemed to be dictator to the company; his talent lay in history, having a particular knack att telling a story. In his narratives he interspersed a particular kind of low wit well known to vulgar understandings. And having a homely carbuncle [pustule] kind of a countenance with a hideous knob of a nose, he screwd it into a hundred different forms while he spoke and gave such a strong emphasis to his words that he merely spit in one's face att three or four foot's distance, his mouth being plentifully bedewed with salival juice, by the force of the liquor which he drank and the fumes of the tobacco which he smoaked. The company seemed to admire him much, but he set me a staring.

After I had sat some time with this polite company, Dr. Colchoun, surgeon to the fort, called in, to whom I delivered letters, and he carried me to the tavern which is kept by one Todd, an old Scotsman, to supp with the Hungarian Club of which he is a member and which meets there every night. . . . They saluted me very civily, and I, as civilly as I could, returned their compliments in neat short speeches such as, "Your very humble servant," "I'm glad to see you," and the like commonplace phrazes used upon such occasions. We went to supper, and our landlord Todd entertained us as he stood waiting with quaint saws [sayings] and jack pudding [clownish] speeches. "Praised be God," said he, "as to cuikry, I defaa ony French cuik to ding me, bot a haggis is a dish I wadna tak the trouble to mak. . . ." He was a going on with this...when, very sasonably for the company, the bell, hastily pulled, called him to another room, and a little after we heard him roaring att the stair head, "Dam ye bitch, wharefor winna ye bring a canle?"

After supper they set in for drinking, to which I was averse and therefor sat upon nettles. They filled up bumpers att each round, but I would drink only three which were to the King, Governour Clinton, and Governour Bladen, which last was my own. Two or three toapers in the company seemed to be of opinion that a man could not have a more sociable quality or enduement than to be able to pour down seas of liquor and remain unconquered while others sunk under the table. I heard this philosophical maxim but silently dissented to it. I left the company att 10 att night pritty well flushed with my three bumpers and . . . ruminating on my folly. . . .

Saturday, June 16. . . . In the afternoon I took a turn thro' severall of the principall streets in town. . . .

The following observations occurred to me: I found this city less in extent but, by the stirr and

frequency upon the streets, more populous than Philadelphia; I saw more shipping in the harbour; the houses are more compact and regular and, in generall, higher built, most of them after the Dutch modell with their gavell [gable] ends fronting the street. There are a few built of stone, more of wood, but the greatest number of brick, and a great many covered with pan tile and glazed tile with the year of God when built figured out with plates of iron upon the fronts of severall of them. The streets, in generall, are but narrow and not regularly disposed [arranged]. The best of them run paralell to the river, for the city is built all along the water. In generall this city has more of an urban appearance than Philadelphia. Their wharfs are mostly built with logs of wood piled upon a stone foundation. In the city are severall large publick buildings. There is a spacious church belonging to the English congregation with a pritty high but heavy, clumsy steeple built of freestone fronting the street called Broadway. There are two Dutch churches, severall other meetings, and a pritty large Town House at the head of Broadstreet. The Exchange stands near the water and is a wooden structure, going to decay. . . . The women of fashion here appear more in publick than in Philadelphia and dress much gayer. They come abroad generally in the cool of the evening and go to the Promenade. . . .

Saturday, June 23. . . . [Hamilton takes ship to sail up the Hudson River.] We went ashore to fill water near a small log cottage on the west side of the river inhabited by one Stanespring and his family. The man was about 37 years of age, and the woman 30. They had seven children, girls and boys. The children seemed quite wild and rustick. They stared like sheep upon M——s [Milne] and I when we entered the house, being amazed att my laced hat and sword. They went out to gather blackberries for us, which was the greatest present they could make us. In return for which, we destributed among them a handfull of copper halfpence. This cottage was very clean and neat but poorly furnished. Yet Mr. M——s [Milne] observed severall superfluous things which showed an inclination to finery in these poor people, such as a looking glass with a painted frame, half a dozen pewter spoons and as many plates, old and wore out but bright and clean, a set of tea dishes, and a tea pot. These, Mr. M——s [Milne] said, were superfluous and too splendid for such a cottage, and therefor they ought to be sold to buy wool to make yarn; that a little water in a wooden pail might serve for a looking glass, and wooden plates and spoons would be as good for use and, when clean, would be almost as ornamental. As for the tea equipage it was quite unnecessary.... [T]he wind coming southerly att eleven a'clock, we weighed anchor and entered the Highlands which presented a wild, romantick scene of rocks and mountains covered with small scraggy wood, mostly oak....

This wild and solitary place, where nothing presents but huge precipices and inaccessible steeps where foot of man never was, infused in my mind a kind of melancholly and filled my imagination with odd thoughts which, att the same time, had some thing pleasant in them. It was pritty to see the springs of water run down the rocks, and what entertained me not a little was to observe some pritty large oaks growing there, and their roots to appearance fixed in nothing but the solid stone where you see not the least grain of mould or earth. The river is so deep in these Narrows of the Highlands that a large sloop may sail close upon the shore. We kept so near that the extremity of our boom frequently rustled among the leaves of the hanging branches from the bank....

Albany

Tuesday, June 26th.... We went a small mile out of town to the house of Jeremiah Ranslaer, who is dignified here with the title of Patroon. He is the principal landed man in these parts, having a large mannor, 48 miles long and 24 broad, bestowed upon his great grandfather by K. Charles the Second.... This mannor is divided into two equall halves by Hudson's River, and the city of Albany stands in the middle of it.... The Patroon is a young man of good mein [appearance] and presence.... He has a great number of tennants upon his mannor, and he told me himself that he could muster 600 men fit to bear arms. Mr. M——s [Milne] and I dined att his house and were handsomly entertained with good viands [food] and wine. After dinner he showed us his garden and parks....

Att 4 a'clock M——s [Milne], and I returned to town where M——s [Milne], having a generall acquaintance, for he had practised physick ten years in the city and was likewise the Church of England minister there, he introduced me into about 20 or 30 houses where I went thro' the farce of kissing most of the women, a manner of salutation which is expected (as M——s [Milne] told me) from strangers coming there. I told him it was very well, if he led the way I should follow, which he did with clericall gravity. This might almost pass for a pennance, for the generality of the women here, both old and young, are remarkably ugly....

Mohooks Town

Wednesday, June 27.... We rid att a pritty hard rate 15 or 16 miles farther to the Mohooks town.... In it there are severall wooden and brick houses, built after the Dutch fashion, and some Indian wigwams or huts, with a church where one Barclay preaches to a congregation of Indians in their own language, for the bulk of the Mohooks up this way are Christians.

Returning from here we dined att Coll. Skuyler's about 4 a'clock in the afternoon, who is naturalized among the Indians, can speak severall of their languages, and has lived for years among them....

Monday, July 2d.... The city of Albany.... consists of three pritty compact streets, two of which run paralell to the river and are pritty broad, and the third cuts the other two att right angles, running up towards the fort, which is a square stone building about 200 foot square with a bastion att each corner, each bastion mounting eight or ten great guns.... There are three market houses in this city and three publick edifices, upon two of which are cupolos or spires, vizt., upon the Town House and the Dutch church. The English church is a great, heavy stone building without any steeple, standing just below the fort. The greatest length of the streets is half a mile. In the fort is kept a garrison of 300 men under the King's pay.... This city is inclosed by a rampart or wall of wooden palisadoes about 10 foot high and a foot thick, being the trunks of pine trees rammed into the ground, pinned close together, and ending each in a point att top. Here they call them stockadoes. Att each 200 foot distance round this wall is a block house, and from the north gate of the city runs a thick stone wall down into the river, 200 foot long, att each end of which is a block house. In these block houses about 50 of the city militia keep guard every night, and the word all's well walks constantly round all night long from centry to centry and round the fort. There are 5 or 6 gates to this city.... In the city are about 4,000 inhabitants, mostly Dutch or of Dutch extract.

The Dutch here keep their houses very neat and clean, both without and within. Their chamber floors are generally laid with rough plank which, in time, by constant rubbing and scrubbing becomes as smooth as if it had been plained. Their chambers and rooms are large and handsom. They have their beds generally in alcoves so that you may go thro all the rooms of a great house and see never a bed. They affect pictures much, particularly scripture history, with which they adorn their rooms. They set out their cabinets and bouffetts much with china. Their kitchens are likewise very clean, and there they hang earthen or delft plates and dishes all round the walls in manner of pictures, having a hole drilled thro the edge of the plate or dish and a loop of ribbon put into it to hang it by. But notwithstanding all this nicety and cleanliness in their houses, they are in their persons slovenly and dirty. They live here very frugally and plain, for the chief merit among them seems to be riches, which they spare no pains or trouble to acquire, but are a civil and hospitable people in their way but, att best, rustick and unpolished.... They trade pritty much with the Indians and have their manufactorys for wampum, a good Indian commodity. It is of two sorts—the black, which is the most valuable, and the white wampum. The first kind is a bead made out of the bluish black part of a clam shell.... The white is made of a conch shell from the W. Indies and is not so valuable. They grind the beads to a shape upon a stone, and then with a well tempered needle dipt in wax and tallow, they drill a hole thro' each bead. This trade is apparently triffling but would soon make an estate to a man that could have a monopoly of it, for being in perpetuall demand among the Indians from their custome of burying quantitys of it with their dead, they are very fond of it, and they will give skins or money or any thing for it, having (tho they first taught the art of making it to the Europeans) lost the art of making it themselves.

They live in their houses in Albany as if it were in prisons, all their doors and windows being perpetually shut. But the reason of this may be the little desire they have for conversation and society, their whole thoughts being turned upon profit and gain which necessarily makes them live retired and frugall. Att least this is the common character of the Dutch every where. But indeed the excessive cold winters here obliges them in that season to keep all snug and close.... As to religion they have little of it among them and of enthusiasm not a grain.... Their women in generall, both old and young, are the hardest favoured ever I beheld. Their old women wear a comicall head dress, large pendants, short petticoats, and they stare upon one like witches....

Friday, July 6th. *New York* [*City*].... [T]he most remarkable person in the whole company [at a tavern] was one Wendal, a young gentleman from Boston. He entertained us mightily by playing on the violin the quickest tunes upon the highest keys, which he accompanied with his voice so as even to drown the violin with such nice shakings and gracings that I thought his voice outdid the instrument. I sat for some time imoveable with surprize. The like I never heard, and

the thing seemed to me next [nearly] a miracle. The extent of his voice is impossible to describe or even to imagine unless by hearing him. The whole company were amazed that any person but a woman or eunuch could have such a pipe [voice] and began to question his virility; but he swore that if the company pleased he would show a couple of as good witnesses as any man might wear. He then imitated severall beasts, as cats, dogs, horses, and cows, with the cackling of poultry, and all to such perfection that nothing but nature could match it. When the landlord (a clumsy, tallow faced fellow in a white jacket) came to receive his reckoning [payment], our mimick's art struck and surprized him in such a manner that...he might have passed for a statue done in white marble. He was so struck that the company might have gone away without paying and carried off all his silver tankards and spoons, and he never would have observed....

Sunday, July 8th.... [A]tt one a'clock went to dine with Mr. Bayard. Among some other gentlemen there was my old friend Dr. McGraa who to day seemed to have more talk and ostentation than usuall, but he did not shine quite bright till he had drank half a dozen glasses of wine after dinner. He spoke now in a very arbitrary tone as if his opinion was to pass for an ipse dixit [a dictum]. He and I unhappily engaged in a dispute which I was sorry for, it being dissonant to good manners before company, and what none but rank pedants will be guilty of. We were obliged to use hard physicall terms, very discordant and dissagreeable to ears not accustomed to them. I wanted much to drop it, but he kept teizing of me. I found my chap to be one of those learned bullys who, by loud talking and an affected sneer, seem to outshine all other men in parts of literature where the company are by no means propper judges, where for the most part the most impudent of the disputants passes for the most knowing man.... The thing that introduced this was an action of McGraa's which exceeded every thing I had seen for nastiness, impudence, and rusticity. He told us he was troubled with the open piles [hemorrhoids] and with that, from his breeches, pulled out a linnen handkercheff all stained with blood and showed it to the company just after we had eat dinner. After my astonishment att this piece of clownish impudence was over, I asked him if that evacuation att any particular times was greater or less, such as the full or change of the moon in the same manner as...in women. I intended only to play upon him. He answered with a sneer that he did not believe the moon had anything to do with us or our distempers and said that such notions were only superstitious nonsense, wondering how I could give credit to any such stuff. We had a great deal of talk about attraction, condensation, gravitation, rarifaction, of all which I found he understood just as much as a goose; and when he began to show his ignorance of the mathematical and astronomical problems of the illustrious [Isaac] Newton and blockishly resolve all my meaning into judiciall astrology, I gave him up as an unintelligent, unintelligible, and consequently inflexible disputant. And the company, being no judges of the thing, imagined, I suppose, that he had got the victory, which did not att all make me uneasy. He pretended to have travelled most countrys in Europe, to have shared the favour and acquaintance of some foreign princes and grandees and to have been att their tables, to be master of severall European languages, tho I found he could not speak good French and he merely murdered the Latin....

Monday, July 9th.... In this city are a mayor, recorder, aldermen, and common council. The goverment is under the English law, but the chief places are possessed by Dutchmen, they composing the best part of the House of Assembly. The Dutch were the first settlers of this province,... and ever since there have been a great number of Dutch here, tho now their language and customs begin pritty much to wear out and would very soon die were it not for a parcell of Dutch domines [clergymen or schoolmasters] here who, in the education of their children, endeavour to preserve the Dutch customs as much as possible. There is as much jarring here betwixt the powers of the legislature as in any of the other American provinces....

There are a great many handsome women in this city. They appear much more in publick than att Philadelphia. It is customary here to ride thro the street in light chairs. When the ladys walk the streets in the day time, they commonly use umbrellas, prittily adorned with feathers and painted....

Saturday, July 14th.... Upon the road here [in Rhode Island] stands a house belonging to an Indian King named George, commonly called King George's house or palace. He possesses twenty or thirty 1000 acres of very fine levell land round this house, upon which he has many tennants and has, of his own, a good stock of horses and other cattle. This King lives after the English mode. His subjects have lost their own goverment policy and laws and are servants or vassals to the English here. His queen goes in a high modish dress in her silks, hoops, stays, and dresses like an English woman. He educates his children to the belles letters [elegant literature] and

is himself a very complaisant [agreeable] mannerly man. We pay'd him a visit, and he treated us with a glass of good wine....

Thursday, July 19th.... *Boston*....

Att 12 o clock I waited upon Mr. Hooper, one of the ministers in Boston, and from thence went to Mr. Lechmere's the surveyor's, to whom my letters of credit were directed. From his house I went to the Change or place of publick rendezvous. Here is a great building called the Townhouse, about 125 foot long and 40 foot broad. The lower chamber of this house, called the Change, is all one apartment, the roof of which is supported all along the middle with a row of wooden pillars about 25 foot high. Upon Change I met Mr. Hutchinson and Captain Wendall to whom I delivered letters....

Sunday, July 22. After breakfast I went with Mr. Hughes to Hooper's meeting where we heard a very good discourse and saw a genteel congregation. The ladys were most of them in high dress. This meeting house is a handsome, new, wooden building with a huge spire or steeple att the north end of it. The pulpit is large and neat with a large sounding board supported att each side with pilasters [columns] of the Dorick order, fluted [grooved], and behind it there is a high arched door over which hangs a green curtain. The pulpit cushion is of green velvet, and all the windows in the meeting are mounted with green curtains....

After dinner I went to the English chappell with Mr. Lechmere and heard a small organ play'd by an indifferent [mediocre] organist. A certain pedantick Irishman preached to us, who had much of the brogue. He gave us rather a philosophicall lecture than a sermon and seemed to be one of those conceited priggs who are fond of spreading out to its full extent all that superficial physicall knowledge which they have acquired more by hearsay than by application or study; but of all places the pulpit is the most impropper for the ostentations of this sort; the language and phraseology of which sacred rostrum [platform] ought to be as plain to the ploughman as the schollar. We had a load of impertinence from him about the specific gravity of air and water, the exhalation of vapours, the expansion and condensation of clouds, the operation of distillation, and the chemistry of nature. In fine it was but a very puerile [silly or childish] physicall lecture and no sermon att all. There sat some Indians in a pew near me who stunk so that they had almost made me turn up my dinner. They made a profound reverence to the parson when he finished; the men bowed, and the squas curtsied....

Tuesday, July 24th....After dinner I went...to an auction of books in King's Street....We were called to the windows in the auction room by a noise in the street which was occasioned by a parade of Indian chiefs marching up the street with Collonell Wendal. The fellows had all laced hats, and some of them laced matchcoats and ruffled shirts, and a multitude of the plebs [ordinary people] of their own complexion followed them. This was one Henrique and some other of the chiefs of the Mohooks who had been deputed to treat with the eastren [sic] Indians bordering upon New England. This Henrique is a bold, intrepid fellow....These Mohooks are a terror to all round them and are certainly a brave warlike people, but they are divided into two nations, Protestants and Roman Catholicks, for the most of them are Christians; the first take part with the English, the latter with the French....

Salem

Monday, July 30....Our conversation [at a Mr. Sewell's] run upon the enthusiasm now prevalent in these parts and the strange madness that had possessed some people att Ipswitch occasioned by one Woodberry, a mad enthusiast, who, pretending to inspiration, uttered severall blasphemous and absurb [sic] speeches, asserting that he was the same to day, yesterday, and for ever, saying he had it in his power to save or damn whom he pleased, falling down upon the ground, licking the dust, and condemning all to hell who would not do the like, drinking healths to King Jesus,...and prosperity to the kingdom of heaven, and a thousand other such mad and ridiculous frolicks. I was quite shoked att these relations, both when I heard them mentioned in conversation and saw them published in the news paper, being surprized that some of the chief clergy there had been so weak as to be drawn away by these follies. This is a remarkable instance to what lengths of madness enthusiasm will carry men once they give it a loose [rein], and tho' excursions may appear shoking to people in their senses, yet so much good may follow them as that the interest and influence of these fanatick preachers will be thereby depressed among all such people as are not quite fools or mad. These extravagancies take all their first root from the labours of that righteous apostle Whitefield who, only for the sake of private lucre and gain, sowed the first seeds of distraction in these unhappy, ignorant parts.

In the afternoon Mr. Malcolm and I rid to the country seat of one Brown, a gentleman who married a daughter of the late Governour Burnet's, a grandaughter of the bishop's. His house stands upon the top of a high hill and is not yet quite finished. It is built in the form of an H with a middle body and two wings: The porch is supported by pillars of the Ionick order about 15 foot high, and betwixt the windows of the front are pilasters of the same. The great hall or parlour is about 40 foot long and 25 wide, with a gallery over the first row of windows, and there is two large rooms upon a floor in each of the wings, about 25 foot square. From this hill you have a most extensive view. To the southwest you see the Blue Hills about 36 miles' distance, to the east the sea and several islands, to the northwest the top of a mountain called Machuset Mountain, like a cloud, about 90 miles' distance towards Albany, and all round you a fine landskip covered with woods, a mixture of hills and valleys, land and water, upon which variety the eye dwells with pleasure....

Newburry Ferry—Hampton

Wednesday, August 1....I was overtaken by a man who bore me company all the way to Portsmouth. He was very inquisitive about where I was going, whence I came, and who I was. His questions were all stated in the rustick civil stile. "Pray sir, if I may be so bold, where are you going?" "Prithee, friend," says I, "where are you going?" "Why, I go along the road here a little way." "So do I, friend," replied I. "But may I presume, sir, whence do you come?" "And from whence do you come, friend?" says I. "Pardon me, from John Singleton's farm," replied he, "with a bag of oats." "And I come from Maryland," said I, "with a portmanteau [suitcase] and baggage." "Maryland!" said my companion, "where the devil is that there place? I have never heard of it. But pray, sir, may I be so free as to ask your name?" "And may I be so bold as to ask yours, friend?" said I. "Mine is Jerry Jacobs, att your service," replied he. I told him that mine was Bombast Huynhym van Helmont, att his service. "A strange name indeed; belike your a Dutchman, sir,—a captain of a ship, belike." "No, friend," says I, "I am a High German alchymist." "Bless us! You don't say so; that's a trade I never heard of; what may you deal in sir?" "I sell air," said I. "Air," said he, "damn it, a strange commodity. I'd thank you for some wholesom air to cure my fevers which have held me these two months." I have noted down this dialogue as a specimen of many of the same tenour [sort] I had in my journey when I met with these inquisitive rusticks....

[Having visited New Hampshire, Hamilton returns to Boston.]

Monday August 13. I made a tour thro the town in the forenoon with Mr. Hughes and, att a certain lady's house, saw a white monkey. It was one of those that are brought from the Muscetto [Mosquito] shore [in Central America] and seemed a very strange creature. It was about a foot long in its body and, in visage, exceeding like an old man, there being no hair upon its face except a little white, downy beard. It laugh'd and grinned like any Christian (as people say), and was exceeding fond of his mistress, bussing [kissing] her and handling her bubbies just like an old rake. One might well envy the brute, for the lady was very handsome; so that it would have been no dissagreeable thing for a man to have been in this monkey's place. It is strange to see how fond these brutes are of women, and, on the other hand, how much the female monkeys affect [like] men. The progress of nature is surprizing in many such instances. She seems by one connected gradation to pass from one species of creatures to another without any visible gap, intervall, or *discontinuum* in her works; but an infinity of her operations are yet unknown to us. . . .

Some children in the street took me for an Indian king upon account of my laced hat and sun burnt vissage.

Tuesday, August 14th. . . . I went in the afternoon with Hughes to the house of Mr. Harding and had some conversation with a very agreeable lady there, Mr. Withered's sister. This lady cannot be deemed handsom, but to supply the want of that naturall accomplishment which the sex are so very fond of, she had a great deal of good sense and acquired knowledge which appeared to the best advantage in every turn of her discourse. The conversation was lively, entertaining, and solid, neither tainted with false or triffling wit nor ill natured satire or reflexion, of late so much the topic of tea tables. . . .

Thursday, August 16. . . . I need scarce take notice that Boston is the largest town in North America, being much about the same extent as the city of Glasgow in Scotland and having much the same number of inhabitants, which is between 20 and 30 thousand. It is considerably larger than either Philadelphia or New York, but the streets are irregularly disposed and, in generall, too narrow. The best street in the town is that which runs down towards the Long Wharff which goes by the name of King's Street. This town is a considerable place for shipping and carrys on a great trade in time of peace . . . tho now, upon account of the war, the times are very dead. The people of this province chiefly follow farming and merchandise. Their staples are shipping, lumber, and fish. The government is so far democratic as that the election of the Governour's Council and the great officers is made by the members of the Lower House, or representatives of the people. . . .

There are many different religions and perswasions here, but the chief sect is that of the Presbyterians. There are above 25 churches, chapells, and meetings in the town, but the Quakers here have but a small remnant, having been banished [from] the province att the first settlement upon account of some disturbances they raised. The people here have latlely been, and indeed are now, in great confusion and much infested with enthusiasm from the preaching of some fanaticks and New Light teachers, but now this humour begins to lessen. . . . It is not by half such a flagrant sin to cheat and cozen one's neighbour as it is to ride about for pleasure on the sabbath day or to neglect going to church and singing of psalms.

The middling sort of people here are to a degree dissingenuous and dissembling, which appears even in their common conversation in which their indirect and dubious answers to the plainest and fairest questions show their suspicions of one another. The better sort are polite, mannerly, and hospitable to strangers, such strangers, I mean, as come not to trade among them (for of them they are jealous). There is more hospitality and frankness showed here to strangers than either att York or at Philadelphia. And in the place there is abundance of men of learning and parts; so that one is att no loss for agreeable conversation nor for any sett of company he pleases. Assemblys of the gayer sort are frequent here; the gentlemen and ladys meeting almost every week att consorts of musick and balls. I was present att two or three such and saw as fine a ring of ladys, as good dancing, and heard musick as elegant as I had been witness to any where. I must take notice that this place abounds with pritty women who appear rather more abroad than they do att York and dress elegantly. They are, for the most part, free and affable as well as pritty. I saw not one prude while I was here. . . .

They have a variety of paper currencys in the provinces; viz., that of New Hampshire, the Massachusets, Rhode Island, and Connecticut, all of different value, divided and subdivided into old and new tenors [issues] so that it is a science to know the nature and value of their moneys, and what will cost a stranger some study and application. . . .

Sunday, August 26. . . . *N[ew] London*

Deacon Green's son came to see me. He entertained me with the history of the behaviour of one [James] Davenport, a fanatick preacher there who told his flock in one of his enthusiastic rhapsodies that in order to be saved they ought to burn all their idols. They began this conflagration with a pile of books in the public street,...and sung psalms and hymns over the pile while it was a burning. They did not stop here, but the women made up a lofty pile of hoop petticoats, silk gowns, short cloaks, cambrick [fine white linen] caps, red heeld shoes, fans, necklaces, gloves and other such aparrell, and what was merry enough, Davenport's own idol with which he topped the pile, was a pair of old, wore out, plush breaches. But this bone fire was happily prevented by one more moderate than the rest, who found means to perswade them that making such a sacrifice was not necessary for their salvation, and so every one carried of[f] their idols again, which was lucky for Davenport who, had fire been put to the pile, would have been obliged to strutt about bare-arsed....

Monday, August 27....*Nantique, an Indian Town....*

A little after I passed this ferry I rid close by an Indian town upon the left hand situated upon the brow of a hill. This town is called Nantique and consists of 13 or 14 hutts or wig-wams made of bark.

Connecticut River....

After dinner there came in a rabble of clowns who fell to disputing upon points of divinity as learnedly as if they had been professed theologues. 'Tis strange to see how this humour prevails, even among the lower class of the people here. They will talk so pointedly about justification, santification, adoption, regeneration, repentance, free grace, reprobation, original sin, and a thousand other such pritty, chimerical knick knacks as if they had done nothing but studied divinity all their life time..., and yet the fellows look as much, or rather more, like clowns than the very riff-raff of our Maryland planters....

Wednesday, August 29th....*Norwalk*

I arrived att Norwalk att seven o clock att night.... [T]he children were frightened att my negroe, for here negroe slaves are not so much in use as with us, their servants being chiefly bound or indentured Indians. The child asked if that negroe was a coming to eat them up. Dromo indeed wore a voracious phiz, for having rid 20 miles without eating, he grinned like a crocodile and showed his teeth most hideously.

Betwixt Taylor's and Norwalk I met a caravan of 18 or 20 Indians. I put up att Norwalk att one

Beelding's, and as my boy was taking off the saddles, I could see one half of the town standing about him making enquiry about his master....

Friday, August 31....*New York [City]....*

The table chat run upon privateering and such discourse as has now become so common that it is tiresome and flat. One there, who set up for a dictator, talked very much to the discredit of Old England, preferring New York to it in every respect whatsoever relating to good living. Most of his propositions were gratis dicta [mere assertions], and it seemed as if he either would not, or did not, know much of that fine country England. He said that the grapes there were good for nothing but to set a man's teeth on edge; but to my knowledge I have seen grapes in gentlemen's gardens there far preferable to any ever I saw in these northeren parts of America. He asserted also that no good apple could be brought up there without a glass and artificiall heat, which assertion was palpably false and glaringly ignorant, for almost every fool knows that apples grow best in northeren climates betwixt the latitudes of 35 and 50, and that in the southern hot climes, within the tropics, they don't grow att all, and therefor the best apples in the world grow in England and in the north of France. He went even so far as to say that the beef in New York was preferable to that of England. When he came there I gave him up as a triffler, and giving no more attention to his discourse, he lost himself, the Lord knows how or where, in a thicket of erroneous and ignorant dogmas....But he was a great person in the place, and therefor none in the company was imprudent enough to contradict him tho some were there that knew better. I have known in my time some of these great dons take upon them to talk in an extravagant and absurd manner: "What a fine temperate climate this is!" says a certain dicting fop, while every body that hears him is conscious that it is fit for none but the devil to live in. "Don't you think them fine oysters," says another exalted prigg, while every body knows he is eating of eggs. This we cannot conceive proceeds from ignorance but from a certain odd pleasure they have in talking nonsense without being contradicted. This disposition may arise from the naturall perverseness of human nature, which is always most absurd and unreasonable when free from curb or restraint....

Wednesday, September 5th....I went in the morning with Mr. Hog to the Jews' sinagogue where was an assembly of about 50 of the seed of Abraham chanting and singing their dolefull hymns, (they had 4 great wax candles lighted, as large as a man's arm, round the sanctuary where was contained the ark of the covenant and Aaron's rod), dressed in robes of white silk. Before the rabbi, who was elevated above the rest, in a kind of desk, stood the seven golden candlesticks transformed into silver gilt. They were all slip shod. The men wore their hats in the synagogue and had a veil of some white stuff which they sometimes threw over their heads in their devotion; the women, of whom some were very pritty, stood up in a gallery like a hen coop. They sometimes paused or rested a little from singing and talked about business. My ears were so filled with their lugubr[i]ous [mournful] songs that I could not get the sound out of my head all day....

Tuesday, September 11....

I was sorry to leave New York upon account of being separated from some agreeable acquaintance I had contracted there.... I knew here severall men of sense, ingenuity, and learning, and a much greater number of fops whom I chuse not to name, not so much for fear of giving offence as because I think their names are not worthy to be recorded either in manuscript or printed journals. These dons commonly held their heads higher than the rest of mankind and imagined few or none were their equals. But this I found always proceeded from their narrow notions, ignorance of the world, and low extraction [origin], which

indeed is the case with most of our aggrandized [exalted] upstarts in these infant countrys of America who never had an opportunity to see, or if they had, the capacity to observe the different ranks of men in polite nations or to know what it is that really constitutes that difference of degrees....

Thursday, September 27....*Annapolis*

I arrived att Annapolis att two o'clock afternoon and so ended my perigrinations [ramblings].

In these my northeren travells I compassed [achieved] my design in obtaining a better state of health, which was the purpose of my journey. I found but little difference in the manners and character of the people in the different provinces I passed thro', but as to constitutions and complexions, air and goverment, I found some variety. Their forms of goverment in the northeren provinces I look upon to be much better and happier than ours, which is a poor, sickly, convulsed state. Their air and living to the northward is likewise much preferable, and the people of a more gygantick size and make. Att Albany, indeed, they are intirely Dutch and have a method of living something differing from the English.

In this itineration I compleated, by land and water together, a course of 1624 miles. The northeren parts I found in generall much better settled than the southeren. As to politeness and humanity, they are much alike except in the great towns where the inhabitants are more civilized, especially att Boston.

CHAPTER 6

Benjamin Franklin Composes His Life

"A young man of promising parts"

Benjamin Franklin (1706–1790) was easily the most famous American of his day. At a time when George Washington was still a tobacco planter, Thomas Jefferson a student at the College of William and Mary, and John Adams an obscure lawyer, Franklin was renowned throughout the Atlantic world. Scientist, inventor, and philosopher, holder of honorary degrees from Harvard, Yale, and Oxford, he was hailed as "the First American."[1] A generation later, when he died in Philadelphia on April 17, 1790, 20,000 people—almost half of that city's population—attended the funeral.

The years since have only added to his stature: Franklin with kite and key braving a lightning storm; Franklin and his ingenious stove; Franklin as *Poor Richard*, offering up such sayings as "Early to bed and early to rise, makes a man healthy, wealthy, and wise"; Franklin the toast of the town in Paris (where he served as a diplomat from 1776 to 1785), the emblematic American in his fur cap. An image of the man, usually sporting spectacles and a bemused smile, is deeply etched into the American mind and memory. The many editions of his classic *Autobiography* available today—in paperback and hardcover volumes, of course, but also as audio cassettes and on the Internet—attest to Franklin's enduring fame and abiding appeal. So, too, do the many recent biographies and his being featured on the cover of *Time*.[2]

Franklin would be delighted that we remember him so well, but not surprised. Certainly during his own lifetime he enjoyed (and cultivated) what he called his "reputation in the world." Moreover, he hoped that what he labeled his "memoirs" or his "life" (the word *autobiography* only appeared in the nineteenth century) would continue to entertain and instruct people long after he was gone.[3] Though the work's beginning reads like a letter to his son, it soon becomes obvious that Franklin was writing for a wider audience that included us. Having begun the work in 1771, then returning to it several times in the 1780s, near the end of his life Franklin tried to ensure that it would be published, sending copies to friends and, in his will, leaving instructions to shepherd the manuscript into print.

The first complete edition, which appeared in 1818, was an instant hit, and it has remained a blockbuster ever since. In that age of the "self-made man," when Americans were on the move and on the make, Franklin's story became an indispensable guidebook. Charting the path to success, it shaped the lives of people from Andrew Carnegie to Jay Gatsby (F. Scott Fitzgerald's fictional Minnesota boy seeking fame and fortune) to Jimmy Carter, the peanut farmer who became president. The book's "influence on American life," writes critic Ormond Seavey, "is really incalculable."[4]

Those who read Franklin's reminiscences as a true story, an instructive, inspirational self-improvement book—especially those who are what one Franklin friend called his target audience,

"American Youth"—are taking this text the way he hoped they would. As a student of America's past, however, you should come to the *Autobiography* from a different angle. For one thing, you should not take him at his word: As Seavey has noted, this memoir, even more than most, is "an elaborate fabrication."[5] Franklin was not necessarily making things up, but he wrote down what he wanted us to know, including (and omitting) chapters of his life in order to paint a particular image of himself. How would you describe that image? Why would a married, elderly, distinguished man admit—first to his son, then to everyone—that he had had "intrigues with low women" that left him fretting about sexually transmitted diseases?

Adopting a more critical stance also helps us to resist being seduced by Franklin's amiable persona, which is as evident in his *Autobiography* as it was in contemporary portraits and in person. He is "all jollity and pleasantry," recalled one who knew him, and a biographer observes how "[h]is contemporaries referred again and again to his half-quizzical smile and to his easy laughter."[6] Beneath that, however, some—during Franklin's lifetime and ever since—have detected a darker side to the man, a cold, calculating detachment that goes against the popular image of a benign, bemused genius. As you read, look for evidence of what various people have called "a black streak" of "bitter anger" in this "crafty and ruthless" loner.[7] Just as in previous chapters I encouraged you to turn the tables on Mary Rowlandson and Dr. Alexander Hamilton by asking what her captors or his contacts might have said about them, so with Franklin it is fruitful (and fun) to imagine what his brother James or his first Philadelphia employer, Samuel Keimer, might have said about young Benjamin had they written memoirs of their own.

But Franklin's text is important not just because it was enormously influential or because it sheds light on an American icon; it has the added advantage of joining (and enriching) conversations that have occupied and will continue to preoccupy us. Franklin was born to Puritan parents in Boston at a time when the shadow of King Philip's War still hung over New England (and the Indian leader's skull still sat on a pole in Plymouth); as a boy, he heard sermons by the minister Increase Mather, the likely author of the Preface to Mary Rowlandson's captivity narrative (Chapter 4). Not surprisingly, some scholars find a "deep and binding" Puritanism in Franklin. Others argue that he shed this heritage by leaving Boston, that he "was born in Philadelphia—at the age of 17."[8] To what extent had Franklin imbibed the personal habits and religious sensibilities, the views of this world and the next, that Mary Rowlandson held?

Franklin's connections with his contemporary, Dr. Alexander Hamilton, are even more pronounced. That he was a prominent figure on the Philadelphia scene when Hamilton passed through there in 1744 and that a decade later he visited the physician's Annapolis club are perhaps the least important of these connections. (Though it is worth pondering how well they would have gotten along had they spent even more time together; you already know what the Edinburgh-trained physician thought of would-be gentlemen; you will soon find out what Franklin said about "men of all sorts that have been bred at Edinborough"!) More interesting and more illuminating are how his religious beliefs correspond to the Scot's. What, for example, did Franklin think of the evangelical movement known as the Great Awakening? Would he have agreed with Dr. Hamilton about the "new light biggots" and "hair brained fanatics"?

As with the spiritual, so with the social: Comparing Franklin with Hamilton yields rich insights into the tension between hierarchy and equality in colonial America. Did the social world Franklin mapped bear any resemblance to Hamilton's? Do you find in Franklin's *Autobiography* any traces of divisions between "the better sort" and "the lower sort"? Or did he not only personify but celebrate what would later be called the "rags-to-riches story"? Pay close attention to how young Benjamin, the son of a soap- and candle-maker, tried to get ahead in the world. What was the secret to his success: Cultivating men like Dr. Hamilton? Striking out on his own? Some other means altogether?

It is clear that Dr. Hamilton and Dr. Franklin would agree on one thing: The pervasive influence, authority, and superiority Great Britain enjoyed over her American colonies for most of the eighteenth century. Franklin started writing this classic *American* story in an *English* country house. He spent the opening pages of this quintessentially *American* tale proudly sketching his *English* family tree. And throughout this drama, England plays a leading role. Moreover, Franklin spent eighteen of the twenty years before 1776 in London as an agent (a combination lobbyist and ambassador) for various colonies. Was he in exile, pining for his "native country"? Hardly. For the most part this "First American," this Founding Father, loved it there, loved it so much that he toyed with the idea of living in England "for ever."[9]

Just as Franklin's *Autobiography* intersects with various other texts you have already read, his long life would intersect with other men and other documents you will encounter soon enough. In London he met Thomas Paine and wrote a letter of recommendation for the Englishman to take to Pennsylvania. Back in Philadelphia himself by the summer of 1775, Franklin went over a draft of Paine's pamphlet, *Common Sense*. The next year found him helping Thomas Jefferson with the Declaration of Independence (Chapter 7).

Thus, both the man himself and his famous memoir are vital keys to unlocking the American experience in colonial times, during the revolutionary era—and in the generations since. You will, I think, find him an agreeable companion on this stage of your travels through America's past.

Questions for Consideration and Conversation

1. Franklin began his text writing to his son William. By the end, he was writing it to…whom? Not William, from whom he was estranged (William remained loyal to Britain during the Revolution). To whom, then, was Franklin writing? Is the change in audience—and, by the 1780s, the changes in Franklin's place in the world—reflected by changes in the text's topics? Its tone?

2. Consider closely the thirteen virtues Franklin listed. Did he include any that surprised you? Did he omit any that he should have included?

3. Some readers have come away from this work thinking of Franklin as an amiable, congenial, amusing, charming fellow, always interested in helping others and improving society; others consider him self-centered, shrewd, ruthless, and materialistic, something of a rogue. Where do you stand in this debate?

4. If Benjamin's brother James wrote his own memoir of "My Life with Ben," what might that have looked like? If Samuel Keimer had left us his own recollections of his relationship with young Franklin, what would the principal themes have been?

5. We know that Franklin and Dr. Alexander Hamilton met in 1754, if not at other times. How would they have gotten along? Would Franklin have admired Hamilton? Would Hamilton have accepted Franklin as a fellow gentleman?

6. Franklin was born in Boston of Puritan stock. Do you see elements of a Puritan way of living in his writing, or did his escape to Philadelphia take his belief and behavior in different directions?

7. What does Franklin *fail* to talk about in his memoir?

8. Why would Franklin admit to such mistakes (he called them *errata*, a printer's term for "errors") as "intrigues with low women"? Why not just leave out what might be called youthful indiscretions?

Endnotes

1. Esmond Wright, *Franklin of Philadelphia* (Cambridge, MA, 1986), 354.
2. *Time*, July 7, 2003.
3. Benjamin Franklin, *The Autobiography of Benjamin Franklin*, ed. Louis P. Masur (Boston, MA, 1993), 2.

4. Ormond Seavey, *Becoming Benjamin Franklin: The Autobiography and the Life* (University Park, PA, 1988), 95; Franklin, *Autobiography*, 17.

5. Seavey, *Becoming Benjamin Franklin*, 7.

6. Wright, *Franklin of Philadelphia*, 350.

7. Ibid., 11 ("bitter anger"), 351 ("black streak"); Franklin, *Autobiography*, 4 ("crafty and ruthless").

8. Wright, *Franklin of Philadelphia*, 24.

9. Jack P. Greene, *Understanding the American Revolution: Issues and Actors* (Charlottesville, VA, 1995), 254.

BENJAMIN FRANKLIN, *AUTOBIOGRAPHY* (1788)

Source: Benjamin Franklin, *The Autobiography*, in J. A. Leo Lemay, ed., *Benjamin Franklin: Writings.* New York: The Library of America, 1987.

Part One

Twyford, at the Bishop of St Asaph's 1771

Dear Son,

...[I]magining it may be...agreable to you to know the Circumstances of *my* Life, many of which you are yet unacquainted with; and expecting a Weeks uninterrupted Leisure in my present Country Retirement, I sit down to write them for you. To which I have besides some other Inducements. Having emerg'd from the Poverty & Obscurity in which I was born & bred, to a State of Affluence & some Degree of Reputation in the World, and having gone so far thro' Life with a considerable Share of Felicity, the conducing Means I made use of, which, with the Blessing of God, so well succeeded, my Posterity may like to know, as they may find some of them suitable to their own Situations, & therefore fit to be imitated.—That Felicity, when I reflected on it, has induc'd me sometimes to say, that were it offer'd to my Choice, I should have no Objection to a Repetition of the same Life from its Beginning, only asking the Advantage Authors have in a second Edition to correct some Faults of the first. So would I if I might, besides corr[ectin]g the Faults, change some sinister Accidents & Events of it for others more favourable, but tho' this were deny'd, I should still accept the Offer. However, since such a Repetition is not to be expected, the Thing most like living one's Life over again, seems to be a *Recollection* of that Life; and to make that Recollection as durable as possible, the putting it down in Writing.—Hereby, too, I shall indulge the Inclination so natural in old Men, to be talking of themselves and their own past Actions, and I shall indulge it, without being troublesome to others who thro' respect to Age might think themselves oblig'd to give me a Hearing, since this may be read or not as any one pleases. And lastly, (I may as well confess it, since my Denial of it will be believ'd by no body) perhaps I shall a good deal gratify my own *Vanity*. Indeed I scarce ever heard or saw the introductory Words, *Without Vanity I may say*, &c. but some vain thing immediately follow'd. Most People dislike Vanity in others whatever Share they have of it themselves, but I give it fair Quarter wherever I meet with it, being persuaded that it is often productive of Good to the Possessor & to others that are within his Sphere of Action: And therefore in many Cases it would not be quite absurd if a Man were to thank God for his Vanity among the other Comforts of Life.—

And now I speak of thanking God, I desire with all Humility to acknowledge, that I owe the mention'd Happiness of my past Life to his kind Providence, which led me to the Means I us'd & gave them Success.—My Belief of This, induces me to *hope*, tho' I must not *presume*, that the same Goodness will still be exercis'd towards me in continuing that Happiness, or in enabling me to bear a fatal Reverso, which I may experience as others have done, the Complexion of my future Fortune being known to him only: and in whose Power it is to bless to us even our Afflictions.

The Notes one of my Uncles (who had the same kind of Curiosity in collecting Family Anecdotes) once put into my Hands, furnish'd me with several Particulars, relating to our Ancestors. From those Notes I learnt that the Family had liv'd in the same Village, Ecton in Northamptonshire, for 300 Years, & how much longer he knew not,...on a Freehold of about 30 Acres, aided by the Smith's Business which had continued in the Family till his Time, the eldest Son being always bred to that Business. A Custom which he & my Father both followed as to their eldest Sons....My Grandfather Thomas, who was born in 1598, lived at Ecton till he grew too old to follow Business longer, when he went to live with his Son John, a Dyer at Banbury in Oxfordshire, with whom my Father serv'd an Apprenticeship. There my Grandfather died and lies buried....

Josiah, my Father, married young, and carried his Wife with three Children unto New England, about 1682. The Conventicles [secret religious services] having been forbidden by Law, & frequently disturbed, induced some considerable Men of his Acquaintance to remove to that Country, and he was prevail'd with to accompany them thither, where they expected to enjoy their Mode of Religion with Freedom.—By the same Wife he had 4 Children more born there, and by a second Wife ten more, in all 17, of which I remember 13 sitting at one time at his Table, who all grew up to be Men & Women, and married;—I was the youngest Son and the youngest Child but two, & was born in Boston, N. England.

My Mother the 2d Wife was Abiah Folger, a Daughter of Peter Folger, one of the first Settlers of New England, of whom honourable mention is made by Cotton Mather, in his Church History of that Country, (entitled Magnalia Christi Americana) as a *godly learned Englishman*, if I remember the Words rightly....

My elder Brothers were all put Apprentices to different Trades. I was put to the Grammar School at Eight Years of Age, my Father intending to devote me as the Tithe [a grant to support one's church] of his Sons to the Service of the Church. My early Readiness in learning to read (which must have been very early, as I do not remember when I could not read) and the Opinion of all his Friends that I should certainly make a good Scholar, encourag'd him in this Purpose....I continu'd however at the Grammar School not quite one Year, tho' in that time I had risen gradually from the Middle of the Class of that Year to be the Head of it, and farther was remov'd into the next Class above it, in order to go with that into the third at the End of the Year. But my Father in the mean time, from a View of the Expence of a College Education which, having so large a Family, he could not well afford, and the mean Living many so educated were afterwards able to obtain, Reasons that he gave to his Friends in my Hearing, altered his first Intention, took me from the Grammar School, and sent me to a School for Writing & Arithmetic....At Ten Years old, I was taken home to assist my Father in his Business, which was that of a Tallow Chandler and Sope-Boiler....Accordingly I was employed in cutting Wick for the Candles, filling the Dipping Mold, & the Molds for cast Candles, attending the Shop, going of Errands, &c.—I dislik'd the Trade and had a strong Inclination for the Sea; but my Father declar'd against it....

I continu'd thus employ'd in my Father's Business for two Years....But my Dislike to the Trade continuing, my Father was under Apprehensions that if he did not find one for me more agreable, I should

break away and get to Sea, as his Son Josiah had done to his great Vexation. He therefore sometimes took me to walk with him, and see Joiners [woodworkers], Bricklayers, Turners [those who make objects using a lathe], Braziers [those who craft items from brass], &c. at their Work, that he might observe my Inclination, & endeavour to fix it on some Trade or other on Land....

From a Child I was fond of Reading, and all the little Money that came into my Hands was ever laid out in Books....

This Bookish Inclination at length determin'd my Father to make me a Printer, tho' he had already one Son, (James) of that Profession. In 1717 my Brother James return'd from England with a Press & Letters to set up his Business in Boston. I lik'd it much better than that of my Father, but still had a hankering for the Sea.—To prevent the apprehended Effect of such an Inclination, my Father was impatient to have me bound to my Brother. I stood out some time, but at last was persuaded and signed the Indentures, when I was yet but 12 Years old.—I was to serve as an Apprentice till I was 21 Years of Age....In a little time I made great Proficiency in the Business, and became a useful Hand to my Brother. I now had Access to better Books. An Acquaintance with the Apprentices of Booksellers, enabled me sometimes to borrow a small one, which I was careful to return soon & clean. Often I sat up in my Room reading the greatest Part of the Night, when the Book was borrow'd in the Evening & to be return'd early in the Morning lest it should be miss'd or wanted.—And after some time an ingenious Tradesman who had a pretty Collection of Books, & who frequented our Printing House, took Notice of me, invited me to his Library, & very kindly lent me such Books as I chose to read....[A]s Prose Writing has been a great Use to me in the Course of my Life, and was a principal Means of my Advancement, I shall tell you how in such a Situation I acquir'd what little Ability I have in that Way.

There was another Bookish Lad in the Town, John Collins by Name, with whom I was intimately acquainted. We sometimes disputed, and very fond we were of Argument, & very desirous of confuting [refuting] one another. Which disputacious Turn, by the way, is apt to become a very bad Habit, making People often extreamly disagreable in Company, by the Contradiction that is necessary to bring it into Practice, & thence, besides souring & spoiling the Conversation, is productive of Disgusts & perhaps Enmities....I had caught it by reading my Father's Books of Dispute about Religion. Persons of good Sense, I have since observ'd, seldom fall into it, except

Lawyers, University Men, and Men of all Sorts that have been bred at Edinborough. A Question was once some how or other started between Collins & me, of the Propriety of educating the Female Sex in Learning, & their Abilities for Study. He was of Opinion that it was improper; & that they were naturally unequal to it. I took the contrary Side, perhaps a little for Dispute sake. He was naturally more eloquent, had a ready Plenty of Words, and sometimes as I thought bore me down more by his Fluency than by the Strengths of his Reasons. As we parted without settling the Point, & were not to see one another again for some time, I sat down to put my Arguments in Writing, which I copied fair & sent to him. He answer'd & I reply'd. Three or four letters of a Side had pass'd, when my Father happen'd to find my Papers, and read them. Without entring into the Discussion, he took occasion to talk to me about the Manner of my Writing, observ'd that tho' I had the Advantage of my Antagonist in correct Spelling & pointing [punctuating] (which I ow'd to the Printing House) I fell far short in elegance of Expression, in method and in Perspicuity, of which he convinc'd me by several Instances. I saw the Justice of his Remarks, & thence grew more attentive to the *Manner* in Writing, and determin'd to endeavour at Improvement.—

About this time I met with an odd Volume of the Spectator [an English magazine]. I had never before seen any of them. I bought it, read it over and over, and was much delighted with it. I thought the Writing excellent, & wish'd if possible to imitate it. With that View, I took some of the Papers, & making short Hints of the Sentiment in each Sentence, laid them by a few Days, and then without looking at the Book, try'd to compleat the Papers again, by expressing each hinted Sentiment at length & as fully as it had been express'd before, in any suitable Words that should come to hand.

Then I compar'd my Spectator with the Original, discover'd some of my Faults & corrected them. But I found I wanted a Stock of Words or a readiness in recollecting & using them.... Therefore I took some of the Tales & turn'd them into Verse: And after a time, when I had pretty well forgotten the Prose, turn'd them back again. I also sometimes jumbled my Collections of Hints into Confusion, and after some Weeks, endeavour'd to reduce them into the best Order, before I began to form the full Sentences & compleat the Paper. This was to teach me Method in the Arrangement of Thoughts. By comparing my Work afterwards with the original, I discover'd many faults and amended them; but I sometimes had the Pleasure of Fancying that in certain Particulars of small Import, I had been lucky enough to improve the Method or the Language and this encourag'd me to think I might possibly in time come to be a tolerable English Writer, of which I was extreamly ambitious.

My Time for these Exercises & for Reading, was at Night after Work, or before Work began in the Morning; or on Sundays, when I contrived to be in the Printing House alone, evading as much as I could the common Attendance on publick Worship, which my Father used to exact of me when I was under his Care:—And which indeed I still thought a Duty; tho' I could not, as it seemed to me, afford the Time to practise it....

My Brother had in 1720 or 21, begun to print a Newspaper. It was the second that appear'd in America, & was called *The New England Courant*.... [A]fter having work'd in composing the Types & printing off the Sheets I was employ'd to carry the papers thro' the Streets to the Customers.—He had some ingenious Men among his Friends who amus'd themselves by writing little Pieces for this Paper, which gain'd it Credit, & made it more in Demand; and these Gentlemen often visited us.—Hearing their Conversations, and their Accounts of the Approbation their Papers were receiv'd with, I was excited to try my Hand among them. But being still a Boy, & suspecting that my Brother would object to printing any Thing of mine in his Paper if he knew it to be mine, I contriv'd to disguise my Hand, & writing an anonymous Paper I put it in at Night under the Door of the Printing House. It was found the Morning & communicated to his Writing Friends when they call'd in as Usual. They read it, commented on it in my Hearing, and I had the exquisite Pleasure, of finding it met with their Approbation, and that in their different Guesses at the Author none were named but Men of some Character among us for Learning & Ingenuity.—...En courag'd...by this, I wrote and convey'd in the same Way to the Press several more Papers, which were equally approv'd, and I kept my Secret till my small Fund of Sense for such Performances was pretty well exhausted, & then I discovered [revealed] it; when I began to be considered a little more by my Brother's Acquaintance[s], and in a manner that did not quite please him, as he thought, probably with reason, that it tended to make me too vain. And perhaps this might be one Occasion of the Differences that we began to have about this Time. Tho' a Brother, he considered himself as my Master, & me as his Apprentice; and accordingly expected the same Services from me as he would from another; while I thought he demean'd me too much in some [things] he requir'd of me, who from a Brother expected more Indulgence. Our Disputes were often brought before our Father, and I fancy I was either generally in the right, or else a better Pleader, because the Judgment was generally in my favour: But my Brother was passionate & had often beaten me, which I took extreamly amiss; and thinking my Apprenticeship very tedious, I was continually wishing for some Opportunity of shortening it, which at length offered in a manner unexpected.

One of the Pieces in our News-Paper, on some political Point which I have now forgotten, gave Offence to the Assembly. He was taken up, censur'd and imprison'd for a Month....During my Brother's Confinement, which I resented a good deal, notwithstanding our private Differences, I had the Management of the Paper, and I made bold to give our Rulers some Rubs in it, which my Brother took very kindly, while others began to consider me in an unfavourable Light, as a young Genius that had a Turn for Libelling & Satyr[e]. My Brother's Discharge was accompany'd with an Order of the House, (a very odd one) *that James Franklin should no longer print the Paper called the New England Courant.* There was a Consultation held in our Printing House among his Friends what he should do in this Case. Some propos'd to evade the Order by changing the Name of the Paper; but my Brother seeing Inconveniences in that, it was finally concluded on as a better Way, to let it be printed for the future under the Name of *Benjamin Franklin.* And to avoid the Censure of the Assembly that might fall on him, as still printing it by his Apprentice, the Contrivance was, that my old Indenture should be return'd to me with a full Discharge on the Back of it, to be shown on Occasion; but to secure to him the Benefit of my Service I was to sign new Indentures for the Remainder of the Term, wch. were to be kept private. A very flimsy Scheme it was, but however it was immediately executed, and the Paper went on accordingly under my Name for several Months. At length a fresh Difference arising between my Brother and me, I took upon me to assert my Freedom, presuming that he would not venture to produce the new Indentures. It was not fair in me to take this Advantage, and this I therefore reckon one of the first Errata of my Life: But the Unfairness of it weigh'd little with me, when under the Impressions of Resentment, for the Blows his Passion too often urg'd him to bestow upon me. Tho' He was otherwise not an ill-natur'd Man: Perhaps I was too saucy & provoking.—

When he found I would leave him, he took care to prevent my getting Employment in any other Printing-House of the Town, by going round & speaking to every Master, who accordingly refus'd to give me Work. I then thought of going to New York as the nearest Place where there was a Printer: and I was the rather inclin'd to leave Boston, when I reflected that I had already made my self a little obnoxious, to the governing Party; & from the arbitrary Proceedings of the Assembly in my Brother's Case it was likely I might if I stay'd soon bring my self into Scrapes; and farther that my indiscrete Disputations about Religion began to make me pointed at with Horror by good People, as an Infidel or Atheist; I deteremin'd on the Point: but my Father now siding with my Brother, I was sensible that if I attempted to go openly, Means would be used to prevent me. My friend Collins therefore undertook to manage a little for me. He agreed with the Captain of a New York Sloop for my Passage, under the Notion of my being a young Acquaintance of his that had got a naughty Girl with Child, whose Friends would compel me to marry her, and therefore I could not appear or come away publickly. So I sold some of my Books to raise a little Money, Was taken on board privately, and as we had a fair Wind, in three Days I found my self in New York near 300 Miles from home, a Boy of but 17, without the least Recommendation to or Knowledge of any Person in the Place, and with very little Money in my Pocket....

[Finding jobs in New York scarce, Franklin proceeds to Philadelphia, and describes] my first Entry into that City, that you may in your Mind compare such unlikely Beginning with the Figure I have since made there. I was in my working Dress, my best Cloaths being to come round by Sea. I was dirty from my Journey; my Pockets were stuff'd out with Shirts & Stockings; I knew no Soul, nor where to look for Lodging. I was fatigu'd with Travelling..., I was very hungry, and my whole Stock of Cash consisted of a Dutch Dollar and about a Shilling in Copper....I walk'd up the Street, gazing about, till near the Market House I met a Boy with Bread. I had made many a Meal on Bread, & inquiring where he got it, I went immediately to the Baker's he directed me to in second Street; and ask'd for Bisket, intending such as we had in Boston, but they it seems were not made in Philadelphia, then I ask'd for a threepenny Loaf, and was told they had none such: so not considering or knowing the Difference of Money & the greater Cheapness nor the Names of his Bread, I bad him give me three pennyworth of any sort. He gave me accordingly three great Puffy Rolls. I was surpiz'd at the Quantity, but took it, and having no Room in my Pockets, walk'd off, with a Roll under each Arm, & eating the other. Thus I went up Market Street as far as fourth Street, passing by the Door of Mr. Read, my future Wife's Father, when she standing at the Door saw me, & thought I made as I certainly did a most awkward ridiculous Appearance.... Thus refresh'd I walk'd again up the Street, which by this time had many clean dress'd People in it who were all walking the same Way; I join'd them, and thereby was led into the great Meeting House of the Quakers near the Market. I sat down among them, and after looking round a while & hearing nothing said, being very drowsy thro' Labour & want of Rest the preceding Night, I fell fast asleep, and continu'd so till the Meeting broke up, when one was kind enough to rouse me. This was therefore the first House I was in or slept in, in Philadelphia....

[Franklin finds work with Samuel Keimer, one of two printers in town, and lodges with the Reads.]

I began now to have some Acquaintance among the young People of the Town, that were Lovers of Reading with whom I spent my Evenings very pleasantly and gaining Money by my Industry & Frugality, I lived very agreably, forgetting Boston as much as I could, and not desiring that any there should know where I resided except my Friend Collins who was in [on] my Secret, & kept it when I wrote to him.—At length an Incident happened that sent me back again much sooner than I had intended.—

I had a Brother-in-law, Robert Holmes, Master of a Sloop, that traded between Boston and Delaware. He being at New Castle 40 Miles below Philadelphia, heard there of me, and wrote me a Letter, mentioning the Concern of my Friends in Boston at my abrupt Departure, assuring me of their Goodwill to me, and that every thing would be accommodated to my Mind if I would return, to which he exhorted me very earnestly.—I wrote an Answer to his Letter, thank'd him for his Advice, but stated my Reasons for quitting Boston fully, & in such a Light as to convince him I was not so wrong as he had apprehended.—Sir William Keith Governor of the Province, was then at New Castle, and Capt. Holmes happening to be in Company with him when my Letter came to hand, spoke to him of me, and show'd him the letter. The Governor read it, and seem'd surpriz'd when he was told my Age. He said I appear'd a young Man of promising Parts, and therefore should be encouraged: The Printers at Philadelphia were wretched ones, and if I would set up there, he made no doubt

I should succeed; for his Part, he would procure me the publick Business, & do me every other Service in his Power. This my Brother-in-Law afterwards told me in Boston. But I knew as yet nothing of it; when one Day Keimer and I being at Work together near the Window, we saw the Governor and another Gentleman (which prov'd to be Col. French, of New Castle) finely dress'd, come directly across the Street to our House, & heard them at the Door. Keimer ran down immediately, thinking it a Visit to him. But the Governor enquir'd for me, came up, & with a Condescension & Politeness I had been quite unus'd to, made me many Compliments, desired to be acquainted with me, blam'd me kindly for not having made my self known to him when I first came to the Place, and would have me away with him to the Tavern where he was going with Col. French to taste as he said some excellent Madeira [a type of wine]. I was not a little surpriz'd, and Keimer star'd like a Pig poison'd. I went however with the Governor & Col. French, to a Tavern the Corner of Third Street, and over the Madeira he propos'd my Setting up my Business, laid beforre me the Probabilities of Success, & both he & Col French, assur'd me I should have their Interest & Influence in procuring the Publick Business of both Governments. On my doubting whether my Father would assist me in it, Sir William said he would give me a Letter to him, in which he would state the Advantages,—and he did not doubt of prevailing with him. So it was concluded I should return to Boston in the first Vessel with the Governor's Letter recommending me to my Father. In the mean time the Intention was to be kept secret, and I went on working with Keimer as usual, the Governor sending for me now & then to dine with him, a very great Honour I thought it, and conversing with me in the most affable, familiar, & friendly manner imaginable. About the End of April 1724. a little Vessel offer'd for Boston. I took leave of Keimer as going to see my Friends. The Governor gave me an ample Letter, saying many flattering things of me to my Father, and strongly recommending the Project of my setting up at Philadelphia, as a Thing that must make my Fortune.... We arriv'd safe...at Boston in about a Fortnight.—I had been absent Seven Months.... My unexpected Appearance surpriz'd the Family; all were however very glad to see me and made me Welcome, except my Brother. I went to see him at his Printing-House: I was better dress'd than ever while in his Service, having a genteel new suit from Head to foot, a Watch, and my Pockets lin'd with near Five Pounds Sterling in Silver. He receiv'd me not very frankly, look'd me all over, and turn'd to his Work again. The Journey-Men were inquisitive where I had been, what sort of a Country it was, and how I lik'd it? I prais'd it much, & the happy Life I led in it; expressing strongly my Intention of returning to it; and one of them asking what kind of Money we had there, I produc'd a handful of Silver, and spread it before them, which was a kind of Raree-Show [peep show] they had not been us'd to, Paper being the Money of Boston. Then I took an Opportunity of letting them see my Watch: and lastly, (my Brother still grum & sullen) I gave them a Piece of Eight to drink & took my Leave.—This Visit of mine offended him extreamly. For when my Mother some time after spoke to him of a Reconciliation, & of her Wishes to see us on good Terms together, & that we might live for the future as Brothers, he said, I had insulted him in such a Manner before his People that he could never forget or forgive it.—In this however he was mistaken.—

My Father receiv'd the Governor's Letter with some apparent Surpize; but said little of it to me for some Days; when Capt. Homes returning, he show'd it to him, ask'd if he knew Keith, and what kind of a Man he was: Adding his Opinion that he must be of small Discretion, to think of setting a Boy up in Business who wanted yet 3 years of being at Man's Estate. Homes said what he could in fav[o]r of the Project; but my Father was clear in the Impropriety of it; and at last gave a flat Denial to it. Then he wrote a civil letter to Sir William thanking him for the Patronage he had so kindly offered me, but declining to assist me as yet in Setting up, I being in his Opinion too young to be trusted with the Management of a Business so important; & for which the Preparation must be so expensive.…

My Father, tho' he did not approve Sir William's Proposition was yet pleas'd that I had been able to obtain so advantageous a Character from a Person of such Note where I had resided, and that I had been so industrious & careful as to equip my self so handsomely in so short a time: therefore seeing no Prospect of an Accommodation between my Brother & me, he gave his Consent to my Returning again to Philadelphia, advis'd me to behave respectfully to the People there, endeavour to obtain the general Esteem, & avoid lampooning & libelling to which he thought I had too much Inclination;—telling me, that by steady Industry and a prudent Parsimony, I might save enough by the time I was One and Twenty to set me up, & that if I came near the Matter he would help me out with the Rest.—This was all I could obtain, except some small Gifts as Tokens of his & my

Mother's Love, when I embark'd again…, now with their Approbation & their Blessing.…

Sir William, on reading his Letter, said he was too prudent. There was great Difference in Persons, and Discretion did not always accompany Years, nor was Youth always without it. And since he will not set you up, says he, I will do it my self. Give me an Inventory of the Things necessary to be had from England, and I will send for them. You shall repay me when you are able; I am resolv'd to have a good Printer here, and I am sure you must succeed. This was spoken with such an Appearance of Cordiality, that I had not the least doubt of his meaning what he said.—I had hitherto kept the Proposition of my Setting up a Secret in Philadelphia, & I still kept it. Had it been known that I depended on the Governor, probably some Friend that knew him better would have advis'd me not to rely on him, as I afterwards heard it as his known Character to be liberal of Promises which he never meant to keep.—Yet unsolicited as he was by me, how could I think his generous Offers insincere? I believ'd him one of the best Men in the World.—

I presented him an Inventory of a little Print[in]g House, amounting by my Computation to about 100£ Sterling. He lik'd it, but ask'd me if my being on the Spot in England to chuse the Types & see that every thing was good of the kind, might not be of some Advantage. Then, says he, when there, you may make Acquaintances & establish Correspondencies in the Bookselling, & Stationary Way. I agreed that this might be advantageous. Then says he, get yourself ready to go with Annis; which was the annual Ship, and the only one at that Time usually passing between London and Philadelphia. But it would be some Months before Annis sail'd, so I continu'd working with Keimer.…

I had made some Courtship during this time to Miss Read, I had a great Respect & Affection for her, and had some Reason to believe she had the same for me: but as I was about to take a long Voyage, and we were both very young, only a little above 18[,] it was thought most prudent by her Mother to prevent our going too far at present, as a Marriage if it was to take place would be more convenient after my Return, when I should be as I expected set up in my Business. Perhaps too she thought my Expectations not so well founded as I imagined them to be.…

The Governor, seeming to like my Company, had me frequently to his House; & his Setting me up was always mention'd as a fix'd thing. I was to take with me Letters recommendatory to a Number of his Friends, besides the Letter of Credit, to furnish me with the necessary Money for purchasing the Press & Types, Paper,

&c. For these Letters I was appointed to call at different times, when they were to be ready, but a future time was still named.—Thus we went on till the Ship whose Departure too had been several times postponed was on the Point of sailing. Then when I call'd to take my Leave & receive the Letters, his Secretary…came out to me and said the Governor was extreamly busy, in writing, but would be down at Newcastle before the Ship, & there the Letters would be delivered to me.…

Having taken leave of my Friends, & interchang'd some Promises with Miss Read, I left Philadelphia in the Ship, which anchor'd at Newcastle. The Governor was there. But when I went to his Lodging, the Secretary came to me from him with the civillest Message in the World, that he could not then see me being engag'd in Business of the utmost Importance, but should send the Letters to me on board, wish'd me heartily a good Voyage and a speedy Return, &c. I return'd on board, a little puzzled, but still not doubting.—

Mr. Andrew Hamilton, a famous Lawyer of Philadelphia, had taken Passage in the same Ship for himself and Son: and with Mr. Denham a Quaker Merchant, & Messrs Onion and Russel Masters of an Iron Work in Maryland, had engag'd the Great Cabin; so that [Franklin's friend James] Ralph and I were forc'd to take up with a Birth [berth] in the Steerage:— And none on board knowing us, were considered as ordinary Persons.—But Mr. Hamilton & his Son (it was James, since Governor) return'd from New Castle to Philadelphia…; And just before we sail'd Col. French coming on board, & showing me great Respect, I was more taken Notice of, and with my Friend Ralph invited by the other Gentlemen to come into the Cabin, there being now Room. Accordingly we remov'd thither.…

When we came into the [English] Channel, the Captain kept his Word with me, & gave me an Opportunity of examining the Bag for the Governor's Letters. I found none upon which my Name was put.…I found my Friend Denham, and opened the whole Affair to him. He let me into Keith's Character, told me there was not the least Probability that he had written any Letters for me, that no one who knew him had the smallest Dependance on him, and he laught at the Notion of the Governor's giving me a Letter of Credit, having as he said no Credit to give.—On my expressing some Concern about what I should do: He advis'd me to endeavour getting some Employment in the Way of my Business. Among the Printers here, says he, you will improve yourself; and when you return to America, you will set up to greater Advantage.…

But what shall we think of a Governor's playing such pitiful Tricks, & imposing so grossly on a poor ignorant Boy! It was a Habit he had acquired. He wish'd to please every body; and having little to give, he gave Expectations.…

[Back in Philadelphia after eighteen months in London, Franklin again finds work as one of the "hands"—that is, workers—in Samuel Keimer's print shop.] I began to live very agreably; for they all respected me, the more as they found Keimer incapable of instructing them, and that from me they learnt something daily.…My Acquaintance with ingenious People in the Town, increased. Keimer himself treated me with great Civility & apparent Regard.…

But however serviceable I might be, I found that my Services became every Day of less Importance, as the other Hands improv'd in the Business. And when Keimer paid my second Quarter's Wages, he let me know that he felt them too heavy, and thought I should make an Abatement [reduction]. He grew by degrees less civil, put on more of the Master, frequently found Fault,…and seem'd ready for an Out-breaking. I went on nevertheless with a good deal of Patience, thinking that his incumber'd Circumstances were partly the Cause. At length a Trifle snapt our Connexion. For a great Noise happening near the Courthouse, I put my Head out of the Window to see what was the Matter. Keimer being in the Street look'd up & saw me, call'd out to me in a loud Voice and angry Tone to mind my Business, adding some reproachful Words, that nettled me the more for their Publicity, all the Neighbours who were looking out on the same Occasion being Witnesses how I was treated. He came up immediately into the Printing-House, continu'd the Quarrel, high Words pass'd on both Sides, he gave me the Quarter's Warning we had stipulated, expressing a Wish that he had not been oblig'd to so long a Warning: I told him his Wish was unnecessary for I would leave him that Instant; and so taking my Hat walk'd out of Doors.…

[Franklin and another Keimer employee, Hugh Meredith, funded by Meredith's father, decide to set up their own shop. Awaiting the printing materials from England,] the Secret [of their scheme] was to be kept till they should arrive, and in the mean time I was to get Work if I could at the other Printing House.—But I found no Vacancy there, and so remain'd idle a few Days, when Keimer, on a Prospect of being employ'd to print some Paper-money, in New Jersey…, sent me a very civil Message, that old Friends should not part for a few Words the Effect of sudden Passion, and wishing me to return.…So I return'd, and we went on more smoothly than for some time before.—The New Jersey Jobb was obtain'd.…

At Burlington [New Jersey] I made an Acquaintance with many principal People of the Province. Several of them had been appointed by the Assembly a Committee to attend the Press, and take Care that no more Bills were printed than the Law directed. They were therefore by Turns constantly with us, and generally he who attended brought with him a Friend or two for Company. My Mind having been much more improv'd by Reading than Keimer's, I suppose it was for that Reason my Conversation seem'd to be more valu'd. They had me to their Houses, introduc'd me to their Friends and show'd me much Civility, while he, tho' the Master, was a little neglected. In truth he was an odd Fish, ignorant of common Life, fond of rudely opposing receiv'd Opinions, slovenly to extream dirtiness, enthusiastic [irrational] in some Points of Religion, and a little Knavish withal.…

Before I enter upon my public Appearance in Business, it may be well to let you know the then State of my Mind, with regard to my Principles and Morals, that you may see how far those influenc'd the future Events of my Life. My Parent's had early given me religious Impressions, and brought me through my Childhood piously in the Dissenting [Puritan] Way. But I was scarce 15 when, after doubting by turns of several Points as I found them disputed in the different Books I read, I began to doubt of Revelation it self.…

I grew convinc'd that *Truth, Sincerity & Integrity* in Dealings between Man & Man, were of the utmost Importance to the Felicity of Life.…And this Persuasion, with the kind hand of Providence, or some guardian Angel, or accidental favourable Circumstances & Situations, or all together, preserved me (thro' this dangerous Time of Youth & the hazardous Situations I was sometimes in among Strangers, remote from the Eye & Advice of my Father,) without any *wilful* gross Immorality or Injustice that might have been expected from my Want of Religion.—I say *wilful*, because the Instances I have mentioned, had something of *Necessity* in them, from my Youth, Inexperience, & the Knavery of others.—I had therefore a tolerable Character to begin the World with, I valued it properly, & determin'd to preserve it.—

We had not been long return'd to Philadelphia, before the New Types arriv'd from London.—We settled with Keimer, & left him by his Consent before he heard of it [that is, heard that his employees had become his competitors].…

[I]n the Autumn of the preceding Year, I had form'd most of my ingenious Acquaintance into a Club, for mutual Improvement, which we call'd the Junto. We met on Friday Evenings. The Rules I drew up, requir'd that every Member in his Turn should produce one or more Queries on any Point of Morals, Politics or Natural Philosophy, to be discuss'd by the Company, and once in three Months produce and read an Essay of his own Writing on any Subject he pleased. Our Debates were to be under the Direction of a President, and to be conducted in the sincere Spirit of Enquiry after Truth, without fondness for Dispute, or Desire of Victory; and to prevent Warmth, all Expressions of Positiveness in Opinion, or of direct Contradiction, were after some time…prohibited under small pecuniary [monetary] Penalties.…[T]he Club…was the best School of Philosophy, Morals & Politics that then existed in the Province; for our Queries which were read the Week preceding their Discussion, put us on reading with Attention upon the several Subjects, that we might speak more to the purpose: and here too we acquired better Habits of Conversation.…[M]y giving this Account of it here, is to show something of the Interest I had, every one of these [Junto members] exerting themselves in recommending Business to us.…[In addition, Franklin found that working late brought many benefits beyond the printing he got done.] [T]his Industry visible to our Neighbours began to give us Character and Credit; particularly I was told, that mention being made of the new Printing Office at the Merchants Every-night-Club, the general Opinion was that it must fail, there being already two Printers in the Place…; but Doctor Baird…gave a contrary Opinion; for the Industry of that Franklin, says he, is superior to any thing I ever saw of the kind: I see him still at work when I go home from Club; and he is at Work again before his Neighbours are out of bed.…

In order to secure my Credit and Character as a Tradesmen [sic], I took care not only to be in *Reality* Industrious & frugal, but to avoid all *Appearances* of the Contrary. I drest plainly; I was seen at no Places of idle Diversion; I never went out a-fishing or shooting; a Book, indeed, sometimes debauch'd me from my Work; but that was seldom, snug, & gave no Scandal: and to show that I was not above my Business, I sometimes brought home the Paper I purchas'd at the Stores, thro' the Streets on a Wheelbarrow. Thus being esteem'd an industrious thriving young Man, and paying duly for what I bought, the Merchants who imported Stationary solicited my Custom [business], others propos'd supplying me with Books, & I went on swimmingly.—In the mean time Keimer's Credit & Business declining daily, he was at last forc'd to sell his Printing-house to satisfy his Creditors. He went to Barbadoes, & there lived some Years, in very poor Circumstances.…

[H]aving turn'd my Thoughts to Marriage, I look'd round me, and made Overtures of Acquaintance…; but soon found that the Business of a Printer being generally thought a poor one, I was not to expect Money with a Wife unless with such a one, as I should not otherwise think agreable.—In the mean time, that hard-to-be-govern'd Passion of Youth, had hurried me frequently into Intrigues with low Women that fell in my Way, which were attended with some Expence & great Inconvenience, besides a continual Risque to my Health by a Distemper which of all Things I dreaded, tho' by great good Luck I escaped it.—

A friendly Correspondence as Neighbours & old Acquaintances, had continued between me & Mrs. Read's Family who all had a Regard for me from the time of my first Lodging in their House. I was often invited there and consulted in their Affairs, wherein I sometimes was of Service.—I pity'd poor Miss Read's unfortunate Situation, who was generally dejected, seldom chearful, and avoided Company. I considered my Giddiness & Inconstancy when in London as in a great degree the Cause of her Unhappiness; tho' the Mother was good enough to think the Fault more her own than mine, as she had prevented our Marrying before I went thither, and persuaded the other Match in my Absence. [When Franklin failed to write Deborah Read from London, she had married another man, who then deserted her.] Our mutual Affection was revived, but there were now great Objections to our Union. That Match [Deborah Read's earlier marriage] was indeed look'd upon as invalid, a preceding Wife being said to be living in England; but this could not easily be prov'd, because of the Distance &c. And tho' there was a Report of his Death, it was not certain. Then, tho' it should be true, he had left many Debts which his Successor might be call'd upon to pay. We ventured however, over all these Difficulties, and I took her to Wife Sept. I. 1730. None of the Inconveniencies happened that we had apprehended, she prov'd a good & faithful Helpmate, assisted me much by attending the Shop, we throve together, and have ever mutually endeavour'd to make each other happy.—Thus I corrected that great *Erratum* as well as I could.…

Memo. Thus far was written with the Intention express'd in the Beginning and therefore contains several little family Anecdotes of no Importance to others. What follows was written many Years after in compliance with the Advice contain'd in these Letters [from friends that Franklin included at the beginning of Part Two, urging him to tell his story to the world], and accordingly intended for the Publick. The Affairs of the Revolution occasion'd the Interruption.

Part Two…

Continuation of the Account of my Life.

Begun at Passy [France] 1784

…I have been too busy till now to [resume writing this account].…It might too be much better done if I were at home among my Papers, which would aid my Memory, & help to ascertain Dates. But my Return being uncertain, and having just now a little Leisure, I will endeavour to recollect & write what I can.…

At the time I establish' my self in Pensylvania, there was not a good Bookseller's Shop in any of the Colonies to the Southward of Boston.…Those who lov'd Reading were oblig'd to send for their Books from England.—The Members of the Junto had each a few. We had left the Alehouse where we first met, and hired a Room to hold our Club in. I propos'd that we should all of us bring our Books to that Room, where they would not only be ready to consult in our Conferences, but become a common Benefit, each of us being at Liberty to borrow such as he wish'd to read at home. This was accordingly done, and for some time contented us. Finding the Advantage of this little Collection, I propos'd to render the Benefit from Books more common by commencing a Public Subscription Library. I drew a Sketch of the Plan and Rules that would be necessary, and…put the whole in Form of Articles of Agreement to be subscribed, by which each Subscriber engag'd to pay a certain Sum down for the first Purchase of Books and an annual Contribution for encreasing them.—So few were the Readers at that time in Philadelphia, and the Majority of us so poor, that I was not able with great Industry to find more than Fifty Persons, mostly young Tradesmen, willing to pay down for this purpose Forty shillings each, & Ten Shillings per Annum. On this little Fund we began. The Books were imported. The Library was open one Day in the Week for lending them to the Subscribers, on their Promisory Notes to pay Double the Value if not duly returned. The Institution soon manifested its Utility, was imitated by other Towns and in other Provinces, the Librarys were augmented by Donations, Reading became fashionable, and our People having no publick Amusements to divert their Attention from Study became better acquainted with Books, and in a few Years were observ'd by Strangers to be better instructed & more intelligent than People of the same Rank generally are in other Countries....

This Library afforded me the Means of Improvement by constant Study, for which I set apart an Hour or two each Day; and thus repair'd in some Degree the Loss of the Learned Education my Father once intended for me. Reading was the only Amusement I allow'd my self. I spent no time in Taverns, Games, or Frolicks of any kind. And my Industry in my Business continu'd as indefatigable as it was necessary. I was in debt for my Printing-house, I had a young Family coming on to be educated, and I had to contend with for Business two Printers who were establish'd in the Place before me. My Circumstances however grew daily easier: my original Habits of Frugality continuing. And My Father having among his Instructions to me when a Boy, frequently repeated a Proverb of Solomon, *"Seest thou a Man diligent in his Calling, he shall stand before Kings, he shall not stand before mean Men."* I from thence consider'd Industry as a Means of obtaining Wealth and Distinction, which encourag'd me; tho' I did not think that I should ever literally stand before Kings, which however has since happened.—for I have stood before five, & even had the honour of sitting down with one, the King of Denmark, to Dinner.

We have an English Proverb that says,

He that would thrive
Must ask his Wife;

it was lucky for me that I had one as much dispos'd to Industry & Frugality as my self. She assisted me chearfully in my Business....We kept no idle Servants, our Table was plain & simple, our Furniture of the cheapest. For instance my Breakfast was a long time Bread & Milk, (no Tea,) and I ate it out of a twopenny earthen Porringer [bowl] with a Pewter Spoon. But mark how Luxury will enter Families, and make a Progress, in Spite of Principle. Being Call'd one Morning to Breakfast, I found it in a China Bowl with a Spoon of Silver. They had been bought for me without my Knowledge by my Wife, and had cost her the enormous Sum of three and twenty Shillings, for which she had no other Excuse or Apology to make, but that she thought *her* Husband deserv'd a Silver Spoon & China Bowl as well as any of his Neighbours....

I had been religiously educated as a Presbyterian; and tho' some of the Dogmas of that Persuasion...appear'd to me unintelligible, others doubtful, & I early absented myself from the Public Assemblies of the Sect, Sunday being my Studying-Day, I never was without some religious Principles; I never doubted, for

instance, the Existance of the Deity, that he made the World, & govern'd it by his Providence; that the most acceptable Service of God was the doing Good to Man; that our Souls are immortal; and that all Crime will be punished & Virtue rewarded either here or hereafter; these I esteeem'd the Essentials of every Religion, and being to be found in all the Religions we had in our Country I respected them all, tho' with different degrees of Respect as I found them more or less mix'd with other Articles which without any Tendency to inspire, promote or confirm Morality, serv'd principally to divide us & make us unfriendly to one another....

Tho' I seldom attended any Public Worship, I had still an Opinion of its Propriety, and of its Utility when rightly conducted, and I regularly paid my annual Subscription for the Support of the only Presbyterian Minister or Meeting we had in Philadelphia....

It was about this time that I conceiv'd the bold and arduous Project of arriving at moral Perfection. I wish'd to live without committing any Fault at any time; I would conquer all that either Natural Inclination, Custom, or Company might lead me into. As I knew, or thought I knew, what was right and wrong, I did not see why I might not *always* do the one and avoid the other. But I soon found I had undertaken a Task of more Difficulty than I had imagined: While my Care was employ'd in guarding against one Fault, I was often surpriz'd by another. Habit took the Advantage of Inattention. Inclination was sometimes too strong for Reason. I concluded at length, that the mere speculative Conviction that it was our Interest to be compleatly virtuous, was not sufficient to prevent our Slipping, and that the contrary Habits must be broken and good Ones acquired and established, before we can have any Dependance on a steady uniform Rectitude of Conduct. For this purpose I therefore contriv'd the following Method....

I included under Thirteen Names of Virtues all that at that time occurr'd to me as necessary or desirable, and annex'd to each a short Precept, which fully express'd the Extent I gave to its Meaning.—

These Names of Virtues with their Precepts were

1. TEMPERANCE.
   Eat not to Dulness
   Drink not to Elevation.
2. SILENCE.
   Speak not but what may benefit others or your self. Avoid trifling Conversation.
3. ORDER.
   Let all your Things have their Places. Let each Part of your Business have its Time.

4. RESOLUTION.

   Resolve to perform what you ought. Perform without fail what you resolve.

5. FRUGALITY.

   Make no Expence but to do good to others or yourself: i.e., Waste nothing.

6. INDUSTRY.

   Lose no Time.—Be always employ'd in something useful.—Cut off all unnecessary Actions.—

7. SINCERITY.

   Use no hurtful Deceit.

   Think innocently and justly; and, if you speak; speak accordingly.

8. JUSTICE.

   Wrong none, by doing Injuries or omitting the Benefits that are your Duty.

9. MODERATION.

   Avoid Extreams. Forbear resenting Injuries so much as you think they deserve.

10. CLEANLINESS.

    Tolerate no Uncleanness in Body, Cloaths or Habitation.—

11. TRANQUILITY.

    Be not disturbed at Trifles, or at Accidents common or unavoidable.

12. CHASTITY.

    Rarely use Venery but for Health or Offspring; Never to Dulness, Weakness, or the Injury of your own or another's Peace or Reputation.—

13. HUMILITY.

    Imitate Jesus and Socrates.—

My intention being to acquire the *Habitude* of all these Virtues, I judg'd it would be well not to distract my Attention by attempting the whole at once, but to fix it on one of them at a time, and when I should be Master of that, then to proceed to another, and so on till I should have gone thro' the thirteen. And as the previous Acquisition of some might facilitate the Acquisition of certain others, I arrang'd them with that View as they stand above. *Temperance* first, as it tends to procure that Coolness & Clearness of Head, which is so necessary where constant Vigilance was to be kept up, and Guard maintained, against the unremitting Attraction of ancient Habits, and the Force of perpetual Temptations. This being acquir'd & establish'd, *Silence* would be more easy, and my Desire being to gain Knowledge at the same time that I improv'd in Virtue, and considering that in Conversation it was obtain'd rather by the use of the Ears than of the Tongue, & therefore wishing to break a Habit I was getting into of Prattling, Punning

& Joking, which only made me acceptable to trifling Company, I gave *Silence* the second Place. This, and the next, *Order*, I expected would allow me more Time for attending to my Project and my Studies; RESOLUTION once become habitual, would keep me firm in my Endeavours to obtain all the subsequent Virtues; *Frugality* & *Industry*, by freeing me from my remaining Debt, & producing Affluence & Independance would make more easy the Practice of *Sincerity* and *Justice*, &c. &c. Conceiving then that…daily Examination would be necessary, I contriv'd the following Method for conducting that Examination.

I made a little Book in which I allotted a Page for each of the Virtues. I rul'd each Page with red Ink so as to have seven Columns, one for each Day of the Week, marking each Column with a Letter for the Day. I cross'd these Columns with thirteen red Lines, marking the Beginning of each Line with the first Letter of one of the Virtues, on which Line & in its proper Column I might mark by a little black Spot every Fault I found upon Examination, to have been committed respecting that Virtue upon that Day.

Form of the Pages

		S	M	T	W	T	F	S
		TEMPERANCE						

	TEMPERANCE. Eat not to Dulness. Drink not to Elevation.						
	S	M	T	W	T	F	S
T							
S	●●	●		●		●	
O	●		●	●		●	●
R			●			●	
F		●		●			
I			●				
S							
J							
M							
Cl.							
T							
Ch							
H							

I determined to give a Week's strict Attention to each of the Virtues successively. Thus in the first Week my great Guard was to avoid every the least Offence against Temperance, leaving the other Virtues to their ordinary Chance, only marking every Evening the Faults of the Day. Thus if in the first Week I could keep my first Line marked T clear of Spots, I suppos'd the Habit of that Virtue so much strengthen'd and its opposite weaken'd, that I might venture extending my Attention to include the next, and for the following Week keep both Lines clear of Spots. Proceeding thus to the last, I could go thro' a Course compleat in Thirteen Weeks, and four Courses in a Year.—And like him who having a Garden to weed, does not attempt to eradicate all the bad Herbs at once, which would exceed his Reach and his Strength, but works on one of the Beds at a time, & having accomplish'd the first proceeds to a second; so I should have, (I hoped) the encouraging Pleasure of seeing on my Pages the Progress I made in Virtue, by clearing successively my Lines of their Spots, till in the End by a Number of Courses, I should be happy in viewing a clear Book after a thirteen Weeks daily Examination....

The Precept of *Order* requiring that *every Part of my Business should have its allotted Time*, one Page in my little Book contain'd the following Scheme of Employment for the Twenty-four Hours of a natural Day,

The Morning Question, What Good shall I do this Day?	5	Rise, wash, and address *Powerful Goodness;* contrive Day's Business and take the Resolution of the Day; prosecute the present Study: and breakfast?—
	6	
	7	
	8	
	9	Work.
	10	
	11	
	12	Read, or overlook my Accounts, and dine.
	1	
	2	
	3	Work.
	4	
	5	
	6	Put Things in their Places, Supper, Musick, or Diversion, or Conversation, Examination of the Day.
	7	
Evening Question, What Good have I done to day?	8	
	9	
	10	
	11	
	12	
	1	Sleep.—
	2	
	3	
	4	

I enter'd upon the Execution of this Plan for Self Examination, and continu'd it with occasional Intermissions for some time. I was surpriz'd to find myself so much fuller of Faults than I had imagined, but I had the Satisfaction of seeing them diminish.... [O]n the whole, tho' I never arrived at the Perfection I had been so ambitious of obtaining, but fell far short of it, yet I was by the Endeavour made a better and a happier Man than I otherwise should have been, if I had not attempted it....

And it may be well my Posterity should be informed, that to this little Artifice, with the Blessing of God, their Ancestor ow'd the constant Felicity of his Life down to his 79th Year in which this is written.... To *Temperance* he ascribes his long-continu'd Health, & what is still left to him of a good Constitution. To *Industry* and *Frugality* the early Easiness of his Circumstances, & Acquisition of his Fortune, with all that Knowledge which enabled him to be an useful Citizen, and obtain'd for him some degree of Reputation among the Learned. To *Sincerity* & *Justice* the Confidence of his Country, and the honourable Employs it conferr'd upon him. And to the joint Influence of the whole Mass of the Virtues, even in their imperfect State he was able to acquire them, all that Evenness of Temper, & that Chearfulness in Conversation which makes his Company still sought for, & agreable even to his younger Acquaintance. I hope therefore that some of my Descendants may follow the Example & reap the Benefit....

My List of Virtues contain'd at first but twelve: But a Quaker Friend having kindly inform'd me that I was generally thought proud; that my Pride show'd itself frequently in Conversation; that I was not content with being in the right when discussing any Point, but was overbearing & rather insolent; of which he convinc'd me by mentioning several Instances;—I determined endeavouring to cure myself if I could of this Vice or Folly among the rest, and I added *Humility* to my List....I cannot boast of much Success in acquiring the *Reality* of this Virtue; but I had a good deal with regard to the *Appearance* of it.—I made it a Rule to forbear all direct Contradiction to the Sentiments of others, and all positive Assertion of my own. I even forbid myself agreable to the old Laws of our Junto, the Use of every Word or Expression in the Language that imported a fix'd Opinion; such as *certainly*, *undoubtedly*, &c. and I adopted instead of them, *I conceive, I apprehend*, or *I imagine* a thing to be so or so, or it so appears to me at present.... I soon found the Advantages of this Change in my Manners. The Conversations I engag'd in went on more pleasantly. The modest way in which I propos'd my Opinions, procur'd them a readier Reception and less Contradiction; I had less Mortification when I was found to be in the wrong, and I more easily prevail'd with others to give up their Mistakes & join with me when I happen'd to be in the right. And this Mode, which I at first put on, with some violence to natural Inclination, became at length so easy & so habitual to me, that perhaps for these Fifty Years past no one has ever heard a dogmatical Expression escape me. And to this Habit (after my Character of Integrity) I think it principally owing, that I had early so much Weight with my Fellow Citizens, when I proposed new Institutions, or Alterations in the old; and so much Influence in public Councils when I became a Member. For I was but a bad Speaker, never eloquent, subject to much Hesitation in my choice of Words, hardly correct in Language, and yet I generally carried my Points.—

In reality there is perhaps no one of our natural Passions so hard to subdue as *Pride.* Disguise it, struggle with it, beat it down, stifle it, mortify it as much as one pleases, it is still alive, and will every now and then peep out and show itself. You will see it perhaps often in this History. For even if I could conceive that I had compleatly overcome it, I should probably be proud of my Humility.—

Thus far written at Passy 1784.

Part Three

I am now about to write at home, Aug[us]t 1788.— but cannot have the help expected from my Papers, many of them being lost in the War....

I began now [in the late 1730s] to turn my Thoughts a little to public Affairs, beginning however with small Matters [such as reforming the City Watch, establishing a Fire Company, founding an academy, and creating a militia, along with serving in the colonial legislature. One of his civic improvement projects involved Philadelphia's streets]....

Our City, tho' laid out with a beautifull Regularity, the Streets large, strait, and crossing each other at right Angles, had the Disgrace of suffering those Streets to remain long unpav'd, and in wet Weather the Wheels of heavy Carriages plough'd them into a Quagmire, so that it was difficult to cross them. And in dry Weather the Dust was offensive. I had liv'd near what was call'd the Jersey Market, and saw with Pain the Inhabitants wading in Mud while purchasing their Provisions. A Strip of Ground down the middle of that Market was at length pav'd with Brick, so that being once in the Market they had firm Footing, but were often over Shoes in Dirt to get there.—By talking and writing on the Subject, I was at length instrumental in getting the Street pav'd with Stone between the Market and the brick'd Foot-Pavement that was on each Side next the Houses. This for some time gave an easy Access to the Market, dry-shod. But the rest of the Street not being pav'd, whenever a Carriage came

out of the Mud upon this Pavement, it shook off and left its Dirt on it, and it was soon cover'd with Mire, which was not remov'd, the City as yet having no Scavengers.—After some Enquiry I found a poor industrious Man, who was willing to undertake keeping the Pavement clean, by sweeping it twice a week & carrying off the Dirt from before all the Neighbours Doors, for the Sum of Sixpence per Month, to be paid by each House. I then wrote and printed a Paper, setting forth the Advantages to the Neighbourhood that might be obtain'd by this small Expence; the greater Ease in keeping our Houses clean, so much Dirt not being brought in by People's Feet; the Benefit to the Shops by more Custom, as Buyers could more easily get at them, and by not having in windy Weather the Dust blown in upon their Goods, &c. &c. I sent one of these Papers to each House, and in a Day or two went round to see who would subscribe an Agreement to pay these Sixpences. It was unanimously sign'd, and for a time well executed. All the Inhabitants of the City were delighted with the Cleanliness of the Pavement that surrounded the Market; it being a Convenience to all; and this rais'd a general Desire to have all the Streets paved; & made the People more willing to submit to a Tax for that purpose....

Some may think these trifling Matters not worth minding or relating: But when they consider, that tho' Dust blown into the Eyes of a single Person or into a single Shop on a windy Day, is but of small Importance, yet the great Number of the Instances in a populous City, and its frequent Repetitions give it Weight & Consequence; perhaps they will not censure very severely those who bestow some of Attention to Affairs of this seemingly low Nature. Human Felicity is produc'd not so much by great Pieces of good Fortune that seldom happen, as by little Advantages that occur every Day. Thus if you teach a poor young Man to shave himself and keep his Razor in order, you may contribute more to the Happiness of his Life than in giving him a 1000 Guineas. The Money may be soon spent, and the Regret only remaining of having foolishly consum'd it. But in the other Case he escapes the frequent Vexation of waiting for Barbers, & of their sometimes, dirty Fingers, offensive Breaths and dull Razors. He shaves when most convenient to him, and enjoys daily the Pleasure of its being done with a good Instrument.—With these Sentiments I have hazarded the few preceding Pages, hoping they may afford Hints which some time or other may be useful to a City I love, having lived many Years in it very happily; and perhaps to some of our Towns in America....

CHAPTER 7

Colonists Declare Independence

"The last cord now is broken"

Wtend to think of American independence as easily declared and easily achieved; the shift from British colonies to American nation seems as inevitable as it does swift and sure. Popular images of the period from the end of the Seven Years' War in 1763 to the break with Britain thirteen years later reinforce this notion. From Patrick Henry's cry of "Liberty or Death" to tarring and feathering, from the Boston Massacre to the Boston Tea Party, from Paul Revere and the Minutemen to Bunker Hill and the Continental Congress, colonists seem eager to march down the road to independence.

That is not how it looked to those colonists at the time. On the contrary: Americans were reluctant rebels. For one thing, the honor and obedience that the Bible and custom accorded parents carried over to what many of them called "the mother country" and their "father," the king. "[T]orn from the body, to which we are united by religion, liberty, laws, affections, relations, language, and commerce," fretted one, "we must bleed at every vein."[1] For another, the deference, even awe, Americans often showed a Briton like Alexander Hamilton (Chapter 5) was deeply rooted. "Natives of Britain were always treated with a particular regard" by colonists, said Benjamin Franklin, whose own pride in his English heritage was clear (Chapter 6); "to be an Old England Man was, of itself, a character of some respect, and gave a kind of rank among us."[2] Franklin himself, in England until 1775, shuddered at the prospect of independence and used all of his personal and political skills to avoid a final rupture.

Like Franklin, most colonists, unhappy with particular British leaders or policies, were loath to forsake Britain. Being part of the British empire was all they had known, after all, and conventional wisdom had it that Britain boasted the best government—a happy balance of King, House of Lords, and House of Commons—in human history. For more than a century that government had protected its colonial "children" from French and Indian raids. Moreover, as those foes had learned the hard way, Britain boasted the most powerful military in the world. Challenging that might, many thought, would be suicidal folly; it would also be treason. When Franklin reportedly said, on the eve of independence, that "we must indeed all hang together, or most assuredly we shall all hang separately," he was only half joking. He knew—they all knew—the fate of traitors.[3]

The glacial pace at which colonists slid toward independence further attests to their reluctance. It took ten full years from the first protests against British tax policies in 1765 to the first battles between Americans and redcoats, at Lexington and Concord on April 19, 1775. And from that bloody day, it was fourteen months more until Americans went from killing redcoats to declaring independence. Think back to where you were and what you were doing fourteen months ago; ponder all that has happened in

America and around the world during that span. Now you can begin to appreciate how slowly Americans went from colonies to nation.

Enter Thomas Paine (1737–1809) and *Common Sense*. At first glance Paine seems an unlikely addition to the roster of Founding Fathers. Born on the outskirts of a village northeast of London, he had *failure*—as shopkeeper, preacher, teacher, tax collector, even as husband—written all over him. At age thirty-seven, his dreams of happiness or success dashed, Paine sought a fresh start in America. Through mutual friends he met and got a letter of recommendation from Benjamin Franklin (who was then still in London). With that, and not much more, Paine embarked for Pennsylvania.

Upon his arrival in Philadelphia late in 1774, Paine found Americans every bit as loyal as Franklin had said they were. "[T]hey might have been led by a thread and governed by a reed," he later wrote. "Their…attachment to Britain was obstinate, and it was at that time a kind of treason to speak against it." True, a "Continental Congress" had convened in Philadelphia that very fall to coordinate American resistance to British policies. But Congress had reconciliation, not revolution, in mind; repeating the commonplace notion that King George III was a "loving father," it beseeched rather than threatened the mother country. Paine himself, at first, "viewed the dispute as a kind of lawsuit….I had no thoughts of independence….But," he went on, Lexington and Concord changed all that: "when the country, into which I had but just set my foot, was set on fire about my ears it was time to stir. It was time for every man to stir."[4]

Stirring people up was not going to be easy, however. Few in the Second Continental Congress, which assembled in May 1775, sought independence. "[T]here is not in the British empire a man who more cordially loves a Union with Gr. Britain than I do," wrote one congressman in November 1775. The author? Thomas Jefferson.[5] The young Virginian was not alone. Many colonies sent their representatives to this session of Congress with explicit instructions *not* to declare independence. In January 1776, when *Common Sense* appeared, probably no more than one congressman in three would have voted for a final break with Britain.

Common Sense would change all that. "[I]t burst from the press with an effect which has rarely been produced by types and papers in any age or country," wrote one excited Philadelphian; another, Franklin, who had perused a draft of it, called the pamphlet's impact "prodigious."[6] At a time when a newspaper might sell two thousand copies and a political pamphlet twice that many, *Common Sense* sold somewhere between 50,000 and 120,000 copies in twenty-five printings, more printings than any other American work before the Civil War era and the equivalent perhaps of a sales figure of ten million today. Just ten days after publication it was "already making 'a great noise' " in Virginia. (No less than George Washington praised its "sound doctrine and unanswerable reasoning.") From Massachusetts, Abigail Adams thanked her husband John, then serving in Congress, for sending it: "tis highly prized here and carries conviction wherever it is read." "[Y]ou have declared the sentiments of Millions," gushed a Connecticut colonist. "Your production may justly be compared to a land-flood that sweeps all before it."[7]

Reading *Common Sense* today is a little like reading Mary Rowlandson's captivity narrative (Chapter 4): It can be hard to fathom what all the excitement was about. Because we come to the text from a profoundly different frame of reference—America is an independent nation and a global power spanning an entire continent—we "just don't get it." Yet—as with Rowlandson's—in this work's popularity lie valuable clues to understanding the American world at the time.

It was, first of all, a world of kings. Scripture, tradition, history, political theory—all held that hereditary monarchy was the best form of government, a time-honored, even sacred system that ensured a nation's stability. And republics, governed by representatives of the people? These had neither Biblical sanction nor historical success.

In 1776, then, "common sense" meant honoring, even worshipping, the king. If Paine was going to move Americans toward independence, he had to convince them that crowns were not to be venerated but scorned.

To accomplish that, Paine also knew, he had to start with the Bible, so long the sacred source of royal power. If God had made kings, how could man question kingship? Here, too, the colonial world differs in important ways from our own. Paine, a sometime preacher brought up by a Quaker father and an Anglican mother, was well versed in the Bible; so, he found, were American colonists. Hence Paine's explication of Biblical passages, which might seem tedious digressions in our more secular age (and which I have omitted or shortened in this excerpt), was part of the pamphlet's appeal.

But it was not just that Paine used the Bible and other tools of demolition—a decidedly revisionist reading of English history, for example—against kingship. It was also the language he employed that got people's attention. Here again, 1776 contrasts with our own era, when cruel barbs, biting sarcasm, and worse fill the airwaves and the Internet. Most pamphlets in Paine's day were written by, and for, men like Dr. Hamilton. Sprinkled with Latin phrases, references to classical Greek or Roman authorities, and quotations from contemporary political theorists, these works were restrained in their tone and limited in their audience; they sought to persuade gentlemen, not rouse a mob. How does *Common Sense* depart from that style? What rhetorical weapons does it add to the American conversation? As you read, consider why some Americans (the "People of Sense & Property"), however they felt about independence, condemned the pamphlet as "[o]ne of the vilest things that ever was published," "nonsensical" and "scandalous," "crude" and "ignorant," "an outrageous insult on the common sense of Americans."[8]

Thin skinned and temperamental, Paine resented the attacks. But he also relished them, because he had little use for those "People of Sense & Property." He sought a different audience, the common folk. Indeed, Paine intended the work to be read aloud so that it would reach the illiterate. Reading passages out loud yourself (such as the last two paragraphs included here) will suggest something of Paine's power, and will also recapture a time when—in streets, taverns, and homes throughout the colonies—*Common Sense* was "read to all ranks" of Americans.[9]

What Paine, as a newcomer, also offered was an identity as "Americans." As Dr. Hamilton learned, Britain's colonies were different in many ways, and that sense of difference endured in the 1760s and 1770s. South Carolina, sneered one New England visitor there, is a land "divided into opulent and lordly planters, poor and spiritless peasants and vile slaves." Meanwhile a New Yorker grumbled that men from Connecticut, "that damd C[o]untry," are "d—d ungreatfull cheating fellows." Independence? A new nation? Never! America would, wrote a Pennsylvanian, end up with "a multitude of Commonwealths, Crimes and Calamities—centuries of mutual Jealousies, hatred, Wars and Devastations."[10] Paine, an outsider ignorant of the long-standing prejudices and accepted wisdom, saw what colonists shared, not what divided them. Nowadays it is commonplace to call ourselves "Americans." In 1776, a time when Franklin called New England his "native country" and Thomas Jefferson thought of Virginia the same way, all this was unheard of, daring, and exciting.

Once you have something of the mind-set of those picking up (or listening to) *Common Sense* in 1776, it is easier to be swept along, as they were, by his work. But be careful: So powerful is Paine's prose, so bold are his claims against the past and for the future, against kings and for republics, against Britain and for America, that it is easy to miss his leaps of faith and lapses in logic. Even as you enjoy what historian Bernard Bailyn considers "the most brilliant pamphlet written during the American Revolution, and one of the most brilliant...ever written in the English language," remember that Paine was out to stir people up, not present an accurate depiction of America's past, present, or future.[11]

Near the end of *Common Sense*, Paine urged that Americans write "a manifesto… setting forth the miseries we have endured, and the peaceable methods we have ineffectually used for redress; declaring, at the same time, that not being able, any longer, to live happily or safely under the cruel disposition of the British court, we had been driven to the necessity of breaking off all connections with her….Such a memorial," Paine concluded, "would produce more good effects to this Continent, than if a ship were freighted with petitions to Britain."

Six months later, Congress authorized the writing of just such a manifesto and appointed a committee that included Franklin, John Adams, and Thomas Jefferson (1743–1826). Recalling many years later his central role in drafting that document, Jefferson, perhaps acknowledging America's debt to Paine, wrote that he intended "[n]ot to find out new principles, or new arguments, never before thought of…; but to place before mankind the *common sense* of the subject."[12]

As historians Joseph Ellis and Pauline Maier have noted, the document Jefferson drafted, Franklin and Adams reviewed, and Congress revised before approving it on July 4 is more often revered than read. Nonetheless, scholars have for a century now been debating its character and meaning. Some look to different European thinkers who influenced Jefferson, some to his previous writings, others to fellow Virginians like George Mason, who was then in Williamsburg helping to draft a state constitution (see Chapter 8). Still others take Jefferson at his word when he wrote that "it was intended to be an expression of the American mind"; Maier recently found some ninety other "declarations of independence" penned by towns, counties, and colonies during that tumultuous time. Some insist that Congress, not Jefferson, was the real author, since that body made no less than eighty-six changes as an unhappy Jefferson sat—fuming and squirming, an amused Franklin at his side—while colleagues "mangled" his text.[13]

Whatever its origins, whatever alterations (Jefferson called them "mutilations") it endured on its journey from Jefferson's desk to the printer's shop and from there to "a candid world," the document deserves close scrutiny, not empty veneration.[14] Like you starting a history essay with a blank computer screen, Jefferson began writing, that June day, with a blank sheet of paper. Like you, he had a specific assignment and a deadline to meet. Like you, he had other tasks to do and other things on his mind. Like you, he sought to make a compelling argument that would persuade readers. Like you, he drew upon his own thinking, his own reading, in structuring and phrasing his paper. Like you (I hope!), he revised and reworked the document.

Consider the result and its use of language, its tone. How would you characterize its mood (or moods)? How does he convey that mood? Is this, like *Common Sense*, designed to "stir" people up? For that matter, what "people," what audience, is it trying to reach? It is easy enough to conclude that *Common Sense* is propaganda; is the Declaration? Imagine that Dr. Alexander Hamilton had still been alive in 1776 (he would have been sixty-four, six years younger than Franklin was then): What would he have had to say about the sentiments expressed here?

The Declaration of Independence can be further illuminated by comparing it with *Common Sense*. Would Paine have been pleased with the "manifesto" Congress produced? One historian argues that in terms of style, at least, "it is difficult to imagine a text less similar to *Common Sense* than Thomas Jefferson's draft of the Declaration of Independence."[15] Do you agree?

Whatever insights comparison yields, the two documents have led very different lives. At the time, the Declaration made nothing like the splash *Common Sense* did. It was what Maier has called a "workaday document," written in haste by busy men with lots of other things on their agenda (for one thing, the rebellion was going badly). True, General Washington ordered it read to the troops, and townsfolk throughout the land heard it that summer. But thereafter it largely sank from sight for decades—except for the occasional conservative condemnation of it as a "false, flatulent, and foolish paper"!—until an aging Jefferson, with others keen to keep alive the patriotic "Spirit of '76," began making the Declaration into the sacred object it is today. *Common Sense*, meanwhile, which in 1776 so stirred American hearts and minds, was all but forgotten. You have probably read the Declaration of Independence before now; had you read *Common Sense*?[16]

One explanation for the different fates of these two texts has to do with the paths Paine and Jefferson followed after 1776. Jefferson's career is well known: From Philadelphia that summer he went on to greatness, becoming the new nation's third president and eventually winning a memorial in Washington, D.C., as well as a place on Mount Rushmore. And Paine? He stayed in Philadelphia for another decade, then went back to Britain briefly before making his way to France, where he became involved in the revolution sweeping that country after 1789. In 1802 he was back in the United States, but he met a cold reception. Having published, since he left America, *The Age of Reason* and *The Age of Man*, he was branded an atheist and a dangerous radical. John Adams, who in 1776 had praised the "elegant simplicity" and "piercing pathos" of *Common Sense* as "very meritorious," now called the work "a poor, ignorant, malicious, short-sighted, crapulous [intemperate] mass." Meanwhile old friends shunned Paine; hostile crowds greeted him; newspapers called him "a lying, drunken, brutal infidel"; innkeepers refused him a bed or a meal. Alone, ill, and embittered, Paine took to drink. When he died in New York City in 1809, only six people attended his funeral. Not for Thomas Paine a Mount Rushmore or a memorial in the nation's capital.[17]

The careers of the two men help explain why the Declaration is worshipped and *Common Sense* neglected; perhaps the documents themselves hold another clue. Just as Americans assume that the road to independence was straight and smooth, we like to think of the Revolution as a tidy affair, a matter of genteel men in white wigs sitting in assembly halls to draft calm, reasoned arguments—like the Declaration of Independence. In fact, the American Revolution was a messy business (some sense of its messiness awaits you in Chapter 9), full of anger and anguish, a sense of betrayal and a thirst for blood. That is Thomas Paine's revolution. His *Common Sense* helps us remember it.

Questions for Consideration and Conversation

1. How would you characterize the tone of *Common Sense*? How did that tone help get Paine's message across?
2. Most early editions of *Common Sense* gave no author, but one had "By an Englishman" on the title page. What impact would this have on colonial readers?
3. It is clear from the texts by Dr. Alexander Hamilton and Benjamin Franklin that American colonists suffered from an inferiority complex compared with Europe in general and Great Britain in particular. How does *Common Sense* speak to this sense of inferiority?
4. Near the end of his pamphlet, Paine called for America to write a "manifesto" explaining its reasons for leaving the empire. Would he have been happy with the "manifesto" written seven months later?
5. How would you characterize the overall tone of the Declaration of Independence? Does that tone shift in different portions of the text?
6. What is the most important part of the Declaration of Independence?
7. How does reading the Declaration—in context, with care, and more than once!—change your view of the document? Of American independence?
8. Everyone agrees that *Common Sense* is propaganda. Is the Declaration of Independence? Why or why not?

Endnotes

1. Pauline Maier, *American Scripture: Making the Declaration of Independence* (New York, 1997), 29.
2. Jack P. Greene, *Understanding the American Revolution: Issues and Actors* (Charlottesville, VA, 1995), 26.
3. H. W. Brands, *The First American: The Life and Times of Benjamin Franklin* (New York, 2000), 512.
4. Thomas Paine, *Common Sense*, ed. Isaac Kramnick (New York, 1976), 25.
5. Julian P. Boyd, ed., *The Papers of Thomas Jefferson*, vol. I (Princeton, NJ, 1950), 269.
6. Paine, *Common Sense*, 8.
7. David Freeman Hawke, *Paine* (New York, 1974), 47 (Virginia); Paine, *Common Sense*, 29 (Washington); Winthrop Jordan, "Familial Politics: Thomas Paine and the Killing of the King, 1776," *Journal of American History*, 60 (1973), 295 (Adams, Connecticut).
8. John Keane, *Tom Paine: A Political Life* (Boston, 1995), 123–28.
9. Hawke, *Paine*, 47.
10. Jack P. Greene, *Imperatives, Behaviors, and Identities: Essays in Early American Cultural History* (Charlottesville, VA, 1992), 269 ("vile slaves"), 296 ("Calamities"); John M. Murrin, "A Roof Without Walls: The Dilemma of American National Identity," in Richard Beeman, Stephen Botein, and Edward C. Carter II, eds., *Beyond Confederation: Origins of the Constitution and American National Identity* (Chapel Hill, NC, 1987), 343 (New York).
11. Bernard Bailyn, "Common Sense," *Fundamental Testaments of the American Revolution* (Washington, DC, 1973), 7.
12. Julian P. Boyd, ed., *The Declaration of Independence: The Evolution of the Text…* (Princeton, NJ, 1945), 2 (emphasis added).
13. Maier, *American Scripture*; Joseph J. Ellis, *American Sphinx: The Character of Thomas Jefferson* (New York, 1997), ch. 1 ("mangled," 60); Boyd, ed., *Declaration of Independence*, 2.
14. Maier, *American Scripture*, 149.
15. Thomas Paine, *Common Sense and Related Writings*, ed. Thomas P. Slaughter (Boston, 2001), 40.
16. Maier, *American Scripture*, xviii ("workaday"); Marshall Smelser, *The Democratic Republic, 1801–1815* (New York, 1968), 18 ("false").
17. Hawke, *Paine*, 48–49 ("simplicity," "pathos," "meritorious," "ignorant"); Eric Foner, *Tom Paine and Revolutionary America* (New York, 1976), 258 ("infidel"); Paine, *Common Sense and Related Writings*, 51–56.

THOMAS PAINE, *COMMON SENSE* (1776)

Source: [Thomas Paine,] *Common Sense: Addressed to the Inhabitants of America.…* Philadelphia: W. & T. Bradford, February 14, 1776.

Introduction

Perhaps the sentiments contained in the following pages, are not yet sufficiently fashionable to procure them general favor; a long habit of not thinking a thing *wrong*, gives it a superficial appearance of being *right*, and raises at first a formidable outcry in defence of custom. But the tumult soon subsides. Time makes more converts than reason.…

The cause of America is in a great measure the cause of all mankind. Many circumstances hath, and will arise, which are not local, but universal, and through which the principles of all Lovers of Mankind are affected.… The laying a Country desolate with Fire and Sword, declaring War against the natural rights of all Mankind, and extirpating the Defenders thereof from the Face of the Earth, is the Concern of every Man to whom Nature hath given the Power of feeling; of which Class, regardless of Party Censure, is the

AUTHOR

Of the Origin and Design of Government in General. With concise Remarks on the English Constitution

Some writers have so confounded society with government, as to leave little or no distinction between them; whereas they are not only different, but have different origins. Society is produced by our wants, and government by our wickedness; the former promotes our happiness *positively* by uniting our affections, the latter *negatively* by restraining our vices.… Society in every state is a blessing, but government even in its best state is but a necessary evil; in its worst state an intolerable one; for when we suffer, or are exposed to the same miseries *by a government*, which we might expect in a country *without government*, our calamities is [*sic*] heightened by reflecting that we furnish the means by which we suffer. Government, like dress, is the badge of lost innocence; the palaces of kings are built on the ruins of the bowers of paradise. For were the impulses of conscience clear, uniform, and irresistibly obeyed, man would need no other lawgiver; but that not being the case, he finds it necessary to surrender up a part of his property to furnish means for the protection of the rest.…*Wherefore*, security being the true design and end of government, it unanswerably follows that whatever *form* thereof appears most likely to ensure it to us, with the least expence and greatest benefit, is preferable to all others.

In order to gain a clear and just idea of the design and end of government, let us suppose a small number of persons, settled in some sequestered part of the earth, unconnected with the rest, they will then represent the first peopling of any country, or of the world. In this state of natural liberty, society will be their first thought. A thousand motives will excite them thereto, the strength of one man is so unequal to his wants, and his mind so unfitted for perpetual solitude, that he is soon obliged to seek assistance and relief of another, who in his turn requires the same. Four or five united would be able to raise a tolerable dwelling in the midst of a wilderness, but *one* man might labour out the common period of life without accomplishing any thing; when he had felled his timber he could not remove it, nor erect it after it was removed; hunger in the mean time would urge him from his work, and every different want call him a different way. Disease, nay even misfortune would be death, for though neither might be mortal, yet either would disable him from living, and reduce him to a state in which he might rather be said to perish than to die.

Thus necessity, like a gravitating power, would soon form our newly arrived emigrants into society, the reciprocal blessings of which, would supercede, and render the obligations of law and government unnecessary while they remained perfectly just to each other; but as nothing but heaven is impregnable to vice, it will unavoidably happen, that in proportion as they surmount the first difficulties of emigration, which bound them together in a common cause, they will begin to relax in their duty and attachment to each other; and this remissness [negligence], will point out

the necessity, of establishing some form of government to supply the defect of moral virtue.

Some convenient tree will afford them a State-House, under the branches of which, the whole colony may assemble to deliberate on public matters.…In this first parliament every man, by natural right will have a seat.

But as the colony increases, the public concerns will increase likewise, and the distance at which the members may be separated, will render it too inconvenient for all of them to meet on every occasion as at first, when their number was small, their habitations near, and the public concerns few and trifling. This will point out the convenience of their consenting to leave the legislative part to be managed by a select number chosen from the whole body, who are supposed to have the same concerns at stake which those have who appointed them, and who will act in the same manner as the whole body would act were they present.…[A]nd that the *elected* might never form to themselves an interest separate from the *electors*, prudence will point out the propriety of having elections often; because…the *elected* might by that means return and mix again with the general body of the *electors* in a few months.…And as this frequent interchange will establish a common interest with every part of the community, they will mutually and naturally support each other, and on this (not on the unmeaning name of king) depends the *strength of government, and the happiness of the governed*.

Here then is the origin and rise of government; namely, a mode rendered necessary by the inability of moral virtue to govern the world; here too is the design and end of government, viz. [namely] freedom and security. And however our eyes may be dazzled with show, or our ears deceived by sound; however prejudice may warp our wills, or interest darken our understanding, the simple voice of nature and of reason will say, it is right.

I draw my idea of the form of government from a principle in nature, which no art can overturn, viz. that the more simple any thing is, the less liable it is to be disordered, and the easier repaired when disordered; and with this maxim in view, I offer a few remarks on the so much boasted constitution of England. That it was noble for the dark and slavish times in which it was erected is granted. When the world was over-run with tyranny the least remove therefrom was a glorious rescue. But that it is imperfect, subject to convulsions, and incapable of producing what it seems to promise, is easily demonstrated.

Absolute governments (tho' the disgrace of human nature) have this advantage with them, that they are simple; if the people suffer, they know the head from which their suffering springs, know likewise the remedy, and are not bewildered by a variety of causes and cures. But the constitution of England is so exceedingly complex, that the nation may suffer for years together without being able to discover in which part the fault lies, some will say in one and some in another, and every political physician will advise a different medicine.

I know it is difficult to get over local or long standing prejudices, yet if we will suffer ourselves to examine the component parts of the English constitution, we shall find them to be the base remains of two ancient tyrannies, compounded with some new republican materials.

First.—The remains of monarchical tyranny in the person of the king.

Secondly.—The remains of aristocratical tyranny in the persons of the peers.

Thirdly.—The new republican materials, in the persons of the commons, on whose virtue depends the freedom of England.

The two first, by being hereditary, are independent of the people; wherefore in a *constitutional sense* they contribute nothing towards the freedom of the state.

To say that the constitution of England is a *union* of three powers reciprocally *checking* each other, is farcical, either the words have no meaning, or they are flat contradictions.

To say that the commons is a check upon the king, presupposes two things.

First.—That the king is not to be trusted without being looked after, or in other words, that a thirst for absolute power is the natural disease of monarchy.

Secondly.—That the commons, by being appointed for that purpose, are either wiser or more worthy of confidence than the crown.

But as the same constitution which gives the commons a power to check the king by withholding the supplies, gives afterwards the king a power to check the commons, by empowering him to reject their other bills; it again supposes that the king is wiser than those whom it has already supposed to be wiser than him. A mere absurdity!

There is something exceedingly ridiculous in the composition of monarchy; it first excludes a man from the means of information, yet empowers him to act in cases where the highest judgment is required. The state of a king shuts him from the world, yet the business of a king requires him to know it thoroughly; wherefore the different parts, unnaturally opposing and destroying each other, prove the whole character to be absurd and useless....

Of Monarchy and Hereditary Succession

Mankind being originally equals in the order of creation, the equality could only be destroyed by some subsequent circumstance....

But there is another and greater distinction [besides rich and poor] for which no truly natural or religious reason can be assigned, and that is, the distinction of men into KINGS and SUBJECTS. Male and female are the distinctions of nature, good and bad the distinctions of heaven; but how a race of men came into the world so exalted above the rest, and distinguished like some new species, is worth enquiring into....

In the early ages of the world, according to the scripture chronology, there were no kings; the consequence of which was there were no wars; it is the pride of kings which throw mankind into confusion. Holland without a king hath enjoyed more peace for this last century than any of the monarchi[c]al governments in Europe. Antiquity favors the same remark; for the quiet and rural lives of the first patriarchs hath a happy something in them, which vanishes away when we come to the history of Jewish royalty.

Government by kings was first introduced into the world by the Heathens, from whom the children of Israel copied the custom. It was the most prosperous invention the Devil ever set on foot for the promotion of idolatry. The Heathens paid divine honors to their deceased kings, and the christian world hath improved on the plan by doing the same to their living ones....

As the exalting one man so greatly above the rest cannot be justified on the equal rights of nature, so neither can it be defended on the authority of scripture; for the will of the Almighty, as declared by Gideon and the prophet Samuel, expressly disapproves of government by kings....

Near three thousand years passed away from the Mosaic account of the creation, till the Jews under a national delusion requested a king. Till then their form of government (except in extraordinary cases, where the Almighty interposed) was a kind of republic administered by a judge and the elders of the tribes. Kings they had none, and it was held sinful to acknowledge any being under that title but the Lord of Hosts. And when a man seriously reflects on the idolatrous homage which is paid to the persons of Kings, he need not wonder, that the Almighty, ever jealous of his honor, should disapprove of a form of government which so impiously invades the prerogative of heaven....

To the evil of monarchy we have added that of hereditary succession; and as the first is a degradation and lessening of ourselves, so the second, claimed as a matter of right, is an insult and an imposition on posterity. For all men being originally equals, no *one* by *birth* could have a right to set up his own family in perpetual preference to all others for ever, and though himself might deserve *some* decent degree of honors of his contemporaries, yet his descendants might be far too unworthy to inherit them. One of the strongest *natural* proofs of the folly of hereditary right in kings, is, that nature disapproves it, otherwise she would not so frequently turn it into ridicule by giving mankind an *ass for a lion.*

Secondly, as no man at first could possess any other public honors than were bestowed upon him, so the givers of those honors could have no power to give away the right of posterity, and though they might say "We choose you for *our* head," they could not, without manifest injustice to their children, say "that your children and your children's children shall reign over *ours* for ever." Because such an unwise, unjust, unnatural compact might (perhaps) in the next succession put them under the government of a rogue or a fool. Most wise men, in their private sentiments, have ever treated hereditary right with contempt; yet it is one of those evils, which when once established is not easily removed; many submit from fear, others from superstition, and the more powerful part shares with the king the plunder of the rest.

This is supposing the present race of kings in the world to have had an honourable origin; whereas it is more than probable, that could we take off the dark covering of antiquity, and trace them to their first rise, that we should find the first of them nothing better than the principal ruffian of some restless gang, whose savage manners or pre-eminence in subtilty obtained him the title of chief among plunderers; and who by increasing in power, and extending his depredations, over-awed the quiet and defenceless to purchase their safety by frequent contributions. Yet his electors could have no idea of giving hereditary right to his descendants, because such a perpetual exclusion of themselves was incompatible with the free and unrestrained principles they professed to live by. Wherefore, hereditary succession in the early ages of monarchy could not take place as a matter of claim, but as something casual or complimental; but as few or no records were extant in those days, and traditionary history stuffed with fables, it was very easy, after the lapse of a few generations, to trump up some superstitious tale, conveniently timed, Mahomet like, to cram hereditary right down the throats of the vulgar. Perhaps the disorders which threatened, or seemed to threaten on the decease of a leader and the choice of a new one (for elections among ruffians could not be very orderly) induced many at first to favor hereditary pretensions; by which means it happened, as it hath happened since, that what at first was submitted to as a convenience, was afterwards claimed as a right.

England, since the [Norman] conquest [of England in 1066], hath known some few good monarchs, but groaned beneath a much larger number of bad ones, yet no man in his senses can say that their claim under William the Conqueror is a very honorable one. A French bastard landing with an armed banditti, and establishing himself king of England against the consent of the natives, is in plain terms a very paltry rascally original.—It certainly hath no divinity in it. However, it is needless to spend much time in exposing the folly of hereditary right, if there are any so weak as to believe it, let them promiscuously [indiscriminately] worship the ass and lion, and welcome. I shall neither copy their humility, nor disturb their devotion....

But it is not so much the absurdity as the evil of hereditary succession which concerns mankind. Did it ensure a race of good and wise men it would have the seal of divine authority, but as it opens a door to the *foolish,* the *wicked,* and the *improper,* it hath in it the nature of oppression. Men who look upon themselves born to reign, and others to obey, soon grow insolent; selected from the rest of mankind their minds are early poisoned by importance; and the world they act in differs so materially from the world at large, that they have but little opportunity of knowing its true interests, and when they succeed to the government are frequently the most ignorant and unfit of any throughout the dominions....

The most plausible plea, which hath ever been offered in favour of hereditary succession, is, that it preserves a nation from civil wars; and were this true, it would be weighty; whereas, it is the most barefaced falsity ever imposed upon mankind. The whole history of England disowns the fact. Thirty kings and two minors have reigned in that distracted kingdom since the conquest, in which time there have been (including the Revolution) no less than eight civil wars and nineteen rebellions....

Thoughts on the present State of American Affairs

In the following pages I offer nothing more than simple facts, plain arguments, and common sense; and have no other preliminaries to settle with the reader, than that he will divest himself of prejudice and prepossession, and suffer his reason and his feelings to determine for themselves; that he will put *on*, or rather that he will not put *off*, the true character of a man, and generously enlarge his views beyond the present day.

Volumes have been written on the subject of the struggle between England and America. Men of all ranks have embarked in the controversy, from different motives, and with various designs; but all have been ineffectual, and the period of debate is closed. Arms, as the last resource, decide the contest; the appeal [to arms] was the choice of the king, and the continent hath accepted the challenge....

The sun never shined on a cause of greater worth. 'Tis not the affair of a city, a county, a province, or a kingdom, but of a continent—of at least one eighth part of the habitable globe. 'Tis not the concern of a day, a year, or an age; posterity are virtually involved in the contest, and will be more or less affected, even to the end of time, by the proceedings now. Now is the seed time of continental union, faith and honor. The least fracture now will be like a name engraved with the point of a pin on the tender rind of a young oak; the wound will enlarge with the tree, and posterity read it in full grown characters.

By referring the matter from argument to arms, a new æra for politics is struck; a new method of thinking hath arisen. All plans, proposals, &c. prior to the nineteenth of April [1775, the battles of Lexington and Concord], *i.e.* to the commencement of hostilities, are like the almanacks of the last year; which, though proper then, are superceded and useless now....

As much hath been said of the advantages of reconciliation, which, like an agreeable dream, hath passed away and left us as we were, it is but right, that we should examine the contrary side of the argument, and inquire into some of the many material injuries which these colonies sustain, and always will sustain, by being connected with, and dependant on Great Britain. To examine that connexion and dependance, on the principles of nature and common sense, to see what we have to trust to, if separated, and what we are to expect, if dependant.

I have heard it asserted by some, that as America hath flourished under her former connexion with Great-Britain, that the same connexion is necessary towards her future happiness, and will always have the same effect. Nothing can be more fallacious than this kind of argument. We may as well assert, that because a child has thrived upon milk, that it is never to have meat; or that the first twenty years of our lives is to become a precedent for the next twenty. But even this is admitting more than is true, for I answer roundly, that America would have flourished as much, and probably much more, had no European power had any thing to do with her. The commerce by which she hath enriched herself are the necessaries of life, and will always have a market while eating is the custom of Europe.

But she has protected us, say some. That she hath engrossed [monopolized] us is true, and defended the continent at our expence as well as her own is admitted, and she would have defended Turkey from the same motive, viz. the sake of trade and dominion....

But Britain is the parent country, say some. Then the more shame upon her conduct. Even Brutes do not devour their young, nor savages make war upon their families; wherefore the assertion, if true, turns to her reproach; but it happens not to be true, or only partly so, and the phrase *parent* or *mother country* hath been jesuitically adopted by the ——— and his parasites, with a low papistical design of gaining an unfair bias on the credulous weakness of our minds. Europe, and not England, is the parent country of America. This new world hath been the asylum for the persecuted lovers of civil and religious liberty from *every part* of Europe. Hither have they fled, not from the tender embraces of the mother, but from the cruelty of the monster; and it is so far true of England, that the same tyranny which drove the first emigrants from home, pursues their descendants still....

But admitting that we were all of English descent, what does it amount to? Nothing. Britain, being now an open enemy, extinguishes every other name and title: And to say that reconciliation is our duty, is truly farcical. The first king of England, of the present line (William the Conqueror) was a Frenchman, and half the peers of England are descendants from the same country; wherefore by the same method of reasoning, England ought to be governed by France....

I challenge the warmest advocate for reconciliation, to shew, a single advantage that this continent can reap, by being connected with Great Britain. I repeat the challenge, not a single advantage is derived. Our corn will fetch its price in any market in Europe, and our imported goods must be paid for buy them where we will.

But the injuries and disadvantages we sustain by that connection, are without number; and our duty to mankind at large, as well as to ourselves, instruct us to renounce the alliance: Because, any submission to, or dependance on Great Britain, tends directly to involve this continent in European wars and quarrels; and sets us at variance with nations, who would otherwise seek our friendship, and against whom, we have neither anger nor complaint. As Europe is our market for trade, we ought to form no partial connection with any part of it....

Europe is too thickly planted with kingdoms to be long at peace, and whenever a war breaks out between England and any foreign power, the trade of America goes to ruin, *because of her connection with Britain*....Every thing that is right or natural pleads for separation. The blood of the slain, the weeping voice of nature cries, 'TIS TIME TO PART. Even the distance at which the Almighty hath placed England and America, is a strong and natural proof, that the authority of the one, over the other, was never the design of Heaven. The time likewise at which the continent was discovered, adds weight to the argument, and the manner in which it was peopled encreases the force of it. The [Protestant] reformation was preceded by the discovery of America, as if the Almighty graciously meant to open a sanctuary to the persecuted in future years, when home should afford neither friendship nor safety.

The authority of Great-Britain over this continent, is a form of government, which sooner or later must have an end: And a serious mind can draw no true pleasure by looking forward, under the painful and positive conviction, that what he calls "the present constitution" is merely temporary. As parents, we can have no joy, knowing that *this government* is not sufficiently lasting to ensure any thing which we may bequeath to posterity: And by a plain method of argument, as we are running the next generation into debt, we ought to do the work of it, otherwise we use them meanly and pitifully. In order to discover the line of our duty rightly, we should take our children in our hand, and fix our station a few years farther into life; that eminence will present a prospect, which a few present fears and prejudices conceal from our sight.

Though I would carefully avoid giving unnecessary offence, yet I am inclined to believe, that all those who espouse the doctrine of reconciliation, may be included within the following descriptions. Interested men, who are not to be trusted; weak men who *cannot* see; prejudiced men who *will not* see; and a certain set of moderate men, who think better of the European world than it deserves; and this last class by an ill-judged deliberation, will be the cause of more calamities to this continent, than all the other three.

It is the good fortune of many to live distant from the scene of sorrow; the evil is not sufficiently brought to *their* doors to make *them* feel the precariousness with which all American property is possessed. But let our imaginations transport us for a few moments to Boston, that seat of wretchedness will teach us wisdom....The inhabitants of that unfortunate city, who but a few months ago were in ease and affluence, have now no other alternative than to stay and starve, or turn out to beg....In their present condition they are prisoners without the hope of redemption....

Men of passive tempers look somewhat lightly over the offences of Britain, and, still hoping for the best, are apt to call out, *"Come, we shall be friends again for all this."* But examine the passions and feelings of mankind. Bring the doctrine of reconciliation to the touchstone of nature, and then tell me, whether you can hereafter love, honour, and faithfully serve the power that hath carried fire and sword into your land? If you cannot do all these, then are you only deceiving yourselves, and by your delay bringing ruin upon posterity. Your future connection with Britain, whom you can neither love nor honour, will be forced and unnatural, and being formed only on the plan of present convenience, will in a little time fall into a relapse more wretched than the first. But if you say, you can still pass the violations over, then I ask, Hath your house been burnt? Hath your property been destroyed before your face? Are your wife and children destitute of a bed to lie on, or bread to live on? Have you lost a parent or a child by their hands, and yourself the ruined and wretched survivor? If you have not, then are you not a judge of those who have. But if you have, and still can shake hands with the murderers, then are you unworthy the name of husband, father, friend, or lover, and whatever may be your rank or title in life, you have the heart of a coward, and the spirit of a sycophant [toady].

This is not inflaming or exaggerating matters, but trying them by those feelings and affections which nature justifies, and without which, we should be incapable of discharging the social duties of life, or enjoying the felicities of it. I mean not to exhibit horror for the purpose of provoking revenge, but to awaken us from fatal and unmanly slumbers, that we may pursue determinately some fixed object. It is not in the power of Britain or of Europe to conquer America, if she do not conquer herself by *delay* and *timidity*. The present winter is worth an age if rightly employed, but if lost or neglected, the whole continent will partake of the misfortune; and there is no punishment which that man will not deserve, be he who, or what, or where he will, that may be the means of sacrificing a season so precious and useful.

It is repugnant to reason, to the universal order of things, to all examples from the former ages, to suppose, that this continent can longer remain subject to any external power....

[T]here is something very absurd, in supposing a continent to be perpetually governed by an island. In no instance hath nature made the satellite larger than its primary planet, and as England and America, with respect to each other, reverses the common order of nature, it is evident they belong to different systems: England to Europe, America to itself....

No man was a warmer wisher for reconciliation than myself, before the fatal nineteenth of April 1775 ["Massacre at Lexington." *Paine's Note*], but the moment the event of that day was made known, I rejected the hardened, sullen tempered Pharoah of —— for ever; and disdain the wretch, that with the pretended title of FATHER OF HIS PEOPLE can unfeelingly hear of their slaughter, and composedly sleep with their blood upon his soul....

If there is any true cause of fear respecting independance, it is because no plan is yet laid down. Men do not see their way out—Wherefore, as an opening into that business, I offer the following hints; at the same time modestly affirming, that I have no other opinion of them myself, than that they may be the means of giving rise to something better. Could the straggling thoughts of individuals be collected, they would frequently form materials for wise and able men to improve to useful matter.

Let the assemblies be annual, with a President only. The representation more equal. Their business wholly domestic, and subject to the authority of a Continental Congress.

Let each colony be divided into six, eight, or ten, convenient districts, each district to send a proper number of delegates to Congress, so that each colony send at least thirty. The whole number in Congress will be least 390. Each Congress to sit and to choose a president [from each colony's delegation in turn]....And in order that nothing may pass into a law but what is satisfactorily just, not less than three fifths of the Congress to be called a majority....

But as there is a peculiar delicacy, from whom, or in what manner, this business must first arise, and as it seems most agreeable and consistent, that it should come from some intermediate body between the governed and the governors, that is between the Congress and the people, let a CONTINENTAL CONFERENCE be held, in the following manner, and for the following purpose.

A committee of twenty-six members of Congress, viz. two for each colony....In this conference, thus assembled, will be united, the two grand principles of business, *knowledge* and *power*. The members of Congress, Assemblies, or Conventions, by having had experience in national concerns, will be able and useful counsellors, and the whole, being impowered by the people, will have a truly legal authority.

The conferring members being met, let their business be to frame a CONTINENTAL CHARTER, or Charter of the United Colonies; (answering to what is called the Magna Charta of England) fixing the number and manner of choosing members of Congress, members of Assembly, with their date of sitting, and drawing the line of business and jurisdiction between them: (Always remembering, that our strength is continental, not provincial:) Securing freedom and property to all men, and above all things the free exercise of religion, according to the dictates of conscience; with such other matter as is necessary for a charter to contain. Immediately after which, the said conference to dissolve, and the bodies which shall be chosen conformable to the said charter, to be the legislators and governors of this continent for the time being: Whose peace and happiness, may God preserve, Amen....

Ye that tell us of harmony and reconciliation, can ye restore to us the time that is past? Can ye give to prostitution its former innocence? Neither can ye reconcile Britain and America. The last cord now is broken, the people of England are presenting addresses against us. There are injuries which nature cannot forgive; she would cease to be nature if she did. As well can the lover forgive the ravisher [rapist] of his mistress, as the continent forgive the murders of Britain. The Almighty hath implanted in us these unextinguishable feelings for good and wise purposes. They are the guardians of his image in our hearts. They distinguish us from the herd of common animals....

O ye that love mankind! Ye that dare oppose, not only the tyranny, but the tyrant, stand forth! Every spot of the old world is over-run with oppression. Freedom hath been hunted round the globe. Asia, and Africa, have long expelled her.—Europe regards her like a stranger, and England hath given her warning to depart. O! receive the fugitive, and prepare in time an asylum for mankind.

In Congress

The Unanimous Declaration of the Thirteen United States of America (July 4, 1776)

Source: The National Archives.

When in the Course of human events, it becomes necessary for one people to dissolve the political bands which have connected them with another, and to assume among the powers of the earth, the separate and equal station to which the Laws of Nature and of Nature's God entitle them, a decent respect to the opinions of mankind requires that they should declare the causes which impel them to the separation.

We hold these truths to be self-evident, That all men are created equal, that they are endowed by their Creator with certain unalienable Rights, that among these are Life, Liberty, and the pursuit of Happiness.— That to secure these rights, Governments are instituted among Men, deriving their just powers from the consent of the governed,—That whenever any Form of Government becomes destructive of these ends, it is the Right of the People to alter or to abolish it, and to institute new Government, laying its foundation on such principles and organizing its powers in such form, as to them shall seem most likely to effect their Safety and Happiness. Prudence, indeed, will dictate that Governments long established should not be changed for light and transient causes; and accordingly all experience hath shewn, that mankind are more disposed to suffer, while evils are sufferable, than to right themselves by abolishing the forms to which they are accustomed. But when a long train of abuses and usurpations, pursuing invariably the same Object evinces a design to reduce them under absolute Despotism, it is their right, it is their duty, to throw off such Government, and to provide new Guards for their future security.—Such has been the

patient sufferance of these Colonies; and such is now the necessity which constrains [forces] them to alter their former Systems of Government. The history of the present King of Great Britain is a history of repeated injuries and usurpations, all having in direct object the establishment of an absolute Tyranny over these States. To prove this, let Facts be submitted to a candid world.

He has refused his Assent to Laws, the most wholesome and necessary for the public good.

He has forbidden his Governors to pass Laws of immediate and pressing importance, unless suspended in their operation till his Assent should be obtained; and when so suspended, he has utterly neglected to attend to them.

He has refused to pass other Laws for the accommodation of large districts of people, unless those people would relinquish the right of Representation in the Legislature, a right inestimable to them and formidable to tyrants only.

He has called together legislative bodies at places unusual, uncomfortable, and distant from the depository of their public Records, for the sole purpose of fatiguing them into compliance with his measures.

He has dissolved Representative Houses repeatedly, for opposing with manly firmness his invasions on the rights of the people.

He has refused for a long time, after such dissolutions, to cause others to be elected; whereby the Legislative powers, incapable of Annihilation, have returned to the People at large for their exercise;

the State remaining in the mean time exposed to all the dangers of invasion from without, and convulsions within.

He has endeavoured to prevent the population of these States; for that purpose obstructing the Laws for Naturalization of Foreigners; refusing to pass others to encourage their migrations hither, and raising the conditions of new Appropriations of Lands.

He has obstructed the Administration of Justice, by refusing his Assent to Laws for establishing Judiciary powers.

He has made Judges dependent on his Will alone, for the tenure of their offices, and the amount and payment of their salaries.

He has erected a multitude of New Offices, and sent hither swarms of Officers to harrass our people, and eat out their substance.

He has kept among us, in times of peace, Standing Armies without the Consent of our legislatures.

He has affected [attempted] to render the Military independent of and superior to the Civil power.

He has combined with others to subject us to a jurisdiction foreign to our constitution, and unacknowledged by our laws; giving his Assent to their Acts of pretended Legislation:

For Quartering large bodies of armed troops among us:

For protecting them, by a mock Trial, from punishment for any Murders which they should commit on the Inhabitants of these States:

For cutting off our Trade with all parts of the world:

For imposing Taxes on us without our Consent:

For depriving us in many cases, of the benefits of Trial by Jury:

For transporting us beyond Seas to be tried for pretended offenses[:]

For abolishing the free System of English Laws in a neighbouring Province, establishing therein an Arbitrary government, and enlarging its Boundaries so as to render it at once an example and fit instrument for introducing the same absolute rule into these Colonies:

For taking away our Charters, abolishing our most valuable Laws, and altering fundamentally the Forms of our Governments:

For suspending our own Legislatures, and declaring themselves invested with power to legislate for us in all cases whatsoever.

He has abdicated Government here, by declaring us out of his Protection and waging War against us.

He has plundered our seas, ravaged our Coasts, burnt our towns, and destroyed the lives of our people.

He is at this time transporting large Armies of foreign Mercenaries to compleat the works of death, desolation and tyranny, already begun with circumstances of Cruelty & perfidy scarcely paralleled in the most barbarous ages, and totally unworthy the Head of a civilized nation.

He has constrained our fellow Citizens taken Captive on the high Seas to bear Arms against their Country, to become the executioners of their friends and Brethren, or to fall themselves by their Hands.

He has excited domestic insurrection amongst us, and has endeavoured to bring on the inhabitants of our frontiers, the merciless Indian Savages, whose known rule of warfare, is an undistinguished destruction of all ages, sexes and conditions.

In every stage of these Oppressions we have Petitioned for Redress in the most humble terms: Our repeated Petitions have been answered only by repeated injury. A Prince whose character is thus marked by every act which may define a Tyrant, is unfit to be the ruler of a free people.

Nor have We been wanting in our attentions to our Brittish brethren. We have warned them from time to time of attempts by their legislature to extend an unwarrantable jurisdiction over us. We have reminded them of the circumstances of our emigration and settlement here. We have appealed to their native justice and magnanimity, and we have conjured [beseeched] them by the ties of our common kindred to disavow these usurpations, which, would inevitably interrupt our connections and correspondence. They too have been deaf to the voice of justice and of consanguinity [kinship]. We must, therefore, acquiesce in the necessity, which denounces [proclaims] our Separation, and hold them, as we hold the rest of mankind, Enemies in War, in Peace Friends.

We, therefore, the Representatives of the united States of America, in General Congress, Assembled, appealing to the Supreme Judge of the world for the rectitude of our intentions, do, in the Name and by Authority of the good People of these Colonies, solemnly publish and declare, That these United Colonies are, and of Right ought to be Free and Independent States; that they are Absolved from all Allegiance to the British Crown, and that all political connection between them and the State of Great Britain, is and ought to be totally dissolved; and that as Free and Independent States, they have full Power to levy War, conclude Peace, contract Alliances, establish Commerce, and to do all other Acts and Things which Independent States may of right do. And for the support of this Declaration, with a firm reliance on the protection of divine Providence, we mutually pledge to each other our Lives, our Fortunes and our sacred Honor.

[Signed by] John Hancock [President]

Button Gwinnett

Lyman Hall

Geo Walton

Wm Hooper,

Joseph Hewes,

John Penn

Edward Rutledge

Thos Hayward Junr.

Thomas Lynch Junr.

Arthur Middleton

Samuel Chase

W^m. Paca

Thos. Stone

Charles Carroll of Carrollton

George Wythe

Richard Henry Lee

Th Jefferson

Benj^a Harrison

Thos Nelson jr.

Francis Lightfoot Lee

Carter Braxton

Robt Morris

Benjamin Rush

Benj^a. Franklin

John Morton

Geo Clymer

Ja^s. Smith

Geo. Taylor

James Wilson

Geo. Ross

Casar Rodney

Geo Read

Tho M:Kean

Wm Floyd

Phil. Livingston

Fran^s. Lewis

Lewis Morris

Richd Stockton

Jno. Witherspoon

Fra^s. Hopkinson

John Hart

Abra Clark

Josiah Bartlett

W^m. Whipple

Saml Adams

John Adams

Robt Treat Paine

Elbridge Gerry

Step Hopkins

William Ellery

Roger Sherman

Sam^{ll} Huntington

Wm Williams

Oliver Wolcott

Matthew Thornton

CHAPTER 8

Rebels Make Up
New States

"Constitutions Employ Every Pen"

Declaring and winning independence was only part of the American rebels' task—and many thought it the least important part. "The independence of America considered merely as a separation from England," declared Thomas Paine, "would have been a matter but of little importance, had it not been accompanied by a revolution in the principles and practise of governments." So vital did Paine consider this phase of the revolution, so certain was he that the shift "from argument to arms" also launched "a new æra for politics," that his pamphlet *Common Sense* (Chapter 7) included helpful "hints" on erecting governments "as an opening to that business."[1]

It is hard now to appreciate what historian Gordon Wood calls this moment's "spine-tingling exhilaration." "Nothing...in the years surrounding the Declaration of Independence," he argues, "engaged the interests of Americans more than the framing of these separate governments." As one American remarked excitedly in the fall of 1776, "*Constitutions* employ every pen." Congress gets little done, griped a Pennsylvanian that October, because "all the *Maryland* Delegates are at home, forming a constitution. This seems to be the present business of all *America*, except the army."[2]

None were more excited (or more busily employed) than John Adams, the Massachusetts lawyer, congressman, and avid student of political science. "You and I, my dear friend," he exclaimed in April 1776, "have been sent into life at a time when the greatest lawgivers of antiquity would have wished to have lived. How few of the human race have ever enjoyed an opportunity of making an election [choice] of government...for themselves or their children!" But Adams also knew that this was a perilous undertaking. "To contrive some Method for the Colonies to glide insensibly, from under the old Government, into a peaceable and contented submission to new ones," he admitted, is "the most difficult and dangerous Part of the Business Americans have to do in this mighty Contest."[3]

"From...the old Government...to new *ones*." The plural seems odd. *Constitution* nowadays usually means the second United States Constitution, a document that, drafted in 1787 and ratified the following year, has been the law of the land ever since. So venerated is this charter—with the Declaration of Independence, it is enshrined in the National Archives—that we forget it was but one of many constitutions Americans wrote in those times—and, for many, the least important one. Rather, these United States (and until after the Civil War Americans stressed *States* more than *United*, the plural more than the singular) were to be, Adams insisted, a mere "Confederacy of States, each of which must have a separate Government."[4]

So vital were these separate governments that Americans started creating new states even before they declared independence. On May 15, 1776, Continental Congress agreed to advise the states to draw up constitutions, a vote the delighted Adams called "the most important Resolution, that ever was taken in America." But even as he had pushed for independence in Philadelphia that spring, Adams himself, the "resident expert" on constitutions, was writing a "model of government" for several states. Compared to that work, Adams "considered" the Declaration of Independence, Joseph Ellis observes, "a merely ornamental afterthought."[5]

Adams's congressional colleague Thomas Jefferson agreed. Reaching Philadelphia in mid-May to join Virginia's delegation, he yearned to be in Williamsburg, where the constitutional convention of his "country" was assembling. "It is a work of the most interesting nature," he wrote of that gathering, "and such as every individual would wish to have his voice in." No individual wished to have a voice more than Jefferson. Believing that founding state governments is "the whole object of the present controversy" with Britain, he spent late May and early June scribbling several drafts of a Virginia constitution, dispatching the last version to Williamsburg just before he took up his pen to write a declaration of independence. (You will see what Jefferson, late in life, called the "similitude" between the famous document [Chapter 7] and the forgotten one produced by the Virginia Convention.)[6]

By then the convention was well underway, in part because Virginians had not waited for the go-ahead from Philadelphia. On May 15, the very day Congress passed its resolution, the Virginia Convention produced some of its own: declaring independence, calling on Congress to do the same, and appointing a committee to write a declaration of rights and a constitution. Realizing this moment's significance, "[a] crowd that was gathered outside the Capitol as the final vote approached immediately hauled down the British flag from the cupola and raised the Grand Union flag of Washington's army."[7]

By the time Virginia representatives had completed their work on June 29, Pennsylvania was moving toward its own "Provincial Convention." On July 15, with Benjamin Franklin presiding, ninety-six delegates gathered in Philadelphia to begin more than two months of deliberations. Maryland, meanwhile, moved more slowly. In fact, on May 21, six days *after* Virginia declared independence, Maryland's conservative leadership sent word to the colony's congressional delegation in Philadelphia, once again *forbidding* them to vote for independence. Not until June 28 did the colony's leaders—fearful of being left to stand alone, faced with revolts by black slaves and white Loyalists alike—finally change their minds. It was August 14 before a constitutional convention assembled in Annapolis and November 8 before that convention finished its business.

Maryland, Pennsylvania, Virginia: These three states were neither the first nor the last to create new governments in those heady days, but they merit our attention for several reasons. For one thing, especially Virginia and Pennsylvania were crucial states, Virginia the most productive and most populous, Pennsylvania the home of what passed in those days for a national government. For another, their three charters suggest the range of constitutional types Americans invented.

At first glance these documents can be as bewildering as Mary Rowlandson's Puritanism or Dr. Alexander Hamilton's elitism. It is easy to get lost in the legalese and minutiae, the various rights and governmental branches. It helps to focus on— even to jot down—a few key variables in the constitutional equation. What might those variables be? It helps, too, to compare the three: Are they variations on a common theme or so different as to be separate species altogether?

It might help to know that during their deliberations the Pennsylvania and Maryland conventions (like Jefferson when he wrote the Declaration of Independence) had in hand Virginia's declaration of rights, published in draft form in Philadelphia on June 12. It might also help to know more about the context of these texts, the different circumstances in which they were written. In Virginia and Maryland, the colonial elite— men resembling Dr. Hamilton—remained in control as independence approached. They opposed Britain's tax policy and felt their rights threatened, yet there was more to it than that. Many were speculators in western lands, but in 1763 England had frustrated their hopes and schemes by halting colonial settlement west of the Appalachian Mountains. Many more were infuriated (and terrified) when in the fall of 1775 Virginia's royal governor, Lord Dunmore, desperate to crush the rebellion, offered liberty to slaves who left rebel masters to fight for the King. Dunmore rattled Maryland, too, sending agents up Chesapeake Bay to turn slaves and poor whites against provincial leaders. Their hold on power even more fragile than their Virginia counterparts', Maryland's political draftsmen were reluctant rebels indeed. One scholar called Maryland's "by far the most conservative" of the new state constitutions. Do you agree?[8]

In Pennsylvania, on the other hand, the provincial elite resisted independence for various reasons. Delaying and equivocating, they found themselves pushed aside by new men of "the middling sort" more like Thomas Paine than Dr. Hamilton. The result was a gathering in Philadelphia unlike those in Williamsburg and Annapolis. Only in Pennsylvania was voting for delegates to the constitutional convention opened up so that, instead of the usual 50–60% of adult white men, perhaps 90% went to the polls. Those new voters tended to elect men like themselves, "plain countrymen" who had never held office, had "[n]ever read a word" about government, but who believed that the convention must, as one member put it, "clear away every part of the old rubbish out of the way and begin upon a clean foundation."[9]

So far did the cleansing go that delegates debated whether to add this clause to the constitution: "That an enormous Proportion of Property vested in a few Individuals is dangerous to the Rights, and destructive of the Common Happiness of Mankind; and therefore every free State hath a Right by its Laws to discourage the Possession of such Property." Stripped of its legal verbiage, this empowered the government to limit how much wealth one person could have. What might America look like today if that provision had passed—and other states had followed suit?[10]

Nor were such notions confined to Pennsylvania: Elsewhere men overthrowing the king's rule were wondering whether the gentry's rule, too, ought to go. One man went around Virginia during the spring of 1776 and "asked the People if they were such fools to go to protect the Gentlemen's houses" from British attack; "he thought it would be better if they were burnt down." That May, George Washington heard from another planter that to some people "Independency" meant "a form of Government...independ[en]t of the rich men." In Maryland that summer, people showed up at polling places during the election for the constitutional convention to demand that every taxpayer be allowed to vote. From one county 885 "freemen" signed "instructions" to their delegates telling them to draft a charter more like Pennsylvania's than Virginia's.[11]

Those instructions were ignored, just as the Virginia voices were silenced and Pennsylvania's property proposal failed. Such setbacks for a more thoroughgoing revolution invite another question about these constitutions: Were they a sharp break with the past, or just politics as usual? Consider, for example, who could vote. Virginia said that voting rights should "remain as exercised at present"; this restricted the franchise (as the colony had done since 1736) to men owning at least 100 acres of unimproved land, or 25 acres that had a house and farm—perhaps 60% of all adult white men. Maryland went further, decreeing not just property requirements for voters but higher ones for those running for office. (Only 11% of Maryland's adult white men had enough wealth to run for a seat in the legislature and just 7.4% for the state senate.)[12] Even Pennsylvania decreed that a man had to pay taxes in order to vote.

All three states were acting upon the widespread belief that a man without property could not be trusted to vote responsibly. Lacking a stake in society, he had no investment in the community's well-being and would not be directly affected by taxation. Moreover, like women (who were thought too emotional) and people of color (who were thought too savage), a white man without property lacked independence of mind. "Such is the Frailty of the human Heart," wrote John Adams, expressing a common view, "that very few Men, who have no Property, have any Judgment of their own. They talk and vote as they are directed by Some Man of property, who has attached their Minds to his Interest." Beware of lowering property requirements, Adams warned. "It tends to…destroy all Distinctions, and prostrate all Ranks, to one common Levell." Does this sound like anyone else you have read in this volume?[13]

Still other planks in these constitutional structures continued colonial customs. For example, in Virginia and Maryland elections were *viva voce* ("live voice"), a long-standing practice in which a man came forward and declared his choice in front of election officials, the candidates, and everyone else who happened to be there. To appreciate how this could inhibit a voter—who might owe a candidate money, say, or hope that a candidate would sponsor his son at the local college—imagine doing evaluations of your courses this way, declaring your opinions aloud, before the whole class (including the teacher!), at semester's end.

These and other features suggest that state constitutions perpetuated forms of government inherited from colonial times and from English precedent. (Even the states' declarations of rights borrowed from England's 1689 "Declaration of Rights.") On the other hand, it can be argued that, considered in the context of their own times, these charters did indeed herald the dawn of a new day. Once again, knowing what *didn't* get included in these constitutions, as well as what did, helps shed light on their character. The Williamsburg convention rejected proposals that the governor have veto power and serve for as long as he exhibited "good behavior," that the upper house be elected by the assembly rather than by voters and that its members serve for life, that (as in Maryland) candidates for office have substantial estates, and that the assembly be elected every three years. Maryland, meanwhile, reduced a senator's term from seven years to five, and an assemblyman's from three years to one. Moreover, all three constitutions ended colonial governors' power to call (or not call) for elections or to dissolve the legislature if it was discussing matters he disliked. Imagine if President Nixon in the 1970s or President Clinton in the 1990s had had the power to adjourn Congress whenever he wished! Imagine if a governor or president today could call for new elections when, and only when, it suited him! Then you can begin to understand why Americans in 1776 thought that they did indeed fashion "new-modell" governments.[14]

Still, not everyone at the time admired the conventions' handiwork. The product of Pennsylvania's "plain countrymen" was a particular target for scorn. This "Villa[i]-nous," "Damned Constitution," written by a bunch of "numsculs," has erected a "mob government" as "absurd" as it is "intolerable," critics cried; the document is "confused, deficient in sense & grammar, and the ridicule of all *America*." It is, in a word, "Excrement." In Williamsburg, Thomas Jefferson (who served as governor under Virginia's constitution) deplored "the endless quibbles, chicaneries, perversions, vexations, and delays of lawyers and demi [half or inferior]-lawyers" elected to the legislature, and ruefully admitted that 173 men (the number of representatives in the state assembly) could be as tyrannical as one.[15]

But the very vituperation and shrill argument surrounding these documents—before, during, and after their writing—attest to the excitement they generated. The wrangling would continue unabated in the years to come. Jefferson in the 1770s and 1780s was proposing major revisions to Virginia's constitution. In 1790, opponents of the Pennsylvania charter would carry the day, writing and passing a new constitution. A generation later, virtually every state would revisit the documents drafted by their fathers, expanding the franchise and otherwise revising the blueprints drafted in the heat of revolution.

By then, what we think of today as "The Constitution" was firmly in place. But back in the founding era, American indifference to a national charter was reflected in the glacial pace at which Congress wrote and states ratified a federal constitution. Even as America moved toward independence and men in Annapolis, Williamsburg, and other capitals scribbled constitutions that spring and summer of 1776, Congress turned to what Paine had termed "a CONTINENTAL CHARTER" for the new nation. As Jefferson later recalled, the same June day Congress established a committee to draft a declaration of independence, it set up another a committee "to prepare a plan of confederation for the colonies." A month later, on July 12, that committee reported its work to Congress, only to have that draft "debated from day to day, & time to time for two years."[16] Not until March 1781 did all thirteen states finally ratify what became known as the Articles of Confederation. As unhappiness with that government grew during the 1780s, another constitution, "The Constitution," took its place. Our devotion to this second document obscures how most Americans at the time considered it less important than its counterparts for states from Georgia to New Hampshire. It has also obscured how far, as Willi Paul Adams notes, "the basic structure of the Federal Constitution of 1787 was that of certain existing state constitutions writ large."[17]

Whether thinking of state or federal constitutions, Americans today tend to take these documents for granted. We do not appreciate how extraordinary that moment of constitution making was, how creative, how rich with promise and fraught with peril—and how important for the world. Finding a way to build a new government that had enough legitimacy to earn people's support, is, as John Adams and his fellow "law-givers" knew, a profoundly important and profoundly difficult task. The many countries across the globe today that look to America's constitutions as touchstones should be sufficient reason to give those documents another, closer look.

Questions for Consideration and Conversation

1. As with the creation stories in Chapter 1, here you have three texts to compare. Consider them carefully: Are you more struck by their similarities or by their differences?
2. What are the crucial variables, the core elements, of these constitutions? Do they share these key planks in their "political architecture," or do these vary?
3. What would Dr. Alexander Hamilton of Annapolis (Chapter 5) have to say about Maryland's constitution? About the other two?
4. Can the requirements for voting set forth in these constitutions be reconciled with the phrase "All Men are created Equal"? If so, how? If not, how can you explain their departure from that creed?
5. Why did Pennsylvania's constitution draw such criticism? Was that criticism justified?
6. True or false: "These state constitutions prove that the American Revolution was not very revolutionary." Explain your answer.
7. How closely do these documents resemble the political system operating in America today?

Endnotes

1. Gordon S. Wood, *The Creation of the American Republic, 1776–1787* (Chapel Hill, NC, 1969), 594 ("little importance"); Thomas Paine, *Common Sense*, ed. Isaac Kramnick (New York, 1976), 82.
2. Wood, *Creation*, 127–28 ("*Constitutions*"); Marc W. Kruman, *Between Authority and Liberty: State Constitution Making in Revolutionary America* (Chapel Hill, NC, 1997), 18 (Maryland).
3. Willi Paul Adams, *The First American Constitutions: Republican Ideology and the Making of the State Constitutions in the Revolutionary Era*, trans. Rita and Robert Kimber (Chapel Hill, NC, 1980), 23–24 ("law-givers"); Wood, *Creation*, 131 ("some Method").
4. Wood, *Creation*, 128.
5. Kruman, *Between Authority and Liberty*, 20 (Adams); John E. Selby, *The Revolution in Virginia, 1775–1783*

(Williamsburg, 1988), 113 ("expert"); Joseph J. Ellis, *American Sphinx: The Character of Thomas Jefferson* (New York, 1997), 55 ("afterthought").

6. David Freeman Hawke, *A Transaction of Free Men: The Birth and Course of the Declaration of Independence*, 2nd ed. (New York, 1989), 6 ("country," "interesting"); Wood, *Creation*, 128 ("whole object"); Julian P. Boyd, ed., *The Papers of Thomas Jefferson*, Volume 1 (Princeton, NJ, 1950), 332 ("similitude"). For the parallels and cross-fertilization, see Ellis, *American Sphinx*, 45–48; Pauline Maier, *American Scripture: Making the Declaration of Independence* (New York, 1997), 55–57, 125–28.

7. Selby, *Revolution in Virginia*, 97.

8. Ronald Hoffman, *A Spirit of Dissension: Economics, Politics, and the Revolution in Maryland* (Baltimore, 1973), 269.

9. Eric Foner, *Tom Paine and Revolutionary America* (New York, 1976), 131 ("plain," "read a word"); Wood, *Creation*, 226–27 ("rubbish").

10. Foner, *Tom Paine*, 133.

11. Woody Holton, *Forced Founders: Indians, Debtors, Slaves, & the Making of the American Revolution in Virginia*

(Chapel Hill, NC, 1999), 185–86, 201; Hoffman, *Spirit of Dissension*, 173 (Maryland).

12. Hoffman, *Spirit of Dissension*, 180.

13. Kruman, *Between Authority and Liberty*, 89–90.

14. Ibid., 4.

15. Steven Rosswurm, *Arms, Country, and Class: The Philadelphia Militia and the "Lower Sort" During the American Revolution, 1775–1783* (New Brunswick, NJ, 1987), 103 ("Villa[i]nous," "Damned"); Foner, *Tom Paine*, 131 ("numsculs"); Wood, *Creation*, 233 ("intolerable," "mob," "confused," "absurd," "Excrement"); Gordon S. Wood, "Interests and Disinterestedness in the Making of the Constitution," in Richard Beeman, Stephen Botein, and Edward C. Carter II, eds., *Beyond Confederation: Origins of the Constitution and American National Identity* (Chapel Hill, NC, 1987), 74 ("quibbles").

16. Thomas Jefferson, "Autobiography," in *Thomas Jefferson: Writings* (New York, 1984), 17, 31.

17. Adams, *First American Constitutions*, 4.

The Constitution of Virginia (June 29, 1776)

Source: The Federal and State Constitutions, Colonial Charters, and Other Organic Laws of the States, Territories, and Colonies Now or Heretofore Forming the United States of America Compiled and Edited Under the Act of Congress of June 30, 1906, by Francis Newton Thorpe. Washington, D.C.: Government Printing Office, 1909.

Bill of Rights; June 12, 1776

A declaration of rights made by the representatives of the good people of Virginia, assembled in full and free convention; which rights do pertain to them and their posterity, as the basis and foundation of government.

SECTION 1. That all men are by nature equally free and independent, and have certain inherent rights, of which, when they enter into a state of society, they cannot, by any compact, deprive or divest their posterity, namely, the enjoyment of life and liberty, with the means of acquiring and possessing property, and pursuing and obtaining happiness and safety.

SEC. 2. That all power is vested in, and consequently derived from, the people; that magistrates are their trustees and servants, and at all times amenable to them.

SEC. 3. That government is, or ought to be, instituted for the common benefit, protection, and security of the people, nation, or community; of all the various modes and forms of government, that is best which is capable of producing the greatest degree of happiness and safety, and is most effectually secured against the danger of maladministration; and that, when any government shall be found inadequate or contrary to these purposes, a majority of the community hath an indubitable, inalienable, and indefeasible [cannot be forfeited] right to reform, alter, or abolish it, in such manner as shall be judged most conducive to the public weal.

SEC. 4. That no man, or set of men, are entitled to exclusive or separate emoluments [profits] or privileges from the community, but in consideration of public services;... neither ought the offices of magistrate, legislator, or judge to be hereditary.

SEC. 5. That the legislative and executive powers of the State should be separate and distinct from the judiciary; and that the members of the two first may be restrained from oppression, by feeling and participating the burdens of the people, they should, at fixed periods, be reduced to a private station, return into that body from which they were originally taken, and the vacancies be supplied by frequent, certain, and regular elections, in which all, or any part of the former members, to be again eligible, or ineligible, as the laws shall direct.

SEC. 6. That elections of members to serve as representatives of the people, in assembly, ought to be free; and that all men, having sufficient evidence of permanent common interest with, and attachment to, the community, have the right of suffrage, and cannot be taxed or deprived of their property for public uses, without their own consent, or that of their representatives so elected, nor bound by any law to which they have not, in like manner, assembled, for the public good.

SEC. 7. That all power of suspending laws, or the execution of laws, by any authority, without consent of the representatives of the people, is injurious to their rights, and ought not to be exercised.

SEC. 8. That in all capital or criminal prosecutions a man hath a right to demand the cause and nature of his accusation, to be confronted with the accusers and witnesses, to call for evidence in his favor, and to a speedy trial by an impartial jury of twelve men of his vicinage [neighborhood], without whose unanimous consent he cannot be found guilty; nor can he be compelled to give evidence against himself; that no man be deprived of his liberty, except by the law of the land or the judgment of his peers.

SEC. 9. That excessive bail ought not to be required, nor excessive fines imposed, nor cruel and unusual punishments inflicted.

SEC. 10. That general warrants, whereby an officer or messenger may be commanded to search suspected places without evidence of a fact committed, or to seize any person or persons not named, or whose offence is not particularly described and supported by evidence, are grievous and oppressive, and ought not to be granted.

SEC. 11. That in controversies respecting property, and in suits between man and man, the ancient trial by jury is preferable to any other, and ought to be held sacred.

SEC. 12. That the freedom of the press is one of the great bulwarks of liberty, and can never be restrained but by despotic governments.

SEC. 13. That a well-regulated militia, composed of the body of the people, trained to arms, is the proper, natural, and safe defence of a free State; that standing armies, in time of peace, should be avoided, as dangerous to liberty; and that in all cases the military should be under strict subordination to, and governed by, the civil power....

SEC. 15. That no free government, or the blessings of liberty, can be preserved to any people, but by a firm adherence to justice, moderation, temperance, frugality, and virtue, and by frequent recurrence to fundamental principles.

SEC. 16. That religion, or the duty which we owe to our Creator, and the manner of discharging it, can be directed only by reason and conviction, not by force or violence; and therefore all men are equally entitled to the free exercise of religion, according to the dictates of conscience; and that it is the mutual duty of all to practise Christian forbearance, love, and charity towards each other.

The Constitution or Form of Government, Agreed To and Resolved Upon By The Delegates and Representatives of The Several Counties and Corporations of Virginia

Whereas George the third, King of Great Britain..., heretofore intrusted with the exercise of the kingly office in this government, hath endeavoured to prevent, the same into a detestable and insupportable tyranny, by putting his negative on laws the most wholesome and necessary for the public good:

By denying his Governors permission to pass laws of immediate and pressing importance, unless suspended in their operation for his assent, and, when so suspended neglecting to attend to them for many years:

By refusing to pass certain other laws, unless the persons to be benefited by them would relinquish the inestimable right of representation in the legislature:

By dissolving legislative Assemblies repeatedly and continually, for opposing with manly firmness his invasions of the rights of the people:

When dissolved, by refusing to call others for a long space of time, thereby leaving the political system without any legislative head:...

By keeping among us, in times of peace, standing armies and ships of war:

By effecting to render the military independent of, and superior to, the civil power:

By combining with others to subject us to a foreign jurisdiction, giving his assent to their pretended acts of legislation:

For quartering large bodies of armed troops among us:

For cutting off our trade with all parts of the world:

For imposing taxes on us without our consent:

For depriving us of the benefits of trial by jury:

For transporting us beyond seas, to be tried for pretended offences:

For suspending our own legislatures, and declaring themselves invested with power to legislate for us in all cases whatsoever:

By plundering our seas, ravaging our coasts, burning our towns, and destroying the lives of our people:

By inciting insurrections of our fellow subjects, with the allurements of forfeiture and confiscation:

By prompting our negroes to rise in arms against us…:

By endeavoring to bring on the inhabitants of our frontiers the merciless Indian savages, whose known rule of warfare is an undistinguished destruction of all ages, sexes, and conditions of existence:

By transporting, at this time, a large army of foreign mercenaries, to complete the works of death, desolation, and tyranny, already begun with circumstances of cruelty and perfidy unworthy the head of a civilized nation:

By answering our repeated petitions for redress with a repetition of injuries: And finally, by abandoning the helm of government and declaring us out of his allegiance and protection.

By which several acts of misrule, the government of this country, as formerly exercised under the crown of Great Britain, is TOTALLY DISSOLVED.

We therefore, the delegates and representatives of the good people of Virginia, having maturely considered the premises, and viewing with great concern the deplorable conditions to which this once happy country must be reduced, unless some regular, adequate mode of civil polity is speedily adopted, and in compliance with a recommendation of the General Congress, do ordain and declare the future form of government of Virginia to be as followeth:

The legislative, executive, and judiciary department, shall be separate and distinct, so that neither exercise the powers properly belonging to the other: nor shall any person exercise the powers of more than one of them, at the same time; except that the Justices of the County Courts shall be eligible to either House of Assembly.

The legislative shall be formed of two distinct branches, who, together, shall be a complete Legislature. They shall meet once, or oftener, every year, and shall be called, *The General Assembly of Virginia*. One of these shall be called, *The House of Delegates*, and consist of two Representatives, to be chosen for each county…annually, of such men as actually reside in, and are freeholders of the same, or duly qualified according to law.…

The other shall be called *The Senate*, and consist of twenty-four members…; for whose election, the different counties shall be divided into twenty-four districts; and each county of the respective district, at the time of the election of its Delegates, shall vote for one Senator, who is actually a resident and freeholder within the district, or duly qualified according to law, and is upwards of twenty-five years of age.…

The right of suffrage in the election of members for both Houses shall remain as exercised at present.…

All laws shall originate in the House of Delegates, to be approved of or rejected by the Senate, or to be amended, with consent of the House of Delegates; except money-bills, which in no instance shall be altered by the Senate, but wholly approved or rejected.

A Governor, or chief magistrate, shall be chosen annually by joint ballot of both Houses.…[He] shall not continue in that office longer than three years successively, nor be eligible, until the expiration of four years after he shall have been out of that office. An adequate, but moderate salary shall be settled on him, during his continuance in office; and he shall, with the advice of a Council of State, exercise the executive powers of government, according to the laws of this Commonwealth; and shall not, under any pretence, exercise any power or prerogative, by virtue of any law, statute or custom of England.…

Either House of the General Assembly may adjourn themselves respectively. The Governor shall not…adjourn the Assembly, during their sitting, nor dissolve them at any time.…

A Privy Council, or Council of State, consisting of eight members, shall be chosen, by joint ballot of both Houses of Assembly, either from their own members or the people at large, to assist in the administration of government. They shall annually choose, out of their own members, a President, who, in case of death, inability, or absence of the Governor from the government, shall act as Lieutenant-Governor. Four members shall be sufficient to act, and their advice and proceedings shall be entered on record, and signed by the members present, (to any part whereof, any member may enter his dissent) to be laid before the General Assembly, when called for by them.… [A]nd they shall be incapable, during their continuance in office, of sitting in either House of Assembly. Two members shall be removed, by Joint ballot of both Houses of Assembly, at the end of every three years, and be ineligible for the three next years.…

The present militia officers shall be continued, and vacancies supplied by appointment of the Governor, with the advice of the Privy Council, on recommendations from the respective County Courts....

The Governor may embody the militia, with the advice of the Privy Council; and when embodied, shall alone have the direction of the militia, under the laws of the country.

The two Houses of Assembly shall, by joint ballot, appoint Judges of the Supreme Court of Appeals, and General Court...[and other courts], and the Attorney-General, to be commissioned by the Governor, and continue in office during good behaviour.... These officers shall have fixed and adequate salaries, and, together with all others, holding lucrative offices, and all ministers of the gospel, of every denomination, be incapable of being elected members of either House of Assembly or the Privy Council.

The Governor, with the advice of the Privy Council, shall appoint Justices of the Peace for the counties....

The Governor, when he is out of office, and others, offending against the State, either by mal-administration, corruption, or other means, by which the safety of the State may be endangered, shall be impeachable by the House of Delegates....If found guilty, he or they shall be either forever disabled to hold any office under government, or be removed from such office *pro tempore*, or subjected to such pains or penalties as the laws shall direct.

If all or any of the Judges of the General Court should on good grounds (to be judged of by the House of Delegates) be accused of any of the crimes or offences above mentioned, such House of Delegates may, in like manner, impeach the Judge or Judges so accused....

Commissions and grants shall run, "*In the name of the Commonwealth of Virginia,*" and bear test by the Governor, with the seal of the Commonwealth annexed....Indictments shall conclude, "*Against the peace and dignity of the Commonwealth.*"...

THE CONSTITUTION OF PENNSYLVANIA (SEPTEMBER 28, 1776)

Source: The Federal and State Constitutions, Colonial Charters, and Other Organic Laws of the States, Territories, and Colonies Now or Heretofore Forming the United States of America Compiled and Edited Under the Act of Congress of June 30, 1906, by Francis Newton Thorpe. Washington, D.C.: Government Printing Office, 1909.

Whereas all government ought to be instituted and supported for the security and protection of the community as such, and to enable the individuals who compose it to enjoy their natural rights, and the other blessings which the Author of existence has bestowed upon man; and whenever these great ends of government are not obtained, the people have a right, by common consent to change it, and take such measures as to them may appear necessary to promote their safety and happiness. AND WHEREAS the inhabitants of this commonwealth have in consideration of protection only, heretofore acknowledged allegiance to the king of Great Britain; and the said king has not only withdrawn that protection, but commenced, and still continues to carry on, with unabated vengeance, a most cruel and unjust war against them, employing therein, not only the troops of Great Britain, but foreign mercenaries, savages and slaves, for the avowed purpose of reducing them to a total and abject submission to

the despotic domination of the British parliament, with many other acts of tyranny, (more fully set forth in the declaration [of Independence] of Congress) whereby all allegiance and fealty to the said king and his successors, are dissolved and at an end, and all power and authority derived from him ceased in these colonies. AND WHEREAS it is absolutely necessary for the welfare and safety of the inhabitants of said colonies, that they be henceforth free and independent States, and that just, permanent, and proper forms of government exist in every part of them, derived from and founded on the authority of the people only, agreeable to the directions of the honourable American Congress. We, the representatives of the freemen of Pennsylvania, in general convention met, for the express purpose of framing such a government, confessing the goodness of the great Governor of the universe (who alone knows to what degree of earthly happiness mankind may attain, by perfecting the arts of government) in permitting the people of this State, by common consent, and without violence, deliberately to form for themselves such just rules as they shall think best, for governing their future society, and being fully convinced, that it is our indispensable duty to establish such original principles of government, as will best promote the general happiness of the people of this State, and their posterity, and provide for future improvements, without partiality for, or prejudice against any particular class, sect, or denomination of men whatever, do, by virtue of the authority vested in us by our constituents, ordain, declare, and establish, the following Declaration of Rights and Frame of Government, to be the CONSTITUTION of this commonwealth, and to remain in force therein for ever, unaltered, except in such articles as shall hereafter on experience be found to require improvement, and which shall by the same authority of the people, fairly delegated as this frame of government directs, be amended or improved for the more effectual obtaining and securing the great end and design of all government, herein before mentioned.

A Declaration of The Rights of The Inhabitants of The Commonwealth or State of Pennsylvania

I. That all men are born equally free and independent, and have certain natural, inherent and inalienable rights, amongst which are, the enjoying and defending life and liberty, acquiring, possessing and protecting property, and pursuing and obtaining happiness and safety.

II. That all men have a natural and unalienable right to worship Almighty God according to the dictates of their own consciences and understanding: And that no man ought or of right can be compelled to attend any religious worship, or erect or support any place of worship, or maintain any ministry, contrary to, or against, his own free will and consent: Nor can any man, who acknowledges the being of a God, be justly deprived or abridged of any civil right as a citizen, on account of his religious sentiments or peculiar mode of religious worship: And that no authority can or ought to be vested in, or assumed by any power whatever, that shall in any case interfere with, or in any manner controul, the right of conscience in the free exercise of religious worship.

III. That the people of this State have the sole, exclusive and inherent right of governing and regulating the internal police of the same.

IV. That all power being originally inherent in, and consequently derived from, the people; therefore all officers of government, whether legislative or executive, are their trustees and servants, and at all times accountable to them.

V. That government is, or ought to be, instituted for the common benefit, protection and security of the people, nation or community; and not for the particular emolument or advantage of any single man, family, or sort of men, who are a part only of that community, And that the community hath an indubitable, unalienable and indefeasible right to reform, alter, or abolish government in such manner as shall be by that community judged most conducive to the public weal [welfare].

VI. That those who are employed in the legislative and executive business of the State, may be restrained from oppression, the people have a right, at such periods as they may think proper, to reduce their public officers to a private station, and supply the vacancies by certain and regular elections.

VII. That all elections ought to be free; and that all free men having a sufficient evident common interest with, and attachment to the community, have a right to elect officers, or to be elected into office.

VIII. That every member of society hath a right to be protected in the enjoyment of life, liberty and property, and therefore is bound to contribute his proportion towards the expence of that protection, and yield his personal service when necessary, or an equivalent thereto: But no part of a man's property can be justly taken from him, or applied to public uses, without his own consent, or that of his legal representatives: Nor can any man who is conscientiously scrupulous of bearing arms, be justly compelled thereto, if he will pay such equivalent, nor are the people bound by any laws, but such as they have in like manner assented to, for their common good.

IX. That in all prosecutions for criminal offences, a man hath a right to be heard by himself and his council, to demand the cause and nature of his accusation, to be confronted with the witnesses, to call for evidence in his favour, and a speedy public trial, by an impartial jury of the country, without the unanimous consent of which jury he cannot be found guilty; nor can he be compelled to give evidence against himself; nor can any man be justly deprived of his liberty except by the laws of the land, or the judgment of his peers.

X. That the people have a right to hold themselves, their houses, papers, and possessions free from search and seizure, and therefore warrants without oaths or affirmations first made, affording a sufficient foundation for them, and whereby any officer...may be commanded or required to search suspected places, or to seize any person or persons, his or their property, not particularly described, are contrary to that right, and ought not to be granted.

XI. That in controversies respecting property, and in suits between man and man, the parties have a right to trial by jury, which ought to be held sacred.

XII. That the people have a right to freedom of speech, and of writing, and publishing their sentiments; therefore the freedom of the press ought not to be restrained.

XIII. That the people have a right to bear arms for the defence of themselves and the state; and as standing armies in the time of peace are dangerous to liberty, they ought not to be kept up; And that the military should be kept under strict subordination to, and governed by, the civil power.

XIV. That a frequent recurrence to fundamental principles, and a firm adherence to justice, moderation, temperance, industry, and frugality are absolutely necessary to preserve the blessings of liberty, and keep a government free: The people ought therefore to pay particular attention to these points in the choice of officers and representatives, and have a right to exact a due and constant regard to them, from their legislatures and magistrates, in the making and executing such laws as are necessary for the good government of the state.

XV. That all men have a natural inherent right to emigrate from one state to another that will receive them, or to form a new state in vacant countries, or in such countries as they can purchase, whenever they think that thereby they may promote their own happiness.

XVI. That the people have a right to assemble together, to consult for their common good, to instruct their representatives, and to apply to the legislature for redress of grievances, by address, petition, or remonstrance.

Plan or Frame of Government For The Commonwealth or State of Pennsylvania

SECTION 1. The commonwealth or state of Pennsylvania shall be governed hereafter by an assembly of the representatives of the freemen of the same, and a president and council, in manner and form following—

SECT. 2. The supreme legislative power shall be vested in a house of representatives of the freemen of the commonwealth or state of Pennsylvania.

SECT. 3. The supreme executive power shall be vested in a president and council....

SECT. 5. The freemen of this commonwealth and their sons shall be trained and armed for its defence under such regulations, restrictions, and exceptions as the general assembly shall by law direct, preserving always to the people the right of choosing their colonels and all commissioned officers under that rank....

SECT. 6. Every freeman of the full age of twenty-one Years, having resided in this state for the space of one whole Year next before the day of election for representatives, and paid public taxes during that time, shall enjoy the right of an elector: Provided always, that sons of freeholders of the age of twenty-one years shall be intitled to vote although they have not paid taxes.

SECT. 7. The house of representatives of the freemen of this commonwealth shall consist of persons most noted for wisdom and virtue, to be chosen by the freemen of every city and county of this commonwealth respectively. And no person shall be elected unless he has resided in the city or county for which he shall be chosen two years immediately before the said election; nor shall any member, while he continues such, hold any other office, except in the militia.

SECT. 8. No person shall be capable of being elected a member to serve in the house of representatives of the freemen of this commonwealth more than four years in seven.

SECT. 9. The members of the house of representatives shall be chosen annually by ballot, by the freemen of the commonwealth, on the second Tuesday in October forever, (except this present year,) and shall meet on the fourth Monday of the same month, and shall be stiled, *The general assembly of the representatives of the freemen of Pennsylvania*, and shall have power to choose their speaker, the treasurer of the state, and their other officers; sit on their own adjournments; prepare bills and enact them into laws; judge of the elections and qualifications of their own members; they...shall have all other powers necessary for the legislature of a free state or commonwealth: But they shall have no power to add to, alter, abolish, or infringe any part of this constitution.

SECT. 10. A quorum of the house of representatives shall consist of two-thirds of the whole number of members elected; and having met and chosen their speaker, shall each of them before they proceed to business take and subscribe, as well the oath or affirmation of fidelity and allegiance hereinafter directed, as the following oath or affirmation, viz [namely]:

> I—do swear (or affirm) that as a member of this assembly, I will not propose or assent to any bill, vote, or resolution, which shall appear to be injurious to the people; nor do or consent to any act or thing whatever, that shall have a tendency to lessen or abridge their rights and privileges, as declared in the constitution of this state; but will in all things conduct myself as a faithful honest representative and guardian of the people, according to the best of my judgment and abilities.

And each member, before he takes his seat, shall make and subscribe the following declaration, viz:

> I do believe in one God, the creator and governor of the universe, the rewarder of the good and the punisher of the wicked. And I do acknowledge the Scriptures of the Old and New Testament to be given by Divine inspiration.

And no further or other religious test shall ever hereafter be required of any civil officer or magistrate in this State....

SECT. 13. The doors of the house in which the representatives of the freemen of this state shall sit in general assembly, shall be and remain open for the admission of all persons who behave decently, except only when the welfare of this state may require the doors to be shut.

SECT. 14. The votes and proceedings of the general assembly shall be printed weekly during their sitting, with the yeas and nays, on any question, vote or resolution, where any two members require it except when the vote is taken by ballot....

SECT. 15. To the end that laws before they are enacted may be more maturely considered, and the inconvenience of hasty determinations as much as possible prevented, all bills of public nature shall be printed for the consideration of the people, before they are read in general assembly the last time for debate and amendment; and, except on occasions of sudden necessity, shall not be passed into laws until the next session of assembly; and for the more perfect satisfaction of the public, the reasons and motives for making such laws shall be fully and clearly expressed in the preambles....

SECT. 17. The city of Philadelphia and each county of this commonwealth respectively, shall [annually]...choose six persons to represent them in general assembly. But as representation in proportion to the number of taxable inhabitants is the only principle which can at all times secure liberty, and make the voice of a majority of the people the law of the land; therefore the general assembly shall cause complete lists of the taxable inhabitants in the city and each county in the commonwealth respectively, to be taken and returned to them,...who shall appoint a representation to each, in proportion to the number of taxables in such returns; which representation shall continue for the next seven years afterwards at the end of which, a new return of the taxable inhabitants shall be made, and a representation agreeable thereto appointed by the said assembly, and so on septennially forever. The wages of the representatives in general assembly, and all other state charges shall be paid out of the state treasury....

SECT. 19. For the present the supreme executive council of this state shall consist of twelve persons chosen in the following manner: The freemen...shall choose by ballot one person for the city [of Philadelphia], and one for each county.... By this mode of election and continual rotation, more men will be trained to public business, there will in every subsequent year be found in the council a number of persons acquainted with the proceedings of the foregoing Years, whereby the business will be more consistently conducted, and moreover the danger of establishing an inconvenient aristocracy will be effectually prevented.... No member of the general assembly or delegate in congress, shall be chosen a member of the council. The president and vice-president shall be chosen annually by the joint ballot of the general assembly and council, of the members of the council. Any person having served as a counsellor for three successive years, shall be incapable of holding that office for four years afterwards....

The council shall meet annually, at the same time and place with the general assembly.

The treasurer of the state, trustees of the loan office, naval officers, collectors of customs or excise, judge of the admiralty, attornies general, sheriffs, and prothonotaries [clerks or recorders in courts], shall not be capable of a seat in the general assembly, executive council, or continental congress.

SECT. 20. The president, and in his absence the vice-president, with the council,...shall have power to appoint...judges, naval officers, judge of the admiralty, attorney general and all other officers, civil and military, except such as are chosen by the general assembly or the people, agreeable to this frame of government.... They are to correspond with other states, and transact business with the officers of government, civil and military; and to prepare such business as may appear to them necessary to lay before the general assembly.... [T]hey are also to take care that the laws be faithfully executed;... and they may draw upon the treasury for such sums as shall be appropriated by the house.... The president shall be commander in chief of the forces of the state, but shall not command in person, except advised thereto by the council, and then only so long as they shall approve thereof. The president and council shall have a secretary, and keep fair books of their proceedings, wherein any counsellor may enter his dissent, with his reasons in support of it.

SECT. 21. All commissions shall be in the name, and by the authority of the freemen of the commonwealth of Pennsylvania, sealed with the state seal, [and] signed by the president or vice-president....

SECT. 22. Every officer of state, whether judicial or executive, shall be liable to be impeached by the general assembly, either when in office, or after his resignation or removal for maladministration: All impeachments shall be before the president or vice-president and council, who shall hear and determine the same.

SECT. 23. The judges of the supreme court of judicature shall have fixed salaries, be commissioned for seven years only, though capable of re-appointment at the end of that term, but removable for misbehaviour at any time by the general assembly; they shall not be allowed to sit as members in the continental congress, executive council, or general assembly, nor to hold any other office civil or military, nor to take or receive fees or perquisites of any kind....

SECT. 25. Trials shall be by jury as heretofore: And it is recommended to the legislature of this state, to provide by law against every corruption or partiality in the choice, return, or appointment of juries.

SECT. 26.... All courts shall be open, and justice shall be impartially administered without corruption or unnecessary delay: All their officers shall be paid an adequate but moderate compensation for their services: And if any officer shall take greater or other fees than the law allows him, either directly or indirectly, it shall ever after disqualify him from holding any office in this state.

SECT. 27. All prosecutions shall commence in the name and by the authority of the freemen of the commonwealth of Pennsylvania; and all indictments shall conclude with these words, *"Against the peace and dignity of the same."* ...

SECT. 28. The person of a debtor, where there is not a strong presumption of fraud, shall not be continued in prison, after delivering up... all his estate real and personal, for the use of his creditors.... All prisoners shall be bailable by sufficient sureties, unless for capital offences, when the proof is evident, or presumption great.

SECT. 29. Excessive bail shall not be exacted for bailable offences: And all fines shall be moderate.

SECT. 30. Justices of the peace shall be elected by the freeholders of each city and county respectively.... No justice of the peace shall sit in the general assembly unless he first resigns his commission; nor shall he be allowed to take any fees, nor any salary or allowance, except such as the future legislature may grant....

SECT. 32. All elections, whether by the people or in general assembly, shall be by ballot, free and voluntary: And any elector, who shall receive any gift or reward for his vote, in meat, drink, monies, or otherwise, shall forfeit his right to elect for that time, and suffer such other penalties as future laws shall direct. And any person who shall directly or indirectly give, promise, or bestow any such rewards to be elected, shall be thereby rendered incapable to serve for the ensuing year....

SECT. 35. The printing presses shall be free to every person who undertakes to examine the proceedings of the legislature, or any part of government.

SECT. 36. As every freeman to preserve his independence, (if without a sufficient estate) ought to have some profession, calling, trade or farm, whereby he may honestly subsist, there can be no necessity for, nor use in establishing offices of profit, the usual effects of which are dependence and servility unbecoming freemen, in the possessors and expectants; faction, contention, corruption, and disorder among the people. But if any man is called into public service, to the prejudice of his private affairs, he has a right to a reasonable compensation: And whenever an office, through increase of fees or otherwise, becomes so profitable as to occasion many to apply for it, the profits ought to be lessened by the legislature....

SECT. 38. The penal laws as heretofore used shall be reformed by the legislature of this state, as soon as may be, and punishments made in... general more proportionate to the crimes.

SECT. 39. To deter more effectually from the commission of crimes by continued visible punishments of long duration...; houses ought to be provided for punishing by hard labour, those who shall be convicted of crimes not capital; wherein the criminals shall be imployed for the benefit of the public, or for reparation of injuries done to private persons: And all persons at proper times shall be admitted to see the prisoners at their labour....

SECT. 41. No public tax, custom or contribution shall be imposed upon, or paid by the people of this state, except by a law for that purpose: And before any law be made for raising it, the purpose for which any tax is to be raised ought to appear clearly to the legislature to be of more service to the community than the money would be, if not collected; which being well observed, taxes can never be burthens.

SECT. 42. Every foreigner of good character who comes to settle in this state, having first taken an oath or affirmation of allegiance to the same, may purchase, or by other just means acquire, hold, and transfer land or other real estate; and after one year's residence, shall be deemed a free denizen thereof, and entitled to all the rights of a natural born subject of this state, except that he shall not be capable of being elected a representative until after two years residence.

SECT. 43. The inhabitants of this state shall have liberty to fowl and hunt in seasonable times on the lands they hold, and on all other lands therein not inclosed; and in like manner to fish in all boatable waters, and others not private property.

SECT. 44. A school or schools shall be established in each county by the legislature, for the convenient instruction of youth, with such salaries to the masters paid by the public, as may enable them to instruct youth at low prices: And all useful learning shall be duly encouraged and promoted in one or more universities.

SECT. 45. Laws for the encouragement of virtue, and prevention of vice and immorality, shall be made and constantly kept in force, and provision shall be made for their due execution: And all religious societies or bodies of men heretofore united or incorporated for the advancement of religion or learning, or for other pious and charitable purposes, shall be encouraged and protected in the enjoyment of the privileges, immunities and estates which they were accustomed to enjoy, or could of right have enjoyed, under the laws and former constitution of this state.

SECT. 46. The declaration of rights is hereby declared to be a part of the constitution of this commonwealth, and ought never to be violated on any pretence whatever.

SECT. 47. In order that the freedom of the commonwealth may be preserved inviolate forever, there shall be chosen by ballot by the freemen in each city and county respectively, on the second Tuesday in October, in the Year one thousand seven hundred and eighty-three, and on the second Tuesday in October, in every seventh year thereafter, two persons in each city and county of this state, to be called the COUNCIL OF CENSORS; who shall meet together on the second Monday of November next ensuing their election;... And whose duty it shall be to enquire whether the constitution has been preserved inviolate in every part; and whether the legislative and executive branches of government have performed their duty as guardians of the people, or assumed to themselves, or exercised other or greater powers than they are intitled to by the constitution: They are also to enquire whether the public taxes have been justly laid and collected in all parts of this commonwealth, in what manner the public monies have been disposed of, and whether the laws have been duly executed. For these purposes they shall have power to send for persons, papers, and records; they shall have authority to pass public censures, to order impeachments, and to recommend to the legislature the repealing such laws as appear to them to have been enacted contrary to the principles of the constitution. These powers they shall continue to have, for and during the space of one year from the day of their election and no longer: The said council of censors shall also have power to call a convention, to meet within two years after their sitting, if there appear to them an absolute necessity of amending any article of the constitution which may be defective, explaining such as may be thought not clearly expressed, and of adding such as are necessary for the preservation of the rights and happiness of the people: But the articles to be amended, and the amendments proposed, and such articles as are proposed to be added or abolished, shall be promulgated at least six months before the day appointed for the election of such convention, for the previous consideration of the people, that they may have an opportunity of instructing their delegates on the subject.

Passed in Convention the 28th day of September, 1776, and signed by their order.

BENJ. FRANKLIN, *Pres[iden]t.*

THE CONSTITUTION OF MARYLAND (NOVEMBER 11, 1776)

Source: The Federal and State Constitutions, Colonial Charters, and Other Organic Laws of the States, Territories, and Colonies Now or Heretofore Forming the United States of America Compiled and Edited Under the Act of Congress of June 30, 1906, by Francis Newton Thorpe. Washington, D.C.: Government Printing Office, 1909.

A Declaration of Rights, and the Constitution and Form of Government agreed to by the Delegates of Maryland, in Free and Full Convention Assembled.

A Declaration of Rights, &C.

The parliament of Great Britain, by a declaratory act [1766], having assumed a right to make laws to bind the Colonies in all cases whatsoever, and, in pursuance of such claim, endeavoured, by force of arms, to subjugate the United Colonies to an unconditional submission to their will and power, and having at length constrained [forced] them to declare themselves independent States, and to assume government under the authority of the people; Therefore we, the Delegates of Maryland, in free and full Convention assembled, taking into our most serious consideration the best means of establishing a good Constitution in this State, for the sure foundation and more permanent security thereof, declare,

I. That all government of right originates from the people, is founded in compact only, and instituted solely for the good of the whole.

II. That the people of this State ought to have the sole and exclusive right of regulating the internal government and police thereof.

III. That the inhabitants of Maryland are entitled to the common law of England, and the trial by Jury, according to that law, and to the benefit of such of the English statutes, as existed at the time of their first emigration, and which, by experience, have been found applicable to their ... circumstances, and of such others as have been since made in England ..., and have been introduced, used and practised by the courts ...; and also to acts of Assembly, in force on the first of June seventeen hundred and seventy-four, except such as may have since expired, or have been or may be altered by acts of Convention, or this Declaration of Rights—subject, nevertheless, to the revision of, and amendment or repeal by, the Legislature of this State: and the inhabitants of Maryland are also entitled to all property, derived to them, from or under the Charter, granted [in 1632] by his Majesty Charles I to Cæcilius Calvert, Baron of Baltimore.

IV. That all persons invested with the legislative or executive powers of government are the trustees of the public, and, as such, accountable for their conduct; wherefore, whenever the ends of government are perverted, and public liberty manifestly endangered, and all other means of redress are ineffectual, the people may, and of right ought, to reform the old or establish a new government. The doctrine of non-resistance, against arbitrary power and oppression, is absurd, slavish, and destructive of the good and happiness of mankind.

V. That the right in the people to participate in the Legislature is the best security of liberty, and the foundation of all free government; for this purpose, elections ought to be free and frequent, and every man, having property in, a common interest with, and an attachment to the community, ought to have a right of suffrage.

VI. That the legislative, executive and judicial powers of government, ought to be forever separate and distinct from each other.

VII. That no power of suspending laws, or the execution of laws, unless by or derived from the Legislature, ought to be exercised or allowed.

VIII. That freedom of speech and debates, or proceedings in the Legislature, ought not to be impeached in any other court or judicature.

IX. That a place for the meeting of the Legislature ought to be fixed, the most convenient to the members thereof, and to the depository of public records; and the Legislature ought not to be convened or held at any other place, but from evident necessity.

X. That, for redress of grievances, and for amending, strengthening and preserving the laws, the Legislature ought to be frequently convened.

XI. That every man hath a right to petition the Legislature, for the redress of grievances, in a peaceable and orderly manner....

XIII. That the levying taxes by the poll [i.e., per person] is grievous and oppressive, and ought to be abolished; that paupers ought not to be assessed for the support of government; but every other person in the State ought to contribute his proportion of public taxes, for the support of government, according to his actual worth, in real or personal property, within the State; yet fines, duties, or taxes, may properly and justly be imposed or laid, with a political view, for the good government and benefit of the community....

XVII. That every freeman, for any injury done him in his person or property, ought to have remedy, by the course of the law of the land, and ought to have justice and right freely without sale, fully without any denial, and speedily without delay, according to the law of the land.

XVIII. That the trial of facts where they arise, is one of the greatest securities of the lives, liberties and estates of the people.

XIX. That, in all criminal prosecutions, every man hath a right to be informed of the accusation against him; to have a copy of the indictment or charge in due time (if required) to prepare for his defence; to be allowed counsel; to be confronted with the witnesses against him; to have process for his witnesses; to examine the witnesses, for and against him, on oath; and to a speedy trial by an impartial jury, without whose unanimous consent he ought not to be found guilty.

XX. That no man ought to be compelled to give evidence against himself, in...any...court, but in such cases as have been usually practised in this State, or may hereafter be directed by the Legislature.

XXI. That no freeman ought to be taken, or imprisoned, or disseized [dispossessed] of his freehold, liberties, or privileges, or outlawed, or exiled, or in any manner destroyed, or deprived of his life, liberty, or property, but by the judgment of his peers, or by the law of the land.

XXII. That excessive bail ought not to be required, nor excessive fines imposed, nor cruel or unusual punishments inflicted, by the courts of law.

XXIII. That all warrants, without oath or affirmation, to search suspected places, or to seize any person or property, are grievous and oppressive....

XXV. That a well-regulated militia is the proper and natural defence of a free government.

XXVI. That standing armies are dangerous to liberty, and ought not to be raised or kept up, without consent of the Legislature.

XXVII. That in all cases, and at all times, the military ought to be under strict subordination to and control of the civil power.

XXVIII. That no soldier ought to be quartered in any house, in time of peace, without the consent of the owner; and in time of war, in such manner only, as the Legislature shall direct....

XXX. That the independency and uprightness of Judges are essential to the impartial administration of Justice, and a great security to the rights and liberties of the people; wherefore...Judges ought to hold commissions during good behaviour; and the said...Judges shall be removed for misbehaviour, on conviction in a court of law, and may be removed by the Governor, upon the address of the General Assembly; *Provided*, That two-thirds of all the members of each House concur in such address. That salaries, liberal, but not profuse, ought to be secured to...the Judges, during the continuance of their Com missions....No...Judge ought to hold any other office, civil or military, or receive fees or perquisites of any kind.

XXXI. That a long continuance, in the first executive departments of power or trust, is dangerous to liberty; a rotation, therefore, in those departments, is one of the best securities of permanent freedom.

XXXII. That no person ought to hold, at the same time, more than one office of profit, nor ought any person, in public trust, to receive any present from any foreign prince or state, or from the United States, or any of them, without the approbation of this State.

XXXIII. That, as it is the duty of every man to worship God in such manner as he thinks most acceptable to him; all persons, professing the Christian religion, are equally entitled to protection in their religious liberty; wherefore no person ought by any law to be molested in his person or estate on account of his religious persuasion or profession, or for his religious practice;...nor ought any person to be compelled to frequent or maintain, or contribute, unless on contract, to maintain any particular place of worship, or any particular ministry; yet the Legislature may, in their discretion, lay a general and equal tax for the support of the Christian religion; leaving to each individual the power of appointing the payment over of the money, collected from him, to the support of any particular place of worship or minister, or for the benefit of the poor of his own denomination, or the poor in general of any particular county....

XXXV. That no other test or qualification ought to be required, on admission to any office of trust or profit, than such oath of support and fidelity to this State, and such oath of office, as shall be directed by this Convention or the Legislature of this State, and a declaration of a belief in the Christian religion.

XXXVI. That the manner of administering an oath to any person, ought to be such, as those of the religious persuasion, profession, or denomination, of which such person is one, generally esteem the most effectual confirmation, by the attestation of the Divine Being. And that the people called Quakers, those called Dunkers [a religious sect], and those called Menonists [Mennonites], holding it unlawful to take an oath on any occasion, ought to be allowed to make their solemn affirmation, in the manner that Quakers have been heretofore allowed to affirm....

XXXVIII. That the liberty of the press ought to be inviolably preserved.

XXXIX. That monopolies are odious, contrary to the spirit of a free government, and the principles of commerce; and ought not to be suffered.

XL. That no title of nobility, or hereditary honours, ought to be granted in this State....

XLII. That this Declaration of Rights, or the Form of Government, to be established by this Convention, or any part or either of them, ought not to be altered, changed or abolished, by the Legislature of this State, but in such manner as this Convention shall prescribe and direct.

This Declaration of Rights was assented to, and passed, in Convention of the Delegates of the freemen of Maryland, begun and held at Annapolis, the 14th day of August, A. D. 1776.

By order of the Convention.

MAT. TILGHMAN, *President.*

The Constitution, or Form of Government, &C.

I. That the Legislature consist of two distinct branches, a Senate and House of Delegates, which shall be styled, *The General Assembly of Maryland.*

II. That the House of Delegates shall be chosen in the following manner: All freemen, above twenty-one years of age, having a freehold of fifty acres of land, in the county in which they offer to vote, and residing therein—and all freemen, having property in this State above the value of thirty pounds current money, and having resided in the county, in which they offer to vote, one whole year next preceding the election, shall have a right of suffrage, in the election of Delegates for such county: and all

freemen, so qualified, shall, on the first Monday of October, seventeen hundred and seventy-seven and on the same day in every year thereafter, assemble in the counties, in which they are respectively qualified to vote, at the court-house, in the said counties; or at such other place as the Legislature shall direct; and, when assembled, they shall proceed to elect, *viva voce* ["live voice"], four Delegates, for their respective counties, of the most wise, sensible, and discreet of the people, residents in the county where they are to be chosen, one whole year next preceding the election, above twenty-one years of age, and having, in the State, real or personal property above the value of five hundred pounds current money....

IX. That the House of Delegates shall judge of the elections and qualifications of Delegates.

X. That the House of Delegates may originate all money bills, propose bills to the Senate, or receive those offered by that body; and assent, dissent, or propose amendments; that they may inquire on the oath of witnesses, into all complaints, grievances, and offences, as the grand inquest of this State; and may commit any person, for any crime, to the public jail, there to remain till he be discharged by due course of law. They may expel any member, for a great misdemeanor, but not a second time for the same cause. They may examine and pass all accounts of the State, relating either to the collection or expenditure of the revenue, or appoint auditors, to state and adjust the same. They may call for all public or official papers and records, and send for persons, whom they may judge necessary in the course of their inquiries, concerning affairs relating to the public interest....

XI. That the Senate may be at full and perfect liberty to exercise their judgment in passing laws— and that they may not be compelled by the House of Delegates, either to reject a money bill, which the emergency of affairs may require, or to assent to some other act of legislation, in their conscience and judgment injurious to the public welfare—the House of Delegates shall not on any occasion, or under any pretence annex to, or blend with a money bill, any matter, clause, or thing, not immediately relating to, and necessary for the imposing, assessing, levying, or applying the taxes or supplies, to be raised for the support of government, or the current expenses of the State: and to prevent altercation about such bills, it is declared, that no bill, imposing duties or customs for the mere regulation of commerce, or inflicting fines for the reformation of morals, or to enforce the execution of the laws, by which an incidental revenue may arise, shall be accounted a money bill: but every bill, assessing, levying, or applying taxes or supplies, for the support of government, or the current expenses of the State, or appropriating money in the treasury, shall be deemed a money bill.

XII. That the House of Delegates may punish, by imprisonment, any person who shall be guilty of a contempt in their view, by any disorderly or riotous behaviour, or by threats to, or abuse of their members, or by any obstruction to their proceedings. They may also punish, by imprisonment, any person who shall be guilty of a breach of privilege, by arresting on civil process, or by assaulting any of their members, during their sitting, or on their way to, or return from the House of Delegates, or by any assault of, or obstruction to their officers, in the execution of any order or process, or by assaulting or obstructing any witness, or any other person, attending on, or on their way to or from the House, or by rescuing any person committed by the House: and the Senate may exercise the same power, in similar cases....

XIV. That the Senate be chosen in the following manner: All persons, qualified as aforesaid to vote for county Delegates, shall, on the first Tuesday of September, 1781, and on the same day in every fifth year forever thereafter, elect, *viva voce*, by a majority of votes, two persons for their respective counties (qualified as aforesaid to be elected county Delegates) to be electors of the Senate....

XV. That the said electors of the Senate meet at the city of Annapolis, or such other place as shall be appointed for convening the legislature, on the third Monday in September, 1781, and on the same day in every fifth year forever thereafter, and they, or any twenty-four of them so met, shall proceed to elect, by ballot, either out of their own body, or the people at large, fifteen Senators (nine of whom to be residents on the western, and six to be residents on the eastern shore [of the Chesapeake Bay]) men of the most wisdom, experience and virtue, above twenty-five years of age, residents of the State above three whole years next preceding the election, and having real and personal property above the value of one thousand pounds current money....

XXI. That the Senate shall judge of the Elections and qualifications of Senators.

XXII. That the Senate may originate any other, except money bills, to which their assent or dissent only shall be given; and may receive any other bills from the House of Delegates, and assent, dissent, or propose amendments.

XXIII. That the General Assembly meet annually, on the first Monday of November, and if necessary, oftener.

XXIV. That each House shall appoint its own officers, and settle its own rules of proceeding.

XXV. That a person of wisdom, experience, and virtue, shall be chosen Governor, on the second Monday of November, seventeen hundred and seventy-seven, and on the second Monday in every year forever thereafter, by the joint ballot of both Houses....

XXVI. That the Senators and Delegates..., annually..., elect by Joint ballot (in the same manner as Senators are directed to be chosen) five of the most sensible, discreet, and experienced men, above twenty-five years of age, residents in the State above three years next preceding the election, and having therein a freehold of lands and tenements [possessions], above the value of one thousand pounds current money, to be the Council to the Governor, whose proceedings shall be always entered on record, to any part whereof any member may enter his dissent; and their advice, if so required by the Governor, or any member of the Council, shall be given in writing, and signed by the members giving the same respectively: which proceedings of the Council shall be laid before the Senate, or House of Delegates, when called for by them or either of them....

XXVIII. That the Senators and Delegates, immediately on their annual meeting, and before they proceed to any business..., shall take an oath of support and fidelity to this State, as aforesaid; and before the election of a governor, or members of the Council, shall take an oath, "elect without favour, affection, partiality, or prejudice, such person as Governor, or member of the Council, as they, in their judgment and conscience, believe best qualified for the office."

XXIX. ...[T]he Governor shall not adjourn the Assembly...at any time.

XXX. That no person, unless above twenty-five years of age, a resident in this State above five years next preceding the election and having in the State real and personal property, above the value of five thousand pounds, current money, (one thousand pounds whereof, at least, to be freehold estate) shall be eligible as governor.

XXXI. That the governor shall not continue in that office longer than three years successively, nor be eligible as Governor, until the expiration of four years after he shall have been out of that office....

XXXIII. That the Governor, by and with the advice and consent of the Council, may embody [organize] the militia; and, when embodied, shall alone have the direction thereof; and shall also have the direction of all the regular land and sea forces, under the laws of this State, (but he shall not command in person, unless advised thereto by the Council, and then, only so long as they shall approve thereof); and may alone exercise all other the executive powers of government, where the concurrence of the Council is not required, according to the laws of this State; and grant reprieves or pardons for any crime, except in such cases where the law shall otherwise direct; and may, during the recess of the General Assembly, lay embargoes, to prevent the departure of any shipping, or the exportation of any commodities, for any time not exceeding thirty days in any one year—summoning the General Assembly to meet within the time of the continuance of such embargo; and may also order and compel any vessel to ride quarantine, if such vessel, or the port from which she may have come, shall, on strong grounds, be suspected to be infected with the plague; but the Governor shall not, under any pretence, exercise any power or prerogative by virtue of any law, statute, or custom of England or Great Britain....

XXXVI. That the Council shall have power to make the Great Seal of this State, which shall be...affixed to all laws, commissions, grants, and other public testimonials, as has been heretofore practised in this State.

XXXVII. That no Senator, Delegate of Assembly, or member of the Council, if he shall qualify as such, shall hold or execute any office of profit, or receive the profits of any office exercised by any other person, during the time for which he shall be elected; nor shall any Governor be capable of holding any other office of profit in this State, while he acts as such. And no person, holding a place of profit or receiving any part of the profits thereof, or receiving the profits or any part of the profits arising on any agency, for the supply of clothing or provisions for the Army or Navy, or holding any office under the United States, or any of them—or a minister, or preacher of the gospel, of any denomination—or any person, employed in the regular land service, or marine, of this or the United States—shall have a seat in the General Assembly or the Council of this State....

XLV. That no field officer of the militia be eligible as a Senator, Delegate, or member of the Council....

XLVIII. That the Governor, for the time being, with the advice and consent of the Council, may appoint the Chancellor, and all Judges and Justices, the Attorney-General, Naval Officers, officers in the regular land and sea service, officers of the militia, Registers of the Land Office, Surveyors, and all other civil officers of government (Assessors, Constables, and Overseers of the roads only excepted) and may also suspend or remove any civil officer who has not a commission, during good behaviour; and may suspend any militia officer, for one month: and may also suspend or remove any regular officer in the land or sea service: and the Governor may remove or suspend any militia officer, in pursuance of the judgment of a Court Martial....

L. That the Governor, every member of the Council, and every Judge and Justice, before they act as such, shall respectively take an oath, "That he will not, through favour, affection or partiality vote for any person to office; and that he will vote for such person as, in his judgment and conscience, he believes most fit and best qualified for the office; and that he has not made, nor will make, any promise or engagement to give his vote or interest in favor of any person."...

LIV. That if any person shall give any bribe, present, or reward, or any promise, or any security for the payment or delivery of any money, or any other thing, to obtain or procure a vote to be Governor, Senator, Delegate to Congress or Assembly, member of the Council, or Judge, or to be appointed to any of the said offices, or to any office of profit or trust, now created or hereafter to be created in this State—the person giving, and the person receiving the same (on conviction in a court of law) shall be forever disqualified to hold any office of trust or profit in this State.

LV. That every person, appointed to any office of profit or trust, shall, before he enters on the execution thereof, take the following oath; to wit: "I, A. B., do swear, that I do not hold myself bound in allegiance to the King of Great Britain, and that I will be faithful, and bear true allegiance to the State of Maryland;" and shall also subscribe a declaration of his belief in the Christian religion....

LVII. That the style of all laws run thus; "*Be it enacted by the General Assembly of Maryland:*" that all public commissions and grants run thus; "*The State of Maryland,*" &c. and shall be signed by the Governor, and attested by the Chancellor, with the seal of the State annexed—except military commissions...: that all writs shall run in the same style, and be attested, sealed and signed a usual: that all indictments shall conclude, "*Against the peace, government, and dignity of the State.*"

LVIII. That all penalties and forfeitures, heretofore going to the King or proprietary [ruler of the colony], shall go to the State—save only such, as the General Assembly may abolish or otherwise provide for.

LIX. That this Form of Government, and the Declaration of Rights, and no part thereof, shall be altered, changed, or abolished, unless a bill so to alter, change or abolish the same shall pass the General Assembly, and be published at least three months before a new election, and shall be confirmed by the General Assembly, after a new election of Delegates, in the first session after such new election; provided that nothing in this form of government, which relates to the eastern shore particularly, shall at any time hereafter be altered, unless for the alteration and confirmation thereof at least two-thirds of all the members of each branch of the General Assembly shall concur. . . .

This Form of Government was assented to, and passed in Convention of the Delegates of the freemen of Maryland, begun and held at the city of Annapolis, the fourteenth of August, A. D. one thousand seven hundred and seventy-six.

By order of the Convention.

M. TILGHMAN, *President.*

CHAPTER 9

Private Martin
Tells War Stories

"Great men get great praise, little men, nothing"

The American Revolution included, entangled, and profoundly affected many more Americans than the elite white men you met in the last two chapters, the men who wrote pamphlets and petitions, declarations and constitutions. On the frontier, the Iroquois you encountered in Chapter 1 were among many native peoples declaring (or, since they already were sovereign nations, perhaps a better word is *defending*) their independence from distant powers in Philadelphia and London. On plantations, meanwhile, the chaos of war and the talk of *liberty* prompted many African American slaves to declare their own independence in what Gary Nash calls "the largest slave uprising in our history."[1] Among white women, too, the rebellion opened new possibilities. Protests before 1776 already had given women a political role, boycotting British goods and making homespun clothing; now, with husbands and fathers in the army or the assembly for long stretches of time, wives and daughters ran family farms or businesses.

Entire volumes have been devoted to the Revolution's large cast of characters. Unable to embrace all of these Americans, this book invites you to get acquainted with yet another forgotten, often despised group that had a vital role in shaping "the course of human events": The Continental Army soldier.

Our guide on that journey into the ranks is a New Englander named Joseph Plumb Martin (1760–1850). Martin, the son of an "unsuccessful" and "quarrelsome" clergyman, grew up on his grandfather's farm in Milford, Connecticut. He was not quite sixteen when he joined the rebel forces on July 6, 1776, just two days after Congress officially declared independence. Except for one season between enlistments, he stayed until war's end. The length of his service makes him unusual enough: Historian James Kirby Martin estimates that "no more than 1 out of every 250 people" in America matched young Joseph's record of devotion to the cause. But what makes this teenage soldier "unique" is that he later wrote at length about those years. This "priceless account of the Revolutionary era" is not just an "authentic American classic," Professor Martin declares; it is also "the only detailed memoir of the Revolutionary War by a common soldier."[2]

Joseph Plumb Martin's war stories are also invaluable because they focus attention on the war itself. It is not as if we have altogether forgotten that conflict. The battles of Lexington and Concord, of Bunker Hill and Saratoga; the depths of despair at Valley Forge and the height of jubilation at Yorktown: These are prominently featured in American lore. When, as civil war loomed in 1861, President Abraham Lincoln stood on the steps of the nation's capitol and begged his "dissatisfied fellow countrymen" to listen still to "the mystic chords of memory, stretching from every battle-field, and patriot grave, to every heart and hearthstone, all over this broad land," these names were among those he was calling to mind (Chapter 18).

Lexington and Concord, Bunker Hill, Saratoga, Valley Forge, Yorktown: The very words still have the power to move Americans today, even if few remember their exact dates and details. They remind us that it was one thing to *declare* independence, quite another to *acquire* it. All of the ink spilled in writing pamphlets, manifestoes, and constitutions was nothing compared to the blood spilled in backing up words with deeds. Today, with the government maintaining the sites as sacred ground, with a film like Mel Gibson's *The Patriot* to fire the imagination, memory of the War for Independence is sure to live on.

The popular version, however, is so slanted that some call it a myth. Its origins can be traced to the very first armed clash, at Lexington and Concord in the spring of 1775. Everyone knows how the "Minutemen"—alerted by Paul Revere and other riders that "the British are coming!"—left home and family on a moment's notice to face the redcoats. From that point forward, the story goes, patriotic citizen-soldiers by the thousands, reluctant warriors determined to defend their liberties and their communities against tyranny, met British professionals (and German mercenaries) in battle after battle, with glorious results known to all. The chorus of adulation has sung more or less the same tune for more than two centuries.

Lately, however, some scholars—without denying Americans rebels' courage, sacrifice, and ultimate success—have begun to paint this picture of the War for Independence in darker colors. They point out, for example, that this was the longest war in American history before Vietnam: Fully six-and-a-half years stretched from the first shots fired at Lexington and Concord (April 19, 1775) to Lord Cornwallis's surrender at Yorktown (October 19, 1781), and peace did not come for two years more.

The new scholarship has also revealed that one reason the struggle dragged on so long was the poor quality of the American fighting force. George Washington's Continental Army "was never a very good army by European standards," writes historian John Shy, and "it never won a battle in open field." Rebel forces also struggled because neither *Common Sense* nor the Declaration of Independence persuaded every colonist. Perhaps 20% of the white population remained loyal to King George III. When many of those Loyalists joined the fight against "the rebels," the contest became a brutal civil war. "[T]his country is the scene of the most cruel events," reported a German officer serving with the British forces. "Neighbors are on opposite sides, children are against their fathers. Anyone who differs with the opinions of Congress in thought or in speech is regarded as an enemy and turned over to the hangman, or else he must flee" to British lines. Armed and supplied by imperial forces, "these refugees" then head back home "to take revenge by pillaging, murdering, and burning."[3]

Given the searing heat of the hatred and the interminable length of the war, no wonder casualties were so high—another aspect of the conflict, like its duration and intensity, that has largely escaped notice. The figures alone—an estimated 25,000 American rebels dead, 8,000 more wounded, 1,500 missing in action—might not seem like much. After all, some 58,000 American troops lost their lives in Vietnam, 300,000 perished in World War II, and more than twice that many (North and South) fell in the Civil War. But as with King Philip's War a century before Lexington and Concord (Chapter 4), we need to calculate how small the population was in the mid-1770s: *Proportionally*, as a percentage of the American population at the time, the Revolutionary War's casualty count is staggering; if the United States today suffered the same proportion of losses, Shy notes, the death toll would be well above two million.[4]

In short, Shy concludes, "[t]he bedrock facts of the American Revolutionary struggle...are not pretty."[5] Those facts would have been even uglier had the rebels lost, and—another unpleasant fact too rarely recalled—they almost did. Thomas Paine's experience in the six months after Congress heeded his call and declared independence reveals this neglected part of the saga. On July 9, the day after the Declaration was read to a large and clamorous Philadelphia crowd, Paine joined a band of Pennsylvania volunteers bound for the New Jersey coast across from New York City. There they were to bolster rebel defenses against the British, who were using their formidable fleet to land tens of thousands of soldiers. The very sight of this vast armada prompted some of Paine's comrades to desert. He handed out copies of *Common Sense* to bolster the spirits of the rest, while in New York City General Washington also tried to boost morale by ordering the Declaration read to the troops.

Neither document helped much: Through the summer and fall Paine watched as American forces in and around New York City—outnumbered, outgunned, and outmaneuvered—suffered one disaster after another. "[T]he rebels fled like scared rabbits," sneered a British officer that November after taking a fort Paine had been in. By December, what was left of Washington's army had retreated all the way to Pennsylvania, where it found that Congress, fearing that Philadelphia soon would fall, had left town. The outlook seemed hopeless. If we cannot get more troops, George Washington confided to his brother on December 18, "I think the game is pretty near up."[6]

Paine, like Washington, was not ready to surrender just yet. Urged by army officers to pen something that would rally the dejected rebels, he sat down in early December and, in "a passion of patriotism," hammered out a pamphlet called *The Crisis*. If you thought *Common Sense* sounded angry, listen to what Paine said a year later. Loyalists? "Every Tory is a coward" full of "a servile, slavish, self-interested fear." The king? "[A] sottish, stupid, stubborn, worthless, brutish man." That man and his henchmen *must* be defeated, Paine insisted, and they *can* be defeated if we do not despair. "These are the times that try men's souls," he wrote. "The summer soldier and the sunshine patriot will, in this crisis, shrink from the service of his country; but he that stands it *now*, deserves the thanks of man and woman. Tyranny, like hell, is not easily conquered: yet…the harder the conflict, the more glorious the triumph."[7]

The pamphlet appeared on December 23. Two days later, at the American camp, officers read it aloud to their men. Then, under cover of darkness, those soldiers crossed back over the Delaware and struck an enemy post at Trenton, killing and wounding more than a hundred while capturing almost a thousand. This stunning success, and another at Princeton a week later, kept the cause of independence alive. Washington and his men would fight another day.[8]

So would Joseph Plumb Martin. Young Martin's initial enlistment was up in December, so he headed home to Connecticut, thus missing Trenton and Princeton. But come spring he was back in the army, this time "for the duration" of the war. Had he known how long the conflict would last and how much he would suffer, Martin might have thought twice about reenlisting. Certainly many other men who had raced to America's rescue in 1775 and 1776 were having second thoughts about risking their lives in the cause of independence; as the war ground on, relatively few followed him back into the army.

This striking loss of enthusiasm is another dimension of the war that Americans, then and since, have covered up and forgotten. In the days and months after Lexington, men had flocked to the front lines. "The ardour of our people is such," wrote a Connecticut man two days after the first blood was shed, "that they can't be kept back" from marching to Boston. Nor was commitment to the rebellion confined to New England in those early days; from Philadelphia came word that "the Rage Militaire, as the French call a passion for arms, has taken possession of the whole Continent."[9]

Behind this devotion was a belief in the American cause and a serene confidence that patriotism and virtue would triumph—and quickly—even over the greatest military power in the world. "Our Troops are animated with the Love of Freedom," boasted one writer in February 1776. True, "they have not the Advantages arising from Experience and Discipline....But...native Courage warmed with Patriotism, is sufficient to counterbalance these [military] Advantages." As the years passed, however, more and more Americans elected to stay home. One disgusted French officer serving in the Continental Army even claimed that "[t]here is a hundred times more enthusiasm for this Revolution in any Paris café than in all the colonies together."[10]

It was, of course, easier to be a patriot in a Paris café than in the American army, where if a British bayonet or bullet did not kill you, disease might. Still, as early as 1776 it began to look like Americans were indeed "summer soldiers and sunshine patriots." Once, so many men clamored to fight the British that they had to be sent home; now army recruiters beat the bushes for recruits in vain. Once, those recruiters had sounded like Thomas Paine as they appealed to patriotism ("we are engaged...in the cause of virtue, of liberty, of *God*") and to common sense (asking "whether we will see our wives and children, with everything that is dear to us, subjected to the merciless rage of uncontrolled despotism"); now, Congress appealed to men's pockets rather than their patriotism, offering a bounty (a cash bonus) for enlisting and 100 acres of land for those who fought until war's end.[11]

Even these rewards were not enough. Bounties served merely "to hire the populace to visit the army," wrote one cynic; recruits took the money, paid a courtesy call on an encampment, then headed home. "[S]o great was the aversion to military service" in one part of North Carolina that most men there were said to be suffering from an "artificial hernia." The states, asked by Congress to send a set number of men to the Continental ranks, tried desperately to fill their quota. Many resorted to a draft, then let a rich man pay a fine for refusing to go or buy a substitute soldier—like Joseph Plumb Martin. Servants and slaves sent in their masters' place; vagrants snatched off the street; debtors and criminals; prisoners of war and Loyalists; boys even younger than sixteen-year-old Joseph—all these and more joined Joseph in the ranks. As a result, the War for Independence was fought and won by men who bore little resemblance to the bands of sturdy yeomen and artisans protecting home and hearth that have long been celebrated as Revolutionary heroes. Young and poor, Irish and German, Native American and African American, these men were not defending "home and family because they rarely had either."[12]

Nor, as you will see in Martin's account, were they entirely happy with the soldier's life. The army suffered from chronic shortages of everything from shoes and shirts to flour and beef, in part because civilians often sold supplies to the British army for gold and silver rather than to rebel forces for almost-worthless paper money issued by Congress. "I despise my countrymen," a Connecticut officer named Ebenezer Huntington stormed to his father in 1780. "I wish I could say I was not born in America....The insults and neglects which the army have met with from the country beggars all description."[13]

To Martin and his mates, though, officers like Huntington could be part of the problem, part of what made a soldier's life hard. Fancying themselves officers *and* gentlemen in the days when the term "gentleman" meant something (recall Dr. Alexander Hamilton's views in Chapter 5), these men tended to look down on their troops as "miserable...lean fac'd Villains" or "a wretched motley Crew." Those troops, in turn, resented the contempt, pretension, and harsh commands emanating from on high.[14]

Small wonder, then, that a rash of mutinies broke out in the Continental ranks, yet another chapter of the Revolutionary War story largely unwritten and unread. These rebellions were not against independence or in favor of the enemy, but against officers and civilian officials deemed unsympathetic to common soldiers' suffering. In December 1783, when General Washington went to deliver his sword and resign his command to Congress, he found the nation's government in Annapolis. Why Annapolis? Because the previous summer angry troops demanding back pay had surrounded Independence Hall in Philadelphia, where Congress was in session, forcing the national government to go on the road yet again, this time to escape not its foe but its own men.[15]

Hunger and anger, arrogant officers and indifferent civilians, *rage militaire* and reliance on substitutes—Joseph Plumb Martin experienced all of this, and much more besides. As you read the excerpts below, ask both why he enlisted and why, given all that he endured, he stayed. Look, too, for signs of tension between the egalitarian rhetoric of the Declaration of Independence and the enduring grip of the hierarchical social views of Dr. Hamilton. In addition, Martin's memoir, like Hamilton's diary, offers glimpses of vivid scenes and snatches of conversation that speak to other important issues we have considered, such as racial attitudes, gender relations, or the poles of localism and nationalism competing for people's loyalty. To what extent did the divisions Hamilton detected in the 1740s endure?

Consider, finally, perhaps the most important question of all: Was there an "American Revolution" for Joseph Plumb Martin? Did his life, his world, change in fundamental ways? His adventures after leaving the army in 1783 send a mixed message. On the one hand, there are signs that Martin not only pursued happiness, he found it. Settling on a farm in Maine, he married, raised four children, and was elected to several local offices as well as to the legislature. Some who knew him recalled that, with "his lively, social disposition, and ready wit," he was "a highly entertaining and instructive companion."[16]

On the other hand, in 1818, applying for a pension under the new federal program to help veterans, Martin testified (and his neighbors confirmed) that he was in dire straits. "I have no real nor personal estate" beyond clothes, bedding, and some livestock, he reported, "nor any income whatever." Worse, he was "unable to work" "by reason of age and infirmity."[17] He had sold, unseen and for a pittance, the 100 acres of land in Ohio the government had finally given him in 1797; apparently by 1818 his Maine farm was gone, too.

Historian Alan Taylor, chronicling Martin's later years, argues that the veteran "lost the revolution he had sought."[18] Whether or not you agree, one thing is clear: A sort of historical amnesia about Martin and his Continental Army comrades soon swept the land. That it took thirty-five years for the government to pass a law aiding veterans testifies to the nation's neglect. With independence won, Americans began forgetting the darker side of the conflict—not just the fury of *Common Sense* (Chapter 7) but also the draft resisters and the deserters, the mutineers who disobeyed haughty officers and the civilians who closed their doors to a hungry soldier.

If Joseph Plumb Martin's goal in writing this book was to set the record straight, he must have been disappointed. If his hope was to make money, he must have been doubly disappointed. Published in 1830 in Hallowell, Maine, the *Narrative* sold few copies, then sank from sight even more completely than did *Common Sense* and Thomas Paine. As you will see, America in 1830 was far removed from "the times that tried men's souls"; the nation was busy celebrating rags-to-riches tales like Benjamin Franklin's (Chapter 6) and the sunnier version of Revolutionary history that Mason Locke Weems created in his *Life of Washington* (Chapter 10). There was little appetite for a rags-to-rags account that cast doubt on the accepted version of the Revolutionary War. We still live with that accepted version and its happy ending; we should also learn to live with the war stories of an old soldier like Private Martin.

Questions for Consideration and Conversation

1. Why did Joseph Plumb Martin write this account? Why did he publish it in 1830 rather than, say, 1790 or 1810?
2. Why did Martin join the army? Why did he stay in the army?
3. How do Martin's memories compare with the reminiscences you might have heard or read by veterans of World War II, Korea, Vietnam, Iraq, or Afghanistan?
4. How much can we trust war stories told by an aged veteran—stories of events, people, and impressions that were, by the time he wrote them down, fifty years old?

5. Some of the questions posed regarding Dr. Alexander Hamilton's travel account (Chapter 5) can also be posed for Martin's memoir: Is there, in this text, evidence of a *unified* American nation? Of an egalitarian ethos?
6. Was there a "revolution" for Martin? Could one argue that his life would have been more or less the same even if 1776 had never happened?
7. How does Martin's discussion of the way veterans were treated two hundred years ago compare with the way veterans of more recent American wars have been treated?

Endnotes

1. Gary B. Nash, *Race and Revolution* (Madison, WI, 1990), 57.
2. James Kirby Martin, ed., *Ordinary Courage: The Revolutionary War Adventures of Joseph Plumb Martin* (St. James, NY, 1993), viii, x, xii.
3. John Shy, *A People Numerous and Armed: Reflections on the Military Struggle for American Independence*, revised edition (Ann Arbor, MI, 1990), 23 (German), 127 ("never won").
4. Ibid., 249.
5. Ibid., 23.
6. David Freeman Hawke, *Paine* (New York, 1974), 58 ("rabbits"); James Kirby Martin and Mark Edward Lender, *A Respectable Army: The Military Origins of the Republic, 1763–1789* (Arlington Heights, IL, 1982), 59 (Washington).
7. Thomas Paine, *Common Sense and Related Writings*, ed. Thomas P. Slaughter (Boston, 2001), 126–32.
8. For dramatic accounts of these military affairs, see David Hackett Fischer, *Washington's Crossing* (New York, 2004); David McCullough, *1776* (New York, 2005).
9. Richard Buel, Jr., *Dear Liberty: Connecticut's Mobilization for the Revolutionary War* (Middletown, CT, 1980), 36 ("ardour"); Charles Royster, *A Revolutionary People at War: The Continental Army and American Character, 1775–1783* (Chapel Hill, NC, 1979), 25 ("Rage Militaire").
10. Martin and Lender, *Respectable Army*, 32 ("animated"); Shy, *People Numerous and Armed*, 21 ("Paris café").
11. Martin and Lender, *Respectable Army*, 70.
12. Royster, *Revolutionary People*, 326 ("visit," "hernia"); Martin and Lender, *Respectable Army*, 90 ("home and family"). For recent work that further complicates the story, see John Resch and Walter Sargent, eds., *War and Society in the American Revolution: Mobilization and Home Fronts* (Dekalb, IL, 2007).
13. Martin and Lender, *Respectable Army*, 147.
14. Charles Patrick Neimeyer, *America Goes to War: A Social History of the Continental Army* (New York, 1996), 9.
15. Ibid., 155–57.
16. Martin, ed., *Ordinary Courage*, vii.
17. Ibid., xi.
18. Alan Taylor, *Liberty Men and Great Proprietors: The Revolutionary Settlement on the Maine Frontier, 1790–1820* (Chapel Hill, NC, 1990), 247.

Joseph Plumb Martin, *A Narrative of a Revolutionary Soldier*: *Some of the Adventures, Dangers, and Sufferings of Joseph Plumb Martin* (1830)

Source: Joseph Plumb Martin, *A Narrative of a Revolutionary Soldier: Some of the Adventures, Dangers, and Sufferings of Joseph Plumb Martin*. New York: Signet, 2001 [originally published Hallowell, ME, 1830].

Preface

... [M]y intention is to give a succinct account of some of my adventures, dangers and sufferings during my several campaigns in the revolutionary army. My readers, (who, by the by, will, I hope, none of them be beyond the pale [boundary] of my own neighbourhood,) must not expect any great transactions to be exhibited to their notice, ... but they are here, once for all, requested to bear it in mind, that they are not the achievements of an officer of high grade which they are perusing, but the common transactions of one of the lowest in station in an army, a private soldier.

Should the reader chance to ask himself this question, (and I think it very natural for him to do so,) how could any man of common sense ever spend his precious time in writing such a rhapsody of nonsense?—to satisfy his inquiring mind, I would inform him, that ... every private soldier in an army thinks his particular services as essential to carry on the war he is engaged in, as the services of the most influential general; and why not? what could officers do without such men? Nothing at all....

But ... the real cause of my ever undertaking to rake up circumstances and actions that have so long rested in my own mind, and to spread them upon paper, was this:—my friends, and especially my juvenile friends have often urged me to do so; to oblige such, I undertook it, hoping it might save me often the trouble of verbally relating them.

The critical grammarian may find enough to feed his spleen upon, if he peruses the following pages; but I can inform him beforehand, I do not regard his sneers; if I cannot write grammatically, I can think, talk and feel like other men. Besides, if the common readers can understand it, it is all I desire; and to give them an idea, though but a faint one, of what the army suffered that gained and secured our independence, is all I wish. I never studied grammar an hour in my life, when I ought to have been doing that, I was forced to be studying the rules and articles of war....

But lest I should make my preface longer than my story, I will here bring it to a close.

Chapter I

Introductory

... Time passed smoothly on with me till the year 1774 arrived, the smell of war began to be pretty strong, but I was determined to have no hand in it, happen when it might; I felt myself to be a real coward. What—venture my carcass where bullets fly! that will never do for me....

[T]he spring of 1775 arrived. Expectation of some fatal event seemed to fill the minds of most of the considerate [thoughtful] people throughout the country. I was ploughing in the field about half a mile from home, about the twenty-first day of April, when all of a sudden the bells fell to ringing, and three guns were repeatedly fired in succession down in the village; what the cause was we could not conjecture. I had some fearful forebodings that something ... was in the wind. The regulars are coming in good earnest, thought I....I sat off to see what the cause of the commotion was. I found most of the male kind of the people together; soldiers for Boston were in requisition. A dollar deposited upon the drum head was taken up by some one as soon as placed there, and the holder's name taken, as he enrolled, with orders to equip himself as quick as possible. My spirits began to revive at the sight of the money offered; the seeds of courage began to sprout; for, contrary to my knowledge, there was a scattering of them sowed, but they had not as yet germinated; I felt a strong inclination, when I found I had them, to cultivate them. O, thought I, if I were but old enough to put myself forward, I would be the possessor of one dollar, the dangers of war to the contrary notwithstanding....

The men that had engaged "to go to war" went as far as the next town, where they received orders to return, as there was a sufficiency of men already engaged, so that I should have had but a short campaign had I have gone.

This year there were troops raised both for Boston and New-York. Some from the back [interior] towns were billeted at my grandsire's; their company and conversation began to warm my courage to such a degree, that I resolved at all events to "go a sogering."...I was as earnest now to call myself, and be called a soldier, as I had been a year before *not* to be called one. I thought over many things, and formed many plans, but they all fell through, and poor disconsolate I was forced to set down and gnaw my finger nails in silence.

I said but little more about "soldiering," until the troops raised in and near the town in which I resided, came to march off for New-York, then I felt bitterly again; I accompanied them as far as the town line, and it was hard parting with them, my heart and soul went with them, but my mortal part must stay behind. By and by they will come swaggering back, thought I, and tell me of all their exploits, all their "hairbreadth 'scapes."...

The thoughts of service still haunted me after the troops were gone, and the town clear of them....

Chapter II

Campaign of 1776

...During the winter of 1775–6, by hearing the conversation and disputes of the good old farmer politicians of the times, I collected pretty correct ideas of the contest between this country and the mother country, (as it was then called.) I thought I was as warm a patriot as the best of them....I felt more anxious than ever, if possible, to be called a defender of my country....

In the month of June, this year, orders came out for enlisting men for six months....The troops were stiled new levies, they were to go to New-York; and notwithstanding I was told that the British army at that place was reinforced by fifteen thousand men, it made no alteration in my mind; I did not care if there had been fifteen times fifteen thousand, I should have gone just as soon as if there had been but fifteen hundred. I never spent a thought about numbers, the Americans were invincible, in my opinion....

[Despite lingering doubts,] I one evening went off with a full determination to enlist at all hazards. When I arrived at the place of rendezvous I found a number of young men of my acquaintance there; the old bantering began—come, if you will enlist I will, says one, you have long been talking about it, says another—come, now is the time. "Thinks I to myself," I will not be laughed into it or out of it, at any rate; I will act my own pleasure after all. But what did I come here for tonight? why, to enlist; then enlist I will. So seating myself at the table, enlisting orders were immediately presented to me; I took up the pen, loaded it with the

fatal charge, made several mimic imitations of writing my name, but took especial care not to touch the paper with the pen until an unlucky wight who was leaning over my shoulder gave my hand a stroke, which caused the pen to make a woful scratch on the paper. "O, he has enlisted," said he, "he has made his mark, he is fast enough now." Well, thought I, I may as well go through with the business now as not; so I wrote my name fairly upon the indentures. And now I was a *soldier*, in name at least, if not in practice....

I went, with several others of the company, on board a sloop, bound to New-York,...marched up into the city, and joined the rest of the regiment that were already there....

I was called out every morning at reveille beating, which was at daybreak, to go to our regimental parade, in Broad-street, and there practice the manual exercise, which was the most that was known in our new levies, if they knew even that. I was brought to an allowance of provisions, which, while we lay in New-York was not bad....

[On August 27, Martin's regiment goes to reinforce American lines during a battle.] We soon landed at Brooklyn, upon the [Long] Island, marched up the ascent from the ferry, to the plain. We now began to meet the wounded men, another sight I was unacquainted with, some with broken arms, some with broken legs, and some with broken heads. The sight of these a little daunted me, and made me think of home, but the sight and thought vanished together. We marched a short distance, when we halted to refresh ourselves....[T]he Americans and British were warmly engaged within sight of us. What were the feelings of most or all the young soldiers at this time, I know not, but I know what were mine;— but let mine or theirs be what they might, I saw a Lieutenant who appeared to have feelings not very enviable; whether he was actuated by fear or the canteen I cannot determine now; I thought it fear at the time; for he ran round among the men of his company, snivelling and blubbering, praying each one if he had aught against him, or if *he* had injured any one that they would forgive him, declaring at the same time that he, from his heart, forgave them if they had offended him....A fine soldier you are, I thought, a fine officer, an exemplary man for young soldiers! I would have then suffered any thing short of death rather than have made such an exhibition of myself....

We were soon called upon to fall in and proceed. We had not gone far...when I heard one in the rear ask another where his musket was; I looked round and saw one of the soldiers stemming off without his gun, having left it where we last halted; he was inspecting his side as if undetermined whether he had it or not, he then fell out of the ranks to go in search of it: one of the company, who had brought it on (wishing to see how far he would go before he missed it) gave it to him....

By the time we arrived [at the battlefield], the enemy had driven our men into the creek, or rather mill-pond, (the tide being up,) where such as could swim got across; those that could not swim, and could not procure any thing to buoy them up, sunk. The British having several fieldpieces stationed by a brick house, were pouring the canister [-shot] and grape [-shot] upon the Americans like a shower of hail....

[After this defeat, Martin's regiment spends several days in New York City.] And now was coming on the famous Kipp's Bay affair [the British invasion of the city], which has been criticized so much by the Historians of the Revolution. I was there, and will give a true statement of all that *I* saw during that day.

It was on a Sabbath morning, the day in which the British were always employed about their deviltry, if possible; because, they said, they had the prayers of the church on that day. We lay very quiet in our ditch, waiting their motions, till the sun was an hour or two high;...all of a sudden, there came such a peal of thunder from the British shipping that I thought my head would go with the sound. I made a frog's leap for the ditch, and lay as still as I possibly could, and began to consider which part of my carcass was to go first....We kept the lines till they were almost levelled upon us, when our officers, seeing we could make no resistance, and no orders coming from any superior officer, and that we must soon be entirely exposed to the rake of their guns, gave the order to leave the lines. In retreating we had to cross a level clear spot of ground, forty or fifty rods wide [a rod is 16.5 feet], exposed to the whole of the enemy's fire; and they gave it to us in prime order; the grape shot and language flew merrily, which served to quicken our motions. When I had gotten a little out of the reach of their combustibles, I found myself in company with one who was a neighbour of mine when at home, and one other man belonging to our regiment; where the rest of them were I knew not. We went into a house by the highway, in which were two women and some small children, all crying most bitterly; we asked the women if they had any spirits [liquor] in the house; they placed a case bottle of rum upon the table, and bid us help ourselves. We each of us drank a glass, and bidding them good bye, betook ourselves to the highway again....

We had not long been on this road before we saw another party, just ahead of us, whom we know to be Americans; just as we overtook these, they were fired upon by a party of British from a cornfield, and all was immediately in confusion again. I believe the enemies' party was small; but our people were all militia, and the demons of fear and disorder seemed to take full possession of all and every thing on that day. When I came to the spot where the militia were fired upon, the ground was literally covered with arms, knapsacks, staves, coats, [and] hats....We had to advance slowly, for my comrade having been sometime unwell, was now so overcome by heat, hunger and fatigue that he became suddenly and violently sick. I took his musket and endeavoured to encourage him him on....I was loath to leave him behind, although I was anxious to find the main part of the regiment, if possible, before night....

After proceeding about half a mile we came to a place where our people had begun to make a stand. A number, say two or three hundred, had collected here, having been stopped by the artillery officers....[and] a sentinel...placed in the road to prevent our going any further. I felt very much chagrined to be thus hindered from proceeding, as I felt confident that our regiment, or some considerable part of it, was not far ahead....I remonstrated with the officer who detained us....I told him I had a sick man with me who was wet and would die if exposed all night to the damp cold air, hoping by this to move his compassion; but it would not do, he was inexorable. I shall not soon forget the answer he gave me...."Well," said he, "if he dies the country will be rid of one who can do it no good." Pretty fellow! thought I, a very compassionate gentleman! When a man has got his bane [death] in his country's cause, let him die like an old horse or dog, because he can do no more!—The *only wish* I would wish such men, would be, to let them have exactly the same treatment which they would give to others....

[Sneaking past that evening, Martin rejoins his regiment.]...And here ends the "Kipp's Bay" affair, which caused at the time, and has since caused much "inkshed." Anecdotes, jests, imprecations and sarcasms, have been multiplied; and even the grave writers of the revolution have said and written more about it than it deserved. I could make some observations, but it is beyond my province....

[E]very man that I saw was endeavouring by all sober means to escape from death or captivity, which, at that period of the war was almost certain death. The men were confused, being without officers to command them....How could the men fight without officers?...

We remained here [the northern end of Manhattan Island] till sometime in…October, without any thing very material transpiring, excepting starvation, and *that* had by this time become quite a secondary matter; hard duty and nakedness were considered the prime evils, for…we lost all our clothing in the Kipp's Bay affair.…It now began to be cool weather, especially the nights. To have to lie, as I did, almost every other night,…on the cold and often wet ground, without a blanket, and with nothing but thin summer clothing, was tedious. I have often, while upon guard, lain on one side until the upper side smarted with cold, then turned that side down to the place warmed by my body, and let the other take its turn at smarting, while the one on the ground warmed; thus alternately turning for four or six hours, till called upon to go on sentry [duty]…; in the morning, the ground as white as snow, with hoar frost.…

[The army moves up the Hudson River to White Plains, where a major battle takes place in late October. Afterward,] a number of our sick were sent off to Norwalk, in Connecticut, to recruit [recuperate]. I was sent with them as a nurse. We were billetted among the inhabitants.…The inhabitants here were almost entirely what were in those days termed tories. An old lady, of whom I often procured milk, used always, when I went to her house, to give me a lecture on my opposition to our good king George. She had always said, (she told me,) that the regulars would make us fly like pigeons.…

The man of the house where I was quartered had a smart looking negro man, a great politician; I chanced one day to go into the barn where he was threshing. He quickly began to upbraid me with my opposition to the British. The king of England was a very powerful prince, he said,—a very powerful prince; and it was a great pitty that the colonists had fallen out with him; but as we had, we must abide by the consequences. I had no inclination to waste the shafts [arrows or missiles] of my rhetoric upon a negro slave. I concluded he had heard his betters say so. As the old cock crows so crows the young one; and I thought, as the white cock crows so crows the black one. He ran away from his master, before I left there, and went to Long-Island to assist king George; but it seems the king of terrors was more potent than king George, for his master had certain intelligence that poor Cuff was laid flat on his back.

[On] the twenty-fifth day of December, 1776…, I was discharged, (my term of service having expired,).…

Here ends my first campaign. I had learned something of a soldier's life; enough, I thought, to keep me at home for the future.…

Chapter III

Campaign of 1777

…The spring of 1777 arrived; I had got recruited during the winter, and begun to think again about the army. In the month of April…, the young men began to enlist. Orders were out for enlisting men for three years, or during the war. The general opinion of the people was, that the war would not continue three years longer; what reasons they had for making such conjectures I cannot imagine, but so it was;—perhaps it was their wish that it *might* be so, induced them to think that it *would* be so.…

The inhabitants of the town were about this time put into what were called squads, according to their rateable property. Of some of the most opulent, one formed a squad,—of others, two or three, and of the lower sort of the people, several formed a squad. Each of these squads were to furnish a man for the army, either by hiring or by sending one of their own number.…

[A friend] had a Lieutenant's commission in the standing army.…One of the above-mentioned squads, wanting to procure a man, the Lieutenant told them that he thought they might persuade me to go for them, and they accordingly attacked me, front, rear and flank. I thought…, I might as well endeavour to get as much for my skin as I could;—accordingly, I told them that I would go for them, and fixed upon a day when I would meet them and clinch the bargain. The day, which was a muster-day of the militia of the town, arrived;—I went to the parade, where all was liveliness, as it generally is upon such occasions; but poor *I* felt miserably; my execution-day was come. I kept wandering about till the afternoon, among the crowd, when I saw the Lieutenant, who went with me into a house where the men of the squad were, and there I put my name to enlisting indentures for the last time.…The men gave me what they agreed to, I forget the sum, perhaps enough to keep the blood circulating during the short space of time which I tarried at home after I had enlisted. They were now freed from any further trouble, at least for the present, and I had become the scape-goat for them.

Well, I was again a soldier!…

[In September, Martin's regiment is ordered toward Philadelphia, where the British army is concentrated. They arrive in time for the Battle of Germantown on October 4.] We marched slowly all night; in the morning there was a low vapour lying on the land which made it very difficult to distinguish objects at any considerable distance. About daybreak our advanced guard and the British outposts came in contact. The curs began to bark first and then the bull-dogs. Our brigade moved off to the right into the fields. We saw a body of the enemy drawn up behind a rail fence on our right flank; we immediately formed a line and advanced upon them,—our orders were, not to fire till we could see the buttons upon their clothes; but they were so coy that they would not give us an opportunity to be so curious, for they hid their clothes in fire and smoke before we had either time or leisure to examine their buttons. They soon fell back and we advanced, when the action became general. The enemy were driven quite through their camp. They left their kettles, in which they were cooking their breakfasts, on the fires, and some of their garments were lying on the ground, which the owners had not time to put on. Affairs went on well for sometime; the enemy were retreating before us, until the first division that was engaged had expended their ammunition; some of the men unadvisedly calling out that their ammunition was spent, the enemy were so near that they overheard them, when they first made a stand and then returned upon our people, who, for want of ammunition and reinforcements, were obliged in their turn to retreat, which ultimately resulted in the route [rout] of the whole army....

When...it had become dark [some days after the battle], we met the Quartermasters, who had come out to meet us with wagons and hogsheads of whiskey! (thinking, perhaps, that we might take cold by being so much exposed in the cold water;) they had better have brought us something more substantial, but we thought that better than nothing. The...Quartermaster-sergeants stood in the wagons and dealt out the liquor to the platoons....The intention...was, to give to each man a gill [four ounces] of liquor, but as measuring it out by gills was tedious, it was dealt out to us in pint measures, with directions to divide a pint between four men; but as it was dark and the actions of the men could not be well seen by those who served out the liquor, each one drank as much as he pleased....We again moved on for the camp, distant about five miles. We had not proceeded far before we entered a lane fenced on either side with rails, in which was a...puddle. The fence was taken down on one side of the road to enable us to pass round the water...;—here was fun....[O]ur stomachs being empty the whiskey took rank hold, and the poor brain fared accordingly. When the men came to the fence, not being able...to keep a regular balance between head and heels, they would pile themselves up on each side of the fence, swearing and hallooing;

some losing their arms, some their hats, some their shoes, and some themselves. Had the enemy come upon us at this time, there would have been an action worth recording....

We halted for the night at a village called Haddington [New Jersey]; we had nothing to eat.... We were put into the houses for quarters during the night. Myself and about a dozen more of the company were put into a chamber....There was no other furniture in the room excepting an old quill-wheel and an old chair frame; we procured a thick board and placed the ends upon the wheel and chair and all sat down to regale ourselves with the warmth, when the cat happening to come under the bench to partake of the bounty, the board bending by the weight upon it, both ends slipped off at once and brought us all slap to the floor; upon taking up the board to replace it again we found the poor cat, pressed as flat as a pancake, with her eyes started out two inches from her head. We did not eat her although my appetite was sharp enough to have eaten almost any thing that could be eaten....

[T]wo of the club went out [foraging] and shortly after returned with a Hissian, a cant [lively, merry] word with the soldiers, for a goose....We dressed her and then divided her amongst us; if I remember rightly, I got *one wing*....After this sumptuous repast, I lay down and slept as well as a gnawing stomach would permit....

[Martin joins a garrison on an island in the Delaware River below Philadelphia. Pounded by British cannon, they are forced to abandon the fort in mid-November.] Here ends the account of as hard and fatiguing a job, for the time it lasted, as occurred during the revolutionary war. Thomas Paine, in one of his political essays, speaking of the siege and defence of this post, says, "they had nothing but their bravery and good conduct to cover them." He spoke the truth. I was at the siege and capture of lord Cornwallis, and the hardships of that were no more to be compared with this, than the sting of a bee is to the bite of a rattlesnake. But there has been but little notice taken of it; the reason of which is, there was no Washington...there. Had there been, the affair would have been extolled to the skies. No, it was only a few officers and soldiers who accomplished it in a remote quarter of the army. Such circumstances and such troops generally get but little notice taken of them, do what they will. Great men get great praise, little men, nothing. But it always was so and always will be....

We arrived early in the morning, at a pretty village called Milltown or Mount-holly [New Jersey].... I was as near starved with hunger, as ever I wish to be. I strolled into a large yard where…was a plenty of geese, turkeys, ducks, and barn-door fowls; I obtained a piece of an ear of Indian corn, and seating myself on a pile of boards began throwing the corn to the fowls which soon drew a fine battalion of them about me, I might have taken as many as I pleased, but I took up one only, wrung off its head, dressed and washed it in the stream…, and stalked into the first house that fell in my way, invited myself into the kitchen, took down the gridiron and put my fowl to cooking upon the coals. The women of the house were all the time going and coming to and from the room; they looked at me but said nothing.…When my game was sufficiently broiled, I took it by the *hind* leg and made my exit from the house with as little ceremony as I had made my entrance. When I got into the street I devoured it after a *very* short grace.…

But, lest the reader should be disgusted at hearing so much said about "starvation," I will give him something that, perhaps, may in some measure alleviate his ill humour.

While we lay here [near Philadelphia] there was a Continental thanksgiving ordered by Congress;…we were ordered to participate in it. We had nothing to eat for two or three days previous, except what the trees of the fields and forests afforded us. But we must now have what Congress said— a sumptuous thanksgiving to close the year of high living, we had now nearly seen brought to a close. Well—to add something extraordinary to our present stock of provisions, our country, ever mindful of its suffering army, opened her sympathizing heart so wide, upon this occasion, as to give us something to make the world stare. And what do you think it was, reader?—Guess.—You cannot guess.…I will tell you: it gave each and every man *half* a gill of rice, and a *table spoon full* of vinegar!! After we had made sure of this extraordinary superabundant donation, we were ordered out to attend a meeting, and hear a sermon delivered upon the happy occasion…, a "thanksgiving sermon," what sort of one I do not know…, I had something else to think upon.…

The army was now not only starved but naked; the greatest part were not only shirtless and barefoot, but destitute of all other clothing, especially blankets. I procured a small piece of raw cowhide and made myself a pair of moccasons, which kept my feet (while they lasted) from the frozen ground, although, as I well remember, the hard edges so galled my ancles, while on a march, that it was with much difficulty and pain that I could wear them afterwards; but the only alternative I had, was to endure this inconvenience or to go barefoot, as hundreds of my companions had to, till they might be tracked by their blood upon the rough frozen ground.…

The army…marched for the Valley Forge in order to take up our winter-quarters. We were now in a truly forlorn condition,—no clothing, no provisions and as disheartened as need be. We arrived, however, at our destination a few days before christmas. Our prospect was indeed dreary.…However, there was no remedy,—no alternative but this or dispersion;—but dispersion, I believe, was not thought of,—at least, I did not think of it,—we had engaged in the defence of our injured country and were willing, nay, we were determined to persevere as long as such hardships were not altogether intolerable.…But we were now absolutely in danger of perishing, and that too, in the midst of a plentiful country. We then had but little, and often nothing to eat for days together; but now we had nothing and saw no likelihood of any betterment of our condition. Had there fallen deep snows (and it was the time of year to expect them) or even heavy and long rain-storms, the whole army must inevitably have perished. Or had the enemy, strong and well provided as he then was, thought fit to pursue us, our poor emaciated carcas[s]es must have "strewed the plain." But a kind and holy Providence took more notice and better care of us than did the country in whose service we were wearing away our lives by piecemeal.…

Chapter IV

Campaign of 1778

…As there was no cessation of duty in the army, I must commence another campaign as soon as the succeeding one ended. There was no going home and spending the winter season among friends, and procuring a new recruit of strength and spirits. No—it was one constant drill, summer and winter, like an old horse in a mill, it was a continual routine.…

[In May] I was sent off from camp in a detachment…of about three thousand men.…We marched to Barren hill, about twelve miles from Philadelphia.… We halted here…and waited for—I know not what.— A company of about a hundred Indians, from some northern tribe [Iroquois], joined us here,—there were three or four young Frenchmen with them. The Indians were stout [proud, fierce] looking fellows, and remarkably neat [elegant] for that race of mortals, (but they were Indians.) There was upon the hill…an old church built of stone, entirely divested of all its entrails [insides]. The Indians were amusing themselves and the soldiers by shooting with their bows, in and about the church. I observed something in a corner of the roof which did not appear to belong to the building, and desired an Indian who was standing near me, to shoot an arrow at it; he did so and it proved to be a cluster of bats; I should think there were nearly a bushel of them, all hanging upon one another. The house was immediately alive with them, and it was likewise instantly full of Indians and soldiers. The poor bats fared hard, it was sport for all hands....

[Pursuing the British across New Jersey in June,] we marched again and came up with the rear of the British army. We followed them several days, arriving upon their camping ground within an hour after their departure from it. We had ample opportunity to see the devastation they made in their rout[e]; cattle killed and lying about the fields and pastures, some just in the position they were in when shot down, others with a small spot of skin take off their hind quarters and a mess of steak taken out; household furniture hacked and broken to pieces; wells filled up and mechanic's and farmer's tools destroyed. It was in the height of the season of cherries, the innocent industrious creatures could not climb the trees for the fruit, but universally cut them down. Such conduct did not give the Americans any more agreeable feelings toward them than they entertained before....

[After the Battle of Monmouth in late June, the army moves to White Plains, New York.] There were three regiments of Light Infantry, composed of men from the whole main army,—it was a motly group,—Yankees, Irishmen, Buckskins and what not. The regiment that I belonged to, was made up of about one half New-Englanders and the remainder were chiefly Pennsylvanians,—two setts of people as opposite in manners and customs as light and darkness, consequently there was not much cordialty subsisting between us; for, to tell the sober truth, I had in those days, as lief [willingly] have been incorporated with a tribe of western Indians, as with any of the southern troops; especially of those which consisted mostly (as the Pennsylvanians did,) of foreigners. But I *was* among them and in the same regiment too, and under their officers, (but the officers, in general, were gentlemen,) and had to do duty with them; to make a bad matter worse, I was often, when on duty, the only Yankee that happened to be on the same tour for several days together. "The bloody Yankee," or "the d——d Yankee," was the mildest epithets that they would bestow upon me at such times....

Chapter VI

Campaign of 1780

...The guard kept at Woodbridge [New Jersey], being so small, and so far from the troops, and so near the enemy [on Staten Island] that they were obliged to be constantly on the alert. We had three different houses that we occupied alternately, during the night; the first was an empty house, the second the parson's house, and the third a farmer's house; we had to remove from one to the other of these houses three times every night, from fear of being surprised by the enemy. There was no trusting the inhabitants, for many of them were friendly to the British, and we did not know who were or who were not, and consequently, were distrustful of them all, unless it were one or two....

[One night,] about the time the moon was setting, which was about ten o'clock, they [Loyalist "Refugees"] came....The first sentinel that occupied that post had not stood out his trick [turn], before he saw them coming; he immediately hailed them by the usual question, "who comes there?" they answered him, that if he would not discharge his piece, they would not hurt him, but if he did they would kill him. The sentinel being true to his trust, paid no regard to their threats, but fired his piece and ran for the house to alarm the guard; in his way he had to cross a hedge fence, in passing which, he got entangled in the bushes, as it was supposed, and the enemy coming up thrust a bayonet through him, they then inflicted twelve more wounds upon him with bayonets, and rushed on for the house, to massacre the remainder of the guard, but they had taken the alarm and left the house....Mr. Holstead [owner of the point where the enemy landed] had two young daughters in the house, one of which secreted herself in a closet and remained throughout the whole transaction undiscovered; the other they caught, and compelled to light a candle, and attend them about the house in search of the Rebels, but without finding any, or offering any other abuse to the young lady, (which was indeed a wonder.) When they could find none to wreak their vengeance upon, they cut open the knapsacks of the guard, and strewed the Indian meal about the floor, laughing at the poverty of the Yankee soldiery, who had nothing but hog's fodder, as they termed it, to eat; after they had done all the mischief they could in the house, they proceeded to the barn and drove off five or six head of Mr. Holstead's young cattle, took them down upon the point and killed them, and went off in their boats, that had come across from the island for that purpose, to their den among the British....

Such manoeuvres the British continued to exhibit the whole time we were stationed here, but could never do any other damage to us than killing the poor Twist, (the name of the young man.) Unfortunate young man! I could not restrain my tears, when I saw him the next day, with his breast like a sieve, caused by the wounds. He lost his own life by endeavouring to save the lives of others; massacred by his own country-men, who ought to have been fighting in the common cause of the country, instead of murdering him. I have been more particular in relating this circumstance, that the reader may be informed what people there were in the times of the revolution. Mr. Holstead told me that almost the whole of his neighborhood had joined the enemy and that his next door neighbour was in this very party....

For several days after we rejoined the army [at Basking Ridge, New Jersey, in late May], we got a lit-tle musty bread, and a little beef, about every other day, but this lasted only a short time and then we got nothing at all. The men were now exasperated beyond endurance; they could not stand it any longer; they saw no other alternative but to starve to death, or break up the army, give all up and go home. This was a hard matter for the soldiers to think upon; they were truly patriotic; they loved their country, and they had already suffered every thing short of death in its cause; and now, after such extreme hardships to give up all, was too much; but to starve to death was too much also. What was to be done?—Here was the army starved and naked, and there their coun-try sitting still and expecting the army to do notable things while fainting from sheer starvation. All things considered, the army was not to be blamed. Reader, suffer what we did and you will say so too.

We had borne as along as human nature could endure, and to bear longer we considered folly. Accordingly, one pleasant day, the men spent the most of their time upon the parade, growling like soreheaded dogs; at evening roll-call they began to show their dissatisfaction, by snapping at the offi-cers, and acting contrary to their orders; after their dismissal from the parade, the officers went, as usual, to their quarters, except the Adjutant, who happened to remain, giving details for next day's duty to the orderly sergeants, or some other business, when the men (none of whom had left the parade) began to make him sensible that they had something in train [planned]; he said something that did not altogether accord with the soldiers' ideas of propriety, one of the men retorted, the Adjutant called him a mutinous rascal, or some such epithet, and then left the parade.

This man, then stamping the butt of his musket upon the ground, as much as to say, I am in a passion, called out, "who will parade with me?" The whole regiment immediately fell in and formed. We had made no plans for our future operations, but while we were consult-ing how to proceed, the fourth regiment, which lay on our left, formed, and came and paraded with us. We now concluded to go in a body to the other two regiments that belonged to our brigade, and induce them to join with us; these regiments lay forty or fifty rods in front of us, with a brook and bushes between. We did not wish to have any one in particular to com-mand, lest he might be singled out for a Court Martial to exercise its clemency upon; we therefore gave directions to the drummers to give certain signals on the drums; at the first signal we shouldered our arms, at the second we faced, at the third we began our march to join with the other two regiments, and went off with music playing. By this time our officers had obtained knowledge of our military manoeuvre-ing, and some of them had run across the brook, by a nearer way than we had taken, (it being now quite dark,) and informed the officers of those regiments of our approach and supposed intentions. These officers ordered their men to parade as quick as possible *with-out* arms; when that was done, they stationed a camp guard, that happened to be near at hand, between the men and their huts, which prevented them from entering and taking their arms, which they were very anxious to do....

When we found the officers had been too crafty for us we returned with grumbling instead of music, the officers following in the rear growling in con-cert. One of the men in the rear calling out, "halt in front," the officers seized upon him like wolves on a sheep, and dragged him out of the ranks, intending to make an example of him, for being a "mutinous rascal," but the bayonets of the men pointing at their breasts as thick as hatchel teeth [a farming tool], com-pelled them quickly to relinquish their hold of him. We marched back to our own parade and then formed again; the officers now began to coax us to disperse to our quarters, but that had no more effect upon us than their threats....

Our stir did us some good in the end, for we had provisions directly after, so we had no great cause for complaint for some time....

Another affair happened...which did not set very well on my stomach at the time. I had been on a detached party for four of five days and had had nothing to eat, for at least eight and forty hours of the latter part of the time. When I came to camp there was nothing there; I strolled off to where some butchers were killing cattle, as I supposed, for the General officers, (for they must have victuals, let the poor men fare as they would,) and by some means procured an old ox's liver; I then went home and soon had a quantity of it in my kettle; the more I seethed [boiled] it the harder it grew, but I soon filled my empty stomach with it, and, it being night, I turned in; I had not slept long before I awoke, feeling... "dreadfully." I worried it out till morning, when, as soon as I thought I could call upon the doctors, without too much disturbing their honours, I applied to one for relief; he gave me a large dose of tartar-emetic [a substance to cause vomiting], the usual remedy in the army for all disorders, even sore eyes....I waited sometime for it [to take effect], but growing impatient, I wandered off into the fields and bushes to see what effect exercise would have; I had not strolled a half or three fourths of a mile from camp, when it took full hold of my gizzard; I then sat down...and discharged the hard junks of liver like grapeshot from a fieldpiece....O, I thought I *must* die in good earnest. The liver still kept coming, and I looked at every heave for my own liver to come next, but that happened to be too well fastened to part from its moorings. Perhaps the reader will think this a trifling matter, happening in the ordinary course of things, but I think it a "suffering," and not a small one neither, "of a revolutionary soldier."...

Chapter VII

Campaign of 1781

...[Camped on the Lower Hudson in May, Martin joins a scouting party to look for armed Loyalists known as "Cowboys."] [W]e set out, and had but just entered the wood when we found ourselves flanked by thirty or forty Cowboys, who gave us a hearty welcome to their assumed territories and we returned the compliment; but a kind Providence protected every man of us from injury although we were within ten rods of the enemy. They immediately rushed from their covert, before we had time to reload our pieces; consequently, we had no other alternative but to get off as well and as fast as we could. They did not fire upon us again, but gave us chase, for what reason I know not. I was soon in the rear of my party, which had to cross the fence composed of old posts and rails with trees plashed [bent and interwoven] down upon it. When I arrived at the fence, the foremost of the enemy was not more than six or eight rods distant, all running after us helter-skelter, without any order; my men had all crossed the fence in safety, I alone was to

suffer. I endeavoured to get over the fence across two or three of the trees that were plashed down; some how or other, I blundered and fell over, and caught my right foot in a place where a tree had split partly from the stump, here I hung as fast as though my foot had been in the stocks..., while my body hung down perpendicularly; I could barely reach the ground with my hands, and, of course, could make but little exertion to clear myself from the limbs. The commander of the enemy came to the fence and the first compliment I received from him was a stroke with his hanger [sword] across my leg, just under or below the knee-pan, which laid the bone bare. I could see him through the fence and knew him; he was, when we were boys, one of my most familiar playmates, was with me, a messmate, in the campaign of 1776, had enlisted during the war in 1777, but sometimes before this, had deserted to the enemy, having been coaxed off by an old harridan, to whose daughter he had taken a fancy; the old hag of a mother, living in the vicinity of the British, easily inveigled him away. He was a smart active fellow, and soon got command of a gang of Refugee-cowboy plunderers. When he had had his hack at my shins, I began to think it was "neck or nothing," and making one desperate effort, I cleared my foot by leaving my shoe behind, before he could have the second stroke at me. He knew me as well as I did him, for as soon as he saw me clear of the fence and out of the reach of his sword, he called me by name, and told me to surrender myself and he would give me good quarters [terms of surrender];—thought I, you will wait till I ask them of you. I sprang up and ran till I came to my party who were about a hundred rods ahead....The enemy never fired a shot at me all the time I was running from them....Whether his conscience smote him and he prevented them from firing at me; or, whether they were unprepared, not having had time to reload their pieces in their pursuit of us, or from what other cause, I know not....

[By fall, Martin is outside of Yorktown, Virginia, with "miners" and "sappers," specialists in trench warfare and sieges.] We now began to make preparations for laying close siege to the enemy. We had holed him and nothing remained but to dig him out. Accordingly, after taking every precaution to prevent his escape..., on the fifth of October we began to put our plans into execution....

It was a very dark and rainy night....[T]here came a man alone to us..., and inquired for the Engineers. We now began to be a little jealous [worried] for our safety, being alone and without arms, and within forty rods of the British trenches. The stranger inquired what troops we were; talked familiarly with us a few minutes, when, being informed which way the officers had gone, he went off in the same direction, after strictly charging us, in case we should be taken prisoners, not to discover to the enemy what troops we were. We were obliged to him for his kind advice, but we considered ourselves as standing in no great need of it....

In a short time the Engineers returned and the aforementioned stranger with them; they discoursed together sometime, when, by the officers calling him "Your Excellency," we discovered that it was Gen. Washington. Had we dared, we might have cautioned him for exposing himself so carelessly to danger at such a time, and doubtless he would have taken it in good part if we had. But nothing ill happened to either him or ourselves....

I do not remember, exactly, the number of days we were employed before we got our batteries in readiness to open upon the enemy, but think it was not more than two or three. The French [allies], who were upon our left, had completed their batteries a few hours before us, but were not allowed to discharge their pieces till the American batteries were ready.... I was in the trenches the day that the batteries were to be opened; all were upon the tiptoe of expectation and impatience to see the signal given to open the whole line of batteries, which was to be the hoisting of the American flag.... About noon the much wished for signal went up. I confess I felt a secret pride swell in my heart when I saw the "star spangled banner" waving majestically in the very faces of our implacable adversaries; it appeared like an omen of success to our enterprize, and so it proved in reality. A simultaneous discharge of all the guns in the line followed; the French troops accompanying it with "Huzza for the Americans!" It was said that the first shell sent from our batteries, entered an elegant house, formerly owned or occupied by the Secretary of State under the British government, and burnt directly over a table surrounded by a large party of British officers at dinner, killing and wounding a number of them;— this was a warmday [sic] to the British.

The siege was carried on warmly for several days, when most of the guns in the enemy's works were silenced....[B]efore dark I was informed of the whole plan, which was to storm the redoubts [small forts], the one by the Americans and the other by the French. The Sappers and Miners were furnished with axes, and were to proceed in front and cut a passage for the troops through the abatis [defensive

barricades], which are composed of the tops of trees, the small branches cut off with a slanting stroke which renders them as sharp as spikes....At dark the detachment was formed and advanced beyond the trenches, and lay down on the ground to await the signal for advancing to the attack, which was to be three shells from a certain battery near where we were lying.... Our watchword was "Rochambeau," the commander of the French forces' name, a good watchword, for being pronounced Ro-sham-bow, it sounded, when pronounced quick, like rush-on-boys. We had not lain here long before the expected signal was given, for us and the French..., by the three shells with their fiery trains mounting the air in quick succession. The word up, up, was then reiterated through the detachment. We immediately moved silently on toward the redoubt we were to attack, with unloaded muskets. Just as we arrived at the abatis, the enemy discovered us and directly opened a sharp fire upon us....As soon as the firing began, our people began to cry, "the fort's our own!" and it was "rush on boys." The Sappers and Miners soon cleared a passage for the Infantry, who entered it rapidly. Our Miners were ordered not to enter the fort, but there was no stopping them. "We will go," said they; "then go to the d—l," said the commanding officer of our corps, "if you will." I could not pass at the entrance we had made, it was so crowded; I therefore forced a passage at a place where I saw our shot had cut away some of the abatis; several others entered at the same place. While passing, a man at my side received a ball in his head and fell under my feet, crying out bitterly. While crossing the trench, the enemy threw hand grenades, (small shells) into it; they were so thick that I at first thought them cartridge papers on fire; but was soon undeceived by their cracking. As I mounted the breastwork, I met an old associate hitching himself down into the trench; I knew him by the light of the enemy's musketry, it was so vivid. The fort was taken, and all quiet in a very short time. Immediately after the firing ceased, I went out to see what had become of my wounded friend and the other that fell in the passage—they were both dead....

[U]pon the seventeenth day of October...[Lord Cornwallis] requested a cessation of hostilities for, I think, twenty-four hours, when commissioners from both armies met at a house between the lines, to agree upon articles of capitulation. We waited with anxiety the termination of the armistice, and as the time drew nearer our anxiety increased. The time at length arrived,—it passed, and all remained quiet.— And now we concluded that we had obtained what we had taken so much pains for....Before night we were informed that the British had surrendered and that the siege was ended.

The next day we were ordered to put ourselves in as good order as our circumstances would admit, to see...the British army march out and stack their arms....After breakfast, on the nineteenth, we were marched on to the ground and paraded on the right-hand side of the road, and the French forces on the left. We waited two or three hours before the British made their appearance;...they were compelled at last..., to appear, all armed, with bayonets fixed, drums beating, and faces lengthening..., the Americans and French beating a march as they passed out between them. It was a noble sight to us, and the more so, as it seemed to promise a speedy conclusion to the contest....The British paid the Americans, seemingly, but little attention as they passed them, but they eyed the French with considerable malice....They marched to the place appointed and stacked their arms; they then returned to the town....

During the siege, we saw in the woods herds of Negroes which lord Cornwallis, (after he had inveigled them from their proprietors,) in love and pity to them, had turned adrift with no other recompense for their confidence in his humanity, than the small pox for their bounty and starvation and death for their wages. They might be seen scattered about in every direction, dead and dying, with pieces of ears of burnt Indian corn in the hands and mouths, even of those that were dead. After the siege was ended many of the owners of these deluded creatures, came to our camp and engaged some of our men to take them up....I saw several of those miserable wretches delivered to their master; they came before him under a very powerful fit of the ague [fever and chills]. He told them that he gave them the free choice, either to go with him or remain where they were; that he would not injure a hair of their heads if they returned with him to their duty. Had the poor souls received a reprieve at the gallows, they would not have been more overjoyed than they appeared to be at what he promised them....I had a share in one of them by assisting in taking him up; the fortune I acquired was small, only one dollar....

Chapter IX

Campaign of 1783

[Martin spends the winter of 1782–1783 stationed at New Windsor, an army camp on the west bank of the Hudson River above West Point.]...Time thus passed on to the nineteenth of April, when we had general orders read [that Congress had approved preliminary articles of peace] which satisfied the most skeptical, that the war was over, and the prize won for which we had been contending through eight tedious years. But the soldiers said but very little about it, their chief thoughts were more closely fixed upon their situation as it respected the figure they were to exhibit upon their leaving the army and becoming citizens. Starved, ragged and meagre, not a cent to help themselves with, and no means or method in view to remedy or alleviate their condition; this was appaling in the extreme....

I confess, after all, that my anticipation of the happiness I should experience upon such a day as this, was not realized; I can assure the reader that there was as much sorrow as joy transfused on the occasion. We had lived together as a family of brothers for several years (setting aside some little family squabbles, like most other families,) had shared with each other the hardships, dangers and sufferings incident to a soldier's life, had sympathized with each other in trouble and sickness; had assisted in bearing each other's burdens, or strove to make them lighter by council and advice; had endeavoured to conceal each other's faults, or make them appear in as good a light as they would bear....And now we were to be (the greater part of us) parted forever; as unconditionally separated, as though the grave lay between us....[W]e were young men, and had warm hearts. I question if there was a corps in the army that parted with more regret than ours did, the New-Englanders in particular, Ah! it was a serious time....

....[Discharged at last, Martin teaches school in a Dutch community near West Point through the winter of 1783–84.] When the spring opened I bid my Dutch friends adieu, and set my face to the eastward, and made no material halt till I arrived in the, now, State of Maine, in the year 1784, where I have remained ever since....And here I would make an end of my tedious narrative, but that I deem it necessary to make a few short observations relative to what I have said....

When those who engaged to serve during the war, enlisted, they were promised a hundred acres of land, each, which was to be in their own or the adjoining States. When the country had drained the last drop of service it could screw out of the poor soldiers, they were turned adrift like old worn out horses, and nothing said about land to pasture them upon. Congress did, indeed, appropriate lands under the denomination of "Soldier's lands," in Ohio State, or some State, or a future state; but no care was taken that the soldiers should get them. No agents were appointed to see that the poor fellows ever got possession of their lands; no one ever took the least care about it, except a pack of speculators, who were driving about the country like so many evil spirits, endeavouring to pluck the last feather from the soldiers. The soldiers were ignorant of the ways and means to obtain their bounty lands, and there was no one appointed to inform them. The truth was, none cared for them; the country was served, and faithfully served, and that was all that was deemed necessary....

They were likewise promised...articles of clothing per year....How often have I had to lie whole stormy cold nights in a wood, on a field, or a bleak hill, with such blankets and other clothing like them, with nothing but the canopy of the heavens to cover me, all this too in the heart of winter, when a New-England farmer, if his cattle had been in my situation, would not have slept a wink from sheer anxiety for them. And if I stepped into a house to warm me, when passing, wet to the skin and almost dead with cold, hunger and fatigue, what scornful looks and hard words have I experienced.

Almost every one has heard of the soldiers of the Revolution being tracked by the blood of their feet on the frozen ground. This is literally true; and the thousandth part of their sufferings has not, nor ever will be told. That the country was young and poor, at that time, I am willing to allow; but young people are generally modest, especially females. Now, I think the country, (although of the feminine gender, for we say, she, and her, of it) showed but little modesty at the time alluded to, for she appeared to think her soldiers had no private parts; for on our march from the Valley forge, through the Jerseys, and at the boasted battle of Monmouth, a fourth part of the troops had not a scrip of any thing but their ragged shift-flaps to cover their nakedness....

As to provision of victuals, I have said a great deal already; but ten times as much might be said and not get to the end of the chapter. When we engaged in the service we were promised the following articles for a ration.—One pound of good and wholesome fresh or salt beef, or three fourths of a pound of good salt pork, a pound of good flour, soft or hard bread, a quart of salt to every hundred pounds of fresh beef, quart of vinegar to a hundred rations, a gill of rum, brandy or whiskey per day....But we never received what was allowed us. Oftentimes have I gone one, two, three, and even four days without a morsel....

We were, also, promised six dollars and two thirds a month, to be paid us monthly; and how did we fare in this particular? Why, as we did in every other. I received the six dollars and two thirds, till (if I remember rightly) the month of August, 1777, when paying ceased. And what was six dollars and sixty-seven cents of this "Continental currency" as it was called, worth? it was scarcely enough to procure a man a dinner....I received [from the French] one month's pay in specie [coins]...in the year 1781, and except that, I never received any pay worth the name while I belonged to the army....It is provoking to think of it. The country was rigorous in exacting my compliance to *my* engagements to a punctilio, but equally careless in performing her contracts with me; and why so? One reason was, because she had all the power in her own hands, and I had none. Such things ought not to be....

And now I think it is time to draw to a close, (and so say I, says the reader,) in truth, when I began this narrative, I thought a very few pages would contain it, but as occurrences returned to my memory, and one thing brought another to mind, I could not stop, for as soon as I had let one thought through my mind, another would step up and ask for admittance. And now, dear reader, if any such should be found, I will come to a close and trespass upon your time no longer, time that may, doubtless, be spent to more advantage than reading the "Adventures and Sufferings" of a private soldier. But if you have been really desirous to hear a part, and a part only, of the hardships of some of that army that achieved our Independence, I can say I am sorry you have not had an abler pen than mine to give you the requisite information.

To conclude. Whoever has the patience to follow me to the end of this rhapsody, I will confess that I think he must have almost as great a share of perseverance in reading it as I had to go through the hardships and dangers it records—And now, kind reader, I bid you a cordial and long farewell....

CHAPTER 10

Parson Weems Invents George Washington

"I can't tell a lie, Pa"

Just as we assume that Americans were eager for independence (Chapter 7), just as we overlook how crucial rebels thought writing constitutions was (Chapter 8), just as we forget how brutal and complicated the war was (Chapter 9), so we tend to believe that the Revolutionary era ended with George Washington's inauguration as president in 1789. People at the time, however, were less certain that this chapter of the American saga was closed—much less that the story would have a happy ending. History and political theory alike taught that republics such as the United States were fragile, prone to anarchy or tyranny. The nation's first constitution, the Articles of Confederation, had lived just seven years, after all; few would have predicted that its successor would last thirty-one times longer (and counting).

Many questions awaited answers. The new constitution had barely passed in some states: Would its many opponents now accept it? The document itself gave Congress power to "provide for the...general Welfare of the United States" and "to make all Laws which shall be necessary and proper": Who would decide what such phrases meant? The 1780s had seen scattered rebellions against state governments: Would these subside, or spread? To the west, powerful Indian nations bitterly opposed American encroachment onto their lands: could they be appeased, or conquered? To the east, across the Atlantic, were Britain and France: Would these superpowers leave the fledgling nation alone, or try to recolonize it? Reading his Inaugural Address that spring day in 1789, President Washington's hands trembled and his voice shook, betraying his "anxieties" and "despondence" about "the magnitude and difficulty of the trust to which the voice of my Country called me."[1]

Washington had reason to worry: The next decade would be among the most dangerous in American history. Debates over the Constitution's meaning and the country's very character combined with disagreements over whether to support Britain or France in their European struggles to divide the nation's leaders into Federalist and Republican parties—and this in an age when most considered joining a political party tantamount to treason. Nor was that all: A brawl on the floor of Congress; a close, bitter presidential election in 1800 between the Federalist John Adams and the Republican Thomas Jefferson that had Republican militia units massing for a march on the nation's capital; vicious attacks on that "blasted tyrant of America," that "ruffian deserving the curses of mankind," "the blind, bald, toothless, querulous ADAMS," and on Jefferson, that "contemptible hypocrite," "howling atheist," "red-headed son of a bitch"—these were the political realities of the 1790s. Add to this Indian wars and a tax revolt in western Pennsylvania, and it is clear why Americans still fretted about the state of the union.[2]

One reason for the turmoil, some thought, was that the United States was a nation in name only. The Constitution was in place, but the structure itself remained unfinished because the country lacked a national spirit, a sense of common past and common destiny. European nations could trace their roots back centuries to real or mythical founders, steeped in fables about Romulus and Remus (Rome), Charlemagne and Joan of Arc (France), King Arthur and Camelot (England). They could point to battles and heroes, to poets and artists who sang the praises of those heroes and thereby cultivated, over generations, a sense of national identity. America, born yesterday, had none of these, and Americans knew it. "We are one people in name," lamented South Carolinian David Ramsay in 1792, "but do not know half enough of each other to...cement our friendship....We are too widely disseminated over an extensive country and too much diversified by different customs and forms of government to feel as one people[,] which," he concluded plaintively, "we really are." Ramsay, like other Americans, thirsted for a history and a hero that would help them become a people.[3]

Perhaps no one knew better what Americans wanted and needed than Mason Locke Weems (1759–1825). An itinerant book peddler who, starting in the early 1790s, traveled widely from New York to Georgia selling volumes from what he called "his FLYING LIBRARY," Weems had followed a circuitous path to that occupation. Born in Maryland to a wealthy family, he spent much of the Revolutionary War studying in Edinburgh and London, first to become a physician, then to enter the ministry. Ordained an Anglican clergyman in 1784 (he is often called "Parson Weems"), the young man returned to America at a time when Anglicanism, England's official religion, was—not surprisingly!—unpopular. (It did not help that sermons might not have been his strong suit: Though some commended Weems's "Zeal & Attention to ye Duties of his sacred Office," according to one listener "no one could hear him preach without wanting to laugh.")[4]

Soon enough, Weems found his true calling in the book trade—"this most important of all human pursuits"—an alternative means to advance his aims of reforming morals, promoting nationalism, and making money. A tireless worker, to drum up business he would "toil from door to door throughout Philad[elphi]a & the towns of Jersey" or go "from breakfast till tea constantly engag[e]d in *walking, talking, pleading & preaching* to the Multitudes." A shrewd promoter, he timed his visits to coincide with holidays or court days, then drew a crowd with a sermon or a tune on his fiddle. It paid, once he had their attention, to figure out their tastes in reading; indeed, Weems was a "super-salesman," "a one-man market research enterprise," adept, as he put it, at choosing "subjects calculated to *strike* the Popular Curiosity." Observes historian Marcus Cunliffe, Weems found ordinary Americans "religiously minded," "ferociously patriotic," and "eager for color and excitement." Short books "printed in very large numbers and properly *distributed*," he assured the Philadelphia publisher Mathew Carey in January 1797, "wd prove an immense revenue....If you coud get the life of...Men whose courage and Abilities, whose patriotism and Exploits have won the love and admiration of the American people, printed in small volumes...," Weems concluded, "you wd, without doubt, sell an immense number of them" as long as they were "*cheap*—mighty cheap— monstrous cheap" so that everyone, including "small fry," could afford them. Three years later Weems would write and publish just that kind of book himself: It was about George Washington.[5]

To us, living in the long shadow cast by Washington's legend, he seems the obvious—indeed, the only—choice. To many at the time, too, Washington loomed large in the American hall of fame. Ever since June 1775, when Congress gave the Virginian command of the newly created Continental Army, people had invested in him their most fervent hopes for the American cause. They named children and towns after him, and started calling him "our political Father." "Throughout all the land," reported a French observer in 1781, "he appears like a benevolent god; old men, women, children[,] they all flock eagerly to catch a glimpse of him when he travels." "I have seen him!" exclaimed a young woman in 1789. "I never saw a human being that looked so great and noble as he does. I could fall down on my knees before him."[6]

Given this veneration, it is surprising that, listing possible subjects for heroic treatment in his 1797 letter to Carey, Weems mentioned "Genl. [Anthony] Wayne, [Israel] Putnam, [Nathanael] Green[e] &c."—hardly household names today—but not George Washington.[7] Perhaps this was because Washington, just then leaving the presidency after two terms, had become too controversial. For all the praise, many Americans were not inclined to kneel before him. "[T]hose who knew him well and talked with him," notes historian Gordon Wood, "were often disappointed. He never seemed to have very much to say." John Adams sneered that Washington "was too illiterate, unlearned, [and] unread for his station and reputation," while Thomas Jefferson thought his "colloquial [conversational] talents were not above mediocrity." One visitor felt "a repulsive coldness...under a courteous demeanor."[8]

No less repulsive to some Americans was the tone of Washington's presidency. His preference for bows over handshakes, the celebration of his birthday, his image on coins—all looked uncomfortably like kingship. Add to this his policies—favoring Britain over France, for example—and he made enemies aplenty. "Washington's house [in the capital] was surrounded by an innumerable multitude," reported Adams, "from day to day huzzaing, demanding war against England, cursing Washington." While Thomas Paine labeled him a "treacherous" "hypocrite," newspapers called him everything from a traitor in the war to a "most horrid swearer and blasphemer," from a "usurper with dark schemes of ambition" to a man with "all the insolence of an Emperor of Rome." While some talked impeachment, others—in Virginia, no less—raised their glasses to toast "A speedy Death to General Washington."[9]

It was going to be hard to make this man into a myth. Nonetheless, by the summer of 1799 Weems had chosen his hero and was hard at work on " 'The Beauties of Washington.' Tis artfully drawn up," he boasted, "enlivend with anecdotes, and in my humble opinion"—modesty was not among Weems's virtues—"marvellously fitted, *'ad captandum—gustum populi Americani!!!*[']*"* (for charming the taste of the American people). When Washington died that December, the bookseller was delighted. "I've something to whisper in your lug [ear]," he wrote Carey. "Washington, you know is gone! Millions are gaping to read something about him. I am very nearly primd and cockd for 'em." Soon Weems had a first edition off the press—ever the promoter, he published it on February 22, 1800, his hero's birthday—and into his "Flying Library." More editions and more enlivening anecdotes followed (the cherry tree story first showed up in the 1806 version), for, as he cheerfully reminded Carey, there is "a great deal of money lying in the bones of old George."[10]

Though Weems was delighted with his work, many were not. Reviewers found the "ludicrous" book "full of ridiculous exaggeration," "fanaticism and absurdity." Historians have generally agreed, calling it "pernicious drivel" marred by "absurdities and deliberately false inventions," "silly" "rubbish" and "slush" that is flawed by "grotesque and wholly imaginary stories." Reading the excerpts below, you might be inclined to join the chorus of condemnation, for the writing and stories seem laughably bad: *All those words in italics!! All those exclamation marks!! All that weeping!!*[11]

Ridiculous, too, is Weems's habit of (to put it nicely) stretching the truth. On the 1809 edition's title page, for example, he boasted that he was "Formerly Rector [minister] of Mount-Vernon Parish," figuring few would know that there was no such parish. (After 1795, Weems, when not on the road, lived some twenty miles from Washington's home; they met at least once, in 1787, and exchanged a few letters.)[12] In that edition, Weems also announced that the cherry tree story is "too true to be doubted." Think about that, and imagine the reaction if *you* ever used that phrase to prove a point.

For all its flaws, *The Life of Washington* deserves our attention, if for no other reason than it was, as Weems predicted, a phenomenal best seller. Before his death in 1825, the book went through twenty-nine printings; during the next century there were fifty-one more. "[A]way back in my childhood, the earliest days of my being able to read," recalled Abraham Lincoln in 1861, talking of books that had had a profound impact on him, "I got hold of a small book, Weem[s]'s Life of Washington." In an age of "Biographical Mania," when Americans hungered for stories about famous people that would instruct them in proper ways of living and escort them into the private lives of public figures, *The Life of Washington* was easily the most popular biography of the day. Just as the runaway best seller of the 1770s, *Common Sense* (Chapter 7), helps us understand America on the eve of independence, so the blockbuster of the next generation offers a window onto the new American nation.[13]

From the passages included here (less than 20% of the ninth, and last, edition), it can be hard to appreciate one facet of the book's appeal. Weems went on and on about topics that seem irrelevant in a Washington biography, while slighting other subjects that should have been central. Almost a third of the volume gives a blow-by-blow account of the American Revolution, including many events Washington had no part in. His two terms as president, on the other hand, occupy less than one sixth of the book, and half of that section reproduced Washington's "Farewell Address to the American People," an eloquent plea for national unity. It is worth asking why Weems included—and excluded—what he did.

For all that it omitted, distorted, or simply made up, *The Life of Washington* proves that Weems knew how to draw readers in and then to keep them entranced. Packed with "Curious Anecdotes" (as the title page promised) about parents and children, piety and patriotism, English kings and Indian chiefs, the book was easy to read and as emotionally charged as *Common Sense* (albeit in a different way). It says much about what a true American should be—and, no less important, what a true American should *not* be. *The Life of Washington* spoke to deep and powerful needs in the new and still-fragile American nation. For better or worse, we live with Weems's Washington still.

Questions for Consideration and Conversation

1. Explain the popularity of this work in the new American nation.
2. How does Weems's Washington compare to the man you knew from other sources?
3. What is the most illuminating passage in this text, the one you consider most important or most amusing?
4. Would Dr. Alexander Hamilton (Chapter 5) consider George Washington a gentleman?
5. Did Weems believe that "all men are created equal"? Could anyone, then, become a Washington?
6. We know from other sources that Washington was twenty-something when he recruited Iroquois, Catawba, and other Indian men to face the French in the 1750s, then marched and fought alongside them. So, too, during the Revolutionary War, men from various Indian nations joined Washington's cause, as Joseph Plumb Martin saw (Chapter 9). As late as 1796, a dozen Catawbas dropped in on the president at Mount Vernon. Why do you suppose Weems omitted incidents like these from his collection of "Curious Anecdotes"? What tales about Indians did he put in their place, and what does that substitution reveal about American national identity?
7. Both *The Life of Washington* and Benjamin Franklin's *Autobiography* (Chapter 6) were popular among Americans in the early nineteenth century. Did the two texts teach the same lessons, the same values, or did they contradict one another? Is, for example, Franklin's maxim, "Use no hurtful deceit," the same as Washington's *"I can't tell a lie, Pa"*?

Endnotes

1. Marcus Cunliffe, *George Washington: Man and Monument*, Revised edition (New York, 1982), 118; Barry Schwartz, *George Washington: The Making of an American Symbol* (New York, 1987), 152 (Inaugural speech).

2. John C. Miller, *The Federalist Era, 1789–1801* (New York, 1960), 233 (Adams), 265 ("atheist"), 270 ("hypocrite"); Marshall Smelser, *The Democratic Republic, 1801–1815* (New York, 1968), 1 ("red-headed"). See James Roger Sharp, *American Politics in the Early Republic: The New Nation in Crisis* (New Haven, CT, 1993).

3. Daniel J. Boorstin, *The Americans: The National Experience* (New York, 1965), 338 (other nations); Lawrence J. Friedman, *Inventors of the Promised Land* (New York, 1975), 25 (Ramsay).

4. Marcus Cunliffe, "Introduction," in Mason L. Weems, *The Life of Washington*, ed. Cunliffe (Cambridge, MA, 1962), xlvi ("FLYING"), lv ("laugh"); François Furstenberg, *In the Name of the Father: Washington's Legacy, Slavery, and the Making of a Nation* (New York, 2006), 109 ("Zeal").

5. Boorstin, *National Experience*, 340 ("supersalesman," "market research"); Cunliffe, "Introduction," *Life of Washington*, xiv ("Curiosity," "artfully"), xliii (ordinary Americans); Furstenberg, *In the Name of the Father*, 132 ("cheap," "small fry"), 136–37 ("Jersey," "Multitudes"), 144 ("human pursuits"). For his being interested in more than money, see Furstenberg, *In the Name of the Father*, 111–12.

6. Richard Brookhiser, *Founding Father: Rediscovering George Washington* (New York, 1996), 159 ("political father"); Schwartz, *Washington*, 23 (1781), 49 (1789).

7. Cunliffe, "Introduction," *Life of Washington*, xiv.

8. Gordon S. Wood, "The Greatness of George Washington," in Don Higginbotham, ed., *George Washington Reconsidered* (Charlottesville, VA, 2001), 312 (Wood, Adams, Jefferson); Cunliffe, *Washington*, 149 ("coldness").

9. Schwartz, *Washington*, 66–67 (Adams); John R. Howe, "Republican Thought and the Political Violence of the 1790s," *American Quarterly*, 19 (1967), 149 (Paine, toast).

10. Cunliffe, "Introduction," *Life of Washington*, xiv, xv, xviii–xix. The publication date is noted in Furstenberg, *In the Name of the Father*, 130.

11. Cunliffe, "Introduction," *Life of Washington*, xxiv–xxvi.

12. Furstenberg, *In the Name of the Father*, 110. Furstenberg writes that after their first meeting in March 1787 "Weems occasionally *came into contact* with Washington during the next few years" (110), but he quotes a 1792 Weems letter to the President, saying "I was *once* introduced to your Excellency…some years ago," making it unclear if "came into contact" involved writing letters or actual conversations (284, n. 22, emphasis added).

13. Cunliffe, "Introduction," *Life of Washington*, xxii (Lincoln); Scott E. Casper, *Constructing American Lives: Biography and Culture in Nineteenth-Century America* (Chapel Hill, NC, 1999), 2 ("Mania"); see also Christopher Harris, *Public Lives, Private Virtues: Images of Revolutionary War Heroes, 1782–1832* (New York, 2000).

M. L. WEEMS, *THE LIFE OF GEORGE WASHINGTON; WITH CURIOUS ANECDOTES, EQUALLY HONOURABLE TO HIMSELF AND EXEMPLARY TO HIS YOUNG COUNTRYMEN* (1809)

Source: M. L. Weems, *The Life of George Washington; with Curious Anecdotes, Equally Honourable to Himself and Exemplary to His Young Countrymen.* Ninth Edition…. Greatly Improved. Philadelphia, 1809.

Chapter I…

"*AH, gentlemen!*"—exclaimed [French leader Napoleon] Bonaparte—'twas just as he was about to embark for Egypt…some young Americans happening at Toulon, and anxious to see the mighty Corsican, had obtained the honour of an introduction to him. Scarcely were past the customary salutations, when he eagerly asked, "*how fares your countryman, the great* WASHINGTON?" "He was very well," replied the youths, brightening at the thought that they were the countrymen of Washington; "he was very well, general, when we left America."—"*Ah, gentlemen!*" rejoined he, "*Washington can never be otherwise than well:—The measure of his fame is full—Posterity shall talk of him with reverence as the founder of a great empire, when my name shall be lost in the vortex of Revolutions!*"

Who then that has a spark of virtuous curiosity, but must wish to know the history of him whose name could thus awaken the sigh even of Bonaparte? But is not his history *already* known? Have not a thousand orators spread his fame abroad...? Yes, they have indeed spread his fame...as Generalissimo of the armies, and first President of the councils of his nation. But this is not *half* his fame.... True, he is there seen in *greatness*, but it is only the greatness of public character, which is no evidence of *true greatness*; for a public character is often an artificial one. At the head of an army or nation, where gold and glory are at stake, and where a man feels himself the *burning focus* of unnumbered eyes; he must be a paltry fellow indeed, who does not play his part pretty handsomely...even the common passions of pride, avarice, or ambition, will put him up to his metal [mettle], and call forth his best and bravest doings. But let all this heat and blaze of public situation and incitement be withdrawn; let him be thrust back into the shade of private life, and you shall see how soon, like a forced plant robbed of its hot-bed, he will drop his false foliage and fruit, and stand forth confessed in native stickweed sterility and worthlessness.... There was Benedict Arnold—while strutting a BRIGADIER GENERAL on the public stage, he could play you the *great man*, on a handsome scale...he out-marched Hannibal, and out-fought [British General John] Burgoyne...he chaced the British like curlews [a species of bird], or cooped them up like chickens! and yet in the *private walks of life*, in Philadelphia, he could swindle rum from the commissary's stores, and, with the aid of loose women, retail it by the gill [one-fourth of a pint]!!...

It is not then in the glare of *public*, but in the shade of *private life*, that we are to look for the man. Private life is always *real* life. Behind the curtain, where the eyes of the million are not upon him, and where a man can have no motive but *inclination*, no excitement [*sic*—incitement?] but *honest nature*, there he will always be sure to act *himself*; consequently, if he act greatly, he must be great indeed. Hence it has been justly said, that, "our *private deeds*, if *noble*, are noblest of our lives."

Of these private deeds of Washington very little has been said. In most of the elegant orations pronounced to his praise, you see nothing of Washington below the *clouds*—nothing of Washington the *dutiful son*—the affectionate brother—the cheerful school-boy—the diligent surveyor—the neat draftsman—the laborious farmer—and widow's husband—the orphan's father—the poor man's friend. No! this is

not the Washington you see; 'tis only Washington the HERO, and the Demigod....Washington the *sun beam* in council, or the *storm* in war....

And yet it was to those *old-fashioned virtues* that our hero owed every thing. For they in fact were the food of the great actions of him, whom men call Washington. It was they that enabled him, first to triumph over *himself*, then over the *British*, and uniformly to set such bright examples of *human perfectibility* and *true greatness*....

Since then it is the private virtues that lay the foundation of all human excellence—since it was these that exalted Washington to be *"Columbia's first and greatest Son,"* be it our first care to present these, in all their lustre, before the admiring eyes of our *children*. To *them* his private character is *every thing*; his public, hardly *any thing*. For how glorious soever it may have been in Washington to have undertaken the emancipation of his country;...to have baffled every effort of a wealthy and warlike nation; to have obtained for his countrymen the completest victory, and for himself the most unbounded power; and then to have returned that power, accompanied with all the weight of his own great character and advice to establish a government that should immortalize the blessings of liberty...however glorious, I say, all this may have been to himself, or instructive to future generals and presidents, yet does it but *little* concern our *children*. For who among us can hope that his son shall ever be called, like Washington, to direct the storm of war, or to ravish the ears of deeply listening Senates? To be constantly placing him then, before our children, in this high character, what is it but like springing in the clouds a golden Phœnix, which no mortal calibre can hope to reach? Or like setting pictures of the Mammoth before the *mice* whom "not all the manna of Heaven" can ever raise to equality? Oh no! give us his *private virtues!* In *these*, every youth is interested, because in these every youth may become a Washington—a Washington in piety and patriotism,—in industry and honour—and consequently a Washington, in what alone deserves the name, SELF ESTEEM and UNIVERSAL RESPECT.

Chapter II

Birth and Education...

To this day numbers of good Christians can hardly find faith to believe that Washington was, bona fide [genuinely], *a Virginian!* "What! a buckskin!" say they with a smile, *"George Washington a buckskin! pshaw!*

impossible! he was certainly an European: So great a man could never have been born in America."

So *great a man could never have been born in America!*—Why that's the very *prince of reasons* why he should have been born here! Nature, we know, is fond of *harmonies*; and *paria paribus*, that is, *great things to great*, is the rule she delights to work by. Where, for example, do we look for the *whale* "the biggest born of nature?" not, I trow, in a *mill-pond*, but in the main ocean....

By the same rule, where shall we look for Washington, the greatest among men, but in *America?* That greatest Continent, which, rising from beneath the frozen pole, stretches far and wide to the south, running almost *"whole the length of this vast terrene,"* and sustaining on her ample sides the roaring shock of half the watery globe. And equal to its size, is the furniture of this vast continent, where the Almighty has reared his cloud-capt mountains, and spread his sea-like lakes, and poured his mighty rivers, and hurled down his thundering cataracts in a style of the *sublime*, so far superior to any thing of the kind in the other continents, that we may fairly conclude that great men and great deeds are designed for America.

This seems to be the verdict of honest analogy; and accordingly we find America the honoured cradle of Washington, who was born on Pope's creek, in Westmoreland county, Virginia, the 22d of February, 1732. His father, whose name was Augustin Washington, was also a Virginian, but his grandfather (John) was an Englishman, who came over and settled in Virginia in 1657....

[After Augustin's first wife died,] [f]ully persuaded still, that *"it is not good for man to be alone,"* he renewed, for the second time, the chaste delights of matrimonial love. His consort was Miss Mary Ball, a young lady of fortune, and descended from one of the best families in Virginia.

From his intermarriage with this charming girl, it would appear that our Hero's father must have possessed either a very pleasing person, or highly polished manners, or perhaps *both; for*, from what I can learn, he was at that time at least 40 years old! while she, on the other hand, was universally toasted as the belle of the Northern Neck [of the colony, beside the Potomac River], and in the full bloom and freshness of love-inspiring sixteen. This I have from one who tells me that he has carried down many a sett [country] dance with her; I mean that amiable and pleasant old gentleman, John Fitzhugh, Esq. of Stafford, *who* was, all his life, a neighbour and intimate of the Washington family. By his first

wife, Mr. Washington had two children, both sons—Lawrence and Augustin. By his second wife, he had five children, four sons and a daughter—George, Samuel, John, Charles, and Elizabeth. Those *over delicate* ones, who are ready to faint at thought of a second marriage, might do well to remember, that the greatest man that ever lived was the son of this second marriage!

Little George had scarcely attained his fifth year, when his father left Pope's creek, and came up to a plantation which he had in Stafford [County], opposite to Fredericksburg. The house in which he lived is still to be seen. It lifts its low and modest front of faded red, over the turbid waters of Rappahannock [River]....

The first place of education to which George was ever sent, was a little *"old field school,"* kept by one of his father's tenants, named Hobby; an honest, poor old man, who acted in the double character of sexton [church caretaker] and schoolmaster. On his skill as a grave-digger, tradition is silent; but for a teacher of youth, his qualifications were certainly of the humbler sort; making what is generally called an A. B. C. schoolmaster....

But though George was early sent to a schoolmaster, yet he was not on that account neglected by his father. Deeply sensible of the *loveliness* and *worth* of which human nature is capable, through the *virtues* and *graces* early implanted in the heart, he never for a moment, lost sight of George in those all-important respects.

To assist his son to overcome that selfish spirit which too often leads children to fret and fight about trifles, was a notable care of Mr. Washington. For this purpose, of all the presents, such as cakes, fruit, &c. he received, he was always desired to give a liberal part to his play-mates. To enable him to do this with more alacrity, his father would remind him of the love which he would hereby gain, and the frequent presents which would in return be made *to him*; and also would tell of that great and good God, who delights above all things to see children love one another, and will assuredly reward them for acting so amiable a part....

Never did the wise Ulysses take more pains with his beloved Telemachus, than did Mr. Washington with George, to inspire him with an *early love of truth*. "Truth, George," (said he) "is the loveliest quality of youth. I would ride fifty miles, my son, to see the little boy whose heart is so *honest*, and his lips so *pure*, that we may depend on every word he says. O how lovely does such a child appear in the eyes of every body! His parents doat on him; his relations glory in him; they are constantly praising him to their children, whom they beg to imitate him. They are often sending for him, to visit them; and receive him, when he comes, with as much joy as if he were a little angel, come to set pretty examples to their children.

"But, Oh! how different, George, is the case with the boy who is so given to lying, that nobody can believe a word he says! He is looked at with aversion wherever he goes, and parents dread to see him come among their children. Oh, George! my son! rather than see you come to this pass, dear as you are to my heart, gladly would I assist to nail you up in your little coffin, and follow you to your grave. Hard, indeed, would it be to me to give up my son, whose little feet are always so ready to run about with me, and whose fondly looking eyes and sweet prattle make so large a part of my happiness: but still I would give him up, rather than see him a common liar.["]

"Pa, (said George very seriously) do I ever tell lies?"

"No, George, I *thank God* you do not, my son; and I rejoice in the hope you never will. At least, you shall never, from me, have cause to be guilty of so shameful a thing. Many parents, indeed, even compel their children to this vile practice, by barbarously beating them for every little fault; hence, on the next offence, the little terrified creature slips out a *lie!* just to escape the rod. But as to yourself, George, you know I have *always* told you, and now tell you again, that, whenever by accident, you do any thing wrong, which must often be the case, as you are but a poor little boy yet, without *experience* or *knowledge*, never tell a falsehood to conceal it; but come *bravely* up, my son, like a *little man*, and tell me of it: and instead of beating you, George, I will but the more honour and love you for it, my dear."

This, you'll say, was sowing good seed!—Yes, it was: and the crop, thank God, was, as I believe it ever will be, where a man acts the true parent, that is, the *Guardian Angel*, by his chid.

The following anecdote is a *case in point*. It is too valuable to be lost, and too true to be doubted; for it was communicated to me by…[an] excellent lady.…

"When George," said she, "was about six years old, he was made the wealthy master of a *hatchet!* of which, like most little boys, he was immoderately fond, and was constantly going about chopping every thing that came in his way. One day, in the garden, where he often amused himself hacking his mother's pea-sticks, he unluckily tried the edge of his hatchet on the body of a beautiful young English cherry-tree, which

he barked so terribly, that I don't believe the tree ever got the better of it. The next morning the old gentleman finding out what had befallen his tree, which, by the by, was a great favourite, came into the house, and with much warmth asked for the mischievous author, declaring at the same time, that he would not have taken five guineas for his tree. Nobody could tell him any thing about it. Presently George and his hatchet made their appearance. *George,* said his father, *do you know who killed that beautiful little cherry-tree yonder in the garden?* This was a *tough question*; and George staggered under it for a moment; but quickly recovered himself: and looking at his father, with the sweet face of youth brightened with the inexpressible charm of all-conquering truth, he bravely cried out, *"I can't tell a lie, Pa; you know I can't tell a lie. I did cut it with my hatchet."—Run to my arms, you dearest boy*, cried his father in transports [ecstatically], *run to my arms; glad am I, George, that you killed my tree; for you have paid me for it a thousand fold. Such an act of heroism in my son, is more worth than a thousand trees, though blossomed with silver, and their fruits of purest gold.*["]

It was in this way, by interesting at once both his *heart* and *head*, that Mr. Washington conducted George with great ease and pleasure along the happy paths of virtue.…

Chapter III…

Thus pleasantly…passed away the few short years of little George's and his father's *earthly* acquaintance. Sweetly ruled by the sceptre of REASON, George almost adored his father; thus sweetly *obeyed* with the cheerfulness of LOVE, his father doated on George.…And though very different in their years, yet parental and filial love rendered them so mutually dear, that the old gentleman was often heard to regret, that *the school took his little companion so much from him*—while George, on the other hand, would often quit his playmates to run home and converse with his more beloved father.

But George was not long to enjoy the pleasure or the profit of such a companion; for scarcely had he attained his tenth year, before his father was seized with the gout in the stomach, which carried him off in a few days. George was not at home when his father was taken ill.…George did not reach home until a few hours before his father's death, and then he was speechless! The moment he alighted, he ran into the chamber where he lay. But oh! what were his feelings when he saw the sad change that had passed upon him! when he beheld those eyes, late so *bright* and *fond*, now reft [robbed] of all their lustre, faintly looking on him from their hollow sockets, and through swelling tears, in mute but melting language, bidding him a *LAST, LAST FAREWELL!*...Rushing with sobs and cries, he fell upon his father's neck...he kissed him a thousand and a thousand times, and bathed his clay-cold face with scalding tears....

But, though he had lost his best of friends, yet he never lost those divine sentiments which that friend had so carefully inculcated. On the contrary, interwoven with the fibres of his heart, they seemed to "grow with his growth, and to strengthen with his strength." The *memory* of his father, often bathed with *a tear*..., now sleeping in his grave, was felt to impose a more sacred obligation to do what, 'twas known, would rejoice his departed shade....

Soon after the death of his father, his mother sent him down to Westmoreland [County], the place of his nativity, where he lived with his half-brother Augustin, and went to school to a Mr. Williams, an excellent teacher in that neighbourhood. He carried with him his virtues, *his zeal for unblemished character, his love of truth, and detestation of whatever was false and base*....[I]n a very short time, so completely had his virtues secured the love and confidence of the boys, his *word* was just as current among them as a *law*. A very aged gentleman, formerly a school-mate of his, has often assured me, (while pleasing recollection brightened his furrowed cheeks,) that nothing was more common, when the boys were in high dispute about a question of fact, than for some little shaver among the mimic heroes, to call out *"well boys! George Washington was there; George Washington was there; he knows all about it; and if he don't say it was so, then we will give it up,"*—*"done,"* said the adverse party. Then away they would trot to hunt for George. Soon as his verdict was heard, the party favoured would begin to crow, and then all hands would return to play again.

About five years after the death of his father, he quitted school for ever, leaving the boys in tears for his departure....

Some of his historians have said, and many believe, that Washington was a *Latin scholar!* But 'tis an error. He never learned a syllable of Latin. His second and last teacher, Mr. Williams, was indeed a capital hand—but not at Latin; for of that he understood perhaps as little as Balaam's ass [in the Bible, an animal given the power of speech by God]—but at *reading, spelling, English grammar, arithmetic, surveying, book-keeping and geography*, he was indeed famous. And in these useful arts, 'tis said, he often boasted that he had made *young George Washington as great a scholar as himself.*

Born to be a soldier, Washington early discovered symptoms of nature's intentions towards him....At jumping with a long pole, or heaving heavy weights, for his years he hardly had an equal. And as to running, the swift-footed Achilles could scarcely have matched his speed.

"Egad! he ran wonderfully," said my amiable and aged friend, John Fitzhugh, esq. who knew him well. *"We had nobody here-abouts, that could come near him...."*

Chapter IV...

Happily for America, George Washington was not born with *"a silver spoon in his mouth."*...Seeing...no chance of ever rising in the world but by his own merit, on leaving school he went up to Fairfax [County] to see his brother Lawrence; with whom he found Mr. William Fairfax, one of the governor's council, who was come up on a visit to his sister, whom Lawrence had married. The counsellor presently took a great liking to George, and hearing him express a wish to get employment as a surveyor, introduced him to his relative, Lord Fairfax, the wealthy proprietor of all those lands generally called the *Northern Neck*, lying between the Potomac and the Rappahan[n]ock, and extending from Smith's Point, on the Chesapeake, to the foot of the Great Allegheny. At the instance of the counsellor, Lord Fairfax readily engaged George as a surveyor, and sent him up into the back-woods to work. He continued in his lordship's service till his 20th year, closely pursuing the laborious life of a woodsman....

Little did the old nobleman expect that he was educating a youth, who should one day dismember the British empire, and break his own heart—which truly came to pass. For on hearing that Washington had captured Cornwallis and all his army [at Yorktown in 1781], he called out to his black waiter, *"Come Joe! carry me to my bed! for I'm sure 'tis high time for me to die!"*

...It was his 15th year, according to the best of my information, that Washington first felt the kindlings of his soul for war. The cause was this—In those days, the people of Virginia looked on Great Britain as the *mother country*, and to go thither was in common phrase, *"to go home."* The name of OLD ENGLAND was music in their ears: and the bare mention of a blow meditated against her, never failed to rouse a something at the heart, which instantly flamed on the cheek and flashed in the eye. Washington had his full share of these virtuous feelings: on hearing, therefore, that France and Spain were mustering a black cloud over his MOTHER COUNTRY, his youthful blood took fire, and he instantly tendered what aid *his little arm* could afford. The rank of midshipman was procured for him on board a British ship of war, then lying in our waters, and his trunk and clothes were actually sent on board. But when he came to take leave of his mother, she wept bitterly, and told him *she felt that her heart would break if he left her.* George immediately got his trunk ashore! as he could not, for a moment, bear the idea of inflicting a wound on that dear life which had so long and so fondly sustained his own....

Chapter V...

In the year 1753 the people of Virginia were alarmed by a report that the French, aided by the Indians, were erecting a long line of military posts on the Ohio [River]. This manœuvre, predicting no good to the ANCIENT DOMINION [Virginia], was properly resented by Robert Dinwiddie, the governor, who wished immediately in the name of his king to forbid the measure. But how to convey a letter to the French commandant on the Ohio, *was the question.* For the whole country west of the Blue Mountains, was one immeasurable forest, from time immemorial the gloomy haunts of ravening beasts and of murderous savages. No voices had ever broke the awful silence of those dreary woods, save the hiss of rattlesnakes, the shrieks of panthers, the yells of Indians, and howling tempests. From such scenes, though beheld but by the distant eye of fancy, the hearts of youth are apt to shrink with terror, and to crouch more closely to their safer fire-sides. But in the firmer nerves of Washington, they do not appear to have made the least impression of the agueish [quaking] sort. The moment he heard of the governor's wishes, he waited on him with—*a* tender [offer] *of his services....*

Drenching rains and drowning floods, and snow-covered mountains opposed his course, but opposed in vain. The generous ambition to serve his country, and to distinguish himself, carried him through all, and even at the most trying times, touched his heart with a joy unknown to the VAIN and TRIFLING. On his way home he was way-laid and shot at by an Indian, who, though not fifteen paces distant, happily missed his aim.... The next evening, in attempting to cross a river on a raft, he was within an ace of being drowned, and, the night following, of perishing in the ice: but from both these imminent deadly risks, there was a hand unseen that effected his escape....

Chapter VI...

Swift as the broad-winged packets [ships] could fly across the deep, the news [of French incursions on the Ohio] was carried to England.—Its effect there was like that of a stone rudely hurled against a nest of *hornets.* Instantly...all is rage and bustle...the hive resounds with the maddening insects; dark tumbling from their cells they spread the hasty wing, and shrill whizzing through the air, they rush to find the foe....

The news was brought to Britain's king just as he had dispatched his pudding; and sat, right royally amusing himself with a slice of Gloucester and a nip of ale. From the lips of the king down fell the luckless cheese, alas! not grac'd to comfort the stomach of the Lord's anointed; while crowned with snowy foam, his nut-brown ale stood untasted by his plate. Suddenly, as he heard the news, the monarch darkened in his place...and answering darkness shrouded all his court.

In silence he rolled his eyes of fire on the floor, and twirled his *terrible thumbs!* his pages [servants] shrunk from his presence; for who could stand before the king of thundering ships, when wrath, in gleams of lightning, flashed from his *"dark red eyes?"* Starting, at length, as from a trance, he swallowed his ale, the[n] clenching his fist, he gave the table a tremendous knock, and cursed the wooden-shoed nation by his God! Swift as he cursed, the dogs of war bounded from their kennels, keen for the chace, and snuffing the blood of Frenchmen on every gale, they raised a howl of death which reached these peaceful shores. Orders were immediately issued, by the British government, for the colonies to arm and unite in one confederacy. Virginia took the lead, and raised a regiment, to the second command in which she raised her favourite Washington....

[In June 1755, Washington's Virginians join forces with British General Edward Braddock's redcoats and begin a march toward the French Fort Duquesne, where Pittsburgh stands today.] Washington, with his usual modesty, observed to General Braddock what sort of an enemy he had now to deal with—an enemy who would not, like the Europeans, come forward to a fair contest in the field, but, concealed behind the rocks and trees, carry on a deadly warfare with their rifles. He concluded with these words, *"I beg of your excellency the honor to allow me to lead on with the Virginia Riflemen, and fight them in their own way."*...

General Braddock, who had all along treated the American officers with infinite contempt, rejected

Washington's counsel, and swelling with most unmanly rage, replied, *"High times, by G—d! High times! when a young Buckskin can teach a British General how to fight!"* Instantly the pale, fever-worn cheeks of Washington turned fiery red—but smothering his feelings, he rode towards his men, biting his lip with grief and rage, to think how many brave fellows would draw short breath that day through the pride and obstinacy of one epauletted madman....

[An ambush by French soldiers and Indian warriors takes a terrible toll on the British and colonial troops.] Washington, alone, remained unhurt! Horse after horse had been killed under him. Showers of bullets had lifted his locks or pierced his regimentals [uniform]. But still protected by Heaven; still supported by a strength not his own, he had continued to fly from quarter to quarter, where his presence was most needed, sometimes animating his rangers; sometimes striving, but in vain, to rally the regulars. 'Twas his lot to be close to the brave but imprudent Braddock when he fell.... He died in the arms of Washington, whose pardon he often begged for *having treated him so rudely that fatal morning—heartily wished*, he said, *he had but followed his advice....*

A famous Indian warrior, who acted a leading part in that bloody tragedy, was often heard to swear, that *"Washington was not born to be killed by a bullet! For,"* continued he, *"I had seventeen fair fires at him with my rifle, and after all could not bring him to the ground!"* And indeed whoever considers that a good rifle, levelled by a proper marksman, hardly ever misses its aim, will readily enough conclude with this unlettered savage, that there was some invisible hand, which turned aside his bullets....

Chapter VII...

The French commandant [at Fort Duquesne] took care to make a proper use of his advantage; for soon as the days of savage feasting and drunkenness were over, he sent out deputations of his chiefs with *grand-talks* to several of the neighbouring tribes, who had not yet lifted the hatchet.

The tribes being assembled, and the calumet or pipe of friendship smoked around, the chiefs arose, and in all the pomp of Indian eloquence announced their great victory over *Long Knife* (the Virginians) and his white brothers, (the British)—then with a proud display of the numerous scalps and rich dresses which they had taken, they concluded with inviting the young men to unbury the tomahawk, and rush with them to drink the blood of their enemies.

This was enough—*"Grinning horribly, a ghastly smile,"* at such prospects of blood and plunder, the grim children of the desert [wilds], rose up at once to war. No time was lost in preparation. A pouch of parched corn, and a bear-skin, with a rifle, tomahawk, and scalping knife, were their equipage. And in a few weeks after Braddock's defeat, an armament of at least 1400 of those blood-thirsty people were in full march over hills and mountains, to surprise and murder the Frontier Inhabitants....

[Washington and his men try to defend the frontier against Indian raids.] "One day"—said he to an intimate; though it was but seldom that he mentioned those things, they gave him so much pain—"One day, as we drew near, through the woods, to a dwelling, suddenly we heard the discharge of a gun.... On rushing into the house..., we saw a mournful sight indeed—a young woman lying on the bed floated with blood—her forehead cleft with a hatchet—and on her breast two little children apparently twins, and about nine months old, bathing her bosom with the crimson currents flowing from their deeply gashed heads! I had often beheld the mangled remains of my murdered countrymen, but never before felt what I did on this occasion....

"On tracing back into the corn-field the steps of the barbarians, we found a little boy, and beyond him his father, both weltering [wallowing] in blood. It appeared, from the print of his little feet in the furrows, that the child had been following his father's plough, and, seeing him shot down, had set off with all his might, to get to the house to his mother, but was overtaken, and destroyed!..."

Such were the scenes in which Washington was doomed to spend three years of a wretched life....

'Tis a thing well worth remark, because it happens but to few, that though he often failed of success, he never *once* lost the confidence of his country.... Wherever he went, homage always waited upon him, though always uncourted. The grey-headed rose up to do him honour, when he came into their company; and the young men, with sighs, often wished for a fame like his. Happy was the fairest lady of the land, who, at a crowded ball, could get colonel Washington for her partner....

At the end of all these stood the accomplished Mrs. Martha Custis, the beautiful and wealthy widow of Mr. John Custis. Her *wealth* was equal, at least, to one hundred thousand dollars! But her beauty was a sum far larger still. It was not the shallow boast of a fine skin, which time so quickly tarnishes, nor of those short-lived roses, which sometimes wither almost as soon as blown. But it sprung from the HEART—from the *divine* and *benevolent affections*, which spontaneously gave to her *eyes*, her *looks*, her *voice* and her *manners*, such angel charms....

For two such *kindred souls* to love, it was only necessary that they should meet. Their friendship commenced with the first hour of their acquaintance, and was soon matured into marriage, which took place about the 27th year of Washington's life....

Chapter VIII...

Had it been appointed unto any man to quaff [drink deeply] unmingled happiness in this life, George Washington had been that man. For where is that pleasurable ingredient with which his cup was not full and overflowing?

Crowned with honours—laden with riches—blest with health—and, in *joyous prime* of 27, sharing each *rural* sweet in the society of a charming woman who doated on him, he surely bid fair to spend his days and nights of life in ceaseless pleasure!—But ah!...[I]in the midst of his favourite labours, of the plough and pruning-hook, covering his extensive farms with all the varied delights of delicious fruits and golden grain, of lowing herds and snowy flocks, he was suddenly called on by his *country*, to turn his plough-share into the sword, and go forth to meet a torrent of evils which threatened her....

[T]he British ministry began to look upon the Americans with an evil eye, and to devise ways and means to make us *"bear a part of their burdens!"*...We were not to be treated as *brothers*, but as *slaves!* over whom an unconditional right was claimed to tax and take our property at pleasure!!!

Reader, if you be a Briton, be a Briton still—preserve the characteristic calm and candor of a Briton. I am not about to say one word against your nation. No! I know them too well: and thank God, I can say, *after several years of residence among them*, I believe them to be as *Honest, Charitable*, and *Magnanimous* a people as any on God's earth. I am about to speak of the MINISTRY only, who certainly, at that time, were a most ambitious and intriguing junto, that by *bad means* had *gotten* power, and by *worse* were endeavouring to extend it, even to the destruction of both *American and British Liberty*....

But, alas! what signifies *right* against *might!* When a king wants money for his own pride, or for his hungry relations, and when his ministers want stakes for their gaming tables, or diamond necklaces for their strumpets, they *will* have it, though plundered colonies should lack bread and spelling books

for their children. For in the year '63, when the lamp of God was burning with peculiar brightness in our land, and both Britain and her colonies enjoyed a measure of blessings seldom indulged to the most favoured nations—When, at the very mention of Old-England, our hearts leaped for joy, as at the name of a great and venerable mother....At that happy period, Lord North brought in a bill to tax the colonies, without allowing us a voice in their councils!!....

But the sons of Columbia, though few in number, had too long enjoyed the sweets of Liberty and Property, to part with them so tamely, because a king and his minions had ordered it. No! blessed be God, their conduct was such as to strike the world with this glorious truth, that *a brave people, who know their rights, are not to be enslaved*....

[T]he Americans had too much of British blood, to allow an *unconstitutional* tax in *any shape or size*....Their numerous letters and petitions to the KING, to the PARLIAMENT, and to the PEOPLE of Britain, all, all breathe the full spirit of dutiful children, and of loving brothers. In terms the most modest and pathetic, they state the extreme injustice and barbarity of such measures—their total inconsistency with the spirit of the *British Constitution*—their positive inadmissibility into America—or, in that event, the certainty of a civil war, with all its fatal effects on the two countries....

"Let the Americans," said Lord Gower with a sneer, *"sit talking about their natural rights! their divine rights! and such stuff! we will send them over a few regiments of grenadiers to help their consultations!"* Thus high-toned was the language of ministry, and thus stoutly bent on the submission of the Americans. Indeed, in some instances, they would not honour them so far as to give their "humble petitions" a reading....

The hell-fraught cloud of civil war was now ready to burst: and April the 19th, 1775, was the fatal day marked out by mysterious heaven, for tearing away the stout [proud] infant colonies from the long-loved paps [breasts] of the old mother country....

Chapter X...

[Having devoted many pages to the Revolutionary War, Weems reached war's end and what many Americans considered the most remarkable chapter in the conflict: the military commander's refusal to listen to those suggesting he become a dictator, as so often had happened in times past.] The hostile fleets and armies [of Britain] thus withdrawn; and the Independence of his country acknowledged,

Washington proceeded, at the command of Congress, to disband the army! To this event, though of all others the dearest to his heart, he had ever looked forward with trembling anxiety. Loving his soldiers as his children, how could he tell them the painful truth which the poverty of his country had imposed on him? How could he tell them, that after all that they had done and suffered with him, they must now ground their arms, and return home, many of them without a decent suit on their backs, or a penny in their pockets?...

Having always disliked parade, he wished to make his resignation in writing; but congress, it seems, willed otherwise. To see a man voluntarily giving up *power*, was a spectacle not to be met with every day. And that they might have the pleasure of seeing him in this last, and perhaps greatest, act of his public life, they expressed a wish to receive his resignation from his own hand at a full *audience*. The next day, the 23d of December, 1783, was appointed for the purpose. At an early hour the house was crowded. The members of congress, with the grandees of the land, filled the floors; the ladies sparkled in the galleries. At eleven o'clock, Washington was ushered into the house, and conducted to a seat which had been prepared for him, covered with red velvet. After a becoming pause, and information given by the president [of Congress], that the United States in congress assembled were ready to receive his communication, he arose, and with great brevity and modesty observed, that he had presented himself before them, to resign into their hands with satisfaction the commission which, eight years before, he had accepted with diffidence. He begged to mingle his sincerest congratulations with them, for the glorious result of their united struggles—took no part of the praise to himself, but ascribed all to the blessing of Heaven on the exertions of the nation. Then fervently commending his dearest country to the protection of Almighty God, he bade them an affectionate farewell; and taking leave of all the employments of public life, surrendered up his commission!...

The sight of their great countryman, already so beloved, and now acting so generous, so godlike a part, produced an effect beyond the power of words to express. Their feelings of admiration and affection were too delicious, too big, *for utterance.* Every countenance was swollen with sentiment, and a flood of tears gushed from every eye, which, though a silent, was perhaps the richest offering of veneration and esteem ever paid to a human being....

[After a chapter devoted to Washington's brief retirement and his two terms as president,

Weems followed Washington into retirement once more, describing at length the hero's final illness in December 1799 and his stoicism in the face of death.]

Chapter XII: The Death of Washington...

He is now about to leave his *country!* that dear spot which gave him birth!—that dear spot for which he has so long watched and prayed, so long toiled and fought; and whose beloved children he has so often sought to gather, even as a hen gathereth her chickens under her wings. He sees them now spread abroad like flocks in goodly pastures; like favoured Israel in the land of promise. He remembers how God, by a mighty hand, and by an out-stretched arm, brought their fathers into this good land, a land flowing with milk and honey; and blessed them with the blessings of heaven above, and the earth beneath; with the blessings of LIBERTY and of PEACE, of RELIGION and of LAWS, above all other people. He sees that, through the rich mercies of God, they have now the precious opportunity to continue their country the GLORY of the earth, and a refuge for the poor and for the persecuted of all lands! The transporting sight of such a cloud of blessings, trembling close over the heads of his countrymen, together with the distressing uncertainty whether they will put forth their hands and enjoy them, shakes the *parent soul* of Washington with feelings *too strong* for his *dying frame!* The last tear that he is ever to shed now steals into his eye—the last groan that he is ever to heave is about to issue from his faintly labouring heart....

The news of his death soon reached Philadelphia, where congress was then in session. A question of importance being on the carpet that day, the house, as usual, was much interested. But, soon as it was announced—"GENERAL WASHINGTON IS DEAD"—an instant stop was put to all business—the tongue of the orator was struck dumb—and a midnight silence ensued, save when it was interrupted by deepest sighs of the members, as, with drooping foreheads rested on their palms, they sat, each absorbed in mournful cogitation. Presently, as utterly unfit for business, both houses adjourned; and the members retired slow and sad to their lodgings, like men who had suddenly heard of the death of a father....

Every where throughout the continent, churches and court houses were hung in black, mourning [garb] was put on, processions were made, and sermons preached, while the crowded houses listened with pleasure to the praises of Washington, or sighed and wept when they heard of his toils and battles for his country.

Chapter XIII

Character of Washington

...When the children of the years to come, hearing his great name re-echoed from every lip, shall say to their fathers, *"what was it that raised Washington to such height of glory?"* let them be told that it was HIS GREAT TALENTS, CONSTANTLY GUIDED AND GUARDED BY RELIGION. For how shall man, *frail man*, prone to inglorious ease and pleasure, ever ascend the arduous steps of virtue, unless animated by the *mighty hopes* of religion? Or what shall stop him in his swift descent to infamy and vice, if unawed by that dread power which proclaims to the guilty that their secret crimes are seen, and shall not go unpunished? Hence the wise, in all ages, have pronounced, that *"there never was a truly great man without religion."*...

[D]o we not daily meet with instances, of youth amiable and promising as their fond parents' wishes, who yet, merely for lack of religion, soon make shipwreck of every precious hope, sacrificing their gold to gamblers, their health to harlots, and their glory to grog—making conscience their curse, this life a purgatory, and the next a hell!! In fact, a young man, though of the finest talents and education, without religion, is but like a gorgeous ship without ballast. Highly painted and with flowing canvas, she launches out on the deep; and, during a smooth sea and gentle breeze, she moves along stately as the pride of ocean; but, as soon as the stormy winds descend, and the blackening billows begin to roll, suddenly she is overset, and disappears for ever. But who is this coming, thus gloriously along, with masts towering to heaven, and his sails white, looming like the mountain of snows? Who is it but *"Columbia's first and greatest son!"* whose talents, like the sails of a mighty ship spread far and wide, catching the gales of heaven, while his capacious soul, stored with the rich ballast of religion, remains firm and unshaken as the ponderous rock....

The Reverend Mr. Lee Massey, long a rector of Washington's parish, and from early life his intimate, has assured me a thousand times, that "he never knew so constant a churchman as Washington. And his behaviour in the house of God," added my reverend friend, "was so deeply reverential, that it produced the happiest effects on my congregation, and greatly assisted me in my moralizing labours...."

And while he resided at Philadelphia, as president of the United States, his constant and cheerful attendance on divine service was such as to convince every reflecting mind that he deemed no levee [assembly] so honourable as that of his Almighty Maker; no pleasures equal to those of devotion; and no business a sufficient excuse for neglecting his supreme benefactor.

In the winter of '77, while Washington, with the American army lay encamped at Valley Forge, a certain good old FRIEND [Quaker], of the respectable family and name of Potts, if I mistake not, had occasion to pass through the woods near head-quarters. Treading his way along the venerable grove, suddenly he heard the sound of a human voice, which as he advanced increased on his ear, and at length became like the voice of one speaking much in earnest. As he approached the spot with a cautious step, whom should he behold, in a dark natural bower of ancient oaks, but the commander in chief of the American armies on his knees at prayer! Motionless with surprise, friend Potts continued on the place till the general, having ended his devotions, arose, and, with a countenance of angel serenity, retired to headquarters: friend Potts then went home, and on entering his parlour called out to his wife, "Sarah, my dear! Sarah! All's well! all's well! George Washington will yet prevail!"...

He then related what he had seen, and concluded with this prophetical remark—"If George Washington be not a man of God, I am greatly deceived—and still more shall I be deceived if God do not, through him, work out a great salvation for America."...

Chapter XIV

Washington's Character Continued

HIS BENEVOLENCE ...If ever man rejoiced in the divine administration, and cordially endeavoured to imitate it by doing good, George Washington was that man. Taught by religion that *"God is love,"* he wisely concluded those the most happy, who love the most; and, taught by *experience*, that it is love alone that gives a participation and interest in others, capacitating us to rejoice with those who rejoice, and to weep with those who weep, he early studied that BENEVOLENCE which rendered him so singularly the delight of all mankind.

The marquis De Chastellux [a French general], who visited him in camp, tells us that he was "astonished and delighted to see this great American living among his officers and men as a father among his children, who at once revered and loved him with a filial tenderness."

[Jacques-Pierre] Brissot, another famous French traveller, assures us, that, "throughout the continent every body spoke of Washington as of a father."

That dearest and best of all appellations, *"the father of his country,"* was the natural fruit of that *benevolence*, which he so carefully cultivated through life....

In consequence of his wealth and large landed possessions, he had visits innumerable from the poor. Knowing the great value of time and of good tempers to them, he could not bear that they should lose these by long waiting, and shuffling, and blowing their fingers at his door. He had a room set apart for the reception of such poor persons as had business with him, and the porter had orders to conduct them into it, and to let him know it immediately. And so affectionately attentive was he to them, that if he was in company with the greatest characters on the continent, when his servant informed him that a poor man wished to speak to him, he would instantly beg them to excuse him for a moment, and go and wait on him....

A poor Irishman, wanting a little farm, and hearing that Washington had such a one to rent, waited on him. Washington told him that he was sincerely sorry that he could not assist him, for he had just disposed of it. The poor man took his leave, but not without returning him a thousand thanks! *Ah, do you thank me so heartily for a refusal?* "Yes, upon my shoul, now please your excellency's honour, and I do thank you a thousand times. For many a great man would have kept me waiting like a black negro; but your excellency's honour has told me strait off hand that you are sorry, and God bless you for it, that you can't help me, and so your honour has done my business for me in no time and less."...

Chapter XV

Washington's Character Continued

HIS INDUSTRY ...But of all the virtues that adorned the life of this great man, there is none more worthy of our imitation than his admirable INDUSTRY. It is to this virtue in her Washington, that America stands indebted for services past calculation: and it is from this virtue, that Washington himself snatched a wreath of glory, that will never fade away. O that the good genius of America may prevail! that the example of this, her favourite son, may but be universally adopted! Soon shall our land be free from all those sloth-begotten demons which now haunt and torment us. For whence do all our miseries proceed, but from lack of industry? In a land like this, which heaven has blessed above all lands; a land abounding with the *fish* and *flesh pots* of Egypt, and flowing with the choicest *milk* and *honey* of Canaan; a land where the poorest Lazarus may get his *fifty cents* a day for the commonest labour;...why is any man hungry or thirsty, or naked, or in prison? Why but for his own unpardonable sloth?

But alas!...A notion, from the land of lies, has taken too deep root among some, that *"labour is a low-lived thing, fit for none but poor people and slaves! and that dress and pleasure are the only accomplishments for a gentleman!"* But does it become a *gentleman* to saunter about, living on the charity of his relations—to suffer himself to be dunned by creditors, and like a hunted wolf, to fly from the face of sheriffs and constables? Is it like a *gentleman* to take a generous woman from her parents, and reduce her to beggary—to see even her bed sold from under her, and herself and weeping infants turned out of doors. Is it like a *gentleman* to reduce one's children to rags, and to drive them, like birds of heaven, to hedges and highways, to pick berries, filling their pale bloated bodies with disease? Or is it like a *gentleman* to bring up one's sons in sloth, pleasure, and dress, as young noblemen, and then leave them without estates, profession, or trades, to turn gamblers, sharpers, or horse thieves? *"From such gentlemen, oh save my country, Heaven!"* was Washington's perpetual prayer, the emphatical prayer of his life and great example! In his ear, Wisdom was heard incessantly calling aloud, "He is the real gentleman, who cheerfully contributes his every exertion to accomplish heaven's favourite designs, the *beauty, order*, and *happiness of human life*; whose industry appears in a plentiful house and smiling wife; in the decent apparel of his children, and in their good education and virtuous manners; who is not afraid to see any man on earth, but meets his creditor with a smiling countenance, and with the welcome music of gold and silver in his hand; who exerts an honest industry for wealth, that he may become as a watercourse in a thirsty land, a source of refreshments to a thousand poor."

This was the life, this the example set by Washington. His whole inheritance was but a small tract of poor land in Stafford county, and a few negroes. This appearing utterly insufficient..., he resolved to make up the deficiency by dint of industry and economy. For these virtues, how excellent! how rare in youth! Washington was admirably distinguished when but a boy. At a time when many young men have no higher ambition than a fine coat and a frolic, *"often have I seen him (says the reverend Mr. Lee Massey) riding about the country with his surveying instruments at his saddle,"* enjoying the double satisfaction of obliging his fellow-citizens by surveying their lands and of making money, not meanly to hoard, but generously to lend to any *worthy* object that asked it. This early industry was one of the first steps to Washington's preferment. It attracted on him the notice and admiration of his numerous acquaintance....

[H]e divided his time into four grand departments, *sleep, devotion, recreation,* and *business.* On the hours of business, whether in his own or in his country's service, he would allow nothing to infringe. While in camp, no company, however illustrious; no pleasures, however elegant; no conversation, however agreeable, could prevail on him to neglect his business....

Knowing how little is generally done before breakfast, he made it a rule to rise so early as to have breakfast over, and be on horseback by the time the sun was up. Let the rising generation remember that he then was sixty years of age!

On his farm, his husbandry of time was equally exemplary....

How delicious must it have been, to a man of Washington's feelings, to reflect that, even in the very worst of weather, every creature, on his extensive farms, was warmly and comfortably provided; to have seen his numerous flocks and herds, gamboling around him through excess of joy, and fullness of fat; to have beheld his steps washed with butter, and his dairies floated with rivers of milk; to have seen his once naked fields and frog-croaking swamps, now, by clearance or manure, converted into meadows, standing thick with heavy crops of timothy and sweet-scented clover; while his farm-yards were piled with such quantities of litter and manure as afforded a constantly increasing fertility to his lands....

[H]is mornings were always his own. Long before the sun peeped into the chambers of the sluggard, Washington was on horseback, and out among his overseers and servants, and neither himself nor any about him were allowed to eat the bread of idleness. The happy effects of such industry were obvious....

Oh! divine Industry! queen mother of all our virtues and of all our blessings! what is there of GREAT or of GOOD in this wide world that springs not from thy royal bounty? And thou, O! infernal Sloth! fruitful fountain of all our crimes and curses! what is there of mean or of miserable in the lot of man that flows not from thy hellish malice?

What was it that betrayed David, otherwise the best of kings, into the worst of crimes? IDLENESS.

Sauntering about *idly* on the terrace of his palace, he beheld the naked beauties of the distant Bathsheba. Lust, adultery, and murder were the consequences.

What was it that brought on a ten years war between the Greeks and Trojans? IDLENESS. Young Paris, the coxcomb [foolish, conceited person] of Troy, having nothing to do, strolls over to the court of Menelaus (a Greek prince), whose beauteous wife Helen, the black-eyed queen of love, he corrupts and runs off with to Troy. A bloody war ensues; Paris is slain; his father, brothers, and myriads of wretched subjects are slaughtered; and Troy, the finest city of Asia, is reduced to ashes!...

What is it that braces the nerves, purifies the blood, and hands down the flame of life, bright and sparkling, to old age? What, but *rosy-cheeked industry....*

What is it that preserves the morals of young men unsoiled, and secures the blessings of unblemished character and unbroken health? What, but *snow-robed industry....*

And what is it that raises a young man from poverty to wealth, from obscurity to never-dying fame? What, but *industry?* See Washington, born of humble parents, and in humble circumstances—born in a narrow nook and obscure corner of the British plantations! yet lo! what great things wonder-working industry can bring out of this unpromising Nazareth....

Since the day that God created man on the earth, none ever displayed the power of industry more signally than did George Washington.... [T]hat a poor young man with no king, lords, nor commons to back him—with no princes, nor strumpets of princes, to curry favour for him—with no gold but his virtue, no silver but his industry, should, with this old-fashioned coin, have stolen away the hearts of all the American Israel, and from a sheep-cot [small shelter] have ascended the throne of his country's affections, and gotten himself a name above the mighty ones of the earth! this is marvellous indeed! It is surely the noblest panegyric [a speech full of praise] ever yet paid to that great virtue, industry....

YOUNG READER! go thy way, think of Washington, and HOPE. Though humble thy birth, low thy fortune, and few thy friends, still think of Washington, and HOPE. Like him, honour thy God, and delight in glorious toil; then, like him, "thou shalt stand before kings; thou shalt not stand before common men."

Chapter XVI

Washington's Character Continued

HIS PATRIOTISM ... In this grand republican virtue, with pleasure we can compare our Washington with the greatest worthies of ancient or modern times.

The patriotism of the Roman emperor, Alexander, has been celebrated through all ages, because he was never known to give any place through *favour* or *friendship*, but employed those only whom he believed to be the best qualified to serve his country. In our Washington we meet this great and honest emperor over again. For, in choosing men to serve his country, Washington knew no recommendation but merit—had no *favourite* but worth. No relations, however near, no friends, however dear, stood any chance for places under him, provided he *knew* men *better qualified....*

Little did that illustrious patriot suspect, that, in so short a time after his death, the awful idea of DISUNION should have become familiar to the public eye!—so familiar as to have worn off half its horrors from the minds of many of our deluded citizens! *Disunion!* Merciful God! what good man can think of it but as of *treason*, and as a very Pandora's box, replete with every curse that can give up our dear country to desolation and havoc!

This disorganizing scheme has been three times brought forward, by what Washington terms *"cunning, ambitious, and unprincipled men,"* making use of a thousand arts to shut the eyes of the citizens on that yawning gulph to which they were so wickedly misleading them. And each time, Lucifer-like, these ministers of darkness have clothed themselves over as *"angels of light"* with the captivating plea of *public good.—"The disadvantages of the union! the disadvantages of the union!"* is their constant cry. Now admitting it to be true, that this so much *hated* union *has* its disadvantages, and where is there any human institution, even the noblest, that is free from them, yet is it not the parent of *blessings so many and great*, that no good man, as Washington says, "can *think of them without gratitude and rejoicing?"* and is it not equally true, that these disadvantages of the union would not, in fifty years, equal the ruinous consequences of a *disunion*, in probably, half a year....

But, O ye favoured countrymen of Washington! your republic is not lost yet; yet there is hope. The arm that wrought your political salvation is still stretched out to save; then hear his voice and live! Hear the voice of the Divine Founder of your republic: "Little children love one another." Hear his voice from the lips of his servant Washington. "Above all things hold dear your NATIONAL UNION; accustom yourselves to estimate its immense, its infinite value to your individual and national happiness. Look on it as the palladium [safeguard] of your tranquillity at home; of your peace abroad; of your safety; of your prosperity; and even of that very liberty which you so highly prize!"...

CHAPTER 11

Monsieur Tocqueville Visits America

"The general equality of condition among the people"

"What, then, is the American, this new man?" This question, posed by the Frenchman J. Hector St. John de Crévecoeur in his popular 1782 book, *Letters from an American Farmer*, would puzzle and provoke Europeans from that day forward.[1] After the United States won independence, curious folk headed west across the Atlantic Ocean to explore this strange new world. With the coming of peace to Europe and America in 1815 after a generation of war, the flow of curiosity seekers became a flood. Whether these tourists were complimentary or condescending (or both), insightful or infuriating (or both!), Europeans visiting America was as popular then as American undergraduates studying in Europe is now.

In the spring of 1831, two more Europeans, Alexis de Tocqueville (1805–1859) and Gustave de Beaumont (1802–1866), slipped into that stream of visitors bound for America. Tocqueville was a Frenchman whose family's noble roots were so deep and so distinguished that they made Dr. Alexander Hamilton, the Scottish physician you met in Chapter 5, seem of low birth indeed. Unfortunately for Tocqueville, it was a tough time for aristocrats. Once the French Revolution began in 1789, the well-born were under attack: Men proclaiming *liberté, egalité, fraternité* guillotined many members of Tocqueville's family and jailed the rest, including his parents. With Napoleon Bonaparte's defeat in 1815, however, the terrible times seemed at an end. Tocqueville's father became a count and served in the restored royal government; Tocqueville himself studied law and in 1827 won a position as "juge auditeur" (a sort of "apprentice magistrate").[2]

It was during these years that young Tocqueville met his future traveling companion, Gustave de Beaumont, like him of noble birth, like him a law student and aspiring magistrate. The two hit it off at once. Tocqueville was "shy" and "aloof," anxious and insecure; Beaumont was, as William Pierson notes, "less wracked by doubts and self-questionings and so more calm and cheerful."[3] With a common background and complementary personalities, the two found that they had similar views. Both were "liberals" who, while horrified by the violence of the French Revolution, nonetheless believed in reform. Both believed, too, that powerful historical forces were undermining the hierarchical notions that had for so long ruled European society, that *egalité* would inevitably triumph, and that this was something to be welcomed rather than feared, encouraged rather than opposed. Thus began a lifelong friendship.

In 1830 that friendship would take an unexpected turn when revolution returned to France, ousting King Charles X and replacing him with Louis Philippe. Unlike his father and older brothers, Tocqueville did not resign his government post: Both he and Beaumont—still ambitious, still believing in reform and in France—took oaths of allegiance to the new regime. "I am at war with myself," he moaned as he took the step that even his friends thought displayed "cowardice and self-interest."[4]

Still, the new government was suspicious (it made Tocqueville take a loyalty oath twice), so the two men began to think of ways they could escape the perilous, uncertain situation for a while without confirming those suspicions. It was at this point that the two came up with what Tocqueville called a "pretext": They would go to America, with their government's blessing, to study prison reform there and report back on how France, too, could improve its treatment of criminals. "I have long had the greatest desire to visit North America," Tocqueville claimed in August 1830, though the idea had only "just occurred to him" and he had never even met any Americans.[5]

In fact, the two had a more ambitious agenda: They would explain America to the world in general and to France in particular. "We are leaving with the intention of examining, in detail and as scientifically as possible, all the mechanisms of that vast American society which every one talks of and no one knows," Tocqueville admitted privately in February 1831. Not only that, but "we are counting on bringing back the elements of a fine work or, at the very least, of a new work; for there is nothing on this subject." "Would not that be a fine book," Beaumont asked his father, "which would give an exact conception of the American people, would paint its character in bold strokes, would analyze its social conditions...?"[6]

Arriving in Newport, Rhode Island, on May 9, the visitors stepped into a particularly turbulent moment in American life. As historian Sean Wilentz argues, this era (and this year in particular) was "a turning point in American history." That January William Lloyd Garrison published the first issue of his newspaper, *The Liberator*, demanding "immediate emancipation" of all slaves and raising American conversations about slavery to a fever pitch (see Chapter 14). That summer Nat Turner led the bloodiest slave rebellion in the nation's history. Meanwhile the U.S. government, bent on Indian Removal, was rounding up thousands of natives and shipping them beyond the Mississippi River. Add to these events the election of Andrew Jackson in 1828 (which heralded "the age of the common man") and the nullification crisis of 1832 (which threatened civil war), and it is clear that Tocqueville and Beaumont were in the United States at a tumultuous, revealing time.[7]

Before heading home on February 20, 1832, these two avid students of America would travel some 7,400 miles through seventeen of the twenty-four states then making up the United States. Over "infernal" paths and "fearful, detestable" roads, in "carriages...so rough that it's enough to break the toughest bones," they endured swarms of annoying *"mosticos"* and stifling heat in summer, in winter "horrible cold" and a "perpetual tornado of snow." They swam in the Hudson River on purpose and in the Ohio by accident (their steamboat sank). They visited Boston when the Pequot minister William Apess was probably in town to arrange for publication of his autobiography (Chapter 13). They were in Baltimore when the young slave Frederick Bailey (later Frederick Douglass) was there, learning to read and yearning for freedom (Chapter 16). On the frontier they saw bears serving as "watchdogs" and Indians being herded from their homeland.[8]

Everywhere they went, the two looked up prominent men (some two hundred in all) and launched at these locals a barrage of questions about Indians and slaves, equality and elections, manners and morals, North and South, and much more besides. Meeting and greeting governors and mayors; dining with former president John Quincy Adams; shaking hands in the White House with the man who had defeated Adams, Andrew Jackson; sitting down with the aged Charles Carroll, the last surviving signer of the Declaration of Independence (see Chapter 7), to discuss Maryland's revised constitution (see Chapter 8)—it seemed that Beaumont and Tocqueville went almost everywhere, saw almost everything, and met almost everyone.

And at the end of every day, they sat down to write about it. Tocqueville filled fourteen notebooks with his thoughts while also penning long letters to family and friends crammed with still more information that he would consult upon his return to France. When he did head home after more than nine months in America, Tocqueville embarked upon what James Schleifer calls his "second voyage," a "mental return to America." Though Tocqueville called some of his notes "rub[b]ish," in fact they were the building blocks of *De la Démocratie en Amérique*. Even with all his material—or perhaps *because* of all his material—writing was torture for this sensitive soul. What he called his "American monomania" sometimes made him ill. "There are moments," he confessed, "when I am seized by a sort of panic terror."[9]

One thing that scared Tocqueville was the sheer size of the assignment he had given himself. By the time its second volume came out in 1840, *Democracy in America* was a massive work: In one modern edition, the Table of Contents alone is eleven pages long; the text runs to 676 pages. In that vast compilation of materials (you only glimpse its riches here) can be found not only politics and religion but reflections on democratic poetry and the place that study of Latin and Greek should have in a democracy, not only social customs and state constitutions (Tocqueville was very interested in these) but thoughts on what sort of historians democracies breed and what kind of lease is best.

Tocqueville's breathtaking range and penetrating insights won immediate applause when the first volume came out in 1835. "I am confounded by its success," he wrote a friend; "for I feared, if not failure, at least a cold reception....I am...altogether stupefied by the praises which buzz in my ears." In the United States (where an English translation appeared in 1838), *Democracy in America* also met "with amazement and delight," as well as "astonishment...that a foreigner could so clearly comprehend and portray the peculiar political institutions of our country."[10]

Since then, *Democracy in America* has been a staple of American conversations, making Tocqueville a household name, quoted (and misquoted) by left and right, as well as by one president after another. "Scarcely a week passes," notes one observer, "without some quotation from *Democracy in America* appearing in the popular media or in literary reviews." Writers retrace the Frenchman's route and report on what they find there; television crews follow Tocqueville's trail, beaming into our living rooms pictures of places he visited, pondering what has changed since his day—and what has not. Scholars, too, have joined the chorus of praise. An expert on Andrew Jackson concludes that "Tocqueville remains the surest and best key to unlocking the mysteries of Jacksonian America." *Democracy in America* is more than that, insists a recent edition: It "is at once the best book ever written on democracy and the best book ever written on America."[11]

The high praise, the air time, the endless quoting—all this can lead us to forget that *Democracy in America* does not offer a mirror image of American reality. Coming to excerpts from the book, it is vital to keep in mind the limits to the man and his text. One of those limits was the new nation's sheer size. As Tocqueville himself confessed to his father near the end of his stay in America, "[t]o try to present a complete picture of the Union would be an enterprise absolutely impracticable for a man who has passed but a year in this immense country."[12]

Then there was the language barrier. Tocqueville wrote his mother shortly after his arrival in America that "[o]ne great difficulty, which we encountered the moment we left France..., is the language. We thought we knew English at Paris...," he said rue-fully, but we were wrong. "Often it's pitiful to hear us." "[I]t happens to us every day to confuse things strangely," he admitted almost a month later. "We are never entirely certain of what we are told."[13]

To a lack of time and a lack of English should be added biases and blind spots, blanks in the American canvas that either Tocqueville's itinerary or his tempera-ment left unfilled. He never spent enough time in the Southern states to know the region well. "I have only a superficial idea of the South of the Union," Tocqueville acknowledged. But South or North, his image of America, like Dr. Alexander Hamilton's almost a century earlier, was shaped by his aristocratic background. Most Americans he got to know were leading men ("if Tocqueville and Beaumont ever had a serious conversation with an American woman," notes one biographer, "no record of it survives"), not ordinary folk in this Age of the Common Man. Though Tocqueville liked the *idea* of democracy and equality, scholars point out, he "woefully lacked the common touch." "Every time that a person does not strike me by something rare in his mind or sentiments," he confessed, sounding very much like Dr. Hamilton, "I so to speak do not see him....I am constantly asking the names of these unknowns whom I see every day, and I constantly forget them....[T]hey bore me profoundly." Even President Jackson failed to impress this visitor: "not a man of genius," Tocqueville sniffed; "[f]ormerly he was celebrated as a...hot-head."[14]

Not surprisingly, the two young aristocrats could not help mentioning—more in private letters than in their publications—that much about America disgusted them. Newport women are "extraordinarily ugly," and American women in general are not only morally lax ("respectable" ones walk the streets alone!), they are also "detestable musicians" who nonetheless insist upon "always playing music." The men are no better. New York City "is bizarre and not very agreeable." Dinners there are an ordeal: the food is terrible, the endless solemn toasts made the French guests snicker, the whole evening is, "[i]n a word, complete barbarism." "[T]he inhabitants...are not all the most agreeable company," Tocqueville concluded. "A great number smoke, chew, [and] spit in your beard....[T]hey lack refinement, grace, and elegance." The two were amazed to find people in the United States "excessively vain," positively "stinking with national conceit." Clearly, Tocqueville would have been more comfortable with Dr. Alexander Hamilton than with most Americans.[15]

Saddled with such attitudes, no wonder Tocqueville missed or misrepresented important features of American life. He caught something of the spirit of the age, the ethos of equality in America, to be sure. This new set of values had made Benjamin Franklin's memoirs a best seller (Chapter 6), transformed George Washington from gentleman to Weems's humble farmer (Chapter 10), and put Andrew Jackson in the White House. But Tocqueville's enthusiasm for this key variable in the American equation obscured the very real—and growing—gap between rich and poor, along with the rise of an American working class in that era. *Democracy in America* mistakenly suggests, as historian John Higham noted, "that all Americans are basically alike."[16]

If Tocqueville missed much about white Americans, he was even farther off the mark when it came to native peoples and African Americans. Looking for the "noble savages" that Thedor de Bry and other Europeans had pictured for centuries (Chapter 3), he was disappointed in the Indians he saw. Moreover, he imbibed the white American convic-tion that Native Americans were destined to "melt away in the presence of European Civilization as the snow before the rays of the sun." What would he have made of Reverend Apess (Chapter 13) had the two met in Boston that year?[17]

As with Indians, so with African Americans: Tocqueville hated slavery and lamented the condition of blacks, but he was blind to the vitality of African American culture. He was unable to see them as anything more than victims, made brutes by racism and slavery. Here, too, consider what he would have thought of young Frederick Bailey (Douglass) had the two crossed paths in Baltimore, perhaps while the young slave was on his way to the African American church he had joined or the East Baltimore Mental Improvement Society he had helped found (Chapter 16).

Nonetheless, for all that Tocqueville found disagreeable, for all that he got wrong, there was much that he admired about the American experiment and much that he got right. "Never before has a people found for itself such a happy and fruitful basis of life," he wrote after only a week in the United States. "Here freedom is unrestrained." "The greatest equality seems to reign," he went on, amazed that New York's governor "was staying at a *boarding house* and . . . received us in the parlor without any ceremony whatever." Nothing in his travels changed these first impressions. "There reigns an unbelievable outward equality in America," he noted some months later. "All classes are constantly meeting and there does not appear the least arrogance resulting from different social positions. Everybody shakes hands," something unheard of in Europe. Americans are also, he found, extraordinarily optimistic. "The immense majority have *faith* in the wisdom and good sense of human kind, faith in the doctrine of human perfectibility." For all their faults, "they . . . form," he concluded, "a race of very remarkable men."[18]

Admiring Americans, Tocqueville also understood them. He had a knack for penetrating to the heart of things, for seeing, better than other travelers from the Old World (and better than many Americans), what made this country tick. "The new society in which we are does not at all resemble our European societies," he informed his father. "We are most certainly in another world here." That world had abandoned aristocracy and embraced democracy, it celebrated equality rather than hierarchy, its hallmark was *individualism* (then a new word), not community.[19]

But Alexis de Tocqueville deserves our consideration not only because his book was a best seller, not only because he earns so much attention today, not only because he "got" America at this pivotal moment in the nation's history. He also rewards us because his concerns connect to themes you have come upon already in this volume. Like John White and Theodor de Bry (Chapter 3), like Mary Rowlandson (Chapter 4), Tocqueville pondered the Indians' place in America's future: could they become "civilized," or must they be hunted down and ousted? Like Dr. Hamilton (Chapter 5), Tocqueville was attuned to questions of hierarchy and equality, including such seemingly mundane matters as who shook hands with whom. Like Benjamin Franklin (Chapter 6), Tocqueville picked up on how Americans celebrated individual initiative even as they formed voluntary associations to get things done.

And like Mason Locke Weems, Tocqueville wondered about American heroes in general and George Washington in particular. Having noticed that "prints of Washington dark with smoke" were "firmly pasted over the hearths of . . . many American homes," while staying in the nation's capital near the end of his trip the Frenchman jotted down notes for "A separate chapter on Washington." Americans' "historical memories" of the man were "badly applied . . . ," he wrote. "Why has Washington, whom the majority finally deserted while he was alive, why has Washington become a superman since his death?"[20]

Finally, Tocqueville's classic work merits our time because many now consider him not merely an astute observer of America in 1831 but something of a prophet about the country's future prospects. Sean Wilentz wonders if "one might even claim that *Democracy* presents a more accurate rendering of our own time than it does of Andrew Jackson's." Wilentz then retreats, noting "how different we are from the America Tocqueville described."[21] Nonetheless, it is worth considering how much of what you are about to read rings true of America today.

Questions for Consideration and Conversation

1. What are the advantages and disadvantages of a text written by a foreign traveler, someone not fluent in the language and who stayed in one place for only a short time? What can we learn from such accounts? What *can't* we learn?

2. How much did Tocqueville's aristocratic background shape his itinerary and his observations?

3. What did Tocqueville mean when he wrote that "freedom of opinion does not exist in America"? How, in a democracy that includes a Bill of Rights protecting free speech, is it possible to make such a claim?

4. What role does Tocqueville believe American geography, the American landscape, play in the character of American society? Is he the first to suggest such a connection in the chapters you have read?

5. According to Tocqueville, what role does religion play in American life? How does his view of that faith compare with the piety noted by Mason Locke Weems or Dr. Alexander Hamilton?

6. Some have argued that Tocqueville was as much a prophet—seeing America's future—as he was an astute observer of the United States in 1831. How closely does his portrait of the United States in 1831 resemble the America that you know today?

Endnotes

1. J. Hector St. John de Crèvecoeur, *Letters from an American Farmer and Sketches of 18th-Century America*, ed. Albert E. Stone (New York, 1981), 69.

2. George Wilson Pierson, *Tocqueville in America* (Baltimore, 1996 [originally published 1938]), 18.

3. Pierson, *Tocqueville in America*, 3, 22; Hugh Brogan, *Tocqueville* (Bungay, England, 1973), 3 ("shy").

4. Pierson, *Tocqueville in America*, 29.

5. Alexis de Tocqueville, *Democracy in America*, ed. and trans. Harvey C. Mansfield and Delba Winthrop (Chicago, 2000), xxii ("pretext"); Pierson, *Tocqueville in America*, 31 ("desire," "occurred"); Hugh Brogan, *Alexis de Tocqueville: A Life* (New Haven, CT, 2007), 146 (never met).

6. Pierson, *Tocqueville in America*, 32, 47–48.

7. Sean Wilentz, "Many Democracies: On Tocqueville and Jacksonian America," in Abraham S. Eisenstadt, ed., *Reconsidering Tocqueville's* Democracy in America (New Brunswick, NJ, 1988), 214. For an excellent portrait of America at the time, see Louis P. Masur, *1831: Year of Eclipse* (New York, 2001).

8. Pierson, *Tocqueville in America*, 189, 192, 259, 269, 543, 545.

9. James T. Schleifer, *The Making of Tocqueville's* Democracy in America (Chapel Hill, NC, 1980), xxi, 9, 20, 24. Sometime during their travels, Beaumont had decided that instead of coauthoring a book with his friend he wanted to write a novel about race relations in the United States; *Marie, ou l'Esclavage aux États-Unis*, was published in 1835. (The two did submit their assigned report on prisons.)

10. Pierson, *Tocqueville in America*, 6–7.

11. Sheldon S. Wolin, *Tocqueville Between Two Worlds: The Making of a Political and Theoretical Life* (Princeton, 2001), 3 ("scarcely a week"). See Richard Reeves, *American Journey: Traveling with Tocqueville in Search of* Democracy in America (New York, 1982); David Cohen, *Chasing the Red, White, and Blue: A Journey in Tocqueville's Footsteps Through Contemporary America* (New York, 2001); Anne Bentzel, *Traveling Tocqueville's America: Retracing the 17-State Tour that Inspired Alexis de Tocqueville's Political Classic* Democracy in America (Baltimore, 1998); Wilentz, "Many Democracies," in Eisenstadt, ed., *Reconsidering Tocqueville's* Democracy in America, 208 ("best key"); Tocqueville, *Democracy in America*, ed. Mansfield and Winthrop, xvii ("best book").

12. Pierson, *Tocqueville in America*, 675.

13. Ibid., 68, 110.

14. Ibid., 639n ("superficial idea"), 664 (Jackson); Tocqueville, *Democracy in America*, ed. Mansfield and Winthrop, xxii (scholars, "bore me"); Brogan, *Tocqueville*, 158 ("serious conversation").

15. Pierson, *Tocqueville in America*, 54, 68, 73, 90–91, 478; Bentzel, *Traveling Tocqueville's America*, 8 ("bizarre").

16. Wilentz, "Many Democracies," in Eisenstadt, *Reconsidering Tocqueville's* Democracy in America, 207.

17. Pierson, *Tocqueville in America*, 191–92.

18. Ibid., 65–66, 76, 153, 373, 478.

19. Ibid., 70, 81.

20. Mark E. Neely, Jr. and Harold Holzer, *The Union Image: Popular Prints of the Civil War North* (Chapel Hill, NC, 2000), 26, quoting Beaumont; Pierson, *Tocqueville in America*, 674 ("superman").

21. Wilentz, "Many Democracies," in Eisenstadt, ed., *Reconsidering Tocqueville's* Democracy in America, 227.

ALEXIS DE TOCQUEVILLE, *DEMOCRACY IN AMERICA* (1840)

Source: Alexis de Tocqueville, *Democracy in America.* Henry Reeve, translator. Cambridge: Sever and Francis, 1863.

VOLUME I

Author's Introduction

Among the novel objects that attracted my attention during my stay in the United States, nothing struck me more forcibly than the general equality of condition among the people. I readily discovered the prodigious influence that this primary fact exercises on the whole course of society....

I soon perceived that the influence of this fact extends far beyond the political character and the laws of the country, and that it has no less effect on civil society than on the government; it creates opinions, gives birth to new sentiments, founds novel customs, and modifies whatever it does not produce....

I then turned my thoughts to our own hemisphere, and thought that I discerned there something analogous to the spectacle which the New World presented to me. I observed that equality of condition, though it has not there reached the extreme limit which it seems to have attained in the United States, is constantly approaching it; and that the democracy which governs the American communities appears to be rapidly rising into power in Europe.

Hence I conceived the idea of the book that is now before the reader.

It is evident to all alike that a great democratic revolution is going on among us, but all do not look at it in the same light. To some it appears to be novel but accidental, and, as such, they hope it may still be checked; to others it seems irresistible....

The whole book that is here offered to the public has been written under the influence of a kind of religious awe produced in the author's mind by the view of that irresistible revolution which has advanced for centuries in spite of every obstacle and which is still advancing in the midst of the ruins it has caused. It is not necessary that God himself should speak in order that we may discover the unquestionable signs of his will. It is enough to ascertain what is the habitual course of nature and the constant tendency of events....

There is one country in the world where the great social revolution that I am speaking of seems to have nearly reached its natural limits....

How It can be Strictly said that the People Govern in the United States....

In America the people appoint the legislative and the executive power and furnish the jurors who punish all infractions of the laws. The institutions are democratic, not only in their principle, but in all their consequences; and the people elect their representatives directly, and for the most part annually, in order to ensure their dependence. The people are therefore the real directing power; and although the form of government is representative, it is evident that the opinions, the prejudices, the interests, and even the passions of the people are hindered by no permanent obstacles from exercising a perpetual influence on the daily conduct of affairs. In the United States the majority governs in the name of the people....

Political Associations in the United States....

In no country in the world has the principle of association been more successfully used or applied to a greater multitude of objects than in America. Besides the permanent associations which are established by law under the names of townships, cities, and counties, a vast number of others are formed and maintained by the agency of private individuals.

The citizen of the United States is taught from infancy to rely upon his own exertions in order to resist the evils and the difficulties of life; he looks upon the social authority with an eye of mistrust and anxiety, and he claims its assistance only when he is unable to do without it. This habit may be traced even in the schools, where the children in their games are wont to submit to rules which they have themselves established, and to punish misdemeanors which they have themselves defined. The same spirit pervades every act of social life. If a stoppage occurs in a thoroughfare and the circulation of vehicles is hindered, the neighbors immediately form themselves into a deliberative body; and this extemporaneous assembly gives rise to an executive power which remedies the inconvenience before anybody has thought of recurring to a pre-existing authority superior to that of the persons immediately concerned....Societies are formed to resist evils that are exclusively of a moral nature, as to diminish the vice of intemperance. In the United States associations are established to promote the public safety, commerce, industry, morality, and religion....

Government of the Democracy in America...

Many people in Europe are apt to believe without saying it, or to say without believing it, that one of the great advantages of universal suffrage is that it entrusts the direction of affairs to men who are worthy of the public confidence. They admit that the people are unable to govern of themselves, but they aver that the people always wish the welfare of the state and instinctively designate those who are animated by the same good will and who are the most fit to wield the supreme authority. I confess that the observations I made in America by no means coincide with these opinions. On my arrival in the United States I was surprised to find so much distinguished talent among the citizens and so little among the heads of the government. It is a constant fact that at the present day the ablest men in the United States are rarely placed at the head of affairs.... The race of American statesmen has evidently dwindled most remarkably in the course of the last fifty years....

There are certain laws of a democratic nature which contribute, nevertheless, to correct in some measure these dangerous tendencies of democracy. On entering the House of Representatives at Washington, one is struck by the vulgar demeanor of that great assembly.... Its members are almost all obscure individuals,... mostly village lawyers, men in trade, or even persons belonging to the lower classes of society. In a country in which education is very general, it is said that the representatives of the people do not always know how to write correctly.

At a few yards' distance is the door of the Senate, which contains within a small space a large proportion of the celebrated men of America. Scarcely an individual is to be seen in it who has not had an active and illustrious career....

How comes this strange contrast...? ...The only reason which appears to me adequately to account for it is that the House of Representatives is elected by the people directly, while the Senate is elected by elected bodies [this changed in 1913].... The Senators are elected by an indirect application of the popular vote; for the [state] legislatures which appoint them are... chosen by the totality of the citizens.... [T]his transmission of the popular authority through an assembly of chosen men operates an important

change in it by refining its discretion and improving its choice. Men who are chosen in this manner accurately represent the majority of the nation which governs them; but they represent only the elevated thoughts that are current in the community and the generous propensities that prompt its nobler actions rather than the petty passions that disturb or the vices that disgrace it....

Public officers in the United States are not separate from the mass of citizens; they have neither palaces nor guards nor ceremonial costumes. This simple exterior of persons in authority is connected not only with the peculiarities of the American character, but with the fundamental principles of society. In the estimation of the democracy a government is not a benefit, but a necessary evil. A certain degree of power must be granted to public officers.... The public officers themselves are well aware that the superiority over their fellow citizens which they derive from their authority they enjoy only on condition of putting themselves on a level with the whole community by their manners. A public officer in the United States is uniformly simple in his manners, accessible to all the world, attentive to all requests, and obliging in his replies....

Tyranny of the Majority

...In my opinion, the main evil of the present democratic institutions of the United States does not arise, as is often asserted in Europe, from their weakness, but from their irresistible strength. I am not so much alarmed at the excessive liberty which reigns in that country as at the inadequate securities which one finds there against tyranny....

Power Exercised by the Majority in America Upon Opinion...

It is in the examination of the exercise of thought in the United States that we clearly perceive how far the power of the majority surpasses all the powers with which we are acquainted in Europe. Thought is an invisible and subtle power that mocks all the efforts of tyranny. At the present time the most absolute monarchs in Europe cannot prevent certain opinions hostile to their authority from circulating in secret through their dominions and even in their courts. It is not so in America; as long as the majority is still undecided, discussion is carried on; but as soon as its decision is irrevocably pronounced, everyone is silent, and the friends as well as the opponents of the measure unite in assenting to its propriety....

The authority of a king is physical and controls the actions of men without subduing their will. But the majority possesses a power that is physical and moral at the same time, which acts upon the will as much as upon the actions and represses not only all contest, but all controversy.

I know of no country in which there is so little independence of mind and real freedom of discussion as in America.…

In America the majority raises formidable barriers around the liberty of opinion; within these barriers an author may write what he pleases, but woe to him if he goes beyond them. Not that he is in danger of an *auto-da-fé* [execution by burning at the stake], but he is exposed to continued obloquy and persecution. His political career is closed forever, since he has offended the only authority that is able to open it.… Before making public his opinions he thought he had sympathizers; now it seems to him that he has none any more since he has revealed himself to everyone; then those who blame him criticize loudly and those who think as he does keep quiet and move away without courage. He yields at length, overcome by the daily effort which he has to make, and subsides into silence, as if he felt remorse for having spoken the truth.

Fetters and headsmen [executioners] were the coarse instruments that tyranny formerly employed; but the civilization of our age has perfected despotism itself.… Monarchs had, so to speak, materialized oppression; the democratic republics of the present day have rendered it as entirely an affair of the mind as the will which it is intended to coerce. Under the absolute sway of one man the body was attacked in order to subdue the soul; but the soul escaped the blows which were directed against it and rose proudly superior. Such is not the course adopted by tyranny in democratic republics; there the body is left free, and the soul is enslaved. The master no longer says: "You shall think as I do or you shall die"; but he says: "You are free to think differently from me and to retain your life, your property, and all that you possess; but you are henceforth a stranger among your people. You may retain your civil rights, but they will be useless to you, for you will never be chosen by your fellow citizens if you solicit their votes; and they will affect to scorn you if you ask for their esteem.… Your fellow creatures will shun you like an impure being; and even those who believe in your innocence will abandon you, lest they should be shunned in their turn. Go in peace! I have given you your life, but it is an existence worse than death."

…If America has not as yet had any great writers, the reason is…there can be no literary genius without freedom of opinion, and freedom of opinion does not exist in America.…

Principal Causes which Tend to Maintain the Democratic Republic in the United States…

The Americans have no neighbors and consequently they have no great wars, or financial crises, or inroads, or conquest, to dread; they require neither great taxes, nor large armies, nor great generals; and they have nothing to fear from a scourge which is more formidable to republics than all these evils combined: namely, military glory. It is impossible to deny the inconceivable influence that military glory exercises upon the spirit of a nation. General Jackson, whom the Americans have twice elected to be the head of their government, is a man of violent temper and very moderate talents; nothing in his whole career ever proved him qualified to govern a free people; and, indeed, the majority of the enlightened classes of the Union has always opposed him. But he was raised to the Presidency, and has been maintained there, solely by the recollection of a victory which he gained, twenty years ago, under the walls of New Orleans; a victory which was, however, a very ordinary achievement and which could only be remembered in a country where battles are rare.…

The chief circumstance which has favored the establishment and the maintenance of a democratic republic in the United States is the nature of the territory that the Americans inhabit. Their ancestors gave them the love of equality and of freedom; but God himself gave them the means of remaining equal and free, by placing them upon a boundless continent. General prosperity is favorable to the stability of all governments, but more particularly of a democratic one, which depends upon the will of the majority, and especially upon the will of that portion of the community which is most exposed to want. When the people rule, they must be rendered happy or they will overturn the state.… The physical causes, independent of the laws, which promote general prosperity are more numerous in America than they ever have been in any other country in the world, at any other period of history. In the United States not only is legislation democratic, but Nature herself favors the cause of the people.

In what part of human history can be found anything similar to what is passing before our eyes in North America? The celebrated communities of antiquity were all founded in the midst of hostile nations, which they were obliged to subjugate before they could flourish in their place. . . . But North America was inhabited only by wandering tribes . . .; that vast country was still, properly speaking, an empty continent, a desert [wild] land awaiting its inhabitants.

Everything is extraordinary in America, the social condition of the inhabitants as well as the laws; but the soil upon which these institutions are founded is more extraordinary than all the rest. When the earth was given to men by the Creator, the earth was inexhaustible; but men were weak and ignorant, and when they had learned to take advantage of the treasures which it contained, they already covered its surface and were soon obliged to earn by the sword an asylum for repose and freedom. Just then North America was discovered, as if it had been kept in reserve by the Deity and had just risen from beneath the waters of the Deluge.

That continent still presents, as it did in the primeval time, rivers that rise from never failing sources, green and moist solitudes, and limitless fields which the plowshare of the husbandman has never turned. In this state it is offered to man, not barbarous, ignorant, and isolated, as he was in the early ages, but already in possession of the most important secrets of nature, united to his fellow men, and instructed by the experience of fifty centuries. At this very time thirteen millions of civilized Europeans are peaceably spreading over those fertile plains. . . . Three or four thousand soldiers drive before them the wandering races of the aborigines; these are followed by the pioneers, who pierce the woods, scare off the beasts of prey, explore the courses of the inland streams, and make ready the triumphal march of civilization across the desert [wilderness]. . . .

It would be difficult to describe the avidity with which the American rushes forward to secure this immense booty that fortune offers. In the pursuit he fearlessly braves the arrow of the Indian and the diseases of the forest; he is unimpressed by the silence of the woods; the approach of beasts of prey does not disturb him, for he is goaded onwards by a passion stronger than the love of life. Before him lies a boundless continent, and he urges onward as if time pressed and he was afraid of finding no room for his exertions. . . . The desire of prosperity has become an ardent and restless passion in their minds, which grows by what it feeds on. They early broke the ties that bound them to their natal earth, and they have contracted no fresh ones on their way. Emigration was at first necessary to them; and it soon

becomes a sort of game of chance, which they pursue for the emotions it excites as much as for the gain it procures. . . .

In Europe we are wont to look upon a restless disposition, an unbounded desire of riches, and an excessive love of independence as propensities very dangerous to society. Yet these are the very elements that ensure a long and peaceful future to the republics of America. Without these unquiet passions the population would collect in certain spots and would soon experience wants like those of the Old World, which it is difficult to satisfy. . . .

Indirect Influence of Religious Opinions Upon Political Society in the United States . . .

The sects that exist in the United States are innumerable. They all differ in respect to the worship which is due to the Creator; but they all agree in respect to the duties which are due from man to man. Each sect adores the Deity in its own peculiar manner, but all sects preach the same moral law in the name of God. . . .

[T]here is no country in the world where the Christian religion retains a greater influence over the souls of men than in America. . . .

I do not question that the great austerity of manners that is observable in the United States arises, in the first instance, from religious faith. Religion is often unable to restrain man from the numberless temptations which chance offers; nor can it check that passion for gain which everything contributes to arouse; but its influence over the mind of woman is supreme, and women are the protectors of morals. There is certainly no country in the world where the tie of marriage is more respected than in America or where conjugal happiness is more highly or worthily appreciated. . . . [W]hen the American retires from the turmoil of public life to the bosom of his family, he finds in it the image of order and of peace. There his pleasures are simple and natural, his joys are innocent and calm; and . . . he finds that an orderly life is the surest path to happiness. . . .

The imagination of the Americans, even in its greatest flights, is circumspect and undecided; its impulses are checked and its works unfinished. These habits of restraint recur in political society and are singularly favorable both to the tranquillity of the people and to the durability of the institutions they have established. Nature and circumstances have made the inhabitants of the United States bold, as is sufficiently attested by the enterprising spirit with which they seek for fortune. If the mind of the

Americans were free from all hindrances, they would shortly become the most daring innovators and the most persistent disputants in the world. But the revolutionists of America are obliged to profess an ostensible respect for Christian morality and equity, which does not permit them to violate wantonly the laws that oppose their designs; nor would they find it easy to surmount the scruples of their partisans even if they were able to get over their own.... Thus, while the law permits the Americans to do what they please, religion prevents them from conceiving, and forbids them to commit, what is rash or unjust.

Religion in America takes no direct part in the government of society, but it must be regarded as the first of their political institutions.... I do not know whether all Americans have a sincere faith in their religion—for who can search the human heart?—but I am certain that they hold it to be indispensable to the maintenance of republican institutions....

The Americans combine the notions of Christianity and of liberty so intimately in their minds that it is impossible to make them conceive the one without the other....

The Present and Probable Future Condition of the Three Races that Inhabit the Territory of the United States

...The human beings who are scattered over this space do not form, as in Europe, so many branches of the same stock. Three races, naturally distinct, and, I might almost say, hostile to each other, are discoverable among them at the first glance. Almost insurmountable barriers had been raised between them by education and law, as well as by their origin and outward characteristics, but fortune has brought them together on the same soil, where, although they are mixed, they do not amalgamate, and each race fulfills its destiny apart.

Among these widely differing families of men, the first that attracts attention, the superior in intelligence, in power, and in enjoyment, is the white, or European, the MAN pre-eminently so called, below him appear the Negro and the Indian. These two unhappy races have nothing in common, neither birth, nor features, nor language, nor habits. Their only resemblance lies in their misfortunes. Both of them occupy an equally inferior position in the country they inhabit; both suffer from tyranny; and if their wrongs are not the same, they originate from the same authors.

If we reason from what passes in the world, we should almost say that the European is to the other races of mankind what man himself is to the lower animals: he makes them subservient to his use, and when he cannot subdue he destroys them. Oppression has, at one stroke, deprived the descendants of the Africans of almost all the privileges of humanity. The Negro of the United States has lost even the remembrance of his country; the language which his forefathers spoke is never heard around him; he abjured [gave up] their religion and forgot their customs when he ceased to belong to Africa, without acquiring any claim to European privileges. But he remains half-way between the two communities, isolated between two races; sold by the one, repulsed by the other; finding not a spot in the universe to call by the name of country, except the faint image of a home which the shelter of his master's roof affords.

The Negro has no family: woman is merely the temporary companion of his pleasures, and his children are on an equality with himself from the moment of their birth. Am I to call it a proof of God's mercy, or a visitation of his wrath, that man, in certain states, appears to be insensible to his extreme wretchedness and almost obtains a depraved taste for the cause of his misfortunes? The Negro, plunged in this abyss of evils, scarcely feels his own calamitous situation. Violence made him a slave, and the habit of servitude gives him the thoughts and desires of a slave, he admires his tyrants more than he hates them, and finds his joy and his pride in the servile imitation of those who oppress him. His understanding is degraded to the level of his soul....

If he becomes free, independence is often felt by him to be a heavier burden than slavery; for, having learned in the course of his life to submit to everything except reason, he is too unacquainted with her dictates to obey them. A thousand new desires beset him, and he has not the knowledge and energy necessary to resist them: these are masters which it is necessary to contend with, and he has learned only to submit and obey. In short, he is sunk to such a depth of wretchedness that while servitude brutalizes, liberty destroys him.

Oppression has been no less fatal to the Indian than to the Negro race, but its effects are different. Before the arrival of white men in the New World, the inhabitants of North America lived quietly in their woods, enduring the vicissitudes and practicing the virtues and vices common to savage nations. The Europeans having dispersed the Indian tribes and driven them into the deserts, condemned them to a wandering life, full of inexpressible sufferings.

Savage nations are only controlled by opinion and custom. When the North American Indians had lost the sentiment of attachment to their country; when their families were dispersed, their traditions obscured, and the chain of their recollections broken; when all their habits were changed, and their wants increased beyond measure, European tyranny rendered them more disorderly and less civilized than they were before. The moral and physical condition of these tribes continually grew worse, and they became more barbarous as they became more wretched. Nevertheless, the Europeans have not been able to change the character of the Indians; and though they have had power to destroy, they have never been able to subdue and civilize them....

The Negro makes a thousand fruitless efforts to insinuate himself among men who repulse him; he conforms to the tastes of his oppressors, adopts their opinions, and hopes by imitating them to form a part of their community....

The Indian, on the contrary, has his imagination inflated with the pretended nobility of his origin, and lives and dies in the midst of these dreams of pride. Far from desiring to conform his habits to ours, he loves his savage life as the distinguishing mark of his race and repels every advance to civilization, less, perhaps, from hatred of it than from a dread of resembling the Europeans.

While he has nothing to oppose to our perfection in the arts but the resources of the wilderness, to our tactics nothing but undisciplined courage, while our well-digested plans are met only by the spontaneous instincts of savage life, who can wonder if he fails in this unequal contest?

The Negro, who earnestly desires to mingle his race with that of the European, cannot do so; while the Indian, who might succeed to a certain extent, disdains to make the attempt. The servility of the one dooms him to slavery, the pride of the other to death....

The Present and Probable Future Condition of the Indian Tribes that Inhabit the Territory Possessed by the Union

...NONE of the Indian tribes which formerly inhabited the territory of New England, the Narragansetts, the Mohicans, the Pequots, have any existence but in the recollection of man....I myself met with the last of the Iroquois, who were begging alms. The nations I have mentioned formerly covered the country to the seacoast; but a traveler at the present day must penetrate more than a hundred leagues [around 300 miles] into the interior of the continent to find an Indian....

It is impossible to conceive the frightful sufferings that attend these forced migrations [of Indians who retreat when European intrusion drives them and the game animals away]. They are undertaken by a people already exhausted and reduced; and the countries to which the newcomers betake themselves are inhabited by other tribes, which receive them with jealous hostility. Hunger is in the rear, war awaits them, and misery besets them on all sides.... [T]hey have no longer a country, and soon they will not be a people; their very families are obliterated; their common name is forgotten; their language perishes; and all traces of their origin disappear. Their nation has ceased to exist except in the recollection of the antiquaries of America and a few of the learned of Europe.

I should be sorry to have my reader suppose that I am coloring the picture too highly; I saw with my own eyes many of the miseries that I have just described....

At the end of the year 1831, while I was on the left bank of the Mississippi, at a place named by Europeans Memphis, there arrived a numerous band of Choctaws....These savages had left their country and were endeavoring to gain the right bank of the Mississippi, where they hoped to find an asylum that had been promised them by the American government. It was then the middle of winter, and the cold was unusually severe; the snow had frozen hard upon the ground, and the river was drifting huge masses of ice. The Indians had their families with them, and they brought in their train the wounded and the sick, with children newly born and old men upon the verge of death. They possessed neither tents nor wagons, but only their arms and some provisions. I saw them embark to pass the mighty river, and never will that solemn spectacle fade from my remembrance. No cry, no sob, was heard among the assembled crowd; all were silent. Their calamities were of ancient date, and they knew them to be irremediable. The Indians had all stepped into the bark [boat] that was to carry them across, but their dogs remained upon the bank. As soon as these animals perceived that their masters were finally leaving the shore, they set up a dismal howl and, plunging all together into the icy waters of the Mississippi, swam after the boat.

The expulsion of the Indians often takes place at the present day in a regular and, as it were, a legal manner. When the European population begins to approach the limit of the desert inhabited by a savage tribe, the government of the United States usually sends forward envoys who assemble the Indians in a large plain and, having first eaten and drunk with them, address them thus: "What have you to do in the land of your fathers? Before long, you must dig up their bones in order to live. In what respect is the country you inhabit better than another? Are there no woods, marshes, or prairies except where you dwell? And can you live nowhere but under your own sun? Beyond those mountains which you see at the horizon, beyond the lake which bounds your territory on the west, there lie vast countries where beasts of the chase are yet found in great abundance; sell us your lands, then, and go to live happily in those solitudes."...[Then] they spread before the eyes of the Indians firearms, woolen garments, kegs of brandy, glass necklaces, bracelets of tinsel, earrings, and looking-glasses. If, when they have beheld all these riches, they still hesitate, it is insinuated that they cannot refuse the required consent and that the government itself will not long have the power of protecting them in their rights. What are they to do? Half convinced and half compelled, they go to inhabit new deserts, where the importunate [demanding, persistent] whites will not let them remain ten years in peace. In this manner do the Americans obtain, at a very low price, whole provinces, which the richest sovereigns of Europe could not purchase.

These are great evils; and it must be added that they appear to me to be irremediable. I believe that the Indian nations of North America are doomed to perish....The Indians had only the alternative of war or civilization; in other words, they must either destroy the Europeans or become their equals.

At the first settlement of the colonies they might have found it possible, by uniting their forces, to deliver themselves from the small bodies of strangers who landed on their continent. They several times attempted to do it, and were on the point of succeeding [in a footnote Tocqueville mentions Metacom (King Philip); see chapters 4 and 13]; but the disproportion of their resources at the present day, when compared with those of the whites, is too great to allow such an enterprise to be thought of....

There is no Indian so wretched as not to retain under his hut of bark a lofty idea of his personal worth;...while he acknowledges our ascendancy, he still believes in his own superiority....

Situation of the black Population in the United States, and Dangers with which Its Presence Threatens the Whites

...The Indians will perish in the same isolated condition in which they have lived, but the destiny of the Negroes is in some measure interwoven with that of the Europeans. These two races are fastened to each other without intermingling; and they are alike unable to separate entirely or to combine. The most

formidable of all the ills that threaten the future of the Union arises from the presence of a black population upon its territory; and in contemplating the cause of the present embarrassments, or the future dangers of the United States, the observer is invariably led to this as a primary fact....

[Unlike in the ancient world,] among the moderns the abstract and transient fact of slavery is fatally united with the physical and permanent fact of color. The tradition of slavery dishonors the race, and the peculiarity of the race perpetuates the tradition of slavery....Thus the Negro transmits the eternal mark of his ignominy to all his descendants; and although the law may abolish slavery, God alone can obliterate the traces of its existence....

You may set the Negro free, but you cannot make him otherwise than an alien to the European. Nor is this all: we scarcely acknowledge the common features of humanity in this stranger whom slavery has brought among us....

I see that in a certain portion of the territory of the United States at the present day the legal barrier which separated the two races is falling away, but not that which exists in the manners of the country, slavery recedes, but the prejudice to which it has given birth is immovable. Whoever has inhabited the United States must have perceived that in those parts of the Union in which the Negroes are no longer slaves they have in no wise drawn nearer to the whites. On the contrary, the prejudice of race appears to be stronger in the states that have abolished slavery than in those where it still exists; and nowhere is it so intolerant as in those states where servitude has never been known.

It is true that in the North of the Union marriages may be legally contracted between Negroes and whites; but public opinion would stigmatize as infamous a man who should connect himself with a Negress, and it would be difficult to cite a single instance of such a union. The electoral franchise has been conferred upon the Negroes in almost all the states in which slavery has been abolished, but if they come forward to vote, their lives are in danger. If oppressed, they may bring an action at law, but they will find none but whites among their judges; and although they may legally serve as jurors, prejudice repels them from that office. The same schools do not receive the children of the black and of the European. In the theaters gold cannot procure a seat for the servile race beside their former masters; in the hospitals they lie apart; and although they are allowed to invoke the same God as the whites, it must be at a different altar and in their own churches, with their own clergy. The gates of heaven are not closed against them, but their inferiority is continued to the very confines of the other world. When the Negro dies, his bones are cast aside, and the distinction of condition prevails even in the equality of death. Thus the Negro is free, but he can share neither the rights, nor the pleasures, nor the labor, nor the afflictions, nor the tomb of him whose equal he has been declared to be; and he cannot meet him upon fair terms in life or in death.

In the South, where slavery still exists, the Negroes are less carefully kept apart; they sometimes share the labors and the recreations of the whites; the whites consent to intermix with them to a certain extent, and although legislation treats them more harshly, the habits of the people are more tolerant and compassionate. In the South the master is not afraid to raise his slave to his own standing, because he knows that he can in a moment reduce him to the dust at pleasure. In the North the white no longer distinctly perceives the barrier that separates him from the degraded race, and he shuns the Negro with the more pertinacity [determination] since he fears lest they should some day be confounded together....

[American history shows that] in general, the colonies in which there were no slaves became more populous and more prosperous than those in which slavery flourished....

But this truth was most satisfactorily demonstrated when civilization reached the banks of the Ohio...[,] one of the most magnificent valleys which have ever been made the abode of man. Undulating lands extend upon both shores..., whose soil affords inexhaustible treasures to the laborer; on either bank the air is equally wholesome and the climate mild.... [Kentucky and Ohio] differ only in a single respect: Kentucky has admitted slavery, but...Ohio has prohibited the existence of slaves within its borders. Thus the traveler who floats down the current of the Ohio...may be said to sail between liberty and servitude; and a transient inspection of surrounding objects will convince him which of the two is more favorable to humanity.

Upon the left bank of the stream the population is sparse; from time to time one descries [sees] a troop of slaves loitering in the half-desert [half-wild] fields; the primeval forest reappears at every turn; society seems to be asleep, man to be idle, and nature alone offers a scene of activity and life.

From the right bank, on the contrary, a confused hum is heard, which proclaims afar the presence of industry; the fields are covered with abundant harvests; the elegance of the dwellings announces the taste and activity of the laborers; and man appears to be in the enjoyment of that wealth and contentment which is the reward of labor....

The influence of slavery extends still further: it affects the character of the master and imparts a peculiar tendency to his ideas and tastes. Upon both banks of the Ohio the character of the inhabitants is enterprising and energetic, but this vigor is very differently exercised in the two states. The white inhabitant of Ohio, obliged to subsist by his own exertions, regards temporal prosperity as the chief aim of his existence; and as the country which he occupies presents inexhaustible resources to his industry..., his acquisitive ardor surpasses the ordinary limits of human cupidity [greed]: he is tormented by the desire of wealth, and he boldly enters upon every path that fortune opens to him;...the resources of his intelligence are astonishing, and his avidity in the pursuit of gain amounts to a species of heroism.

But the Kentuckian scorns not only labor but all the undertakings that labor promotes; as he lives in an idle independence, his tastes are those of an idle man; money has lost a portion of its value in his eyes; he covets wealth much less than pleasure and excitement; and the energy which his neighbor devotes to gain turns with him to a passionate love of field sports and military exercises; he delights in violent bodily exertion, he is familiar with the use of arms, and is accustomed from a very early age to expose his life in single combat. Thus slavery prevents the whites not only from becoming opulent, but even from desiring to become so....

[A]lmost all the differences which may be noticed between the characters of the Americans in the Southern and in the Northern states have originated in slavery....

If, on the one hand, it be admitted (and the fact is unquestionable) that the colored population perpetually accumulate in the extreme South and increase more rapidly than the whites; and if, on the other hand, it be allowed that it is impossible to foresee a time at which the whites and the blacks will be so intermingled as to derive the same benefits from society, must it not be inferred that the blacks and the whites will, sooner or later, come to open strife in the Southern states?...

Whatever may be the efforts of the Americans of the South to maintain slavery, they will not always succeed. Slavery, now confined to a single tract of the civilized earth, attacked by Christianity as unjust and by political economy as prejudicial, and now contrasted with democratic liberty and the intelligence of our age, cannot survive. By the act of the master, or by the will of the slave, it will cease; and in either case great calamities may be expected to ensue. If liberty be refused to the Negroes of the South, they will in the end forcibly seize it for themselves; if it be given, they will before long abuse it....

VOLUME II

Section 2. Influence of Democracy on the Feelings of Americans

Of Individualism in Democratic Countries

...*Individualism* is a novel expression, to which a novel idea has given birth. Our fathers were only acquainted with *egoisme* (selfishness). Selfishness is a passionate and exaggerated love of self, which leads a man to connect everything with himself and to prefer himself to everything in the world. Individualism is a mature and calm feeling, which disposes each member of the community to sever himself from the mass of his fellows and to draw apart with his family and his friends, so that after he has thus formed a little circle of his own, he willingly leaves society at large to itself....

Among aristocratic nations, as families remain for centuries in the same condition, often on the same spot, all generations become, as it were, contemporaneous. A man almost always knows his forefathers and respects them; he thinks he already sees his remote descendants and he loves them. He willingly imposes duties on himself towards the former and the latter, and he will frequently sacrifice his personal gratifications to those who went before and to those who will come after him. Aristocratic institutions, moreover, have the effect of closely binding every man to several of his fellow citizens. As the classes of an aristocratic people are strongly marked and permanent, each of them is regarded by its own members as a sort of lesser country, more tangible and more cherished than the country at large. As in aristocratic communities all the citizens occupy fixed positions, one above another, the result is that each of them always sees a man above himself whose patronage is necessary to him, and below himself another man whose co-operation he may claim....In democratic times, on the contrary, when the duties of each individual to the race are much more clear, devoted service to any one man becomes more rare; the bond of human affection is extended, but it is relaxed.

Among democratic nations new families are constantly springing up, others are constantly falling away, and all that remain change their condition; the woof of time is every instant broken and the track of generations effaced. Those who went before are soon forgotten; of those who will come after, no one has any idea: the interest of man is confined to those in close propinquity [proximity] to himself....Aristocracy had made a chain of all the members of the community, from the peasant to the king; democracy breaks that chain and severs every link of it....

Thus not only does democracy make every man forget his ancestors, but it hides his descendants and separates his contemporaries from him; it throws him back forever upon himself alone and threatens in the end to confine him entirely within the solitude of his own heart....

Of the Taste for Physical well-being in America

In America the passion for physical well-being...is felt by all. The effort to satisfy even the least wants of the body and to provide the little conveniences of life is uppermost in every mind....

In aristocratic communities the wealthy, never having experienced a condition different from their own, entertain no fear of changing it; the existence of such conditions hardly occurs to them. The comforts of life are not to them the end of life, but simply a way of living; they regard them as existence itself, enjoyed but scarcely thought of....

If I turn my observation from the upper to the lower classes, I find analogous effects produced by opposite causes. Among a nation where aristocracy predominates in society and keeps it stationary, the people in the end get as much accustomed to poverty as the rich to their opulence. The [poor]...do not think of things which they despair of obtaining and which they hardly know enough of to desire....

When, on the contrary, the distinctions of ranks are obliterated and privileges are destroyed, when hereditary property is subdivided and education and freedom are widely diffused, the desire of acquiring the comforts of the world haunts the imagination of the poor, and the dread of losing them that of the rich. Many scanty fortunes spring up; those who possess them have a sufficient share of physical gratifications to conceive a taste for these pleasures, not enough to satisfy it. They never procure them without exertion, and they never indulge in them without apprehension. They are therefore always straining to pursue or to retain gratifications so delightful, so imperfect, so fugitive.

If I were to inquire what passion is most natural to men who are stimulated and circumscribed by the obscurity of their birth or the mediocrity of their fortune, I could discover none more peculiarly appropriate to their condition than this love of physical prosperity. The passion for physical comforts is essentially a passion of the middle classes; with those classes it grows and spreads, with them it is preponderant. From them it mounts into the higher orders of society and descends into the mass of the people.

I never met in America any citizen so poor as not to cast a glance of hope and envy on the enjoyments of the rich or whose imagination did not possess itself by anticipation of those good things that fate still obstinately withheld from him.

On the other hand, I never perceived among the wealthier inhabitants of the United States that proud contempt of physical gratifications which is sometimes to be met with even in the most opulent and dissolute aristocracies. Most of these wealthy persons were once poor; they have felt the sting of want; they were long a prey to adverse fortunes; and now that the victory is won, the passions which accompanied the contest have survived it; their minds are, as it were, intoxicated by the small enjoyments which they have pursued for forty years....

The taste for physical gratifications leads a democratic people into no...excesses. The love of well-being is there displayed as a tenacious, exclusive, universal passion, but its range is confined. To build enormous palaces, to conquer or to mimic nature, to ransack the world in order to gratify the passions of a man, is not thought of, but to add a few yards of land to your field, to plant an orchard, to enlarge a dwelling, to be always making life more comfortable and convenient, to avoid trouble, and to satisfy the smallest wants without effort and almost without cost. These are small objects, but the soul clings to them; it dwells upon them closely and day by day, till they at last shut out the rest of the world and sometimes intervene between itself and heaven....

Why Among the Americans All Honest Callings are Considered Honorable

Among a democratic people, where there is no hereditary wealth, every man works to earn a living, or has worked, or is born of parents who have worked. The notion of labor is therefore presented to the mind, on every side, as the necessary, natural, and honest condition of human existence. Not only is labor not dishonorable among such a people, but it is held in honor; the prejudice is not against it, but in its favor. In the United States a wealthy man thinks that he owes it to public opinion to devote his leisure to some kind of industrial or commercial pursuit or to public

business. He would think himself in bad repute if he employed his life solely in living....

No profession exists in which men do not work for money; and the remuneration that is common to them all gives them all an air of resemblance.

This serves to explain the opinions that the Americans entertain with respect to different callings. In America no one is degraded because he works, for everyone about him works also; nor is anyone humiliated by the notion of receiving pay, for the President of the United States also works for pay. He is paid for commanding, other men for obeying orders. In the United States professions are more or less laborious, more or less profitable; but they are never either high or low: every honest calling is honorable....

Section 3. Influence of Democracy on Manners Properly so Called

Influence of Democracy on the Family

...It has been universally remarked that in our time the several members of a family stand upon an entirely new footing towards each other; that the distance which formerly separated a father from his sons has been lessened; and that paternal authority, if not destroyed, is at least impaired. Something analogous to this, but even more striking, may be observed in the United States. In America the family, in the Roman and aristocratic signification of the word, does not exist. All that remains of it are a few vestiges in the first years of childhood, when the father exercises, without opposition, that absolute domestic authority which the feebleness of his children renders necessary and which their interest, as well as his own incontestable superiority, warrants. But as soon as the young American approaches manhood, the ties of filial obedience are relaxed day by day; master of his thoughts, he is soon master of his conduct. In America there is, strictly speaking, no adolescence: at the close of boyhood the man appears and begins to trace out his own path.

It would be an error to suppose that this is preceded by a domestic struggle in which the son has obtained by a sort of moral violence the liberty that his father refused him. The same habits[,] the same principles, which impel the one to assert his independence predispose the other to consider the use of that independence as an incontestable right....It may perhaps be useful to show how these changes which take place in family relations are closely connected with the social and political revolution that is approaching its consummation under our own eyes....

When men live more for the remembrance of what has been than for the care of what is, and when they are more given to attend to what their ancestors thought than to think themselves, the father is the natural and necessary tie between the past and the present, the link by which the ends of these two chains are connected. In aristocracies, then, the father is not only the civil head of the family, but the organ of its traditions, the expounder of its customs, the arbiter of its manners. He is listened to with deference, he is addressed with respect, and the love that is felt for him is always tempered with fear....

In a democratic family the father exercises no other power than that which is granted to the affection and the experience of age; his orders would perhaps be disobeyed, but his advice is for the most part authoritative. Though he is not hedged in with ceremonial respect, his sons at least accost him with confidence; they have no settled form of addressing him, but they speak to him constantly and are ready to consult him every day. The master and the constituted ruler have vanished; the father remains....

Education of Young Women in the United States

...Long before an American girl arrives at the marriageable age, her emancipation from maternal control begins: she has scarcely ceased to be a child when she already thinks for herself, speaks with freedom, and acts on her own impulse. The great scene of the world is constantly open to her view; far from seeking to conceal it from her, it is every day disclosed more completely and she is taught to survey it with a firm and calm gaze. Thus the vices and dangers of society are early revealed to her; as she sees them clearly, she views them without illusion and braves them without fear, for she is full of reliance on her own strength, and her confidence seems to be shared by all around her....

I have been frequently surprised and almost frightened at the singular address [way of speaking] and happy boldness with which young women in America contrive to manage their thoughts and their language amid all the difficulties of free conversation;...even amid the independence of early youth an American woman is always mistress of herself; she indulges in all permitted pleasures without yielding herself up to any of them, and her reason never allows the reins of self-guidance to drop, though it often seems to hold them loosely....

Although the Americans are a very religious people, they do not rely on religion alone to defend the virtue of woman; they seek to arm her reason also....

I am aware that an education of this kind is not without danger; I am sensible that it tends to invigorate the judgment at the expense of the imagination and to make cold and virtuous women instead of affectionate wives and agreeable companions to man. Society may be more tranquil and better regulated, but domestic life has often fewer charms....

The Young Woman in the Character of a Wife

In America the independence of woman is irrecoverably lost in the bonds of matrimony. If an unmarried woman is less constrained there than elsewhere, a wife is subjected to stricter obligations. The former makes her father's house an abode of freedom and of pleasure; the latter lives in the home of her husband as if it were a cloister. Yet these two different conditions of life are perhaps not so contrary as may be supposed, and it is natural that the American women should pass through the one to arrive at the other.

Religious communities and trading nations entertain peculiarly serious notions of marriage: the former consider the regularity of woman's life as the best pledge and most certain sign of the purity of her morals; the latter regard it as the highest security for the order and prosperity of the household. The Americans are at the same time a puritanical people and a commercial nation; their religious opinions as well as their trading habits consequently lead them to require much abnegation on the part of woman and a constant sacrifice of her pleasures to her duties, which is seldom demanded of her in Europe. Thus in the United States the inexorable opinion of the public carefully circumscribes woman within the narrow circle of domestic interests and duties and forbids her to step beyond it.

Upon her entrance into the world a young American woman finds these notions firmly established; she sees the rules that are derived from them; she is not slow to perceive that she cannot depart for an instant from the established usages of her contemporaries without putting in jeopardy her peace of mind, her honor, nay, even her social existence; and she finds the energy required for such an act of submission in the firmness of her understanding and in the virile habits which her education has given her. It may be said that she has learned by the use of her independence to surrender it without a struggle and without a murmur when the time comes for making the sacrifice.

But no American woman falls into the toils of matrimony as into a snare held out to her simplicity and ignorance. She has been taught beforehand what is expected of her and voluntarily and freely enters upon this engagement. She supports her new condition with courage because she chose it. As in America paternal discipline is very relaxed and the conjugal tie very strict, a young woman does not contract the latter without considerable circumspection and apprehension....American women do not marry until their understandings are exercised and ripened, whereas in other countries most women generally begin to exercise and ripen their understandings only after marriage....

How the Americans Understand the Equality of the Sexes

I have shown how democracy destroys or modifies the different inequalities that originate in society; but is this all, or does it not ultimately affect that great inequality of man and woman which has seemed, up to the present day, to be eternally based in human nature? I believe that the social changes that bring nearer to the same level the father and son, the master and servant, and, in general, superiors and inferiors will raise woman and make her more and more the equal of man....

There are people in Europe who, confounding [mixing] together the different characteristics of the sexes, would make man and woman into beings not only equal but alike. They would give to both the same functions, impose on both the same duties, and grant to both the same rights; they would mix them in all things—their occupations, their pleasures, their business. It may readily be conceived that by thus attempting to make one sex equal to the other, both are degraded, and from so preposterous a medley of the works of nature nothing could ever result but weak men and disorderly women.

It is not thus that the Americans understand that species of democratic equality which may be established between the sexes. They admit that as nature has appointed such wide differences between the physical and moral constitution of man and woman, her manifest design was to give a distinct employment to their various faculties; and they hold that improvement does not consist in making beings so dissimilar do pretty nearly the same things, but in causing each of them to fulfill their respective tasks in the best possible manner...in order that the great work of society may be the better carried on.

In no country has such constant care been taken as in America to trace two clearly distinct lines of action for the two sexes and to make them keep pace one with the other....American women never manage the outward concerns of the family or conduct a

business or take a part in political life; nor are they, on the other hand, ever compelled to perform the rough labor of the fields or to make any of those laborious efforts which demand the exertion of physical strength. No families are so poor as to form an exception to this rule....Hence it is that the women of America, who often exhibit a masculine strength of understanding and a manly energy, generally preserve great delicacy of personal appearance and always retain the manners of women although they sometimes show that they have the hearts and minds of men.

Nor have the Americans ever supposed that one consequence of democratic principles is the subversion of marital power or the confusion of the natural authorities in families. They hold that every association must have a head in order to accomplish its object, and that the natural head of the conjugal association is man. They do not therefore deny him the right of directing his partner....

This opinion is not peculiar to one sex and contested by the other; I never observed that the women of America consider conjugal authority as a fortunate usurpation of their rights, or that they thought themselves degraded by submitting to it. It appeared to me, on the contrary, that they attach a sort of pride to the voluntary surrender of their own will and make it their boast to bend themselves to the yoke, not to shake it off. Such, at least, is the feeling expressed by the most virtuous of their sex; the others are silent; and in the United States it is not the practice for a guilty wife to clamor for the rights of women while she is trampling on her own holiest duties....

[T]he Americans do not think that man and woman have either the duty or the right to perform the same offices, but they show an equal regard for both their respective parts; and though their lot is different, they consider both of them as beings of equal value. They do not give to the courage of woman the same form or the same direction as to that of man, but they never doubt her courage; and if they hold that man and his partner ought not always to exercise their intellect and understanding in the same manner, they at least believe the understanding of the one to be as sound as that of the other, and her intellect to be as clear. Thus, then, while they have allowed the social inferiority of woman to continue, they have done all they could to raise her morally and intellectually to the level of man....

As for myself, I do not hesitate to avow that although the women of the United States are confined within the narrow circle of domestic life, and their situation is in some respects one of extreme dependence, I have nowhere seen woman occupying a loftier position; and if I were asked, now that I am drawing to the close of this work, in which I have spoken of so many important things done by the Americans, to what the singular prosperity and growing strength of that people ought mainly to be attributed, I should reply: To the superiority of their women....

Why the National Vanity of the Americans is more Restless and Captious [apt to find fault] than that of the English

All free nations are vainglorious, but national pride is not displayed by all in the same manner. The Americans, in their intercourse with strangers, appear impatient of the smallest censure and insatiable of praise. The most slender eulogy is acceptable to them, the most exalted seldom contents them; they unceasingly harass you to extort praise, and if you resist their entreaties, they fall to praising themselves. It would seem as if, doubting their own merit, they wished to have it constantly exhibited before their eyes....

   If I say to an American that the country he lives in is a fine one, "Ay," he replies, "there is not its equal in the world." If I applaud the freedom that its inhabitants enjoy, he answers: "Freedom is a fine thing, but few nations are worthy to enjoy it." If I remark on the purity of morals that distinguishes the United States, "I can imagine," says he, "that a stranger, who has witnessed the corruption that prevails in other nations, would be astonished at the difference." At length I leave him to the contemplation of himself; but he returns to the charge and does not desist till he has got me to repeat all I had just been saying. It is impossible to conceive a more troublesome or more garrulous [talkative] patriotism; it wearies even those who are disposed to respect it.

   Such is not the case with the English. An Englishman calmly enjoys the real or imaginary advantages which, in his opinion, his country possesses.... The censure of foreigners does not affect him, and their praise hardly flatters him; ... his pride requires no sustenance; it nourishes itself. It is remarkable that two nations so recently sprung from the same stock should be so opposite to each other in their manner of feeling and conversing....

   When ... social conditions differ but little, the slightest privileges are of some importance; as every man sees around himself a million people enjoying precisely similar or analogous advantages, his pride becomes craving and jealous, he clings to mere trifles and doggedly defends them. In democracies, as

the conditions of life are very fluctuating, men have almost always recently acquired the advantages which they possess; the consequence is that they feel extreme pleasure in exhibiting them, to show others and convince themselves that they really enjoy them. As at any instant these same advantages may be lost, their possessors are constantly on the alert and make a point of showing that they still retain them. Men living in democracies love their country just as they love themselves, and they transfer the habits of their private vanity to their vanity as a nation....

How the Aspect of Society in the United States is at once Excited and Monotonous

It would seem that nothing could be more adapted to stimulate and to feed curiosity than the aspect [appearance] of the United States. Fortunes, opinions, and laws are there in ceaseless variation; it is as if immutable Nature herself were mutable, such are the changes worked upon her by the hand of man. Yet in the end the spectacle of this excited community becomes monotonous, and after having watched the moving pageant for a time, the spectator is tired of it.

   Among aristocratic nations every man is pretty nearly stationary in his own sphere, but men are astonishingly unlike each other; their passions, their notions, their habits, and their tastes are essentially different: nothing changes, but everything differs. In democracies, on the contrary, all men are alike and do things pretty nearly alike. It is true that they are subject to great and frequent vicissitudes, but as the same events of good or adverse fortune are continually recurring, only the name of the actors is changed, the piece is always the same. The aspect of American society is animated because men and things are always changing, but it is monotonous because all these changes are alike.

   Men living in democratic times have many passions, but most of their passions either end in the love of riches or proceed from it. The cause of this is not that their souls are narrower, but that the importance of money is really greater.... When the reverence that belonged to what is old has vanished, birth, condition, and profession no longer distinguish men, or scarcely distinguish them; hardly anything but money remains to create strongly marked differences between them and to raise some of them above the common level....

   The love of wealth is therefore to be traced, as either a principal or an accessory motive, at the bottom of all that the Americans do; this gives to all their passions a sort of family likeness and soon renders the survey of them exceedingly wearisome. This perpetual recurrence of the same passion is monotonous; the peculiar methods by which this passion seeks its own gratification are no less so....

The remark I here apply to America may indeed be addressed to almost all our contemporaries. Variety is disappearing from the human race; the same ways of acting, thinking, and feeling are to be met with all over the world. This is not only because nations work more upon each other and copy each other more faithfully, but as the men of each country relinquish more and more the peculiar opinions and feelings of a caste, a profession, or a family, they simultaneously arrive at something nearer to the constitution of man, which is everywhere the same. Thus they become more alike, even without having imitated each other. Like travelers scattered about some large wood, intersected by paths converging to one point, if all of them keep their eyes fixed upon that point and advance towards it, they insensibly draw nearer together, though they do not seek, though they do not see and know each other; and they will be surprised at length to find themselves all collected at the same spot. All the nations which take, not any particular man, but Man himself as the object of their researches and their imitations are tending in the end to a similar state of society, like these travelers converging at the central spot of the forest....

CHAPTER 12

Cole and Company Paint Nature's Nation

"The thoroughly American branch of painting"

In May 1831, just as Alexis de Tocqueville was setting foot on American soil (Chapter 11), a painter named Thomas Cole (1801–1848) arrived in France. Cole was, that spring, almost halfway through a long sojourn from his New York home. Eager to expand his artistic horizons and hone his skills, he had spent the last two years in England, visiting museums and exhibitions to study the "works of the Old Masters," talking to artists and experts; he would do the same in Paris, then head to Italy before returning to the United States in November 1832. Some of Cole's American friends fretted that Europe's spectacular scenery and rich artistic heritage would seduce him. "To Cole, The Painter, Departing for Europe," wrote the poet William Cullen Bryant[1]:

> *Fair scenes shall greet thee where thou goest—fair,*
> *But different—everywhere the trace of men....*
> *Gaze on them, till the tears shall dim thy sight,*
> *But keep that earlier, wilder image bright.*

Bryant need not have worried. Cole was impressed by what he saw in the Old World, and he painted many European landscapes (as well as Biblical scenes). But he remained true to the "wilder" America that had made him the country's best-known painter. "I have found...no natural scenery yet which has affected me so powerfully as that which I have seen in the wilderness places of America," he wrote from Italy. So closely were Cole's paintings identified with the new nation that in 1833 one observer demanded that "every American is bound to prove his love of country by admiring Cole."[2]

At first glance, Thomas Cole seems an unlikely candidate for the part of America's painter. Born in England in 1801, he had no formal artistic training either before or after he came to the United States with his family in 1818. For years the Coles struggled to get by, moving from Philadelphia to Ohio to Pittsburgh to New York while his father's business ventures failed time and again. By 1825, however, young Thomas had found his calling and his destiny: He would capture on canvas the American landscape in all of its glory. A trip up the Hudson River in the autumn of that year brought the obscure, penniless artist to the Catskill Mountains at the peak of their fall colors. Back in New York City, his depictions of that scenery "caused a sensation" and "his fame spread like fire" (Figure 12-1).[3]

It takes nothing away from Cole's ability or his ambition to say that he happened along at just the right time. As Mason Locke Weems knew (Chapter 10), in those days Americans sought—eagerly, even desperately—to construct a stronger sense of national identity. They were all too aware that the United States was a nation in name only, lacking the history and heroes, the language and literature, the art and music that in Europe were key ingredients of nationalism. "In the four quarters of the globe," sneered a British critic in 1820, sounding like he was channeling Dr. Alexander Hamilton (Chapter 5), "who reads an American book? Or goes to an American play? Or looks at an American picture or statue?"[4]

It was enough to give the young country an inferiority complex (one that, some say, continues to this day). To counter such snide remarks, Americans began to argue that the United States had something that Europe lacked: Vast tracts of untouched, untamed "Nature" that could become what one scholar calls "an effective substitute for a missing national tradition." Thus the boasting heard in Weems's *The Life of Washington* and bemoaned by Tocqueville (Chapter 11) grew louder. "[C]an there be a country in the world better calculated than ours to exercise and to exalt the imagination...?" asked one nationalist at the founding of the American Academy of the Fine Arts in 1816. "Here Nature has conducted her operations on a magnificent scale: extensive and elevated mountains—lakes of oceanic size—rivers of prodigious magnitude...—and boundless forests filled with wild beasts and savage men." Even as Cole was capturing the Catskills in the fall of 1825, another speaker at the American Academy in New York City exclaimed: "Come then, son of art, the genius of your country points you to its...enchanting scenery. There, where Nature needs no fictitious charms,...place on the canvass [*sic*] the lovely landscape and adorn our houses with American prospects and American skies."[5]

Instead of apologizing for being uncivilized, Americans now bragged about it. Living close to Nature makes us better, they insisted, more virtuous than those confined to sordid cities and dreary farms. "[I]n civilized Europe," Cole wrote in 1835, "the primitive features of scenery have long since been destroyed or modified—the extensive forests...have been felled—rugged mountains have been smoothed, and impetuous rivers turned from their courses to accommodate the tastes and necessities of a dense population—the once tangled wood is now a grassy lawn." Not so in America: Here "nature is still predominant," here "scenes of solitude...affect the mind with a more deep toned emotion than aught [anything] which the hand of man has touched."[6]

No wonder Cole's paintings of "unspoiled Nature" generated such excitement. His images brought Americans together in what one scholar calls "a set of common experiences and...reference points shared by people otherwise unconnected." And Cole was only the first: His friend and disciple Asher B. Durand (1796–1886), his pupil Frederic Edwin Church (1826–1900), along with Albert Bierstadt (1830–1902) and still others would follow over the next several decades, so many of them inspired by Cole and by the Hudson Valley that they later came to be called "the Hudson River School." Some forty years after Cole burst on the scene, one observer noted that "[t]he thoroughly American branch of painting, based upon the facts and tastes of the country and people, is the landscape. It surpasses all others in popular favor." Not only that, argues Matthew Baigell; this genre is "the most profound visual embodiment of the nineteenth-century American psyche."[7] What would Álvar Nuñez Cabeza de Vaca or Mary Rowlandson (Chapters 2 and 4) say about this celebration of "boundless forests filled with wild beasts and savage men"?

Nor were folks content to look at pictures. Many middle- and upper-class Americans with time on their hands and money in their pockets began leaving New York, Boston, and other cities to head for the Catskills, the Berkshire Mountains in western Massachusetts (where Mary Rowlandson had been held captive), and other spots where "Nature" could be enjoyed and "the hand of man" hidden. These tourists went for more than a nice view; scenery not only had a national, political meaning, it also had a profoundly spiritual dimension. As Weems knew, Americans were a deeply religious people. And those people took seriously the talk of "Nature's God" in the Declaration of Independence: They believed that the deity could be found not just by reading the Bible but by communing with Nature, that "scenes of solitude" were important because, as Cole put it, "they are" the Lord's "undefiled works." As it had been in Biblical times, so today "the wilderness is YET a fitting place to speak to God."[8]

Nor was this all that Cole and his contemporaries read into their wilderness. That the new nation had *so much* Nature, that it boasted such *abundant* natural resources, led many to conclude (as Puritans had, two centuries before) that this land was particularly close to God, particularly favored by God—perhaps even a new Garden of Eden. Indeed, echoing Theodor de Bry (Chapter 3), Cole insisted that "We are still in Eden." Just as Cole's canvases gave the country a national symbol, so they also proclaimed the artist's belief that God, Nature, and America were close relatives.[9]

Connecting people to the divine, advancing the cause of American identity—these tasks gave the landscape artist a fervent sense of mission. "My highest ambition lies in excelling in the art" of landscape painting, wrote a teenaged Frederic Church to Cole when applying to work with the master. "I pursue it not as a source of gain or merely as an amusement; I trust I have higher aims than these." Those aims included being society's "soul and conscience," as art historian Angela Miller puts it. And society, delighted, made these men into celebrities: newspapers reported their comings and goings, their current projects and future prospects; guidebooks invited tourists to their studios; thousands paid to view their paintings.[10]

We should not assume, however, that those crowds saw "reality." Despite claims about Nature needing "no fictitious charms," despite one patron telling Cole that "[a]bove all things…*truth*…in *drawing* the scenes of our own country is essential" because "I prefer *real American* scenes," landscape artists had other ideas. Cole, for example, neither would nor could give an exact likeness. (Even America's first photographers, as you will see in Chapter 19, embellished reality.) "If the imagination is shackled," he replied to his patron, "and nothing is described but what we see, seldom will anything truly great be produced…in Painting." "I believe with you," he admitted, "that…a painter [must] always have his mind upon Nature." But, he went on, "the most lovely and perfect parts of Nature may be brought together [on one canvas], and combined in a whole that shall surpass in beauty and effect any picture painted from a single view."[11]

To achieve that effect, Cole went on forays into the woods not with paints, brushes, and canvas but with pencil, paper, and ink to sketch scenes that he could "compose" later. Once back in his studio, he waited a while before beginning, for he did not want what he had seen to be too fresh in his memory. "I never succeed in painting scenes, however beautiful, immediately upon returning from them," he wrote. "I must wait for time to draw a veil over the common details, the unessential parts, which shall leave the great features…dominant in the mind." In short, Cole took what we would call artistic license.[12]

Cole's pictures, whether he admitted it or not, were also shaped by contemporary American tastes. Like Weems, he had to have his finger on America's pulse. He might chafe at the demands of patrons and public, but to earn a living Cole had to sell paintings, and to sell paintings he could not stray too far from what people wanted. Thus there was a complex relationship between an artist *mirroring* popular likes and dislikes and actually *shaping* them. "I long for the time when I can paint whatever my imagination would dictate," he confided to his diary late in life, "without fear of running into pecuniary difficulties. This painting for money, and to please the many, is sadly repulsive to me." That time never came, however: Cole, having known poverty in his youth, had no desire to return to it.[13]

These variables—reality and imagination, art and business—shaped every canvas Cole composed. As you study these texts, look for patterns, signatures, in his perch and perspective, in his foregrounds and backgrounds, in his waters and skies, in his trees and figures, in what he included and what he left out. Scholars write that some aspects of Cole's scenes are "obviously exaggerations" contrived to tell a story and convey a moral, to heighten "visual drama" while offering a "sense of danger and revelation."[14] Can you identify some of those contrivances? Some of the stories and morals? Compare Figure 12-2, Cole's 1836 treatment of the *View from Mount Holyoke, Northampton, Massachusetts, After a Thunderstorm (The Oxbow)*, with another treatment of the same view at almost the same time (Figure 12-3). What do the similarities and differences reveal about Cole's vision?

Closer to home, Cole's treatment of his beloved Catskills also holds clues to his agenda. To profit from the growing tourist trade, in 1824 some enterprising men built Catskill Mountain House near Kaaterskill Falls, erected a lookout tower, and put in steps and railings so that visitors could approach the falls safely. A decade later other enterprising men began building railroad lines through these hills and valleys. Yet Cole's later canvases often obscured or omitted the railings and railroads, the tourists and train tracks.

The artist's views on America's past, present, and future have been the subject of considerable debate. On the one hand, there is evidence that Cole, profoundly upset with those railroads and tourists invading "scenes of solitude," was pessimistic about America's future prospects. "Nothing is more disagreeable to me," he wrote in 1829, "than the sight of lands that are just clearing with its prostrate trees—black stumps—burnt and deformed." Soon the tree-cutters were in Cole's Catskills backyard. "[T]hey are cutting down all the trees in the beautiful valley on which I have looked so often with a loving eye," he moaned, penning poems with titles like "Complaint of the Forest" and "On seeing that a favorite tree of the Author's had been cut down." In 1835 he told a New York City audience that "I cannot but express my sorrow that the beauty of such landscapes is quickly passing away—the ravages of the axe are daily increasing—the most noble scenes are made destitute, and oftentimes with a wantonness and barbarism scarcely credible in a civilized nation."[15]

On the other hand, there are signs that Cole, on canvas and on paper, considered the American advance across the continent to be progress. In olden times, he wrote, the country's "primaeval forests" had a "gloom [that] was peopled by savage beasts, and scarcely less savage men." Now the continent held "an enlightened and increasing people" who, "with activity and power," have "wrought changes that seem magical." And so it would continue. "Where the wolf roams," Cole predicted, "the plough shall glisten; on the gray crag shall rise temple and tower—mighty deeds shall be done in the now pathless wilderness; and poets yet unborn shall sanctify the soil."[16] Having studied his paintings with care, which interpretation of his take on the future do you find more convincing?

That Thomas Cole's paintings touched Americans deeply helps to explain the reaction to his unexpected death in 1848 at age forty-seven. Newspapers mourned this "national calamity." His Catskill home became a shrine. "Though the great man has departed," wrote the landscape painter Jasper Cropsey, who had made the pilgrimage to Cole's house, "yet he has left a spell behind him that is not broken."[17]

Over the next two decades, Cropsey would join Church, Durand, Bierstadt, and others who followed in Cole's footsteps, personifying "the artist who becomes the public voice of a culture, summarizing its beliefs, embodying its ideas, and confirming its assumptions." Though rooted in New York City studios and Hudson Valley environs (Church eventually built a home directly across the river from Cole's), these men ventured farther afield—Church to Jamaica and South America, Bierstadt to the West (Figures 12-5–12-7, 12-9, 12-10).[18]

Scholars disagree on whether these artists went farther than Cole in other ways as well. Some argue that these men employed a similar "stylistic vocabulary" and viewed the country through the same national and spiritual lenses as Cole. Bierstadt's *Rocky Mountains*, for example (Figure 12-9)—"eminently national," one critic called it—can be read as carrying familiar ways of depicting the American land into the unfamiliar territory of the Far West, of capturing (and therefore commanding) the wilderness, thereby helping make real Thomas Paine's fiction about the country being a *continent* (Chapter 7). Others, however, see "marked differences between Cole and those who followed."[19] Setting Cole alongside his heirs, which argument is more persuasive?

Whatever their differences, all of these painters shared with one another—and with us—a veneration of nature. Yet they are at most distant cousins to Americans today. We find it ironic—at best—that men professing a deep love for wilderness were so celebrated by a society intent on conquering that wilderness. Cole produced work for railroad men who wanted "to possess a picture showing what the valley of the Catskill was *before* the art of modern improvement"—such as their own railroads—"found footing there."[20] Church, too, had patrons among rail barons, while Bierstadt not only took trains west to paint, his first visit there was with a U.S. Army surveying and road-building expedition. Most of us share with the Hudson River School the notion that wilderness is a vital part of American identity (witness our National Parks and National Forests, our wilderness areas and wildlife refuges). Some nowadays question blind faith in the gospel of "progress" or in the idea that it is America's destiny to expand across the continent, to obey the divine decree to "subdue the earth" (Chapter 1). What would they say about America's being "Nature's nation" today?

Questions for Consideration and Conversation

1. From the creation stories in Chapter 1 forward, the landscape and people's relations with that landscape have been a central part of *American Conversations.* How do the landscapes depicted here contribute to that conversation? Do they take it in entirely new directions, or continue along the same paths?

2. Why did paintings like these emerge when they did rather than, say, a century or two earlier, in Dr. Alexander Hamilton's or Mary Rowlandson's day?

3. What role does the human figure play in these images?

4. As you know, artists took pains to construct images of the landscape, not merely to "reproduce" what they saw. What themes, what images, what "characters," were they drawn to? Why?

5. Compare Thomas Cole's image of Mount Holyoke with William Bartlett's. What differences do you see? What might be the significance of those differences?

6. What messages are contained in the paintings that move beyond the "wilderness" to include people moving into that wilderness? Is the end of wilderness being celebrated? Mourned?

7. How closely did the painters who came after Cole—Church, Durand, Bierstadt—follow in his footsteps? How far did they depart from his style, his subjects, his themes?

8. Is it correct to include Bierstadt's images of the Rocky Mountains and Yosemite, painted in the 1860s, in a "school" that was rooted in the Hudson Valley a generation earlier?

Endnotes

1. Louis Legrand Noble, *The Life and Works of Thomas Cole*, ed. Elliot S. Vesell (Cambridge, MA, 1964), 89; Earl A. Powell, *Thomas Cole* (New York, 1990), 49–50.

2. Noble, *Life and Works*, 101 (Cole); Oswaldo Rodriguez Roque, "The Exaltation of American Landscape Painting," in John K. Howat, ed., *American Paradise: The World of the Hudson River School* (New York, 1987), 24 ("every American").

3. Roque, "Exaltation," 24 ('sensation'); Noble, *Life and Works*, 36.

4. Roque, "Exaltation," 21.

5. Barbara Novak, *Nature and Culture: American Landscape Painting, 1825–1875*, Revised edition (New York, 1995), 20 ("substitute"); Roque, "Exaltation," 22 (1816); Albert Boime, *The Magisterial Gaze: Manifest Destiny and American Landscape Painting, c. 1830–1865* (Washington, DC, 1991), 49 (1825).

6. Thomas Cole, "Essay on American Scenery," in Cole, *The Collected Essays and Prose Sketches*, ed. Marshall Tymn (St. Paul, MN, 1980), 8.

7. Angela Miller, *The Empire of the Eye: Landscape Representation and American Cultural Politics, 1825–1875* (Ithaca, NY, 1993), 8 ("unconnected"); Roque, "Exaltation," 45 ("surpasses"); Matthew Baigell, *Albert Bierstadt* (New York, 1981), 12 ("psyche").

8. Cole, "American Scenery," 5, 8.

9. Ibid., 17.

10. Franklin Kelly, *Frederic Edwin Church and the National Landscape* (Washington, DC, 1988), 1; Miller, *Empire of the Eye*, 63.

11. Powell, *Cole*, 28 ("truth"); Roque, "Exaltation," 24–25.

12. Roque, "Exaltation," 31.

13. Noble, *Life and Works*, 274.

14. Roque, "Exaltation," 24.

15. Cole, "American Scenery," 8 ("wildness"), 17 ("sorrow"); Miller, *Empire of the Eye*, 60 ("disagreeable"); Novak, *Nature and Culture*, 160 (poems), 163 ("loving eye").

16. Cole, "American Scenery," 7–8, 17.

17. J. Gray Sweeney, "The Advantages of Genius and Virtue: Thomas Cole's Influence, 1848–1858," in William H. Truettner and Alan Wallach, eds., *Thomas Cole: Landscape into History* (New Haven, CT and Washington, DC, 1994), 113 ("calamity"); Kelly, *Church and the National Landscape*, ix (Cropsey).

18. Barbara Novak, quoted in Kelly, *Church and the National Landscape*, viii ("public voice").

19. William H. Truettner, "Ideology and Image: Justifying Westward Expansion," in Truettner, ed., *The West as America: Reinterpreting Images of the Frontier, 1820–1920* (Washington, DC, 1991), 30 ("vocabulary"); Novak, *Nature and Culture*, 25 ("national"); Miller, *Empire of the Eye*, 21 ("marked").

20. Alan Wallach, "Thomas Cole: Landscape and the Course of Empire," in Truettner and Wallach, eds., *Cole*, 74.

PAINTINGS BY THOMAS COLE, FREDERIC CHURCH, WILLIAM BARTLETT, ASHER DURAND, AND ALBERT BIERSTADT

FIGURE 12-1 *Falls of Kaaterskill*, 1826, by Thomas Cole.   *Source:* Wadsworth Atheneum Museum of Art/Art Resource, NY.

FIGURE 12-2 *View from Mount Holyoke, Northampton, Massachusetts, After a Thunderstorm (The Oxbow)*, 1836, by Thomas Cole.   *Source:* Metropolitan Museum of Art/Art Resource, NY.

FIGURE 12-3 *View from Mount Holyoke,* 1840, by William Bartlett.   *Source:* Milstein Division of United States History, Local History & Genealogy, The New York Public Library, Astor, Lenox and Tilden Foundations.

FIGURE 12-4 *The Pic-Nic,* 1846, by Thomas Cole.   *Source:* Brooklyn Museum.

FIGURE 12-5 *The Catskill Creek*, c. 1845, by Frederic Church.   *Source:* The Catskill Creek, Oil painting on panel, 1845, by Frederic Edwin Church OL.1980.1873.

FIGURE 12-6 *New England Scenery*, 1851, by Frederic Church.   *Source:* George Walter Vincent Smith Art Museum.

FIGURE 12-7 *Twilight in the Wilderness*, 1860, by Frederic Church.   *Source:* The Cleveland Museum of Art.

FIGURE 12-8 *Oregon City on the Willamette River*, 1850, John Mix Stanley.   *Source:* Amon Carter Museum.

FIGURE 12-9 *The Rocky Mountains, Lander's Peak*, 1863, by Albert Bierstadt.   *Source:* Metropolitan Museum of Art/Art Resource, NY.

FIGURE 12-10 *Dome of the Yosemite*, 1867, by Albert Bierstadt.   *Source:* St. Johnsbury Athenaeum.

CHAPTER 13

Reverend Apess Rewrites American History

*"Let every man of color wrap himself in mourning, for the 22nd of December
and the 4th of July are days of mourning and not of joy"*

T he America that Alexis de Tocqueville toured and Thomas Cole painted had come a long way
from its colonial and revolutionary beginnings. A bustling nation of some thirteen million people
in 1830, it stretched from the Atlantic to the Mississippi and beyond. The end of the War of 1812,
the country's "second war for independence," enabled the young republic to feel more secure than ever
before: British troops might have burned the nation's capital, but they had not conquered the nation.
With that conflict ended, the new country could, for the first time, fully turn its gaze from east across the
ocean to west across the continent.

With that shift came a corresponding change in tone and mood. Having bowed to or gawked
at gentlemen like Dr. Alexander Hamilton in colonial times (Chapter 5) and followed Joseph Plumb
Martin's "great men" into battle against the British in 1776 (Chapter 9), Americans now celebrated the
common man. Mason Locke Weems's George Washington—not the aspiring young gentleman but the
plain, pious farmer—was the hero of the day (Chapter 10). Alongside him in the national hall of fame
stood Benjamin Franklin, whose *Autobiography*, first published in 1817, enshrined the self-made man as
an American icon (Chapter 6). At almost the same time, a flesh-and-blood hero burst on the American
scene. With his stunning victory over the British at the Battle of New Orleans in January 1815, Andrew
Jackson catapulted to national prominence, the very personification of a man of the people, a man of
humble origins who made himself rich and famous. Jackson's election to the presidency in 1828 seemed
to confirm that a new age had now begun.

Voting for Jackson, reading about Washington and Franklin, admiring Cole, Americans also began
celebrating a glorious past. The years after 1815 helped by supplying lots of anniversaries. The bicenten-
nials of the Pilgrims' landing at Plymouth (1820) and the Puritans' founding of Massachusetts (1830),
the deaths of John Adams and Thomas Jefferson on the very same Independence Day (July 4, 1826), the
centennial of Washington's birth (1832)—the country marked these and other milestones with songs and
speeches, solemn ceremonies and marble monuments that boasted of America's past and promised still
greater things to come.

As this chapter and others ahead of you demonstrate, however, not everyone was celebrating.
Amid the congratulations and commemorations, the boasts and the toasts, one can hear voices singing
of America in a very different key. The Indian William Apess, the abolitionists and feminists Sarah and
Angelina Grimké, the former slave Frederick Douglass—each challenged the upbeat tempo of the age.
As you read them, compare their views on the new nation's past, present, and future. Were they aiming
at the same targets, using the same rhetoric, deploying the same weapons? Were their songs of protest

harmonious or discordant? Would you agree that Apess's texts resemble the antislavery writings of the Grimkés and Douglass? These works merit comparison, too, with voices of protest already familiar to you, such as *Common Sense* and the Declaration of Independence (Chapter 7).

The first of these protesters is also the least well known: William Apess (1798–1839), a Pequot Indian and Methodist minister. So obscure is Apess that most of what we know about him comes from his autobiography, *A Son of the Forest*, portions of which you will read below. Born in western Massachusetts, he was the son of William and Candace Apes (he later added the second "s"), Pequots who soon after William's birth returned to their people's traditional homelands in southeastern Connecticut.

Thus began a hard childhood. When the boy was three, his parents separated for a time, leaving him with his maternal grandparents. A year later, a vicious beating by his grandmother brought the authorities, who placed young William in the care of a local white couple. This was the first of several white families—some cruel, some kind—who would take the Pequot boy in and see to his upbringing in exchange for his labor, a common practice for children of poor families in those times. Besides getting him a few winters of schooling, these masters and mistresses introduced William to Christianity, thereby setting him on a long spiritual journey.

The account of this journey can seem to modern readers, as one student of Apess has written, "formulaic and monotonous." But it would have been familiar, and exciting, to readers in his own day, steeped as they were in evangelical Christianity and the popular literature of "conversion narratives," gripping tales of sin and redemption in which anguish and joy intermingle in a soul's search for salvation. (Mary Rowlandson's account [Chapter 4] is a variant of the conversion narrative, and one scholar suggests that *Son of the Forest* is not only a *conversion* narrative but also, like Rowlandson's, a *captivity* narrative. Do you agree?)[1]

In 1813, the teenager's life began a new chapter when he converted to Methodism and ran away from the last of his masters. His wanderings led him to New York City, then with the United States Army to northern New York and Canada to fight the British. Discharged from the service, Apess spent time with native "brethren" (possibly Iroquois) in the U.S.–Canada borderlands, then began to make his way "home" (note his use of that word).

By 1820, back among his people, Apess's story began yet another chapter when he married and started a family while also beginning to speak at Methodist meetings, a sect that many "respectable" Christians found subversive because it welcomed poor as well as rich, "colored" as well as white. By the end of that decade, Apess was a licensed Methodist minister preaching throughout New England and eastern New York. Those travels took him to the Mashpee Indian community on Cape Cod, where in 1833 he helped lead a protest against attempts by Massachusetts authorities to control Mashpee political and religious life. Arrested, jailed, and fined, nonetheless Apess helped Mashpees regain the right to govern themselves. After delivering and publishing his *Eulogy on King Philip* in Boston in 1836, Apess, hounded by creditors, went to New York City, where he died in 1839.

Brutal beatings by kin and master alike, battles with the bottle and other sins, a wandering and impoverished existence—it was clearly a hard life. Yet Apess, in finding a calling and a community, in finding his voice and his pen, was luckier than most Native Americans of his day. The period of his life's span, roughly 1800 to 1840, was a dark time in Indian America. This era is most famous (or infamous) for the forced government "removal" of thousands of natives—Cherokees, Creeks, and others—from their homelands to regions west of the Mississippi River. In fact, however, Indians were being removed from American life in a whole variety of ways in that period. During the Revolutionary era, for example, an Indian was the most common symbol used to represent *America*; soon thereafter, classical figures like "Columbia" and caricatures like Uncle Sam replaced the native.

Other kinds of erasures went hand in hand with this shift. Historian Ruth Herndon has shown how, in New England after the Revolution, local officials began labeling native people "colored" or "mulatto," refusing to consider them Indian any more. So, too, with historical memory: Allied, some of them (including Pequots and Mashpees), with British colonists in the Seven Years' War (1756–1763) and again with the rebels against Britain during the Revolutionary War (1775–1783), that alliance was forgotten. In its place were the gruesome tales of bloody Indian savagery that Weems told (Chapter 10), horror stories that Apess himself heard growing up in white Connecticut households.[2]

By 1830, then, the Indian's place in American life had changed forever. Álvar Nuñez Cabeza de Vaca, Theodor de Bry, and others all the way through Thomas Jefferson had considered Indians human beings at an earlier stage of social development, capable of becoming "civilized." In Apess's day, on the other hand, most whites thought Native Americans were irredeemable savages whose extinction was at once inevitable and imminent. From the common feature of the social landscape that Dr. Hamilton toured in 1744 (Chapter 5), Indians were now, as Alexis de Tocqueville and many others wrote (and Thomas Cole painted), "doomed to perish."

Merely by existing, then, William Apess in particular and the Pequot people in general defied those who put Indians on the edge of extinction. For two centuries, whites had been trying to render Pequots invisible. After a devastating war in the 1630s, when colonists killed or enslaved most of that nation, the victors forbade use of the nation's very name "so that," one Puritan wrote, "the name of the Pequots . . . is blotted out from under heaven."[3] But the tribe refused to disappear. In Apess's time, perhaps one hundred of them lived on two small Connecticut reservations; many more were, like his parents in 1798, scattered throughout New England, moving from place to place in search of work, intermarrying with Indians from other nations as well as with whites, African Americans, even Spanish and Portuguese sailors. The result was a people diverse in culture and appearance—often speaking English, dressing like poor whites, and otherwise "passing" as white—yet firmly grounded in an enduring native identity. Pequots today, best known for their casino and museum near Mystic, Connecticut, are heirs to that tradition of camouflage, adaptation, and resilience.

Like his people, William Apess shatters stereotypes about Indians that were prevalent then—and still are now. Upon starting *A Son of the Forest*, you are likely to think that the author does not "sound Indian," at least when compared with Hollywood movies. His spiritual travels and travails resemble Mary Rowlandson's, prompting the question: Can someone be both an Indian *and* a Christian, or is embracing the conqueror's foreign faith a form of surrender? Not only that, but *Son of the Forest* sounds a bit like Ben Franklin and George Washington; compare it with their stories for the values it espouses and the messages it contains. Some scholars even wonder whether this, the first published autobiography by an American Indian, can be considered an "authentic" native voice at all: It is written in English, not Algonquian; its central concern is Christianity, not a native faith; even its subject—a man's life—is alien to native oral traditions, which generally do not structure narratives around one person.[4]

Apess would be delighted by our confusion. From his title onward, one of his goals was to undermine assumptions about how a "real Indian" ought to sound. Many popular stories, poems, and plays penned by whites of his day talked of Indians in just these terms, *children of nature* who would disappear when their woodland haunts fell to the axes and plows of white farmers. Apess lured readers in with the title, then surprised them with the announcement that the story was "Written by Himself"—surely no "real" Indian can write?—and with the news that he was born in a Massachusetts town, far from any "forest." What passages in the rest of the work further his demolition of stereotypes about Indians?

In the second excerpt here, *Eulogy on King Philip*, Apess turned from his own history to America's. His subject, largely forgotten nowadays (except by readers of this book!), would have been well known to Apess's audience in 1836. You will recall from Chapter 4 that Philip (Metacom), son of the Pilgrims' friend Massasoit, was a Wampanoag leader most famous (or, to Puritans, infamous) for leading a revolt in 1675–76 against colonists, since called "King Philip's War."

In resurrecting Philip, Apess hoped to counter the congratulatory commemorations enthusiastic New Englanders put on during his day. In this, the *Eulogy* is kin to *Common Sense* (Chapter 7). Like Thomas Paine trying to destroy colonial veneration for the King and transform Americans from weak and divided colonies into a strong and united nation, Apess wanted people to think twice about who were the heroes, and who the villains. What tools did Apess use, what "buttons" did he push, to bring this about?

The Pequot clergyman was not alone in his interpretation of American history. Some white authors at the time had kind things to say about Philip as a noble warrior, a tragic hero, and cruel words for the Puritans who fought him. Where Apess differed, writes his modern editor Barry O'Connell, was in how he linked past with present: Arguing that the children of those first colonists were continuing that grim legacy in 1836, he demanded that they mend their ways. "For him," O'Connell concludes, "history was to be not an excuse for nostalgia or vain regret but an accounting of what had been and what might yet be done differently."[5]

Accustomed to pondering what Americans remember and what we forget—as you did in Chapter 7 with Paine and Jefferson or in Chapter 9 with Joseph Plumb Martin—it is worth considering why Apess, like Martin and Paine, languished in obscurity until recently. Americans in the 1830s devoured James Fenimore Cooper's *Last of the Mohicans*, flocked to plays about the doomed "Metacomet," and clamored for a glimpse of defeated warriors from the west such as the Sauk leader Black Hawk; yet they relegated Apess and his writings to the shadowy sidelines of American life. Why?

Questions for Consideration and Conversation

1. What makes William Apess an Indian? What casts doubt on his Indian identity?
2. How does Apess's spiritual journey compare with others you have read, such as Mary Rowlandson's?
3. Some have argued that a native cannot be Christian *and* Indian, that adopting the faith of the colonizers is a form of surrender. How would Apess respond to that argument?
4. What were the principal obstacles in Apess's journey through life? What were his main sources of support?
5. Which text did you find more engaging, more powerful, more illuminating: *Son of the Forest* or *Eulogy on King Philip*? Which do you think white Americans at the time would have found more engaging, more powerful, and more illuminating?
6. Alexis de Tocqueville wrote that Pequots in particular had vanished and that Native Americans in general soon would be gone. If he had met Apess during his visit to the United States or read Apess's work, would he have revised his opinions? If so, how? If not, why not?
7. Why has Apess been forgotten for so long?

Endnotes

1. Barry O'Connell, ed., *On Our Own Ground: The Complete Writings of William Apess, A Pequot* (Amherst, MA, 1992), lv; Hilary E. Wyss, *Writing Indians: Literacy, Christianity, and Native Community in Early America* (Amherst, MA, 2000), 157–58.
2. Ruth Wallis Herndon, *Unwelcome Americans: Living on the Margin in Early New England* (Philadelphia, PA, 2001).
3. Quoted in O'Connell, ed., *On Our Own Ground*, xxv.
4. Ibid., xlv; Wyss, *Writing Indians*, 4–6, 155–56; Cheryl Walker, *Indian Nation: Native American Literature and Nineteenth-Century Nationalisms* (Durham, NC, 1997), 13.
5. O'Connell, ed., *On Our Own Ground*, 276.

WILLIAM APESS, *A SON OF THE FOREST* (1831)

Source: William Apess, *A Son of the Forest*, in *A Son of the Forest and Other Writings*, ed. Barry O'Connell. Amherst: University of Massachusetts Press, 1997. [Originally published 1831.]

...Chapter I

...My grandfather was a white man and married a female attached to the royal family of Philip, king of the Pequot tribe of Indians, so well known in that part of American history which relates to the wars between the whites and the natives. My grandmother was, if I am not misinformed, the king's granddaughter and a fair and beautiful woman. This statement is given not with a view of appearing great in the estimation of others—what, I would ask, is *royal* blood?—the blood of a king is no better than that of the subject. We are in fact but one family; we are all the descendants of one great progenitor—Adam....

[M]y father was of mixed blood, his father being a white man and his mother a native or, in other words, a red woman. On attaining a sufficient age to act for himself, he joined the Pequot tribe, to which he was maternally connected. He was well received, and in a short time afterward married a female of the tribe, in whose veins a single drop of the white man's blood never flowed. Not long after his marriage, he removed to what was then called the back settlements..., where he pitched his tent in the woods of...Colrain, near the Connecticut River....In this, the place of my birth, he continued some time and afterward removed to Colchester,...Connecticut. At the latter place, our little family lived for nearly three years in comparative comfort.

Circumstances, however, changed with us, as with many other people, in consequence of which I was taken together with my two brothers and sisters into my grandfather's family. One of my uncles dwelt in the same hut. Now my grandparents were not the best people in the world—like all others who are wedded to the beastly vice of intemperance, they would drink to excess whenever they could procure rum, and as usual in such cases, when under the influence of liquor, they would not only quarrel and fight with each other but would at times turn upon their unoffending grandchildren and beat them in a most cruel manner. It makes me shudder, even at this time, to think how frequent and how great have been our sufferings in consequence of the introduction of this "cursed stuff" into our family—and I could wish, in the sincerity of my soul, that it were banished from our land.

Our fare was of the poorest kind, and even of this we had not enough. Our clothing also was of the worst description: Literally speaking, we were clothed with rags, so far only as rags would suffice to cover our nakedness. We were always contented and happy to get a cold potato for our dinners..., and many a night have we gone supperless to rest, if stretching our limbs on a bundle of straw, without any covering against the weather, may be called rest....Some of our white neighbors, however, took pity on us and measurably administered to our wants, by bringing us frozen milk, with which we were glad to satisfy the calls of hunger....Happily, we did not continue in this very deplorable condition for a great length of time. Providence smiled on us, but in a particular manner.

Our parents quarreled, parted, and went off to a great distance, leaving their helpless children to the care of their grandparents. We lived at this time in an old house, divided into two apartments—one of which was occupied by my uncle. Shortly after my father left us, my grandmother, who had been out among the whites, returned in a state of intoxication and, without any provocation whatever on my part, began to belabor me most unmercifully with a club; she asked me if I hated her, and I very innocently answered in the affirmative as I did not then know what the word meant and thought all the while that I was answering aright; and so she continued asking me the same question, and I as often answered her in the same way, whereupon she continued beating me, by which means one of my arms was broken in three different places. I was then only four years of age....[M]y uncle...., being alarmed for my safety, came down to take me away, when my grandfather made toward him with a firebrand, but very fortunately he succeeded in rescuing me and thus saved my life, for had he not come at the time he did, I would most certainly have been killed. My grandparents who acted in this unfeeling and cruel manner were by my mother's side—those by my father's side were Christians, lived and died happy in the love of God....

The next morning, when it was discovered that I had been most dangerously injured, my uncle determined to make the whites acquainted with my condition. He accordingly went to a Mr. Furman, the person who had occasionally furnished us with milk, and the good man came immediately to see me. He found me dreadfully beaten, and the other children in a state of absolute suffering; and as he was extremely anxious that something should be done for our relief, he applied to the selectmen of the town in our behalf, who after duly considering the application adjudged that we should be severally taken and bound out [as servants]. Being entirely disabled in consequence of the wounds I had received, I was supported at the expense of the town for about twelve months....

I presume that the reader will exclaim, "What savages your grandparents were to treat unoffending, helpless children in this cruel manner." But this cruel and unnatural conduct was the effect of some cause. I attribute it in a great measure to the whites, inasmuch as they introduced among my countrymen that bane of comfort and happiness, ardent spirits— seduced them into a love of it and, when under its unhappy influence, wronged them out of their lawful possessions—that land, where reposed the ashes of their sires.... Now many of them were seen reeling about intoxicated with liquor, neglecting to provide for themselves and families, who before were assiduously engaged in supplying the necessities of those depending on them for support....

After I had been nursed for about twelve months, I had so far recovered that it was deemed expedient to bind me out, until I should attain the age of twenty-one years. Mr. Furman...was a poor man....As I was only five years old, he at first thought that his circumstances would not justify him in keeping me, as it would be some considerable time before I could render him much service. But such was the attachment of the family toward me that he came to the conclusion to keep me until I was of age, and he further agreed to give me so much instruction as would enable me to read and write. Accordingly, when I attained my sixth year, I was sent to school, and continued for six successive winters.... This was all the instruction of the kind I ever received....

Chapter II...

I well remember the conversation that took place between Mrs. Furman and myself when I was about six years of age; she was attached to the Baptist church and was esteemed as a very pious woman.... [S]he spoke to me respecting a future state of existence and told me that I might die and enter upon it, to which I replied that I was too young—that old people only died. But she assured me that I was not too young, and in order to convince me..., she referred me to the graveyard, where many younger and smaller persons than myself were laid to molder in the earth.... About this time I was taken to meeting.... This was the first time I had ever entered a house of worship,

and instead of attending to what the minister said, I was employed in gazing about the house or playing with the unruly boys with whom I was seated in the gallery. On my return home, Mr. Furman, who had been apprised of my conduct, told me that I had acted very wrong. He did not, however, stop here. He went on to tell me how I ought to behave in church, and to this very day I bless God for such wholesome and timely instruction....

[S]o completely was I weaned from the interests and affections of my [native American] brethren that a mere threat of being sent away among the Indians into the dreary woods had a much better effect in making me obedient to the commands of my superiors than any corporal punishment that they ever inflicted. I had received a lesson in the unnatural treatment of my own relations, which could not be effaced, and I thought that, if those who should have loved and protected me treated me with such unkindness, surely I had no reason to expect mercy or favor at the hands of those who knew me in no other relation than that of a cast-off member of the tribe....

I cannot perhaps give a better idea of the dread which pervaded my mind on seeing any of my brethren of the forest than by relating the following occurrence. One day several of the [Furman] family went into the woods to gather berries, taking me with them. We had not been out long before we fell in with a company of white females, on the same errand—their complexion was, to say the least, as *dark* as that of the natives. This circumstance filled my mind with terror, and I broke from the party with my utmost speed, and I could not muster courage enough to look behind until I had reached home. By this time my imagination had pictured out a tale of blood, and as soon as I regained breath sufficient to answer the questions which my master asked, I informed him that we had met a body of the natives in the woods, but what had become of the party I could not tell. Notwithstanding the manifest incredibility of my tale of terror, Mr. Furman was agitated; my very appearance was sufficient to convince him that I had been terrified by something, and...he sallied out in quest of the absent party.... The whole mystery was soon unraveled. It may be proper for me here to remark that the great fear I entertained of my brethren was occasioned by the many stories I had heard of their cruelty toward the whites—how they were in the habit of killing and scalping men, women, and children. But the whites did not tell me that they were in a great majority of instances the aggressors—that they had imbrued their hands in the lifeblood of my brethren, driven them from their once peaceful and happy homes—that they introduced among them the fatal and exterminating diseases of civilized life. If the whites had told me how cruel they had been to the "poor Indian," I should have apprehended as much harm from them.

Shortly after this occurrence I relapsed into my former bad habits—was fond of the company of boys—and in a short time lost in a great measure that spirit of obedience which had made me the favorite of my mistress. I was easily led astray....

Chapter III

About the time that I had attained my eighth year a sect called the Christians [a Methodist sect] visited our neighborhood....I took great delight in hearing them sing the songs of Zion....I listened to the word of God with the greatest degree of attention. It was not long before I resolved to mend my ways and become a better boy. By my strict attendance on divine worship and my orderly behavior, I attracted the notice of some of the people....

I became very fond of attending meetings, so much so that Mr. Furman forbid me. He supposed that I only went for the purpose of seeing the boys and playing with them. This thing caused me a great deal of grief; I went for many days with my head and heart bowed down....By day and by night I was in a continual ferment....

Nothing very extraordinary occurred until I had attained my eleventh year. At this time it was fashionable for boys to run away, and the wicked one [the devil] put it into the head of the oldest boy on the farm to persuade me to follow the fashion. He told me that I could take care of myself and get my own living. I thought it was a very pretty notion to be a man.... Like a fool, I concluded to make the experiment and accordingly began to pack up my clothes....I had been once or twice at New London, where I saw, as I thought, everything wonderful: Thither I determined to bend my course, as I expected that on reaching the town I should be metamorphosed into a person of consequence..., when behold, my companion, who had persuaded me to act thus, informed my master that I was going to run off. At first he would not believe the boy, but my clothing already packed up was ample evidence of my intention. On being questioned I acknowledged the fact. I did not wish to leave them—told Mr. Furman so; he believed me but thought best that for a while I should have another master. He accordingly agreed to transfer my indentures [servant's contract] to Judge Hillhouse for the sum of twenty dollars. Of course, after the bargain was made, my consent was

to be obtained....After some persuasion, I agreed to try it for a fortnight, on condition that I should take my dog with me, and my request being granted I was soon under the old man's roof, as he only lived about six miles off. Here everything was done to make me contented, because they thought to promote their own interests by securing my services. They fed me with knickknacks, and soon after I went among them I had a jackknife presented to me....Like other boys, I spent my time either in whittling or playing with my dog and was withal very happy. But I was homesick at heart, and as soon as my fortnight had expired I went home without ceremony. Mr. Furman's family were surprised to see me....

The joy I felt on returning home...was turned to sorrow on being informed that I had been *sold* to the judge and must instantly return. This I was compelled to do. And, reader, all this sorrow was in consequence of being led away by a bad boy: If I had not listened to him I should not have lost my home....

After a little while the conduct of my new guardians was changed toward me. Once secured, I was no longer the favorite. The few clothes I had [soon]...were all "tattered and torn" and I was not fit to be seen in decent company....I now became quite anxious to attend evening meetings a few miles off: I asked the judge if I should go and take one of the horses, to which he consented. This promise greatly delighted me—but when it was time for me to go..., the judge had changed his mind. I was not to be foiled so easily; I watched the first opportunity and slipped off with one of the horses, reached the meeting, and returned in safety....[B]eing successful in one grand act of disobedience, I was encouraged to make another similar attempt...; for the very next time I wished to go to meeting, I thought I would take the horse again, and in the same manner too, without the knowledge of my master. As he was by some means apprised of my intention, he prevented my doing so and had the horses locked up in the stable. He then commanded me to give him the bridle; I was obstinate for a time, then threw it at the old gentleman and run off. I did not return until the next day, when I received a flogging for my bad conduct, which determined me to run away. Now, the judge was partly to blame for all this. He had in the first place treated me with the utmost kindness until he had made sure of me. Then the whole course of his conduct changed, and I believed he fulfilled only one item of the transferred indentures, and that was work. Of this there was no lack. To be sure I had enough to eat, such as it was, but he did not send me to school as he had promised.

A few days found me on my way to New London, where I stayed a while. I then pushed on to Waterford, and as my father lived about twenty miles off, I concluded to go and see him. I got there safely and told him I had come on a visit and that I should stay one week. At the expiration of the week he bid me go home, and I obeyed him. On my return I was treated rather coolly, and this not suiting my disposition, I run off again but returned in a few days. Now, as the judge found he could not control me, he got heartily tired of me and wished to hand me over to someone else, so he obtained a place for me in New London. I knew nothing of it, and I was greatly mortified to think that I was sold in this way. If my consent had been solicited as a matter of form, I should not have felt so bad. But to be sold to and treated unkindly by those who had got our fathers' lands for nothing was too much to bear. When all things were ready, the judge told me that he wanted me to go to New London with a neighbor, to purchase salt. I was delighted and went with the man, expecting to return that night. When I reached the place I found my mistake. The name of the person to whom I was transferred this time was Gen. William Williams, and as my treatment at the judge's was none of the best, I went home with him contentedly. Indeed, I felt glad that I had changed masters and more especially that I was to reside in the city. The finery and show caught my eye and captivated my heart.... In a little time I was furnished with good new clothes. I had enough to eat..., and my work was light. The whole family treated me kindly, and the only difficulty of moment was that they all wished to be masters. But I would not obey all of them. There was a French boy in the family, who one day told Mr. Williams a willful lie about me, which he believed and gave me a horsewhipping, without asking me a single question about it. Now, I do not suppose that he whipped so much on account of what the boy told him as he did from the influence of the judge's directions. He used the falsehood as a pretext for flogging me, as from what he said he was determined to make a good boy of me at once—as if stripes were calculated to effect that which love, kindness, and instruction can only successfully accomplish....

Everything went on smoothly for two or three years. About this time the Methodists began to hold meetings in the neighborhood, and consequently a storm of persecution gathered..., and every evil report prejudicial to this pious people was freely circulated.... Indeed, the stories circulated about them were bad enough to deter people of "character!" from attending the Methodist ministry. But it had no effect on me. I thought I had no character to lose in the estimation of those who were accounted great. For what cared they for me? They had possession of the red man's inheritance and had deprived me of liberty; with this they were satisfied and could do as they pleased; therefore, I thought I could do as I pleased.... I therefore went to hear the *noisy Methodists*. When I reached the house I found a clever [agreeable] company. They did not appear to differ much from "respectable" people. They were neatly and decently clothed, and I could not see that they differed from other people except in their behavior, which was more kind and gentlemanly. Their countenance was heavenly, their songs were like sweetest music— in their manners they were plain.... The exercises were accompanied by the power of God. His people shouted for joy—while sinners wept....

[M]any people went to these meetings to make fun. This was a common thing, and I often wondered how persons who professed to be considered great, i.e., "ladies and gentlemen," would so far disgrace themselves as to scoff in the house of God and at his holy services....

But notwithstanding the people were so wicked, the Lord had respect unto the labors of his servants.... In a little time the work rolled onward like an overwhelming flood.... [A]ll opposition had no other effect than of cementing the brethren more closely together.... I felt convinced that Christ died for all mankind—that age, sect, color, country, or situation made no difference....

After meeting I returned home with a heavy heart, determined to seek the salvation of my soul. This night I slept but little—at times I would be melted down to tenderness and tears, and then again...I fancied that evil spirits stood around my bed...and I longed for the day to break.... But sin was the cause of this, and no wonder I groaned and wept. I had often sinned, and my accumulated transgressions had piled themselves as a rocky mountain on my heart.... The weight thereof seemed to crush me down.... I continued in this frame of mind for more than seven weeks.

My distress finally became so acute that the family took notice of it. Some of them persecuted me because I was serious and fond of attending meeting.... But, in the midst of difficulties so great to one only fifteen years of age, I ceased not to pray for the salvation of my soul....

I went on from day to day with my head and heart bowed down.... It seemed as if I were friendless, unpitied, and unknown.... I now hung all my hope on the Redeemer and clung with indescribable tenacity to the cross on which he purchased salvation for the *"vilest of the vile."* The result was such as is always to be expected when a lost and ruined sinner throws himself entirely on the Lord—*perfect freedom.* On the fifteenth day of March, in the year of our Lord, eighteen hundred and thirteen, I heard a voice in soft and soothing accents saying unto me, *Arise, thy sins which were many are all forgiven thee, go in peace and sin no more!*

...I had been sent into the garden to work, and while there I lifted up my heart to God, when all at once my burden and fears left me—my heart melted into tenderness—my soul was filled with love—love to God, and love to all mankind....There was not only a change in my heart but in everything around me....

I enjoyed great peace of mind, and that peace was like a river, full, deep, and wide, and flowing continually; my mind was employed in contemplating the wonderful works of God and in praising his holy name, dwelt so continually upon his mercy and goodness that I could praise him aloud even in my sleep. I continued in this happy frame of mind for some months....

Chapter IV

The calm and sunshine did not, however, continue uninterrupted for any length of time; my peace of mind...was disturbed....It was considered by some members of the family that I was too young to be religiously inclined and consequently that I was under a strong delusion. After a time, Mr. Williams came to the conclusion that it was advisable for me to absent myself entirely from the Methodist meetings....

Sometimes I would get permission to attend meetings in the evening, and once or twice on the Sabbath....But the waves of persecution and affliction and sorrow rolled on, and gathered strength in their progress, and for a season overwhelmed my dispirited soul. I was flogged several times very unjustly for what the maid said respecting me. My treatment in this respect was so bad that I could not brook [tolerate] it, and in an evil hour I listened to the suggestions of the devil....He put it into my head to abscond from my master, and I made arrangements with a boy of my acquaintance to accompany me....While my companion was getting ready I hid my clothes in a barn and went to buy some bread and cheese, and while at the store, although I had about four dollars in my pocket, I so far forgot myself as to buy a pair of shoes on my master's account. Then it was that I began to lose sight of religion and of God. We now set out; it being a rainy night, we bought a bottle of rum, of which poisonous stuff I drank heartily. Now the shadows of spiritual death began to gather around my soul. It was half-past nine o'clock at night when we started, and to keep up our courage we took another drink of the liquor....

The next morning we started for my father's.... I told him that we had come to stay only one week, and when that week had expired he wished me to redeem my promise and return home. So I had seemingly to comply, and when we had packed up our clothes, he said he would accompany us part of the way; and when we parted I thought he had some suspicions of my intention to take another direction, as he begged me to go straight home. He then sat down on the wayside and looked after us as long as we were to be seen. At last we descended a hill, and as soon as we lost sight of him, we struck into the woods. I did not see my father again for eight years. At this time, I felt very much disturbed. I was just going to step out on the broad theater of the world, as it were, without father, mother, or friends....

[Traveling from Hartford through New Haven to New York City, Apess joins the army, though he "could not think why I should risk my life and limbs in fighting for the white man, who had cheated my forefathers out of their land." In addition, among the soldiers,] I became almost as bad as any of them, could drink rum, play cards, and act as wickedly as any....

Chapter V...

[North of Albany, an officer "promoted" Apess from drummer boy to soldier.] As I had only enlisted for a drummer, I thought that this change...was contrary to law and, as the bond was broken, liberty was granted me; therefore, being heartily tired of a soldier's life, and having a desire to see my father once more, I went off very deliberately; I had no idea that they had a lawful claim on me and was greatly surprised as well as alarmed when arrested as a deserter....We shortly after marched for Canada, and during this dreary march the officers tormented me by telling me that it was their intention to make a fire in the woods, stick my skin full of pine splinters, and after having an Indian powwow over me, burn me to death....

As soon as it was known that the war had terminated..., I...obtained my release. Now, according to the act of enlistment, I was entitled to forty dollars bounty money and one hundred and sixty acres of land. The government also owed me for fifteen months' pay. I have not seen anything of bounty money, land, or arrearages [overdue pay], from that day to this. I am not, however, alone in this—hundreds were served in the same manner. But I could never think that the government acted right toward the *"Natives,"* not merely in refusing to pay us but in claiming our services in cases of perilous emergency, and still deny us the right of citizenship; and as long as our nation is debarred the privilege of voting for civil officers, I shall believe that the government has no claim on our services.

Chapter VI…

When I left the army, I had not a shilling in my pocket. I depended upon the precarious bounty of the inhabitants, until I reached the place where some of my brethren dwelt. I tarried with them but a short time and then set off for Montreal. I was anxious, in some degree, to become steady and went to learn the business of a baker. My bad habits now overcome my good intentions. I was addicted to drinking rum and would sometimes get quite intoxicated. As it was my place to carry out the bread, I frequently fell in company, and one day, being in liquor, I met one of the king's soldiers, and after abusing him with my tongue, I gave him a sound flogging. In the course of the affair I broke a pitcher which the soldier had, and as I had to pay for it, I was wicked enough to take my master's money, without his knowledge, for that purpose. My master liked me, but he thought, if I acted so once, I would a second time, and he very properly discharged me.…

[After a series of short-term jobs as a farmhand, a cook on a boat, and a merchant's assistant,] I shifted my quarters to another place and agreed with a Dutch farmer to stay with him all winter at five dollars a month. With this situation I was much pleased. My work was light—I had very little to do except procuring firewood. I often went with them on hunting excursions; besides, my brethren were all around me, and it therefore seemed like home.…

Chapter VII…

In the spring the old gentleman set us to making maple sugar. This took us into the woods, which were vocal with the songs of the birds; all nature seemed to smile and rejoice in the freshness and beauty of spring. My brethren appeared very cheerful on account of its return and enjoyed themselves in hunting, fishing, basket making, etc. After we had done making sugar, I told the old gentleman I wished to go and see my friends in the East, as I had been

absent about three years: He consented, though he wished me to tarry longer with him.… [Only after another year of temporary jobs, however, does Apess head to "the East."]

[A]t last I arrived in safety at the home of my childhood. At first my people looked upon me as one risen from the dead. Not having heard from me since I left home, being more than four years, they thought I must certainly have died, and the days of mourning had almost passed. They were rejoiced to see me once more in the land of the living, and I was equally rejoiced to find all my folks alive. The whites with whom I had been acquainted were also very glad to see me. After I had spent some time with my relations in Groton and visited all my old friends, I concluded to go to work and be steady. Accordingly, I hired myself to a Mr. Geers, for a month or two. I served him faithfully, but when I wanted my pay he undertook to treat me as he would a degraded African slave. He took a cart stake in order to pay me, but he soon found out his mistake, as I made him put it down as quick as he had taken it up. I had been cheated so often that I determined to have my rights this time, and forever after.

Chapter VIII

I was now about nineteen years of age and had become quite steady. I attended meetings again quite often and my mind was powerfully wrought upon.… I would think upon the varied scenes of my life—how often the Lord had called me, and how for a season I attended to that call—of the blessed and happy times I had experienced in the house of God, and in secret devotion—and the days of darkness and nights of sorrowful anguish since those days when the Spirit of God breathed upon my soul. *Then*, I enjoyed happiness in a preeminent degree! *Now*, I was miserable, I had offended God—violated his laws—abused his goodness.… I was pressed down by a load of shame and a weight of guilt too intolerable to be borne. Hour after hour, and day after day, did I endeavor to lift my heart to God, to implore forgiveness of my sins.… But the Holy Spirit flew not to my relief. I then thought that I must die and go to hell.…

Being determined to persevere in the way of well-doing, I united with the Methodist Society…, on trial, for six months. I had never been at a camp meeting and, of course, knew nothing about it. It far exceeded my expectations. I never witnessed so great a body of Christians assembled together before—I was also astonished with their proceedings, was affected by their prayers, charmed by their songs of praise, and stood gazing at them like a brainless clown. However, I soon solicited the prayers of this body of Christians, for my poor soul was greatly troubled. But behold, one of the brethren called on me to pray. I began to make excuse, but nothing would do; he said, pray, and I thought I must. I trembled through fear and began to wish myself at home; I soon got on my knees.... While endeavoring to pray, it appeared as if my words would choke me—the cold chills run over my body—my feelings were indescribably awful. This, however, had a very good effect upon me, as it learned me not to please man so much as God. The camp meeting was a very happy one; I found some comfort and enjoyed myself tolerably well....

When I returned home, I began to tell the family all about the camp meeting, what a blessed time we had, etc., but they ridiculed me, saying we were only deluded....

When the time for which I engaged had expired, I went among my tribe at Groton. I lived this winter with my aunt, who was comfortably situated. She was the handmaid of the Lord, and being a widow, she rented her lands to the whites, and it brought her in enough to live on. While here we had some very good times. Once in four weeks we had meeting, which was attended by people from Rhode Island, Stonington, and other places and generally lasted three days. These seasons were glorious. We observed particular forms, although we knew nothing about the dead languages [Latin or Greek], except that the knowledge thereof was not necessary for us to serve God. We had no house of divine worship, and believing "that the groves were God's first temples," thither we would repair when the weather permitted....

My aunt could not read, but she could almost preach and, in her feeble manner, endeavor to give me much instruction. Poor dear woman, her body slumbers in the grave, but her soul is in the paradise of God—she has escaped from a world of trouble. The whites were anxious to have the honor of burying her; she was interred very decently, the whites being as numerous as the natives. Indeed, all who knew her wished to show the veneration in which they held her by following her remains to their last earthly resting place. Her name was Sally George, and she was deservedly esteemed for her piety. In her sphere she was a very useful woman and greatly beloved by all who knew her. She was very attentive to the sick, kind to the unfortunate, good and benevolent to the poor and the fatherless. She would often pour into the ear of the sin-sick soul the graciously reviving promises of the Gospel. While she lay sick, she

expressed a desire to go and see her brethren, who lived about eight miles off; she said the Lord would give her the strength, and so he did. She then visited her friends, and after enjoying some religious conversation, she returned home to die. The fear of death was now taken away, and she exhorted all around her to be faithful and serve the Lord. She died in the full triumphs of the faith, on the 6th of May, 1824, aged 45 years....

Shortly after this I felt a desire to see my family connections again and therefore left this part of the country, after obtaining a certificate of my standing in society, etc., as is generally done by Methodists when they remove from one place to another. Nothing worthy of special notice occurred during my journey, except losing my way one night. It happened in this manner: Having reached the neighborhood of my father's residence about sundown, and being extremely anxious to complete my journey, I concluded to continue on, as I expected to reach his house by two o'clock in the morning. Unfortunately, I took the wrong road and was led into a swamp.... At every step I became more and more entangled— the thickness of the branches above me shut out the little light afforded by the stars, and to my horror I found that the further I went, the deeper the mire.... This was the hour of peril.... I was shut out from the world and did not know but that I should perish there, and my fate forever remain a mystery to my friends. I raised my heart in humble prayer and supplication to the father of mercies, and behold he stretched forth his hand and delivered me from this place of danger....I found a small piece of solid earth, and then another, so that after much difficulty I succeeded in once more placing my feet upon dry ground. I then fell upon my knees and thanked my blessed master for this singular interposition of his providence and mercy....I did not reach home until daylight. I found my father well, and all the family rejoiced to see me. On this occasion I had an opportunity of making some remarks to the friends who came to see me. My father, who was a member the Baptist church, was much pleased....I now agreed with my father to tarry with him all winter, and he agreed to learn me how to make shoes....

Chapter IX...

While in Colrain the Lord moved upon my heart in a peculiarly powerful manner, and by it I was led to believe that I was called to preach the Gospel of our Lord and Savior Jesus Christ....I began immediately...excusing myself, saying, Lord I cannot. I was nothing but a poor ignorant Indian and thought the people would not hear me.... [B]ut in the evening I would find myself in our little meetings exhorting sinners to repentance and striving to comfort the saints. On these occasions I had the greatest liberty....

I now requested, if the Lord had called me to this holy work, that he would make it manifest by a sign. So one day, after prayer, I went to a friend and told him, if he was willing to give out an appointment for meeting at his house, I would try and exhort. He assented, and in giving out the appointment he made a mistake, as he informed the people that there would be a *sermon* [that is, by a licensed clergyman] instead of an exhortation, and when I attended, in place of finding a few persons at my friend's house, I found a large congregation assembled at the schoolhouse.... When I went in, every eye was fixed on me, and when I was commencing the meeting, it appeared as if my confidence in God was gone; my lips quivered, my voice trembled, my knees smote together, and in short I quaked as it were with fear. But the Lord blessed me.... Soon after this, I received an invitation to hold a meeting in the same place again. I accordingly went, and I found a great concourse of people who had come out to hear the Indian preach, and as soon as I had commenced, the sons of the devil began to show their front—... one of them threw an old hat in my face, and ... others ... threw sticks at me. But in the midst I went on with my sermon, and ... [t]he Lord laid too his helping hand....

Shortly after this, my father began to oppose me—perhaps he thought, with some of the whites, that there were enough preachers in the land already. Be this as it may, I continued to exercise my gift and preached wherever a door was opened and, I trust, with some success.

[Apess, preaching without a license from Methodist leaders, is criticized by his church and told] to confess that I was in error; but I was such a blind Indian that I could not see how I was in error in preaching *Christ Jesus*....

This unkind treatment, as I regarded it, had nearly proved the ruin of my soul.... [H]aving been excluded from ... the church, I viewed myself as an *outcast from society*.... I went then to my native tribe, where meetings were still kept up. I tarried here but a short time and then went to Old Saybrook.... There were ... a few colored people who met regularly for religious worship; with these I sometimes assembled.

About this time I met with a woman of nearly the same color as myself—she bore a pious and exemplary character. After a short acquaintance, we were united in the sacred bonds of marriage; and now I was going on prosperously.... I obtained a situation with a Mr. Hail, in Gloucester, for two months, at twelve dollars a month. It being harvest time, my employer allowed each of his hands a half-pint of spirits every day. I told him I did not want my portion, so he agreed to pay me a little more. *I abstained entirely, and found that I could not only stand labor as well but perform more than those who drank the spirits*. All the hands exclaimed against me and said that I would soon give out; but ... God supported me, and I can truly say that my health was better, my appetite improved, and my mind was calm....

I remembered that I had a sister living in Providence. Thither I went and soon found my sister, who was very kind to me. I had no difficulty in procuring work. The Spirit of the Lord now fell afresh upon me, and I at once entered into the work without conferring with flesh and blood. I appointed meeting for exhortation and prayer—the Lord blessed my feeble efforts, and souls were converted and added to the church. I continued here five months and then, taking a letter of recommendation, returned to my family; and when I had concluded to remove to Providence, as the place of my future residence, the society gave me a certificate to the church in Providence—I there joined, and I was shortly appointed to the office of class leader, which office I filled for two years....

After having been absent six months [preaching in New York and elsewhere] I returned home and found my dear family and friends in the enjoyment of their usual health. After remaining about a fortnight, I went to Boston. Here the Lord blessed my labors among the friends of the cross. While in Boston I met with a professed infidel, who wished to draw me into an argument by hooting at me for believing in Jesus Christ, the Savior of fallen men. I spoke to him about being a *good gentleman*, and he replied that I, in common with my brethren, believed that no man was a gentleman unless he was under the influence of priestcraft; and I told him that I considered every man a gentleman who acted in a becoming manner.... After spending about two months in Boston, I returned home; then I visited New Bedford, Martha's Vineyard, and Nantucket, preaching the word wherever a door was opened—and the Lord ... accompanied me, and I believe that much good was done. Again I visited my family and then ... visited ... different towns, preaching as I went along, until I reached Newburyport, and having taken letters of recommendation from the various preachers, I was kindly received....

From Newburyport I went to Portland, Maine, where I had some gracious times and labored with success, and then returned to my abiding place at Providence, R.I., with a recommendation. I reported myself to the preacher in charge and asked for a certificate; he said that my recommendation was "genuine," but he had heard evil reports respecting me and preferred inquiring into the matter before he granted my request. I felt glad that the brother had promised to make inquiry, as I knew that I should come out well. As this would take some time I crossed over to Long Island, preached at Sag Harbor and other places with success, and then went to New York [City], where I remained but a short time and then proceeded to Albany. Here I was known and was received in a friendly way and continued to preach wherever an opportunity offered; while here, a certificate of my membership was received from the church in Providence, and on the force of it I entered the church. I now applied for license to preach and was recommended to the quarterly Conference as a suitable candidate, but the Conference thought differently; so after improving my gift three months I made another application....

I held meetings in Albany and crowds flocked out, some to *hear* the truth and others to *see* the "Indian."...

Now, my dear reader, I have endeavored to give you a short but correct statement of the leading features of my life. When I think of what I am, and how wonderfully the Lord has led me, I am dumb before him. When I contrast my situation with that of the rest of my family, and many of my tribe, I am led to adore the goodness of God. When I reflect upon my many misdeeds and wanderings, and the dangers to which I was consequently exposed, I am lost in astonishment at the long forbearance and the unmerited mercy of God. I stand before you as a monument of his unfailing goodness. May that same mercy which has upheld me still be my portion—and may author and reader be preserved until the perfect day and dwell forever in the paradise of God.

WILLIAM APESS

WILLIAM APESS, *EULOGY ON KING PHILIP, AS PRONOUNCED AT THE ODEON, IN FEDERAL STREET, BOSTON* (1836)

Source: William Apess, *Eulogy on King Philip,* in *A son of the Forest and Other Writings,* ed. Barry O'Connell Amherst: University of Massachusetts Press, 1997.[Originally published 1836.]

...[A]s the immortal Washington lives endeared and engraven on the hearts of every white in America, never to be forgotten in time—even such is the immortal Philip honored, as held in memory by the degraded but yet grateful descendants who appreciate his character; so will every patriot, especially in this enlightened age, respect the rude yet all-accomplished son of the forest, that died a martyr to his cause, though unsuccessful, yet as glorious as the *American* Revolution....

Justice and humanity for the remaining few prompt me to vindicate the character of him who yet lives in their hearts and, if possible, melt the prejudice that exists in the hearts of those who are in the possession of his soil, and only by the right of conquest—is the aim of him who proudly tells you, the blood of a denominated [so-called] savage runs in his veins....

The first inquiry is: Who is Philip? He was the descendant of one of the most celebrated chiefs in the known world [Massasoit], for peace and universal benevolence toward all men; for injuries upon injuries, and the most daring robberies and barbarous deeds of death that were ever committed by the American Pilgrims, were with patience and resignation borne, in a manner that would do justice to any Christian nation or being in the world—especially when we realize that it was voluntary suffering on the part of the good old chief. His country extensive, his men numerous..., say, a thousand to one of the white men, and they [whites] also sick and feeble—where, then, shall we find one nation submitting so tamely to another, with such a host at their command?...It will be well for us to lay those deeds and depredations committed by whites upon Indians before the civilized world, and then they can judge for themselves.

[Citing published accounts by whites, Apess tells how in 1614 an English expedition captured thirty natives from the area and took them back to London "to be sold for slaves among the Spaniards."] How inhuman it was in those wretches, to come into a country where...those natural sons of an Almighty Being,...whose virtues far surpassed their more enlightened foes, notwithstanding their [colonists'] pretended zeal for religion and virtue. How they could go to work to enslave a free people and call it religion is beyond the power of my imagination.... O thou pretended hypocritical Christian,... to say it was the design of God that we should murder and slay one another....

But notwithstanding the transgression..., yet it does appear that the Indians had a wish to be friendly....[T]he Pilgrims...acknowledge themselves that no people could be used better than they were; that their treatment [by the Indians] would do honor to any nation;...that they [natives] gave them venison and sold them many hogsheads of corn....Had it not been for this humane act of the Indians, every white man would have been swept from the New England colonies. In their [the colonists'] sickness, too, the Indians were as tender to them as to their own children; and for all this, they were denounced as savages by those who had received all the acts of kindness they possibly could show them....

December...1620, the Pilgrims landed at Plymouth, and without asking liberty from anyone they possessed themselves of a portion of the country, and built themselves houses, and then made a treaty, and commanded them [Indians] to accede to it. This, if now done, it would be called an insult, and every white man would be called to go out and act the part of a patriot, to defend their country's rights; and if every intruder were butchered, it would be sung upon every hilltop in the Union that victory and patriotism was the order of the day. And yet the Indians...bore it....

In the history of Massasoit we find that his own head men were not satisfied with the Pilgrims, that they looked upon them to be intruders and had a wish to expel those intruders...; and no wonder that from the least reports the Pilgrims were ready to take it up. A false report was made respecting one Tisquantum [Squanto], that he was murdered by an Indian.... Upon this news, one [Capt. Miles] Standish, a vile and malicious fellow, took fourteen of his lewd Pilgrims with him, and at midnight, when...those children of the woods...had taken their rest,...they were surrounded by ruffians and assassins; yes, assassins, what better name can be given them? At that late hour of the night, meeting a house in the wilderness, whose inmates were nothing but a few helpless females and children; soon a voice is heard—"Move not, upon the peril of your life." I appeal to this audience if there was any righteousness in their proceedings. Justice would say no. At the same time some of the females were so

frightened that some of them undertook to make their escape, upon which they were fired upon....And can it be supposed that these innocent Indians could have looked upon them as good and trusty men? Do you look upon the midnight robber and assassin as being a Christian and trusty man? These Indians had not done one single wrong act to the whites but were as innocent of any crime as any beings in the world. And do you believe that the Indians cannot feel and see, as well as white people? If you think so, you are mistaken....

And who is to account for those destructions upon innocent families and helpless children?...Let the children [descendants] of the Pilgrims blush, while the son of the forest drops a tear and groans over the fate of his murdered and departed fathers. He would say to the sons of the Pilgrims (as Job said about his birthday), let the day be dark, the 22nd day of December 1622 [sic—1620]; let it be forgotten in your celebration, in your speeches, and by the burying of the rock that your fathers first put their foot upon....We say,...let every man of color wrap himself in mourning, for the 22nd of December and the 4th of July are days of mourning and not of joy....

[A]s the seed of iniquity and prejudice was sown in that day, so it still remains; and there is a deep-rooted popular opinion in the hearts of many that Indians were made...on purpose for destruction, to be driven out by white Christians, and they to take their places; and that God had decreed it from all eternity....

But having laid a mass of history...before you, the purpose of which is to show that Philip and all the Indians generally felt indignantly toward whites, whereby they were more easily allied together by Philip, their king and emperor, we come to notice more particularly his history....It is a matter of uncertainty about his age; but his birthplace was at Mount Hope, Rhode Island, where Massasoit, his father, lived till 1656, and died, as also his brother, Alexander, by the governor's ill-treating him..., which caused his death...in 1662; after which, the kingdom fell into the hands of Philip, the greatest man that ever lived upon the American shores....When he came into office it appears that he knew there was great responsibility resting upon himself and country, that it was likely to be ruined by those rude intruders around him, though he appears friendly and is willing to sell them lands for almost nothing....

[Apess goes through these land sales, along with how colonial courts further reduced Indians' territory and power.] Who stood up in those days, and since, to plead Indian rights? Was it the friend of the Indian? No, it was his enemies who rose—his enemies, to judge and pass sentence....

[In 1671 colonial authorities summoned Philip to a treaty council to resolve differences and ease fears of war.] Philip's complaint was that the Pilgrims had injured the planting grounds of his people. The Pilgrims, acting as umpires, say the charges against them were not sustained; and... wanted that Philip should order all his men to bring in his arms and ammunition.... The next thing was that Philip must pay the cost of the treaty.... It appears that Philip did not wish to make war with them but compromised with them; and in order to appease the Pilgrims he actually did order his men... to deliver them [the weapons] up; but his own men withheld [their arms], with the exception of a very few.

Now, what an unrighteous act this was in the people who professed to be friendly and humane and peaceable to all men. It could not be that they were so devoid of sense as to think these illiberal acts would produce peace, but contrawise, continual broils. And, in fact, it does appear that they courted war instead of peace.... [Apess goes through further colonial provocations, arguing that by 1675 an "exasperated King Philip...studied to be revenged of (on) the Pilgrims."]

When the governor finds that His Majesty [Philip] was displeased, he then sends messengers to him and wishes to know why he would make war upon him (as if he had done all right), and wished to enter into a new treaty with him. The king answered them thus: "Your governor is but a subject of King Charles of England; I shall not treat with a subject; I shall treat of peace only with a king, my brother; when he comes, I am ready."

This answer of Philip's...is worthy of note throughout the world. And never could a prince answer with more dignity in regard to his official authority than he did...letting them know...that he felt his independence more than they thought he did.... [I]t is not doubted that he meant to be revenged upon his enemies; for during some time he had been cementing his countrymen together, as it appears that he had sent to all the disaffected tribes, who...were as dissatisfied as Philip himself was with their [colonists'] proceedings....

At this council it appears that Philip made the following speech to his chiefs, counselors, and warriors:

> Brothers, you see this vast country before us, which the Great Spirit gave to our fathers and us; you see the buffalo and deer that now are our

support. Brothers, you see these little ones, our wives and children, who are looking to us for food and raiment [clothing]; and you now see the foe before you, that they have gown insolent and bold; that all our ancient customs are disregarded; the treaties made by our fathers and us are broken, and all of us insulted;...our brothers murdered before our eyes, and their spirits cry to us for revenge. Brothers, these people from the unknown world will cut down our groves, spoil our hunting and planting grounds, and drive us and our children from the graves of our fathers, and our council fires, and enslave our women and children....

The blow had now been struck, the die was cast, and nothing but blood and carnage was before them. And we find Philip as active as the wind, as dexterous as a giant,...fierce as a lion,...and as swift as an eagle.... It must be recollected that this war was legally declared by Philip, so that the colonies had a fair warning. It was no savage war of surprise, as some suppose, but one sorely provoked by the Pilgrims themselves.... [W]e find more manly nobility in him than we do in all the head Pilgrims put together....

At the great fight at Pocasset [July 18, 1675], Philip commanded in person, where he also was discovered with his host in a dismal swamp.... [T]he Pilgrims...were in close pursuit of him, and their numbers were so powerful they thought the fate of Philip was sealed.... The Pilgrims placed a guard around the swamp for 13 days, which gave Philip and his men time to prepare canoes to make good his retreat, in which he did, to the Connecticut River.... We may look upon this move of Philip's to be equal, if not superior, to that of Washington crossing the Delaware. For while Washington was assisted by all the knowledge that art and science could give, together with...edged tools to prepare rafts..., Philip was naked as to any of these things, possessing only what nature, his mother, had bestowed upon him....

[H]e made many successful attempts against the Pilgrims, in surprising and driving them from their posts, during the year 1676, in February and through till August.... It appears that Philip treated his prisoners with a great deal more Christian-like spirit than the Pilgrims did; even Mrs. Rowlandson [see Chapter 4], although speaking with bitterness sometimes of the Indians, yet in her journal she speaks not a word against him. Philip even hires her to work for him, and pays her for her work, and then invites her to dine with him and to smoke with him.

And…when the English wanted to redeem [ransom] Philip's prisoners, they had the privilege.

Now, did Governor Winthrop or any of those ancient divines use any of his [Philip's] men so? No. Was it known that they [colonists] received any of their female captives into their houses and fed them? No, it cannot be found upon history. Were not the [colonial] females [that Indians captured] completely safe, and none of them were violated, as they acknowledged themselves? But was it so when the Indian women fell into the hands of the Pilgrims? No. Did the Indians get a chance to redeem their prisoners? No. But when they were taken they were either compelled to turn traitors and join their enemies or be butchered upon the spot.…

But we have another dark and corrupt deed for the sons of Pilgrims to look at, and that is the fight and capture of Philip's son and wife…; this was in August 1676. But the most horrid act was in taking Philip's son, about ten years of age, and selling him to be a slave away from his father and mother. While I am writing, I can hardly restrain my feelings, to think a people calling themselves Christians should conduct so scandalous, so outrageous, making themselves appear so despicable in the eyes of the Indians; and even now, in the audience, I doubt but there is men honorable enough to despise the conduct of those pretended Christians.…Gentlemen and Ladies, I blush at these tales if you do not.…

Philip's forces had now become very small, so many having been duped away by the whites and killed that it was now easy surrounding him.…When coming out of the swamp, he was fired upon by an Indian [ally of the colonists] and killed dead upon the spot.…

[Commander of the colonial forces] Captain [Benjamin] Church now orders him to be cut up. Accordingly, he was quartered and hung up upon four trees, his head and one hand given to the Indian who shot him, to carry about to show, at which sight it so overjoyed the Pilgrims that they would give him money for it.…After which his head was sent to Plymouth and exposed…for twenty years; and his hand to Boston, where it was exhibited in savage triumph; and his mangled body denied a resting place in the tomb.…

I think that, as a matter of honor, that I can rejoice that no such evil conduct is recorded of the Indians, that they never hung up any of the white warriors who were head men.…

I do not hesitate to say that through the prayers, preaching, and examples of those pretended pious

has been the foundation of all the slavery and degradation in the American colonies toward colored people. Experience has taught me that this has been a most sorry and wretched doctrine to us poor ignorant Indians. I will mention two or three things to amuse you a little; that is, as I was passing through Connecticut, about 15 years ago, where they are so pious that they kill the cats for killing rats, and whip the beer barrels for working upon the Sabbath, that in a severe cold night, when the face of the earth was one glare of ice, dark and stormy, I called at a man's house to know if I could not stay with him, it being about nine miles to the house where I then lived, and knowing him to be a rich man, and withal very pious, knowing if he had a mind he could do it comfortably, and withal we were both members of one church. My reception, however, was almost as cold as the weather, only he did not turn me out-of-doors; if he had, I know not but I should have frozen to death. My situation was a little better than being out, for he allowed a little wood but no bed, because I was an Indian. Another Christian asked me to dine with him and put my dinner behind the door; I thought this a queer compliment indeed.

About two years ago, I called at an inn in Lexington; and a gentleman present, not spying me to be an Indian, began to say they ought to be exterminated. I took it up in our defense, though not boisterous but coolly; and when we came to retire, finding that I was an Indian, he was unwilling to sleep opposite my room for fear of being murdered before morning.… These things I mention to show that the doctrines of the Pilgrims has grown up with the people.

But not to forget Philip.…But who was Philip, that…put an enlightened nation to flight and won so many battles? It was a son of nature, with nature's talents alone. And who did he have to contend with? With all the combined arts of cultivated talents of the Old and New World. It was like putting one talent against a thousand. And yet Philip, with that, accomplished more than all of them.…

How deep, then, was the thought of Philip,… how true his prophecy, that the white people would not only cut down their groves but would enslave them.… [H]e could not have been more correct. Our groves and hunting grounds are gone, our dead are dug up, our council fires are put out, and a foundation was laid in the first Legislature to enslave our people, by taking from them all rights, which has been strictly adhered to ever since. Look at the disgraceful laws, disfranchising us as citizens. Look at the treaties made by Congress, all broken.…A fire, a canker [cancer], created by the

Pilgrims…, to burn and destroy my poor unfortunate brethren, and it cannot be denied. What, then, shall we do? Shall we cease crying and say it is all wrong, or shall we bury the hatchet and those unjust laws and Plymouth Rock together and become friends? And will the sons of the Pilgrims aid in putting out the fire and destroying the canker…?

…Now, while we sum up this subject, does it not appear that…the whites have always been the aggressors, and the wars, cruelties, and bloodshed is a job of their own seeking, and not the Indians?…We often hear of the wars breaking out upon the frontiers, and it is because the same spirit reigns there that reigned here in New England;…and at present, there is no law to stop it.…

[B]y this time you have been enabled to see that Philip's prophecy has come to pass; therefore,…I shall pronounce him the greatest man that was ever in America; and so it will stand, until he is proved to the contrary, to the everlasting disgrace of the Pilgrims' fathers.…

I will appeal to you that are white. Have you any regard for your wives and children…? Would you like to see them slain and lain in heaps, and their bodies devoured by the vultures and wild beasts of prey, and their bones bleaching in the sun and air, till they molder away or were covered by the falling leaves of the forest, and not resist? No. Your hearts would break with grief, and with all the religion and knowledge you have, it would not impede your force to take vengeance upon your foe that had so cruelly conducted thus.…What, then, my dear affectionate friends, can you think of those who have been so often betrayed, routed, and stripped of all they possess, of all their kindred in the flesh? Can you or do you think we have no feelings?…

Our affections for each other are the same as yours; we think as much of ourselves as you do of yourselves. When our children are sick, we do all we can for them; they lie buried deep in our affections; if they die, we remember it long and mourn in after years. Children also cleave to their parents; they look to them for aid; they do the best they know how to do for each other; and when strangers come among us, we use them as well as we know how.…And although I can say that I have some dear, good friends among white people, yet I eye them with a jealous eye, for fear they will betray me. Having been deceived so much by them, how can I help it?…Yes, in vain have I looked for the Christian to take me by the hand and bid me welcome to his cabin, as my fathers did them, before we were born; and if they did, it was only to satisfy curiosity and not to look upon me as a man and a Christian.…

Having now closed, I would say that many thanks is due from me to you, though an unworthy speaker, for your kind attention; and I wish you to understand that we are thankful for every favor; and you and I have to rejoice that we have not to answer for our fathers' crimes; neither shall we do right to charge them one to another. We can only regret it, and flee from it; and from henceforth, let peace and righteousness be written upon our hearts and hands forever, is the wish of a poor Indian.

CHAPTER 14

The Grimké Sisters Upset America

"We Abolition Women are turning the world upside down"

In March 1838, shortly after William Apess delivered his *Eulogy on King Philip* at the Odeon, Boston's largest auditorium (Chapter 13), Sarah Grimké (1792–1873) and her sister Angelina (1805–1879) walked onto the same stage to give a series of lectures. Apess, offering his alternative version of America's past, had met with "some dissatisfaction"; the Grimkés, who sketched an alternative vision of America's future—a future without slavery or racism—heard "hissing and noise" before the packed crowd of 2800 quieted down. "[W]hen I rose [to speak,]" Angelina recalled, sounding like Apess delivering his first sermon or Frederick Douglass (Chapter 16) his first oration, "I trembled so exceedingly for 10 minutes I could hardly stand on my feet." Soon, however, "[m]y tongue was loosed, my spirit unfettered[,]…and I spoke…with…power and authority."

Many in the audience agreed. "I shall never forget the wonderful manifestation of this power," recalled one man years later. In an age when oratory was popular entertainment, Angelina came to be known as among the best orators in the land. Her "phenomenal voice" held listeners in "painful silence and breathless interest [that] told the deep effect and lasting impression her words were making."[1]

The Odeon lectures were the last of many Grimké speeches in New England. Since arriving in Boston the previous spring, the Grimkés had delivered talks in sixty-seven different towns to crowds totaling more than 40,000. Everywhere they went, controversy followed. Like William Apess—an *Indian* preaching the *gospel*?—a woman speaking in public was a curiosity sure to draw a crowd.

But the sisters Grimké were no mere freak show: To many, they were a menace. Clergymen, calling the two "unnatural," warned of widespread "degeneracy and ruin" if they were not stopped. People tore down notices advertising their lectures. So many churches and town halls were closed to them that they had to give some talks in a barn. Amid the boos were epithets such as "notorious," "infamous," "infidel," and "female fanatic." Sarah and Angelina (or "*Devil*-ina," as some called her) were branded, their biographer Gerda Lerner writes, "old maids anxious to attract men, abnormal creatures lusting for the degenerate pleasures of 'amalgamation' [sex with African-American men], embittered spinsters venting their frustrated emotions by public attacks on the sacred and time-honored institutions of society, or, simply and most frequently, as cranks."[2]

A quick search for the Grimkés' pictures on the Internet will show that they do not look much like cranks; moreover, they were a pious pair from a respectable family. Why, then, were people so mad at them? One reason had to do with what they said: Ending slavery was a profoundly unpopular idea in those times. Most Northern whites—despising African Americans, fearing civil war, economically or politically entangled in Southern slavery and its "Cotton Kingdom"—considered abolitionists a bunch of troublemakers. Throughout the North mobs threatened, roughed up, even killed people advocating an end to slavery and racism.

It did not help that the Grimkés' brand of antislavery was particularly inflammatory, for they were disciples of a New Englander named William Lloyd Garrison. In 1831, Garrison—tired of the talk about gradually ending slavery, compensating owners for loss of their "property," and shipping freed blacks out of the country (colonization)—set out to change the tone of the national discussion. With the first issue of his newspaper, *The Liberator*, Garrison launched a moral crusade aimed at persuading people that slavery was a sin, that slaves must be freed immediately (without reimbursing masters) and then woven, as citizens, into the fabric of American life. Like Thomas Paine (Chapter 7), Garrison wanted to shake people up. "On this subject, I do not wish to think, or speak, or write, moderation. No! no!" he exclaimed in that first *Liberator*. "Tell a man whose house is on fire, to give a moderate alarm; tell him to moderately rescue his wife from the hands of the ravisher [rapist]; tell the mother to gradually extricate her babe from the fire into which it has fallen;—but urge me not to use moderation in a cause like the present. I am in earnest—...," he concluded, "I will not retreat a single inch—AND I WILL BE HEARD." Garrison, though plenty loud, was by no means the first to raise his voice against slavery: two years earlier another Bostonian, a free African American named David Walker, wrote *David Walker's Appeal...to the Coloured Citizens of the World, But in Particular...to those of the United States of America*; two years before that, African Americans in New York City started *Freedom's Journal*, an antislavery newspaper that proclaimed "We wish to plead our own cause. Too long have others spoken for us"; and for a generation before *that*, as Timothy Patrick McCarthy and John Stauffer write, "Northern free blacks created a range of institutions and media—including African American churches, annual freedom celebrations, political pamphlets, and serial newspapers—to assert their opposition to both slavery and colonization as part of the broader struggle for freedom and racial equality." Nonetheless, Garrison's "conversion" was crucial to the movement's growing power and scope. Inspired by his rhetoric, during the 1830s Northerners by the thousands founded antislavery societies, then began flooding Congress with petitions demanding freedom for slaves and clogging the mails with pamphlets condemning slavery.[3]

Among those who rallied to Garrison's banner were the Grimkés. Though they were hardly the first to join—not until the spring of 1834 did Angelina note in her journal that "I have become deeply interested in the subject of abolition," and Sarah waited two years longer—they were soon among its leading figures. One reason for that prominence was their background: Almost all abolitionists, white and black, were Northerners with no direct experience of slavery. Not the Grimkés. Having grown up in a prominent South Carolina slaveholding family before fleeing to Philadelphia in the 1820s, they knew slavery's horrors firsthand and were eager to share their knowledge.[4]

Hence, in the fall of 1836, Angelina wrote *Appeal to the Christian Women of the Southern States*, which made her famous (or infamous) throughout the country. The *Liberator* called it "eloquent and powerful"; the Charleston postmaster publicly burned every copy mailed to the sisters' hometown, then the mayor warned that if she ever showed up in South Carolina again she would be imprisoned and shipped back North—if she managed to escape a lynch mob. By the end of that year, now in lifelong exile, the sisters became the first women hired as lecturers by the American Anti-Slavery Society.[5]

And here was the second reason these two so upset people. It was not just *what they said*, it was *who they were*: No woman in those days was supposed to speak in public. "We have given great offense on account of our womanhood," Angelina wrote during their New England tour, "which seems to be as objectionable as our abolitionism." It was, to many, blasphemy; did not the Bible itself say "suffer not a woman to teach,…but to be in silence"? Thought to be ruled by emotion rather than reason (like children, "savages," and slaves), by heart and womb instead of head, a woman in those times could neither vote nor hold office, neither sue nor be sued. What she *could* do, conventional wisdom had it, what she *must* do, was use the extra measure of religious piety and sexual purity God and Nature had given her to make her family home "a private enclave, a retreat from the 'world.' " As America grew ever more competitive and individualistic, men and women alike agreed that keeping house and raising children were vital to the nation's well-being. It is to the home, proclaimed a popular woman's magazine, that "the church and state must come for their origin and support." Taking care of her husband and nurturing virtuous children was woman's proper place. Despite the many exceptions to this ideology—slave women, of course, but also "mill girls" in textile factories or servants in well-to-do households—its hold over men and women alike in those days was powerful, as Alexis de Tocqueville observed in 1831 (Chapter 11). (Some today might argue, paging through *Good Housekeeping* and *Ladies' Home Journal*, that this ideology endures. Would you agree?[6])

This mindset had no room for women traveling around giving speeches. One antislavery clergyman announced that "he would as soon be caught robbing a hen roost as encouraging a woman to lecture." The Grimkés themselves could scarcely believe it when abolitionists invited them to become agents. After much agonizing, they agreed, partly because they thought they would be talking only to small groups of women in private homes, a venue well within a woman's "proper sphere." When the sisters drew larger crowds that required churches and auditoriums, Angelina was amazed. "I don't know in fact what to call such novel proceedings," she wrote to a friend. "How little! how *very little* I supposed, when I used to say, 'I wish I was a *man*, that I might go out and lecture,' that *I* would ever do such a thing. The idea never crossed my mind that *as a woman* such work could possibly be assigned me."[7]

It was bad enough, many thought, that these two women were in the pulpit and on the stage. Worse, soon they were lecturing to "promiscuous assemblies" of women *and* men. As the word *promiscuous* suggests, this was scandalous, even to many abolitionists. Antislavery societies themselves were divided by sex: The American Anti-Slavery Society (AAS), founded in 1833, was restricted to men; women formed local "auxiliaries." The first national convention of these auxiliaries, which met in New York City in May 1837, was scheduled to run parallel to the men's annual meeting, assembled there at the same time.

One result of that historic convention of women reformers was the publication of Angelina's *Appeal to the Women of the Nominally Free States*, excerpted below.[8] This is your first in-depth encounter with the debate over slavery, a debate that would preoccupy America for several decades—as it preoccupies *American Conversations* for several chapters. How "radical" does this document seem, in its views on slavery and on blacks, on women's rights and women's roles? Since Northern women owned no slaves and could neither vote nor hold office, why bother to address them directly? And why insert "nominally"—that is, *in name only*, not *in fact*—before "free states"? Some see condescension toward African American women here; others disagree, noting that the Grimkés formed close friendships with women of color, defied segregated pews in church to sit with them, and insisted that they be included in the convention. What are the *Appeal*'s racial views?

Just two weeks after the convention adjourned, the Grimké sisters headed to New England on their antislavery lecture tour—and another sort of awakening. The same journey they had taken on slavery—first accepting it as a fact of life, then quietly questioning it, then loathing and leaving it before finally speaking out against it—they now took on women's rights and roles. "I verily believed in *female subordination until* very recently," Angelina admitted that summer. Now, "[w]hat an untrodden path we have entered upon!" "If in calling us thus publicly to advocate the cause of the downtrodden slave," Sarah wrote toward summer's end, "God has unexpectedly placed us in the forefront of the battle which is to be waged against the rights and duties and responsibilities of woman, it would ill become us to shrink from such a contest."[9] With Angelina in greater demand as a public speaker than she was, Sarah had time to prepare *Letters on the Equality of the Sexes, and the Condition of Woman*.

Starting that excerpt, you might feel as if you're beginning this volume all over again, for Grimké begins where *American Conversations* began: with the Book of Genesis. Why did she start there, and what does that say about change and continuity in American spirituality? What other sources of authority does *Letters* summon? How "radical" does *Letters* seem? Would it be considered "feminist" now?

Whatever you think of Sarah Grimké's arguments, you should know that, at the time, even their closest male friends and allies were appalled when the sisters added women's rights to antislavery. "Does it not *look*, dear sisters," wrote one, "like abandoning in some degree the cause of the poor and miserable slave...? Is it not forgetting the great and dreadful wrongs of the slave in a selfish crusade against some paltry grievance of our own?" "[W]e *fully agree in principle*...," wrote another, but "I do most deeply regret" your introducing "the rights of woman" this summer. Just by lecturing on slavery, you advance women's rights, for "[t]housands hear you every week who have all their lives held that woman must not speak in public." Beyond that, you should "leave the *lesser* work to others."[10]

Angelina, known for being what people then called "wrathy," was furious. "[C]an you not see," she replied, "that women *could* do, and *would* do a hundred times more for the slave if she were not fettered?" "If we surrender the right to *speak* to the public this year, we must surrender the right to petition next year and the right to *write* the year after and so on. What *then* can *woman* do for the slave when she is herself under the feet of man and shamed into *silence*?"[11]

Such talk might seem a long way from prevailing notions that women were divinely ordained to be silent, submissive creatures best kept at home. In fact, however, a logical series of steps connected women speaking, petitioning, and writing to women cooking, cleaning, and child rearing. During the early nineteenth century, many white women, without rejecting the conventional wisdom, actually used that ideology (which scholars call "domestic feminism") as a vehicle for moving out into the world. How can a woman run a household correctly and raise children properly if she was not educated? Women's schools and academies sprang up. How can a woman protect her family from the evils of the world if sin spilled onto her very doorstep and even over her threshold? Women crossed that threshold to battle vice of all sorts, from poverty to paganism, from prostitution to alcohol. Since "WOMAN" is "God's appointed agent of *morality*," men and women alike agreed, such reforms are "her task, her lot, her ministry, her special destination."[12]

How could women accomplish these tasks? They started organizations to promote piety (by distributing Bibles and religious tracts, by teaching Sunday school) and purity (by aiding the poor, reforming prostitutes, attacking taverns). All of a sudden, it seemed, women were drafting constitutions, lobbying legislatures, raising and spending money, visiting prisons and poorhouses, collecting signatures on petitions—all while claiming they were merely upholding "traditional" values.

Powerful social currents underlay this remarkable change. Middle- and upper-class white women in Northern cities and towns (where most of the reform energy originated) were not just better educated than their mothers or grandmothers; they also had more time to devote to a cause. The shift from farms to factories, from a household economy to an industrial economy, meant that more men left home in the morning to work elsewhere, leaving women behind, women who—with immigrants supplying cheap labor as servants—had less to do around the house than ever before. Meanwhile the growth of cities at once brought large numbers of these women in closer contact with each other and concentrated in one place poverty, taverns, prostitutes, and other ills, thereby making vice more visible—and more threatening. Add to this a religious revival, now called the Second Great Awakening, which particularly appealed to women and gave spiritual sanction to the idea of redeeming a sinful world, and the ingredients for a fundamental shift in women's activities were at hand.

But it was one thing to hand out Bibles and clothes, condemn whoredom and poverty, or aid widows and orphans, quite another to denounce slavery and racism. Everyone could agree that Bibles were good, widows and orphans deserved help, and prostitution was sinful. As the Grimkés discovered, hardly anyone agreed that slavery should be abolished and that blacks should be equal to whites. Those women who did join—often against the wishes of husbands, fathers, ministers, and politicians—faced, one wrote, "ridicule, persecution and danger." Nonetheless, join they did, in such numbers that Frederick Douglass would later remark: "When the true history of the antislavery cause shall be written, women will occupy a large space in its pages."[13]

If the number of women making the leap from moral reform to abolition was smaller, the number joining the Grimkés in moving even further, from abolitionism to feminism, was smaller still. It would be another decade before a group of women and some men (including Douglass) gathered at Seneca Falls, New York, in July 1848 to write a "Declaration of Sentiments" that included the phrase "all men *and women* are created equal."

The Grimkés were not at Seneca Falls; by then they led a different life. A month after their Odeon lectures, Angelina married the abolitionist Theodore Dwight Weld. With Sarah along to tend house and help with the children who soon arrived, the three spent the rest of their long lives mostly farming and teaching. "The Grimkés, I think, are extinct," wrote one disappointed admirer.[14]

In fact, their agitation never ceased: Both worked with Weld on his monumental bestseller, *Slavery As It Is*; Sarah researched how state laws discriminated against women; in the early 1870s the sisters were marching for woman's suffrage and going door-to-door selling a book entitled *The Subjection of Women*. Still, packed lecture halls and incendiary pamphlets were a thing of the past. "We...are filling up 'the appropriate sphere of woman' to admiration...," Angelina wrote two months after the wedding, "in the kitchen with baking pans & pots..., & in the parlor & chambers with the broom & the duster. Indeed," she went on, "I think our enemies w[ou]ld rejoice, could they only look in upon us...& see us toiling in domestic life, instead of lecturing to *promiscuous* audiences. Now I verily believe that we are *thus* doing *as much* for the cause of woman as we did by public speaking. For it is absolutely necessary that we should show that we are *not* ruined as domestic characters, but so far from it, *as soon* as duty calls us home, we can & do rejoice in the release from public service, & are as anxious to make good bread as we were to deliver a good lecture." Faced with the same hard choices women today confront—home and children vs. career—Angelina and Sarah made their peace with their short time in the limelight. What does this say about their views on relations between the sexes?[15]

Whatever we think of the Grimké sisters' "retirement," they had made an indelible mark on American life. Shortly before the Odeon lectures, Angelina exulted that "We Abolition Women are turning the world upside down." After her last appearance on that stage, one inspired member of the audience remarked that "a fire had been kindled which would never go out." He was right. The Grimkés—by their speeches and their writings, by their very existence—served as role models for young women who would go on to become lead actors in the women's rights movement for the rest of the century, and beyond.[16]

Questions for Consideration and Conversation

1. Women in the North neither owned slaves nor voted. Why did Angelina Grimké bother to direct her pamphlet to them?
2. What did Grimké mean by "nominally free" (i.e., free in name only)?
3. Why, according to Grimké, was slavery wrong? What arguments did she deploy to convince her readers? What arguments against slavery might she have used but did not?
4. What did Grimké want her audience to do about slavery? About racism?
5. Some have seen in this text a certain tone of condescension toward women of color. Do you agree with that assessment?
6. On what grounds did Sarah Grimké base her analysis of relations between the sexes? Why did she choose these grounds rather than some others?
7. What did she mean when she closed her letter with the phrase "Thine in the bonds of womanhood"?
8. Some call the Grimké sisters "feminists"; others suggest that they are far from modern feminists in a variety of ways. Which side of the argument do you favor? (You'll have to begin, of course, by defining the term *feminist*.)
9. How does Sarah Grimké's description of women's place in America compare to Alexis de Tocqueville's?

Endnotes

1. Barry O'Connell, ed., *On Our Own Ground: The Complete Writings of William Apess, a Pequot* (Amherst, MA, 1992), 275 (Apess); Gilbert H. Barnes and Dwight L. Dumond, eds., *Letters of Theodore Dwight Weld, Angelina Grimké Weld, and Sarah Grimké, 1822–1844* (New York, 1934), II, 611 ("trembled"), 625 ("unfettered"); Gerda Lerner, *The Grimké Sisters from South Carolina: Rebels Against Slavery* (Boston, 1967), 231 ("noise"), 233 ("never forget"); Katharine Du Pre Lumpkin, *The Emancipation of Angelina Grimké* (Chapel Hill, 1974), x ("phenomenal"); Stephen Howard Browne, *Angelina Grimké: Rhetoric, Identity, and the Radical Imagination* (East Lansing, MI, 1999), 170 ("breathless").
2. Kathryn Kish Sklar, ed., *Women's Rights Emerges within the Antislavery Movement, 1830–1870* (Boston, 2000), 120–21 ("unnatural," "ruin"); Lumpkin, *Emancipation of Grimké*, 120 ("incendiary," "infidel," "fanatic"), 139 (*Devil*-ina); Lerner, *Grimké Sisters*, 226 ("cranks").
3. William E. Cain, ed., *William Lloyd Garrison and the Fight against Slavery: Selections from* The Liberator (Boston, 1995), 72 (Garrison quotations); *David Walker's Appeal, Together with a Preamble, To the Coloured Citizens of the World, but in Particular, and Very Expressly, to those of the United States of America* (New York, 1965 [orig. pub. 1829]); Timothy Patrick McCarthy, "'To Plead Our Own Cause': Black Print Culture and the Origins of American Abolitionism," in McCarthy and John Stauffer, eds., *Prophets of Protest: Reconsidering the History of American Abolitionism* (New York, 2006), 115 (*Freedom's Journal*); McCarthy and Stauffer, "Introduction," ibid., xviii–xix ("range," "conversion").
4. Larry Ceplair, ed., *The Public Years of Sarah and Angelina Grimké: Selected Writings, 1835–1839* (New York, 1989), 19.
5. Lerner, *Grimké Sisters*, 146.
6. Ibid., 165 ("suffer not"), 183 ("great offense"); Nancy Woloch, *Women and the American Experience* (New York, 1984), 114–15 ("refuge, "support").
7. Barnes and Dumond, eds., *Letters*, I, 430 ("hen roost"); Lumpkin, *Emancipation*, 100–01 ("novel proceedings").
8. Scholars differ on whether Angelina was the sole author of this pamphlet. Most attribute it to her, but some argue that it was a committee report, a committee that included African-American women as well as whites.
9. Lumpkin, *Emancipation*, 106 ("verily believed"); Ceplair, ed., *Public Years*, 142 ("untrodden path"); Blanche Glassman Hersh, *The Slavery of Sex: Feminist-Abolitionists in America* (Urbana, IL, 1978), 20 (Sarah).
10. Barnes and Dumond, eds., *Letters*, I, 424–26.
11. Browne, *Angelina Grimké*, 8 ("wrathy"); Barnes and Dumond, eds., *Letters*, I, 429–30.
12. Michael D. Pierson, *Free Hearts and Free Homes: Gender and American Antislavery Politics* (Chapel Hill, NC, 2003), 11–13 ("domestic feminism"); Lori D. Ginzberg, *Women and the Work of Benevolence: Morality, Politics, and Class in the Nineteenth-Century United States* (New Haven, CT, 1990), 14 ("special destination").
13. Julie Roy Jeffrey, *The Great Silent Army of Abolitionism: Ordinary Women in the Antislavery Movement* (Chapel Hill, NC, 1998), xiii.
14. Mark Perry, *Lift Up Thy Voice: The Grimké Family's Journey from Slaveholders to Civil Rights Leaders* (New York, 2001), 182.
15. Ceplair, ed., *Public Years*, 326.
16. Hersh, *Slavery of Sex*, 29 ("upside down"); Barnes and Dumond, eds., *Letters*, II, 651 ("fire").

ANGELINA GRIMKÉ, *AN APPEAL TO THE WOMEN OF THE NOMINALLY FREE STATES* (MAY 1837)

Source: Angelina Grimké, *An Appeal to the Women of the Nominally Free States.* Issued by an Anti-Slavery Convention of American Women held May 1837. Second Edition. Boston: Isaac Knapp, 1838.

Beloved Sisters—

The wrongs of outraged millions, and the fore-shadows of coming judgments, constrain us…to press upon your consideration the subject of American Slavery. The women of the North have high and holy duties to perform in the work of emancipation—duties to themselves, to the suffering slave, to the slaveholder, to the church, to their country, and to the world at large; and, above all, to their God. Duties which, if not performed now, may never be performed at all.

Multitudes will doubtless deem such an address ill-timed and ill-directed. Many regard the excitement produced by the agitation of this subject as an evidence of the impolicy of free discussion, and a sufficient excuse for their own inactivity. Others so undervalue the rights and responsibilities of woman, as to scoff…whenever she goes forth to duties beyond the parlor and the nursery. The cry of such is, that the agitation of this subject has rolled back the cause of emancipation 50 or 100, or it may be 200 years, and that this is a *political* subject with which women have nothing to do. To the first, we would reply, that the people of the South are the *best judges* of the effects of Anti-slavery discussions upon their favorite "domestic institution;" and the universal alarm which has spread through the slave States, is conclusive evidence of *their* conviction that *slavery cannot survive discussion.*…

To the second objection, that slavery is a political question, we would say: every citizen should feel an intense interest in the political concerns of the country, because the honor, happiness, and well-being of every class, are bound up in its politics, government and laws. Are we aliens because we are women? Are we bereft of citizenship because we are the *mothers, wives,* and *daughters* of a mighty people? Have *women* no country—no interest staked in the public weal…—no partnership in a nation's guilt and shame?—Has *woman* no…sway with man…, nor voice to cheer, nor hand to raise the drooping and to bind the broken?…

Slavery as a Political Subject

I. …Such incongruous elements as freedom and slavery, republicanism and despotism, cannot long exist together; the unnatural and unhallowed union between these things must sooner or later be broken.…The slaveholding and non-slaveholding States have antagonist interests, which are continually conflicting, and producing jealousies and heart-burnings between the contending parties.… Slavery not only robs the slave of all his rights as a man in thirteen of the States of this Confederacy, but it…swims the Ohio and the Potomac, and bribes Northern citizens to kidnap and enslave freemen of the North—drags them into hopeless bondage, and sells them under the hammer of the auctioneer. Not only so—it outlaws every Northerner who openly avows the sentiments of the Declaration of our Independence, and destroys the free communication of our sentiments through the…mail, so that the daughters of America cannot now send the productions of their pen to the parent who resides in a slaveholding State.…Slavery…threatens to bring down the "exterminating thunders" of divine vengeance upon our guilty heads. "The dark spirit of slavery" rules in our national councils, and menaces the severance of the bonds which bind together these United States, and to shake from our star-spangled banner, as with a mighty wind, those glittering emblems of our country's pre-eminence among the nations of the earth, and to burn our Declaration as a "splendid absurdity," a "rhetorical flourish".…

[I]t is gravely urged, that as it is a *political subject, women* have no concernment with it.…Some, who…are very anxious that *we* should scrupulously maintain the dignity and delicacy of female propriety, continually urge this objection to female effort.… Have women never wisely and laudably exercised political responsibilities?

When the Lord led out his chosen people like a flock into the wilderness, from the house of bondage, was it not a WOMAN whom He sent before them with Moses and Aaron?…And was not the deliverance of Israel from Egyptian bondage a *political concern?*… Miriam then interfered with the *political concerns* of Egypt.…

But are these the doings of olden time alone?…

[L]et us turn over the pages of our own history. When the British army had taken possession of our beautiful city of brotherly love [Philadelphia], who arose at midnight to listen to the plots which were laid in an upper chamber, by [British] General Howe in his council of war? It was a *woman:* and when she stole the secret from their unconscious lips, she kept it locked within her own bosom, until under an ingenious pretext she repaired to Frankford, gained an interview with Washington, and disclosed to him the important intelligence which saved the lives of her countrymen. Did Lydia Darrah confer a benefit upon the American army—did she perform the duties of an American citizen? Or, was this act an impertinent intermeddling with the *political concerns* of her country, with which, as a *woman,* she had nothing to do? Let the daughters of this republic answer the Question....

We do not, then, and cannot concede the position, that because this is a *political subject* women ought to fold their hands in idleness, and close their eyes and ears to the "horrible things" that are practiced in our land. The denial of our duty to act, is a bold denial of our right to act; and if we have no right to act, then may *we* well be termed "the white slaves of the North"—for, like our brethren in bonds, we must seal our lips in silence and despair.

Slavery a Moral Subject

II. This, however, is not merely a political subject; it is highly moral, and as such claims the attention of every *moral* being. Slavery exerts a most deadly influence over the morals of our country, not only over that portion of it where it actually exists..., but like the miasma of some pestilential pool, it spreads its desolating influence far beyond its own boundaries. Who does not know that licentiousness is a crying sin at the North as well as at South? and who does not admit that the manners of the South in this respect have had wide and destructive influence on Northern character?...Can Northern men go down to the well-watered plains of the South to make their fortunes, without...drinking of the waters of that river of pollution which rolls over the plain of Sodom and Gomorrah? Do they return uncontaminated to their homes, or does not many and many a Northerner dig the grave of his virtue in...our Southern States. And can our theological and academic institutions be opened to the sons of the planter without endangering the purity of the morals of our own sons, by associations with men who regard...oppression as no wrong? Impossible!...

Have Northern women, then, nothing to do with slavery, when its demoralizing influence is polluting their domestic circles and blasting the fair character of *their* sons and brothers? Nothing to do with slavery when *their* domestics [house servants] are often dragged by the merciless kidnapper from the hearth of their nurseries and the arms of their little ones? Nothing to do with slavery when Northern women are chained and driven like criminals, and incarcerated in the great prison-house of the South? Nothing to do with slavery?...

Slavery as a Religious Subject

III. It is as a religious question that we regard it as most important. O! it is when we look at the effort made by slaveholders to destroy the *mind* of the slave that we fear and tremble....

Not only are the means of *mental* improvement withheld from the slave, but the opportunities of receiving *moral* culture also....Indeed the slaveholder possesses *legally* supreme dominion over the *soul* of his slave....

Shall we pour our treasures into the funds of the Foreign Missionary Society to send the glad tidings of redeeming love...to Russia and Greece, to China and Burmah, and the coast of Africa, and yet sit down in indifference to the perishing souls of *our own countrymen?*...Nothing to do with slavery!...

We have hitherto addressed you more as moral and responsible beings, than in the distinctive character of women; we have appealed to you on the broad ground of *human rights* and human responsibilities, rather than on that of your peculiar [distinctive] duties as women. We have pursued this course of argument designedly, because, in order to prove that you have any duties to perform, it is necessary first to establish the principle of moral being—for all our rights and all our duties grow out of this principle. *All moral beings have essentially the same rights and the same duties,* whether they be male or female....We will now endeavor to enumerate some reasons why we believe Northern women, as *women,* are solemnly called upon to labor in the great and glorious work of emancipation....

II. Women the Victims of Slavery

Out of the millions of slaves who have been stolen from Africa, a very great number must have been women who were torn from the arms of their fathers and husbands, brothers and children, and subjected to all the horrors of the middle passage and the still greater sufferings of slavery in a foreign land. Multitudes of these were cast upon our inhospitable shores; some of them now toil out a life of bondage, "one hour of which is fraught with more misery than ages of that" which our fathers rose in rebellion to oppose. But the great mass of female slaves in the southern States are the descendants of these hapless strangers; 1,000,000 of them now wear the iron yoke of slavery in this land of boasted liberty and law. They are our country women—*they are our sisters*; and to us, as women, they have a right to look for sympathy with their sorrows, and effort and prayer for their rescue. Upon those of us especially who have named the name of Christ, they have peculiar claims, and claims which *we must answer, or we shall incur a heavy load of guilt.*

Women, too, are constituted by nature the peculiar guardians of children, and children are the victims of this horrible system. Helpless infancy is robbed of the tender care of the mother and the protection of the father. There are in this Christian land thousands of little children who have been made orphans by the "domestic institution" of the South; and whilst woman's hand is stretched out to gather in the orphans...whom *death* has made in our country, and to shelter them from the storms of adversity, O let us not forget the orphans whom *crime* has made in our midst; but let us plead the cause of *these* innocents. Let us expose the heinous wickedness of the internal slave-trade. It is an organized system for the disruption of family ties, a manufactory of widows and orphans.

III. Women are Slaveholders

Multitudes of the Southern women hold men, women and children as *property. They* are pampered in luxury, and nursed in the school of tyranny; *they* sway the iron rod of power, and *they* rob the laborer of his hire. Immortal beings tremble at *their* nod, and bow in abject submission at *their* word, and under the cowskin too often wielded by *their* own delicate hands. Women at the South hold *their own sisters* and brothers in bondage. Start not at this dreadful assertion—we speak that which some of us do know—we testify that which some of us have seen. Such facts ought to be known, that the women of the North may understand *their* duties, and be incited to perform *them....*

[W]e know that there are *female tyrants* too, who are prompt to lay their complaints of misconduct before their husbands, brothers and sons, and to urge them to commit acts of violence against their helpless slaves. Others still more cruel, place the lash in the hands of some trusty domestic, and stand by whilst he lays the heavy strokes upon the unresisting victim, deaf to the cries for mercy which rend the air, or rather more enraged at such

appeals, which are only answered by the Southern lady with the prompt command of "give her more for that."...Other mistresses who cannot bear that their delicate ears should be pained by the screams of the poor sufferers, write an order to the master of the Charleston work-house, or, the New Orleans calaboose [prison], where they are most cruelly stretched in order to render the stroke of the whip or the blow of the paddle more certain to produce cuts and wounds which cause the blood to flow at every stroke. And let it be remembered that these poor creatures are often *women* who are most indecently divested of their clothing and exposed to the gaze of the executioner of a *woman's* command.

What then, our beloved sisters, must be the effects of such a system upon the domestic character of the white females? Can a corrupt tree bring forth good fruit? Can such despotism mould the character of the Southern woman to gentleness and love?...

[A]nother important consideration is, that in consequence of the dreadful state of morals at the South, the wife and the daughter sometimes find their home a scene of most mortifying, heart-rending preference of the degraded domestic, or the colored daughter of the head of the family....But we forbear to lift the veil of private life any higher; let these few hints suffice to give you some idea of what is daily passing *behind* that curtain which has been so carefully drawn before the scenes of domestic life in Christian America.

And now, dear sisters, let us not forget that *Northern* women are participators in the crime of slavery—too many of *us* have surrendered our hearts and hands to the wealthy planters of the South, and gone down with them to live on the unrequited toil of the slave....

And...some of us have fathers and mothers, sisters and brothers, who are living in the slave States, and are daily served by the unremunerated [unpaid] servant; and for the enlightenment of these *we* are most solemnly bound to labor and to pray without ceasing....

IV. Women Use the Products of Slave Labor

Multitudes of Northern women are daily making use of the products of slave labor. They are clothing themselves and their families in the cotton, and eating the rice and the sugar which they well know has cost the slave his unrequited toil, his blood and his tears; and if the maxim in law be founded in justice and truth, that "the receiver is *as bad* as the thief," how much *greater* the condemnation of those who not merely receive the stolen products of the slave's labor, but *voluntarily* purchase them, and *continually appropriate them to their own use....*

And has the Lord uttered no rebuke to us in these fearful times? Is there *no* lesson for *us* to learn in recent events? Who are the men that now weep and mourn over their broken fortunes—their ruined hopes? Are they not the merchants and manufacturers, who have traded largely in the unrequited labor of the slave?...

We are often told that free articles cannot be obtained; but why not? Our answer is, because there is so little demand for them....We find that those who really wish to obtain such articles, are almost universally able to do so, if they will pay a little higher price, and be satisfied to wear what may not be of quite so good a quality; but it is frequently the case that even this trifling self-denial is not necessary.

We would remind you of the course pursued by our revolutionary fathers and mothers when Great Britain levied upon her colonies what they regarded as unjust taxes. Read the words of the historian, and ponder well the noble self-denial of the men and *women* of this country, when they considered their own liberties endangered by the encroachments of England's bad policy. Look, then, at the influence which their measures produced in making it the interest of the merchants and manufacturers in Great Britain to second the petitions of her colonies for a redress of grievances, and judge for yourselves whether the Southern planters would not gladly second the efforts of the abolitionists, by petitioning their National and State Legislatures for the abolition of slavery, if they found they could no longer sell their slave-grown produce....

Would not a similar effect be produced in *this* country at *this* time, if the *women* of the free States would practice the same self-denial which distinguished our mothers....

Our fathers asserted their right to freedom at the point of the bayonet and the mouth of the cannon, but we repudiate all war and violence—...we wield no other sword than "the sword of the Spirit";...for this is a moral conflict, and we know that "Truth is mighty and will prevail."...

VI. Northern Women Have Deep-Rooted Prejudices Against Our Colored Brethren and Sisters

They gravely talk of their intellectual inferiority and their physical organization, as sufficient reasons why they never should be permitted to rise to an equality with the whites in this country, forgetting

that they have not yet proved the position assumed with regard to mental inferiority. This we utterly deny, and appeal to history and facts to show that the colored is equal in capacity to the white man....

We must remember, that if in this country he has not risen to an equality with the whites, it is solely because he has not had the same advantages. In schools for colored children, we have witnessed the same ability and anxiety to learn; and our experience is...corroborated by the testimony of many living teachers....

But what further evidence of the intellectual capacities of colored men do we need, than the attainments of those who are now living in our free States, and occupying the station of ministers of the gospel....

Now, beloved sisters, what do you say to these proofs of the intellectual abilities of our colored brethren? Can you *rejoice* to find out that you were mistaken in your opinion of their inferiority? Are you ready to extend to them the hand of a sister, to welcome them upon that platform of equal rights, social, civil and religious, on which they are as much entitled to stand erect as any white man in our land?

Physical Organization. But we will now endeavor to answer the second objection urged against the colored man's equality, which is his physical organization. He has a black, or it may be a yellow skin. From these peculiarities, it is argued that he belongs to a *different race.* This we confess we cannot understand, if the Bible account of man's creation is authentic; for there we are told that Eve was the "mother of all living." There can therefore be but *one race* of human beings, as they have all sprung from one common parentage. This holy book speaks of different nations, people, kindreds, and tongues, but tells us nothing of different *races*; so far from it that it expressly declares "God hath made of one blood all the nations, to dwell on all the face of the earth."...

If then the black skin is *not* the mark of a distinct *race,* but merely the peculiarity incident to climate and food, what shall we say about it—how shall we regard it? As an insuperable barrier between our colored brethren and sisters and ourselves—as a sufficient reason for their being deprived of valuable privileges and social enjoyments among us—or a trivial distinction, as unworthy of our notice as the difference of color in the hair and the eyes of our fairer companions and friends? Is it not wonderful and humiliating to us as Republicans and Christians, that we should ever have made the sinful distinction and silly assertions which we have, because some of our fellow-creatures wear a skin not colored like our own?...Women ought to feel a peculiar sympathy in the colored man's wrongs, for like him, *she* has been accused of mental inferiority, and denied the privileges of liberal education....

VIII. The Colored Women of the North are Oppressed

The eighth reason we would urge for the interference of northern women with the system of slavery is, that in consequence of the odium which the degradation of slavery has attached to *color* even in the free States, our *colored sisters* are dreadfully oppressed here. Our seminaries of learning are closed to them..., and even in the house of God they are separated from their white brethren and sisters as though we were afraid to come in contact with a colored skin....

Here, then, are some of the bitter fruits of that inveterate prejudice which the vast proportion of northern women are cherishing towards their colored sisters; and let us remember that every one of us who denies the sinfulness of this prejudice, under the false pretext of its being "an ordination [arrangement] of Providence" "no more to be changed than the laws of nature," and fixed beyond the control of any *human power;...every one of us...* is awfully guilty in the sight of Him who is no respecter of persons....Yes, our sisters,...whenever we treat a colored brother or sister in a way different from that in which we would treat them were they white, we do virtually *reproach our Maker* for having dyed their skins of a sable hue....

But our colored sisters are oppressed in other ways. As they walk the streets of our cities, they are continually liable so be insulted with the vulgar epithet of "nigger"; no matter how respectable or wealthy, they cannot visit the Zoological Institute of New-York except in the capacity of nurses or servants—no matter how worthy, they cannot gain admittance into or receive assistance from any of the charities of this city..., though into these are gathered the very offscouring of our population. These are only specimens of that soul-crushing influence from which the colored women of the north are daily suffering....If they attempt to travel, they are exposed to great indignities and great inconveniences. Instances have been known of their actually dying in consequence of the exposure to which they were subjected on board of our steamboats. No money could purchase the use of a berth for a delicate female because she had a colored skin....Shall *we* be silent at such a time as this?...

How Northern Woman can Help the Cause of Emancipation

We come next to the second grand division of our subject: we are now to show you *how* Northern women can help the cause of abolition....We would answer, they can organize themselves into Anti-Slavery Societies, and thus add to the number of those beaming stars which are already pouring their cheering rays upon the dreary pathway of the slave....By joining an Anti-Slavery Society we assume a responsibility...—we declare that slavery is a crime against God and against man—and we swell the tide of that public opinion which in a few years is to sweep from our land this vast system of oppression and robbery and licentiousness and heathenism. But be not satisfied with merely setting your names to a constitution—this is a very little thing: read on the subject—none of us have yet learned half the abominations of slavery....

Read, then, beloved sisters; and as many of you as are able, subscribe for one or more Anti-Slavery papers or periodicals, and exert your influence to induce your friends to do the same; and when memory has been stored with interesting facts, lock them not up in her store-house, but tell them from house to house, and strive to awaken interest and sympathy and action in others....

By spreading correct information on the subject of slavery, you will prepare the way for the circulation of numerous petitions, both to the ecclesiastical and civil authorities of the nation..., beseeching and entreating that they would banish slavery from the communion table and the pulpit, and rebuke iron-hearted prejudice from our places of worship. Such memorials must ultimately produce the desired effect.

Every woman, of every denomination, whatever may be her color or her creed, *ought to sign* a petition to Congress for the abolition of slavery and the slave-trade in the district of Columbia..., and the inter-state slave traffic. Seven thousands of our brethren and sisters are now languishing in the chains of servitude in the capital of this republican despotism:...they have heard what the women of England did for the slaves of the West-Indies—800,000 women signed the petition which broke the fetters of 800,000 slaves; and when there are as many signatures to the memorials sent up by the women of the United States to Congress as there are slaves in our country, oh! then will the prison-doors of the South be opened by the earthquake of public opinion.

We believe you may also help this cause, by refraining from the use of slave-grown products. Wives and mothers, sisters and daughters, can exert a very extensive influence in providing for the wants of a family....

Much may be done, too, by sympathizing with our oppressed colored sisters, who are suffering in our very midst. Extend to them the right hand of fellowship on the broad principles of humanity and Christianity, treat them as *equals*, visit them as *equals*, invite them to co-operate with you in Anti-Slavery and Temperance and Moral Reform Societies—in Maternal Associations and Prayer Meetings and Reading Companies.... Opportunities frequently occur in travelling, and in other public situations, when your countenance, your influence, and your hand might shield a sister from contempt and insult, and procure for her comfortable accommodations. Then again you can do a great deal towards the elevation of our free colored population, by visiting their day-schools, and teaching in their Sabbath and evening schools, and shedding over them the smile of your approbation, and aiding them with pecuniary contributions. Go to their places of worship; or, if you attend others, sit not down in the highest seats, among the white aristocracy, but go down to the despised colored woman's pew, and sit side by side with her. Multitudes of instances will continually occur in which you will have the opportunity of *identifying yourselves with this injured class* of our fellow beings: embrace these opportunities at all times and in all places, in the true nobility of our great Exemplar, who was ever found among the *poor and the despised*, elevating and blessing them with his counsels and presence. In this way, and this alone, will you be enabled to subdue that deep-rooted prejudice which is doing the work of oppression in the free States to a most dreadful extent.

When this demon has been cast out of your own hearts, when you can recognize the colored woman as a WOMAN—*then* will you be prepared to send out an appeal to our Southern sisters, entreating them to "go and do likewise."...

And since we have set before our white sisters of the North their duties to our sisters of color, so now we would tenderly solicit their indulgence whilst we throw out some suggestions to them. *You*, beloved sisters, have important duties to perform at this crisis, duties no less dignified and far more delicate and difficult. You daily feel the sorrowful effects of the prejudice...towards...you. It is your allotment to bear the cruel scorn and aversion in a thousand different ways....[Y]ou feel afraid to come into our presence unless assured that we can greet you as human beings, as women, as sisters; and often, perhaps, when duty calls you into associations with us, you shrink back and refuse to come, lest haply some among us may be too delicate to sit beside you, too fastidious to bear the contact. We know such things must be mortifying, and hard, very hard to endure, especially from your *professed friends*; but we entreat you to "bear with us a little in *our folly*," for we have so long indulged this prejudice, that some of us find it exceedingly difficult to divest our minds of it. We fully believe that it is *not* a plant of our Father's planting, we are striving to root it up.... You must be willing to mingle with us whilst we have the prejudice, because it is only by associating with you that we shall ever be able to overcome it.... We know that we have not the same mind in us which was in Christ Jesus, and you can confer no greater favor upon us than in thus for a season "bearing all things, believing all things, hoping all things, enduring all things."... We crave your sympathy and prayers: we deeply feel our need of them.

But there is one thing which above all others we beseech you to do for this glorious cause. *Pray for it.* Pray without ceasing.... We have no confidence in *effort without prayer*, and no confidence in *prayer without effort*....

Ah! But we are told—the measures, the measures we cannot unite with. What is the matter with the measures? Why, there is such a daring of public opinion—such a determination to carry on this work in spite of opposition when you see that the public are not prepared for it—when you know that they have so often produced mobs.

And how, we would ask, is the public to be prepared for the reception of these great doctrines? By throwing a bushel over the candle of truth, because the organs of spiritual vision are pained by its radiance in consequence of the moral darkness with which they have so long been involved?—or, by still continuing to *hold forth* the word of life until the eye gradually becomes accustomed to the light, and at last receives it without pain. What did our Lord mean by calling his disciples *the light of the world*, and by commanding them *to let their lights so shine before men*, that they might *see* their good works. Did he mean they must cease to preach the truth as soon as wicked and deceitful men opposed the truth, and blasphemed it? Let us learn his meaning from his actions, for *He* embodied all his principles in his glorious *life*.... Let us then trace the history of Jesus—let us see whether he propagated doctrines obnoxious to public opinion, adverse to the views of the dignitaries of Church and of State, and whether, when he was traduced [slandered] and opposed, he bowed to popular tumult and clamor, or stood erect, uprearing the light of truth in the tempest of passion which howled around him....

It is the Province of Woman to Labor in this Cause

If our brethren...have suffered and dared so much in the cause of bleeding humanity, shall *we* not stand side by side with them in the bloodless contest?...[S]hall American women refuse to follow their husbands, fathers and brothers into the wide field of moral enterprise and holy aggressive conflict with the master sin of the American republic, and the American church? Oh, no! we know the hearts of our sisters too well—we see them already girding on the whole armor of God, already gathering in the plain and on the mountain, in the crowded cities of our seaboard, and the little villas and hamlets of the country; we see them cheering with their smiles and strengthening with their prayers and aiding with their efforts that noble band of patriots, philanthropists and Christians, who have come up to the help of the Lord against the mighty. We see them meekly bowing to the obloquy [verbal abuse] and uncovering their heads to the curses which are heaped by Southern slaveholders upon all who remember those who are in bonds. Woman is now rising, in her womanhood, to throw from her, with one hand the paltry privileges with which *man* has invested her, of conquering by fashionable charms and winning by personal attractions, whilst with the other she grasps the right of woman to unite in holy copartnership with man, in the renovation of a fallen world....

SARAH M. GRIMKÉ, *LETTERS ON THE EQUALITY OF THE SEXES, AND THE CONDITION OF WOMAN, ADDRESSED TO MARY S. PARKER, PRESIDENT OF THE BOSTON FEMALE ANTI-SLAVERY SOCIETY* (1837)

Source: Sarah Grimké, *Letters on the Equality of the Sexes and Other Essays,* ed. Elizabeth Ann Bartlett. New Haven: Yale University Press, 1988. [Originally published 1838.]

LETTER I The Original Equality of Woman
Amesbury, 7th Mo. 11th, 1837
My Dear Friend,

In attempting to comply with thy request to give my views on the Province of Woman, I feel that I am venturing on nearly untrodden ground, and that I shall advance arguments in opposition to a corrupt public opinion, and to the perverted interpretation of Holy Writ, which has so universally obtained. But I am in search of truth; and no obstacle shall prevent my prosecuting that search, because I believe the welfare of the world will be materially advanced by every new discovery we make of the designs of Jehovah in the creation of woman. It is impossible that we can answer the purpose of our being, unless we understand that purpose. It is impossible that we should fulfil our duties, unless we comprehend them; or live up to our privileges, unless we know what they are.

In examining this important subject, I shall depend solely on the Bible to designate the sphere of woman, because I believe almost every thing that has been written on this subject, has been the result of a misconception of the simple truths revealed in the Scriptures, in consequence of the false translation of many passages of Holy Writ. My mind is entirely delivered from the superstitious reverence which is attached to the English version of the Bible. King James's translators certainly were not inspired. I therefore claim the original as my standard, *believing that to have been inspired*, and I also claim to judge for myself what is the meaning of the inspired writers, because I believe it to be the solemn duty of every individual to search the Scriptures for themselves, with the aid of the Holy Spirit, and not be governed by the views of any man, or set of men.

We must first view woman at the period of her creation. "And God said, Let us make man in our own image, after our likeness; and let them have dominion over the fish of the sea, and over the fowl of the air, and over the cattle, and over all the earth, and over every creeping thing that creepeth upon the earth. So God created man in his own image, in the image of God created he him, male and female created he them" [Gen. 1:26-27]. In all this sublime description of the creation of man, (which is a generic term including man and woman), there is not one particle of difference intimated as existing between them. They were both made in the image of

God; dominion was given to both over every other creature, but not over each other. Created in perfect equality, they were expected to exercise the vicegerence intrusted to them by their Maker, in harmony and love.

Let us pass on now to the recapitulation of the creation of man—"The Lord God formed man of the dust of the ground, and breathed into his nostrils the breath of life; and man became a living soul. And the Lord God said, it is not good that man should be alone, I will make him an help meet for him" [Gen. 2:7-18]. All creation swarmed with animated beings capable of natural affection, as we know they still are; it was not, therefore, merely to give man a creature susceptible of loving, obeying, and looking up to him, for all that the animals could do and did do. It was to give him a companion, *in all respects* his equal; one who was like himself *a free agent*, gifted with intellect and endowed with immortality; not a partaker merely of his animal gratifications, but able to enter into all his feelings as a moral and responsible being. If this had not been the case, how could she have been an help meet for him?...

This blissful condition was not long enjoyed by our first parents. Eve, it would seem from the history, was wandering alone amid the bowers of Paradise, when the serpent met with her. From her reply to Satan, it is evident that the command not to eat "of the tree that is in the midst of the garden," was given to both, although the term man was used when the prohibition was issued by God. "And the woman said unto the serpent, WE may eat of the fruit of the trees of the garden, but of the fruit of the tree which is in the midst of the garden, God hath said, YE shall not eat of it, neither shall YE touch it, lest YE die" [Gen. 3:3]....Through the subtlety of the serpent, she was beguiled. And "when she saw that the tree was good for food, and that it was pleasant to the eyes, and a tree to be desired to make one wise, she took of the fruit thereof and did eat" [Gen. 3:6].

We next find Adam involved in the same sin, not through the instrumentality of a supernatural agent, but through that of his equal....Had Adam tenderly reproved [corrected] his wife, and endeavored to lead her to repentance instead of sharing in her guilt, I should be much more ready to accord to man that superiority which he claims; but as the facts stand disclosed by the sacred historian, it appears to me that to say the least, there was as much weakness exhibited by Adam as by Eve. They both fell from innocence, and consequently from happiness, *but not from equality*.

Let us next examine the conduct of this fallen pair, when Jehovah interrogated them respecting their fault. They both frankly confessed their guilt. "The man said, the woman whom thou gavest to be with me, she gave me of the tree and I did eat. And the woman said, the serpent beguiled me and I did eat" [Gen. 3:12]. And the Lord God said unto the woman, "Thou wilt be subject unto thy husband, and he will rule over thee" [Gen. 3:16]. That this did not allude to the subjection of woman to man is manifest....The truth is that the curse, as it is termed, which was pronounced by Jehovah upon woman, is a simple prophecy. The Hebrew, like the French language, uses the same word to express shall and will. Our translators having been accustomed to exercise lordship over their wives, and seeing only through the medium of a perverted judgment, very naturally, though I think not very learnedly or very kindly, translated it *shall* instead of *will*, and thus converted a prediction to Eve into a command to Adam; for observe, it is addressed to the woman and not to the man. The consequence of the fall was an immediate struggle for dominion, and Jehovah foretold which would gain the ascendency....

Here then I plant myself. God created us equal;...and to him alone is woman bound to be in subjection....

Thine for the oppressed in the bonds of womanhood,

Sarah M. Grimké

LETTER II Woman Subject Only To God...

[W]oman I am aware stands charged to the present day with having brought sin into the world. I shall not repel the charge by any counter assertions, although...Adam's ready acquiescence with his wife's proposal, does not savor much of that superiority *in strength of mind*, which is arrogated [claimed] by man....But I ask no favors for my sex....All I ask our brethren is, that they will take their feet from off our necks, and permit us to stand upright on that ground which God designed us to occupy. If he has not given us the rights which have, as I conceive, been wrested from us, we shall soon give evidence of our inferiority, and shrink back into that obscurity, which the high souled magnanimity of man has assigned us as our appropriate sphere....

The lust of dominion was probably the first effect of the fall; and as there was no other intelligent being over whom to exercise it, woman was the first victim of this unhallowed passion....Here we see the origin...of slavery, which sprang up immediately after the fall, and has spread its pestilential branches over the whole face of the known world. All history attests that man has subjected woman to his will, used her as a means to promote his selfish gratification, to minister to his sensual pleasures, to be instrumental in promoting his comfort; but never has he desired to elevate her to that rank she was created to fill. He has done all he could to debase and enslave her mind; and now he looks triumphantly on the ruin he has wrought, and says, the being he has thus deeply injured is his inferior. . . .

LETTER III The Pastoral Letter of the General Association of Congregational Ministers of Massachusetts [Against Women Speaking in Public] . . .

No one can desire more earnestly than I do, that woman may move exactly in the sphere which her Creator has assigned her; and I believe her having been displaced from that sphere has introduced confusion into the world. . . . The New Testament has been referred to, and I am willing to abide by its decisions, but must enter my protest against the false translation of some passages by the MEN who did that work. . . . I am inclined to think, when we are admitted to the honor of studying Greek and Hebrew, we shall produce some various readings of the Bible a little different from those we now have.

The Lord Jesus defines the duties of his followers in his Sermon on the Mount. He lays down grand principles by which they should be governed, without any reference to sex or condition. . . . I follow him through all his precepts, and find him giving the same directions to women as to men, never even referring to the distinction now so strenuously insisted upon between masculine and feminine virtues. . . . Men and women were CREATED EQUAL; they are both moral and accountable beings, and whatever is *right* for man to do, is *right* for woman. . . .

How monstrous, how anti-christian, is the doctrine that woman is to be dependent on man! Where, in all the sacred Scriptures, is this taught? . . .

But we are told, "the power of woman is in her dependence, flowing from a consciousness of that weakness which God has given her for her protection." If physical weakness is alluded to, I cheerfully concede the superiority; if brute force is what my brethren are claiming, I am willing to let them have all the honor they desire; but if they mean to intimate, that mental or moral weakness belongs to woman, more than to man, I utterly disclaim the charge. . . .

LETTER IV Social Intercourse of the Sexes . . .

We approach each other, and mingle with each other, under the constant pressure of feeling that we are of different sexes. . . . Hence our intercourse, instead of being elevated and refined, is generally calculated to excite and keep alive the lowest propensities of our nature. . . . The idea that she is sought as an intelligent and heaven-born creature, whose society will cheer, refine and elevate her companion, and that she will receive the same blessings she confers, is rarely held up to her view. On the contrary, man almost always addresses himself to the weakness of woman. By flattery, by an appeal to her passions, he seeks access to her heart; and when he has gained her affections, he uses her as the instrument of his pleasure—the minister of his temporal comfort. He furnishes himself with a housekeeper, whose chief business is in the kitchen, or the nursery. And whilst he goes abroad and enjoys the means of improvement afforded by collision of intellect with cultivated minds, his wife is condemned to draw nearly all her instruction from books, if she has time to peruse them; and if not, from her meditations, whilst engaged in those domestic duties which are necessary for the comfort of her lord and master. . . .

The apostle beautifully remarks, ". . . There is neither Jew nor Greek, there is neither bond nor free, there is neither *male* nor *female*; for ye are all one in Christ Jesus" [Gal. 3:28]. . . .

The woman who goes forth, clad in the panoply of God, to stem the tide of iniquity and misery, which she beholds rolling through our land, goes not forth . . . as a female. She goes as the dignified messenger of Jehovah. . . .

So far from woman losing any thing of the purity of her mind, by visiting the wretched victims of vice in their miserable abodes, by talking with them, or of them, she becomes more and more elevated and refined in her feelings and views. While laboring to cleanse the minds of others from the malaria of moral pollution, her own heart becomes purified, and her soul rises to nearer communion with her God. Such a woman is infinitely better qualified to fulfil the duties of a wife and a mother, than the woman whose *false delicacy* leads her to shun her fallen sister and brother, and shrink from *naming those sins* which she knows exist, but which she is too fastidious to labor by deed and by word to exterminate. . . .

LETTER VII Condition in Some Parts of Europe and America . . .

[N]ow that her attention is solicited to the subject of her rights, her privileges and her duties, I would entreat her to double her diligence in the performance of all her obligations as a *wife,* a *mother,* a *sister* and a *daughter.* Let us remember that our claim to stand on perfect equality with our brethren, can only be substantiated by a scrupulous attention to our domestic duties, as well as by aiding in the great work of moral reformation—a work which is now calling for the energies and consecrated powers of every man and woman who desires to see the Redeemer's kingdom established on earth....

[B]ut now a new and vast sphere of usefulness is opened to her, and she is pressed by surrounding circumstances to come up to the help of the Lord against the giant sins which desolate our beloved country. Shall woman shrink from duty in this exigency [urgency]...? Shall she rejoice in her home, her husband, her children, and forget her brethren and sisters in bondage, who know not what it is to call a spot of earth their own, whose husbands and wives are torn from them by relentless tyrants, and whose children are snatched from their arms by their unfeeling taskmasters...? Shall woman disregard the situation of thousands of her fellow creatures, who are the victims of intemperance and licentiousness, and...be satisfied that her whole duty is performed, when she can exhibit "her children well clad and smiling, and her table neatly spread with wholesome provisions?"...Ah no! for every such blessing, God demands a grateful heart; and woman must be recreant [unfaithful] to her duty, if she can quietly sit down in the enjoyments of her own domestic circle, and not exert herself to procure the same happiness for others....

LETTER VIII On the Condition of Women in the United States...

During the early part of my life, my lot was cast among the butterflies of the *fashionable* world; and of this class of women, I am constrained to say, both from experience and observation, that their education is miserably deficient; that they are taught to regard marriage as the one thing needful, the only avenue to distinction; hence to attract the notice and win the attentions of men, by their external charms, is the chief business of fashionable girls. They seldom think that men will be allured by intellectual acquirements, because they find, that where any mental superiority exists, a woman is generally shunned and regarded as stepping out of her "appropriate sphere," which, in their view, is to dress, to dance, to set out to the best possible advantage her person....Fashionable women regard themselves, and are regarded by men, as pretty toys or as mere instruments of pleasure; and the vacuity of mind, the heartlessness, the frivolity

which is the necessary result of this false and debasing estimate of women, can only be fully understood by those who have mingled in the folly and wickedness of fashionable life; and who have been called from such pursuits by the voice of the Lord Jesus....

There is another and much more numerous class in this country, who are withdrawn by education or circumstances from the circle of fashionable amusements, but who are brought up with the dangerous and absurd idea, that...to be able to keep their husband's house, and render his situation comfortable, is the end of her being....For this purpose more than for any other, I verily believe the majority of girls are trained. This is demonstrated by the imperfect education which is bestowed upon them, and the little pains taken to cultivate their minds, after they leave school....In most families, it is considered a matter of far more consequence to call a girl off from making a pie, or a pudding, than to interrupt her whilst engaged in her studies....

Let no one think, from these remarks, that I regard a knowledge of housewifery as beneath the acquisition of women. Far from it: I believe that a complete knowledge of household affairs is an indispensable requisite in a woman's education....All I complain of is, that our education consists so almost exclusively in culinary and other manual operations....

The influence of women over the minds and character of *children* of both sexes, is allowed to be far greater than that of men. This being the case by the very ordering of nature, women should be prepared by education for the performance of their sacred duties, as mothers and as sisters....

There is another way in which the general opinion, that women are inferior to men, is manifested, that bears with tremendous effect on the laboring class, and indeed on almost all who are obliged to earn a subsistence,...—I allude to the disproportionate value set on the time and labor of men and of women. A man who is engaged in teaching, can always, I believe, command a higher price for tuition than a woman—even when he teaches the same branches, and is not in any respect superior to the woman. This...is so in every occupation in which the sexes engage indiscriminately....In those employments which are peculiar to women, their time is estimated at only half the value of that of men. A woman who goes out to wash, works as hard in proportion as a wood sawyer..., but she is not generally able to make more than half as much by a day's work....

[Having discussed the plight of slave women, Grimké goes on:] I cannot close this letter, without saying a few words on the benefits to be derived by men, as well as women, from the opinions I advocate relative to the equality of the sexes. Many women are now supported, in idleness and extravagance, by the industry of their husbands, fathers, or brothers, who are compelled to toil out their existence…while the wife and daughters and sisters take no part in the support of the family, and appear to think that their sole business is to spend the hard bought earnings of their male friends.…Our brethren may reject my doctrine, because it runs counter to common opinions, and because it wounds their pride; but I believe they would be "partakers of the benefit" resulting from the Equality of the Sexes, and would find that woman, as their equal, was unspeakably more valuable than woman as their inferior.…

LETTER XII Legal Disabilities of Women…

There are few things which present greater obstacles to the improvement and elevation of woman to her appropriate sphere of usefulness and duty, than the laws which have been enacted to destroy her independence, and crush her individuality; laws which, although they are framed for her government, she has had no voice in establishing, and which rob her of some of her *essential rights.*… I shall confine myself to the laws of our country. These laws bear with peculiar rigor on married women. [Sir William] Blackstone [1723–1780, influential English jurist], in the chapter entitled "Of husband and wife," says:—

> By marriage, the husband and wife are one person in law; that is, *the very being,* or *legal existence of the woman* is suspended during the marriage, or at least is incorporated and consolidated into that of the husband under whose wing, protection and cover she performs everything.…

Here now, the very being of a woman, like that of a slave, is absorbed in her master. All contracts made with her, like those made with slaves by their owners, are a mere nullity. Our kind defenders have legislated away almost all our legal rights, and in the true spirit of such injustice and oppression, have kept us in ignorance of those very laws by which we are governed. They have persuaded us, that we have no right to investigate the laws, and that, if we did, we could not comprehend them; they alone are capable of understanding the mysteries of Blackstone, &c.…

[W]omen, who have brought their husbands handsome fortunes, have been left, in consequence of the wasteful and dissolute habits of their husbands, in straitened circumstances, and compelled to toil for the support of their families.…

The wife's property is, I believe, equally liable for her husband's debts contracted before marriage.

> If the wife be injured in her person or property, she can bring no action for redress without her husband's concurrence, and his name as well as her own: neither can she be sued, without making her husband a defendant.

This law that "a wife can bring no action," &c., is similar to the law respecting slaves.…So if any damages are recovered for an injury committed on a wife, the husband pockets it; in the case of the slave, the master does the same.…

> The husband, by the old law, might give his wife moderate correction, as he is to answer for her misbehavior.…The courts of law will still permit a husband to restrain a wife in her liberty, in case of any gross misbehavior.

What a mortifying proof this law affords, of the estimation in which woman is held! She is placed completely in the hands of a being subject like herself to the outbursts of passion, and therefore unworthy to be trusted with power. Perhaps I may be told respecting this law, that it is a dead letter, as I am sometimes told about the slave laws; but this is not true in either case. The slaveholder does kill his slave by moderate correction, as the law allows; and many a husband, among the poor, exercises the right given him by the law, of degrading woman by personal chastisement. And among the higher ranks, if actual imprisonment is not resorted to, women are not unfrequently restrained of the liberty of going to places of worship by irreligious husbands, and of doing many other things.…

> A woman's personal property by marriage becomes absolutely her husband's, which, at his death, he may leave entirely away from her.

And further, all…that she acquires by her industry is his.…I know an instance of a woman…, who by great industry had acquired a little money which she deposited in a bank for safe keeping. She had saved this pittance whilst able to work, in hopes that when age or sickness disqualified her for exertion, she might have something to render life comfortable, without being a burden to her friends. Her husband, a worthless, idle man, discovered this hid treasure, drew her little stock from the bank, and expended it all in extravagance and vicious indulgence....

> With regard to the property of women, there is taxation without representation; for they pay taxes without having the liberty of voting for representatives.

And this taxation, without representation, be it remembered, was the cause of our Revolutionary war..., yet the daughters of New England, as well as of all the other States of this free Republic, are suffering a similar injustice....

The various laws...leave women very little more liberty, or power, in some respects, than the slave.... I do not wish by any means to intimate that the condition of free women can be compared to that of slaves in suffering, or in degradation; still, I believe the laws which deprive married women of their rights and privileges, have a tendency to lessen them in their own estimation as moral and responsible beings, and that their being made by civil law inferior to their husbands, has a debasing and mischievous effect upon them, teaching them practically the fatal lesson to look unto man for protection and indulgence....

LETTER XV Man Equally Guilty with Woman in the Fall...

I should not mention this subject again, if it were not to point out to my sisters what seems to me an irresistible conclusion from the literal interpretation of St. Paul, without reference to the context, and the peculiar circumstances and abuses which drew forth the expressions, "I suffer not a woman to teach"— "Let your women keep silence in the church," [I Cor. 14:34], i.e., congregation. It is manifest, that if the apostle meant what his words imply, when taken in the strictest sense, then women have no right to *teach* Sabbath or day schools, or to open their lips to sing in the assemblies of the people; yet young and delicate women are engaged in all these offices; they are expressly trained to exhibit themselves, and raise their voices to a high pitch in the choirs of our places of worship. I do not intend to sit in judgment on my sisters for doing these things; I only want them to see, that they are as really infringing a *supposed* divine command, by instructing their pupils in the Sabbath or day schools, and by singing in the congregation, as if they were engaged in preaching....Why, then, are we permitted to break this injunction in some

points, and so sedulously [diligently] warned not to overstep the bounds set for us by our *brethren* in another? Simply, as I believe, because in the one case we subserve *their* views and *their* interests, and act *in subordination to them*; whilst in the other, we come in contact with their interests, and claim to be on an equality with them in the highest and most important trust ever committed to man, namely, the ministry of the world. It is manifest, that if women were permitted to be ministers of the gospel, as they unquestionably were in the primitive ages of the Christian church, it would interfere materially with the present organized system of spiritual power and ecclesiastical authority, which is now vested solely in the hands of men....I do not ask any one to believe my statements, or adopt my conclusions, because they are mine; but I do earnestly entreat my sisters to lay aside their prejudices, and examine these subjects for themselves, regardless of the "traditions of men"....

Duties of Women

One of the duties which devolve upon women in the present interesting crisis, is to prepare themselves for more extensive usefulness, by making use of those religious and literary privileges and advantages that are within their reach, if they will only stretch out their hands and possess them. By doing this, they will become better acquainted with their rights as moral beings, and with their responsibilities growing out of those rights; they will regard themselves, as they really are, FREE AGENTS, immortal beings..., bound not to submit to any restriction imposed for selfish purposes, or to gratify that love of power which has reigned in the heart of man from Adam down to the present time. In contemplating the great moral reformations of the day, and the part which they are bound to take in them, instead of puzzling themselves with...how far they may go without overstepping the bounds of propriety, which separate male and female duties, they will only inquire, "Lord, what wilt thou have us to do?" They will be enabled to see the simple truth, that God has made no distinction between men and women as moral beings; that the distinction now so much insisted upon between male and female virtues is as absurd as it is unscriptural, and has been the fruitful source of much mischief—granting to man a license for the exhibition of brute force and conflict on the battle field; for sternness, selfishness, and the exercise of irresponsible power in the circle of home—and to woman a permit to...regard modesty and delicacy, and all the kindred virtues, as peculiarly appropriate to her. Now to me it is perfectly clear, that WHATSOEVER IT IS MORALLY RIGHT FOR A MAN TO DO, IT IS MORALLY RIGHT FOR A WOMAN TO DO; and that confusion must exist in the moral world, until woman takes her stand on the same platform with man, and feels that she is clothed by her Maker with the *same rights*, and, of course, that upon her devolve the *same duties*....

There is a vast field of usefulness before them. The signs of the times give portentous evidence, that a day of deep trial is approaching; and I urge them...to come to the rescue of a ruined world, and to be found co-workers with Jesus Christ....

Conclusion

I have now, my dear sister, completed my series of letters. I am aware, they contain some new views; but I believe they are based on the immutable truths of the Bible. All I ask for them is, the candid and prayerful consideration of Christians. If they strike at some of our bosom sins, our deep-rooted prejudices, our long cherished opinions, let us not condemn them on that account, but investigate them fearlessly and prayerfully, and not shrink from the examination; because, if they are true, they place heavy responsibilities upon women. In throwing them before the public, I have been actuated solely by the belief, that if they are acted upon, they will exalt the character and enlarge the usefulness of my own sex, and contribute greatly to the happiness and virtue of the other. That there is a root of bitterness continually springing up in families and troubling the repose of both men and women, must be manifest to even a superficial observer; and I believe it is the mistaken notion of the inequality of the sexes. As there is an assumption of superiority on the one part, which is not sanctioned by Jehovah, there is an incessant struggle on the other to rise to that degree of dignity, which God designed women to possess in common with men, and to maintain those rights and exercise those privileges which every woman's common sense, apart from the prejudices of education, tells her are inalienable....

Thine in the bonds of womanhood,

Sarah M. Grimké

CHAPTER 15

José Enrique de la Peña Remembers the Alamo

"A series of unfortunate incidents"

"Remember the Alamo!" The cry has a prominent place in American lore alongside "Remember the *Maine!*" and "Remember Pearl Harbor!" It calls to mind March 6, 1836, the day William Barret Travis, Jim Bowie, Davy Crockett, and almost two hundred others defending a makeshift fort (really an old Spanish mission) in San Antonio, Texas, were slain to the last man by a Mexican army led by General Antonio López de Santa Anna. Two weeks earlier, as Santa Anna's 2,500-man force surrounded the place, Colonel Travis had written to "the People of Texas & all Americans in the world," calling for reinforcements but insisting that, whether help came or not, "*I shall never surrender or retreat*": it would be either "VICTORY or DEATH."[1] Some six weeks after death found Travis and his men, Texas General Sam Houston rallied his troops on the eve of his own fight against Santa Anna by shouting "soldiers remember the Alamo! the Alamo! the Alamo!" The cry "was caught up by every man in the army," Houston recalled. Mexican forces heard it themselves on April 21 at the Battle of San Jacinto, where Texans killed some 630 *soldados* and took another 730 prisoner, including Santa Anna, effectively ending the war and giving Texas its independence from Mexico.[2]

Even today, more than 150 years after the Texas Republic became part of the United States in 1845, Americans remember the Alamo. The site is a shrine visited by millions. Hollywood has told the story many times, from silent films to blockbusters by Walt Disney (1955) and John Wayne (1960) to *The Alamo* (2004), starring Billy Bob Thornton as Davy Crockett. Many presidents (Franklin Roosevelt, John Kennedy) have campaigned in its shadow, and many others (Ronald Reagan, George H. W. Bush) have invoked it to advance one cause or another. In the 1960s, Texan Lyndon Baines Johnson, who claimed (falsely) that one of his ancestors died in the battle, sent more U.S. troops to Vietnam in part because "Vietnam is just like the Alamo. Hell, it's just like if you were…surrounded and you damn well needed somebody." In 1999, another Texan, Governor George W. Bush, read "Travis's 'VICTORY or DEATH' letter to America's Ryder Cup golf team" to inspire them in their upcoming match against Europe. (They won.)[3]

All of the energy spent remembering the Alamo would have surprised people in 1836. Many Texans thought it was not worth defending and many Mexicans thought it not worth taking: Houston had ordered Travis to blow it up and retreat; Santa Anna's officers considered capturing it a waste of time and troops. Afterward, Santa Anna dismissed the battle as "but a small affair." San Antonio residents apparently agreed, for—unlike Gettysburg, hallowed ground soon after the battle there in July 1863 (Chapter 19)—the Alamo drifted toward ruin, its stones carted away by locals, its walls covered in graffiti, its floor speckled with bird droppings. Only the founding of the Daughters of the Republic of Texas in 1892—part of a national craze for U.S. history that spawned countless monuments, pageants, and historic sites—put the Alamo on the road to its starring role as an American icon.[4]

But remembering the Alamo is not as simple as it sounds. People view this symbol in different ways, making it a place for protests as well as parades. The contest over what gets remembered (and what forgotten) is so intense that it can be called the second Battle of the Alamo.[5] With San Antonio now over half Hispanic, more people argue that the focus on "Anglos" (who in 1836 were called "Texians") is both misleading and demeaning, for it lumps anyone of Hispanic heritage with the killers of Crockett and the rest. In fact, many "Tejanos" (Texans of Hispanic origin) were active in the resistance to Santa Anna's rule. More than one hundred joined cavalry companies, earning praise from their Texian comrades because they "uniformly acquitted themselves to their credit as patriots and soldiers." In the political realm, meanwhile, José Francisco Ruiz and José Antonio Navarro, Tejanos from San Antonio, signed the Texas Declaration of Independence on March 2. When Travis, Bowie, and Crockett fell at the Alamo four days later, Juan Abamillo, Juan Antonio Badillo, and José Esparza died fighting beside them. And at San Jacinto, amid the shouts "Remember the Alamo!" by triumphant *norte-americanos* could be heard their Tejano comrades-in-arms "bellowing '*Recuerden el Alamo*!'"[6]

Another way of contesting the Alamo's memory is to tarnish Texas leaders. *A fight for liberty?* It was actually a "land grab" by a gang of unscrupulous slaveowners from the United States, most of them illegal immigrants who responded to Mexico's generosity—free land, no taxes, slavery allowed there while it was outlawed in the rest of the nation—with constant complaints and, ultimately, rebellion.[7] *Heroes?* More like men drowning in debt, drink, and defeat who were desperate to salvage their reputation. Sam Houston drank too much (his Cherokee friends called him *Oo-tse-tee Ar-dee-tah-skee*, "Big Drunk"), as did Jim Bowie, whom some San Antonio locals called "*fanfarrón* Santiago Bowie" (James Bowie the braggart). Travis had abandoned his wife, his children, and his creditors back in Alabama, while the celebrated Crockett, campaigning for reelection to Congress back in Tennessee, told his constituents that if he lost "They might go to hell, and I would go to Texas"; beaten at the polls, he got there just two months before the battle.[8] *Stalwart soldiers?* These men, ignoring Tejano scouts who warned of Santa Anna's approach, were caught "lounging in town" when he showed up and "barely had time to grab a few provisions and fall back into the Alamo." Moreover, while proclaiming "VICTORY or DEATH" to the world, they parleyed with Santa Anna about surrender. When Mexican troops attacked early on March 6, the entire garrison (including the sentries) was asleep.[9]

Thus, while the first Battle of the Alamo lasted less than an hour, its modern counterpart—noisy but nonviolent—has been going on for decades. No skirmish in this contemporary combat has been more bitterly fought than how Davy Crockett died. Hollywood's Crockett—Fess Parker in the Disney version, John Wayne five years later—went down fighting, but ever since 1836, when various American newspapers mentioned it, there had been another scenario: Crockett and several others had surrendered when further resistance was suicidal; taken to Santa Anna, the folk hero tried to talk his way out of trouble, but the Mexican leader, adhering to his "take no prisoners" policy, ordered the survivors executed on the spot.

Imagine the ruckus this version of Crockett's end stirred up. Those who think it sounds just like the celebrated wit and storyteller point out that the fellow was known for his quick thinking and glib tongue. "Few could eclipse him in conversation," wrote one Texan who met him. "He was fond of talking, and had an ease and grace about him which…rendered him irresistible." Is it far-fetched to imagine Crockett trying to charm Santa Anna, as the "Canebrake Congressman" had so many Americans? But others insist that this sort of talk is "blasphemy." Proponents of the surrender story have been met with articles about "smarty-pants historians," along with "late-night phone calls" and "hate mail" calling them everything from "gutless wonders" to Communists, from "smut peddler" to "mealy-mouthed intellectual" who ought to "have his mouth washed out with soap."[10]

At the center of this storm sits a long-forgotten account of the Alamo by an obscure Mexican Army officer, José Enrique de la Peña (1807-*c.* 1842). First published in English in 1975 by Texas A & M University Press, its appearance set off what historian James E. Crisp calls "one of the most intense historical controversies of recent times."[11] Is it a modern fake? Could it be authentic but wrong about Crockett? The debate has brought this man and this text into the spotlight.

Despite all the recent attention, de la Peña remains little known. A professional soldier since 1825, he was part of the Mexican Army's effort to crush the Texas rebellion, seeing action at the Alamo. Deeply disillusioned with Santa Anna as both general and president (Santa Anna had become dictator of Mexico in 1834), after leaving Texas he joined other officers opposed to his nation's government. When in 1838 that opposition landed de la Peña in prison, he drew on his own diary of the Texas campaign and on material from other veterans to craft his account.

De la Peña claimed at the outset that he wrote to set the record straight about that "series of unfortunate incidents": as "an eyewitness" and "impartial observer," he insisted, "I have described" the campaign "with accuracy" because "[m]y chief purpose is to relate facts." Nonetheless, de la Peña's text makes it clear that he was an angry man with scores to settle and too much time to brood about "the cruel faction that has submerged our country in an abyss of misfortunes." Santa Anna "never took a step that was not the wrong one," he sneered. Another general was "an insignificant being," "a despicable buffoon." He even turned his pen on his ex-girlfriend, who apparently left him because of his politics, calling her "deceitful," "fickle," "cruel," and "treacherous."

"I was gifted with extreme sensitivity, a passionate soul, and a vivid imagination," de la Peña admitted, prompting some to dismiss his work as either genuine but unreliable or a fake concocted in the twentieth century.[12]

In fact, however, those fixated on Crockett's demise, which gets just a paragraph in almost two hundred pages of this remarkable account, miss the significance of de la Peña's text. He helps shift our point of view in valuable ways, getting us to consider these famous events not from Washington, D.C., but from Mexico City, not from the Alamo's ramparts but from the ground below, where de la Peña and his men crept through the predawn darkness on March 6. Such vantage points, historian Daniel Flores suggests, reveal that the so-called Texas Revolution started out as "both Mexicans and Anglo-Americans [there] seeking to restore a federalist government in Mexico" that would give them more autonomy. When that failed and fighting began, Flores goes on, "Santa Anna's actions can be viewed as an effort to quash an internal uprising in his own country." Just as Álvar Nuñez Cabeza de Vaca's account of his wanderings through this same region three centuries earlier helps call into question conventional ideas about what constitutes "American History" (Chapter 2), so de la Peña's memories remind us that the Alamo was as much a part of the history of New Spain (Mexico) as of the United States, that "the Texas Revolution" might better be termed "the war of Texas secession."[13]

Looking outward from Mexico City, it becomes clear that unrest in Texas was just one of many problems the fragile new nation faced. Ever since winning independence from Spain in 1821, Mexico had endured several coups. Whoever was in charge had, among the biggest challenges (as it was at the time in the United States), working out the balance of power between the states ("federalists") and the national government ("centralists"). When Santa Anna took over in 1834 and made himself dictator—suspending the 1824 Federal Constitution, dissolving Congress, shutting down state legislatures—Texas was only one of many Mexican regions that resisted: New Mexico and California were also restive, and rebellions erupted in Yucatán, Coahuilla, and Zacatecas.

But Texas was different. Its 1836 population of perhaps 40,000 non-Indians consisted of just 3,500 Tejanos; the rest were recent arrivals from the United States (and their slaves) who, even if they had become Mexican citizens, never forgot where they came from. Mexican leaders had long seen trouble coming. "[T]he colonists in Texas will not be Mexicans more than in name," fretted one in 1825. For the next decade, the chorus of concern grew louder. "[I]t is necessary to build dams to contain these restless peoples—scheming, haughty, and rash," another wrote. Otherwise these "shrewd and unruly" Americans, many of them "turbulent characters," will "one day...revolt and join with their former country."[14]

An important item in the baggage these immigrants hauled with them into Texas was pride in their former country's heritage and a tendency to see things through a lens fashioned by Thomas Paine, Thomas Jefferson, and Mason Locke Weems (Chapters 7 and 10). "Citizens of Texas," cried Governor Henry Smith in February 1836, rallying people to the cause, "descendents of Washington, awake! arouse yourself!" That same month the Texas provisional government proclaimed themselves "*the sons* of the BRAVE PATRIOTS of '76." Meanwhile, at the Alamo on the evening of February 22, with Santa Anna's army approaching, "the garrison and the townspeople...held a *fandango* [dance] celebrating George Washington's birthday." On March 2, as Mexican forces prepared to storm the Alamo, a rebel convention gathered in *Washington*-on-the-Brazos.[15]

The Declaration of Independence approved that very day resembled the document that (as a Texan put it) "old Tom Jefferson" had penned sixty years earlier. From rhetoric about "appealing to a candid world" to the cadence of the charges against Mexico's government (*It has dissolved...It has demanded...It has invaded*) to the stress on tyranny being met with patience and petitions, the parallels were close, and significant. But no less significant were the differences. As one Texian observed, in 1776 colonists had rebelled against a nation with "kindred blood, language, and institutions"; "we," on the other hand, "separate from a people one half of whom are the most depraved of the different races of Indians, different in color, pursuits[,] and character." As the 1836 Declaration bluntly put it, "the Mexican people...are unfit to be free, and incapable of self government." Such talk was by then common. It was not just the "utter dissimilarity of character between the two people," Anglos explained, but that Mexicans are inferior, "a mongrel race of degenerate Spaniards and Indians more depraved than they." Indeed, "the great mass" of them are "incapable of appreciating or even comprehending the Blessings of free institutions."[16]

Given such talk, no wonder most people since have preferred to "remember the Alamo" as what Paul Hutton calls "a conflict of civilizations: freedom versus tyranny, democracy versus despotism, Protestantism versus Catholicism, the New World culture of the United States versus the Old World culture of Mexico, Anglo-Saxons versus the mongrelized mixture of Indian and Spanish races, and ultimately, the forces of good and evil." This storyline would have come as a surprise to Tejanos and Texians, who had been living together more or less in peace for over a decade before the rebellion. Intermarriage was common, the most famous union being between Jim Bowie and Ursula de Veramendi, daughter of San Antonio's *alcalde* (mayor) in 1831. Over the next four years, the petitions Texians sent to Mexico City asking redress of their grievances were echoed by similar documents—including one by the San Antonio *ayuntamiento* (city council)—drafted by Tejanos. When those petitions failed and fighting erupted in the fall of 1835, Tejanos not only joined the rebel army and signed the Texas Declaration of Independence, they went on to play a prominent role in the Republic of Texas as jurors, rangers, mayors, congressmen, and much more besides.[17]

Consider Juan Nepomuceno Seguín (1806–1889) of San Antonio, a man so well known at the time that even José Enrique de la Peña singled him out by name as one of only three "intelligent men who incurred the name of traitor [to Mexico], a label both ugly and deserved." As *alcalde* in the early 1830s Seguín had signed petitions on behalf of his Texian friends and business partners. During the rebellion he led a company of Tejano cavalry (those celebrated "patriots and soldiers" mentioned earlier), followed orders to slip out of the Alamo on February 28 to seek reinforcements, and, two months later, demanded that he and his Tejano company be allowed to join the rebel force at San Jacinto. With the Lone Star Republic won, its new president, Sam Houston—writing that "I rely on your ability, patriotism, and watchfulness"—made Lieutenant Colonel Seguín commandant at San Antonio, where he delivered the eulogy at the formal burial of the Alamo's defenders. In 1838, Seguín won election to a three-year term in the Texas Senate before returning home to again become mayor.[18]

By then, however, the Texas climate had turned cold for men like Seguín. The chill began as early as 1835 when hundreds, even thousands, of recently arrived men from the United States, lacking experience with Tejanos as neighbors, friends, wives, and trading partners, considered them inferiors who doubtless favored Santa Anna in the rebellion—and then treated them as such. As in 1776, some did indeed support the rebellion, others did not, and most simply wanted to stay out of it, but all were now suspect. Despite the language in their 1836 Declaration, the split between Texians and Tejanos was, as James Crisp points out, "not so much an immediate *cause* as it was an eventual *consequence* of Texas's separation from Mexico." When Mexico sought to retake Texas in 1842, even someone with Seguín's resumé was no longer welcome. Charged with treason, his plantation plundered, he had "to resign as mayor and flee across the Rio Grande—where he was immediately put under arrest as a traitor to Mexico!" Lamenting that he had become "a foreigner in my native land," in the fall of 1842 Seguín returned to San Antonio to shepherd south hundreds of other Tejanos who felt the same way.[19]

That same year (or the year before), José Enrique de la Peña died, perhaps still in prison but certainly in poverty, obscurity, and disgrace, his account forgotten—along with so much about the Texas Rebellion. Indeed, as Crisp notes, " 'Remember the Alamo' became a formula for forgetfulness. The voices of Seguín and his men…were all but silenced; for decades the Tejanos were virtually erased from standard histories of the war against Mexico and from the historical memories of most Texans"—not to mention most Americans. Like Joseph Plumb Martin and Mason Locke Weems before him, José Enrique de la Peña joins the contest for memory and meaning, a contest that is still being fought at the Alamo—and across America.[20]

Questions for Consideration and Conversation

1. Why did de la Peña write this? How did his agenda shape, even distort, his text?

2. As with Joseph Plumb Martin (Chapter 9), so with José Enrique de la Peña: How much can we trust the reminiscences of an embittered veteran?

3. Why, according to de la Peña, did the Mexican assault on the Alamo succeed? Why did the Mexican army campaign overall fail? What would he have done differently had he been in charge?

4. How does reading his account alter your perceptions of American history? Of the history of Texas?

5. Why does it matter so much to so many people whether Davy Crockett died fighting or was executed after surrendering? If this account were universally accepted, beyond a shadow of a doubt, to be *true*, how would American history be changed? If this account were universally accepted, beyond a shadow of a doubt, to be *false*, how would American history be changed?

6. The head note mentions that some call many of the Americans who ventured into Texas in the 1820s and 1830s "illegal immigrants," because they settled there without asking or receiving permission from the Mexican government. Is that a fair characterization? How does thinking of them as "illegals" influence your views on the contemporary debates about immigration in the United States?

Endnotes

1. Randy Roberts and James S. Olson, *A Line in the Sand: The Alamo in Blood and Memory* (New York, 2001), 126–27.

2. Randolph B. Campbell, *Gone to Texas: A History of the Lone Star State* (New York, 2003), 153–54, 157.

3. Roberts and Olson, *Line in the Sand*, 224 (Roosevelt), 254–57 (Kennedy), 279–81 (Johnson), 312 (Reagan, Bush).

4. Ibid., 184 (Santa Anna), 200–09.

5. See Holly Beachley Brear, *Inherit the Alamo: Myth and Ritual at an American Shrine* (Austin, TX, 1995); Paul Andrew Hutton, "The Alamo as Icon," in Joseph G. Dawson III, ed., *The Texas Military Experience: From the Texas Revolution through World War II* (College Station, TX, 1995), 14–31; Richard R. Flores, *Remembering the Alamo: Memory, Modernity, and the Master Symbol* (Austin, TX, 2002).

6. Paul D. Lack, *The Texas Revolutionary Experience: A Political and Social History, 1835–1836* (College Station, TX, 1992), 185 ("patriots and soldiers"); Roberts and Olson, *Line in the Sand*, 189 ("el Alamo").

7. Gary Clayton Anderson, *The Conquest of Texas: Ethnic Cleansing in the Promised Land, 1820–1875* (Norman, OK, 2005), 5 ("land grab"); Campbell, *Gone to Texas*, ch. 5.

8. James E. Crisp, *Sleuthing the Alamo: Davy Crockett's Last Stand and Other Mysteries of the Texas Revolution* (New York, 2005), 29 ("Big Drunk"); Roberts and Olson, *Line in the Sand*, 111 (Bowie), 93 (Crockett).

9. Crisp, *Sleuthing the Alamo*, 63 ("lounging"); Roberts and Olson, *Line in the Sand*, 160 (asleep); Stephen L. Hardin, *Texian Iliad: A Military History of the Texas Revolution, 1835–1836* (Austin, TX, 1994), 137 (parleying), 139 (asleep).

10. Crisp, *Sleuthing the Alamo*, 72 ("smut peddler"); Hutton, "Alamo as Icon," 26 ("hate mail," "phone calls"), 27 ("soap"), 29 ("blasphemy"), 30 ("gutless wonders"); Roberts and Olson, *Line in the Sand*, 114 ("irresistible"), 291 ("smarty-pants").

11. Crisp, *Sleuthing the Alamo*, 65.

12. José Enrique de la Peña, *With Santa Anna in Texas: A Personal Narrative of the Revolution*, trans. and ed. by Carmen Perry, expanded edition (College Station, TX, 1997), xxvii ("impartial," "accuracy"), xxix ("incidents"), 79 ("wrong one"), 137 ("being"), 140 ("buffoon"), 152 ("facts"), 167 ("misfortunes," girlfriend, "gifted").

13. Flores, *Remembering the Alamo*, 31; Raúl A. Ramos, *Beyond the Alamo: Forging Mexican Ethnicity in San Antonio, 1821–1861* (Chapel Hill, NC, 2008), 4 ("Texas secession").

14. David J. Weber, *The Mexican Frontier, 1821–1846: The American Southwest Under Mexico* (Albuquerque, 1982), 163 ("one day"), 166 ("more than name"), 175 ("rash"); Anderson, *Conquest of Texas*, 72 ("unruly"); Lack, *Texas Revolutionary Experience*, 44 ("turbulent").

15. Roberts and Olson, *Line in the Sand*, 118–19 (*fandango*), 139 (Smith), 144–47 (declaration and constitution); Lack, *Texas Revolutionary Experience*, xiv (government), ch. 5 (convention); William C. Davis, *Lone Star Rising: The Revolutionary Birth of the Texas Republic* (New York, 2004), 212 (*fandango*).

16. Roberts and Olson, *Line in the Sand*, 56 ("old Tom Jefferson"); "The Unanimous Declaration of Independence Made by the Delegates of the People of Texas in General Convention at the Town of Washington on the 2nd day of March 1836," http://www.yale.edu/lawweb/avalon/texdec.htm, accessed January 16, 2008; Lack, *Texas Revolutionary Experience*, 78 ("incapable"), 86 ("depraved," "dissimilarity," "mongrel").

17. Crisp, *Sleuthing the Alamo*, 47 (Republic), 146 (Hutton); Roberts and Olson, *Line in the Sand*, 111 (Bowie); Anderson, *Conquest of Texas*, 87 (petitions); and see Flores, *Remembering the Alamo*, 31.

18. Anderson, *Conquest of Texas*, 87; Weber, *Mexican Frontier*, 176 (*alcalde*); Crisp, *Sleuthing the Alamo*, 44 (Alamo, San Jacinto, eulogy); Timothy M. Matovina, ed., *The Alamo Remembered: Tejano Accounts and Perspectives* (Austin, TX, 1995), 19–21 (eulogy).

19. Crisp, *Sleuthing the Alamo*, 41 (cause), 47–48 ("put under arrest"); Weber, *Mexican Frontier*, 253 ("foreigner").

20. Crisp, *Sleuthing the Alamo*, 59.

José Enrique De la Peña, Review and Journal of the Texas Campaign (1836)

[Original Title: *Reseña y diario de la campaña de Texas*.]
Source: José Enrique de la Peña, *With Santa Anna in Texas: A Personal Narrative of the Revolution*, trans. and ed. Carmen Perry. Expanded edition. Introduction by James E. Crisp. College Station: Texas A & M University Press, 1997.

Prologue

The diversity of opinions expressed concerning the Texas campaign; the accumulation of lies told to falsify the events, published in national as well as international newspapers, but especially in the latter, and the cheap adulation the former have rendered to the men least deserving of it; the ignorance, stupidity, and cruelty displayed by the ministry and the commander in chief in this war; the honor of the army, unjustly censured even by its own members, who without adequate knowledge have superficially or inaccurately passed judgment; the honor and self-esteem of every military man who participated, so deeply hurt by the great inaccuracies in the official records as to dates, deeds, and places; and above all the honor of the country, deeply compromised by its leaders and no less by the truth and the atrocity of its crimes—these are the principal causes which compelled me to publish the diary I kept during the time I served in this unfortunate campaign....

I shall pour out the diary just as I have written it, and whenever I see the need I shall make those observations which could not be made on the march, for at times I had to write on horseback, at other times exhausted from the journey, and always uncomfortable and unsheltered....

I would like to conceal my name to avoid the criticism it will draw toward me and so that nothing will distract from the reasons I give and the thoughts I explain, for I do not pretend to be a historian; but no one in the army of operations in Texas would not know who I am, and it could be interpreted that I did this out of weakness.

As concerns General Santa Anna, one would have to write nothing at all to avoid censuring his conduct. He created the sad situation in which he now finds himself, and he would be less vulnerable if, in his misfortune, he had not dragged with him so many worthy of a better fate.

Convinced of my limitations, which I am not ashamed to admit, I would desist from my goal were I not so aware that events are being distorted to the point that we who actually witnessed them will soon fail to recognize them. This has been furthered by some documents which have been published making accusations and at the same time trying to justify them. I have written as an eyewitness to these same events. I have described them with accuracy and have recorded them not from memory, but as they took place. I should be judged as an impartial observer because I have had no ulterior interest in distorting the facts, as has been done and will continue to be done by those who have written and who persist in writing to justify their mistakes. I do not have to answer any charges; I am free to be candid and I wish to be so....

In undertaking this modest, but for me arduous, effort, I find myself far from any pretensions of imitating the artistic style with which the French military men have portrayed their admirable feats, for I do not have the talents nor can I recount anything but errors, which is very sad for a Mexican soldier. Let no one expect to find in my narrative flowery rhetoric or a sublime and lofty style or ornate descriptions, even though the material is appropriate and abundant enough to fill volumes; what I would like to do, were I given the chance to speak with the passion I feel, is to write a historical novel, depicting scenes that could make the dead weep. But since this is not possible, I offer instead accuracy in describing events, as I have previously said; nearly all the army will serve as my witness, and I think that even the guilty will not dare deny them.

The infamies that have occurred in this campaign, infamies that must have horrified the civilized world and whose memory will continue to provoke pain for many years hence, should not remain hidden. In referring to them, I shall thrust aside my personal feelings, and my friends will cease to be friends from the moment that I publish the evils committed against my country and the deeds perpetrated against humanity....

I am well aware...that as I set out to vindicated the corrupted honor of the army, I will at the same time incur enemies within its ranks. I know that the inept never forgive having their errors published. Perhaps I shall incur further persecution and provoke fresh injustices in addition to those already perpetrated against me. But has this not always happened to those who swerve from the path of adulation and abide solely by the truth? I am determined to tell it, knowing full well that I cannot flatter everyone, but, schooled in adversity, I am prepared for anything, entrenched behind the bulwark of a clear conscience and the wise conviction of the Mexicans that nothing can frighten a man of honor.

I have heard some military personnel, especially those with rank, say that whatever happened in Texas should remain buried in the deepest silence because it is shameful; but those writers who have preceded me have surely convinced them that this is impossible. Others, who have heard about my diary, have been cruel enough to say that for the writing of it alone, I should be condemned to isolation in a fortress, and when they see that I have published it, they will no doubt think I should be shot. You and other sensible persons who read this will judge those who think thus as they deserve. As for me, I do not think that I should subject my ideas to those of everyone else....

Through a series of unfortunate incidents detrimental to the [Mexican] Republic, one has been led to believe that only those in command have a right to think. It is taken for granted that men in high posts reason best, as if one did not know how these positions have been obtained up to now, pretending that the favoritism lavished on them could also endow them with talents. This sort of fanaticism engendered among members of the army and even among other classes of society produces a situation in which deeds are evaluated according to who is involved rather than by their own merits. Thus, my observations will have among other shortcomings that of not being those of a general....

I could have published my notes a few days after I returned from the campaign, but I was convinced that in order to be impartial I had to take some time to verify those acts to which I was not an eyewitness and to obtain more accurate information about others, important objectives which I achieved by collecting the day-books from the various sections that constituted the army....

If in bringing forth my notes I accomplished the noble objectives I have pursued in vindicating the honor of this unfortunate nation and its army, which has recently been tarnished, believe me, I shall feel amply rewarded for the insignificant services that I have been able to render it during my career and for the painful missions of this unfortunate campaign. I am well aware how difficult it is to write for the public and to fulfill the mission of a historian, but I also know that in order to narrate facts it is necessary to have integrity and steadfastness, qualities which, though it may be immodest to say, I do not lack.

JOSÉ ENRIQUE DE LA PEÑA
Matamoros, Tam[auli]p[a]s, [Mexico].
15 September 1836

Chapter One

The political change which followed after eleven years of the [Mexican] nation's rule under a liberal system, and likewise the extension of its territory and the differences in climate and customs, were what provoked the Texas war or, better stated, were the pretexts of which the colonists [from the United States] took advantage. They would have legitimately presented to the nation a problem of justice in doing so under the banner of the 1824 Constitution, had it not been for the fact that their previous behavior had betrayed their distorted aims.

The federal system, destroyed no less by the errors and the evils of its own liberals than by the ignorance and bad faith of her antagonists, had established significant roots and created many interests, and there remained a strong and numerous party opposed to the new regime, which sooner or later would overcome its adversaries. It was this party which the revolutionaries in Texas attempted to flatter in order to encourage it to return anew to the cause in which it had just been overcome by perfidy after a long and bloody struggle in which it had always been victorious. Obviously they wished for us to destroy ourselves, the better to assure the success of their designs; but they were mistaken, because those same men to whom their cooperation was being offered rejected it, considering the offer ignominious since it came from "newcomers." And in effect, it was, because after the triumph they would have demanded indemnities that would have been opprobrious to grant and that it would have appeared ungrateful to deny, had enough strength remained to do so. Those who had given themselves a country needed no help from foreigners in order to gain their freedom.

Circumstances forced them to remove their masks when it was least convenient; on the 2nd of March 1836, when the army had already invaded the territory, they declared the independence of Texas, because without this declaration the land speculators in New York and New Orleans and other points in the United States would have blocked the subsidies offered for the pursuit of the war.

This declaration was also useful to the Mexicans, for, once they saw these incidents in proper perspective, they knew exactly where they stood. The cry of independence darkened the magic of liberty that had misled some of the less careful thinkers, and the few who had cast their lot with the colonists, believing them to be acting in good faith, disassociated themselves immediately, there remaining with the colonists only Don Lorenzo de Zavala and the [San Antonio de] Béjar natives, Don Antonio Navarro and Don Juan N. Seguín, the only intelligent men who incurred the name of traitor, a label both ugly and deserved. At least they are the only ones that we know about.

Public documents had analyzed the events in Texas during the last months in 1835 and the telling of them alone sufficed to prove the injustice of the colonists' aggression. The insults lavished upon the nation as represented by the customs officials and commanders of military detachments, the disregard for laws, and the attitudes with which the colonists looked upon those who had given them a country were more than sufficient cause to justify war on our part. They were the aggressors and we the attacked, they the ingrates, we the benefactors. When they were in want we had given them sustenance, yet as soon as they gained strength they used it to destroy us.

The neglect, the apathy, or, even more, the criminal indifference with which all governments without exception have watched over the national interests; the failure to enforce colonization laws; the lack of sympathy with which the colonists had been regarded and the loyalty that these still had for their native country [the United States]; these things led us into these circumstances. Because of all this, war was inevitable, for between war and dishonor there was no doubt as to the choice; however, it was necessary to prepare for it with mature judgment and to carry it out cautiously because the national honor was in the balance and it was less harmful to postpone the campaign than to expose the nation to ridicule by trying to carry it out contrary to the rules of the game.

It was necessary for all Mexicans of all classes and political parties to rally around the government in order to bring it forth successfully out of an undertaking that concerned everyone equally; but unfortunately this could not be.

The political scene had hardly changed when the cry of war was heard. The vanquished had been many; their wounds were still oozing blood. Directing affairs were the men least able to inspire confidence. The Ministries of the Treasury and of War were the most important posts at this time, but their duties were poorly discharged. The chief of the former [Rafael Mangino] was busy paying himself past-due debits which he maintained were long owed him; yet he claimed that there were no funds to cover the demands of the budget or to give the current pay to the corps and officers assigned to the campaign, when everyone knew that forced loans and taxes were being arrogantly demanded. There were several officers who, although designated to march with the army, did not do so, due to the lack of equipment. The latter ministry, it is true, was headed by a man of talent [José María Tornel], who is proficient in several subjects, who has lovely manners and a gift for captivating the good will of the people with whom he comes in contact, and who, in spite of his many inconsistencies and great defects, is gifted with other good qualities, such as that of expressing himself with ease, as well as his dramatic talent and oratory that have the appeal of a good actor on the stage. But he was not the ideal man to conduct the business of war. Having reached the rank of general without having gone through the lesser ranks, without having practiced his profession, without ever having seen the horrible scenes of the battlefield (except those depicted in paintings), he could hardly be aware of the needs of the soldier during campaigns, estimate their sacrifices, temper the resilience of punishments and rewards, or select leaders who might better lead them in the presence of danger.

With such elements, the government found it impossible to exercise the necessary moral influence; to this one must add the thoughtless violence with which forced recruiting was carried out and with which the other essentials needed by the army were taken. In spite of all this, it would have been more advantageous for the army had it first raised the curtain on the scene as represented on the 2nd of March. Nevertheless, enthusiasm was not lacking, and among the military classes it was great. As a whole, they were solidly behind the government because, united with the clergy and the friars, they had contributed the most toward the destruction of the old order.

War was the thing that could least frighten Mexicans, who seemed to have sworn not to live without it, but the distance of the country in which it would be waged, its climate, and the local conditions, not only in the general but in the particular topography as well, were factors of considerable weight in the eyes of the thinking person. It was the first time that our soldiers would be dealing with men of a different language and a different religion, men whose character and habits were likewise different from theirs. All was new in this war, and although it was happening on our own soil, it seemed as if it were being waged in a foreign land; but the government did not consider it so, for, as we shall see, it left everything to chance....

[R]esources were not lacking; what was lacking was prudence, planning, order, foresight, clear and precise judgment....[I]t is certain that no one utilized the wealth that the territory contained and that only an effort to destroy it was in evidence, as we shall see in time. The ministry and those in command deceived themselves and have endeavored to mislead the nation. Let us undeceive her!

The army had been infiltrated by a demoralizing force, which unfortunately was present in all classes. Although it absorbed all the taxes, leaving only meager crumbs for its employees, it was only a nominal army. It had been destroyed during the civil war, particularly during the years of 1832, 1833, and 1834. The flower of our veterans had perished without glory, killing each other, at times to uphold freedom, at others abuses, but most frequently tyranny; the errors and ambitions of the leaders of different parties have brought the country to ultimate ruin. Nonetheless, the same causes that had destroyed some soldiers had created others, perhaps less trained, less expert, less accustomed to withstanding dangers and labors. There were still experienced officers among the battalions and regiments, courageous and honorable and capable of leading their men to victory, but everything fell apart as one mistake led to another, and from error to error we went, giving new proof that as a thing is begun so will it end.

The organization of the army that was to have performed brilliantly and was to have given the whole world an idea of the nation's power was generally defective. Its losses were filled by recruits snatched away from the crafts and from agriculture, by heads of families, who usually do not make good soldiers, by men in cells awaiting punishment of their crimes, at times by men condemned by one [army] corps yet finding themselves as part of another. Since so many men had been taken by force, the order for the commander in chief to execute any deserters was considered barbarous. These objections also were due to the fact that the government needed strong garrisons; its power had been created by bayonets and now had to be upheld by them.

Among the many abuses found within the army was the anxious desire of the commanders to increase their number, regardless of how weak or how incapable of resisting the hardships of a campaign these men might be; this occasion gave definite proof that

numerical force did not correspond to individual force. There were many too young, some too old, some of these succumbing under the weight of their weapons and knapsacks, and although some have been transferred out and have returned again to their own ranks, this has become only a burden. How could these men withstand the long and tedious marches and rapid maneuvers they had to execute?...

Chapter Two

...The enemy did not expect our forces until the middle of March, and since our march had been accelerated by a month, the enemy was taken by surprise, an added reason why he could have been vanquished. He expected us to march on Goliad, the key position that would have opened the door to the principal theater of war. In fact, we should have attacked the enemy at the heart instead of weakening ourselves by going to Béjar, a garrison without any political or military importance. This was the unanimous opinion of all the military, and the commander in chief heard it from all those of any significance in the army; but he was not willing to gain the devotion of his subordinates by persuasion and by convincing them; he disdained their approval and contented himself with their obedience. General Santa Anna becomes irritable with discussions....

The armies of all nations, no matter how disciplined, always carry licentiousness with them wherever they march, and the greater their number, the greater the disorders committed and the greater the difficulties in preventing them.

General Ramírez y Sesma had preceded us in these things; permitting many violent acts [against the locals] and committing some himself, he had left behind him grim memories that were still fresh. As we went along, we heard only bitter complaints against this commander and were looked upon as enemies. At least three-fifths or one-half the number of our soldiers were squadrons composed of women, muledrivers, wagon-train drivers, boys, and sutlers [provisioners]; a family much like the locusts that destroy everything in their path, these people perpetrated excesses difficult to remedy, and naturally all hatred fell on the army and those who commanded it....

Chapter Four

...On the 23rd General Ramírez y Sesma advanced at dawn toward Béjar with one hundred horsemen; although he had approached them at three o'clock in the morning, the enemy was unaware of our arrival. The rest of the division came within sight between twelve and one, but by then the enemy had sounded the call to arms and had withdrawn to his fortification at the Alamo. There they had fifteen pieces of artillery, but not all were mounted and ready to use because of a shortage of cannon balls.... The president [Santa Anna], unaware upon entering Béjar that the church was abandoned, ordered Colonel Miñón to take it with half the chasseurs [elite troops]. As the column entered the plaza, from the Alamo came a cannon shot from the eighteen-pounder; immediately the artillery commander was ordered to set up two howitzers and to fire four grenades, which caused the enemy to raise a white flag. The firing ceased and [James] Bowie sent a written communication addressed to the commander of the invading troops of Texas, stating that he had wished to enter into agreements. The president ordered a verbal answer that he would not deal with bandits, leaving them no alternative but to surrender unconditionally. Then he ordered the placement of the troops....

On the 17th of February the commander in chief had proclaimed to the army: "Comrades in arms," he said, "our most sacred duties have brought us to these uninhabited lands and demanded our engaging in combat against a rabble of wretched adventurers to whom our authorities have unwisely given benefits that even Mexicans did not enjoy, and who have taken possession of this vast and fertile area, convinced that our own unfortunate internal divisions have rendered us incapable of defending our soil. Wretches! Soon will they become aware of their folly! Soldiers, our comrades have been shamefully sacrificed at Anáhuac, Goliad, and Béjar, and you are those destined to punish these murderers. My friends: we will march as long as the interests of the nation that we serve demand. The claimants to the acres of Texas land will soon know to their sorrow that their reinforcements from New Orleans, Mobile, Boston, New York, and other points north, whence they should never have come, are insignificant, and that Mexicans, generous by nature, will not leave unpunished affronts resulting in injury or discredit to their country, regardless of who the aggressors may be."

This address was received enthusiastically, but the army needed no incitement; knowing that it was about to engage in the defense of the country and to avenge less fortunate comrades was enough for its ardor to become as great as the noble and just cause it was about to defend. Several officers from the Aldama and Toluca sappers [troops who build forts or field-works] were filled with joy and congratulated each other when they were ordered to hasten

their march, for they knew that they were about to engage in combat. There is no doubt that some would have regretted not being among the first to meet the enemy, for it was considered an honor to be counted among the first. For their part, the enemy leaders had addressed their own men in terms not unlike those of our commander. They said that we were a bunch of mercenaries, blind instruments of tyranny; that without any right we were about to invade their territory; that we would bring desolation and death to their peaceful homes and would seize their possessions; that we were savage men who would rape their women, decapitate their children, destroy everything, and render into ashes the fruits of their industry and their efforts. Unfortunately they did partially foresee what would happen, but they also committed atrocities that we did not commit, and in this rivalry of evil and extermination, I do not dare to venture who had the ignominious advantage, they or we!

In spirited and vehement language, they called on their compatriots to defend the interests so dear to them and those they so tenderly cherished. They urged mothers to arm their sons, and wives not to admit their consorts in their nuptial beds until they had taken up arms and risked their lives in defense of their families. The word liberty was constantly repeated in every line of their writings; this magical word was necessary to inflame the hearts of the men, who rendered tribute to this goddess, although not to the degree they pretend.

When our commander in chief haughtily rejected the agreement that the enemy had proposed, [William] Travis became infuriated at the contemptible manner in which he had been treated, and expecting no honorable way of salvation, chose the path that strong souls choose in crisis, that of dying with honor, and selected the Alamo for his grave. It is possible that this might have been his first resolve, for although he was awaiting the reinforcements promised him, he must have reflected that he would be engaged in battle before these could join him, since it would be difficult for him to cover their entry into the fort with the small force at his disposal. However, this was not the case, for about sixty men did enter one night, the only help that came. They passed through our lines unnoticed until it was too late. My opinion is reinforced by the certainty that Travis could have managed to escape during the first nights, when vigilance was much less, but this he refused to do. It has been said that General Ramírez y Sesma's division was not sufficient to have formed a circumventing line on the first day, since the Alamo is a small place, one of its sides fronting the San Antonio River and clear and open fields. The heroic language in which Travis addressed his compatriots during the days of the conflict finally proved that he had resolved to die before abandoning the Alamo or surrendering unconditionally. He spoke to them thus: "Fellow citizens and compatriots, I am besieged by a thousand or more of the Mexicans under Santa Anna. I have sustained bombardment and cannonade for twenty-four hours and have not lost a man. The enemy has demanded a surrender at discretion, otherwise the garrison are to be put to the sword, if the fort is taken. I have answered the demand with a cannon shot, and our flag still waves proudly over the walls. *I shall never surrender or retreat*. Then, I call on you in the name of Liberty, of patriotism, and everything dear to the American character, to come to our aid. If this call is neglected, I am determined to sustain myself as long as possible and die as a soldier who never forgets what is due to his own honor and that of his country."

…Our commander became more furious when he saw that the enemy resisted the idea of surrender. He believed as others did that the fame and honor of the army were compromised the longer the enemy lived.…It was therefore necessary to attack him in order to make him feel the vigor of our souls and the strength of our arms. But prudent men, who know how to measure the worth of true honor, those whose tempered courage permits their venturing out only when they know beforehand that the destruction they are about to wreak will profit them and who understand that the soldier's glory is the greater, the less bloody the victory and the fewer the victims sacrificed; these men, though moved by the same sentiments as the army and its commander, were of the opinion that victory over a handful of men concentrated in the Alamo did not call for a great sacrifice. In fact, it was necessary only to await the artillery's arrival at Béjar for these to surrender; undoubtedly they could not have resisted for many hours the destruction and imposing fire from twenty cannon. The sums spent by the treasury on the artillery equipment brought to Texas are incalculable; the transportation alone amounts to thousands of pesos. Either they did not wish or did not know how to make use of such weaponry; had it been judiciously employed, it would have saved us many lives, and the success of the campaign would have been very different indeed.

There was no need to fear that the enemy would be reinforced, for even though reinforcements had entered because of our lack of vigilance, we were situated so as to do battle with any other possible arrivals one by one. We were in a position to advance, leaving a small force on watch at the Alamo, the holding of which was unimportant either politically or militarily, whereas its acquisition was both costly and very bitter in the end. If [Sam] Houston had not received news of the fall of the Alamo, it would have been very easy to surprise and defeat him.

During a council of war held on the 4th of March at the commander in chief's quarters, he expounded on the necessity of making the assault. Generals Sesma, Cos, and Castrillón, Colonels Almonte, Duque, Amat, Romero, and Salas, and the interim mayor of San Luis were present and gave their consent. The problem centered around the method of carrying it out. Castrillón, Almonte, and Romero were of the opinion that a breach should be made, and that eight or ten hours would suffice to accomplish this. Field pieces were coming up and Colonel Bringas, aide to the president-general, had left with the idea of activating them. It was agreed to call the artillery commandant and to alert him to this, and although the artillery would not arrive for a day or so, and that solution was still pending, on the 5th the order was given for the assault. Some, though approving this proposal in the presence of the commander in chief, disagreed in his absence, a contradiction that reveals their weakness; others chose silence, knowing that he would not tolerate opposition, his sole pleasure being in hearing what met with his wishes, while discarding all admonitions that deviated from those wishes. None of these commanders was aware that there were no field hospitals or surgeons to save the wounded, and that for some it would be easier to die than to be wounded, as we shall see after the assault.

When in this or some other discussion, the subject of what to do with prisoners was brought up, in case the enemy surrendered before the assault, the example of Arredondo was cited; during the Spanish rule he had hanged eight hundred or more colonists after having triumphed in a military action, and this conduct was taken as a model. General Castrillón and Colonel Almonte then voiced principles regarding the rights of men, philosophical and humane principles which did them honor; they reiterated these later when General [José] Urrea's prisoners were ordered executed, but their arguments were fruitless.…

[Intelligence] made clear to us the limited strength of the garrison at the Alamo and the shortage of supplies and munitions at their disposal. They had walled themselves in so quickly that they had not had time to supply themselves with very much.

Travis's resistance was on the verge of being overcome; for several days his followers had been urging him to surrender, giving the lack of food and the scarcity of munitions as reasons, but he had quieted their restlessness with the hope of quick relief, something not difficult for them to believe since they had seen some reinforcements arrive. Nevertheless, they had pressed him so hard that on the 5th he promised them that if no help arrived on that day they would surrender the next day or would try to escape under cover of darkness; these facts were given to us by a lady from Béjar, a Negro who was the only male who escaped, and several women who were found inside and were rescued by Colonels Morales and Miñón. The enemy was in communication with some of the Béjar townspeople who were their sympathizers, and it was said as a fact during those days that the president-general had known of Travis's decision, and that it was for this reason that he precipitated the assault, because he wanted to cause a sensation and would have regretted taking the Alamo without clamor and without bloodshed, for some believed that without these there is no glory.

Once the order was issued, even those opposing it were ready to carry it out; no one doubted that we would triumph, but it was anticipated that the struggle would be bloody, as indeed it was. All afternoon of the 5th was spent on preparations. Night came, and with it the most sober reflections. Our soldiers, it was said, lacked the cool courage that is demanded by an assault, but they were steadfast and the survivors will have nothing to be ashamed of. Each one individually confronted and prepared his soul for the terrible moment, expressed his last wishes, and silently and coolly took those steps which precede an encounter. It was a general duel from which it was important to us to emerge with honor. No harangue preceded this combat, but the example given was the most eloquent language and the most absolute order. Our brave officers left nothing to be desired in the hour of trial, and if anyone failed in his duty, if anyone tarnished his honor, it was so insignificant that his shortcomings remained in the confusion of obscurity and disdain. Numerous feats of valor were seen in which many fought hand to hand; there were also some cruelties observed.

The Alamo was an irregular fortification without flank fires which a wise general would have taken with insignificant losses, but we lost more than three hundred brave men....

Beginning at one o'clock in the morning of the 6th, the columns were set in motion, and at three they silently advanced toward the river, which they crossed marching two abreast over some narrow wooden bridges. A few minor obstacles were explored in order to reach the enemy without being noticed, to a point personally designated by the commander in chief, where they stationed themselves, resting with weapons in hand. Silence was again ordered and smoking was prohibited. The moon was up, but the density of the clouds that covered it allowed only an opaque light in our direction, seeming thus to contribute to our designs. This half-light, the silence we kept, hardly interrupted by soft murmurs, the coolness of the morning air, the great quietude that seemed to prolong the hours, and the dangers we would soon have to face, all of this rendered our situation grave; we were still breathing and able to communicate; within a few moments many of us would be unable to answer questions addressed to us, having already returned to the nothingness whence we had come; others, badly wounded, would remain stretched out for hours without anyone thinking of them, each still fearing perhaps one of the enemy cannonballs whistling overhead would drop at his feet and put an end to his sufferings. Nevertheless, hope stirred us and within a few moments this anxious uncertainty would disappear; an insult to our arms had to be avenged, as well as the blood of our friends spilled three months before within these same walls we were about to attack. Light began to appear on the horizon, the beautiful dawn would soon let herself be seen behind her golden curtain; a bugle call to attention was the agreed signal and we soon heard that terrible bugle call of death, which stirred our hearts, altered our expressions, and aroused us all suddenly from our painful meditations. Worn out by fatigue and lack of sleep, I had just closed my eyes to nap when my ears were pierced by this fatal note. A trumpeter of the sappers (José María González) was the one who inspired us to scorn life and to welcome death. Seconds later the horror of this sound fled from among us, honor and glory replacing it.

The columns advanced with as much speed as possible; shortly after beginning the march they were ordered to open fire while they were still out of range, but there were some officers who wisely disregarded the signal. Alerted to our attack by the given signal, which all columns answered, the enemy vigorously returned our fire, which had not even touched him but had retarded our advance. Travis, to compensate for the reduced number of the defenders, had placed three or four rifles by the side of each man, so that the initial fire was very rapid and deadly. Our columns left along their path a wide trail of blood, of wounded, and of dead. The bands from all the corps, gathered around our commander, sounded the charge; with a most vivid ardor and enthusiasm, we answered that call which electrifies the heart, elevates the soul, and makes others tremble. The second column, seized by this spirit, burst out in acclamations for the Republic and for the president-general. The officers were unable to repress this act of folly, which was paid for dearly. His attention drawn by this act, the enemy seized the opportunity, at the moment that light was beginning to make objects discernible around us, to redouble the fire on this column, making it suffer the greatest blows. It could be observed that a single cannon volley did away with half the company of chasseurs from Toluca, which was advancing a few paces from the column; Captain José María Herrera, who commanded it, died a few moments later and Vences, its lieutenant, was also wounded. Another volley left many gaps among the ranks at the head, one of them being Colonel Duque, who was wounded in the thigh; there remained standing, not without surprise, one of the two aides to this commander, who marched immediately to his side, but the other one now cannot testify to this. Fate was kind on this occasion to the writer, who survived, though Don José María Macotela, captain from Toluca, was seriously wounded and died shortly after.

It has been observed what the plan of attack was, but various arrangements made to carry it out were for the most part omitted; the columns had been ordered to provide themselves with crow-bars, hatchets, and ladders, but not until the last moment did it become obvious that all this was insufficient and that the ladders were poorly put together.

The columns, bravely storming the fort in the midst of a terrible shower of bullets and cannon-fire, had reached the base of the walls, with the exception of the third, which had been sorely punished on its left flank by a battery of three cannon on a barbette [a platform or mound] that cut a serious breach in its ranks; since it was being attacked frontally at the same time from the height of a position, it was forced to seek a less bloody entrance, and thus changed its course toward the right angle of the north front. The few poor ladders that we were bringing had not arrived, because their bearers had either perished on the way or had escaped. Only one was seen of all those that were planned. General Cos, looking for a starting point from which to climb, had advanced frontally with his column to where the second and third were. All united at one point, mixing and forming a confused mass. Fortunately the wall reinforcement on this front was of lumber, its excavation was hardly begun, and the height of the parapet was eight or nine feet; there was therefore a starting point, and it could be climbed, though with some difficulty. But disorder had already begun; officers of all ranks shouted but were hardly heard. The most daring of our veterans tried to be the first to climb, which they accomplished, yelling wildly so that room could be made for them, at times climbing over their own comrades. Others, jammed together, made useless efforts, obstructing one another, getting in the way of the more agile ones and pushing down those who were about to carry out their courageous effort. A lively rifle fire coming from the roof of the barracks and other points caused painful havoc, increasing the confusion of our disorderly mass. The first to climb were thrown down by bayonets already waiting for them behind the parapet, or by pistol fire, but the courage of our soldiers was not diminished as they saw their comrades falling dead or wounded, and they hurried to occupy their places and to avenge them, climbing over their bleeding bodies. The sharp reports of the rifles, the whistling of bullets, the groans of the wounded, the cursing of the men, the sighs and anguished cries of the dying, the arrogant harangues of the officers, the noise of the instruments of war, and the inordinate shouts of the attackers, who climbed vigorously, bewildered all and made of this moment a tremendous and critical one. The shouting of those being attacked was no less loud and from the beginning had pierced our ears with desperate, terrible cries of alarm in a language we did not understand.

From his point of observation, General Santa Anna viewed with concern this horrible scene and, misled by the difficulties encountered in the climbing of the walls and by the maneuver executed by the third column, believed we were being repulsed; he therefore ordered Colonel Amat to move in with the rest of the reserves; the Sapper Battalion, already ordered to move their column of attack, arrived and began to climb at the same time. He then also ordered into battle his general staff and everyone at his side. This gallant reserve merely added to the noise and the victims, the more regrettable since there was no necessity for them to engage in the combat. Before the Sapper Battalion, advancing through a shower of bullets and volley of shrapnel, had a chance to reach the foot of the walls, half their officers had been wounded. Another one of these officers, young Torres, died within the fort at the very moment of taking a flag. He died at one blow without uttering a word, covered in glory and lamented by his comrades....

A quarter of an hour had elapsed, during which our soldiers remained in a terrible situation, wearing themselves out as they climbed in quest of a less obscure death than that visited on them, crowded in a single mass; later and after much effort, they were able in sufficient numbers to reach the parapet, without distinction of ranks. The terrified defenders withdrew at once into quarters placed to the right and the left of the small area that constituted their second line of defense. They had bolted and reinforced their doors, but in order to form trenches they had excavated some places inside that were now a hindrance to them. Not all of them took refuge, for some remained in the open, looking at us before firing, as if dumbfounded at our daring. Travis was seen to hesitate, but not about the death that he would choose. He would take a few steps and stop, turning his proud face toward us to discharge his shots; he fought like a true soldier. Finally he died, but he died after having traded his life very dearly. None of his men died with greater heroism, and they all died. Travis behaved as a hero; one must do him justice, for with a handful of men without discipline, he resolved to face men used to war and much superior in numbers, without supplies, with scarce munitions, and against the will of his subordinates. He was a handsome blond, with a physique as robust as his spirit was strong.

In the meantime Colonel Morelos with his chasseurs, having carried out instructions received, was just in front of us at a distance of a few paces, and, rightly fearing that our fire would hurt him, he had taken refuge in the trenches he had overrun trying to inflict damage on the enemy without harming us. It was a good thing that other columns could come together in a single front, for because of the small area the destruction among ourselves could be partially avoided; nevertheless, some of our men suffered the pain of falling from shots fired by their comrades, a grievous wound indeed, and a death even more lamentable. The soldiers had been overloaded with munition, for the reserves and all the select companies carried seven rounds apiece. It seems that the purpose of this was to convey the message to the soldier not to rely on his bayonet, which is the weapon generally employed in assault while some of the chasseurs support the attackers with their fire; however, there are always errors committed on these occasions, impossible to remedy. There remains no consolation other than regret for those responsible on this occasion, and there were many.

Our soldiers, some stimulated by courage and others by fury, burst into the quarters where the enemy had entrenched themselves, from which issued an infernal fire. Behind these came others, who, nearing the doors and blind with fury and smoke, fired their shots against friends and enemies alike, and in this way our losses were most grievous. On the other hand, they turned the enemy's own cannon to bring down the doors to the rooms or the rooms themselves; a horrible carnage took place, and some were trampled to death. The tumult was great, the disorder frightful; it seemed as if the furies had descended upon us; different groups of soldiers were firing in all directions, on their comrades and on their officers, so that one was as likely to die by a friendly hand as by an enemy's. In the midst of this thundering din, there was such confusion that orders could not be understood, although those in command would raise their voices when the opportunity occurred. Some may believe that this narrative is exaggerated, but those who were witnesses will confess that this is exact....

It was thus time to end the confusion that was increasing the number of our victims, and on my advice and at my insistence General Cos ordered the fire silenced; but the bugler Tamayo of the sappers blew his instrument in vain, for the fire did not cease until there was no one left to kill and around fifty thousand cartridges had been used up. Whoever doubts this, let him estimate for himself, as I have done, with data that I have given.

Among the defenders there were thirty or more colonists; the rest were pirates, used to defying danger and to disdaining death, and who for that reason fought courageously; their courage, to my way of thinking, merited them the mercy for which, toward the last, some of them pleaded; others, not knowing the language, were unable to do so. In fact, when these men noted the loss of their leader and saw that they were being attacked by superior forces, they faltered. Some, with an accent hardly intelligible, desperately cried, *Mercy, valiant Mexicans*; others poked the points of their bayonets through a hole or a door with a white cloth, the symbol of cease-fire, and some even used their socks. Our trusting soldiers, seeing these demonstrations, would confidently enter their quarters, but those among the enemy who had not pleaded for mercy, who had no thought of surrendering, and who relied on no other recourse than selling their lives dearly, would meet them with pistol shots and bayonets. Thus betrayed, our men rekindled their anger and at every moment fresh skirmishes broke out with renewed fury. The order had been given to spare no one but the women and this was carried out, but such carnage was useless and had we prevented it, we would have saved much blood on our part. Those of the enemy who tried to escape fell victims to the sabers of the cavalry, which had been drawn up for this purpose, but even as they fled they defended themselves. An unfortunate father with a young son in his arms was seen to hurl himself from a considerable height, both perishing at the same blow.

This scene of extermination went on for an hour before the curtain of death covered and ended it: shortly after six in the morning it was all finished; the corps were beginning to reassemble and to identify themselves, their sorrowful countenances revealing the losses in the thinned ranks of their officers and comrades, when the commander in chief appeared. He could see for himself the desolation among his battalions and that devastated area littered with corpses, with scattered limbs and bullets, with weapons and torn uniforms. Some of these were burning together with the corpses, which produced an unbearable and nauseating odor. The bodies, with their blackened and bloody faces disfigured by a desperate death, their hair and uniforms burning at once, presented a dreadful and truly hellish sight. What trophies—those of the battlefield! Quite soon some of the bodies were left naked by fire, others by disgraceful rapacity [aggressive greed], especially among our men. The enemy could be identified by their whiteness, by their robust and bulky shapes. What a sad spectacle, that of the dead and dying! What a horror, to inspect the area and find the remains of friends—! With what anxiety did some seek others and with what ecstasy did they embrace each other! Questions followed one after the other, even while the bullets were still whistling around, in the midst of the groans of the wounded and the last breaths of the dying.

The general then addressed the crippled battalions, lauding their courage and thanking them in the name of their country. But one hardly noticed in his words the magic that Napoleon expresses in his, which, Count Ségur assures us, was impossible to resist. The *vivas* were seconded icily, and silence would hardly have been broken if I, seized by one of those impulses triggered by enthusiasm or one formed to avoid reflection, which conceals the feelings, had not addressed myself to the valiant chasseurs of Aldama, hailing the Republic and them, an act which, carried out in the presence of the commander on whom so much unmerited honor had been bestowed, proved that I never flatter those in power.

Shortly before Santa Anna's speech, an unpleasant episode had taken place, which, since it occurred after the end of the skirmish, was looked upon as base murder and which contributed greatly to the coolness that was noted. Some seven men had survived the general carnage and, under the protection of General Castrillón, they were brought before Santa Anna. Among them was one of great stature, well proportioned, with regular features, in whose face there was the imprint of adversity, but in whom one also noticed a degree of resignation and nobility that did him honor. He was the naturalist David Crockett, well known in North America for his unusual adventures, who had undertaken to explore the country and who, finding himself in Béjar at the very moment of surprise, had taken refuge in the Alamo, fearing that his status as a foreigner might not be respected. Santa Anna answered Castrillón's intervention in Crockett's behalf with a gesture of indignation and, addressing himself to the sappers, the troops closest to him, ordered his execution. The commanders and officers were outraged at this action and did not support the order, hoping that once the fury of the moment had blown over these men would be spared; but several officers who were around the president and who, perhaps, had not been present during the moment of danger, became noteworthy by an infamous deed, surpassing the soldiers in cruelty. They thrust themselves forward, in order to flatter their commander, and with swords in hand, fell upon these unfortunate, defenseless men just as a tiger leaps upon his prey. Though tortured before they were killed, these unfortunates died without complaining and without humiliating themselves before their torturers. It was rumored that General Sesma was one of them; I will not bear witness to this, for though present, I turned away horrified in order not to witness such a barbarous scene. Do you remember, comrades, that fierce moment which struck us all with dread, which made our souls tremble, thirsting for vengeance just a few moments before? Are your resolute hearts not stirred and still full of indignation against those who so ignobly dishonored their swords with blood? As for me, I confess that the very memory of it makes me tremble and that my ear can still hear the penetrating, doleful sound of the victims.

To whom was this sacrifice useful and what advantage was derived by increasing the number of victims? It was paid for dearly, though it could have been otherwise had these men been required to walk across the floor carpeted with the bodies over which we stepped, had they been rehabilitated generously and required to communicate to their comrades the fate that awaited them if they did not desist from their unjust cause. They could have informed their comrades of the force and resources that the enemy had. According to documents found among these men and to subsequent information, the force within the Alamo consisted of 182 men; but according to the number counted by us it was 253. Doubtless the total did not exceed either of these two, and in any case the number is less than that referred to by the commander in chief in his communiqué, which contends that in the excavations and the trenches alone more than 600 bodies had been buried. What was the object of this misrepresentation? Some believe that it was done to give greater importance to the episode, others, that it was done to excuse our losses and to make it less painful.

Death united in one place both friends and enemies; within a few hours a funeral pyre rendered into ashes those men who moments before had been so brave that in a blind fury they had unselfishly offered their lives and had met their ends in combat. The greater part of our dead were buried by their comrades, but the enemy, who seems to have some respect for the dead, attributed the great pyre of their dead to our hatred. I, for one, wishing to count the bodies for myself, arrived at the moment the flames were reddening, ready to consume them.

When calm opens the way for reflection, what sad and cruel thoughts rush to the sensitive soul contemplating the field of battle! Would anyone be the object of reproach, who, after having risked his life to comply with his duty and honor, for a brief period unburdens his feelings and devotes some time to charitable thoughts?

The reflections after the assault, even a few days after it had taken place, were generally well founded; for instance, it was questioned why a breach had not been opened? What had been the use of bringing up the artillery if it were not to be used when necessity required, and why should we have been forced to leap over a fortified place as if we were flying birds? Why, before agreeing on the sacrifice, which was great indeed, had no one borne in mind that we had no means at our disposal to save our wounded? Why were our lives uselessly sacrificed in a deserted and totally hostile country if our losses could not be replaced? These thoughts were followed by others more or less well based, for the taking of the Alamo was not considered a happy event, but rather a defeat that saddened us all. In Béjar one heard nothing but laments; each officer who died aroused compassion and renewed reproaches. Those who arrived later added their criticism to ours, and some of these, one

must say, regretted not having been present, because those who obeyed against their own judgment nonetheless attained eternal glory.

All military authors agree that battles should be undertaken only in extreme situations, and I will take full advantage of these opinions; they affirm that as a general rule, so long as there is a way to weaken and overcome the enemy without combat, it should be adopted and combat avoided. Civilization has humanized man and thanks to its good effects the more barbarous methods that were prevalent before, to kill the greatest number of men in the least possible time, have been abandoned; murderous maneuvers to destroy a whole army at a single blow have been discarded. It has been established as an axiom that a general entrusted with the command of an army should devote as much zeal to sparing the blood of his army as to the enemy. The opinion of the military sages, together with that of the moralists, states that the general who is frugal with the blood of his soldiers is the savior of his country, whereas he who squanders and sacrifices it foolishly is the murderer of his compatriots. One of these authors states that [the French King] Louis XIV, at the time of his death [in 1715], was inconsolable because of the blood spilled during his reign; that the memorable [Vicomte de] Turenne [a French military leader serving Louis XIV], in the last moments of his life, could not be quieted by the priests, in spite of all the consolation religion offers. As a matter of fact, false feelings of glory are not sufficient to suppress the remorse that the useless spilling of blood always brings about. If General Santa Anna were to see gathered together at one place the bodies of all the Mexicans he has sacrificed in all the revolutions he has promoted and in all the ill-directed battles over which he has presided, he would be horrified, no matter how insensitive he may be. The most renowned captains have always feared the day of battle, not so much because of danger to their lives as because of the interests and the soldiers entrusted to their care; but ignorance fears nothing because it foresees nothing. Some of our generals, particularly the conqueror of the Alamo, seemed not to have heeded these authors, for the latter, in his long career, has always separated himself from principles and has cast aside wise counsel. He has acted capriciously, uselessly sacrificing the life of the soldier, the honor and interests of the Republic, and the decorum of its arms, certain that no accounting will be required of him, or else that were this to be brought about, he would be acquitted, as experience has demonstrated. He would certainly act differently were he to be punished for his errors, but since he is lavished with honors even after his defeats, regardless of how shameful these may be, he could care less about losing or winning battles so long as they serve the interest of his party.

The responsibility for the victims sacrificed at the Alamo must rest on General Ramírez y Sesma rather than on the commander in chief. He knew that the enemy was at Béjar in small numbers and in the greatest destitution; he had scarcely had news of our march before our vanguard reached the gates of the city; he ordered the vanguard to surprise the enemy with a force of sixty horsemen, and to effect the march quickly and without the enemy's knowledge; he ordered the officers at the Medina River to yield their horses to the dragoons that lacked good mounts. When General Ramírez y Sesma sighted the town, the enemy was still engaged in the pleasures of a dance given the night before; he therefore could have and should have prevented their taking refuge in the Alamo. Several came to inform him, indicating to him the points through which he might enter and the orders he should give, and urging him earnestly, but he turned down these recommendations and the repeated requests, conducting himself with extraordinary uncertainty and weakness; we have seen how dearly his indecision was paid for. At the very moment that General Ramírez y Sesma was advised to enter Béjar, there were only ten men at the Alamo, and it would have required an equal number to take it. Had he just placed himself at the bridge over the San Antonio [River] that connects the fort to the city, as he was advised, he would have prevented the enemy from taking refuge there, thus avoiding the painful catastrophe that we witnessed....[T]he commander in chief noticed his lack of skill too late, although it was common knowledge among the expeditionary army, for he had certainly revealed his worthlessness through the censurable conduct we have just described....

Chapter Seven...

General Santa Anna...displayed the most unfortunate ideas regarding Texas, expressing in the strongest way his opinion that it should be razed to the ground, so that this immense desert, he said, might serve as a wall between Mexico and the United States....

[S]ome of us who witnessed this act [speech] could only be astonished and saddened to think that such a man was at the head of a great people. When he spoke thus, he was completely ignoring the importance of the country, its prodigious fertility, its geographic situation, and its channels of communication to the sea. When Texas is populated and governed by good laws, it will be one of the most enviable places in the world, in which it doubtless will play a brilliant role. Often, as I admired its beauty, I had the thought, perhaps not so preposterous, that military colonies should have been established, a distribution made among those members of the army who wished to participate in the plan of part of the land and equipment that had served only to encourage pillage and rapacity among certain commanders, some of the Béjar townspeople, and others of the sparsely inhabited places close to the colonies. Among the army there were many individuals who desired it, and they would have been satisfied, because the land was inviting.

Doubtless politics should have influenced the success of the campaign more than arms, but that pursued by the cabinet and the commander in chief was stupid, miserly, ill-conceived, and censurable from all angles. The war to the death that the latter undertook to follow left the enemy the harsh alternatives of vanquishing or perishing, and forced the colonists to unite with the enemy, though the majority were not for independence but rather for the re-establishment of the 1824 Constitution. These were in disagreement with the adventurers who had come from the north because they would attack the colonists' possessions, since, as they had nothing to lose, for them everything was a gain. If General Urrea's pattern of behavior had been followed, the colonists would have submitted without any difficulties, for by his policy he had gained their good will, and as a consequence they gave him important information that lead [*sic*] to the success of his campaign, and offered to contribute, by persuading and convincing those of their comrades who still remained in the ranks to leave the armed bands. How much more honorable and expedient would this have been for us than to kill, desolate, and destroy....

CHAPTER 16

Frederick Douglass Constructs a Life

"I felt a degree of freedom"

Ⅰn August 1841, a young man of twenty-three boarded a ship bound for the island of Nantucket, off the Massachusetts coast. He claimed that, like so many who have headed to Nantucket since, he was going on vacation. In fact, however, this was no mere holiday. The island was to host a convention of people opposed to slavery, a subject close to this man's heart, for by the law of the land he was a slave, a fugitive from justice. The man's name was Frederick Douglass (1818–1895); he was about to become famous, indeed the most famous African American of his century.

The Nantucket meeting of the Massachusetts Anti-Slavery Society followed the usual script for such gatherings: speeches to a mostly white crowd by abolitionist leaders (also white), resolutions condemning Southern slavery and Northern racism. Then, one evening, feeling "strongly moved to speak" and "much urged to do so" by a local abolitionist, the young fugitive approached the platform. Douglass felt much as William Apess and Angelina Grimké had when they first stood to speak their mind: "I trembled in every limb," he recalled, and could scarcely put "two words" together without "hesitation and stammering." Why? "The truth was, I felt myself a slave, and the idea of speaking to white people weighed me down." Anyone today who has given a speech before a crowd of strangers, especially powerful strangers (a student speaking to a roomful of teachers, say), can only begin to imagine what it was like for Douglass to step up to that podium.[1]

The hesitation was short-lived. Soon after he started to talk, Douglass "felt a degree of freedom," the very freedom he had so long sought, and electrified the crowd with his story. "Flinty hearts were pierced," observed one listener, "and cold ones melted by his eloquence." His "great power" gave the "multitude...mingled emotions of admiration, pity, and horror." In the Preface you will read below, the Grimké sisters' friend William Lloyd Garrison, perhaps America's foremost abolitionist, vividly remembered how the "crowded auditory," "completely taken by surprise," filled the hall with "applause...from the beginning to the end of his felicitous remarks." After that night, neither abolition nor Frederick Douglass would ever be the same.[2]

The campaign against slavery desperately needed a Frederick Douglass. More than a decade had passed since Garrison had helped raise the crusade to a higher pitch, yet for all the time, money, and energy that thousands had devoted to the cause, "[b]y 1840," historian James Brewer Stewart notes, "2.5 million black Southerners seemed no closer to freedom than they had been a decade earlier"; indeed, their numbers had increased 25% since Garrison first wrote. Moreover, some Americans feared (and others hoped) that abolitionist fervor was waning. Congress ignored antislavery petitions; mobs ransacked post offices to intercept antislavery tracts and threatened antislavery activists, calling them "scum," "lunatics," and "madmen." Abolitionists themselves squabbled over tactics: Should we include women in our ranks? Should we run for office? Should we condone violence? Should we ally with other reform movements?[3]

The cause was further weakened because, lacking firsthand knowledge of slavery, abolitionists had a harder time refuting Southern masters' claims that slaves were in fact perfectly content (Chapter 17). "[T]he north is so blinded," wailed one abolitionist, "it will not *believe* what we say about slavery"; only "facts and testimony as to the actual condition of the Slaves" would have an impact, would "thrill the land with Horror." The Grimkés (Chapter 14), Southerners from a slaveowning family, certainly helped, but only "narratives of slaves" themselves would "go right to the hearts of men." No wonder abolitionists hearing Douglass speak at Nantucket offered him a job on the spot.[4]

For this young man from the Slave South, it had been a long, hard road to that momentous summer day in 1841. Born on Maryland's Eastern Shore in 1818, named Frederick Augustus Washington Bailey, the child who became Frederick Douglass was the son of a slave named Harriet Bailey and an unknown white man. The Baileys (perhaps derived from a common African name, "Belali") had been living as slaves in that land for more than a century. But if his roots ran deep in Maryland soil (there probably was Native American ancestry, too), like William Apess (Chapter 13) Frederick Bailey grew up in a fractured kin network. Raised until the age of six in his maternal grandmother's cabin, he never learned who his father was and almost never laid eyes on his mother, who died when he was about seven. At almost the same time, his grandmother was compelled to deposit him at the Lloyd family's plantation, where his master, Aaron Anthony, was an overseer.[5]

Thus began a series of journeys and, with them, a series of awakenings to a wider world, a world of cruelty and kindness, despair and hope, villains and heroes. Various Eastern Shore farms were crucial classrooms, teaching young Frederick Bailey about hard labor and harder lashings, about the wisdom of lying to whites and the sorrows buried in slave songs. But no trips were more important than two sojourns in the thriving port city of Baltimore across the Chesapeake Bay. There, Frederick Bailey learned to read and write; there, he found Christ at a revival meeting and first heard the word *abolitionist*; there, he helped start "a secret debating club" called the East Baltimore Mental Improvement Society and held "secret classes" at night to teach others; there, he met Anna Murray, the free black woman who would become his wife; and there, in September 1838, he outfitted himself with money from Murray, forged papers saying he was a free man, and a sailor's outfit, then boarded the train that would carry him north toward freedom. Within a month, he had a new name, a new wife (Murray had followed him north), and a new home, New Bedford, where William Apess had preached, a prosperous Massachusetts coastal town of 12,000, including some Wampanoag Indians (descendants of King Philip's people; see Chapter 4) and about 1,000 African Americans. Nantucket was not far away.[6]

Douglass ended his autobiography with that speech in 1841, when he began a new chapter in his life. Between the day he agreed to become an antislavery speaker and the day in the spring of 1845 when he published his book, the fugitive slave traveled far and wide, from New England to Indiana, giving two and sometimes three speeches a day to crowds ranging from a handful to several thousand. "All the American people needed, I thought, was light," he wrote later; he intended to shed that light on the grim realities of American slavery and racism.[7]

Alas, it was not to be so easy. The August 1841 antislavery meeting itself hinted at the difficulties ahead. That ferryboat's captain refused to set out for Nantucket unless Douglass and the other African Americans stayed on the upper deck, segregated from white passengers. Once on the island, Douglass needed a bodyguard to protect him from hostile whites. Less than a month later, on a train to New Hampshire, an irate conductor and several more white men hauled Douglass out of his seat and roughly deposited him in the "negro car" when he declined to go there of his own accord. Hecklers and death threats, a mob in Indiana that hurled rocks and eggs before yelling "Kill the nigger, kill the damn nigger" and attacking with clubs—these were common fare for any abolitionist on the road, but none faced the dangers more often than Douglass, who "at every step" ran into what he called "illustrations of the dark spirit of slavery."[8]

Despite everything, Douglass went on lecturing. Nantucketers were only the first of many white audiences to be overwhelmed by his skill as a public speaker. Remember that this was an age when oratory was popular entertainment, something like rock concerts today (and orators something like rock stars). Like Angelina Grimké, Douglass had, as one who heard him that fall of 1841 reported, "few equals." "He seemed to move the audience at his will," wrote another listener a year later, "and they at times would hang upon his lips with staring eyes and open mouths,...eager to catch every word." "Go on! Go on," shouted a Philadelphia crowd when Douglass stopped—after only two hours![9]

Sheer physical presence was one secret of his success at the podium. More than six feet tall, with an imposing demeanor and bearing, before he even said a word Douglass struck people as "bold" and "massive," with "the bearing of a king." To that commanding first impression he added a voice "of unequaled depth and volume and power," along with techniques—gesture and cadence, sarcasm and mimicry, pathos and humor—picked up from many places: tales told, songs sung, and sermons preached in the slave quarters; diction picked up from elite Maryland whites and a how-to book, *The Columbian Orator*, which he read while still a slave; practice at his Sabbath school and the East Baltimore Mental Improvement Society in Maryland and, in New Bedford, at black antislavery meetings and the African Methodist Episcopal Church. Though he credited William Lloyd Garrison (compare Garrison's Preface and Douglass's *Narrative*), Douglass drew from many sources when he approached a stage and launched into another assault on slavery.[10]

His skill invited charges of fraud. Many whites doubted that any slave—indeed, any African American—could be so eloquent. "Douglass was unusual," historian John W. Blassingame remarks, "because he did not use the halting, stammering dialect...commonly associated with fugitives." Sympathetic whites recorded their "absolute astonishment," calling his ability "a matter of wonder"; unsympathetic ones thought him a fake. "[M]y manner was such," he later recalled, "as to create a suspicion that I was not a runaway slave, but some educated free negro, whom the abolitionists had sent forth to attract attention." He also reported that white friends, fretting about such claims, advised him that "'tis not best that you seem too learned" and suggested that he keep "a *little* of the plantation manner in your speech."[11]

To silence the skeptics, in the fall of 1844—a century after another Marylander, Dr. Alexander Hamilton, penned his account of a very different journey (Chapter 5)—Douglass sat down to write his life. Convinced that a man bent on changing things not only needed "a tongue that could 'sting like a thousand scorpions' " but also "a pen that could 'manufacture words of fire,' " he produced his own declaration of independence—from his master, from prejudiced, paternalistic Northern whites, from the chains of his past.[12]

The book, when it appeared that spring of 1845, was an immediate bestseller. Henry David Thoreau's *Walden*, Herman Melville's *Moby-Dick*, Walt Whitman's *Leaves of Grass*—none of these classics from that era had sales even approaching *Narrative of the Life of Frederick Douglass*. By summer's end, it had sold 4,500 copies; soon there were nine different U.S. editions, nine more in England, and translations into French, German, and Dutch. Of some one hundred slave narratives published in the nineteenth century, this one was by far the most widely read. Reviewers of the book echoed listeners to the speeches, calling it an "unspeakably affecting" tale written with "great eloquence and power." "It is," concluded one, "the most thrilling work which the American press has ever issued—and the most important." Even those who hated the book knew its power. A Virginia grand jury indicted a man for "feloniously and knowingly circulating" copies of the *Narrative*, which was "intended to cause slaves to rebel…and denying the right of property of masters in their slaves."[13]

Love it or hate it, the tale Douglass told did indeed "go right to the hearts of men." It also offers a window onto slavery. As you read, be alert to plantation power relations: Did whites enjoy total mastery, or did slaves have weapons they could deploy? What made slavery bearable to slaves, and what made it unbearable? One argument defenders of slavery trotted out was the lack of revolts by African Americans; if slavery is so inhumane, these defenders argued, why don't slaves rebel? How would Douglass have answered that question? More particularly, why were there so few Frederick Douglasses among the slave population?

The *Narrative* is useful not only for the light it sheds on slavery but for what it reveals about *anti*slavery. Why include a Preface by Garrison? Does Garrison's resemble the Preface to Mary Rowlandson's book? In the text itself, consider how Douglass went about appealing to, and affecting, his readers, most of whom were Northern whites who knew nothing about slavery and little about blacks. As with William Apess's autobiography, pay attention to what strategies the author used to reach his audience, *and* to what issues, people, or events he omitted.

As with other best-selling authors you have read in this volume—from Mary Rowlandson and Benjamin Franklin to Thomas Paine and Mason Locke Weems—the work's very popularity merits attention. Some scholars argue that one source of the *Narrative*'s appeal was its resemblance to books already familiar to Americans, including captivity narratives (Rowlandson), success stories (Franklin), sentimental tales about growing up (Weems), and spiritual autobiographies (William Apess). Other critics, however, believe that the differences are more pronounced, and more important, that equating Douglass with, say, Franklin, obscures as much as it reveals. What similarities do you see, and what differences? What are their sources? Their implications?

Another reason for the *Narrative*'s success is that its themes preoccupied Americans at the time. As biographer William S. McFeely observes, like Whitman's *Leaves of Grass* (1855), the *Narrative* "is a song of myself"; like Melville's *Moby-Dick* (1851), "it is a story…of survival in a world at sea with evil"; like Ralph Waldo Emerson's essays, the book trumpets a "message of growing self-confidence, of self-reliance." "But perhaps," McFeely continues, "Douglass's telling of his odyssey is closest cousin to [Henry David] Thoreau's account of his altogether safe escape to Walden Pond," an escape that took place the very spring Douglass's book appeared and might have been inspired, in part, by hearing the fugitive's story. Both men were concerned with "self-emancipation," both called for "radical repudiation of a corrupt society," yet both were, ultimately, hopeful about reforming America, of bringing it more in line with its highest ideals.[14]

Unlike Thoreau, Douglass risked everything by publishing his experience. Most slave narratives up to that time were anonymous tracts that remained studiously vague about where and when the author had been held in captivity so that masters could not identify the runaway, hunt him down, and drag him back south. Not Douglass: He proclaimed his authorship, named names, mentioned specific places and events, and broadcast where he lived in Massachusetts; he even sent his former master a copy of the book! So risky was this that when the fugitive read a draft to a white friend, he was advised to "throw the manuscript into the fire" because its publication might mean re-enslavement.[15]

Partly to avoid that fate, Garrison and others arranged for Douglass to go on a lecture tour of Britain in August 1845. The trip was a huge success: Thousands flocked to hear him and to buy his book. Shortly after British supporters purchased his freedom for £150 (about $1250) in December 1846, Douglass returned to America. In the decades to come, he would not only carry forward his war against slavery and racism but also join other reform movements, particularly the campaign for women's rights (he attended the famous convention at Seneca Falls, New York, in 1848).

Scholars studying Douglass's *Narrative* (and two more versions of his life's story that he wrote later) have noted biases and blind spots, what David W. Blight calls "avoidances and silences." Though Dickson J. Preston, after thorough study of the Maryland records, concludes that "in the main his story checked out," he also finds exaggerations and discrepancies. Some might have been due to faulty memory. Some can be explained by a certain reticence, as McFeely suggests, about including "private torments and horrors too deep in the well to be drawn up." And some were doubtless due to the book's purpose, which was to instill in readers a hatred of slavery and change their minds and hearts about the place of blacks in American life. Like any author, Douglass—aware of his agenda and his audience—carefully constructed a self and a story to further that agenda by moving that audience.[16]

The attention here to one person's story is a common theme in *American Conversations*, from Álvar Nuñez Cabeza de Vaca and Benjamin Franklin through George Washington and William Apess to Douglass. Do so many *individual*—indeed, idiosyncratic—accounts inhibit study of a *national* experience? On the contrary, they enhance, enrich, and enliven that study. As Blight has argued, there is an intimate, vital "relationship between autobiography and history. The *one* becomes the source of the individual narratives out of which we construct a sometimes coherent, sometimes conflicted, story about the *many*." "Slave narratives" in particular "are, of course, personal testimonies," Blight goes on; "but they are also the individual stories by which we begin to discern patterns of a collective experience that we can comprehend as *history*." Blight then quotes the novelist Ralph Ellison, who "argued that autobiographical works…both emerge from history and allow us access to it. 'One of the reasons we exchange experiences,' says Ellison, 'is in order to discover the repetitions and coincidences which amount to a common group experience. We tell ourselves our individual stories so as to become aware of our *general* story.' " Frederick Douglass, like Cabeza de Vaca and those who lived and died between these two famous captives, believed that his tale was intimately connected to the fate of his country. We should read all of these self-portraits with that larger American canvas in mind.[17]

Questions for Consideration and Conversation

1. Why, according to Frederick Douglass, was slavery wrong? What arguments did he deploy in his *Narrative* to make his case? What arguments might he have used, but did not?

2. Why does this work include a Preface by the white abolitionist William Lloyd Garrison? How does Garrison's Preface shape your reading of what is to follow? Compare the language of that Preface with the language of the *Narrative*. Is it fair to say, as some readers did at the time, that Douglass was imitating white abolitionist rhetoric (or even that a white abolitionist had actually written the *Narrative*)?

3. What does Douglass's *Narrative* reveal about the character of slave life and culture? About the nature of the slave–master relationship?

4. Some scholars have argued that slavery all but destroyed African American culture, that the masters' power was so great that slave families, slave customs, and slave resistance were seriously compromised. Others have found that, despite the power of the master class, that power was not total, that slaves were remarkably resilient and creative, that they were able to carve out space within the slave regime for a degree of autonomy and a vital cultural life largely hidden from the prying eyes of whites. Which view finds most support in these excerpts of Douglass's *Narrative*?

5. How does the attack on slavery here compare with critiques of the institution you have read elsewhere in this volume, such as Alexis de Tocqueville's and Angelina Grimké's?

6. The *Narrative* has been compared to other popular texts from that era, including Franklin's *Autobiography* and Weems's *Life of Washington*. Others have noted its resemblance to travel accounts and captivity narratives like Cabeza de Vaca's or Mary Rowlandson's. To what extent do such comparisons illuminate Douglass's work? To what extent do they do a disservice to understanding of that work?

7. If Alexis de Tocqueville had met Douglass in Baltimore during the Frenchman's tour of America, would that encounter have changed Tocqueville's views on slavery and race in America? If so, how? If not, why not?

Endnotes

1. Quoted in Waldo E. Martin, Jr., *The Mind of Frederick Douglass* (Chapel Hill, NC, 1984), 21.
2. Ibid., 21 ("hearts," "power"); John W. Blassingame, ed., *The Frederick Douglass Papers. Series One: Speeches, Debates, and Interviews. Volume I: 1841–1846* (New Haven, 1979), xlvi ("horror").
3. James Brewer Stewart, *Holy Warriors: The Abolitionists and American Slavery* (New York, 1976), 75; Blassingame, ed., *Douglass Papers*, ser. 1, vol. I, xxvii.
4. William L. Andrews, *To Tell a Free Story: The First Century of Afro-American Autobiography, 1760–1865* (Urbana, IL, 1986), 5 ("hearts"), 62 ("horror").
5. William S. McFeely, *Frederick Douglass* (New York, 1991), 5 ("Belali").
6. Dickson J. Preston, *Young Frederick Douglass: The Maryland Years* (Baltimore, 1980), 148–49.
7. Quoted in Martin, *Mind of Douglass*, 22.
8. McFeely, *Douglass*, 87 (bodyguard), 110 ("kill"); Blassingame, ed., *Douglass Papers*, ser. 1, vol. I, xxvi ("dark spirit").
9. Martin, *Mind of Douglass*, 24 ("few equals"); Gregory P. Lampe, *Frederick Douglass: Freedom's Voice, 1818–1845* (East Lansing, MI, 1998), viii ("eager"); Blassingame, ed., *Douglass Papers*, ser. 1, vol. I, xxviii (Philadelphia).
10. Blassingame, ed., *Douglass Papers*, ser. 1, vol. I, xxii–xxxiii, xxix–xxxiv; Lampe, *Douglass*.
11. Blassingame, ed., *Douglass Papers*, ser. 1, vol. I, xlvii ("limited contacts"), xlviii ("plantation manner"); John W. Blassingame *et al.*, eds., *The Frederick Douglass Papers. Series Two: Autobiographical Writings. Volume I: Narrative* (New Haven, 1999), xxx ("my manner").
12. Blassingame, ed., *Douglass Papers*, ser. 1, vol. I, xxv.
13. Martin, *Mind of Douglass*, 25 ("thrilling"); Blassingame, ed., *Douglass Papers*, ser. 2, vol. I, xxxix–xli (all other quotations).
14. McFeely, *Douglass*, 115.
15. Quoted in Peter Ripley, "The Autobiographical Writings of Frederick Douglass," in William L. Andrews and William S. McFeely, eds., *Narrative of the Life of Frederick Douglass, An American Slave, Written by Himself* (New York, 1997), 137.
16. David W. Blight, ed., *Narrative of the Life of Frederick Douglass, An American Slave, Written by Himself* (Boston, 1993), 19; Preston, *Young Douglass*, xiv; McFeely, *Douglass*, 116.
17. Blight, ed., *Narrative*, 15, 20.

FREDERICK DOUGLASS, *NARRATIVE OF THE LIFE OF FREDERICK DOUGLASS, AN AMERICAN SLAVE, WRITTEN BY HIMSELF* (1845)

Source: Frederick Douglass, *Narrative of the Life of Frederick Douglass, An American Slave, Written by Himself.* Excerpts downloaded from the University of Virginia Library Charlottesville, Va. Copyright 1999, by the Rector and Visitors of the University of Virginia—http://etext.lib.virginia.edu/

Preface

In the month of August, 1841, I attended an anti-slavery convention in Nantucket, at which it was my happiness to become acquainted with FREDERICK DOUGLASS, the writer of the following Narrative....

I shall never forget his first speech at the convention—the extraordinary emotion it excited in my own mind—the powerful impression it created upon a crowded auditory, completely taken by surprise—the applause which followed from the beginning to the end of his felicitous remarks. I think I never hated slavery so intensely as at that moment....

A beloved friend...prevailed on Mr. DOUGLASS to address the convention. He came forward to the platform with a hesitancy and embarrassment, necessarily the attendants of a sensitive mind in such a novel position. After apologizing for his ignorance, and reminding the audience that slavery was a poor school for the human intellect and heart, he proceeded to narrate some of the facts in his own history as a slave, and in the course of his speech gave utterance to many noble thoughts and thrilling reflections. As soon as he had taken his seat, filled with hope and admiration, I rose, and declared that PATRICK HENRY, of revolutionary fame, never made a speech more eloquent in the cause of liberty, than the one we had just listened to from the lips of that hunted fugitive.... I reminded the audience of the peril which surrounded this self-emancipated young man at the North,—even in Massachusetts, on the soil of the Pilgrim Fathers, among the descendants of revolutionary sires; and I appealed to them, whether they would ever allow him to be carried back into slavery.... The response was unanimous and in thunder-tones—"NO!"...

Mr. DOUGLASS has very properly chosen to write his own Narrative, in his own style, and according to the best of his ability, rather than to employ some one else. It is, therefore, entirely his own production; and, considering how long and dark was the career he had to run as a slave,—how few have been his opportunities to improve his mind since he broke his iron fetters,—it is, in my judgment, highly creditable to his head and heart. He who can peruse it without a tearful eye, a heaving breast, an afflicted spirit,—without being filled with an unutterable abhorrence of slavery and all its abettors, and animated with a determination to seek the immediate overthrow of that execrable system,—without trembling for the fate of this country in the hands of a righteous God, who is ever on the side of the oppressed...,—must have a flinty heart, and be qualified to act the part of a trafficker "in slaves and the souls of men." I am confident that it is essentially true in all its statements; that nothing has been...exaggerated, nothing drawn from the imagination.... The experience of FREDERICK DOUGLASS, as a slave, was not...especially a hard one;...slaves in Maryland...are better fed and less cruelly treated than in Georgia, Alabama, or Louisiana.... Yet how deplorable was his situation! what terrible chastisements were inflicted upon his person! what still more shocking outrages were perpetrated upon his mind! with all his noble powers and sublime aspirations, how like a brute was he treated, even by those professing to have the same mind in them that was in Christ Jesus!...how he thought, reasoned, felt, under the lash of the driver, with the chains upon his limbs! what perils he encountered in his endeavors to escape from his horrible doom! and

how signal have been his deliverance and preservation in the midst of a nation of pitiless enemies!...

Reader! are you with the man-stealers in sympathy and purpose, or on the side of their down-trodden victims? If with the former, then are you the foe of God and man. If with the latter, what are you prepared to do and dare in their behalf? Be faithful, be vigilant, be untiring in your efforts to break every yoke, and let the oppressed go free. Come what may—cost what it may—inscribe on the banner which you unfurl to the breeze, as your religious and political motto—"NO COMPROMISE WITH SLAVERY! NO UNION WITH SLAVEHOLDERS!"

WM. LLOYD GARRISON

BOSTON, *May* 1, 1845...

Chapter I

I was born in Tuckahoe, near Hillsborough, and about twelve miles from Easton, in Talbot county, Maryland. I have no accurate knowledge of my age.... By far the larger part of the slaves know as little of their ages as horses know of theirs.... I do not remember to have ever met a slave who could tell of his birthday.... A want of information concerning my own was a source of unhappiness to me even during childhood. The white children could tell their ages. I could not tell why I ought to be deprived of the same privilege. I was not allowed to make any inquiries of my master concerning it. He deemed all such inquiries on the part of a slave improper and impertinent, and evidence of a restless spirit. The nearest estimate I can give makes me now between twenty-seven and twenty-eight years of age. I come to this, from hearing my master say, some time during 1835, I was about seventeen years old.

My mother was named Harriet Bailey. She was the daughter of Isaac and Betsey Bailey, both colored, and quite dark. My mother was of a darker complexion than either my grandmother or grandfather.

My father was a white man. He was admitted to be such by all I ever heard speak of my parentage. The opinion was also whispered that my master was my father; but of the correctness of this opinion, I know nothing; the means of knowing was withheld from me. My mother and I were separated when I was but an infant—before I knew her as my mother. It is a common custom, in the part of Maryland from which I ran away, to part children from their mothers at a very early age. Frequently, before the child has reached its twelfth month, its mother is taken from it, and hired out on some farm a considerable distance off, and the child is placed under the care of an old woman, too old for field labor. For what this separation is done, I do not know, unless it be to hinder the development of the child's affection toward its mother, and to blunt and destroy the natural affection of the mother for the child. This is the inevitable result.

I never saw my mother, to know her as such, more than four or five times in my life; and each of these times was very short in duration, and at night. She was hired by a Mr. Stewart, who lived about twelve miles from my home. She made her journeys to see me in the night, travelling the whole distance on foot, after the performance of her day's work. She was a field hand, and a whipping is the penalty of not being in the field at sunrise....I do not recollect of ever seeing my mother by the light of day. She was with me in the night. She would lie down with me, and get me to sleep, but long before I waked she was gone. Very little communication ever took place between us....She died when I was about seven years old.... I was not allowed to be present during her illness, at her death, or burial. She was gone long before I knew any thing about it. Never having enjoyed, to any considerable extent, her soothing presence, her tender and watchful care, I received the tidings of her death with much the same emotions I should have probably felt at the death of a stranger....

I have had two masters. My first master's name was Anthony. I do not remember his first name....He was a cruel man, hardened by a long life of slave-holding. He would at times seem to take great pleasure in whipping a slave....I remember the first time I ever witnessed this horrible exhibition. I was quite a child, but I well remember it. I never shall forget it whilst I remember any thing. It was the first of a long series of such outrages, of which I was doomed to be a witness and a participant. It struck me with awful force. It was the blood-stained gate, the entrance to the hell of slavery, through which I was about to pass.... I wish I could commit to paper the feelings with which I beheld it.

This occurrence took place...under the following circumstances. Aunt Hester went out one night..., and happened to be absent when my master desired her presence. He had ordered her not to go out evenings, and warned her that she must never let him catch her in company with a young man, who was paying attention to her[,] belonging to Colonel Lloyd. The young man's name was Ned Roberts, generally called Lloyd's Ned. Why master was so careful of her, may be safely left to conjecture. She was a woman of noble form, and of graceful proportions, having very

few equals, and fewer superiors, in personal appearance, among the colored or white women of our neighborhood.

Aunt Hester had not only disobeyed his orders in going out, but had been found in company with Lloyd's Ned; which circumstance, I found, from what he said while whipping her, was the chief offence. Had he been a man of pure morals himself, he might have been thought interested in protecting the innocence of my aunt; but those who knew him will not suspect him of any such virtue. Before he commenced whipping Aunt Hester, he took her into the kitchen, and stripped her from neck to waist, leaving her neck, shoulders, and back, entirely naked. He then told her to cross her hands, calling her at the same time a d—d b—h. After crossing her hands, he tied them with a strong rope, and led her to a stool under a large hook in the joist, put in for the purpose. He made her get upon the stool, and tied her hands to the hook. She now stood fair for his infernal purpose. Her arms were stretched up at their full length, so that she stood upon the ends of her toes. He then said to her, "Now, you d—d b—h, I'll learn you how to disobey my orders!" and after rolling up his sleeves, he commenced to lay on the heavy cowskin, and soon the warm, red blood (amid heart-rending shrieks from her, and horrid oaths from him) came dripping to the floor. I was so terrified and horror-stricken at the sight, that I hid myself in a closet, and dared not venture out till long after the bloody transaction was over....I had never seen any thing like it before. I had always lived with my grandmother on the outskirts of the plantation, where she was put to raise the children of the younger women. I had therefore been, until now, out of the way of the bloody scenes that often occurred on the plantation.

Chapter II

My master's family consisted of two sons, Andrew and Richard; one daughter, Lucretia, and her husband, Captain Thomas Auld. They lived in one house, upon the home plantation of Colonel Edward Lloyd. My master was Colonel Lloyd's clerk and superintendent. He was what might be called the overseer of the overseers. I spent two years of childhood on this plantation....

Colonel Lloyd kept from three to four hundred slaves on his home plantation, and owned a large number more on the neighboring farms belonging to him....The overseers of...all the...farms, numbering over twenty, received advice and direction from the managers of the home plantation....

Here, too, the slaves of all the other farms received their monthly allowance of food, and their yearly clothing. The men and women slaves received…monthly…eight pounds of pork, or its equivalent in fish, and one bushel of corn meal. Their yearly clothing consisted of two coarse linen shirts, one pair of linen trousers, like the shirts, one jacket, one pair of trousers for winter, made of coarse negro cloth, one pair of stockings, and one pair of shoes…. The children unable to work in the field had neither shoes, stockings, jackets, nor trousers, given to them; their clothing consisted of two coarse linen shirts per year. When these failed them, they went naked until the next allowance-day. Children from seven to ten years old, of both sexes, almost naked, might be seen at all seasons of the year.

There were no beds given the slaves, unless one coarse blanket be considered such, and none but the men and women had these…. They find less difficulty from the want of beds, than from the want of time to sleep; for when their day's work in the field is done, the most of them having their washing, mending, and cooking to do…; and when this is done, old and young, male and female, married and single, drop down side by side, on one common bed,—the cold, damp floor,—each covering himself or herself with their miserable blankets; and here they sleep till they are summoned to the field by the driver's horn. At the sound of this, all must rise, and be off to the field…. [W]oe betides them who hear not this morning summons to the field….

The home plantation of Colonel Lloyd wore the appearance of a country village…. It was called by the slaves the *Great House Farm*. Few privileges were esteemed higher, by the slaves of the out-farms, than that of being selected to do errands at the Great House Farm…. A representative could not be prouder of his election to a seat in the American Congress, than a slave on one of the out-farms would be of his election to do errands at the Great House Farm. They regarded it as evidence of great confidence reposed in them by their overseers; and it was on this account, as well as a constant desire to be out of the field from under the driver's lash, that they esteemed it a high privilege, one worth careful living for. He was called the smartest and most trusty fellow, who had this honor conferred upon him the most frequently….

The slaves selected to go to the Great House Farm, for the monthly allowance for themselves and their fellow-slaves, were peculiarly enthusiastic. While on their way, they would make the dense old woods, for miles around, reverberate with their wild songs, revealing at once the highest joy and the deepest sadness. They would compose and sing as they went along, consulting neither time nor tune. The thought that came up, came out—if not in the word, in the sound.… They would sometimes sing the most pathetic sentiment in the most rapturous tone, and the most rapturous sentiment in the most pathetic tone….

I did not, when a slave, understand the deep meaning of those rude and apparently incoherent songs…. They told a tale of woe which was then altogether beyond my feeble comprehension; they were tones loud, long, and deep; they breathed the prayer and complaint of souls boiling over with the bitterest anguish. Every tone was a testimony against slavery, and a prayer to God for deliverance from chains. The hearing of those wild notes always depressed my spirit, and filled me with ineffable sadness. I have frequently found myself in tears while hearing them. The mere recurrence to those songs, even now, afflicts me; and while I am writing these lines, an expression of feeling has already found its way down my cheek…. Those songs still follow me, to deepen my hatred of slavery, and quicken my sympathies for my brethren in bonds. If any one wishes to be impressed with the soul-killing effects of slavery, let him go to Colonel Lloyd's plantation, and, on allowance-day, place himself in the deep pine woods, and there let him, in silence, analyze the sounds that shall pass through the chambers of his soul….

I have often been utterly astonished, since I came to the north, to find persons who could speak of the singing, among slaves, as evidence of their contentment and happiness. It is impossible to conceive of a greater mistake. Slaves sing most when they are most unhappy. The songs of the slave represent the sorrows of his heart; and he is relieved by them, only as an aching heart is relieved by its tears….

Chapter IV

Mr. Hopkins [an overseer at Great House Farm] was succeeded by Mr. Austin Gore, a man possessing, in an eminent degree, all those traits of character indispensable to what is called a first-rate overseer….

Mr. Gore was proud, ambitious, and persevering. He was artful, cruel, and obdurate. He was just the man for such a place, and it was just the place for such a man. It afforded scope for the full exercise of all his powers, and he seemed to be perfectly at home in it. He was one of those who could torture the slightest look, word, or gesture, on the part of the slave, into impudence, and would treat it accordingly. There must be no answering back to him; no explanation was allowed a slave, showing himself to have been wrongfully accused....To be accused was to be convicted, and to be convicted was to be punished; the one always following the other with immutable certainty....He was, of all the overseers, the most dreaded by the slaves. His presence was painful;...and seldom was his sharp, shrill voice heard, without producing horror and trembling in their ranks....

His savage barbarity was equalled only by the consummate coolness with which he committed the grossest and most savage deeds upon the slaves under his charge. Mr. Gore once undertook to whip one of Colonel Lloyd's slaves, by the name of Demby. He had given Demby but few stripes, when, to get rid of the scourging, he [Demby] ran and plunged himself into a creek, and stood there at the depth of his shoulders, refusing to come out. Mr. Gore told him that he would give him three calls, and that, if he did not come out at the third call, he would shoot him. The first call was given. Demby made no response, but stood his ground. The second and third calls were given with the same result. Mr. Gore then, without consultation or deliberation with any one, not even giving Demby an additional call, raised his musket to his face, taking deadly aim at his standing victim, and in an instant poor Demby was no more. His mangled body sank out of sight, and blood and brains marked the water where he had stood.

A thrill of horror flashed through every soul upon the plantation, excepting Mr. Gore. He alone seemed cool and collected. He was asked by Colonel Lloyd and my old master, why he resorted to this extraordinary expedient. His reply was, (as well as I can remember,) that Demby had become unmanageable. He was setting a dangerous example to the other slaves,—one which, if suffered to pass without some such demonstration on his part, would finally lead to the total subversion of all rule and order upon the plantation. He argued that if one slave refused to be corrected, and escaped with his life, the other slaves would soon copy the example; the result of which would be, the freedom of the slaves, and the enslavement of the whites. Mr. Gore's defence was satisfactory. He was continued in his station as overseer upon the home plantation. His fame as an overseer went abroad. His horrid crime was not even submitted to judicial investigation. It was committed in the presence of slaves, and they of course could neither institute a suit, nor testify against him; and thus the guilty perpetrator of one of the bloodiest and most foul murders goes unwhipped of justice, and uncensured by the community in which he lives. Mr. Gore lived in St. Michael's, Talbot county, Maryland, when I left there; and if he is still alive, he very probably lives there now; and if so, he is now, as he was then, as highly esteemed and as much respected as though his guilty soul had not been stained with his brother's blood.

I speak advisedly when I say this,—that killing a slave, or any colored person, in Talbot county, Maryland, is not treated as a crime, either by the courts or the community....

Chapter V

As to my own treatment while I lived on Colonel Lloyd's plantation, it was very similar to that of the other slave children. I was not old enough to work in the field....The most I had to do was to drive up the cows at evening, keep the fowls out of the garden, keep the front yard clean, and run of errands for my old master's daughter, Mrs. Lucretia Auld....

I was seldom whipped by my old master, and suffered little from any thing else than hunger and cold. I suffered much from hunger, but much more from cold. In hottest summer and coldest winter, I was kept almost naked....I must have perished with cold, but that, the coldest nights, I used to steal a bag which was used for carrying corn to the mill. I would crawl into this bag, and there sleep on the cold, damp, clay floor, with my head in and feet out. My feet have been so cracked with the frost, that the pen with which I am writing might be laid in the gashes.

...Our food was coarse corn meal boiled. This was called *mush*. It was put into a large wooden tray or trough, and set down upon the ground. The children were then called, like so many pigs, and like so many pigs they would come and devour the mush; some with oyster-shells, others with pieces of shingle, some with naked hands, and none with spoons.... [F]ew left the trough satisfied.

I was probably seven or eight years old when I left Colonel Lloyd's plantation....I shall never forget the ecstasy with which I received the intelligence that my old master (Anthony) had determined to let me go to Baltimore, to live with Mr. Hugh Auld, brother to my old master's son-in-law, Captain Thomas Auld. I received this information about three days before my departure. They were three of the happiest days I ever enjoyed. I spent the most part of all these three days in the creek, washing off the plantation scurf, and preparing myself for my departure....

The ties that ordinarily bind children to their homes were all suspended in my case....My home...

was not home to me....My mother was dead, my grandmother lived far off, so that I seldom saw her. I had two sisters and one brother, that lived in the same house with me; but the early separation of us from our mother had well nigh blotted the fact of our relationship from our memories....

We arrived at Baltimore early on Sunday morning....Mr. and Mrs. Auld were both at home, and met me at the door with their little son Thomas.... And here I saw what I had never seen before; it was a white face beaming with the most kindly emotions; it was the face of my new mistress, Sophia Auld. I wish I could describe the rapture that flashed through my soul as I beheld it. It was a new and strange sight to me, brightening up my pathway with the light of happiness. Little Thomas was told, there was his Freddy,—and I was told to take care of little Thomas; and thus I entered upon the duties of my new home with the most cheering prospect ahead.

...It is possible, and even quite probable, that but for the mere circumstance of being removed from that plantation to Baltimore, I should have to-day, instead of being here seated by my own table, in the enjoyment of freedom and the happiness of home, writing this Narrative, been confined in the galling chains of slavery. Going to live at Baltimore laid the foundation, and opened the gateway, to all my subsequent prosperity. I have ever regarded it as the first plain manifestation of that kind Providence which has ever since attended me, and marked my life with so many favors....There were a number of slave children that might have been sent from the plantation to Baltimore....I was chosen from among them all....

I may be deemed superstitious, and even egotistical, in regarding this event as a special interposition of divine Providence in my favor....

Chapter VI

My new mistress proved to be all she appeared when I first met her at the door,—a woman of the kindest heart and finest feelings. She had never had a slave under her control previously to myself, and prior to her marriage she had been dependent upon her own industry for a living. She was by trade a weaver; and by constant application to her business, she had been in a good degree preserved from the blighting and dehumanizing effects of slavery. I was utterly astonished at her goodness....She was entirely unlike any other white woman I had ever seen. I could not approach her as I was accustomed to approach other white ladies....The crouching servility, usually so acceptable a quality in a slave, did not answer when

manifested towards her. Her favor was not gained by it; she seemed to be disturbed by it. She did not deem it impudent or unmannerly for a slave to look her in the face....Her face was made of heavenly smiles, and her voice of tranquil music.

But, alas! this kind heart had but a short time to remain such. The fatal poison of irresponsible power was already in her hands, and soon commenced its infernal work. That cheerful eye, under the influence of slavery, soon became red with rage; that voice, made all of sweet accord, changed to one of harsh and horrid discord; and that angelic face gave place to that of a demon. Thus is slavery the enemy of both the slave and the slaveholder.

Very soon after I went to live with Mr. and Mrs. Auld, she very kindly commenced to teach me the A, B, C. After I had learned this, she assisted me in learning to spell words of three or four letters.... Mr. Auld found out what was going on, and at once forbade Mrs. Auld to instruct me further, telling her, among other things, that it was unlawful, as well as unsafe, to teach a slave to read. To use his own words, further, he said, "...A nigger should know nothing but to obey his master—to do as he is told to do. Learning would *spoil* the best nigger in the world. Now," said he, "if you teach that nigger (speaking of myself) how to read, there would be no keeping him. It would forever unfit him to be a slave. He would at once become unmanageable, and of no value to his master. As to himself, it...would make him discontented and unhappy." These words sank deep into my heart, stirred up sentiments within that lay slumbering, and called into existence an entirely new train of thought....From that moment, I understood the pathway from slavery to freedom....What he most dreaded, that I most desired. What he most loved, that I most hated. That which to him was a great evil, to be carefully shunned, was to me a great good, to be diligently sought; and the argument which he so warmly urged, against my learning to read, only served to inspire me with a desire and determination to learn. In learning to read, I owe almost as much to the bitter opposition of my master, as to the kindly aid of my mistress....

Chapter VII

I lived in Master Hugh's family about seven years. During this time, I succeeded in learning to read and write. In accomplishing this, I was compelled to resort to various stratagems....

The plan which I adopted...was that of making friends of all the little white boys whom I met in the street. As many of these as I could, I converted into teachers. With their kindly aid, obtained at different times and in different places, I finally succeeded in learning to read. When I was sent of errands, I always took my book with me, and…found time to get a lesson before my return.…

I was now about twelve years old, and the thought of being *a slave for life* began to bear heavily upon my heart. Just about this time, I got hold of a book entitled "The Columbian Orator." Every opportunity I got, I used to read this book.…

The more I read, the more I was led to abhor and detest my enslavers. I could regard them in no other light than a band of successful robbers, who had left their homes, and gone to Africa, and stolen us from our homes, and in a strange land reduced us to slavery.…As I read and contemplated the subject, behold! that very discontentment which Master Hugh had predicted would follow my learning to read had already come, to torment and sting my soul to unutterable anguish. As I writhed under it, I would at times feel that learning to read had been a curse rather than a blessing. It had given me a view of my wretched condition, without the remedy. It opened my eyes to the horrible pit, but to no ladder upon which to get out. In moments of agony, I envied my fellow-slaves for their stupidity. I have often wished myself a beast.…Any thing, no matter what, to get rid of thinking!…

[Having learned to read, Douglass sets about learning to write.] [W]hen I met with any boy who I knew could write, I would tell him I could write as well as he. The next word would be, "I don't believe you. Let me see you try it." I would then make the letters which I had been so fortunate as to learn, and ask him to beat that. In this way I got a good many lessons in writing, which it is quite possible I should never have gotten in any other way. During this time, my copy-book was the board fence, brick wall, and pavement; my pen and ink was a lump of chalk.… [M]y little Master Thomas had gone to school, and learned how to write, and had written over a number of copy-books. These had been brought home, and shown to some of our near neighbors, and then laid aside.…When left thus [alone], I used to spend the time in writing in the spaces left in Master Thomas's copy-book, copying what he had written.…

Chapter IX

I have now reached a period of my life when I can give dates. I left Baltimore, and went to live with Master Thomas Auld, at St. Michael's [on the Eastern Shore], in March, 1832. It was now more than seven years since I lived with him in the family of my old master, on Colonel Lloyd's plantation. We of course were now almost entire strangers to each other.…

My master and myself had quite a number of differences. He found me unsuitable to his purpose. My city life, he said, had had a very pernicious effect upon me.…[After nine months and many whippings, Auld] resolved to put me out, as he said, to be broken; and, for this purpose, he let [rented] me for one year to a man named Edward Covey. Mr. Covey was a poor man, a farm-renter. He…had acquired a very high reputation for breaking young slaves, and this reputation was of immense value to him. It enabled him to get his farm tilled with much less expense to himself than he could have had it done without such a reputation. Some slaveholders thought it not much loss to allow Mr. Covey to have their slaves one year, for the sake of the training to which they were subjected, without any other compensation.…Added to the natural good qualities of Mr. Covey, he was a professor of religion—a pious soul—a member and a class-leader in the Methodist church. All of this added weight to his reputation as a "nigger-breaker."…

Chapter X

…I was now, for the first time in my life, a field hand.…I had been at my new home but one week before Mr. Covey gave me a very severe whipping, cutting my back, causing the blood to run, and raising ridges on my flesh as large as my little finger. The details of this affair are as follows: Mr. Covey sent me, very early in the morning of one of our coldest days in the month of January, to the woods, to get a load of wood. He gave me a team of unbroken oxen.…I had never driven oxen before, and of course I was very awkward. I, however, succeeded in getting to the edge of the woods with little difficulty; but I had got a very few rods [one rod is 16.5 feet] into the woods, when the oxen took fright, and started full tilt, carrying the cart against trees, and over stumps, in the most frightful manner.…After running thus for a considerable distance, they finally upset the cart, dashing it with great force against a tree, and threw themselves into a dense thicket.…After a long spell of effort, I succeeded in getting my cart righted, my oxen disentangled, and again yoked to the cart. I now proceeded with my team to the place where I had, the day before, been chopping wood, and loaded my cart pretty heavily, thinking in this way to tame my oxen. I then proceeded on my way home.…I stopped my oxen to open the gate; and just as I did so,…the oxen again started, rushed through the gate, catching it between the wheel and the body of the cart, tearing it to pieces, and coming within a few inches of crushing me against the gate-post. Thus twice, in one short day, I escaped death by the merest chance. On my return, I told Mr. Covey what had happened, and how it happened. He ordered me to return to the woods again immediately. I did so, and he followed on after me. Just as I got into the woods, he came up and told me to stop my cart, and that he would teach me how to trifle away my time, and break gates. He then went to a large gum-tree, and with his axe cut three large switches, and, after trimming them up neatly with his pocket-knife, he ordered me to take off my clothes. I made him no answer, but stood with my clothes on. He repeated his order. I still made him no answer, nor did I move to strip myself. Upon this he rushed at me with the fierceness of a tiger, tore off my clothes, and lashed me till he had worn out his switches, cutting me so savagely as to leave the marks visible for a long time after. This whipping was the first of a number just like it, and for similar offences.

I lived with Mr. Covey one year. During the first six months, of that year, scarce a week passed without his whipping me....

There was no deceiving him....Such was his cunning, that we used to call him, among ourselves, "the snake." When we were at work in the cornfield, he would sometimes crawl on his hands and knees to avoid detection, and all at once he would rise nearly in our midst, and scream out, "Ha, ha! Come, come! Dash on, dash on!" This being his mode of attack, it was never safe to stop a single minute....He was under every tree, behind every stump, in every bush, and at every window....

If at any one time of my life more than another, I was made to drink the bitterest dregs of slavery, that time was during the first six months of my stay with Mr. Covey. We were worked in all weathers. It was never too hot or too cold; it could never rain, blow, hail, or snow, too hard for us to work in the field. Work, work, work, was scarcely more the order of the day than of the night. The longest days were too short for him, and the shortest nights too long for him. I was somewhat unmanageable when I first went there, but a few months of this discipline tamed me. Mr. Covey succeeded in breaking me. I was broken in body, soul, and spirit. My natural elasticity was crushed, my intellect languished, the disposition to read departed, the cheerful spark that lingered about my eye died; the dark night of slavery closed in upon me; and behold a man transformed into a brute!

Sunday was my only leisure time. I spent this in a sort of beast-like stupor, between sleep and wake, under some large tree. At times I would rise up, a flash of energetic freedom would dart through my soul, accompanied with a faint beam of hope, that flickered for a moment, and then vanished. I sank down again, mourning over my wretched condition. I was sometimes prompted to take my life, and that of Covey, but was prevented by a combination of hope and fear. My sufferings on this plantation seem now like a dream rather than a stern reality....

The circumstances leading to the change in Mr. Covey's course toward me form an epoch in my humble history. You have seen how a man was made a slave; you shall see how a slave was made a man. On one of the hottest days of the month of August, 1833, Bill Smith, William Hughes, a slave named Eli, and myself, were engaged in fanning [winnowing] wheat....The work was simple, requiring strength rather than intellect; yet, to one entirely unused to such work, it came very hard. About three o'clock of that day, I broke down; my strength failed me; I was seized with a violent aching of the head, attended with extreme dizziness; I trembled in every limb. Finding what was coming, I nerved myself up, feeling it would never do to stop work. I stood as long as I could stagger....When I could stand no longer, I fell, and felt as if held down by some immense weight....

Mr. Covey...came to the spot where we were. He hastily inquired what the matter was. Bill answered that I was sick....I had by this time crawled away under the side of the post and rail-fence by which the yard was enclosed, hoping to find relief by getting out of the sun. He then asked where I was. He was told by one of the hands. He came to the spot, and, after looking at me awhile, asked me what was the matter. I told him as well as I could, for I scarce had strength to speak. He then gave me a savage kick in the side, and told me to get up. I tried to do so, but fell back in the attempt. He gave me another kick, and again told me to rise. I again tried, and succeeded in gaining my feet; but...I again staggered and fell. While down in this situation, Mr. Covey took up [a] hickory slat..., and with it gave me a heavy blow upon the head, making a large wound, and the blood ran freely; and with this again told me to get up. I made no effort to comply, having now made up my mind to let him do his worst. In a short time after receiving this blow, my head grew better. Mr. Covey had now left me to my fate....

[Douglass seeks protection from his master, Thomas Auld, but Auld ordered him to return.] All went well till Monday morning....Long before daylight, I was called to go and rub, curry, and feed, the horses. I obeyed, and was glad to obey. But whilst thus engaged, whilst in the act of throwing down some blades [leaves] from the loft, Mr. Covey entered the stable with a long rope; and just as I was half out of the loft, he caught hold of my legs, and was about tying me. As soon as I found what he was up to, I gave a sudden spring, and as I did so, he holding to my legs, I was brought sprawling on the stable floor. Mr. Covey seemed now to think he had me, and could do what he pleased; but at this moment—from whence came the spirit I don't know—I resolved to fight;...I seized Covey hard by the throat; and as I did so, I rose. He held on to me, and I to him. My resistance was so entirely unexpected, that Covey seemed taken all aback. He trembled like a leaf. This gave me assurance, and I held him uneasy, causing the blood to run where I touched him with the ends of my fingers....He asked me if I meant to persist in my resistance. I told him I did, come what might; that he had used me like a brute for six months, and that I was determined to be used so no longer. With that, he strove to drag me to a stick that was lying just out of the stable door. He meant to knock me down. But just as he was leaning over to get the stick, I seized him with both hands by his collar, and brought him by a sudden snatch to the ground....We were at it for nearly two hours. Covey at length let me go, puffing and blowing at a great rate, saying that if I had not resisted, he would not have whipped me half so much. The truth was, that he had not whipped me at all....The whole six months afterwards, that I spent with Mr. Covey, he never laid the weight of his finger upon me in anger....

This battle with Mr. Covey was the turning-point in my career as a slave. It rekindled the few expiring embers of freedom, and revived within me a sense of my own manhood. It recalled the departed self-confidence, and inspired me again with a determination to be free. The gratification afforded by the triumph was a full compensation for whatever else might follow, even death itself....I felt as I never felt before. It was a glorious resurrection, from the tomb of slavery, to the heaven of freedom. My long-crushed spirit rose, cowardice departed, bold defiance took its place; and I now resolved that, however long I might remain a slave in form, the day had passed forever when I could be a slave in fact. I did not hesitate to let it be known of me, that the white man who expected to succeed in whipping, must also succeed in killing me....

It was for a long time a matter of surprise to me why Mr. Covey did not immediately have me taken by the constable to the whipping-post, and there regularly whipped for the crime of raising my hand against a white man in defence of myself. And the only explanation I can now think of does not entirely satisfy me; but such as it is, I will give it. Mr. Covey enjoyed the most unbounded reputation for being a first-rate overseer and negro-breaker. It was of considerable importance to him. That reputation was at stake; and had he sent me—a boy about sixteen years old—to the public whipping-post, his reputation would have been lost; so, to save his reputation, he suffered me to go unpunished....

On the first of January, 1834, I left Mr. Covey, and went to live with Mr. William Freeland, who lived about three miles from St. Michael's....

Mr. Freeland was himself the owner of but two slaves. Their names were Henry Harris and John Harris. The rest of his hands he hired. These consisted of myself, Sandy Jenkins, and Handy Caldwell. Henry and John were quite intelligent, and in a very little while after I went there, I succeeded in creating in them a strong desire to learn how to read. This desire soon sprang up in the others also. They very soon mustered up some old spelling-books, and nothing would do but that I must keep a Sabbath school....

I had at one time over forty scholars,...ardently desiring to learn. They were of all ages, though mostly men and women. I look back to those Sundays with an amount of pleasure not to be expressed. They were great days to my soul. The work of instructing my dear fellow-slaves was the sweetest engagement with which I was ever blessed. We loved each other, and to leave them at the close of the Sabbath was a severe cross indeed....I kept up my school nearly the whole year I lived with Mr. Freeland....

It is sometimes said that we slaves do not love and confide in each other. In answer to this assertion, I can say, I never loved any or confided in any people more than my fellow-slaves, and especially those with whom I lived at Mr. Freeland's. I believe we would have died for each other....

At the close of the year 1834, Mr. Freeland again hired me of my master, for the year 1835. But, by this time, I began to want to live *upon free land* as well as *with Freeland*....I therefore resolved that 1835 should not pass without witnessing an attempt, on my part, to secure my liberty. But I was not willing to cherish this determination alone. My fellow-slaves were dear to me. I was anxious to have them participate with me in this....I therefore, though with great prudence, commenced early to ascertain their views and feelings in regard to their condition, and to imbue their minds with thoughts of freedom....I talked to them of our want of manhood, if we submitted to our enslavement without at least one noble effort to be free. We met often, and consulted frequently, and told our hopes and fears, recounted the difficulties, real and imagined, which we should be called on to meet....

In coming to a fixed determination to run away, we did more than Patrick Henry, when he resolved upon liberty or death. With us it was a doubtful liberty at most, and almost certain death if we failed....

[His plan betrayed, Douglass is captured and jailed. After a week,] my master, to my surprise and utter astonishment, came up, and took me out, with the intention of sending me, with a gentleman of his acquaintance, into Alabama. But, from some cause or other, he...concluded to send me back to Baltimore, to live again with his brother Hugh, and to learn a trade....

[Once Douglass reaches Baltimore,] Master Hugh...took me into the ship-yard of which he was foreman....There I was immediately set to calking, and very soon learned the art of using my mallet and irons....In the course of one year...I was able to command the highest wages given to the most experienced calkers....After learning how to calk, I sought my own employment, made my own contracts, and collected the money which I earned. My...condition was now much more comfortable....

I was now getting...one dollar and fifty cents per day. I contracted for it; I earned it; it was paid to me; it was rightfully my own; yet, upon each returning Saturday night, I was compelled to deliver every cent of that money to Master Hugh. And why? Not because he earned it...,—not because I owed it to him,—nor because he possessed the slightest shadow of a right to it; but solely because he had the power to compel me to give it up. The right of the grim-visaged pirate upon the high seas is exactly the same.

Chapter XI

I now come to that part of my life during which I planned, and finally succeeded in making, my escape from slavery....

In the early part of the year 1838, I became quite restless. I could see no reason why I should, at the end of each week, pour the reward of my toil into the purse of my master. When I carried to him my weekly wages, he would, after counting the money, look me in the face with a robber-like fierceness, and ask, "Is this all?" He was satisfied with nothing less

than the last cent. He would, however, when I made him six dollars, sometimes give me six cents, to encourage me. It had the opposite effect. I regarded it as a sort of admission of my right to the whole.... My discontent grew upon me. I was ever on the lookout for means of escape; and, finding no direct means, I determined to try to hire my time, with a view of getting money with which to make my escape....

I applied to Master Hugh for the privilege of hiring my time....He...proposed the following terms: I was to be allowed all my time, make all contracts with those for whom I worked, and find my own employment; and, in return for this liberty, I was to pay him three dollars at the end of each week; find myself in calking tools, and in board and clothing. My board was two dollars and a half per week. This, with the wear and tear of clothing and calking tools, made my regular expenses about six dollars per week. This amount I was compelled to make up, or relinquish the privilege of hiring my time. Rain or shine, work or no work, at the end of each week the money must be forthcoming, or I must give up my privilege. This arrangement, it will be perceived, was decidedly in my master's favor. It relieved him of all need of looking after me. His money was sure. He received all the benefits of slaveholding without its evils; while I endured all the evils of a slave, and suffered all the care and anxiety of a freeman. I found it a hard bargain. But, hard as it was, I thought it better than the old mode of getting along. It was a step towards freedom to be allowed to bear the responsibilities of a freeman, and I was determined to hold on upon it. I bent myself to the work of making money. I was ready to work at night as well as day, and by the most untiring perseverance and industry, I made enough to meet my expenses, and lay up a little money every week. I went on thus from May till August. Master Hugh then refused to allow me to hire my time longer. The ground for his refusal was a failure on my part, one Saturday night, to pay him for my week's time. This failure was occasioned by my attending a camp meeting [a religious gathering] about ten miles from Baltimore. During the week, I had entered into an engagement with a number of young friends to start from Baltimore to the camp ground early Saturday evening; and being detained by my employer, I was unable to get down to Master Hugh's without disappointing the company. I knew that Master Hugh was in no special need of the money that night. I therefore decided to go to camp meeting, and upon my return to pay him the three dollars. I staid at the camp meeting one day longer than I intended when I left.

But as soon as I returned, I called upon him to pay him what he considered his due. I found him very angry; he could scarce restrain his wrath. He said he had a great mind to give me a severe whipping. He wished to know how I dared go out of the city without asking his permission. I told him I hired my time and while I paid him the price which he asked for it, I did not know that I was bound to ask him when and where I should go. This reply troubled him; and, after reflecting a few moments, he turned to me, and said I should hire my time no longer; the next thing he should know of, I would be running away. Upon the same plea, he told me to bring my tools and clothing home forthwith. I did so; but instead of seeking work, as I had been accustomed to do previously to hiring my time, I spent the whole week without the performance of a single stroke of work. I did this in retaliation. Saturday night, he called upon me as usual for my week's wages. I told him I had no wages; I had done no work that week. Here we were upon the point of coming to blows. He raved, and swore his determination to get hold of me. I did not allow myself a single word; but was resolved, if he laid the weight of his hand upon me, it should be blow for blow. He did not strike me, but told me that he would find me in constant employment in future. I thought the matter over during the next day, Sunday, and finally resolved upon the third day of September, as the day upon which I would make a second attempt to secure my freedom. I now had three weeks during which to prepare for my journey. Early on Monday morning, before Master Hugh had time to make any engagement for me, I went out and got employment....At the end of the week, I brought him between eight and nine dollars. He seemed very well pleased....My object in working steadily was to remove any suspicion he might entertain of my intent to run away; and in this I succeeded admirably. I suppose he thought I was never better satisfied with my condition than at the very time during which I was planning my escape. The second week passed, and again I carried him my full wages; and so well pleased was he, that he gave me twenty-five cents, (quite a large sum for a slaveholder to give a slave,) and bade me to make good use of it. I told him I would.

Things went on without very smoothly indeed, but within there was trouble. It is impossible for me to describe my feelings as the time of my contemplated start drew near. I had a number of warm-hearted friends in Baltimore,—friends that I loved almost as I did my life,—and the thought of being separated from them forever was painful beyond expression. It is my opinion that thousands would escape from slavery, who now remain, but for the strong cords of affection that bind them to their friends....Besides the pain of separation, the dread and apprehension of a failure exceeded what I had experienced at my first attempt. The appalling defeat I then sustained returned to torment me. I felt assured that, if I failed in this attempt, my case would be a hopeless one—it would seal my fate as a slave forever....But I remained firm, and, according to my resolution, on the third day of September, 1838, I left my chains, and succeeded in reaching New York without the slightest interruption of any kind....

I have been frequently asked how I felt when I found myself in a free State. I have never been able to answer the question with any satisfaction to myself. It was a moment of the highest excitement I ever experienced....In writing to a dear friend, immediately after my arrival at New York, I said I felt like one who had escaped a den of hungry lions. This state of mind, however, very soon subsided; and I was again seized with a feeling of great insecurity and loneliness....There I was in the midst of thousands, and yet a perfect stranger; without home and without friends....I dared not to unfold to any one... my sad condition. I was afraid to speak to any one for fear of speaking to the wrong one, and thereby falling into the hands of money-loving kidnappers, whose business it was to lie in wait for the panting fugitive, as the ferocious beasts of the forest lie in wait for their prey. The motto which I adopted when I started from slavery was this—"Trust no man!" I saw in every white man an enemy, and in almost every colored man cause for distrust. It was a most painful situation; and, to understand it, one must needs experience it, or imagine himself in similar circumstances. Let him be a fugitive slave in a strange land—a land given up to be the hunting-ground for slaveholders—whose inhabitants are legalized kidnappers—where he is every moment subjected to the terrible liability of being seized upon by his fellow-men, as the hideous crocodile seizes upon his prey!—I say, let him place himself in my situation—without home or friends—without money or credit—wanting shelter, and no one to give it—wanting bread, and no money to buy it,—and at the same time let him feel that he is pursued by merciless men-hunters, and in total darkness as to what to do, where to go, or where to stay...,—in the midst of plenty, yet suffering the terrible gnawings of hunger,—in the midst of houses, yet having no home...,—I say, let him be placed in this most trying situation...,—then, and not till then, will he fully appreciate the hardships of, and know how to sympathize with, the toil-worn and whip-scarred fugitive slave.

Thank Heaven, I remained but a short time in this distressed situation. I was relieved from it by the humane hand of Mr. DAVID RUGGLES, whose vigilance, kindness, and perseverance, I shall never forget. I am glad of an opportunity to express, as far as words can, the love and gratitude I bear him.... I had been in New York but a few days, when Mr. Ruggles sought me out, and very kindly took me to his boarding-house....Mr. Ruggles was then very deeply engaged in...attending to a number of other fugitive slaves, devising ways and means for their successful escape; and, though watched and hemmed in on almost every side, he seemed to be more than a match for his enemies....

At this time, Anna ["She was free"—Douglass's note], my intended wife, came on; for I wrote to her immediately after my arrival at New York,...informing her of my successful flight, and wishing her to come on forthwith. In a few days after her arrival, Mr. Ruggles called in the Rev. J. W. C. Pennington, who...performed the marriage ceremony....

[Ruggles suggests that they go to New Bedford, Massachusetts, where Douglass might find work as a caulker.] Upon reaching New Bedford, we were directed to the house of Mr. Nathan Johnson, by whom we were kindly received....

On the morning after our arrival at New Bedford, while at the breakfast-table, the question arose as to what name I should be called by. The name given me by my mother was, "Frederick Augustus Washington Bailey." I, however, had dispensed with the two middle names long before I left Maryland so that I was generally known by the name of "Frederick Bailey." I started from Baltimore bearing the name of "Stanley." When I got to New York, I again changed my name to "Frederick Johnson," and thought that would be the last change. But when I got to New Bedford, I found it necessary again to change my name. The reason of this necessity was, that there were so many Johnsons in New Bedford, it was already quite difficult to distinguish between them. I gave Mr. Johnson the privilege of choosing me a name, but told him he must not take from me the name of "Frederick." I must hold on to that, to preserve a sense of my identity. Mr. Johnson had just been reading the "Lady of the Lake," and at once suggested that my name be "Douglass." From that time until now I have been called "Frederick Douglass;" and as I am more widely known by that

name than by any of the others, I shall continue to use it as my own.

I was quite disappointed at the general appearance of things in New Bedford. The impression which I had received respecting the character and condition of the people of the north, I found to be singularly erroneous. I had very strangely supposed, while in slavery, that few of the comforts, and scarcely any of the luxuries, of life were enjoyed at the north, compared with what were enjoyed by the slaveholders of the south....I had somehow imbibed the opinion that, in the absence of slaves, there could be no wealth, and very little refinement. And upon coming to the north, I expected to meet with a rough, hard-handed, and uncultivated population..., knowing nothing of the ease, luxury, pomp, and grandeur of southern slaveholders. Such being my conjectures, any one acquainted with the appearance of New Bedford may very readily infer how palpably I must have seen my mistake.

In the afternoon of the day when I reached New Bedford, I visited the wharves, to take a view of the shipping. Here I found myself surrounded with the strongest proofs of wealth....Upon the right and left, I was walled in by granite warehouses of the widest dimensions, stowed to their utmost capacity with the necessaries and comforts of life. Added to this, almost every body seemed to be at work, but noiselessly so, compared with what I had been accustomed to in Baltimore. There were no loud songs heard from those engaged in loading and unloading ships. I heard no deep oaths or horrid curses on the laborer. I saw no whipping of men; but all seemed to go smoothly on. Every man appeared to understand his work, and went at it with a sober, yet cheerful earnestness, which betokened the deep interest which he felt in what he was doing, as well as a sense of his own dignity as a man. To me this looked exceedingly strange. From the wharves I strolled around and over the town, gazing with wonder and admiration at the splendid churches, beautiful dwellings, and finely-cultivated gardens; evincing an amount of wealth, comfort, taste, and refinement, such as I had never seen in any part of slaveholding Maryland.

Every thing looked clean, new, and beautiful. I saw few or no dilapidated houses, with poverty-stricken inmates; no half-naked children and barefooted women, such as I had been accustomed to see in Hillsborough, Easton, St. Michael's, and Baltimore. The people looked more able, stronger, healthier, and happier, than those of Maryland. I was for once made glad by a view of extreme wealth, without being saddened by seeing extreme poverty. But the most astonishing as well as the most interesting thing to me was the condition of the colored people, a great many of whom, like myself, had escaped thither as a refuge from the hunters of men. I found many, who had not been seven years out of their chains, living in finer houses, and evidently enjoying more of the comforts of life, than the average of slaveholders in Maryland.... I found the colored people much more spirited than I had supposed they would be. I found among them a determination to protect each other from the blood-thirsty kidnapper, at all hazards....

I found employment, the third day after my arrival, in stowing a sloop with a load of oil. It was new, dirty, and hard work for me; but I went at it with a glad heart and a willing hand. I was now my own master. It was a happy moment, the rapture of which can be understood only by those who have been slaves. It was the first work, the reward of which was to be entirely my own. There was no Master Hugh standing ready, the moment I earned the money, to rob me of it. I worked that day with a pleasure I had never before experienced. I was at work for myself and newly-married wife. It was to me the starting-point of a new existence. When I got through with that job, I went in pursuit of a job of calking; but such was the strength of prejudice against color, among the white calkers, that they refused to work with me, and of course I could get no employment.... Finding my trade of no immediate benefit, I...prepared myself to do any kind of work I could get to do.... There was no work too hard—none too dirty. I was ready to saw wood, shovel coal, carry the hod, sweep the chimney, or roll oil casks,—all of which I did for nearly three years in New Bedford, before I became known to the anti-slavery world.

[Within a few months, Douglass joins the anti-slavery movement.] I...never felt happier than when in an anti-slavery meeting. I seldom had much to say at the meetings, because what I wanted to say was said so much better by others. But, while attending an anti-slavery convention at Nantucket, on the 11th of August, 1841, I felt strongly moved to speak, and was at the same time much urged to do so by Mr. William C. Coffin, a gentleman who had heard me speak in the colored people's meeting at New Bedford. It was a severe cross, and I took it up reluctantly. The truth was, I felt myself a slave, and the idea of speaking to white people weighed me down. I spoke but a few moments, when I felt a degree of freedom, and said what I desired with considerable ease. From that time until now, I have been engaged in pleading the cause of my brethren—with what success, and with what devotion, I leave those acquainted with my labors to decide....

Sincerely and earnestly hoping that this little book may do something toward throwing light on the American slave system, and hastening the glad day of deliverance to the millions of my brethren in bonds—faithfully relying upon the power of truth, love, and justice, for success in my humble efforts—and solemnly pledging my self anew to the sacred cause,—I subscribe myself,

FREDERICK DOUGLASS

LYNN, *Mass., April* 28, 1845.

CHAPTER 17

George Fitzhugh Defends Slavery

"Negro slaves are the happiest people in the world"

Painful as it is to read about the ordeals that Frederick Douglass suffered as a slave (Chapter 16), it is comforting to know that his personal story has a happy ending: Freedom. Comforting, too, is the knowledge that American slavery itself ended just two decades after Douglass published his *Narrative*. It is hard to imagine a time when countless intelligent, patriotic, God-fearing people could not only own slaves but sincerely and strenuously argue *against* abolition.

Yet that was the America of Frederick Douglass—and of Angelina and Sarah Grimké, Abraham Lincoln, and everyone else before 1860. Few in number and remote from the American mainstream, abolitionists, write Timothy McCarthy and John Stauffer, "were sharply criticized in the press, denounced from the pulpit, punished in the courtroom, and effectively marginalized in politics. Many of their would-be sympathizers—people who opposed slavery on moral grounds but who were nonetheless uncomfortable with abolitionist appeals to racial equality—were wary of their heated rhetoric and aggressive tactics."[1] Most white Americans, North and South (among them Abraham Lincoln early in his career), considered these reformers dangerously deluded, a fanatical fringe group bent on destroying the sacred Union and demolishing the entire social order.

Not only that, white Americans—again, North as well as South—met abolitionists head on, developing an ideology in defense of slavery. Far from the feverish racist rantings of a few eccentric Southerners—often dismissed as "unhappy men" with "personal problems"—in fact, as Larry Tise (a leading student of this subject) argues, "proslavery ideology was a mode of thinking...that expressed the social, cultural, and moral values of a large portion of the population of America in the first half of the nineteenth century." That very popularity—startling and troubling as it is—demands that we try to understand slavery's apologists.[2]

Historian Drew Gilpin Faust observes that these writers wove the fabric of proslavery thought from several strands, summoning religion, history, and science to their cause.[3] Was owning slaves a sin? Far from it: "Both Old and New Testaments sanctioned human bondage," and Jesus Christ had never condemned the slave societies of his own time. Was slavery, as many called it, a "peculiar institution"? Nonsense: Slaveholding had been the norm around the globe and across the centuries, including the much-admired classical civilizations of ancient Greece and Rome. What was "peculiar," these writers argued, was the notion that "all men are created equal," a hopelessly wrongheaded idea that defied common sense and everyday experience. Turning to what passed then for science—including the measurement of skulls to calibrate brain size—anti-abolitionists argued that Africans, inferior beings incapable of freedom, were actually better off in slavery, where masters could look after them. Instead of individual rights, slavery's proponents stressed mutual duties and obligations: A slave's obedience in exchange for a master's care. Instead of equality, advocates of slavery harked back to hierarchical notions that resemble Dr. Alexander Hamilton's views (Chapter 5) and echo passages of Alexis de Tocqueville (Chapter 11).

These arguments had been well worked out before the Virginian George Fitzhugh (1806–1881) added his voice to the proslavery chorus around 1850. Born into a distinguished but impoverished old family, Fitzhugh married in 1829 and settled down in the backwater village of Port Royal on the Rappahannock River, dabbling in law and local politics. Weary of his legal practice and on the lookout for some other career, at mid-century Fitzhugh began to write pamphlets and newspaper articles in defense of slavery. In 1854, he collected his thoughts in *Sociology for the South, or The Failure of Free Society*; three years later came his second book, *Cannibals All! Or, Slaves Without Masters*.

Those who met George Fitzhugh thought him a "genial," "retiring" "homebody," but in his writings Fitzhugh delighted in provoking people. "[I] have whole files of infidel and abolition papers, like the…Liberator [William Lloyd Garrison's abolitionist newspaper]…," he boasted. Because radicals like "Tom Paine…are [my] daily companions,… [g]ood people give [my] office a wide berth as they pass it." Rather than just reading about his foes, Fitzhugh penned open letters to Northern abolitionists to stir things up, and in 1855 ventured there to debate them. *Sociology for the South,* he wrote a friend that same year, "sells the better because it is odd, eccentric, extravagant, and disorderly."[4]

Ever eager to engage opponents in discussion, Fitzhugh speaks to many others in *American Conversations.* His assault on prevailing wisdom about equality and freedom was like Paine's blistering denunciation of monarchy (Chapter 7). Not content to defend slavery, he went on the attack against free labor, then considered one of the bedrock values of American life (think of how both Benjamin Franklin and Mason Locke Weems celebrated it in Chapters 6 and 10). Moreover, he "borrowed freely from the tactics northern abolitionists employed in their propaganda against Southern slavery," argues historian C. Vann Woodward. "The criminology of the subject was employed as a fair description of conditions, and the occasional instance of sadism and depravity presented as the prevailing practice."[5] Do you agree with Woodward's assessment?

Another weapon in Fitzhugh's arsenal was revisionist history. Independence from England was a good idea, the Virginian admitted, but the sacred Declaration itself? "[B]ombastic absurdity" that "had about as much to do with the occasion [of independence] as would a sermon or oration on the teething of a child or the kittening of a cat." The sainted Jefferson? "[T]houghtless" and "half-informed." The genial Franklin? "His sentiments and his philosophy are low, selfish, atheistic, and material." All men created equal? Nonsense. It is obvious that "men are not born physically, morally, or intellectually equal.… It would be far nearer the truth to say, 'that some were born with saddles on their backs, and others booted and spurred to ride them,'—and the riding does them good."[6]

If it was controversy Fitzhugh sought with such talk, he found it. Garrison, pronouncing *Sociology for the South* "a shallow, impudent, and thoroughly satanic work," diagnosed its author as a "demented," "crack-brained," "moral lunatic." Abraham Lincoln often quoted Fitzhugh in campaign speeches during the 1850s; *Sociology for the South,* reported Lincoln's law partner, "aroused the ire of Lincoln more than most pro-slavery books." Even Southerners who agreed with Fitzhugh thought he went too far. These men fretted about the "want of moderation," the views "too…incautiously asserted," the "utter recklessness of both statement and expression" that, by rendering his writings "incendiary and dangerous," risked giving proslavery thinking a bad name.[7]

Fitzhugh has been as controversial among historians now as he was among Americans then. Some consider his views so atypical as to be "a mutant strain" of proslavery thought. Others believe that he was a "central figure" who "loomed large" at the time because his arguments were a "logical outcome" of others' ideas. His work, argues

Eugene Genovese, "was not so much new as a more rigorous and mature presentation of a line of thought which had been steadily gaining favor for years."[8]

Typical or not, it is clear that Fitzhugh got people's attention. In 1857 *De Bow's Review*, the most influential Southern newspaper of the time and a leading proslavery voice, reported that his views are being "adopted by many." A British visitor writing of a journey through the United States in the same year "explained to his English readers...[that] it was necessary to understand Fitzhugh's position in order to comprehend the American scene."[9]

The irony, the tragedy, is that Fitzhugh loved the Union and shrank from the prospect of secession or civil war. Working in Washington, D.C., for the federal government during the late 1850s, he clung to the hope that the gathering storm could be averted. "[W]hat heart [is] so cold, what mind so dull," he wondered in a newspaper article, "as to be insensible to the progress and the glory of United America?" Having visited the North (he was among the many awed by Hudson River scenery; Chapter 12), he could with authority say: "We are one people." At the same time, however, the propagandist kept his doubts to himself to most effectively make his points about slavery and freedom. "I assure you, Sir," he confided to a friend, "I see great evils in Slavery, but in a controversial work I ought not to admit them." Imagine Thomas Paine privately admitting to a certain affection for King George III.[10]

In putting forth such strident, uncompromising views, Fitzhugh was playing with fire; no wonder he, along with the rest of America, was burned once war came. When his beloved Port Royal went from backwater to battleground, he headed for Richmond, the Confederate capital, and took a government post. After the war, Fitzhugh was a lost soul. Once easygoing, he was now embittered. Once famous (or infamous), he was now forgotten. Once unwilling to go along with those who argued that African Americans were an altogether different species (note his views of African Americans), he now insisted that not only were they another species, but "[t]here never lived one single full-blooded negro who could manage successfully all the details of a large farm. Nay, there never was a negro...who could manage his own family." After 1870, this prolific author wrote no more. Penniless and enfeebled, he moved in with one child or another before dying in Texas in 1881, an obscure figure buried in oblivion.[11]

After 1865 Americans—even Southern whites who had read and celebrated his works—quickly forgot George Fitzhugh. Why, then, read him today? One reason, already noted, is the very popularity of proslavery and antiblack views in America. Another is that, as you will see (Chapter 20), Southern whites after 1865 remained committed to racial supremacy. Still another reason, Woodward suggests, is his critique of industrial America: The very questions Fitzhugh asked about who would care for workers when they became sick, injured, or elderly would be posed by American reformers in later years. A final reason to read him is best captured by Faust, who writes of proslavery authors generally:[12]

> While we can continue to abhor the system of human bondage that flourished in the Old South, there is much we can learn from a more dispassionate examination of the arguments used to defend it. We have sought to distance the slaveholders and their creed, to define them as very unlike ourselves. Yet their processes of rationalization and self-justification were not so very different from our own, or from those of any civilization of human actors. The persistence of modern racism is but one forceful reminder of the ways that human beings always view the world in terms of inherited systems of belief and explanation that only partially reflect the reality they are meant to describe. By understanding how others have fashioned and maintained their systems of meaning, we shall be better equipped to evaluate, criticize, and perhaps even change our own.

Questions for Consideration and Conversation

1. What were the key elements of Fitzhugh's argument in favor of slavery? However convincing you find them, why did most white Americans at the time find them convincing?

2. Imagine that you were invited to debate Fitzhugh and to demolish his argument. How would you go about doing so?

3. What did Fitzhugh mean by the phrase "Cannibals All"? What was his point in using that phrase?

4. What were Fitzhugh's views of Africans and African Americans?

5. Consider Fitzhugh's portrait of the manufacturing society that was developing in the North, as it had in England. Does his critique of that social system have any validity?

6. How does his assessment of slavery, labor, and race relations, North and South, compare with Tocqueville's observations a generation before?

7. What role did two core values of American life, religion and family, play in Fitzhugh's work?

Endnotes

1. Timothy Patrick McCarthy and John Stauffer, eds., "Introduction," in *Prophets of Protest: Reconsidering the History of American Abolitionism* (New York, 2006), xiv.

2. Drew Gilpin Faust, ed., *The Ideology of Slavery: Proslavery Thought in the Antebellum South* (Baton Rouge, LA, 1981), 7 ("unhappy," "personal"); Larry E. Tise, *Proslavery: A History of the Defense of Slavery in America, 1701–1840* (Athens, GA, 1987), xv.

3. Faust, ed., *Ideology of Slavery* (Introduction).

4. Harvey Wish, *George Fitzhugh: Propagandist of the Old South* (Baton Rouge, LA, 1943), 11 ("genial"), 12 ("retiring"), 126–27 ("odd"), 172–73 ("daily companions"); C. Vann Woodward, "George Fitzhugh, *Sui Generis*," in Fitzhugh, *Cannibals All! or, Slaves Without Masters*, ed. Woodward (Cambridge, MA, 1960), xiii ("homebody").

5. Woodward, "Fitzhugh," xxvi.

6. Ibid., xxxiii–xxxiv; George Fitzhugh, *Sociology for the South, Or The Failure of Free Society* (Richmond, 1854), 90 (Franklin).

7. Wish, *Fitzhugh*, 168 ("lunatic"), 200 ("satanic," "demented," "crack-brained"); Woodward, "Fitzhugh," xxx (Lincoln); Drew Gilpin Faust, *A Sacred Circle: The Dilemma of the Intellectual in the Old South, 1840–1860* (Baltimore, 1977), 127 (Southerners).

8. Faust, *Sacred Circle*, 129 ("mutant"); Eugene D. Genovese, *The World the Slaveholders Made: Two Essays in Interpretation* (New York, 1969), 118 ("logical"), 119 ("figure"), 130 ("rigorous").

9. Genovese, *World the Slaveholders Made*, 128 ("adopted"); Wish, *Fitzhugh*, 204 (British visitor).

10. Wish, *Fitzhugh*, 111 ("evils"), 158 ("insensible").

11. Ibid., 325.

12. Faust, ed., *Ideology of Slavery*, 20.

GEORGE FITZHUGH, SOCIOLOGY FOR THE SOUTH (1854)

Source: George Fitzhugh, *Sociology for the South, Or the Failure of Free Society.* Richmond, 1854. http://docsouth.unc.edu/fitzhughsoc. Academic Affairs Library, UNC-CH. University of North Carolina at Chapel Hill, 1998. © *Documenting the American South, or, The Southern Experience in 19th-century America.*

To the People of the South

We dedicate this little work to you, because it is a zealous and honest effort to promote your peculiar [distinctive] interests. Society has been so quiet and contented in the South—it has suffered so little from crime or extreme poverty, that its attention has not been awakened to the revolutionary tumults, uproar, mendicity [beggary] and crime of free society....

From some peculiarity of taste, we have for many years been watching closely the perturbed workings of free society. Its crimes, its revolutions, its sufferings and its beggary, have led us to investigate its past history, as well as to speculate on its future destiny. This pamphlet has been hastily written, but is the result of long observation, some research and much reflection. Should it contain suggestions that will enlist abler pens to show that free society is a failure and its philosophy false, our highest ambition will be gratified....

The ancients took it for granted that slavery was right, and never attempted to justify it. The moderns assume that it is wrong, and forthwith proceed to denounce it. The South can lose nothing, and may gain, by the discussion. She has, up to this time, been condemned without a hearing....

Chapter V. Negro Slavery

...[I]t has been the practice in all countries and in all ages, in some degree, to accommodate the amount and character of government control to the wants, intelligence, and moral capacities of the nations or individuals to be governed. A highly moral and intellectual people, like the free citizens of ancient Athens, are best governed by a democracy. For a less moral and intellectual one, a limited and constitutional monarchy will answer. For a people either very ignorant or very wicked, nothing short of military despotism will suffice. So among individuals, the most moral and well-informed members of society require no other government than law. They are capable of reading and understanding the law, and have sufficient self-control and virtuous disposition to obey it. Children cannot be governed by mere law; first, because they do not understand it, and secondly, because they are so much under the influence of impulse, passion and appetite, that they want sufficient self-control to be deterred or governed by the distant and doubtful penalties of the law. They must be constantly controlled by parents or guardians, whose will and orders shall stand in the place of law for them. Very wicked men must be put into penitentiaries; lunatics into asylums, and the most wild of them into straight jackets, just as the most wicked of the sane are manacled with irons; and idiots must have committees to govern and take care of them. Now, it is clear the Athenian democracy would not suit a negro nation, nor will the government of mere law suffice for the individual negro. He is but a grown up child, and must be governed as a child, not as a lunatic or criminal. The master occupies towards him the place of parent or guardian. We shall not dwell on this view, for no one will differ with us who thinks as we do of the negro's capacity, and we might argue till dooms-day, in vain, with those who have

a high opinion of the negro's moral and intellectual capacity.

Secondly. The negro is improvident; will not lay up in summer for the wants of winter; will not accumulate in youth for the exigencies of age. He would become an insufferable burden to society. Society has the right to prevent this, and can only do so by subjecting him to domestic slavery.

In the last place, the negro race is inferior to the white race, and living in their midst, they would be far outstripped or outwitted in the chase of free competition. Gradual but certain extermination would be their fate. We presume the maddest abolitionist does not think the negro's providence of habits and money-making capacity at all to compare to those of the whites. This defect of character would alone justify enslaving him, if he is to remain here. In Africa or the West Indies, he would become idolatrous, savage and cannibal, or be devoured by savages and cannibals. At the North he would freeze or starve.

We would remind those who deprecate and sympathize with negro slavery, that his slavery here relieves him from a far more cruel slavery in Africa, or from idolatry and cannibalism, and every brutal vice and crime that can disgrace humanity; and that it christianizes, protects, supports and civilizes him; that it governs him far better than free laborers at the North are governed. There, wife murder has become a mere holiday pastime; and where so many wives are murdered, almost all must be brutally treated. Nay, more: men who kill their wives or treat them brutally, must be ready for all kinds of crime, and the calendar of crime at the North proves the inference to be correct. Negroes never kill their wives. If it be objected that legally they have no wives, then we reply, that in an experience of more than forty years, we never yet heard of a negro man killing a negro woman. Our negroes are not only better off as to physical comfort than free laborers, but their moral condition is better.

But abolish negro slavery, and how much of slavery still remains. Soldiers and sailors in Europe enlist for life; here, for five years. Are they not slaves who have not only sold their liberties, but their lives also? And they are worse treated than domestic slaves. No domestic affection and self-interest extend their ægis [protection] over them. No kind mistress, like a guardian angel, provides for them in health, tends them in sickness, and soothes their dying pillow....The kind of slavery is adapted to the men enslaved. Wives and apprentices are slaves; not in theory only, but often in fact. Children are slaves to their parents, guardians and teachers. Imprisoned culprits are slaves. Lunatics and idiots are slaves also. Three-fourths of free society are slaves, no better treated, when their wants and capacities are estimated, than negro slaves.... "In the sweat of thy face shalt thou earn thy bread!" made all men slaves, and such all *good men* continue to be....

Would the abolitionists approve of a system of society that set white children free, and remitted [surrendered] them at the age of fourteen, males and females, to all the rights, both as to person and property, which belong to adults? Would it be criminal or praiseworthy to do so? Criminal, of course. Now, are the average of negroes equal in information, in native intelligence, in prudence or providence, to well-informed white children of fourteen? We who have lived with them for forty years, think not. The competition of the world would be too much for the children. They would be cheated out of their property and debased in their morals. Yet they would meet every where with sympathizing friends of their own color, ready to aid, advise and assist them. The negro would be exposed to the same competition and greater temptations, with no greater ability to contend with them, with these additional difficulties. He would be welcome nowhere; meet with thousands of enemies and no friends. If he went North, the white laborers would kick him and cuff him, and drive him out of employment. If he went to Africa, the savages would cook him and eat him. If he went to the West Indies, they would not let him in, or if they did, they would soon make of him a savage and idolater....

The earliest civilization of which history gives account is that of Egypt. The negro was always in contact with that civilization. For four thousand years he has had opportunities of becoming civilized. Like the wild horse, he must be caught, tamed and domesticated. When his subjugation ceases he again runs wild, like the cattle on the Pampas of the South, or the horses on the prairies of the West. His condition in the West Indies proves this....

We deem this peculiar question of negro slavery of very little importance. The issue is made throughout the world on the general subject of slavery in the abstract. The argument has commenced. One set of ideas will govern and control after awhile the civilized world. Slavery will everywhere be abolished, or every where be reinstituted.... We have introduced the subject of negro slavery to afford us a better opportunity to disclaim the purpose of reducing the white man any where to the condition of negro slaves here. It would be very unwise and unscientific to govern white men as you would negroes. Every shade and variety of slavery has existed in the world. In some cases there has been much of legal regulation, much restraint of the master's authority; in others, none at all. The character of slavery necessary to protect the whites in Europe should be much milder than negro slavery, for slavery is only needed to protect the white man, whilst it is more necessary for the government of the negro even than for his protection. But even negro slavery should not be outlawed. We might and should have laws in Virginia, as in Louisiana, to make the master subject to presentment by the grand jury and to punishment, for any inhuman or improper treatment or neglect of his slave.

We abhor the doctrine of the "Types of Mankind" [an 1854 book by Josiah C. Nott arguing that whites and blacks were separate species]; first, because it is at war with scripture, which teaches us that the whole human race is descended from a common parentage; and, second, because it encourages and incites brutal masters to treat negroes, not as weak, ignorant and dependent brethren, but as wicked beasts, without the pale [outside the boundary] of humanity. The Southerner is the negro's friend, his only friend. Let no intermeddling abolitionist, no refined philosophy, dissolve this friendship.

Chapter VI. Scriptural Authority for Slavery

We find slavery repeatedly instituted by God, or by men acting under his immediate care and direction.... Nowhere in the Old or New Testament do we find the institution condemned, but frequently recognized and enforced.... It is probably no cause of regret that men are so constituted as to require that many should be slaves. Slavery opens many sources of happiness and occasions and encourages the exercise of many virtues and affections which would be unknown without it. It begets friendly, kind and affectionate relations, just as equality engenders antagonism and hostility on all sides. The condition of slavery in all ages and in all countries has been considered in the general disgraceful, but so to some extent have hundreds of the necessary trades and occupations of freemen. The necessity which often compels the best of men to resort to such trades and occupations in no degree degrades their character, nor does the necessity which imposes slavery degrade the character of the slave. The man who acts well his part, whether as slave or free laborer, is entitled to and commands the esteem and respect of all good men....

Ham, a son of Noah, was condemned to slavery and his posterity after him. We do not adopt the theory that he was the ancestor of the negro race. The Jewish slaves were not negroes, and to confine the justification of slavery to that race would be to weaken its scriptural authority, and to lose the whole weight of profane authority, for we read of no negro slavery in ancient times....

Chapter XIX. Declaration of Independence and Virginia Bill of Rights

An essay on the subject of slavery would be very imperfect, if it passed over without noticing these instruments. The abstract principles which they enunciate, we candidly admit, are wholly at war with slavery; we shall attempt to show that they are equally at war with all government, all subordination, all order. Men's minds were heated and blinded when they were written, as well by patriotic zeal, as by a false philosophy, which, beginning with [seventeenth-century English philosopher John] Locke, in a refined materialism, had ripened on the Continent into open infidelity. In England, the doctrine of prescriptive government, the divine right of kings, had met with signal overthrow, and in France there was faith in nothing, speculation about everything. The human mind became extremely presumptuous, and undertook to form governments on exact philosophical principles, just as men make clocks, watches or mills....Society seemed to them a thing whose movement and action could be controlled with as much certainty as the motion of a spinning wheel, provided it was organized on proper principles. It would have been less presumptuous in them to have attempted to have made a tree, for a tree is not half so complex as a society of human beings, each of whom is fearfully and wonderfully compounded of soul and body, and whose aggregate, society, is still more complex and difficult of comprehension than its individual members. Trees grow and man may lop, trim, train and cultivate them, and thus hasten their growth, and improve their size, beauty and fruitfulness. Laws, institutions, societies, and governments grow, and men may aid their growth, improve their strength and beauty, and lop off their deformities and excrescences, by punishing crime and rewarding virtue. When society has worked long enough, under the hand of God and nature, man observing its operations, may discover its laws and constitution. The common law of England and the constitution of England, were discoveries of this kind. Fortunately for us, we adopted, with little change, that common law and that constitution. Our institutions and our ancestry were English. Those institutions were the growth and accretions of many ages, not the work of legislating philosophers.

The abstractions contained in the various instruments on which we professed, but professed falsely, to found our governments, did no harm, because, until abolition arose, they remained a dead letter. Now, and not till now, these abstractions have become matters of serious practical importance, and we propose to give some of them a candid, but fearless examination. We find these words in the preamble and Declaration of Independence,

"We hold these truths to be self-evident, that all men are created equal; that they are endowed by their Creator with certain inalienable rights, that among them, are life, liberty, and the pursuit of happiness; that to secure these rights governments are instituted among men, deriving their just powers from the consent of the governed...."

It is, we believe, conceded on all hands, that men are not born physically, morally or intellectually equal,—some are males, some females, some from birth, large, strong and healthy, others weak, small and sickly—some are naturally amiable, others prone to all kinds of wickednesses—some brave, others timid. Their natural inequalities beget inequalities of rights. The weak in mind or body require guidance, support and protection; they must obey and work for those who protect and guide them—they have a natural right to guardians, committees, teachers or masters. Nature has made them slaves; all that law and government can do, is to regulate, modify and mitigate their slavery. In the absence of legally instituted slavery, their condition would be worse under that natural slavery of the weak to the strong, the foolish to the wise and cunning. The wise and virtuous, the brave, the strong in mind and body, are by nature born to command and protect, and law but follows nature in making them rulers, legislators, judges, captains, husbands, guardians, committees and masters. The naturally depraved class, those born prone to crime, are our brethren too; they are entitled to education, to religious instruction, to all the means and appliances proper to correct their evil propensities, and all their failings; they have a right to be sent to the penitentiary,—for there, if they do not reform, they cannot at least disturb society....

We are but stringing together truisms, which every body knows as well as ourselves, and yet if men are created unequal in all these respects; what truth or what meaning is there in the passage under consideration? Men are not created or born equal, and circumstances, and education, and association, tend to increase and aggravate inequalities among them, from generation to generation. Generally, the rich associate and intermarry with each other, the poor do the same; the ignorant rarely associate with or intermarry with the learned, and all society shuns contact with the criminal, even to the third and fourth generations.

Men are not "born entitled to equal rights!" It would be far nearer the truth to say, "that some were born with saddles on their backs, and others booted and spurred to ride them,"—and the riding does them good. They need the reins, the bit and the spur. No two men by nature are exactly equal or exactly alike. No institutions can prevent the few from acquiring rule and ascendency over the many. Liberty and free competition invite and encourage the attempt of the strong to master the weak; and insure their success.

"Life and liberty" are not "inalienable;" they have been sold in all countries, and in all ages, and must be sold so long as human nature lasts. It is an inexpedient and unwise, and often unmerciful restraint, on a man's liberty of action, to deny him the right to sell himself when starving, and again to buy himself when fortune smiles. Most countries of antiquity, and some, like China at the present day, allowed such sale and purchase. The great object of government is to restrict, control and punish man "in the pursuit of happiness." All crimes are committed in its pursuit. Under the free or competitive system, most men's happiness consists in destroying the happiness of other people. This, then, is no inalienable right.

The author of the Declaration may have, and probably did mean, that all men were created with an equal title to property. Carry out such a doctrine, and it would subvert every government on earth.

In practice, in all ages, and in all countries, men had sold their liberty either for short periods, for life, or hereditarily; that is, both their own liberty and that of their children after them. The laws of all countries have, in various forms and degrees, in all times recognized and regulated this right to *alien* or sell liberty. The soldiers and sailors of the revolution had aliened both liberty and life, the wives in all America had aliened their liberty, so had the apprentices and wards at the very moment this verbose, newborn, false and unmeaning preamble was written.

Mr. Jefferson was an enthusiastic speculative philosopher; Franklin was wise, cunning and judicious; he made no objection to the Declaration, as prepared by Mr. Jefferson, because, probably, he saw it would suit the occasion and supposed it would be harmless for the future. But even Franklin was too much of a physical philosopher, too utilitarian and material in his doctrines, to be relied on in matters of morals or government. We may fairly conclude, that liberty is alienable, that there is a natural right to alien it, first, because the laws and institutions of all countries have recognized and regulated its alienation; and secondly, because we cannot conceive of a civilized society, in which there were no wives, no wards, no apprentices, no sailors and no soldiers; and none of these could there be in a country that practically carried out the doctrine, that liberty is inalienable.

The soldier who meets death at the cannon's mouth, does so because he has aliened both life and liberty. Nay, more, he has aliened the pursuit of happiness, else he might desert on the eve of battle, and pursue happiness in some more promising quarter than the cannon's mouth. If the pursuit of happiness be inalienable, men should not be punished for crime, for all crimes are notoriously committed in the pursuit of happiness. If these abstractions have some hidden…meaning, which none but the initiated can comprehend, then the Declaration should have been accompanied with a translation, and a commentary to fit it for common use.…

But philosophy then was in the chrysalis state. She has since deluged the world with blood, crime and pauperism. She has had full sway, and has inflicted much misery, and done no good. The world is beginning to be satisfied, that it is much safer and better, to look to the past, to trust to experience, to follow nature, than to be guided by the…speculations of closet philosophers. If all men had been created equal, all would have been competitors, rivals, and enemies. Subordination, difference of caste and classes, difference of sex, age and slavery beget peace and good will.

We were only justified in declaring our independence, because we were sufficiently wise, numerous and strong to govern ourselves, and too distant and distinct from England to be well governed by her.…

Chapter XXIV. Infidelity and Abolitionism

Every one who reads the newspapers must have observed that open-mouthed infidelity is never seen or heard in this country except in abolition meetings and conventions, and in women's rights conventicles [assemblies]. On such occasions some woman unsexes herself, and…pours out false and foul execrations against slavery and the Bible, aided by men with sharper tongues and duller courage than the women themselves.…

Liberty, infidelity, and abolition, are three words conveying but one idea. Infidels who dispute the authority of God will not respect or obey the government of man. Abolitionists, who make war upon slavery, instituted by God and approved by Holy

Writ, are in a fair way to denounce the Bible that stands in the way of the attainment of their purpose. Marriage is too much like slavery not to be involved in its fate; and the obedience which the Bible inculcates, furnishes a new theme for infidelity in petticoats or in Bloomers [loose-fitting women's clothing] to harp

on. Slavery, marriage, religion, are the pillars of the social fabric....

If ever the abolitionists succeed in thoroughly imbuing the world with their doctrines and opinions, all religion, all government, all order, will be slowly but surely subverted and destroyed....

GEORGE FITZHUGH, *CANNIBALS ALL! OR, SLAVES WITHOUT MASTERS* (1857)

Source: George Fitzhugh, *Cannibals All! Or, Slaves Without Masters.* 1857. http://docsouth.unc.edu/fitzhughcan/ fitzcan.html. Academic Affairs Library, UNC-CH. University of North Carolina at Chapel Hill, 1998. © *Documenting the American South, or, The Southern Experience in 19th Century America.*

Chapter I. The Universal Trade

We are, all, North and South, engaged in the White Slave Trade, and he who succeeds best, is esteemed most respectable. It is far more cruel than the Black Slave Trade, because it exacts more of its slaves, and neither protects nor governs them. We boast, that it exacts more, when we say, "that the *profits* made from employing free labor are greater than those from slave labor." The profits, made from free labor, are the amount of the products of such labor, which the employer, by means of the command which capital or skill gives him, takes away, exacts or "exploitates" from the free laborer. The profits of slave labor are that portion of the products of such labor which the power of the master enables him to appropriate. These profits are less, because the master allows the slave to retain a larger share of the results of his own labor, than do the employers of free labor.... [T]he White Slave Trade is...also...more cruel, in leaving the laborer to take care of himself and family out of the pittance which skill or capital have allowed him to retain. When the day's labor is ended, he is free, but is overburdened with the cares of family and household, which make his freedom an empty and delusive mockery. But his employer is really free, and may enjoy the profits made by others' labor, without a care, or a trouble, as to their well-being. The negro slave is free, too, when the labors of the day are over, and free in mind as well as body; for the master provides food, raiment [clothes], house, fuel, and everything else necessary to the physical well-being of himself and family. The master's labors commence just when the slave's end....

Now, reader, if you wish to know yourself[,]... read on. But if you would cherish self-conceit, self-esteem, or self-appreciation, throw down our book; for we will dispel illusions which have promoted your happiness, and shew you that what you have considered and practiced as virtue, is little better than moral Cannibalism. But you will find yourself in numerous and respectable company; for all good and respectable people are "Cannibals all," who do not labor, or who are successfully trying to live without labor, on the unrequited labor of other people:— Whilst low, bad, and disreputable people, are those who labor to support themselves, and to support said respectable people besides. Throwing the negro slaves out of the account, and society is divided in Christendom into four classes: The rich, or independent respectable people, who live well and labor not at all; the professional and skillful respectable people, who do a little light work, for enormous wages; the poor hard-working people, who support every body, and starve themselves; and the poor thieves, swindlers and sturdy beggars, who live like gentlemen, without labor, on the labor of other people. The gentlemen exploitate, which being done on a large scale, and requiring a great many victims, is highly respectable....

The respectable way of living is, to make other people work for you, and to pay them nothing for so doing—and to have no concern about them after their work is done. Hence, white slave-holding is much more respectable than negro slavery—for the master works nearly as hard for the negro, as he for the master. But you, my virtuous, respectable reader, exact three thousand dollars per annum from white labor, (for your income is the product of white labor,) and make not one cent of return in any form. You retain your capital, and never labor, and yet live in luxury on the labor of others. Capital commands labor, as the master does the slave.... You, with the command over labor which your capital gives you, are a slave owner—a master, without the obligations of a master. They who work for you, who create your income, are slaves, without the rights of slaves. Slaves without a master! Whilst you were engaged in amassing your capital, in seeking to become independent, you were in the White Slave Trade. To become independent, is to be able to make other people support you, without being obliged to labor for *them*. Now, what man in society is not seeking to attain this situation? He who attains it, is a slave owner, in the worst sense. He who is in pursuit of it, is engaged in the slave trade. You, reader, belong to the one or other class....

The negro slaves of the South are the happiest, and, in some sense, the freest people in the world. The children and the aged and infirm work not at all, and yet have all the comforts and necessaries of life provided for them. They enjoy liberty, because they are oppressed neither by care nor labor. The women do little hard work, and are protected from the despotism of their husbands by their masters. The negro men and stout boys work, on the average, in good weather, not more than nine hours a day. The balance of their time is spent in perfect abandon. Besides, they have their Sabbaths and holidays. White men, with so much of license and liberty, would die of ennui [boredom]; but negroes luxuriate in corporeal [bodily] and mental repose. With their faces upturned to the sun, they can sleep at any hour; and quiet sleep is the greatest of human enjoyments.... 'Tis happiness in itself—and results from contentment with the present, and confident assurance of the future. We do not know whether free laborers ever sleep. They are fools to do so; for, whilst they sleep, the wily and watchful capitalist is devising means to ensnare and exploitate them. The free laborer must work or starve....

Chapter II. Labor, Skill and Capital...

Public opinion unites with self-interest, domestic affection and municipal law to protect the slave. The man who maltreats the weak and dependent, who abuses his authority over wife, children or slaves, is universally detested. That same public opinion, which shields and protects the slave, encourages the oppression of free laborers—for it is considered more honorable and praiseworthy to obtain large fees than small ones, to make good bargains than bad

ones, ... —to live without work, by the exactions of accumulated capital, than to labor at the plough or the spade, for one's living. It is the interest of the capitalist and the skillful to allow free laborers the least possible portion of the fruits of their own labor; for all capital is created by labor, and the smaller the allowance of the free laborer, the greater the gains of his employer. To treat free laborers badly and unfairly, is universally inculcated as a moral duty, and the selfishness of man's nature prompts him to the most rigorous performance of this cannibalish duty.... [A]ll competition is but the effort to enslave others, without being encumbered with their support....

The able-bodied, industrious poor are compelled by the rich and skillful to support the weak, and too often, the idle poor. In addition to defraying the necessary expenses and the wanton luxuries of the rich, to supporting government, and supporting themselves, capital compels them to support its poor houses. In collection of the poor rates, in their distribution, and in the administration of the poor-house system, probably half the tax raised for the poor is exhausted.... Masters, in like manner, support the sick, infant and aged slaves from the labor of the strong and healthy. But nothing is wasted in collection and administration, and nothing given to unworthy objects.... Masters treat their sick, infant and helpless slaves well, not only from feeling and affection, but from motives of self-interest. Good treatment renders them more valuable.... Besides, masters are always in place to render needful aid to the unfortunate and helpless slaves. Thousands of the poor starve out of reach of the poor house, or other public charity.

A common charge preferred against slavery is, that it induces idleness with the masters. The trouble, care and labor, of providing for wife, children and slaves, and of properly governing and administering the whole affairs of the farm, is usually borne on small estates by the master. On larger ones, he is aided by an overseer or manager. If they do their duty, their time is fully occupied. If they do not, the estate goes to ruin. The mistress, on Southern farms, is usually more busily, usefully and benevolently occupied than any one on the farm. She unites in her person, the offices of wife, mother, mistress, housekeeper, and sister of charity. And she fulfills all these offices admirably well. The rich men, in free society, may, if they please, lounge about town, visit clubs, attend the theatre, and have no other trouble than that of collecting rents, interest and dividends of stock. In a well constituted slave society, there should be no idlers.... The master labors for the slave, they exchange industrial value.

But the capitalist, living on his income, gives nothing to his subjects. He lives by mere exploitation.

It is objected that slavery permits or induces immorality. This is a mistake. The intercourse of the house-servants with the white familiar [family], assimilates, in some degree, their state of information, and their moral conduct, to that of the whites. The house-servants, by their intercourse with the field hands, impart their knowledge to them. The master enforces decent morality in all. Negroes are never ignorant of the truths of Christianity, all speak intelligible English, and are posted up in the ordinary occurrences of the times. The reports to the British Parliament shew, that the agricultural and mining poor of England scarce know the existence of God, do not speak intelligible English, and are generally depraved and ignorant. They learn nothing by intercourse with their superiors, as negroes do. They abuse wives and children, because they have no masters to control them, and the men are often dissipated and idle, leaving all the labor to be done by the women and children—for the want of this same control.

Slavery, by separating the mass of the ignorant from each other, and bringing them in contact and daily intercourse with the well-informed, becomes an admirable educational system—no doubt a necessary one. By subjecting them to the constant control and supervision of their superiors, interested in enforcing morality, it becomes the best and most efficient police system....

If we prove that domestic slavery is, in the general, a natural and necessary institution, we remove the greatest stumbling block to belief in the Bible; for whilst texts, detached and torn from their context, may be found for any other purpose, none can be found that even militates against slavery. The distorted and forced construction of certain passages, for this purpose, by abolitionists, if employed as a common rule of construction, would reduce the Bible to a mere allegory, to be interpreted to suit every vicious taste and wicked purpose.

But we have been looking merely to one side of human nature, and to that side rendered darker by the false, antagonistic and competitive relations in which so-called liberty and equality place man.

Man is, by nature, the most social and gregarious, and, therefore, the least selfish of animals. Within the family there is little room, opportunity or temptation to selfishness—and slavery leaves but little of the world without [outside of] the family. Man loves that nearest to him best. First his wife, children and parents, then his slaves, next his neighbors and fellow-countrymen. But his unselfishness does not stop here. He is ready and anxious to relieve a famine in Ireland, and shudders when he reads of a murder at the antipodes [the opposite side of the globe]. He feels deeply for the sufferings of domestic animals, is rendered happy by witnessing the enjoyments of the flocks, and herds, and carroling birds that surround him. He sympathizes with all external nature. A parched field distresses him, and he rejoices as he sees the groves, and the gardens, and the plains flourishing, and blooming, and smiling about him. All men are philanthropists, and would benefit their fellowmen if they could. But we cannot be sure of benefiting those whom we cannot control. Hence, all actively good men are ambitious, and would be masters, in all save the name.

Benevolence, the love of what is without, and the disposition to incur pain or inconvenience to advance the happiness and well-being of what is without self, is as universal a motive of human conduct, as mere selfishness—which is the disposition to sacrifice the good of others to our own good.

The prevalent philosophy of the day takes cognizance of but half of human nature—and that the worst half. Our happiness is so involved in the happiness and well-being of everything around us, that a mere selfish philosophy, like political economy, is a very unsafe and delusive guide.

We employ the term Benevolence to express our outward affections, sympathies, tastes and feelings; but it is inadequate to express our meaning.... Philosophy has been so busy with the worst feature of human nature, that it has not even found a name for this, its better feature. We must fall back on Christianity, which embraces man's whole nature, and though not a code of philosophy, is something better; for it proposes to lead us through the trials and intricacies of life, not by the mere cool calculations of the head, but by the unerring instincts of a pure and regenerate heart. The problem of the Moral World is too vast and complex for the human mind to comprehend; yet the pure heart will, safely and quietly, feel its way through the mazes that confound the head....

Chapter VII. The World Is *Too Little* Governed...

Mobs, secret associations, insurance companies, and social and communistic experiments, are striking features and characteristics of our day, outside of slave society. They are all attempting to supply the defects of regular governments, which have carried the "Let alone" practice so far, that one-third of mankind are let alone to indulge in such criminal immoralities as they please, and another third to starve. Mobs... supply the deficiencies of a defective police, and insurance companies and voluntary unions and associations afford that security and protection which government, under the lead of political economy, has ceased to render.

A lady remarked to us, a few days since, "that society was like an army, in which the inferior officers were as necessary as the commander in chief. Demoralization and insubordination ensue if you dispense with sergeants and corporals in an army, and the same effects result from dispensing with guardians, masters and heads of families in society."... Slavery is an indispensable police institution;—especially so, to check the cruelty and tyranny of vicious and depraved husbands and parents. Husbands and parents have, in theory and practice, a power over their subjects more despotic than kings; and the ignorant and vicious exercise their power more oppressively than kings. Every man is not fit to be king, yet all must have wives and children. Put a master over them to check their power, and we need not resort to the unnatural remedies of woman's rights, limited marriages, voluntary divorces, and free love, as proposed by the abolitionists....

We agree with Mr. Jefferson, that all men have natural and inalienable rights. To violate or disregard such rights, is to oppose the designs and plans of Providence, and cannot "come to good." The order and subordination observable in the physical, animal and human world, show that some are formed for higher, others for lower stations—the few to command, the many to obey. We conclude that about nineteen out of every twenty individuals have "a natural and inalienable right" to be taken care of and protected; to have guardians, trustees, husbands, or masters; in other words, they have a natural and inalienable right to be slaves. The one in twenty are as clearly born or educated, or some way fitted for command and liberty. Not to make them rulers or masters, is as great a violation of natural right, as not to make slaves of the mass. A very little individuality is useful and necessary to society,—much of it begets discord, chaos and anarchy....

Chapter X. Our Best Witnesses and Masters In the Art of War...

[T]he actual leaders and faithful exponents of abolition... [have as] their object... not only to abolish Southern slavery, but to abolish also, or greatly to modify, the relations of husband and wife, parent and child, the institution of private property of all kinds, but especially separate ownership of lands, and the institution of Christian churches as now existing in America. We further charge, that whilst actively engaged in attempts to abolish Southern slavery, they are busy, with equal activity and more promise of success, in attempts to upset and reorganize society at the North....

[W]e are actuated by no feelings of personal ill will or disrespect. We admire them all, and have had kindly intercourse and correspondence with some of them. They are historical characters, who would seek notoriety in order to further their schemes of setting the world to rights. We have no doubt of their sincere philanthropy, and as little doubt, that they are only "paving hell with good intentions." We speak figuratively.... Indeed, we should be ungrateful and discourteous in the extreme, if we did not entertain kindly remembrance and make gentlemanly return for the generous reception and treatment we received, especially from leading abolitionists, when we went north to personate Satan by defending Slavery....

Mr. Garrison... heads the extreme wing of the Socialist, Infidel, Woman's Right,... and Abolition party, who are called Garrisonians. He edits the *Liberator*, which is conducted with an ability worthy of a better cause. He and his followers seem to admit that the Bible and the Constitution recognize and guarantee Slavery, and therefore denounce both, and propose disunion and no priests or churches, as measures to attain abolition. Mr. Garrison usually presides at their meetings, and we infer, in part, their principles and doctrines, from the materials that compose those meetings. A Wise-Woman will rise and utter a philippic [bitter attack] against Marriage, the Bible, and the Constitution,—and will be followed by negro [Charles Lenox] Remond, who "spits upon Washington".... These Garrisonians are as intellectual men as any in the nation. They lead the Black Republican party, and control the politicians. Yet are they deadly enemies of Northern as well as of Southern institutions.

Now, gentlemen, all of you are philosophers, and most zealous philanthropists, and have for years been roaring, at the top of your voice, to the Oi Polloi [rabble] rats, that the old crazy edifice of society, in which they live, is no longer fit for human dwelling, and is imminently dangerous. The rats have taken you at your word, and are rushing headlong... into every hole that promises shelter—into "any port in a storm." Some join the Rappists and Shakers [religious sects]..., many more... to villages in the far West...; and a select few to the salons of Free Love.... But the greater number are waiting (very impatiently)...for Mr. Garrison...to inaugurate their Millenium.

Why, Gentlemen!...[W]hy none of this panic, confusion and flight, in Slave Society? Are we suffering, and yet contented? Is our house tumbling about our heads, and we sitting in conscious security amidst the impending ruin? No! No! Our edifice is one that never did fall, and never will fall; for Nature's plastic hand reared it, supports it, and will forever sustain it.

Have we not shewn, in this single chapter, that the North has as much to apprehend from abolition as the South, and that it is time for conservatives every where to unite in efforts to suppress and extinguish it?...

[After devoting ten chapters to aspects of English, French, and European history and economics stretching back to the Protestant Reformation of the sixteenth century, Fitzhugh returns to contemporary America.]

Chapter XX. The Family

All modern philosophy converges to a single point— the overthrow of all government, the substitution of the untrammelled "Sovereignty of the Individual," for the Sovereignty of Society, and the inauguration of anarchy. First domestic slavery, next religious institutions, then separate property, then political government, and, finally, family government and family relations, are to be swept away. This is the distinctly avowed programme of all able abolitionists and socialists; and towards this end the doctrines and the practices of the weakest and most timid among them tend....

Love and veneration for the family is with us not only a principle, but probably a prejudice and a weakness. We were never two weeks at a time from under the family roof, until we had passed middle life, and now that our years almost number half a century, we have never been from home for an interval of two months. And our historical reading, as well as our habits of life, may have unfitted us to appreciate...communist and fusion [several political parties backing the same candidate] theories....In attempting to vindicate and justify the ways of God and Nature, against the progressiveness of Black Republicanism in America, and Red Republicanism in Europe, we would forewarn the reader that we are a prejudiced witness. We are the enthusiastic admirer of the social relations exhibited in the [biblical] histories of Abraham, Isaac and Jacob. The social relations established in Deuteronomy; and 25th chapter Leviticus, and as practiced by the Jews to this day, elicit our unfeigned admiration and approval. Moses is with us the Prince of Legislators, and the twenty-fifth Leviticus the best of political platforms. The purity of the family seems to be his paramount object....

Abolition contemplates the total overthrow of the Family and all other existing social, moral, religious and governing institutions....The Family is threatened, and all men North or South who love and revere it, should be up and a doing.

Chapter XXI. Negro Slavery

Until the lands of America are appropriated by a few, population becomes dense, competition among laborers active, employment uncertain, and wages low, the personal liberty of all the whites will continue to be a blessing. We have vast unsettled territories; population may cease to increase, or increase slowly, as in most countries, and many centuries may elapse before the question will be practically suggested, whether slavery to capital be preferable to slavery to human masters. But the negro has neither energy nor enterprise, and, even in our sparser population, finds, with his improvident habits, that his liberty is a curse to himself, and a greater curse to the society around him. These considerations, and others equally obvious, have induced the South to attempt to defend negro slavery as an exceptional institution, admitting, nay asserting; that slavery, in the general or in the abstract, is morally wrong, and against common right. With singular inconsistency, after making this admission, which admits away the authority of the Bible, of profane history, and of the almost universal practice of mankind—they turn round and attempt to bolster up the cause of negro slavery by these very exploded authorities. If we mean not to repudiate all divine, and almost all human authority in favor of slavery, we must vindicate that institution in the abstract.

To insist that a status of society, which has been almost universal, and which is expressly and continually justified by Holy Writ, is its natural, normal, and necessary status, under the ordinary circumstances, is on its face a plausible and probable proposition. To insist on less, is to yield our cause, and to give up our religion; for if white slavery be morally wrong, be a violation of natural rights, the Bible cannot be true. Human and divine authority do seem in the general to concur, in establishing the expediency of having masters and slaves of different races.... [It is a] general truth that master and slave should be of different national descent. In some respects, the wider the difference the better, as the slave will feel less mortified by his position. In other respects, it may be that too wide a difference hardens the hearts and brutalizes the feelings of both master and slave. The civilized man hates the savage, and the savage returns the hatred with interest. Hence, West India slavery, of newly caught negroes, is not a very humane, affectionate or civilizing institution. Virginia negroes have become moral and intelligent. They love their master and his family, and the attachment is reciprocated. Still, we like the idle, but intelligent house-servants, better than the hard-used, but stupid outhands [field hands]; and we like the mulatto better than the negro; yet the negro is generally more affectionate, contented and faithful.

The world at large looks on negro slavery as much the worst form of slavery; because it is only acquainted with West India slavery. Abolition never arose till negro slavery was instituted; and now abolition is only directed against negro slavery. There is no philanthropic crusade attempting to set free the white slaves of Eastern Europe and of Asia. The world, then, is prepared for the defence of slavery in the abstract—it is prejudiced only against negro slavery. These prejudices were in their origin well founded. The Slave Trade, the horrors of the Middle Passage, and West India slavery, were enough to rouse the most torpid philanthropy.

But our Southern slavery has become a benign and protective institution, and our negroes are confessedly better off than any free laboring population in the world.

How can we contend that white slavery is wrong, whilst all the great body of free laborers are starving; and slaves, white or black, throughout the world, are enjoying comfort?

We write in the cause of Truth and Humanity, and will not play the advocate for master or for slave.

The aversion to negroes, the antipathy of race, is much greater at the North than at the South; and it is very probable that this antipathy to the person of the negro, is confounded with or generates hatred of the institution with which he is usually connected. Hatred to slavery is very generally little more than hatred of negroes.

There is one strong argument in favor of negro slavery over all other slavery: that he, being unfitted for the mechanic arts, for trade, and all skillful pursuits, leaves those pursuits to be carried on by the whites; and does not bring all industry into disrepute, as in Greece and Rome, where the slaves were not only the artists and mechanics, but also the merchants.

Whilst, as a general and abstract question, negro slavery has no other claims over other forms of slavery, except that from inferiority, or rather peculiarity, of race, almost all negroes require masters, whilst only the children, the women, the very weak, poor, and ignorant, &c., among the whites, need some protective and governing relation of this kind....

Chapter XXII. The Strength of Weakness

An unexplored moral world stretches out before us, and invites our investigation; but neither our time, our abilities, nor the character of our work will permit us to do more than glance at its loveliness.

It is pleasing, however, to turn from the world of political economy, in which "might makes right," and strength of mind and of body are employed to oppress and exact from the weak, to the other and better, and far more numerous world, in which weakness rules, clad in the armor of affection and benevolence. It is delightful to retire from the outer world, with its competitions, rivalries, envyings, jealousies, and selfish war of the wits, to the bosom of the family, where the only tyrant is the infant—the greatest slave the master of the house hold. You feel at once that you have exchanged the keen air of selfishness, for the mild atmosphere of benevolence. Each one prefers the good of others to his own, and finds most happiness in sacrificing selfish pleasures, and ministering to others' enjoyments. The wife, the husband, the parent, the child, the son, the brother and the sister, usually act towards each other on scriptural principles. The infant, in its capricious dominion over mother, father, brothers and sisters, exhibits, in strongest colors, the "strength of weakness," the power of affection. The wife and daughters are more carefully attended by the father, than the sons, because they are weaker and elicit more of his affection.

The dependent exercise, because of their dependence, as much control over their superiors, in most things, as those superiors exercise over them. Thus, and thus only, can conditions be equalized. This constitutes practical equality of rights, enforced not by human, but by divine law. Our hearts bleed at the robbing of a bird's nest; and the little birds, because they are weak, subdue our strength and command our care. We love and cherish the rose, and sympathize with the lily, which some wanton boy has bruised and broken. Our faithful dog shares our affections, and we will risk our lives to redress injustice done to him.

Man is not all selfish. "Might does not always make right." Within the family circle, the law of love prevails, not that of selfishness.

But, besides wife and children, brothers and sisters, dogs, horses, birds and flowers—slaves, also, belong to the family circle. Does their common humanity, their abject weakness and dependence, their great value, their ministering to our wants in childhood, manhood, sickness, old age, cut them off from that affection which everything else in the family elicits? No; the interests of master and slave are bound up together, and each in his appropriate sphere naturally endeavors to promote the happiness of the other.

The humble and obedient slave exercises more or less control over the most brutal and hardhearted master. It is an invariable law of nature, that weakness and dependence are elements of strength, and generally sufficiently limit that universal despotism, observable throughout human and animal nature. The moral and physical world is but a series of subordinations, and the more perfect the subordination, the greater the harmony and the happiness. Inferior and superior act and re-act on each other through agencies and media too delicate and subtle for human apprehensions; yet, looking to usual results, man should be willing to leave to God what God only can regulate. Human law cannot beget benevolence, affection, maternal and paternal love; nor can it supply their places; but it may, by breaking up the ordinary relations of human beings, stop and disturb the current of these finer feelings of our nature. It may abolish slavery; but it can never create between the capitalist and the laborer, between the employer and employed, the kind and affectionate relations that usually exist between master and slave.

Chapter XXV. In What Anti-Slavery Ends…

The materials, as well as the proceedings of the infidel, woman's rights, negro's rights, free-everything and anti-every school,…show that they…are busy…loosening the whole frame of society, and preparing for the glorious advent of Free Love and No-Government. All the Infidel and Abolition papers in the North betray a similar tendency….Probably half the Abolitionists at the North expect a great social revolution soon to occur by the advent of the Millenium. If they would patiently await that event, instead of attempting to get it up themselves, their delusions, however ridiculous, might at least be innocuous….They are…intent and busy in pulling down the priesthood, and abolishing or dividing all property—seeing that whether the denouement be Free Love or a Millenium, the destruction of all existing human relations and human institutions is pre-requisite to their full fruition.…

The Political Economists, Let Alone, for a fair fight, for universal rivalry, antagonism, competition and cannibalism. They say, the eating up the weaker members of society, the killing them out by capital and competition, will improve the breed of men and benefit society. They foresee the consequences of their doctrine, and are consistent.…The Socialists promise that when society is wholly disintegrated and dissolved, by inculcating good principles and "singing fraternity over it," all men will co-operate, love, and help one another.

They place men in positions of equality, rivalry, and antagonism, which must result in extreme selfishness of conduct, and yet propose this system as a cure for selfishness. To us their reasonings seem absurd.…

Chapter XXVI. Christian Morality Impracticable In Free Society—But the Natural Morality of Slave Society

It is strange that theories, self-evidently true so soon as suggested, remain undiscovered for centuries. What more evident, obvious, and axiomatic, than that equals must from necessity be rivals, antagonists, competitors, and enemies. Self-preservation, the first law of human and animal nature, makes this selfish course of action essential to preserve existence. It is almost equally obvious, that in the natural, social, or family state, unselfishness, or the preference of others' good and happiness, is the dictate of nature and policy. Nature impels the father and husband to self-abnegation and self-denial to promote the happiness of wife and children, because his reflected enjoyments will be a thousand times greater than any direct pleasure he can derive by stinting or maltreating them. Their misery and their complaints do much more to render him wretched than what he has denied them can compensate for. Wife and children, too, see and feel that in denying themselves and promoting the happiness of the head of the family, they pursue true policy, and are most sensibly selfish when they seem most unselfish. Especially, however, is it true with slaves and masters, that to "do as they would be done by" is mutually beneficial. Good treatment and proper discipline renders the slave happier, healthier, more valuable, grateful, and contented. Obedience, industry and loyalty on the part of the slave, increases the master's ability and disposition to protect and take care of him. The interests of all the members of a natural family, slaves included, are identical. Selfishness finds no place, because nature, common feelings and self-interest dictate to all that it is their true interest "to love their neighbor as themselves," and "to do as they would be done by,"—at least, within the precincts of the family. To throw off into the world wife, children, and slaves, would injure, not benefit them. To neglect to punish children or slaves when they deserved it, would not be to do as we would be done by. Such punishment is generally the highest reach of self-abnegation and self-control. 'Tis easy and agreeable to be indulgent and remiss—hard to exact and enforce duty. Severe disciplinarians are the best officers, teachers, parents, and masters, and most revered and loved by their subordinates. They sacrifice their time and their feelings to duty, and for the ultimate good of others. Easy, lax, indulgent men are generally selfish and sensual, and justly forfeit the respect and affection of those whom they neglect to punish, because to do so would disturb their Epicurean [luxurious] repose. Christian morality is neither difficult nor unnatural where dependent, family, and slave relations exist, and Christian morality was preached and only intended for such.

The whole morale of free society is, "Every man, woman and child for himself and herself." Slavery in every form must be abolished. Wives must have distinct, separate, and therefore antagonistic and conflicting interests from their husbands, and children must as soon as possible be remitted to the rights of manhood. Is it not passing strange, wonderful, that such men…did not see that their world of universal liberty was a world of universal selfishness, discord, competition, rivalry, and war of the wits.…But the family, including slaves, which the Abolitionists would destroy, has been almost universal, and is therefore natural. Christian morality is the natural morality in slave society, and slave society is the only natural society.…In such society it is natural for men to love one another. The ordinary relations of men are not competitive and antagonistic as in free-society; and selfishness is not general, but exceptionable. Duty to self is the first of duties: free society makes it the only duty. Man is not naturally selfish or bad, for he is naturally social. Free society dissociates him, and makes him bad and selfish from necessity.

It is said in Scripture, that it is harder for a rich man to enter the kingdom of heaven than for a camel to pass through the eye of a needle. We are no theologian; but do know from history and observation that wealthy men who are sincere and devout Christians in free society, feel at a loss what to do with their wealth, so as not to make it an instrument of oppression and wrong.…If you endow colleges, you rear up cunning,

voracious exploitators to devour the poor. If you give it to tradesmen or land owners, 'tis still an additional instrument, always employed to oppress laborers. If you give it to the really needy, you too often encourage idleness, and increase the burdens of the working poor who support every body. We cannot possibly see but one safe way to invest wealth, and that is to buy slaves with it, whose conduct you can control, and be sure that your charity is not misapplied, and mischievous.…

Chapter XXVII. Slavery—Its Effects On the Free

Beaten at every other quarter, we learn that a distinguished writer at the North, is about to be put forward by the Abolitionists, to prove that the influence of slavery is deleterious on the whites who own no slaves.

Now, at first view it elevates those whites; for it makes them not the bottom of society, as at the North—not the menials, the hired day laborer, the work scavengers and scullions [lowest servants]—but privileged citizens, like Greek and Roman citizens, with a numerous class far beneath them. In slave society, one white man does not lord it over another; for all are equal in privilege, if not in wealth; and the poorest would not become a menial—hold your horse and then extend his hand or his hat for a gratuity, were you to proffer him the wealth of the Indies. The menial, the exposed and laborious, and the disgraceful occupations, are all filled by slaves. But filled they must be by some one, and in free society, half of its members are employed in occupations that are not considered or treated as respectable. Our slaves till the land, do the coarse and hard labor on our roads and canals, sweep our streets, cook our food, brush our boots, wait on our tables, hold our horses, do all hard work, and fill all menial offices. Your freemen at the North do the same work and fill the same offices. The only difference is, we love our slaves, and we are ready to defend, assist and protect them; you hate and fear your white servants, and never fail, as a moral duty, to screw down their wages to the lowest, and to starve their families, if possible, as evidence of your thrift, economy and management—the only English and Yankee virtues.

In free society, miscalled freemen fulfill all the offices of slaves for less wages than slaves, and are infinitely less liked and cared for by their superiors than slaves. Does this elevate them and render them happy?

The trades, the professions, the occupations that pay well, and whose work is light, is reserved for freemen in slave society. Does this depress them?

The doctor, the lawyer, the mechanic, the dentist, the merchant, the overseer, every trade and profession, in fact, live from the proceeds of slave labor at the South. They divide the profits with the owner of the slaves. He has nothing to pay them except what his slaves make. But you Yankees and Englishmen more than divide the profits—you take the lion's share. You make more money from our cotton, and tobacco, and sugar, and indigo, and wheat, and corn, and rice, than we make ourselves. You live by slave labor—would perish without it—yet you abuse it. Cut off England and New England from the South American, East and West India and our markets, from which to buy their food, and in which to sell their manufactures, and they would starve at once. You live by our slave labor. It elevates your whites as well as ours, by confining them, in a great degree, to skillful, well-paying, light and intellectual employments—and it feeds and clothes them. Abolish slavery, and you will suffer vastly more than we, because we have all the lands of the South, and can *command* labor as you do, and a genial soil and climate, that require less labor. But while in the absence of slavery, we could support ourselves, we should cease to support you. We would neither send you food and clothing, nor buy your worse than useless notions....

Chapter XXXVI. Warning to the North...

We warn the North, that every one of the leading Abolitionists is agitating the negro slavery question merely as a means to attain ulterior ends, and those ends nearer home. They would not spend so much time and money for the mere sake of the negro or his master, about whom they care little. But they know that men once fairly committed to negro slavery agitation—once committed to the sweeping principle, "that man being a moral agent, accountable to God for his actions, should not have those actions controlled and directed by the will of another," are, in effect, committed to Socialism and Communism, to the most ultra doctrines...—to no private property, no church, no law, no government,—to free love, free lands, free women and free churches.

There is no middle ground—not an inch of ground of any sort, between the doctrines which we hold and those which Mr. Garrison holds. If slavery, either white or black, be wrong in principle or practice, then is Mr. Garrison right—then is all human government wrong.

Socialism, not Abolition, is the real object of Black Republicanism. The North, not the South, the true battle-ground....

CHAPTER 18

President Lincoln Articulates America

"Let us strive on to finish the work we are in"

P resident Abraham Lincoln "is tall and strong," said Frederick Douglass in the spring of 1862, "but he is not done growing." The former slave and leading abolitionist (see Chapter 16) was not referring here to the president's height, but to a hope that Lincoln finally would realize it was time to end slavery. Other observers, then and since, also have remarked upon Lincoln's "enormous capacity for growth," which was, writes historian Eric Foner, "the essence of Lincoln's greatness."[1]

The readings here help you chart that growth, to see how far Lincoln changed his mind about American facts of life like race and slavery, state and nation. This chapter is different from others in *American Conversations*: It contains nine texts, spanning the last decade of Lincoln's life. Together they comprise a moving picture (in both senses of the word) of how one man grappled with the meaning of *America*, and of *American*.

No one can come to Lincoln free of the aura, even the halo, that envelopes him. From Mount Rushmore to Washington, D.C., from the penny to the five-dollar bill, Lincoln and his legacy are everywhere. He is, writes James McPherson, "our most cherished historical possession," so cherished indeed that another Lincoln expert, David Donald, calls the veneration of him a "cult" that is "almost an American religion." "More has been written in the English language about Abraham Lincoln," McPherson observes, "than about anyone else except Jesus of Nazareth and William Shakespeare"— perhaps 14,000 books in all (and counting), including *Lincoln Never Smoked a Cigarette* and *Abraham Lincoln on the Coming of the Caterpillar Tractor.* No wonder everyone tries, in Donald's phrase, to "Get Right with Lincoln." Republicans and Democrats, Communists and conservatives, brewers and temperance advocates, the Ku Klux Klan and Martin Luther King, Jr.—all claim kinship with this American icon. Meanwhile other enthusiasts collect everything from Lincoln's chamber pot to his wife's underwear, and groups across the country—Boston and Washington, Fort Wayne and Chicago, Seattle and Los Angeles—meet to share their passion for Lincoln's life and times.[2]

All of the attention, all of the devotion, can obscure more than it reveals. One hidden feature of Lincoln's story is what he himself called "the blues." "[A]s a young man," writes Douglas L. Wilson, "he suffered from periods of deep depression and moments of suicidal desperation." Law and politics brought him fame and fortune, but Lincoln still struggled, enduring bouts of deep melancholy bordering on despair.[3]

Another dimension of Lincoln's life that often gets overlooked is the very idea that he could change. Monuments of marble and granite do not change; neither do copper pennies and $5 bills. But Lincoln did. Indeed, he had already undergone profound changes before Frederick Douglass in 1862 hoped for still more.

Born in 1809 to poor frontier folk, he lived a hardscrabble existence for most of his first thirty years as his family moved from Kentucky to Indiana and finally to Illinois. Abandoning farm and family when he came of age, to make ends meet Lincoln tried everything from selling firewood to clerking in a store to surveying, from taking a flat-boat to New Orleans to blacksmithing to running a store. Nothing worked out until he hit upon law and politics as an outlet for his abilities and ambitions.

Those abilities, those ambitions, were evident from the very first. In a frontier world where books were scarce and schools scarcer (his mother was illiterate; his father could barely scrawl a signature), this boy was widely known as "a Constant and vora-cious reader." Before or after chores, he could be found atop a woodpile or (his favorite position) stretched out on the floor, reading so much that some folks wondered if, with all that studying, "he would craze himself."[4]

Among the works Lincoln picked up were some that will be familiar: the Bible (Chapter 1); Benjamin Franklin's *Autobiography* (Chapter 6); Thomas Paine's *Common Sense* (Chapter 7); and Mason Locke Weems's *The Life of Washington* (Chapter 10). Like many young men of his day, he followed Franklin's formula for getting ahead, and he admired Washington as "the Greatest of all." Like Franklin, Lincoln did more than simply read: He reread books until he had memorized them, copied favorite passages, even put them into his own words to hone his writing skills. Aware that a successful man had to be an orator as well as a writer, Lincoln joined debating clubs reminiscent of Franklin's "junto" a century before and the East Baltimore Mental Improvement Society Frederick Douglass helped start. (He also pored over *The Columbian Orator*, the very treatise on public speaking that Douglass was reading at about the same time. Some scholars note that the two shared a "rhetorical bond"; do you see a resemblance?[5])

All the hard work paid off: In the 1830s Lincoln won election to the Illinois legislature and in the 1840s to the U.S. Congress; by 1850, back in Illinois, he was a leading political figure in the state and a prosperous lawyer. But president? Here, too, the Lincoln legend hides how preposterous this idea seemed to many—including the man himself. "I must, in candor, say I do not think myself fit for the Presidency," he admitted in 1859. False modesty? Hardly. Lincoln's political experience consisted of a few elections to the state assembly twenty years before, one forgotten term in Congress more than a decade earlier, and unsuccessful campaigns for the U.S. Senate in 1854 and 1858.[6]

Nonetheless, the speeches Lincoln gave in the 1850s—particularly debates with his Democratic opponent, the incumbent Stephen A. Douglas, in the 1858 senate campaign—made the untested politician a leading figure in the newly founded Republican Party and a likely candidate for president in 1860. His election to the presidency did nothing to banish people's doubts, however. Here, too, the halo obscures how bitterly many Americans—North as well as South—opposed, even despised Lincoln. "[O]bscene clown" and "orangutan," a "half-witted," "unmentionable disease," he "had Negro blood in his veins." Men of his own party called him a "timid and ignorant" "political coward," an "unfit," "awful, woeful ass" who was "shattered, dazed, utterly foolish." "I do wish A. Lincoln told fewer dirty stories," admitted one supporter. "I am personally attached to the President," sighed an Illinois friend in 1864, "and have…tried to…make him respectable," but "I fear he is a failure." Many Americans agreed: Lincoln won just 39% of the national vote in 1860; four years later, with only Northerners casting ballots, no less than 45% opposed him.[7]

That Lincoln, having risen from poverty to the presidency, then managed to defeat his enemies, North and South, is testimony not to divine favor but to his ability. Steadfast in pursuing his goals—stopping slavery's expansion and, when war came, preserving the Union—he was flexible about how to reach those goals. A shrewd politician and a painstaking writer, he had a way with words, a gift for conveying the meaning of the terrible conflict and of the nation that conflict sought to save, and a growing awareness of "how effective he could be" in swaying public opinion by the power of his prose. The documents here—if you can "resist our modern impatience and read slowly," as one Lincoln student puts it—help you to see his skills, to understand how Americans of all persuasions could later claim him as their own, and to consider if Abraham Lincoln indeed "was not done growing."[8]

SECTION ONE: THE ROAD TO WASHINGTON, 1854–1860

In the fall of 1854, Lincoln was what he had been for some two decades: a lawyer and politician of little renown. In the fall of 1860, he was president-elect of the United States. The speeches in this section are important landmarks on that remarkable path from Springfield, Illinois, to Washington, D.C. They represent Lincoln's deepening concern with the nation's course, concern arising out of a series of events that convinced him—and many others—that America was on the road to ruin.

The first of these events was the 1854 Kansas-Nebraska Act, which Senator Douglas had authored even though he knew it would cause "a hell of a storm."[9] The gale arose because the act repealed the Missouri Compromise, to many a sacred compact vital to maintaining the balance of power between free and slave states, thereby preserving the Union. That 1820 arrangement had prohibited slavery in western federal territory above Missouri's southern boundary. Now Douglas, eager to develop those lands (and to run railroads there from Chicago, a huge benefit to his state), worked out a deal with Southerners: In exchange for a vote in favor of the northern railroad terminus, the Kansas-Nebraska lands would become either free or slave, depending upon how people who moved there voted; "popular sovereignty" would decide.

Elections might seem fair enough, but Lincoln was not alone in feeling "thunderstruck and stunned." A vast stretch of land that for a generation had been thought forever free might now well become (as antislavery congressmen put it) "a dreary region of despotism, inhabited by masters and slaves." Should that happen, of course, Northern states would be hemmed in by slaveholders and outvoted in Congress, endangering the cherished ideology of free labor—a belief in the virtues of hard work that Weems and Franklin (among others) had celebrated. That frightening prospect not only brought Lincoln back into politics (Document 1) in a "breakthrough speech" that was "the keystone of Lincoln's public career," it also gave birth two years later to a new political party, the Republicans, dedicated to stopping slavery's expansion. *What next?* Would masters haul their slaves to every corner of the land, crowding out free laborers and freedom itself?[10]

That nightmare seemed closer to reality three years later, when a Supreme Court dominated by Southerners handed down its decision in the *Dred Scott* case. Scott, a slave, had been brought north by his master some years earlier—first to Illinois, then to Minnesota Territory—before being taken back to Missouri. Scott sued to obtain his freedom, arguing that Illinois was a free state and Minnesota a free territory. The Court not only found against Scott, it went on to decree that African Americans "had no rights which the white man was bound to respect," that they were omitted from both the Declaration of Independence and the Constitution, and that Congress could not prohibit slavery in any federal domain. Once again the Illinois politician was profoundly troubled: "It would be hard," writes James Oakes, "to name anything in Lincoln's political life that made him angrier than *Dred Scott.*"[11] Now a leading voice in the Republican Party, he delivered a speech to denounce the decision and forecast a bleak future (Document 2).

That address, like the 1854 speech against the Kansas-Nebraska Act, was directed at Douglas, who had vigorously defended the act and the ruling. Both times, Lincoln was positioning himself for a Senate race against Douglas, a man whose political prowess and success Lincoln had long admired—and envied. Documents 3–5 give you a taste of that legendary 1858 election contest. The first of them, since famous as his "House Divided" speech, is an excerpt of Lincoln's words to Illinois Republicans when they nominated him to face Douglas. (Even Lincoln's own friends and advisers thought it a "d—n fool utterance" that was "too far in advance of the times"; can you see why?) Documents 4 and 5 give some of his words at two of the seven debates he and Douglas had during the campaign. Some say that though Lincoln lost the *battle* (the 1858 Senate election), he won the *war* (the presidency in 1860; Douglas was also a candidate), because his speeches brought him national attention.[12]

Opinions on Lincoln's ability as an orator varied. Some listeners found his accent strange, his voice shrill, and his gestures awkward, especially at the beginning when he was invariably nervous. But if he was no Frederick Douglass or Angelina Grimké, many found him compelling once he relaxed; his voice "became harmonious—melodious—musical," and the words flowed, leaving an audience "spell bound." Lincoln chose those words with care (he was never good at impromptu speeches), always seeking the one, his law partner recalled, that contained "the exact coloring, power, and shape of his ideas." Other admirers point out that his high voice carried far, and that Lincoln was "an expert raconteur and mimic" who "knew a good deal about rhythmic delivery and meaningful inflections"—and about how to use humor and humility, stories and jokes, to make his point.[13]

The points Lincoln fixed upon again and again in these speeches were two: what the Founding Fathers intended America to be and (related to that) what place slavery and African Americans had in the nation's past, present, and future. On both subjects, he joined a conversation that had been going on for decades, carried forward not just by Thomas Jefferson and Thomas Paine but by Angelina Grimké and George Fitzhugh, Frederick Douglass and William Apess. How do his views on American history and America's destiny, on slavery and on people of color, compare with theirs?

As you tackle these questions, it might be comforting to know that experts disagree on the answers! The disagreement stems from the fact that Lincoln was careful about what he said and how he said it. Scholars have noted that Lincoln was famous for "clever evasions and key silences" (even friends called him "the most reticent—Secretive man I Ever Saw—or Expect to See"), that he "was especially indirect and hard to interpret on the subject of slavery," and that for much of his life "Lincoln said even less about blacks than he did about slavery."[14]

Certainly Lincoln's defenders have plenty of evidence. "I am naturally anti-slavery," the president wrote in 1864. "If slavery is not wrong, nothing is wrong. I cannot remember when I did not so think, and feel." As early as 1837 he joined another state assemblyman to declare "that the institution of slavery is founded on both injustice and bad policy," and (with just four others, out of eighty) "he voted against a set of resolutions condemning abolitionism and defending the constitutionality of slavery." Visiting Kentucky four years later, Lincoln crossed paths with a dozen slaves bound for sale in the deep South. Chained "together like so many fish upon a trot-line," they had been "separated forever from the scenes of their childhood, their friends, their fathers and mothers, and brother and sisters, and many of them, from their wives and children." The "sight," he remembered more than a decade later, "was a continual torment to me." By the mid-1850s he was calling slavery a "cancer" and a "poison," "a great national crime" to be "resisted as a wrong." Having read George Fitzhugh's work, Lincoln could not help remarking that "[a]lthough volume upon volume is written to prove slavery a very good thing, we never hear of the man who wishes to take the good of it, *by being a slave himself.*"[15]

Defenders of Lincoln further insist that the words you read below must be understood in the context of those times and that place. Remember that Alexis de Tocqueville (Chapter 11) found that "the prejudice of race appears to be stronger in the states that have abolished slavery than in those where it still exists; and nowhere is it so intolerant as in those states where servitude has never been known"—states like Illinois. Lincoln courted votes where some parts were, as one scholar points out, "farther south than most of the [slave] states of Kentucky and Virginia." Another reports that in Lincoln's day Illinois law "forbade interracial marriage, kept blacks off juries and out of the state militia, banned black testimony against whites, [and] denied blacks the vote." Accenting that antipathy, in 1848 70% of Illinois voters endorsed a constitutional amendment prohibiting free blacks from so much as entering the state, an amendment that went into effect in 1853—just before Lincoln resumed his political career. No wonder, his admirers say, Lincoln said some of the things he did.[16]

Those critical of Lincoln also have plenty of evidence, however. After all, his 1837 attack on slavery as an "injustice" went on to condemn "the promulgation of abolition doctrines" because such views tend "rather to increase than to abate its evils." Similarly, his report of that 1841 encounter with chained African Americans in Kentucky, penned *at the time*, said nothing about his "continual torment," mentioning instead the slaves' apparent contentment. It is also true that Lincoln, employing what James Oakes terms "strategic racism" to win followers, told "darky jokes in Negro dialect" and sometimes used "racial epithets."[17]

Keep in mind these contexts, contradictions, and contentions while you read Lincoln's views. One way to sort through those views is simply to ask: What would George Fitzhugh have said in response? Or Frederick Douglass?

SECTION TWO: THE ROAD TO EMANCIPATION, 1861–1865

Before Lincoln became president, he admitted that "[i]f all earthly power were given me, I should not know what to do" about slavery. In 1860, American voters gave Lincoln not all earthly power, but a considerable share of it. While at first he still did not know what to do, during the Civil War he figured it out: The institution of slavery, embedded in American soil for more than two hundred years, would be uprooted in just four.[18]

That was not Lincoln's plan when he won the presidency. He believed, as he had said in the 1850s, that the Constitution forbade the federal government from killing or wounding slavery in any state where it already lived. He wanted only to forbid slavery in the west, federal territory where the national government had sole jurisdiction. Perhaps this "conservative" stance explains the president-elect's surprise when, shortly after the returns were in, one Southern state after another seceded from the Union and formed the Confederate States of America. Lincoln was convinced that secession was a bluff, the work of a few troublemakers in a sea of Southerners loyal to the Union. Be patient, he counseled; the whole thing will blow over. Hence Lincoln said little in the months between the November election and his inauguration the following March (presidents did not take office the January after their election until 1937).

By the time he arrived in Washington, D.C., however, the crisis had deepened, not disappeared. Maryland, a slave state, might well join the secessionists, leaving the national capital surrounded by enemies. Assassination plots abounded. In an age when presidents had nothing like the protection they get today, sharpshooters dotted the rooftops and other soldiers were everywhere as Lincoln made his way to the capitol to take the oath of office and deliver his first speech as president (Document 6).

That speech got mixed reviews. Southern newspapers claimed that it "inaugurates civil war," while in New York City it was said that Southern sympathizers there "approved and applauded it as pacific and likely to prevent collision." If Republican newspapers called it "able, firm, [and] conciliatory," "strong, straightforward[,] and manly," Northern Democrats dismissed it as "rambling" and "loose-jointed," full of "obscurely stated qualifications" that muddled his meaning. Where do you stand in this range of opinion? Can you see why Frederick Douglass was deeply disappointed? Do you detect any parallels between this text and the Declaration of Independence (Chapter 7), which sought not to *stop* a secession movement, as Lincoln did, but to *start* one? How might the men who wrote the Declaration have responded if Britain's King George III had delivered a speech like this one?[19]

For a year and more after the inauguration, the national crisis went from bad to worse. Confederate armies pounded Union troops at almost every turn. Northern morale was low. England and France seemed about to recognize the Confederacy as an independent nation. For a year and more, too, Lincoln for the most part maintained the public silence that he had kept since the election. Hard as it might be to imagine, in those days presidents rarely addressed the public. Though Lincoln eventually would begin to change this, to use his rhetorical gifts to advance his cause—the Gettysburg Address is one example (Document 8)—early in his presidency he largely labored out of the public eye.

For a year and more, too, that labor was devoted to saving the Union, not abolishing slavery. Lincoln's hope for putting down the rebellion rested on a fragile coalition of Republicans, Northern Democrats, politicians in key border states (Maryland, Kentucky, Missouri) who opposed secession, and Unionists he still believed abounded in the deep South. A war to save the Union would keep these unlikely allies together; a war to end slavery would not. When army commanders in the field like John C. Frémont took it upon themselves to set runaway slaves free, Lincoln overruled them; this is "a war for a great national idea, the Union," he insisted, "and…General Frémont should not have dragged the Negro into it."[20]

But "the Negro" would not stay out of it. Slaves by the thousands ran to Union lines, refusing to be returned to bondage. In the North, Frederick Douglass and others pressed for emancipation. Meanwhile the border states seemed safely in the Union camp, those phantom loyalists in the South could not be found, and slave labor was helping the rebel cause by freeing Southern white men to trounce Union armies. By the summer of 1862, things had changed. "My paramount object in this struggle *is* to save the Union," the president wrote to a newspaper that summer, "and is *not* either to save or to destroy slavery. If I could save the Union without freeing *any* slave I would do it, and if I could save it by freeing *all* the slaves I would do it; and if I could save it by freeing some and leaving others alone I would also do that." By then, however, he had become convinced that "[w]e must free the slaves or ourselves be subdued."[21]

But how? It turned out to be a slow process. Lincoln told his Cabinet in July that he had decided to proclaim emancipation in rebel states. They convinced him to wait until after Union troops won a battle or it would "be viewed as…a cry for help," "our last *shriek* on the retreat." When something like victory came in September at the Battle of Antietam (where Union forces halted a Confederate advance into Maryland), Lincoln issued a proclamation saying that emancipation would go into effect if the rebellion did not cease by year's end.[22]

When it finally came, the proclamation (Document 7) disappointed many. Can you explain that disappointment? Can you see why Frederick Douglass nonetheless termed it "the greatest event in our nation's history"? In Boston on January 1, 1863, he anxiously waited with other African Americans for word that Lincoln had signed it. When at last the news came in by telegraph after 11 p.m., pandemonium ensued. "I never saw Joy before," Douglass remembered a month later. "Men, women, young and old, were up; hats and bonnets were in the air."[23]

Yet 1863, which began in celebration, drew to a close with neither emancipation nor peace in sight. Union troops had won spectacular victories in July, gaining control of the Mississippi River by taking Vicksburg and stopping Robert E. Lee's invasion of the North at Gettysburg. Nonetheless, that fall the war ground on. Some (including some in Lincoln's own administration) were talking of a negotiated peace and "a return to 'the Union as it was.' " The president, meanwhile, was looking for ways to "explain to the American people the significance of the huge war into which they had stumbled."[24]

One opportunity came in early November. Officials at Gettysburg had been busy in the months since the battle arranging for proper reburial of the remains. On November 19, the cemetery would be formally dedicated, with Edward Everett—widely known as the nation's greatest orator—delivering the main address. Would the president add "a few appropriate remarks"?

Like Lincoln himself, his Gettysburg address is encrusted with legend. Recent scholarship has helped dispel some of the myths, but not all. It turns out that the invitation was no afterthought, nor was the president insulted that Everett got top billing. Moreover, far from scribbling something on the back of an envelope as his train headed to Pennsylvania (like some student scrambling to write a paper an hour before it is due), Lincoln worked long and hard on the speech. On the crowd's reaction, however, opinions (then and since) differ. Some said that the audience liked what they heard, interrupting with applause several times. Others heard no ovations, only lots of "expressions of disappointment." "So short a time was Mr. Lincoln before them," wrote one, "that the people could scarcely believe their eyes when he disappeared from their view. They were almost dazed." Lincoln might have sensed that disappointment—"it is a flat failure," he reportedly said to a dignitary on stage with him—but he had a bigger audience in mind: Not the thousands listening at the cemetery that afternoon but the millions across the continent who would read his words in newspapers during the days and weeks ahead.[25]

As with the Declaration of Independence, so with the Gettysburg Address: What people heard or read has been celebrated more often than studied. Like Jefferson "four score and seven years" earlier, Lincoln had a lot of other things on his mind, as well as a deadline, a vague assignment—and a blank sheet of paper. Reading what Lincoln wrote to fill that space, pay attention to his selection of words and phrases, to what he chose to say—and, no less important, what he chose not to say. How many of the themes and issues he had been wrestling with for a decade—and Americans had been discussing for far longer—are treated here?

A year after returning to Washington from Gettysburg, Lincoln won reelection. It had been a close call: As late as August, he had been among the many who thought he had no chance at a second term. " 'You think I don't know I am going to be beaten,' he said to a friend, *'but I do* and unless some great change takes place *badly beaten.'*" The war seemed never-ending; casualties mounted; many opposed emancipation with the same fervor that they favored a negotiated peace that would end the Union. But that fall "great change" did take place: Stunning Union victories gave him victory at the polls.[26]

Still, much remained to be done. Without waiting for the newly elected Congress to convene, the president pressed the lame-duck House of Representatives to pass the Thirteenth Amendment abolishing slavery and send it to the states for approval. And still the war dragged on through the winter. March 4, Inauguration Day, dawned rainy, cold, and crowded. (Among the crowd was John Wilkes Booth.) Perhaps half of the enormous throng were African Americans (including Frederick Douglass and four companies of black soldiers); they had come to hear the man who had done so much to end slavery.

Douglass told Lincoln that the speech (Document 9) was "a sacred effort." The president, too, was pleased. "I expect," he wrote, it will "wear as well as—perhaps better than—any thing I have produced." Reading his words—almost three times longer than the Gettysburg Address, but among the shortest inaugural speeches in American history—can you see why? Note, as at Gettysburg, not just *what* Lincoln said and *how* he said it, but also what he did *not* say. As you become acquainted with this text, too, consider why Lincoln, on March 15, wrote a friend that "I believe it is not immediately popular. Men are not flattered by being shown that there has been a difference of purpose between the Almighty and them.... [But] [i]t is a truth which I thought needed to be told; and as whatever of humiliation there is in it, falls most directly on myself, I thought others might afford for [i.e., allow] me to tell it."[27]

Speaking of the Almighty, it is also worth asking whether Lincoln's views here echo another author's at the end of another terrible conflict that some call a civil war: Mary Rowlandson (Chapter 4). Not deeply religious before the war (he never joined a church), during his presidency Lincoln, becoming convinced that he was "an instrument in God's hands," could often be found reading the Bible and pondering its meaning. In this he joined the vast majority of Americans—and joined, too, Mary Rowlandson and other Puritans—in seeing personal or national catastrophe as a sign of God's wrath.[28]

With Lincoln as president, the United States survived its most perilous passage. That very sentence speaks of the deep change mere survival wrought in the American conversation. Before the war, most people considered "the United States" plural ("the United States survived *their* most perilous passage"); afterward, the three words became "it," not "them"; the *unum* triumphed over *e pluribus* in the famous phrase *e pluribus unum* ("out of many, one").

Beyond saving the nation and ending slavery, however, much about Lincoln's legacy remains in dispute. Nothing is more controversial than his views on African Americans; speculation abounds as to what more he would have done had he lived. Some believe that Lincoln would have gone on "growing" and fought for true black equality: "in the end...," concludes James Oakes, he "moved toward a radical position on equal rights...[and] even began to awaken from his lifelong insensitivity to racial injustice." Richard Current points out that Lincoln welcomed African American "visitors [to the White House] as no President had done before"—including, on several occasions, Frederick Douglass. Their last meeting, Current continues, illuminates both abiding racism and Lincoln's efforts to swim against that tide. When Douglass tried to get into the inaugural reception at the White House, "policemen manhandled him and forced him out. Making his way in again, he managed to catch Lincoln's eye. 'Here comes my friend Douglass,' the President exclaimed, and, leaving the circle of guests he had been conversing with, he took Douglass by the hand and began to chat with him." "I am glad to see you," Lincoln said, adding, "there is no man in the country whose opinion I value more than yours." "In all my interviews with Mr. Lincoln," Douglass recalled, "I was impressed with his entire freedom from popular prejudice against the colored race."[29]

Nonetheless, others suggest that Lincoln, and Douglass's take on Lincoln, was more complex. While the president did meet with African American leaders, he did not meet with them often, and rarely sought their advice. Douglass himself was frequently at odds with Lincoln. In 1862, he called the president a "genuine representative of American prejudice and Negro hatred," a man whose policy "has been calculated in a marked and decided way to shield and protect slavery." Two years later, he, for a time, favored other Republican candidates for president. In an 1876 speech, Douglass concluded that Lincoln "was preeminently the white man's President, entirely devoted to the welfare of white men. He was ready and willing at any time during the first years of his administration to deny, postpone, and sacrifice the rights of humanity in the colored people in order to promote the welfare of the white people of this country.... You are the children of Abraham Lincoln," he told his white audience. "We are at best his step-children." Even so, Douglass mused, it all depended on one's perspective. "Viewed from the genuine abolition ground, Mr. Lincoln seemed tardy, cold, dull, and indifferent; but measuring him by the sentiment of his country, a sentiment he was bound as a statesman to consult, he was swift, zealous, radical, and determined."[30]

The Second Inaugural Address captures Lincoln's ambiguous legacy. On the one hand, the bloodshed came because God was punishing whites, North and South, for enslaving blacks; the national sin of slavery that abolitionists had been hammering home for a generation had now been acknowledged—and by the President of the United States, no less. On the other, it was hard to see how "malice toward none" and "charity for all" could be extended both to former slaves and their former masters.[31] Working out the meaning of Lincoln's words, of the Civil War, and of America itself— with Lincoln's assassination on April 15 that was left for others, including us.

Questions for Consideration and Conversation

1. Which is more striking about Lincoln's speeches over time, continuity or change?

2. What can you learn of Lincoln's views on slavery in these speeches? Is it fair to say that he was an abolitionist, as some of his political opponents claimed?

3. What were Lincoln's views on African Americans? In the debate about those views—did he consider them equal or inferior?—which side do you favor?

4. What role does American history in general and the American founding in particular play in Lincoln's speeches, and in his view of America's present and future?

5. Frederick Douglass was disappointed in Lincoln's First Inaugural Address. Why?

6. Read the Emancipation Proclamation with care. What strikes you about the tone of this text? On what grounds did Lincoln claim the right to emancipate slaves? Was he going back on promises he made in his First Inaugural? Why were Frederick Douglass and other abolitionists so jubilant when this appeared on January 1, 1863, and why have so many since condemned this document as too little, too late?

7. What besides its brevity makes the Gettysburg Address so acclaimed? What elements of the Civil War and of America did Lincoln choose to focus on, and why? What did he omit, and why?

8. Why did Frederick Douglass call Lincoln's Second Inaugural "a sacred effort"? What would a supporter of secession have said about its tone? Its promises?

Endnotes

1. William S. McFeely, *Frederick Douglass* (New York, 1991), 214 (Douglass); David Herbert Donald, *Lincoln* (New York, 1995), 14 ("capacity"); Eric Foner, *The Fiery Trial: Abraham Lincoln and American Slavery* (New York, 2010), 336.

2. James M. McPherson, ed., *"We Cannot Escape History": Lincoln and the Last Best Hope of Earth* (Urbana, IL, 1995), 1 ("possession"); McPherson, *Drawn with the Sword: Reflections on the Civil War* (New York, 1996), 177–78 (Shakespeare); David Donald, *Lincoln Reconsidered: Essays on the Civil War Era* (Westport, CT, 1981 [orig. pub. 1956]), 3 (book titles), 144 ("cult"); Donald, *Lincoln Reconsidered: Essays on the Civil War Era*, 3rd ed. (New York, 2001), xiii (kinship); Andrew Ferguson, *Land of Lincoln:* *Adventures in Abe's America* (New York, 2007), ix (14,000), 7 (brewers), 130 (chamber pot), 133 (underwear), 141 (groups).

3. Douglas L. Wilson, *Honor's Voice: The Transformation of Abraham Lincoln* (New York, 1998), 5. See Donald Wolf Shenk, *Lincoln's Melancholy: How Depression Challenged a President and Fueled His Greatness* (New York, 2005).

4. Wilson, *Honor's Voice*, 55; Donald, *Lincoln*, 55.

5. Wilson, *Honor's Voice*, 59 ("Greatest"); David W. Blight, *Frederick Douglass and Abraham Lincoln: A Relationship in Language, Politics, and Memory*, Frank L. Klement Lectures, No. 10 (Milwaukee, 2001), 9 ("rhetorical bond"). See also Douglas L. Wilson, *Lincoln's Sword: The Presidency and the Power of Words* (New York, 2007), 20–27.

6. Michael P. Johnson, ed., *Abraham Lincoln, Slavery, and the Civil War: Selected Writings and Speeches* (Boston, 2001), 81.

7. Frank J. Williams, "Abraham Lincoln—Our Ever-Present Contemporary," in McPherson, ed., *"We Cannot Escape History,"* 139–40 ("obscene clown," "orangutan," "unmentionable disease"); William E. Gienapp, "Abraham Lincoln and Presidential Leadership," ibid., 80 ("failure"); Donald, *Lincoln Reconsidered*, 1st ed., 61–63 ("ass," "Negro blood," "coward," "unfit," "timid and ignorant," "half-witted," "shattered"); Wilson, *Lincoln's Sword*, 244 ("dirty stories").

8. Wilson, *Lincoln's Sword*, 9 ("effective"); John Channing Briggs, *Lincoln's Speeches Reconsidered* (Baltimore, 2005), 2 ("read slowly").

9. William E. Gienapp, *Abraham Lincoln and Civil War America: A Biography* (New York, 2002), 49.

10. Donald, *Lincoln*, 168 ("stunned," "dreary"); Wilson, *Lincoln's Sword*, 37 ("keystone"), 203 ("breakthrough").

11. James Oakes, *The Radical and the Republican: Frederick Douglass, Abraham Lincoln, and the Triumph of Antislavery Politics* (New York, 2007), 74.

12. Briggs, *Lincoln's Speeches Reconsidered*, 167 ("fool"); Donald, *Lincoln*, 209 ("too far").

13. Donald, *Lincoln*, 174 ("musical"); Foner, *The Fiery Trial*, 79 ("spell bound"); Garry Wills, *Lincoln at Gettysburg: The Words That Remade America* (New York, 1992), 36 ("mimic"), 164 ("coloring").

14. Wills, *Lincoln at Gettysburg*, 91 ("evasions," "indirect"); Wilson, *Lincoln's Sword*, 79 ("reticent"); Oakes, *The Radical and the Republican*, 120 ("even less").

15. Johnson, ed., *Lincoln, Slavery, and the Civil War*, 20, n. 14 ("bad policy"), 51 ("trot-line"), 285 ("cannot remember"); Oakes, *The Radical and the Republican*, 42 ("voted against"), 57 (mid-1850s); Donald, *Lincoln*, 187 ("a slave himself").

16. Wills, *Lincoln at Gettysburg*, 91 ("farther south"); Philip S. Paludan, "Emancipating the Republic: Lincoln and the Means and Ends of Antislavery," in McPherson, ed., *"We Cannot Escape History,"* 55 ("forbade").

17. Johnson, ed., *Lincoln, Slavery, and the Civil War*, 20, n. 14, 51, n. 9 (1837, 1841); Oakes, *The Radical and the Republican*, 119 ("darky jokes," "racial epithets"). See Lerone Bennett, *Forced into Glory: Abraham Lincoln's White Dream* (Chicago, 2000).

18. Donald, *Lincoln*, 167.

19. Ibid., 284 (newspapers and Democrats); Wilson, *Lincoln's Sword*, 69 (New York City). For a scholarly assessment, see Lois J. Einhorn, *Abraham Lincoln the Orator: Penetrating the Lincoln Legend*, Great American Orators, No. 16 (Westport, CT, 1992), 66–69.

20. Donald, *Lincoln*, 315.

21. Johnson, ed., *Lincoln, Slavery, and the Civil War*, 205 ("object"); Donald, *Lincoln*, 362 ("be subdued").

22. Donald, *Lincoln*, 366.

23. Don E. Fehrenbacher, *Lincoln in Text and Context: Selected Essays* (Stanford, 1987), 109 ("greatest event"); McFeely, *Douglass*, 215 ("Joy").

24. Donald, *Lincoln*, 459 ("stumbled"), 462.

25. Wills, *Lincoln at Gettysburg*; Wilson, *Lincoln's Sword*, ch. 8 and Appendix (quotations on 226–27).

26. Donald, *Lincoln*, 529.

27. Ibid., 568 ("sacred effort"); Johnson, ed., *Lincoln, Slavery, and the Civil War*, 322.

28. Donald, *Lincoln*, 354.

29. Oakes, *The Radical and the Republican*, xviii ("radical"), 242 ("no man"); Richard Current, *The Lincoln Nobody Knows* (New York, 1958), 234–35.

30. Blight, *Douglass and Lincoln*, 10 ("Negro hatred"); Oakes, *The Radical and the Republican*, 188 ("calculated"); Douglass, *The Life and Times of Frederick Douglass, Written by Himself: His Early Life as a Slave, His Escape From Bondage, and His Complete History* (New York, 1962 [orig. pub. 1892]), 484–85, 489.

31. I thank my Vassar colleague Rebecca Edwards for this insight.

DOCUMENT 1

Speech at Peoria, Illinois (October 16, 1854)

Source: Roy P. Basler, ed., *The Collected Works of Abraham Lincoln*. New Brunswick, NJ, 1953–1955. http://www.hti.umich.edu/l/lincoln/.

The repeal of the Missouri Compromise, and the propriety of its restoration, constitute the subject of what I am about to say....

And, as this subject is no other, than part and parcel of the larger general question of domestic-slavery, I wish to MAKE and to KEEP the distinction between the EXISTING institution, and the EXTENSION of it, so broad, and so clear, that no honest man can misunderstand me, and no dishonest one, successfully misrepresent me....

[During the 1780s,] We were then living under the Articles of Confederation, which were superceded by the Constitution several years afterwards. The question of ceding these territories [between the Appalachian Mountains and the Mississippi River] to the general government was set on foot. Mr. Jefferson, the author of the Declaration of Independence, and otherwise a chief actor in the revolution; then a delegate in Congress; afterwards twice President; who was, is, and perhaps will continue to be, the most distinguished politician of our history;…and withal, a slave-holder; conceived the idea of taking that occasion, to prevent slavery ever going into the north-western territory [above the Ohio River]. He prevailed on the Virginia Legislature to adopt his views, and to cede the territory….Congress accepted the cession…; and in the first Ordinance (which the acts of Congress were then called) for the government of the territory, provided that slavery should never be permitted therein. This is the famed ordinance of '87 so often spoken of. Thenceforward, for sixty-one years, and until in 1848, the last scrap of this territory came into the Union as the State of Wisconsin, all parties acted in quiet obedience to this ordinance. It is now what Jefferson foresaw and intended—the happy home of teeming millions of free, white, prosperous people, and no slave amongst them.

Thus, with the author of the declaration of Independence, the policy of prohibiting slavery in new territory originated. Thus, away back of the constitution, in the pure fresh, free breath of the revolution, the State of Virginia, and the National congress put that policy in practice. Thus…, in those five states, and five millions of free, enterprising people, we have before us the rich fruits of this policy. But *now* new light breaks upon us. Now congress declares this ought never to have been; and the like of it, must never be again….Oh, how difficult it is to treat with respect, such assaults upon all we have ever really held sacred.

But to return to history….[Lincoln then surveys the period from the 1803 Louisiana Purchase forward in time.]

During this long period of time Nebraska had remained, substantially an uninhabited country, but now emigration to, and settlement within it began to take place. It is about one third as large as the present United States, and its importance[,] so long overlooked, begins to come into view. The restriction of slavery by the Missouri Compromise directly applies to it; in fact, was first made, and has since been maintained, expressly for it….[In early 1854 Congress passed a "bill to give Nebraska territorial government," with a provision "to declare the Missouri Compromise inoperative and void; and, substantially, that the People

who go and settle there may establish slavery, or exclude it, as they may see fit."]

This is the repeal of the Missouri Compromise…. I think, and shall try to show, that it is wrong; wrong in its direct effect, letting slavery into Kansas and Nebraska—and wrong in its prospective principle, allowing it to spread to every other part of the wide world, where men can be found inclined to take it.

This *declared* indifference, but as I must think, covert *real zeal* for the spread of slavery, I can not but hate. I hate it because of the monstrous injustice of slavery itself. I hate it because it deprives our republican example of its just influence in the world—enables the enemies of free institutions, with plausibility, to taunt us as hypocrites—causes the real friends of freedom to doubt our sincerity, and especially because it forces so many really good men amongst ourselves into an open war with the very fundamental principles of civil liberty—criticising the Declaration of Independence, and insisting that there is no right principle of action but *self-interest*….

When southern people tell us they are no more responsible for the origin of slavery, than we; I acknowledge the fact. When it is said that the institution exists; and that it is very difficult to get rid of it, in any satisfactory way, I can understand and appreciate the saying. I surely will not blame them for not doing what I should not know how to do myself. If all earthly power were given me, I should not know what to do, as to the existing institution. My first impulse would be to free all the slaves, and send them to Liberia [a West African nation founded by former slaves],—to their own native land. But a moment's reflection would convince me, that whatever of high hope, (as I think there is) there may be in this, in the long run, its sudden execution is impossible….What then? Free them all, and keep them among us as underlings? Is it quite certain that this betters their condition? I think I would not hold one in slavery, at any rate; yet the point is not clear enough for me to denounce people upon. What next? Free them, and make them politically and socially, our equals? My own feelings will not admit of this; and if mine would, we well know that those of the great mass of white people will not. Whether this feeling accords with justice and sound judgment, is not the sole question, if indeed, it is any part of it. A universal feeling, whether well or ill-founded, can not be safely disregarded. We can not, then, make them equals….

Equal justice to the south, it is said, requires us to consent to the extending of slavery to new countries. That is to say, inasmuch as you do not object to my taking my hog to Nebraska, therefore I must not object to you taking your slave. Now, I admit this is perfectly logical, if there is no difference between hogs and negroes. But while you thus require me to deny the humanity of the negro, I wish to ask whether you of the south yourselves, have ever been willing to do as much?...The great majority, south as well as north, have human sympathies....These sympathies...manifest in many ways, their sense of the wrong of slavery, and their consciousness that, after all, there is humanity in the negro. If they deny this, let me address them a few plain questions. In 1820 you joined the north, almost unanimously, in declaring the African slave trade piracy, and in annexing to it the punishment of death. Why did you do this? If you did not feel that it was wrong, why did you join in providing that men should be hung for it? The practice was no more than bringing wild negroes from Africa, to sell to such as would buy them. But you never thought of hanging men for catching and selling wild horses, wild buffaloes or wild bears.

Again, you have amongst you, a sneaking individual, of the class of native tyrants, known as the "SLAVE-DEALER." He watches your necessities, and crawls up to buy your slave, at a speculating price. If you cannot help it, you sell to him; but if you can help it, you drive him from your door. You despise him utterly. You do not recognize him as a friend, or even as an honest man. Your children must not play with his; they may rollick freely with the little negroes, but not with the "slave-dealers" children. If you are obliged to deal with him, you try to get through the job without so much as touching him. It is common with you to join hands with the men you meet; but with the slave dealer you avoid the ceremony—instinctively shrinking from the snaky contact....Now why is this? You do not so treat the man who deals in corn, cattle or tobacco....

And now, why will you ask us to deny the humanity of the slave? and estimate him only as the equal of the hog? Why ask us to do what you will not do yourselves?...

But one great argument in the support of the repeal of the Missouri Compromise, is still to come. That argument is "the sacred right of self government."...

The doctrine of self government is right—absolutely and eternally right—but it has no just application, as here attempted. Or perhaps I should rather say that whether it has such just application depends upon whether a negro is *not* or *is* a man. If he is *not* a man, why in that case, he who *is* a man may, as a matter of self-government, do just as he pleases with him. But if the negro *is* a man, is it not to that extent, a total destruction of self-government, to say that he too shall not govern *himself*? When the white man governs himself that is self-government; but when he governs himself, and also governs *another* man, that is *more* than self-government—that is despotism. If the negro is a *man*, why then my ancient faith teaches me that "all men are created equal;"...

[N]o man is good enough to govern another man, *without that other's consent*. I say this is the leading principle—the sheet anchor of American republicanism. Our Declaration of Independence says:

"We hold these truths to be self evident: that all men are created equal; that they are endowed by their Creator with certain inalienable rights; that among these are life, liberty and the pursuit of happiness. That to secure these rights, governments are instituted among men, DERIVING THEIR JUST POWERS FROM THE CONSENT OF THE GOVERNED."

...[A]ccording to our ancient faith, the just powers of governments are derived from the consent of the governed. Now the relation of masters and slaves is...a total violation of this principle....

In support of his application of the doctrine of self-government, Senator Douglas has sought to bring to his aid the opinions and examples of our revolutionary fathers. I am glad he has done this. I love the sentiments of those old-time men; and shall be most happy to abide by their opinions. He shows us that when it was in contemplation for the colonies to break off from Great Britain, and set up a new government for themselves, several of the states instructed their delegates to go for the measure PROVIDED EACH STATE SHOULD BE ALLOWED TO REGULATE ITS DOMESTIC CONCERNS IN ITS OWN WAY....This was right....I also think it probable that it had some reference to the existence of slavery amongst them. I will not deny that it had. But had it, in any reference to the carrying of slavery into NEW COUNTRIES? That is the question; and we will let the fathers themselves answer it.

This same generation of men, and mostly the same individuals of the generation, who declared this principle—who declared independence—who fought the war of the revolution through—who afterwards made the constitution under which we still live—these same men passed the ordinance of '87, declaring that slavery should never go to the north-west territory. I have no doubt Judge Douglas thinks they were very inconsistent in this. It is a question of discrimination between them and him. But there is not an inch of ground left for his claiming that their opinions—their example—their authority—are on his side in this controversy....

Whether slavery shall go into Nebraska, or other new territories, is not a matter of exclusive concern to the people who may go there. The whole nation is interested that the best use shall be made of these territories. We want them for the homes of free white people. This they cannot be, to any considerable extent, if slavery shall be planted within them. Slave States are places for poor white people to remove FROM; not to remove TO. New free States are the places for poor people to go to and better their condition. For this use, the nation needs these territories....

Some men...who condemn the repeal of the Missouri Compromise, nevertheless hesitate to go for its restoration, lest they be thrown in company with the abolitionist. Will they allow me...to tell them good humoredly, that I think this is very silly? Stand with anybody that stands RIGHT. Stand with him while he is right and PART with him when he goes wrong. Stand WITH the abolitionist in restoring the Missouri Compromise; and stand AGAINST him when he attempts to repeal the fugitive slave law.... [S]tand on middle ground....To desert such ground, because of any company, is to be less than...a man— less than an American.

I particularly object to the NEW position which the avowed principle of this Nebraska law gives to slavery in the body politic. I object to it because it assumes that there CAN be MORAL RIGHT in the enslaving of one man by another....I object to it because the fathers of the republic eschewed, and rejected it. The argument of "Necessity" was the only argument they ever admitted in favor of slavery; and so far, and so far only as it carried them, did they ever go. They found the institution existing among us, which they could not help....BEFORE the constitution, they prohibited its introduction into the north-western Territory—the only country we owned, then free from it. AT the framing and adoption of the constitution, they forbore to so much as mention the word "slave" or "slavery" in the whole instrument.... Thus, the thing is hid away, in the constitution, just as an afflicted man hides away a wen [a lump or wart] or a cancer, which he dares not cut out at once, lest he bleed to death; with the promise, nevertheless, that the cutting may begin at the end of a given time.... But this is not all. The earliest Congress, under the constitution, took the same view of slavery. They hedged and hemmed it in to the narrowest limits of necessity....[To prove this point, Lincoln lists five laws passed between 1794 and 1820.]

Thus we see, the plain unmistakable spirit of that age, towards slavery, was hostility to the PRINCIPLE, and toleration, ONLY BY NECESSITY.

But NOW it is to be transformed into a "sacred right." Nebraska brings it forth, places it on the high road to extension and perpetuity....Little by little, but steadily as man's march to the grave, we have been giving up the OLD for the NEW faith. Near eighty years ago we began by declaring that all men are created equal; but now from that beginning we have run down to the other declaration, that for SOME men to enslave OTHERS is a "sacred right of self-government." These principles can not stand together....[W]hoever holds to the one, must despise the other. When [Indiana Senator John] Pettit, in connection with his support of the Nebraska bill, called the Declaration of Independence "a self-evident lie" he only did what consistency and candor require all other Nebraska men to do....If this had been said...in old Independence Hall, seventy-eight years ago, the very door-keeper would have throttled the man, and thrust him into the street.

Let no one be deceived. The spirit of seventy-six and the spirit of Nebraska, are utter antagonisms; and the former is being rapidly displaced by the latter.

Fellow countrymen—Americans south, as well as north, shall we make no effort to arrest this? Already the liberal party throughout the world, express the apprehension "that the one retrograde institution in America, is undermining the principles of progress, and fatally violating the noblest political system the world ever saw." This is not the taunt of enemies, but the warning of friends. Is it quite safe to disregard it—to despise it? Is there no danger to liberty itself, in discarding the earliest practice, and first precept of our ancient faith?...

Our republican robe is soiled, and trailed in the dust. Let us repurify it. Let us turn and wash it white, in the spirit, if not the blood, of the Revolution. Let us turn slavery from its claims of "moral right," back upon its existing legal rights, and its arguments of "necessity." Let us return it to the position our fathers gave it; and there let it rest in peace. Let us re-adopt the Declaration of Independence, and with it, the practices, and policy, which harmonize with it. Let north and south—let all Americans—let all lovers of liberty everywhere—join in the great and good work. If we do this, we shall not only have saved the Union; but we shall have so saved it, as to make, and to keep it, forever worthy of the saving. We shall have so saved it, that the succeeding millions of free happy people, the world over, shall rise up, and call us blessed, to the latest generations....

DOCUMENT 2

SPEECH AT SPRINGFIELD, ILLINOIS (JUNE 26, 1857)

...And now as to the Dred Scott decision. That decision declares...that Congress cannot prohibit slavery in the Territories. It was made by a divided court....Judge [Stephen] Douglas...denounces all who question the correctness of that decision, as offering violent resistance to it. But who resists it? Who has, in spite of the decision, declared Dred Scott free, and resisted the authority of his master over him?

Judicial decisions have two uses—first, to absolutely determine the case decided, and secondly, to indicate to the public how other similar cases will be decided when they arise....

We believe, as much as Judge Douglas, (perhaps more) in obedience to, and respect for the judicial department of government. We think its decisions on Constitutional questions, when fully settled, should control, not only the particular cases decided, but the general policy of the country, subject to be disturbed only by amendments of the Constitution as provided in that instrument itself. More than this would be revolution. But we think the Dred Scott decision is erroneous. We know the court that made it, has often over-ruled its own decisions, and we shall do what we can to have it to over-rule this. We offer no *resistance* to it.

Judicial decisions are of greater or less authority as precedents, according to circumstances....

If this important decision had been made by the unanimous concurrence of the judges, and without any apparent partisan bias, and in accordance with legal public expectation, and with the steady practice of the departments throughout our history, and had been in no part, based on assumed historical facts which are not really true; or, if wanting in some of these, it had been before the court more than once, and had there been affirmed and re-affirmed through a course of years, it then might be, perhaps would be, factious, nay, even revolutionary, to not acquiesce in it as a precedent.

But when, as it is true we find it wanting in all these claims to the public confidence, it is not resistance, it is not factious, it is not even disrespectful, to treat it as not having yet quite established a settled doctrine for the country....

I have said...that the Dred Scott decision was, in part, based on assumed historical facts which were not really true....Chief Justice [Roger] Taney, in delivering the opinion of the majority of the Court, insists at great length that negroes were no part of the people who made, or for whom was made, the Declaration of Independence, or the Constitution of the United States.

On the contrary, Judge [Benjamin R.] Curtis, in his dissenting opinion, shows that in five of the then thirteen states, to wit, New Hampshire, Massachusetts, New York, New Jersey and North Carolina, free negroes were voters, and, in proportion to their numbers, had the same part in making the Constitution that the white people had....

[T]he Chief Justice does not directly assert, but plainly assumes, as a fact, that the public estimate of the black man is more favorable now than it was in the days of the Revolution. This assumption is a mistake.... [A]s a whole, in this country, the change between then and now is decidedly the other way; and their ultimate destiny has never appeared so hopeless as in the last three or four years. In two of the five States— New Jersey and North Carolina—that then gave the free negro the right of voting, the right has since been taken away; and in a third—New York—it has been greatly abridged; while it has not been extended, so far as I know, to a single additional State, though the number of the States has more than doubled. In those days, as I understand, masters could, at their own pleasure, emancipate their slaves; but since then, such legal restraints have been made upon emancipation, as to amount almost to prohibition....In those days, by common consent, the spread of the black man's bondage to new countries was prohibited; but now, Congress decides that it will not continue the prohibition, and the Supreme Court decides that it [Congress] could not if it would. In those days, our Declaration of Independence was held sacred by all, and thought to include all; but now, to aid in making the bondage of the negro universal and eternal, it is assailed, and sneered at, and construed, and hawked at, and torn, till, if its framers could rise from their graves, they could not at all recognize it. All the powers of earth seem rapidly combining against him....They have him in his prison house....One after another they have closed the heavy iron doors upon him, and now they have him, as it were, bolted in with a lock of a hundred keys, which can never be unlocked without the concurrence of every key; the keys in the hands of a hundred different men, and they scattered to a hundred different and distant places; and they stand musing as to what invention, in all the dominions of mind and matter, can be produced to make the impossibility of his escape more complete than it is.

It is grossly incorrect to say or assume, that the public estimate of the negro is more favorable now than it was at the origin of the government....

There is a natural disgust in the minds of nearly all white people, to the idea of an indiscriminate amalgamation of the white and black races; and Judge Douglas evidently is basing his chief hope, upon the chances of being able to appropriate the benefit of this disgust to himself. If he can, by much drumming and repeating, fasten the odium of that idea upon his adversaries, he thinks he can struggle through the storm. He therefore clings to this hope, as a drowning man to the last plank. He makes an occasion for lugging it in from the opposition to the Dred Scott decision. He finds the Republicans insisting that the Declaration of Independence includes ALL men, black as well as white; and forth-with he boldly denies that it includes negroes at all, and proceeds to argue gravely that all who contend it does, do so only because they want to vote, and eat, and sleep, and marry with negroes!...Now I protest against that counterfeit logic which concludes that, because I do not want a black woman for a *slave* I must necessarily want her for a *wife*. I need not have her for either, I can just leave her alone. In some respects she certainly is not my equal; but in her natural right to eat the bread she earns with her own hands without asking leave of any one else, she is my equal, and the equal of all others.

Chief Justice Taney, in his opinion in the Dred Scott case, admits that the language of the Declaration is broad enough to include the whole human family, but he and Judge Douglas argue that the authors of that instrument did not intend to include negroes, by the fact that they did not at once, actually place them on an equality with the whites. Now this grave argument comes to just nothing at all, by the other fact, that they did not at once, *or ever afterwards*, actually place all white people on an equality with one or another....I think the authors of that notable instrument intended to include *all* men, but they did not intend to declare all men equal *in all respects.* They did not mean to say all were equal in color, size, intellect, moral developments, or social capacity. They defined with tolerable distinctness, in what respects they did consider all men created equal—equal in "certain inalienable rights, among which are life, liberty, and the pursuit of happiness." This they said, and this meant. They did not mean to assert the obvious untruth, that all were then actually enjoying that equality, nor yet, that they were about to confer it immediately upon them. In fact they had no power to confer such a boon. They meant simply to declare the *right*, so that the *enforcement* of it might follow as fast as circumstances should permit. They meant to set up a standard maxim for free society, which should be familiar to all, and revered by all; constantly looked to, constantly labored for, and even though never perfectly attained, constantly approximated, and thereby constantly spreading and deepening its influence, and augmenting the happiness and value of life to all people of all colors everywhere. The assertion that "all men are created equal" was of no practical use in effecting our separation from Great Britain; and it was placed in the Declaration, not for that, but for future use. Its authors meant it to be, thank God, it is now proving itself, a stumbling block to those who in after times might seek to turn a free people back into the hateful paths of despotism. They knew the proneness of prosperity to breed tyrants, and they meant when such should re-appear in this fair land and commence their vocation they should find left for them at least one hard nut to crack....

[A]re you really willing that the Declaration shall be thus frittered away?—thus left no more at most, than an interesting memorial of the dead past?...

I have said that the separation of the races is the only perfect preventive of amalgamation....Such separation, if ever effected at all, must be effected by colonization....The enterprise is a difficult one; but "when there is a will there is a way;" and what colonization needs most is a hearty will....The children of Israel, to such numbers as to include four hundred thousand fighting men, went out of Egyptian bondage in a body.

How differently the respective courses of the Democratic and Republican parties incidentally bear on the question of forming a will—a public sentiment—for colonization, is easy to see....

DOCUMENT 3

Speech at Springfield, Illinois (June 16, 1858)

Mr. PRESIDENT and Gentlemen of the Convention.

If we could first know *where* we are, and *whither* we are tending, we could then better judge *what* to do, and *how* to do it.

We are now far into the *fifth* year, since a policy was initiated, with the *avowed* object, and *confident* promise, of putting an end to slavery agitation.

Under the operation of that policy, that agitation has not only, *not ceased*, but has *constantly augmented*.

In *my* opinion, it *will* not cease, until a *crisis* shall have been reached, and passed.

"A house divided against itself cannot stand."

I believe this government cannot endure, permanently half *slave* and half *free*.

I do not expect the Union to be *dissolved*—I do not expect the house to *fall*—but I *do* expect it will cease to be divided.

It will become *all* one thing, or *all* the other.

Either the *opponents* of slavery, will arrest the further spread of it, and place it where the public mind shall rest in the belief that it is in course of ultimate extinction; or its *advocates* will push it forward, till it shall become alike lawful in *all* the States, *old* as well as *new*—North as well as *South*.

Have we no *tendency* to the latter condition?

Let any one who doubts, carefully contemplate that now almost complete legal combination—piece of *machinery* so to speak—compounded of the Nebraska doctrine, and the Dred Scott decision. Let him consider not only *what work* the machinery is adapted to do, and *how well* adapted; but also, let him study the *history* of its construction, and trace, if he can, or rather *fail*, if he can, to trace the evidences of design, and concert of action, among its chief bosses, from the beginning....

The new year of 1854 found slavery excluded from more than half the States by State Constitutions, and from most of the national territory by Congressional prohibition.

Four days later, commenced the struggle, which ended in repealing that Congressional prohibition.

This opened all the national territory to slavery; and was the first point gained....

While the Nebraska bill was passing through congress, a *law case*, involving the question of a negroe's freedom, by reason of his owner having voluntarily taken him first into a free state and then a territory covered by the congressional prohibition, and held him as a slave, for a long time in each, was passing through the U.S. Circuit Court for the District of Missouri; and both Nebraska bill and law suit were brought to a decision in the same month of May, 1854. The negroe's name was "Dred Scott," which name now designates the decision finally made in the case.

Before the *then* next Presidential election, the law case came *to*, and was argued *in* the Supreme Court of the United States; but the *decision* of it was deferred until *after* the election....

The election came. Mr. Buchanan was elected, and the *indorsement*, such as it was, secured. That was the *second* point gained....

The several points of the Dred Scott decision, in connection with Senator Douglas' "care not" policy [about "whether slavery is voted up or down"], constitute the piece of machinery, in its *present* state of advancement. This was the third point gained.

The *working* points of that machinery are:

First, that no negro slave, imported as such from Africa, and no descendant of such slave can ever be a *citizen* of any State, in the sense of that term as used in the Constitution of the United States.

This point is made in order to deprive the negro, in every possible event, of the benefit of this provision of the United States Constitution, which declares that—

"The citizens of each State shall be entitled to all privileges and immunities of citizens in the several States."

Secondly, that "subject to the Constitution of the United States," neither *Congress* nor a *Territorial Legislature* can exclude slavery from any United States territory.

This point is made in order that individual men may *fill up* the territories with slaves, without danger of losing them as property, and thus to enhance the chances of *permanency* to the institution through all the future....

[W]e may, ere long, see...another Supreme Court decision, declaring that the Constitution of the United States does not permit a *state* to exclude slavery from its limits.

And this may especially be expected if the doctrine of "care not whether slavery be voted *down* or voted *up*," shall gain upon the public mind sufficiently to give promise that such a decision can be maintained when made.

Such a decision is all that slavery now lacks of being alike lawful in all the States.

Welcome or unwelcome, such decision *is* probably coming, and will soon be upon us, unless the power of the present political dynasty shall be met and overthrown.

We shall *lie down* pleasantly dreaming that the people of *Missouri* are on the verge of making their State *free*; and we shall *awake* to the *reality*, instead, that the *Supreme* Court has made *Illinois* a *slave* State.

To meet and overthrow the power of that dynasty, is the work now before all those who would prevent that consummation.

That is *what* we have to do.

But *how* can we best do it?...

Two years ago the Republicans of the nation mustered over thirteen hundred thousand strong.

We did this under the single impulse of resistance to a common danger, with every external circumstance against us.

Of *strange, discordant,* and even, *hostile* elements, we gathered from the four winds, and *formed* and fought the battle through, under the constant hot fire of a disciplined, proud, and pampered enemy.

Did we brave all *then*, to *falter* now?...

The result is not doubtful. We shall not fail—if we stand firm, we shall not fail.

Wise councils may *accelerate* or *mistakes delay* it, but, sooner or later the victory is *sure* to come.

DOCUMENT 4

FIRST DEBATE WITH STEPHEN A. DOUGLAS AT OTTAWA, ILLINOIS (AUGUST 21, 1858)

MY FELLOW-CITIZENS: When a man hears himself somewhat misrepresented, it provokes him—at least, I find it so with myself; but when the misrepresentation becomes very gross and palpable, it is more apt to amuse him. [Laughter.]...

Now gentlemen,... this is the true complexion of all I have ever said in regard to the institution of slavery and the black race. This is the whole of it, and anything that argues me into his idea of perfect social and political equality with the negro, is but a specious and fantastic arrangement of words, by which a man can prove a horse chestnut to be a chestnut horse. [Laughter.]... I have no purpose directly or indirectly to interfere with the institution of slavery in the States where it exists. I believe I have no lawful right to do so, and I have no inclination to do so. I have no purpose to introduce political and social equality between the white and the black races. There is a physical difference between the two, which in my judgment will probably forever forbid their living together upon the footing of perfect equality, and inasmuch as it becomes a necessity that there must be a difference, I, as well as Judge Douglas, am in favor of the race to which I belong, having the superior position. I have never said anything to the contrary,

but I hold that notwithstanding all this, there is no reason in the world why the negro is not entitled to all the natural rights enumerated in the Declaration of Independence, the right to life, liberty and the pursuit of happiness. [Loud cheers.] I hold that he is as much entitled to these as the white man. I agree with Judge Douglas he is not my equal in many respects—certainly not in color, perhaps not in moral or intellectual endowment. But in the right to eat the bread, without leave of anybody else, which his own hand earns, *he is my equal and the equal of Judge Douglas, and the equal of every living man.* [Great applause.]...

He has read from my speech in Springfield, in which I say that "a house divided against itself cannot stand." Does the Judge say it can stand? [Laughter.]...If he does, then there is a question of veracity, not between him and me, but between the Judge and an authority of a somewhat higher character. [Laughter and applause.]...

When I made my speech at Springfield, of which the Judge complains,...I had no thought in the world that I was doing anything to bring about a war between the free and slave States. I had no thought in the world that I was doing anything to bring about a political and social equality of the black and white races.... [C]an it be true, that placing this institution upon the original basis—the basis upon which our fathers placed it—can have any tendency to set the Northern and the Southern States at war with one another, or that it can have any tendency to make the people of Vermont raise sugar cane, because they raise it in Louisiana, or that it can compel the people of Illinois to cut pine logs on the Grand Prairie, where they will not grow, because they cut pine logs in Maine, where they do grow? [Laughter.]... I am fighting it upon these "original principles"—fighting it in the Jeffersonian, Washingtonian, and Madisonian fashion. [Laughter and applause.]...

DOCUMENT 5

FIFTH DEBATE WITH STEPHEN A. DOUGLAS, AT GALESBURG, ILLINOIS (OCTOBER 7, 1858)

MY FELLOW CITIZENS...

The Judge has alluded to the Declaration of Independence, and insisted that negroes are not included in that Declaration; and that it is a slander upon the framers of that instrument, to suppose that negroes were meant therein; and he asks you: Is it possible to believe that Mr. Jefferson, who penned the immortal paper, could have supposed himself applying the language of that instrument to the negro race, and yet held a portion of that race in slavery? Would he not at once have freed them? I only have to remark upon this part of the Judge's speech... that I believe the entire records of the world, from the date of the Declaration of Independence up to within three years ago, may be searched in vain for one single affirmation, from one single man, that the negro was not included in the Declaration of Independence. I think I may defy Judge Douglas to show that he ever said so, that Washington ever said so, that any President ever said so, that any member of Congress ever said so, or that any living man upon the whole earth ever said so, until the necessities of the present policy of the Democratic party, in regard to slavery, had to invent that affirmation. [Tremendous applause.] And I will remind Judge Douglas and this audience, that while Mr. Jefferson was the owner of slaves, as undoubtedly he was, in speaking upon this very subject, he used the strong language that "he trembled for his country when he remembered that God was just"....[Great applause and cries of "Hit him again," "good," "good."]...

[T]he Judge will have it that if we do not confess that there is a sort of inequality between the white and black races, which justifies us in making them slaves, we must, then, insist that there is a degree of equality that requires us to make them our wives. [Loud applause, and cries, "Give it to him;" "Hit him again."]... I have all the while maintained, that in so far as it should be insisted that there was an equality between the white and black races that should produce a perfect social and political equality, it was an impossibility.... I have said, that in their right to "life, liberty and the pursuit of happiness," as proclaimed in that old Declaration, the inferior races are our equals. [Long-continued cheering.]...

DOCUMENT 6

FIRST INAUGURAL ADDRESS (MARCH 4, 1861)

Fellow citizens of the United States:

In compliance with a custom as old as the government itself, I appear before you to address you briefly, and to take, in your presence, the oath prescribed by the Constitution of the United States, to be taken by the President "before he enters on the execution of his office."...

Apprehension seems to exist among the people of the Southern States, that by the accession of a Republican Administration, their property, and their peace, and personal security, are to be endangered. There has never been any reasonable cause for such apprehension. Indeed, the most ample evidence to the contrary has all the while existed, and been open to their inspection. It is found in nearly all the published speeches of him who now addresses you.

I do but quote from one of those speeches when I declare that "I have no purpose, directly or indirectly, to interfere with the institution of slavery in the States where it exists. I believe I have no lawful right to do so, and I have no inclination to do so." Those who nominated and elected me did so with full knowledge that I had made this, and many similar declarations, and had never recanted them....

There is much controversy about the delivering up of fugitives from service or labor. The clause I now read is as plainly written in the Constitution as any other of its provisions:

"No person held to service or labor in one State, under the laws thereof, escaping into another, shall, in consequence of any law or regulation therein, be discharged from such service or labor, but shall be delivered up on claim of the party to whom such service or labor may be due."

It is scarcely questioned that this provision was intended by those who made it, for the reclaiming of what we call fugitive slaves; and the intention of the law-giver is the law. All members of Congress swear their support to the whole Constitution—to this provision as much as to any other. To the proposition, then, that slaves whose cases come within the terms of this clause, "shall be delivered up," their oaths are unanimous....

It is seventy-two years since the first inauguration of a President under our national Constitution. During that period fifteen different and greatly distinguished citizens, have, in succession, administered the executive branch of the government. They have conducted it through many perils; and, generally, with great success. Yet, with all this scope for precedent, I now enter upon the same task for the brief constitutional term of four years, under great and peculiar difficulty. A disruption of the Federal Union heretofore only menaced, is now formidably attempted.

I hold, that in contemplation of universal law, and of the Constitution, the Union of these States is perpetual. Perpetuity is implied, if not expressed, in the fundamental law of all national governments. It is safe to assert that no government proper, ever had a provision in its organic law for its own termination. Continue to execute all the express provisions of our national Constitution, and the Union will endure forever—it being impossible to destroy it, except by some action not provided for in the instrument itself.

Again, if the United States be not a government proper, but an association of States in the nature of contract merely, can it, as a contract, be peaceably unmade, by less than all the parties who made it? One party to a contract may violate it—break it, so to speak; but does it not require all to lawfully rescind it?

Descending from these general principles, we find the proposition that, in legal contemplation, the Union is perpetual, confirmed by the history of the Union itself. The Union is much older than the Constitution. It was formed in fact, by the Articles of Association in 1774. It was matured and continued by the Declaration of Independence in 1776. It was further matured and the faith of all the then thirteen States expressly plighted and engaged that it should be perpetual, by the Articles of Confederation in 1778. And finally, in 1787, one of the declared objects for ordaining and establishing the Constitution, was *"to form a more perfect union."*

But if destruction of the Union, by one, or by a part only, of the States, be lawfully possible, the Union is *less* perfect than before the Constitution, having lost the vital element of perpetuity.

It follows from these views that no State, upon its own mere motion, can lawfully get out of the Union,—that *resolves* and *ordinances* to that effect are legally void; and that acts of violence, within any State or States, against the authority of the United States, are insurrectionary or revolutionary, according to circumstances.

I therefore consider that, in view of the Constitution and the laws, the Union is unbroken; and, to the extent of my ability, I shall take care, as the Constitution itself expressly enjoins upon me, that the laws of the Union be faithfully executed in all the States. Doing this I deem to be only a simple duty on my part; and I shall perform it, so far as practicable, unless my rightful masters, the American people, shall withhold the requisite means, or, in some authoritative manner, direct the contrary. I trust this will not be regarded as a menace, but only as the declared purpose of the Union that it *will* constitutionally defend, and maintain itself.

In doing this there needs to be no bloodshed or violence; and there shall be none, unless it be forced upon the national authority. The power they confided to me, will be used to hold, occupy, and possess the property, and places belonging to the government, and to collect the duties and imposts; but beyond what may be necessary for these objects, there will be no invasion—no using of force against, or among the people anywhere. Where hostility to the United States, in any interior locality, shall be so great and so universal, as to prevent competent resident citizens from holding the Federal offices, there will be no attempt to force obnoxious strangers among the people for that object. While the strict legal right may exist in the government to enforce the exercise of these offices, the attempt to do so would be so irritating, and so nearly impracticable with all, that I deem it better to forego, for the time, the uses of such offices....

So far as possible, the people everywhere shall have that sense of perfect security which is most favorable to calm thought and reflection. The course here indicated will be followed, unless current events, and experience, shall show a modification, or change, to be proper; and in every case and exigency, my best discretion will be exercised, according to circumstances actually existing, and with a view and a hope of a peaceful solution of the national troubles, and the restoration of fraternal sympathies and affections.

That there are persons in one section, or another who seek to destroy the Union at all events, and are glad of any pretext to do it, I will neither affirm or deny; but if there be such, I need address no word to them. To those, however, who really love the Union, may I not speak?

Before entering upon so grave a matter as the destruction of our national fabric, with all its benefits, its memories, and its hopes, would it not be wise to ascertain precisely why we do it? Will you hazard so desperate a step, while there is any possibility that any portion of the ills you fly from, have no real existence? Will you, while the certain ills you fly to, are greater than all the real ones you fly from? Will you risk the commission of so fearful a mistake?

All profess to be content in the Union, if all constitutional rights can be maintained. Is it true, then, that any right, plainly written in the Constitution, has been denied? I think not.... Think, if you can, of a single instance in which a plainly written provision of the Constitution has ever been denied.... All the vital rights of minorities, and of individuals, are so plainly assured to them, by affirmations and negations, guarranties and prohibitions, in the Constitution, that controversies never arise concerning them. But no organic law can ever be framed with a provision specifically applicable to every question which may occur in practical administration. No foresight can anticipate, nor any document of reasonable length contain express provisions for all possible questions. Shall fugitives from labor be surrendered by national or by State authority? The Constitution does not expressly say. *May* Congress prohibit slavery in the territories? The Constitution does not expressly say. *Must* Congress protect slavery in the territories? The Constitution does not expressly say.

From questions of this class spring all our constitutional controversies, and we divide upon them into majorities and minorities. If the minority will not acquiesce, the majority must, or the government must cease. There is no other alternative; for continuing the government, is acquiescence on one side or the other. If a minority, in such case, will secede rather than acquiesce, they make a precedent which, in turn, will divide and ruin them; for a minority of their own will secede from them, whenever a majority refuses to be controlled by such minority. For instance, why may not any portion of a new confederacy, a year or two hence, arbitrarily secede again, precisely as portions of the present Union now claim to secede from it. All who cherish disunion sentiments, are now being educated to the exact temper of doing this. Is there such perfect identity of interests among the States to compose a new Union, as to produce harmony only, and prevent renewed secession?

Plainly, the central idea of secession, is the essence of anarchy. A majority, held in restraint by constitutional checks, and limitations, and always changing easily, with deliberate changes of popular opinions and sentiments, is the only true sovereign of a free people. Whoever rejects it, does, of necessity, fly to anarchy or to despotism....

One section of our country believes slavery is *right*, and ought to be extended, while the other believes it is *wrong*, and ought not to be extended. This is the only substantial dispute....

Physically speaking, we cannot separate. We cannot remove our respective sections from each other, nor build an impassable wall between them. A husband and wife may be divorced, and go out of the presence, and beyond the reach of each other; but the different parts of our country cannot do this. They cannot but remain face to face; and intercourse, either amicable or hostile, must continue between them....

This country, with its institutions, belongs to the people who inhabit it. Whenever they shall grow weary of the existing government, they can exercise their *constitutional* right of amending it, or their *revolutionary* right to dismember, or overthrow it. I can not be ignorant of the fact that many worthy, and patriotic citizens are desirous of having the national constitution amended....I fully recognize the rightful authority of the people over the whole subject, to be exercised in either of the modes prescribed in the instrument itself; and I should, under existing circumstances, favor, rather than oppose, a fair oppertunity being afforded the people to act upon it....

I understand a proposed amendment to the Constitution—which amendment, however, I have not seen, has passed Congress, to the effect that the federal government, shall never interfere with the domestic institutions of the States, including that of persons held to service. To avoid misconstruction of what I have said, I...say that, holding such a provision to now be implied constitutional law, I have no objection to its being made express, and irrevocable.

The Chief Magistrate derives all his authority from the people, and they have conferred none upon him to fix terms for the separation of the States. The people themselves can do this also if they choose; but the executive, as such, has nothing to do with it. His duty is to administer the present government, as it came to his hands, and to transmit it, unimpaired by him, to his successor.

Why should there not be a patient confidence in the ultimate justice of the people? Is there any better, or equal hope, in the world? In our present differences, is either party without faith of being in the right? If the Almighty Ruler of nations, with his eternal truth and justice, be on your side of the North, or on yours of the South, that truth, and that justice, will surely prevail, by the judgment of this great tribunal, the American people.

By the frame of the government under which we live, this same people have wisely given their public servants but little power for mischief; and have, with equal wisdom, provided for the return of that little to their own hands at very short intervals.

While the people retain their virtue, and vigilence, no administration, by any extreme of wickedness or folly, can very seriously injure the government, in the short space of four years.

My countrymen, one and all, think calmly and *well*, upon this whole subject. Nothing valuable can be lost by taking time....Such of you as are now dissatisfied, still have the old Constitution unimpaired, and, on the sensitive point, the laws of your own framing under it; while the new administration will have no immediate power, if it would, to change either. If it were admitted that you who are dissatisfied, hold the right side in the dispute, there still is no single good reason for precipitate action. Intelligence, patriotism, Christianity, and a firm reliance on Him, who has never yet forsaken this favored land, are still competent to adjust, in the best way, all our present difficulty.

In *your* hands, my dissatisfied fellow countrymen, and not in *mine*, is the momentous issue of civil war. The government will not assail *you*. You can have no conflict, without being yourselves the aggressors. *You* have no oath registered in Heaven to destroy the government, while *I* shall have the most solemn one to "preserve, protect and defend" it.

I am loth to close. We are not enemies, but friends. We must not be enemies. Though passion may have strained, it must not break our bonds of affection. The mystic chords of memory, stretching from every battle-field, and patriot grave, to every living heart and hearthstone, all over this broad land, will yet swell the chorus of the Union, when again touched, as surely they will be, by the better angels of our nature.

DOCUMENT 7

EMANCIPATION PROCLAMATION (JANUARY 1, 1863)

By the President of the United States of America:
A Proclamation.

Whereas, on the twenty second day of September, in the year of our Lord one thousand eight hundred and sixty two, a proclamation was issued by the President of the United States, containing, among other things, the following, to wit:

"That on the first day of January, in the year of our Lord one thousand eight hundred and sixty-three, all persons held as slaves within any State or designated part of a State, the people whereof shall then be in rebellion against the United States, shall be then, thenceforward, and forever free; and the Executive Government of the United States, including the military and naval authority thereof, will recognize and maintain the freedom of such persons, and will do no act or acts to repress such persons, or any of them, in any efforts they may make for their actual freedom.

"That the Executive will, on the first day of January aforesaid, by proclamation, designate the States and parts of States, if any, in which the people thereof, respectively, shall then be in rebellion against the United States; and the fact that any State, or the people thereof, shall on that day be, in good faith, represented in the Congress of the United States by members chosen thereto at elections wherein a majority of the qualified voters of such State shall have participated, shall, in the absence of strong countervailing testimony, be deemed conclusive evidence that such State, and the people thereof, are not then in rebellion against the United States."

Now, therefore I, Abraham Lincoln, President of the United States, by virtue of the power in me vested as Commander-in-Chief, of the Army and Navy of the United States in time of actual armed rebellion against authority and government of the United States, and as a fit and necessary war measure for suppressing said rebellion, do, on this first day of January, in the year of our Lord one thousand eight hundred and sixty three, and in accordance with my purpose so to do publicly proclaimed for the full period of one hundred days, from the day first above mentioned, order and designate as the States and parts of States wherein the people thereof respectively, are this day in rebellion against the United States, the following, to wit:

Arkansas, Texas, Louisiana, (except the Parishes of St. Bernard, Plaquemines, Jefferson, St. Johns, St. Charles, St. James[,] Ascension, Assumption, Terrebonne, Lafourche, St. Mary, St. Martin, and Orleans, including the City of New-Orleans) Mississippi, Alabama, Florida, Georgia, South-Carolina, North-Carolina, and Virginia, (except the fortyeight [sic] counties designated as West Virginia, and also the counties of Berkley, Accomac, Northampton, Elizabeth-City, York, Princess Ann,

and Norfolk, including the cities of Norfolk & Portsmouth[)]; and which excepted parts are, for the present, left precisely as if this proclamation were not issued.

And by virtue of the power, and for the purpose aforesaid, I do order and declare that all persons held as slaves within said designated States, and parts of States, are, and henceforward shall be free; and that the Executive government of the United States, including the military and naval authorities thereof, will recognize and maintain the freedom of said persons.

And I hereby enjoin upon the people so declared to be free to abstain from all violence, unless in necessary self-defence; and I recommend to them that, in all cases when allowed, they labor faithfully for reasonable wages.

And I further declare and make known, that such persons of suitable condition, will be received into the armed service of the United States to garrison forts, positions, stations, and other places, and to man vessels of all sorts in said service.

And upon this act, sincerely believed to be an act of justice, warranted by the Constitution, upon military necessity, I invoke the considerate judgment of mankind, and the gracious favor of Almighty God.

In witness whereof, I have hereunto set my hand and caused the seal of the United States to be affixed.

Done at the City of Washington, this first day of January, in the year of our Lord one thousand eight hundred and sixty three, and of the Independence of the United States of America the eighty-seventh.

By the President: ABRAHAM LINCOLN

WILLIAM H. SEWARD, Secretary of State.

DOCUMENT 8

ADDRESS DELIVERED AT THE DEDICATION OF THE CEMETERY AT GETTYSBURG (NOVEMBER 19, 1863)

Four score and seven years ago our fathers brought forth on this continent, a new nation, conceived in Liberty, and dedicated to the proposition that all men are created equal.

Now we are engaged in a great civil war, testing whether that nation, or any nation so conceived and so dedicated, can long endure. We are met on a great battle-field of that war. We have come to dedicate a portion of that field, as a final resting place for those who here gave their lives that that nation might live.

It is altogether fitting and proper that we should do this.

But, in a larger sense, we can not dedicate—we can not consecrate—we can not hallow—this ground. The brave men, living and dead, who struggled here, have consecrated it, far above our poor power to add or detract. The world will little note, nor long remember what we say here, but it can never forget what they did here. It is for us the living, rather, to be dedicated here to the unfinished work which they who fought here have thus far so nobly advanced. It is rather for us to be here dedicated to the great task remaining before us—that from these honored dead we take increased devotion to that cause for which they gave the last full measure of devotion—that we here highly resolve that these dead shall not have died in vain—that this nation, under God, shall have a new birth of freedom—and that government of the people, by the people, for the people, shall not perish from the earth.

November 19. 1863.

ABRAHAM LINCOLN.

DOCUMENT 9

Second Inaugural Address (March 4, 1865)

[Fellow Countrymen:]

At this second appearing to take the oath of the presidential office, there is less occasion for an extended address than there was at the first. Then a statement, somewhat in detail, of a course to be pursued, seemed fitting and proper. Now, at the expiration of four years, during which public declarations have been constantly called forth on every point and phase of the great contest which still absorbs the attention, and engrosses the enerergies [sic] of the nation, little that is new could be presented. The progress of our arms, upon which all else chiefly depends, is as well known to the public as to myself; and it is, I trust, reasonably satisfactory and encouraging to all. With high hope for the future, no prediction in regard to it is ventured.

On the occasion corresponding to this four years ago, all thoughts were anxiously directed to an impending civil-war. All dreaded it—all sought to avert it. While the inaugeral address was being delivered from this place, devoted altogether to saving the Union without war, insurgent agents were in the city seeking to destroy it without war—seeking to dissol[v]e the Union, and divide effects, by negotiation. Both parties deprecated war; but one of them would make war rather than let the nation survive; and the other would accept war rather than let it perish. And the war came.

One eighth of the whole population were colored slaves, not distributed generally over the Union, but localized in the Southern part of it. These slaves constituted a peculiar and powerful interest. All knew that this interest was, somehow, the cause of the war. To strengthen, perpetuate, and extend this interest was the object for which the insurgents would rend the Union, even by war; while the government claimed no right to do more than to restrict the territorial enlargement of it. Neither party expected for the war, the magnitude, or the duration, which it has already attained. Neither anticipated that the cause of the conflict might cease with, or even before, the conflict itself should cease. Each looked for an easier triumph, and a result less fundamental and astounding. Both read the same Bible, and pray to the same God; and each invokes His aid against the other. It may seem strange that any men should dare to ask a just God's assistance in wringing their bread from the sweat of other men's faces; but let us judge not that we be not judged. The prayers of both could not be answered; that of neither has been answered fully. The Almighty has His own purposes. "Woe unto the world because of offences! for it must needs be that offences come; but woe to that man by whom the offence cometh!" If we shall suppose that American Slavery is one of those offences which, in the providence of God, must needs come, but which, having continued through His appointed time, He now wills to remove, and that He gives to both North and South, this terrible war, as the woe due to those by whom the offence came, shall we discern therein any departure from those divine attributes which the believers in a Living God always ascribe to Him? Fondly do we hope—fervently do we pray—that this mighty scourge of war may speedily pass away. Yet, if God wills that it continue, until all the wealth piled by the bond-man's two hundred and fifty years of unrequited toil shall be sunk, and until every drop of blood drawn with the lash, shall be paid by another drawn with the sword, as was said three thousand years ago, so still it must be said "the judgments of the Lord, are true and righteous altogether."

With malice toward none; with charity for all; with firmness in the right, as God gives us to see the right, let us strive on to finish the work we are in; to bind up the nation's wounds; to care for him who shall have borne the battle, and for his widow, and his orphan—to do all which may achieve and cherish a just, and a lasting peace, among ourselves, and with all nations.

CHAPTER 19

Cameramen and Other Artists Picture Gettysburg

*"Photographic presentments will be accepted by posterity
with an undoubting faith"*

"[T]he real war will never get in the books," predicted the poet Walt Whitman after the Civil War; the "seething hell" defied capture. Nonetheless, as if to prove him wrong, even before peace came at Appomattox Courthouse in April 1865, people began trying to get at the war's heart and soul. Those efforts have never ceased: Countless works have been written on every imaginable aspect of America's bloodiest conflict.[1]

But if no words can convey the horror, perhaps pictures can? If there is any truth to the old saying that "a picture is worth a thousand words," maybe the immediacy of an image can do what mere writing cannot. The American Civil War enables us to put this to the test, because several new inventions made it possible, for the first time, to "picture" war. One of these, *photography* ("writing with light"), was barely two decades old when Abraham Lincoln became president. The second, *lithography* ("writing on stone," because an artist wielding a wax tool drew on a slab, which was then inked for printing), was a little older: By the 1820s, it was possible to produce thousands of copies of a scene quickly and cheaply. Finally, newspaper publishers had found an inexpensive way to include illustrations by taking a sketch or a photograph, carving it into a wood block, then copying that image onto copper for printing.

Americans were hungry for the pictures these innovations produced. Hundreds of photographers—then called "operators," their studios "operating rooms"—set up shop throughout the country to take portraits of the famous and the obscure. Lithographs were even more popular. "Pictures are now a necessity," announced Nathaniel Currier happily in 1850 as his company, Currier and Ives, blanketed the land with inexpensive prints of everything from George Washington and Benjamin Franklin to horse races and hunting scenes, from clipper ships and steamboats to Pilgrims landing at Plymouth Rock and the Founding Fathers signing the Declaration of Independence. Meanwhile *Frank Leslie's Illustrated Newspaper* and *Harper's Weekly*, though started only in the late 1850s, were already selling 100,000 copies of each issue by the eve of the Civil War.[2]

No wonder, once that conflict commenced, some thirty-five camera crews and perhaps fifty sketch artists headed out to record the unfolding drama. Currier and Ives alone produced more than two hundred lithographs about the war (not counting their many images of Lincoln). *Leslie's* raced *Harper's* to get a sketch of this general or that battle to newsstands. Photographers not with the troops waited for word of a battle, then packed up their equipment and scurried to the scene. As a result, concludes historian Bryan Le Beau, "the pictorial record of the Civil War was greater than that of any previous American war."[3]

With images everywhere nowadays, it is hard to appreciate the excitement that Americans 150 years ago felt when gazing upon these wonders. People then "minutely scrutinized illustrated newspapers down to the slightest details," observes W. Fletcher Thompson, "and accepted what they saw there as graphic truth." The thousands of Americans hanging a Currier and Ives print on the parlor wall thought it, too, accurately depicted battlegrounds and camp life, generals and corporals, farewells and homecomings; certainly manufacturers boasted that each and every work was an "authentic" and "faithful" reproduction.[4]

If these kinds of pictures looked right, imagine what people thought of a photograph, which seemed magical in its ability to capture and convey a reality that was, insisted the author Edgar Allen Poe, "*infinitely* more accurate in its representation than any painting by human hands." "They are facts," concluded one journalist after perusing photos of famous Americans. When one famous American, Abraham Lincoln, was told that a picture of him "looked very natural, he remarked, 'Yes, that is my objection. The cameras are painfully truthful.' " It would seem, then, that whether or not any picture is worth a thousand words, another old saying is indeed true: "The camera never lies."[5]

Certainly this is what Americans believed in the fall of 1862 after the Battle of Antietam, when photographs of dead soldiers went on display in Mathew Brady's posh New York City studio (Figure 19-1). "For the first time in history," writes Civil War scholar James M. McPherson, "the graphic and grisly sight of bloated corpses killed in action could be seen by those who never came close to the battlefield." At Brady's, crowds of people, some with magnifying glasses in hand, were "stunned...into silence" as they bent over to study "the very features of the slain." Americans then were accustomed to death in ways that we are not, Mark S. Schantz points out. Before modern medicine discovered and then battled the germs that cause disease, death was so common, so ubiquitous, that seeing a corpse—even the photograph of a corpse (taking a picture of, say, a dead child before burial was a thriving business)—would not have been shocking. Nonetheless, those flocking to Brady's exhibit felt that the walls displayed something new, something that touched "the popular heart," something with, a visitor reported, "a terrible fascination about it that draws one near these pictures, and makes him loath to leave them."[6]

Was this Walt Whitman's "real war"? Some who gazed upon the Antietam photographs certainly thought so. A *New York Times* reporter mused how "the dead of the battle-field come up to us very rarely, even in dreams. We see the [casualty] list in the morning paper at breakfast, but dismiss its recollection with the coffee." Here, however, the photographer "has done something to bring home to us the terrible reality...of war. If he has not brought bodies and laid them in our door-yards and along streets, he has done something very like it." "Let him who wishes to know what war is look at this series of illustrations," insisted another visitor, who—having rushed to Antietam after the battle to search for his wounded son—had seen the carnage for himself. "It was so nearly like visiting the battle-field to look over these views, that all the emotions excited by the actual sight of the stained and sordid scene, strewed with rags and wrecks, came back."[7]

Certainly Alexander Gardner (1821–1882), who took those photos when he worked for Brady (1823?–1896), believed in their truth-telling power. "*Verbal* representations of such places, or scenes, may or may not have the merit of accuracy," Gardner wrote in the Preface to his 1866 album of Civil War photos; "but *photographic* presentments of them will be accepted by posterity with an undoubting faith." Even Whitman, who knew both Gardner and Brady, believed that film got at the heart of things. "[H]ow much better it would often be," he told Brady, "rather than having a lot of contradictory records by witnesses or historians...[,] if we could have" photos instead; "...*that* would be history," Whitman exclaimed, "the best history—a history from which there could be no appeal."[8]

Nine months after Gardner's images transfixed visitors to Brady's gallery in October 1862, the two men—one from New York City, the other from Washington, D.C., where he had by then started his own studio—raced to another battlefield, this one at a Pennsylvania town called Gettysburg. On July 1, 1863, General Robert E. Lee's Army of Northern Virginia collided at this country crossroads with its foe, the Army of the Potomac. Three days and 51,000 casualties later, the Southerners (who had lost 28,000 men) were in retreat, and the tide of war had swung forever to the Union side.

By the end of that bloody month Gardner, Brady, and their camera crews would take a series of pictures that William A. Frassanito, the leading authority on Gettysburg cameramen, calls not only "among the first and most dramatic news photographs ever taken" but that also "played a significant role in shaping the nation's image of the war." "[N]o other 19th-century battlefield in the entire world," Frassanito goes on, "can boast of…such a rich, contemporary body of photographic evidence." Gettysburg, is, then, a good spot to consider how well images get at "the real war," to ask whether the camera does indeed "never lie."[9]

Perusing these images today, it is easy to overlook the difficulties cameramen faced. One was combat itself: In 1861, Brady, keen to chronicle the war's first major battle, barely escaped with his equipment and his life. His assistant, Timothy O'Sullivan, got so close to the fighting that an artillery shell demolished his camera and tripod.

No less an obstacle were challenges posed by rudimentary technology. Brady, Gardner, and O'Sullivan would be amazed by equipment today. The small size, the automatic focus, the flash, and other features that enable any amateur, any time, to simply "point and shoot" with camera or cell phone—all this bears little resemblance to the tools available in 1860. Then, the latest advance was "wet-plate" development, an exciting new technology because one could make multiple prints from a single negative. The whole procedure seems, in our digital age, impossibly complicated: Working in a darkroom, the photographer coated a glass plate with a concoction of chemicals, put it in a special holder to keep light out, then hurried to his nearby camera, which he had already set up on a tripod. (He needed that gadget because he had to open the shutter and expose the film for anywhere from five to thirty seconds—no "snap shots" in those days.) Then he tore back to the darkroom to develop the picture before the plate dried out. Every step promised disappointment: The wrong mix of chemicals, improper coating of the plate, a speck of dust, humidity, a passing cloud—any of these (and more) could spell ruin. Imagine if you had to do this every time you wanted to take a picture. Think not only of how skilled a chemist you would have to be with the wet plate but also how hard it would be to get people to hold still for up to half a minute—much less wait around for the ten or twenty minutes between shots.

As the cameramen knew, it was one thing to perform these logistical and chemical feats in a New York or Washington "operating room"; it was quite another to do it on a battlefield. Brady and the rest rigged up portable darkrooms—dubbed "what-is-it wagons" because the contraptions drew such puzzled looks—but driving these down muddy roads or across fields was likely to crack plates and break bottles of chemicals. A slow shutter speed also limited a photographer's choices. Troops marching or charging? Firing a musket or cannon? When a blink or a gust of wind through trees could wreck a photograph, such action shots were out of the question.

But Mathew Brady was a determined man. Born in obscurity in upstate New York, by the 1860s he was celebrated as the "Father of American photography." At fancy studios in New York and Washington, he and a small army of assistants photographed the rich and famous. Once war broke out, Brady, undeterred by arthritis and failing eyesight, knew he must film it for the sake of history—and to make money. But the financial risks were real. "My wife and my most conservative friends had looked unfavorably upon this departure from commercial business to pictorial war correspondence," Brady later admitted, "and I can only describe the destiny that overruled me by saying…, I felt that I had to go. A spirit in my feet said 'Go,' and I went."[10]

At first, Brady's assistants Alexander Gardner and Timothy O'Sullivan went with him. Sometime between Antietam and Gettysburg, however, Gardner decided to go his own way, taking O'Sullivan along. These two men, racing up from the nation's capital, got to the battlefield first, arriving late in the afternoon of July 5. Confederate forces had pulled out only the day before, limping south; much of the Union army was gone, too, in halfhearted pursuit. They left behind "smoking ruins…, fences…leveled," and "a horrible stench" from the rotting carcasses of 3,000 horses and 7,000 men. Over the next two or three days Gardner and O'Sullivan would take almost sixty photographs. A week or so after they left, the site still scarred (not all of the dead had been buried yet, and the smell lingered into the fall), Brady arrived and set to work.[11]

As you study these photos (Figures 19-2–19-5; focus on the images for now, saving the captions for later), consider—as with any text in *American Conversations*—what message or messages the author (in this case, the "operator") sought to convey. Shock? Sorrow? Grief? Solace? Support for the war effort? Opposition to it? Why do you suppose Gardner did not publish an album of the pictures until a year after the war ended? Why did he not include Figure 19-5 in that album?

Ask yourself, too, whether one could argue that the images are as carefully crafted as any painting by Thomas Cole or Frederic Church (Chapter 12). After all, Gardner called himself a "Photographic Artist," and his friend Whitman agreed that he was "a real artist." Just as Cole had insisted that properly depicting "Nature" required "imagination," so Gardner's imagination was hard at work amid the battleground's stench and gore, and not just in selecting scenes, camera angles, and the like. Painstaking research by Frassanito reveals that two photos—one said to be of Southern corpses, the other of Union dead—in fact showed the same bodies (of Union troops) from different angles.

Frassanito has also demonstrated that Gardner's artistry went still further (Figures 19-3 and 19-4): After photographing a Confederate corpse, he dragged it seventy yards to a rocky hideout; then, using a backpack for a pillow and a gun for a prop, he turned the head toward the camera (he also pronounced this a sharpshooter even though the prop was a regular infantry weapon). More generally, Mark S. Schantz argues that *all* of "the images of dead soldiers taken by wartime photographers were carefully staged" and "meticulously posed" in ways that "reflect the studied eye and deliberate hand of the photographer." Do you agree?[12]

At least the figures Gardner photographed were actually dead. A few months after he and Brady left, a local "Photographist" named Peter Weaver had an idea (Figure 19-6). Knowing that a huge crowd—including President Lincoln (Chapter 18)—soon would be descending on Gettysburg for the dedication of the national cemetery, Weaver decided to make some money selling battle photos. Not having any on hand, on November 11 he invited several Union soldiers (still there tending the wounded) to pretend they had fallen in combat. Compare Weaver's picture with Gardner's: Would you have been fooled?[13]

Whatever his sales, Weaver's fakery, like Weaver himself, remained in obscurity. The Gettysburg work done by Mathew Brady and Alexander Gardner, on the other hand, attracted considerable attention at the time and has since become even more renowned. The fame of these photos can hide the fact that relatively few Americans in the 1860s saw them. To be sure, these shots were not confined to a gallery wall in New York or Washington; they could be reproduced and sold, but prints were fairly expensive. Further limiting their audience were the very constraints mentioned earlier: Photographers' cumbersome wagons delayed their arrival at a battlefield; once on the scene, their camera could not convey action. Whatever pictures they took, the technology did not yet exist to reproduce thousands of copies in cheap lithographs or illustrated newspapers.

Hence "[t]he artist's sketch pad, woodcuts, and lithography…continued to rule the market." A talented "battle artist" like Edwin Forbes (1839–1895) or Alfred Waud (1828–1891), armed with only pencil and paper, could sketch a scene, then rush it to New York where it would be made into a woodcut and published in less than two weeks. Most people saw the Civil War not through the lens of a Brady and Gardner but through the reproductions of Currier and Ives, of *Leslie's* and *Harper's*.[14]

Small wonder, then, that when Gardner and his crew arrived at Gettysburg, they crossed paths with Waud, from *Harper's Weekly*, who had been there during the fighting, scurrying about with his sketch pad. (Forbes, *Leslie's* man, had gotten there just after the shooting stopped on July 3.) One of Waud's works, along with the copy redrawn in New York City and published in *Harper's*, is included here (Figures 19-7 and 19-8). One scholar has called them among "the outstanding picture-reports of the war." While studying them, ponder what limitations an artist like Waud faced and what messages he—and *Harper's*—tried to convey. Why did *Harper's* publish Gardner's "Harvest of Death" only in 1865, after the war (Figure 19-9)? How does their rendering compare with the original photograph?[15]

Meanwhile lithographers at Currier and Ives were also busy that summer of 1863, drawing from images and written accounts of the conflict to prepare their own "Battle of Gettysburg" for sale (Figure 19-10). As by far the largest manufacturer of prints suitable for framing and hanging in the home—most of them, scholars suggest, purchased by women—Currier and Ives were intent on selling their own view of the war's character and purpose. Study the scene included here (Figure 19-11), along with their "Battle of Gettysburg." What was their message? How does it compare with the tableaux created by Waud and Forbes, or O'Sullivan and Gardner? Would it surprise you to know that when combat veterans got a look at a Currier and Ives battle print, they often laughed out loud at it? Why did so many Americans, particularly American women, buy these pictures? What would draw their interest in pictures of men who were not dead but dying (Figure 19-12)?

Lithographs, newspaper illustrations, photographs—whatever popularity they enjoyed when they first came out faded rapidly. *Gardner's Photographic Sketch Book of the War*, published in an expensive two-volume edition in 1866, was a disastrous failure, selling less than two hundred copies. Meanwhile, Mathew Brady found out that his wife and friends had been right: With peace he went bankrupt, unable for ten long years to convince the government to buy his vast collection of Civil War photos. Throughout *American Conversations*, we have noted what publications sold (Mary Rowlandson's, *Common Sense*, *The Life of Washington*, Frederick Douglass's), and what did not (Joseph Plumb Martin, William Apess). What conclusions can be drawn from the dismal sales of *Gardner's Sketch Book*? Brady's bankruptcy? How did Gardner's captions, included here, try to shape memories of the war? Do his words add to the photos or detract from them? Some scholars have argued that they neither add nor detract so much as simply contradict the image they are intended to amplify.[16] Do you agree?

Fortunately for Mathew Brady—and for us—Congress eventually relented, insuring that his pictorial archive would reach future generations. We should be grateful as well as critical. True, the photos do not depict "reality": They miss the battle itself; they are the product of "stagecraft," "artistry," even fakery; moreover, Civil War photos rarely include African Americans, and the few pictures of wounded soldiers ended up stashed away in medical archives, not displayed in a New York gallery or a lavish photo album.[17]

Nonetheless, for all their flaws, the images left by this war—particularly the photographs—are haunting, "eloquent testimony" to the terrible conflict. (Alexander Gardner's moving that corpse was, by the way, an "anomaly," perhaps the only time it happened.) If they do not make the Civil War "practically an open book" (as one scholar claimed in 1911), they nonetheless are, as *Harper's Weekly* said of Brady's pictures in 1863, "materials for history of the very highest value." "However composed or staged," concludes historian Alan Trachtenberg, "they bear witness to real events.... The photograph takes us back to the original moment when light fell upon these surfaces, these bodies and guns and fields; we all but feel the same rays of light in our own eyes."[18]

So powerful can images of war be that, ever since Brady, Gardner, and the rest pleaded with Union officers to let them tag along with the army, photographers have quarreled with the military about where they can go and what they can see. It was 1943 before the public again was allowed to view pictures of American troops killed in action—and even then, unlike Antietam and Gettysburg, the faces of the dead were hidden. Many believe that pictures from Vietnam, America's first televised war, had a profound effect on public opinion, so profound indeed that the government now tries to limit "camera operators" in various ways. What kinds of limits are there these days? What images of American troops have you seen—and not seen? Do you agree with restrictions on coverage?[19]

Even with the latest technology and total freedom, though, Whitman was right: Neither in Brady's day nor our own can "the real war get in the books," and not just for the reasons already spelled out. In the fall of 1862 that *New York Times* reporter, after peering at Gardner's Antietam photos in the Brady gallery, hit upon yet another reason, another blind spot of this wondrous new "writing with light": "There is one side of the picture that...has escaped photographic skill," he wrote. "It is the background of widows and orphans....Homes have been made desolate, and the light of life in thousands of hearts has been quenched forever. All of this desolation imagination must paint—broken hearts cannot be photographed."[20]

Questions for Consideration and Conversation

1. Do these photographs speak in support of the Civil War's purpose, or could they be read as antiwar? Do the lithographs support or question the war?

2. Why did some photos find their way to publication in albums, and others did not?

3. Scholars note that Americans then believed firmly that the dead would go to heaven intact, and that families would reunite there. Do the images reinforce that faith, or undermine it?

4. Compare the photographs with the lithographs and magazine images: Do different technologies lead to different pictures of Gettysburg, or are these mere variations on a theme?

5. How do the titles and the captions contribute to the images? Do they enhance the message of those pictures, distort them, contradict them?

6. Are you surprised that the work of Brady and Gardner got so little attention after the Civil War was over? Why do you think that happened?

7. How do these images of Gettysburg compare with images you see—in newspapers and magazines, on television and on the internet—of American battles today?

Endnotes

1. Alan Trachtenberg, *Reading American Photographs: Images as History, Mathew Brady to Walker Evans* (New York, 1989), 76.

2. Mary Panzer, *Mathew Brady and the Image of History* (Washington, DC, 1997), 45 ("operating rooms"); Bryan F. Le Beau, *Currier & Ives: America Imagined* (Washington, DC, 2001), 16 (Currier).

3. Le Beau, *Currier & Ives*, 71. And see Harold Holzer and Mark E. Neely, Jr., *Mine Eyes Have Seen the Glory: The Civil War in Art* (New York, 1993); Neely and Holzer, *The Union Image: Popular Prints of the Civil War North* (Chapel Hill, NC, 2000).

4. W. Fletcher Thompson, Jr., "Pictorial Propaganda and the Civil War," *Wisconsin Magazine of History*, 46 (1962), 21.

5. Mark S. Schantz, *Awaiting the Heavenly Country: The Civil War and America's Culture of Death* (Ithaca, NY, 2008), 180 (Poe); Panzer, *Brady and History*, 84 ("facts"); W. Fletcher Thompson, Jr., *The Image of War: The Pictorial Reporting of the American Civil War* (New York, 1959), 18 (Lincoln).

6. James M. McPherson, *The Crossroads of Freedom: Antietam* (New York, 2002), 7 ("first time"); William F. Stapp, "To...Arouse the Conscience, and Affect

the Heart," in Brooks Johnson, ed., *An Enduring Interest: The Photographs of Alexander Gardner* (Norfolk, VA, 1991), 23 ("stunned"); Trachtenberg, *Reading American Photographs*, 91 ("features"); Schantz, *Awaiting the Heavenly Country*, ch. 1 (death common), 181–84 (postmortem photography), 192 ("fascination").

7. Brooks Johnson, "A Man for an Era," in Johnson, ed., *Enduring Interest*, 5 ("dreams"); Trachtenberg, *Reading American Photographs*, 90 (another visitor).

8. Alexander Gardner, *Gardner's Photographic Sketch Book of the Civil War* (New York, 1959 [orig. pub. 1866 as *Gardner's Photographic Sketch Book of the War*]), no page (emphasis added); Panzer, *Brady and History*, 85 (Whitman; emphasis added).

9. Frassanito, *Gettysburg: A Journey in Time* (New York, 1975), 15 ("dramatic"); Frassanito, *Early Photography at Gettysburg* (Gettysburg, 1995), 406 ("battlefield").

10. Panzer, *Brady and History*, 18 (wife and friends), 115 ("Father").

11. Frassanito, *Early Photography at Gettysburg*, 21. For the stench and the numbers, see Drew Gilpin Faust, *This Republic of Suffering: Death and the American Civil War* (New York, 2008), 69, 81.

12. Johnson, "A Man for an Era," in Johnson, *Enduring Interest*, 6, 8 ("Artist" and "real artist"); Frassanito, *Gettysburg*, 186–95, Chapter 14; Frassanito, *Early Photography at Gettysburg*, 268–78, 315–50; Schantz, *Awaiting the Heavenly Country*, 184 ("staged," "eye"), 186 ("posed").

13. Frassanito, *Early Photography at Gettysburg*, 41–49, 294–307.

14. Le Beau, *Currier & Ives*, 71.

15. Thompson, *Image of War*, 124; Faust.

16. Schantz, *Awaiting the Heavenly Country*, 193–95.

17. Trachtenberg, *Reading American Photographs*, 115–18.

18. Ibid., 72–74; Panzer, *Brady and History*, vii ("materials").

19. Susan Sontag, *Regarding the Pain of Others* (New York, 2003), 70.

20. McPherson, *Crossroads of Freedom*, 7.

PHOTOGRAPHS AND ILLUSTRATIONS OF GETTYSBURG (1863)

FIGURE 19-1 "Confederate Dead Along the Hagerstown Pike [Antietam, September 1862]." Alexander Gardner for the Mathew Brady Studio. *Source:* Library of Congress.

FIGURE 19-2 "A Harvest of Death, Gettysburg, July, 1863." Timothy O'Sullivan and Alexander Gardner. *Source:* Library of Congress.

Caption to this image on the facing page in *Gardner's Photographic Sketch Book of the War* (1866):

Slowly, over the misty fields of Gettysburg—as all reluctant to expose their ghastly horrors to the light—came the sunless morn, after the retreat by Lee's broken army. Through the shadowy vapors, it was, indeed, a "harvest of death" that was presented; hundreds and thousands of torn Union and rebel soldiers—although many of the former were already interred—strewed the now quiet fighting ground, soaked by the rain, which for two days had drenched the country with its fitful showers.

A battle has been often the subject of elaborate description; but it can be described in one simple word, *devilish!* and the distorted dead recall the ancient legends of men torn in pieces by the savage wantonness of fiends. Swept down without preparation, the shattered bodies fall in all conceivable positions. The rebels represented in the photograph are without shoes. These were always removed from the feet of the dead on account of the pressing need of the survivors. The pockets turned inside out also show that appropriation did not cease with the coverings of the feet. Around is scattered the litter of the battle-field, accoutrements, ammunition, rags, cups and canteens, crackers, haversacks, &c., and letters that may tell the name of the owner, although the majority will surely be buried unknown by strangers, and in a strange land. Killed in the frantic efforts to break the steady lines of an army of patriots, whose heroism only excelled theirs in motive, they paid with life the price of their treason, and when the wicked strife was finished, found nameless graves, far from home and kindred.

Such a picture conveys a useful moral: It shows the blank horror and reality of war, in opposition to its pageantry. Here are the dreadful details! Let them aid in preventing such another calamity falling upon the nation.

FIGURE 19-3 "A Sharpshooter's Last Sleep, Gettysburg, July, 1863." Alexander Gardner. *Source:* Library of Congress.

Caption to this image on the facing page in *Gardner's Photographic Sketch Book of the War* (1866):

A burial party, searching for dead on the borders of the Gettysburg battle-field, found, in a secluded spot, a sharpshooter lying as he fell when struck by the bullet. His cap and gun were evidently thrown behind him by the violence of the shock, and the blanket, partly shown, indicates that he had selected this as a permanent position from which to annoy the enemy. How many skeletons of such men are bleaching to-day in out of the way places no one can tell. Now and then the visitor to a battle-field finds the bones of some man shot as this one was, but there are hundreds that will never be known of, and will moulder into nothingness among the rocks....

FIGURE 19-4 "The Home of a Rebel Sharpshooter, Gettysburg, July, 1863." Alexander Gardner. *Source:* Library of Congress.

Caption to this image on the facing page in *Gardner's Photographic Sketch Book of the War* (1866):

On the Fourth of July, 1863, Lee's shattered army withdrew from Gettysburg, and started on its retreat from Pennsylvania to the Potomac. From Culp's Hill, on our right, to the forests that stretched away from Round Top, on the left, the fields were thickly strewn with Confederate dead and wounded, dismounted guns, wrecked caissons [vehicles], and the debris of a broken army. The artist, in passing over the scene of the previous days' engagements, found in a lonely place the covert of a rebel sharpshooter, and photographed the scene presented here. The Confederate soldier had built up between two huge rocks, a stone wall, from the crevices of which he had directed his shots, and, in comparative security, picked off our officers. The side of the rock on the left shows, by the little white spots, how our sharpshooters and infantry had endeavored to dislodge him. The trees in the vicinity were splintered, and their branches cut off, while the front of the wall looked as if just recovering from an attack of geological small-pox. The sharpshooter had evidently been wounded in the head by a fragment of shell which had exploded over him, and had laid down upon his blanket to await death. There was no means of judging how long he had lived after receiving his wound, but the disordered clothing shows that his sufferings must have been intense. Was he delirious with agony, or did death come slowly to his relief, while memories of home grew dearer as the field of carnage faded before him? What visions, of loved ones far away, may have hovered above his stony pillow! What familiar voices may he not have heard, like whispers beneath the roar of battle, as his eyes grew heavy in their long, last sleep!

On the nineteenth of November, the artist attended the consecration of the Gettysburg Cemetery, and again visited the "Sharpshooter's Home." The musket, rusted by many storms, still leaned against the rock, and the skeleton of the soldier lay undisturbed within the mouldering uniform, as did the cold form of the dead four months before. None of those who went up and down the fields to bury the fallen, had found him. "Missing," was all that could have been known of him at home, and some mother may yet be patiently watching for the return of her boy, whose bones lie bleaching, unrecognized and alone, between the rocks at Gettysburg.

FIGURE 19-5 "War, effect of a shell on a Confederate soldier at Battle of Gettysburg." Alexander Gardner.   *Source:* Library of Congress.

FIGURE 19-6 Soldiers at Gettysburg playing dead, November 1863. P. S. Weaver.
Source: Chrysler Museum of Art; The David L. Hack Civil War Photography Collection.

FIGURE 19-7 "The Attack of the Confederate soldiers, known as the Louisiana Tigers. The Battle of Gettysburg in Pennsylvania." Alfred R. Waud. *Source:* Library of Congress.

FIGURE 19-8 "The Battle of Gettysburg—Attack of the Louisiana Tigers on a Battery of the Eleventh Corps." Drawn by Mr. A. R. Waud. *Harper's Weekly*, August 8, 1863. *Source:* Library of Congress.

FIGURE 19-9 "The Harvest of Death—Gettysburg, July 4, 1863—[Photographed by A. Gardner, Washington.]" *Harper's Weekly*, July 22, 1865.   *Source:* Library of Congress.

FIGURE 19-10 "The battle of Gettysburg, Pa., July 3rd 1863." Currier & Ives.   *Source:* Library of Congress.

FIGURE 19-11 "Home from the War, The Soldier's Return." Currier & Ives, 1861. *Source:* Library of Congress.

FIGURE 19-12 "The Dying Soldier." A. Turrell, after a painting by H.B. Simmons, engraving published by Thomas Kelly, New York, 1864. *Source:* Library of Congress.

CHAPTER 20

Congressmen Investigate the Ku Klux Klan

"The terrorism was so great"

On July 22, 1871, three visitors—John Scott from Pennsylvania, along with Job Stevenson and Philadelph Van Trump, both Ohio men—arrived in Yorkville, South Carolina, the seat of York County. They found most of the natives hostile. On the streets, folks muttered *"Damned Yankees"* and *"Yankee sons of bitches"* as the out-of-towners walked by. In the hotel dining room on their first night, one prominent citizen dumped a pitcher of cream on Stevenson—and "was hailed as a hero." Another local hero emerged later that same evening: African American townsfolk, glad to see these Yankees, had gathered outside the hotel to welcome them; as the crowd was breaking up, a constable trying to arrest one of the well-wishers for allegedly blocking the sidewalk ended up shooting the suspect five times. Not only was the officer exonerated, he was "universally praised" by whites.[1]

Scott, Stevenson, and Van Trump attracted such attention because they were no ordinary visitors: They were a congressional subcommittee dispatched south from Washington, D.C., to investigate the racial violence being committed by a secret organization called the Ku Klux Klan. The last stop on their itinerary, Yorkville—population 1,500—was the earthquake's epicenter. "In no Southern county," writes historian Allen Trelease, "did the Klan organize more fully or take over more completely." Since the previous fall, these Klansmen had compiled "a record of sustained brutality that few places in the country ever matched." Not even the arrival of federal troops in March 1871 had halted the epidemic of whipping, arson, rape, and murder. "I never conceived of such a state of social disorganization being possible in any civilized community as exists in this county now," reported Major Lewis M. Merrill, commander of the Yorkville garrison. The pages that follow offer a sense of what Merrill faced, and what South Carolinians, white as well as black, suffered.[2]

The darkness that had descended upon the county, the state, and indeed the entire South by 1871 stands in sharp contrast to the high hopes many Americans had at the Civil War's end. "Never was there a brighter prospect before any people than that presented to the colored people of the Southern states," announced Richard H. Cain, an African American minister who had just moved from New York to South Carolina. Slavery's sudden end brought scenes that freed men and women would long remember: Masters helpless and humiliated; African American troops patrolling the streets of Richmond and Charleston; a slave trader's holding pen turned into a classroom for black children. As that school suggests, freedom was a jewel with many facets. Former slaves could now build churches as well as schools, choose their own names, go in search of work or lost relatives, marry their true love, live where they pleased. They could, as one put it, "belong to ourselves."[3]

And that was just the beginning, for the federal power that had freed the slaves showed signs of carrying the crusade beyond mere freedom toward full equality. On the heels of the constitutional amendment abolishing slavery in 1865 came two more that declared African Americans citizens and gave freedmen the vote. Moreover, after the war Union troops remained in the South, symbols of Confederate defeat. Along with these troops were government officials from the new Bureau of Refugees, Freedmen, and Abandoned Lands (also called the Freedmen's Bureau). These agents fed the hungry and housed the home-less, built schools and hospitals, helped former slaves negotiate labor agreements with former masters, and set up courts to hear disputes.

African Americans did not wait for white bureaucrats, troops, or politicians, however. Soon after the war, Southern blacks held state conventions to collect their thoughts and broadcast their views. They joined the "Union League," a political organi-zation that brought blacks and pro-Union whites together to support one another—and the Republican Party. Before long, more miraculous moments were burned into American memory: Black men voting, helping draft new state constitutions, and running for office. South Carolina's constitutional convention had seventy-six blacks and forty-eight whites, its first assembly eighty-seven blacks and forty whites. As if this were not astonishing enough, in 1870 black South Carolinians enlisted in the new state militia.

That same year brought ratification of the fifteenth amendment aimed at secur-ing black men the vote, an event so momentous that it—not emancipation, not Appomattox—led the American Antislavery Society to declare its work done. "I seem to myself to be living in a new world," Frederick Douglass (Chapter 16) exclaimed at the New York City ceremony marking the organization's end that April. "We have a future," he shouted in Baltimore a month later, "everything is possible to us!" By coin-cidence, down Chesapeake Bay that very year the proslavery writer George Fitzhugh (Chapter 17), who had remained pugnacious and prolific even after the war, published his last article.[4]

But if Fitzhugh fell silent, men like him had not given up—and the person a scornful Fitzhugh called that "bright mulatto, Fred Douglas," knew it only too well. "Slavery has left its poison behind" in America, Douglass admitted that fall. "The set-tled habits of a nation," he warned, are "mightier than a statute"—mightier, even, than a constitutional amendment.[5]

After the war it quickly became clear that the Confederacy, though defeated, remained defiant. A South Carolina man granted that "[w]ith us, the death of slavery is recognized, but," he vowed, "we don't believe that because the nigger is free he ought to be saucy; and we don't mean to have any such nonsense as letting him vote. He's helpless and ignorant, and dependent, and the old masters will still control him." When that "nonsense" came to pass and blacks went to the polls in 1868, other South Carolinians protested to Congress that "[t]he superior race is to be made subservient to the inferior" and to warn that "[t]he white people of our state will never quietly submit to negro rule." "With reference to emancipation," one North Carolinian promised, "we are at the *beginning* of the war."[6]

On this new front, one weapon Southern whites used was the pen, and they used it ferociously. Though few Union troops remained in the region long—just 12,000 in 1868, a mere 4,000 two years later—Southerners denounced hordes of "blue coated dogs of despotism." South Carolina's new constitution? "[T]he work of sixty-odd Negroes, many of them ignorant and depraved, together with fifty white men, outcasts of Northern society, and southern renegades, betrayers of their race and country." That state's first legislature? "[B]aboons and pickpockets."[7]

Mightier than the pen in the postwar South was the sword. Those unwilling to *join* the freedmen, Northerners, and some white Southerners trying to rebuild and reform the region decided to *beat* them instead. Having lost their war, and in fear of losing their world, the bitterness some white Southerners felt spilled over into horrific assaults on former slaves. One black man was shot to death because he "did not remove his hat," another for giving a white person "sarse [sass]." One black woman was beaten for refusing to call her employer "master," another "for crying" when a white man attacked her mother. It was, concludes historian John Hope Franklin, "open season on blacks." It was also increasingly organized. Soon gangs "called 'rangers,' 'moderators,' [or] 'nigger killers' " were abroad in the land, targeting anyone they deemed a danger to white supremacy.[8]

It was out of this toxic atmosphere of rage and racism that the Ku Klux Klan emerged. Founded in Pulaski, Tennessee, about a year after the war ended, it began as a club for young white men of good family, Confederate veterans "'hungering and thirsting' for amusement, as one of them later put it, after the excitements of wartime had given way to the tedium of small-town life." The club came up with a name (*kuklos* is Greek for "circle" or "band") and a set of rituals, along with a penchant for disguise, secrecy, hazing, and crude, cruel practical jokes—sometimes played on one another, sometimes on African Americans.[9]

Over the next two years, as Union Leagues flourished and biracial state assemblies met, the Klan changed dramatically. First, it spread like wildfire across the South as white men of all ranks—mayors, sheriffs, doctors, and professors; poor farmers, bushwhackers, ruffians, and outlaws—founded new "Dens." (Women demonstrated their support by sewing Klan costumes.) Second, its leaders drafted a document that claimed to spell out the group's purpose. "This is an institution of Chivalry, Humanity, Mercy, and Patriotism . . . ," it announced, established "to protect the weak, the innocent, and the defenceless, from the indignities, wrongs, and outrages of the lawless, the violent, and the brutal." Widows and orphans, the lame and the oppressed—all would be enfolded into the Klan's sheltering arms.[10]

Third, the Klan metamorphosed from what Trelease calls "a social fraternity devoted to playing pranks" into "a terrorist organization aiming at the preservation of white supremacy"—particularly, Richard Zuczek adds, in politics. *Terrorist* is a highly charged word, but it was not coined yesterday. During the July 1871 Yorkville hearings Senator Scott talked of how "the terrorism was so great" in those parts, and a visitor that fall mentioned "the Kuklux terrorism." Historians agree that terror was indeed the Klan's stock-in-trade in a ruthless war on America's biracial experiment.[11]

To combat this "reign of terror" and prop up tottering Republican governments in the Southern states, in April 1871 Congress passed the Ku Klux Klan Act. Calling the violence a "rebellion against the government of the United States," for the first time in the nation's history the law made some crimes committed by individuals a *federal* offense and empowered the president to declare martial law in rebellious regions, send in troops, and suspend habeas corpus (in other words, to arrest a suspect without a warrant, then hold him without charges and without trial).[12]

The very day President Ulysses S. Grant signed this controversial bill—Democrats were bitterly opposed, and some Republicans called it "extreme," even "insane"— a joint House and Senate committee composed of thirteen Republicans and eight Democrats met for the first time, its assignment to "inquire into the condition of the late insurrectionary states." In the coming months the committee would hold hearings in the capital, then send subcommittees into the South to learn more. It was an unprecedented example of standard procedure today: A congressional committee having public hearings on an issue of national importance, gathering testimony, then publishing its findings. Through the summer of 1871 it summoned Americans of all sorts—black and white, rich and poor, Northerners and Southerners, Klansmen and freedmen—to tell their stories. The report, published in thirteen volumes early in 1872, was "one of the most extensive that a congressional committee had ever made," clear proof of the growth of federal power during and after the Civil War. Scholars call it "perhaps the richest single source of Southern history for this period."[13]

It was this task that brought to Yorkville that July the committee's chairman, Republican Senator John Scott, along with representatives Stevenson, a fellow Republican, and Van Trump, a Democrat. York County's seat, their last stop, was "the heart of the Kuklux region." "Because it was regarded in a sense as the final straw by the federal government," Trelease writes, "it received more national publicity and governmental attention than any other Southern county." The Klan was ready for them: At a meeting three days before the "Damned Yankees" arrived, the local Den "voted to kill any member who divulged information"; it also talked about waylaying them on their way out of town in order to steal transcripts of the hearings.[14]

As you read the transcripts, ask what the Klan was so afraid of. Keep in mind, too, what witnesses at this public hearing faced. Those ordered to testify "were guaranteed immunity from prosecution for what they said, except in case of perjury," but that did not stop some people from perjuring themselves. Dr. J. Rufus Bratton, the first witness, was a Klan leader who had put a noose around the neck of one victim himself. How did he handle his interrogators? Whatever risks Bratton ran were nothing compared to the perils faced by Elias Hill, Martha Garrison, and other African Americans on the stand. Chairman Scott promised immunity from prosecution; could he immunize them against Klan retaliation? More generally, as you follow the *Question* and *Answer* here, keep a number of questions of your own in mind. What targets did the Klan select, and why? How organized was the Klan? How well did victims and victimizers know one another, and what does that knowledge say about everyday race relations in this corner of the South? Note, too, not only the answers but also the questions: Did Scott, Stevenson, and Van Trump share the same views, the same agenda?[15]

The local Klan's plots against these Northern interlopers notwithstanding, the subcommittee left Yorkville safely after six days, hauling its transcripts back to Washington—and forward to us. That testimony would help put the KKK on the run. In mid-October President Grant declared York and eight other South Carolina counties in rebellion, suspended habeas corpus, and sent more troops, giving Yorkville, one reporter wrote, "the look of a town...recently captured by an invading army." An avalanche of arrests followed: By year's end, 195 York County men were jailed, two hundred more had fled, and over five hundred had "surrendered, given depositions, and been released" because there were neither cells enough to hold them nor courts enough to try them. "Day after day, for weeks, men came in" to "puke" (local slang for *confess*), Major Merrill reported.[16]

In late November, the first trials got underway at a federal court in Columbia, the state capital. In the jury box were black and white men, ready to hear the evidence; in the packed galleries were newspaper reporters from across the nation, ready to wire stories to an eager public. Many of the accused simply pled guilty; the five who stood trial were all from York County, and all were convicted. Fined and sentenced to prison, by early 1872 (as the committee report went to press), twenty-four white South Carolinians arrived at a penitentiary in Albany, New York.[17]

Hundreds arrested, hundreds more surrendering or fleeing, scores brought to justice: It looked to some—then and since—like federal power "broke the back of the Ku Klux Klans" (at least until the KKK resurfaced a generation later).[18] But Klan hunters knew that success remained elusive. For every Klansman imprisoned, hundreds more— particularly leaders—escaped justice. Why? For one thing, the sheer number of suspects overwhelmed the authorities: Of the 220 indicted that November in Columbia, all but 58 had their trials postponed, and the backlog only got worse. For another, the prosecutions met stiff resistance: Local newspapers cried "Tyranny!" and made Klansmen into martyrs; prime suspects fled (including Bratton, to Canada); witnesses vanished; those hauled into court found that leading South Carolinians had hired high-powered defense lawyers from out of state.

In Washington, meanwhile, enthusiasm for wielding federal power flagged. Congress refused to fund the additional personnel and longer court terms needed to deal with the caseload. Instead, the authorities solved the problem of overcrowded jails and overworked prosecutors by issuing pardons, reducing sentences, and dropping charges against some 1,100 South Carolina suspects. Even as violence resumed in 1872, the federal government decided that too many troops were stationed there—having deployed just 900 men in the state, fewer than a county's Klan could summon in an evening—and began withdrawing them. Thus, while the offensive had, one prosecutor observed, "a 'demoralizing effect' on the Klan," that effect was limited and temporary. No one knew this better than Major Merrill. "The causes from which Ku Kluxism sprung are still potent for evil," he wrote the U.S. Attorney General in September 1872. "The blind, unreasoning, bigoted hostility to the results of the war is only smothered, not appeased or destroyed," he went on; with every sign of weakness in federal authority, "the head of the snake may be instantly seen."[19] Whatever the fate of this or that Klan Den, "the spirit which had animated it carried on and soon triumphed by other means." Resorting to constant threats and occasional violence, in the 1876 elections white Democrats wrested control of South Carolina from the Republicans. Soon thereafter, the last troops left the South and Dr. Bratton was back home in Yorkville, "to live out a locally honored old age in perfect safety." "[T]hese days," wrote one man to Frederick Douglass in 1877, "it appears to be growing dark again to the colored man."[20]

In the end, Reconstruction—"America's Unfinished Revolution," historian Eric Foner calls it—foundered on the rocks of localism and racism. The Civil War and its aftermath raised national power to unprecedented heights, so unprecedented indeed that it made many Americans dizzy. Soldiers stationed in the South? Military despotism. The Freedmen's Bureau, arguably the first federal welfare agency? "[A]bnormal to our system of government" (this from its director!)—and soon shut down. The Ku Klux Klan Act? "We are working on the very verge of the Constitution" (this from a Republican)—and many felt the government had crossed that line.[21]

Small wonder, then, that the victorious North not only disappointed freed men and women by refusing to give them land, in the end it could not summon sufficient will to back up its laws and constitutional amendments. Even Republicans believed that, with the ratification of the fifteenth amendment, "the troublesome 'Negro question' had at last been removed from national politics." An Illinois newspaper echoed the views of many when it declared that "[t]he negro is now a voter and a citizen. Let him hereafter take his chances in the battle of life." Five years have passed since the war, said a Republican congressman from that state while the Ku Klux Klan bill was being debated. Enough! "We have reconstructed, and reconstructed, and we are asked to reconstruct again….[W]e are governing the South too much." The North has "grown 'tired of this word reconstruction,' " said one Senator.[22]

Beneath arguments about constitutional constraints and war weariness lurked the racism that Alexis de Tocqueville (Chapter 13), Angelina Grimké (Chapter 14), and Frederick Douglass (Chapter 16) had noticed in the North as well as the South a generation before. "Slavery is dead, the negro is not, there is the misfortune," wrote one Ohio newspaper in May 1865. "For the sake of all parties, would that he were." Unwilling to go that far, Gideon Welles, a member of Lincoln's Cabinet, nonetheless insisted that "the Negro is not, and never can be the equal of the White. He is of an inferior race and must always remain so." Throughout the North, "Negroes…were shunned and separated—in other words, treated like lepers," writes historian William Gillette. The commitment necessary to force black equality on unyielding Southern whites was simply not there. Instead, whites throughout the nation, insistent that blacks were unequal, decided to "bind up the nation's wounds" by pronouncing Reconstruction a failure and a mistake.[23]

Way back in 1862, Frederick Douglass already knew how hard it would be to change the hearts and minds of men. Winning the war will be the easy part, Douglass predicted: After the guns fall silent, *then* "will come the time for the exercise of the highest of all human faculties. A profounder wisdom, a holier zeal, than belongs to the prosecution of war will be required." "The work before us is nothing but a radical revolution in all modes of thought which have flourished under the…slave system," he concluded. Before condemning Americans of the Reconstruction era for their lack of zeal in pursuing that revolution, we should ask how much farther the revolution has been carried forward in the generations since. Does what Douglass called slavery's "poison" linger in American soil, in America's soul, even today?[24]

Questions for Consideration and Conversation

1. Is it fair to call the Ku Klux Klan a terrorist organization?
2. What targets did the Klan select, and why?
3. What methods, what weapons, did the Klan use to achieve its ends? How effective were these methods?
4. What methods, what weapons (if any), did the Klan's targets have to combat the Klan?
5. How well did victims and victimizers know one another, and what does that knowledge say about everyday race relations in this corner of the South?
6. Consider not only the answers but also the questions: Did Scott, Stevenson, and Van Trump share the same views, the same agenda? Why did they ask the questions they did? What questions did they *not* ask that they should have, or might have, posed?
7. How far did fear shape or color the testimony of the witnesses? Where do you see fear show up in the transcripts?
8. Be alert for differences, subtle or obvious, among the various Q and A sessions: Did blacks testify to different things, in different ways, than whites? Did men speak of different topics, or in different ways, from women?

Endnotes

1. U.S. Congress, *Testimony Taken by the Joint Select Committee to Inquire Into the Condition of Affairs in the Late Insurrectionary States*, v. 5 (Washington, D.C., 1872), 1530 (curses); Allen W. Trelease, *White Terror: The Ku Klux Klan Conspiracy and Southern Reconstruction* (New York, 1971), 374–76.
2. Trelease, *White Terror*, 362–63, 365, 370.
3. Leon F. Litwack, *Been in the Storm So Long: The Aftermath of Slavery* (New York, 1979), 226 ("belong"), 515 (Cain).
4. David W. Blight, *Frederick Douglass' Civil War: Keeping Faith in Jubilee* (Baton Rouge, 1989), 207–08.
5. Harvey Wish, *George Fitzhugh: Propagandist of the Old South* (Baton Rouge, 1943), 335; Blight, *Douglass' Civil War*, 208.
6. Litwack, *Storm*, 257 ("helpless"); Trelease, *White Terror*, xxxv ("submit"); Eric Foner, *Reconstruction: America's Unfinished Revolution, 1863–1877* (New York, 1988), 123 ("beginning"; emphasis added).
7. George C. Rable, *But There Was No Peace: The Role of Violence in the Politics of Reconstruction* (Athens, GA, 1984), 11 ("dogs"); John Hope Franklin, *Reconstruction after the Civil War*, 2nd ed. (Chicago, 1994), 104–05; Lou Falkner Williams, *The Great South Carolina Ku*

Klux Klan Trials, 1871–1872 (Athens, GA, 1996), 11 ("pickpockets").
8. Foner, *Reconstruction*, 120 (assaults); Franklin, *Reconstruction*, 51 ("open season"); Trelease, *White Terror*, xlv ("rangers").
9. Trelease, *White Terror*, 3.
10. Ibid., 16–17.
11. Ibid., xi ("terrorist organization"); *Testimony*, v. 5, 1519 (Scott); Louis F. Post, "A 'Carpetbagger' in South Carolina," *Journal of Negro History*, 10 (1925), 41 ("Kuklux terrorism"); Richard Zuczek, *State of Rebellion: Reconstruction in South Carolina* (Columbia, SC, 1996), 55–58.
12. Everette Swinney, *Suppressing the Ku Klux Klan: The Enforcement of the Reconstruction Amendments, 1870– 1877* (New York, 1987), 209 ("reign of terror").
13. Franklin, *Reconstruction*, 164 ("extreme"); Foner, *Reconstruction*, 456 ("insane"); Trelease, *White Terror*, 392 ("richest").
14. Post, "Carpetbagger," 42 ("heart"); Trelease, *White Terror*, 362 ("straw"), 374.
15. Trelease, *White Terror*, 374.
16. Ibid., 403–05.
17. Ibid., 406–08; Williams, *South Carolina Klan Trials*.

18. Trelease, *White Terror*, 418 ("broke the back").

19. Zuczek, *State of Rebellion*, 106 ("demoralizing"), 121 (Merrill).

20. Trelease, *White Terror*, xii ("spirit"), 418 (Bratton); Post, "Carpetbagger," 61 ("old age"); William S. McFeely, *Frederick Douglass* (New York, 1991), 295 ("growing dark").

21. Foner, *Reconstruction*, 152 ("abnormal"); Gillette, *Retreat from Reconstruction*, 52 ("very verge").

22. Foner, *Reconstruction*, 449–50 ("Negro question," "now a voter," "grown tired"); Gillette, *Retreat from Reconstruction*, 53 ("governing too much").

23. Litwack, *Storm*, 233 (Ohio); Gillette, *Retreat from Reconstruction*, 191 (Welles), 193 ("lepers").

24. Blight, *Douglass' Civil War*, 177.

Testimony Taken by the Joint Select Committee to Inquire Into the Condition of Affairs in the Late Insurrectionary States (1871)

Source: U.S. Congress, *Testimony Taken by the Joint Select Committee to Inquire Into the Condition of Affairs in the Late Insurrectionary States*, v. 5. Washington, D.C., 1872.

YORKVILLE, SOUTH CAROLINA, July 25, 1871.
JAMES R. BRATTON sworn and examined.
By the CHAIRMAN:

Question: Do you reside in this place?

Answer: Yes, sir, and have been residing here for twenty-five years.

Question: Are you a native of this State?

Answer: Yes, sir; of this county.

Question: What is your occupation?

Answer: I have been practicing medicine here for twenty-five years.

Question: Have you had an opportunity of becoming acquainted with the people of this county generally?

Answer: Yes, sir, I think I have....

Question: Our purpose is to inquire into the security of life, person, and property through this county, and the manner in which the laws are executed. Have you any knowledge of any offenses against the law, or against the security of person and property, that have not been redressed in the ordinary courts of justice?

Answer: I have no personal knowledge of anything of the kind. I merely hear rumors and reports....

Question: How many persons have you heard of who have been killed in this county within the last six or eight months?

Answer: There was a man up here named Tom Black, or Roundtree, that they say was killed—I cannot tell when. One report says he was killed by negroes for his money; another, that it was by white men in disguise....

Question: Have you heard of any other cases?

Answer: Yes, sir; a negro up here, named [Anderson] Brown, was reported killed....

Question: Was he a militia captain?

Answer: Not that I know of....

Question: Any others?

Answer: Yes, sir; a negro was hung about twelve miles below by some persons, who I cannot tell.

Question: What was his name?

Answer: Williams.

Question: Was he a militia captain?

Answer: He was....

Question: Was that done by men in disguise?

Answer: Yes, sir, it was so reported....

Question: Do you recollect any persons whipped in this county within six or nine months?...

Answer: ...Some gentlemen and myself were counting them up the other night how many negroes to their knowledge or from report had been whipped and we could not make out more than fifteen.... I think one negro man reported himself to Colonel [Lewis M.] Merrill [commander of the federal troops stationed in York] in the last month as having been whipped, and I get from reliable authority that that negro was not touched...; that there was some difference between the negro and his employer...about the crop..., and he not being satisfied came off to Yorkville with this story....

Question: Have you examined the negro?

Answer: No, sir; I do not know him. I have mentioned the case to show you...how easy it is for some people to report themselves here falsely....

Question: Do you discredit the statements of negroes who say they were whipped?

Answer: In many cases I do....[A] great many of these people dislike to work, and if they can get the protection of the State or the United States to relieve them from work they will do it, and I have no faith in their testimony.

Question: In negro testimony?

Answer: I have not.

Question: Is there any concerted arrangement here for the purpose of intimidating the negroes either with regard to their political rights or their making complaints against those who have whipped them or otherwise committed violence upon them?

Answer: I know nothing of the kind. The truth is this, I think it is just the reverse. If ever our people were earnest in anything it is to teach the negro his duty to be quiet and passive and attend to his duty; to let public meetings alone; to go and vote as he pleases, allowing no man to interfere with him. I do not know any cases where a darkey has been interfered with at the polls.

Question: Is attendance at a political meeting considered imprudent or wrong in them?

Answer: When they attend in large numbers they create great confusion and annoyance....I tell you the feeling, the honest purpose of the people of this county and State, so far as I know, are in favor of the negro.

Question: What do you mean?

Answer: For his general good, private and public. They do not wish to take away one particle of the rights of the negro, civil, moral, religious, or political.

Question: Have you no knowledge of this charge, which is so general, as to the existence of this organization called Ku-Klux?

Answer: Only from report and rumor....

Question: From your intercourse with the people here, do you believe that that organization exists in this county?

Answer: I do not believe there was an organization. There may have been assemblages of men to protect person and buildings, but evidently, from the fact of these negroes having been killed, somebody must have done it; but I do not know anything about the organization....

Question: Are you a member of any secret organization?

Answer: I am not. I belong to no Ku-Klux organization....All I know about the Ku-Klux organization is simply from their proclamation.

Question: What do you mean by that?

Answer: Their public proclamation...in the public print....I will read it to you....This is March 9, 1871, from the *Yorkville Enquirer*:

"KU-KLUX MANIFESTO.— Below we publish a document which we received through the post office on Monday last....As to whether or not the paper is genuine, and emanates from the mysterious Ku-Klux Klan, we have no means of knowing, as the handwriting is evidently disguised...:

"ART[ICLE] 2. There shall be no interference with any honest, decent, well-behaved person, whether white or black; and we cordially invite all such to continue at their appropriate labor, and they shall be protected therein by the whole power of this organization. But we do intend that the intelligent, honest white people (the tax-payers) of this county shall rule it! We can no longer put up with negro rule, black bayonets, and a miserably degraded and thievish set of lawmakers,...the scum of the earth, the scrapings of creation. We are pledged to stop it; we are determined to end it, even if we are 'forced, by force, to use force.'...

"By command of the chief.

"Official:

"K.K.K., A.A.G."...

Question: Does that convey to your mind the belief that there is an organization in the county?

Answer: Yes, sir; who constitute that organization I cannot tell....

Question: With this statement, so far as this proclamation is concerned, you indorse it?

Answer: So far as honesty and intelligence is concerned, I do. I do not think the remedy is right. This Ku-Klux business is certainly a terrible remedy; but if the motive be to keep down dishonesty and rascality, and place honest and virtuous men in power, and let them rule the State, without regard to party, we all ought to sanction it....

Question: Has it escaped your attention that the protection accorded to honest people in this proclamation is confined to honest white men?

Answer: White and black....

Question: What construction do you put upon this sentence in it: "But we do intend that the intelligent, honest white people (the tax-payers) of this country shall rule it."

Answer: I mean simply this, that the honest, intelligent white people are the only persons in the county capable of ruling it....

By Mr. VAN TRUMP:

Question: What, in your opinion, have been the causes of whatever disturbances have occurred in this county...?

Answer: Why, sir, my opinion is this: that these burnings of people's houses and barns and [cotton] gin houses produced this disturbance....

Question: What effect on the public mind had this order of [South Carolina's Republican] Governor [Robert Kingston] Scott arming the negroes...all through the State; and what was the extent of that arming in this county?

Answer: ...There were three [companies] in the district. They were well armed and had ammunition, which I was sorry to see; indeed I was....It depressed and discouraged the white man, and made him feel uneasy; it certainly made the negroes more unruly. They had less regard for peace.

Question: Is it the nature of the negro, when put in power, to become arrogant?

Answer: That is so, according to my experience; I have been raised with him....

By the CHAIRMAN:

Question: What is your opinion as to the truth and veracity of the men composing the Ku-Klux?

Answer: I cannot tell; I have no experience or information upon the subject.

Question: Do you believe they would perjure themselves to deny their connection with an order that commits murder and violence?

Answer: If that organization does exist, and is composed of honorable men in this county, I do not believe they would....

Question: You have mentioned...cases of burning in this county....Out of these...cases, is there any evidence to connect the negroes, as a class, with the burning?

Answer: No, sir.

Question: Yet you give these burnings as [the cause of] the outrages against the negroes?

Answer: That is the general impression among the people.

Question: What justice is there in charging the negroes, as a class, with burning, any more than the murderers who are operating through the country?

Answer: Let me tell you. These people are easily excited to action, and when we had the candidates last fall, strange to say, one candidate actually made this speech: "You have to succeed in this county if you have to burn every blade of grass," or something to that effect.

Question: Did you hear it?

Answer: No, sir....

Question: You cannot swear that he said it?

Answer: No, sir.

Question: You are willing to believe it?

Answer: Yes, sir....

Question: You think yourself an impartial witness?

Answer: I have desired to do justice, and I think I have done a little more than justice to the negroes....

****

YORKVILLE, SOUTH CAROLINA, July 25, 1871.
WILLIAM K. OWENS sworn and examined.
By the CHAIRMAN:

Question: Do you live in this place?

Answer: Yes, sir.

Question: What is your occupation?

Answer: I am a carriage-maker by trade.

Question: What is your age?

Answer: I will be twenty-five next February....

Question: How long have you lived in this place?

Answer: I was born and raised right here. I have been here ever since, except a few years from place to place.

Question: Have you any knowledge of any organization in this county, or in this State, which the public call Ku-Klux?

Answer: I have, sir.

Question: Go on and state what knowledge you have of it....

Answer: In the first place, I reckon you want the thing from the jump.

Question: I want to know when you were initiated, who initiated you, what the purpose of the organization is, and all about it.

Answer: I can't exactly recollect the day of the month I was initiated on, but I think it was before last Christmas. I was initiated up town here, in the back room of Avery's store. I was initiated by John Hunter, William Colcock, Rufus McLain, Daniel Williams, and Simon Wallace....Do you want to know the mode of initiation?

Question: I want to know it.

Answer: In the first place, you are blindfolded; then you are required to get down on your knees and take an oath, and the oath reads this way:

"I solemnly swear to never reveal, but always conceal, the secrets of the Invisible Circle; also, to defend and protect our families, our homes, and our firesides; and to be ready at any moment to obey the call of the chief."...I then received the signs and pass-word of the order. Then, if I have to give the sign—

Question: What was the sign?

Answer: The sign of recognition was three strokes with the left hand against the ear. [Illustrating.] The reply or response to that was this: The right hand struck on the pocket, or put in the pocket—done as careless as possible. [Illustrating.] Then there is the grip. [Illustrating, taking the chairman by the hand.]

Question: The fore-finger on the muscle of the arm or wrist, and the little fingers interlaced?

Answer: Yes, sir. Then the pass-word is syllabled; it is not pronounced. If you meet a man at night, and think he belongs to the order, and you wish to find out, you spell the word s-a-y. If he belongs, he will reply n-o-t-h-i-n-g—spelling it....

The organization is divided into clans by tens. I belonged to what is called the Black Panthers. That was the name the club went by. Rufus McLain was chief....

Question: Have you heard any estimate of the number there are in the county?

Answer: I think there are in this county between four and five hundred....

Question: What is the mode of proceeding in this clan...?

Answer: ...Their business is this, I suppose. I have never been on any of their raids and excursions, these murderings, &c., but their plan of operations is to remove obnoxious people, as they have done it, I suppose. The plan is to meet always when they call you, and go, and ask no questions. You are bound to go....

Question: Have any of these occurrences which have taken place in this county ever been discussed in any clan that you were in?

Answer: O, yes, sir, it was generally in my clan—McLain's clan.

Question: Which occurrences?

Answer: This occurrence of the murder of Jim Rainey, down below here....We were just talking about it and making remarks about it, that he was a mean, desperate kind of a negro, and...that they hung him. I got this information from one of the party. I was not there myself....

Question: Who were there?

Answer: The whole clan from York were there, except a few.... Dr. Bratton was there, John Hunter was there, Tomlinson;...

Question: You say this man's name was Jim Rainey?

Answer: That was the name he went by.

Question: No other name?

Answer: I think he went by the name of Williams also....

Question: Was he a captain of a militia company?

Answer: Yes, sir.

Question: Was any other reason given for killing him than that he was a bad negro?

Answer: None, only they said he had been making threats of what he would do if he had the power, &c.

Question: Were there any other cases of murder in this county discussed...?

Answer: Yes, sir. There was a negro—[Pointing to the door partly open, leading into the hall, in which persons were standing.] There's a party standing out there can hear every word that is passing in here; but it makes no difference; I can say this before the world.

By Mr. VAN TRUMP:

Question: Why were you so alarmed because anybody was hearing?

Answer: I am not alarmed.

Question: Why did you make that peculiar motion?

Answer: I didn't know but what this might be a private business....

Question: Are you afraid to speak loud so that we can hear you?

Answer: No, sir. Are you deaf? you must be. Are you slightly deaf?

Question: Not a bit.

Answer: Pardon me.

By the CHAIRMAN:

Question: Go on with your statement.... What did they say about [another murder victim]?

Answer: They said he had made threats of what he would do to white girls if he had the power to do it, and that was the cause of his being removed.

Question: Removed; is that the term they use—removing them?

Answer: Yes, sir....

Question: Was anything said about whipping?

Answer: O, yes, I heard a good deal of it, but I never heard who did it or how many. It was done in the country.... I heard a good many were whipped.

Question: For what purpose?

Answer: I suppose for making threats, &c. There were so many cases like that that I never paid any attention to it....

Question: Was ever anything said about what purpose was finally to be accomplished by this order?

Answer: I think, sir, it is a political thing.

Question: What was said on that subject?

Answer: There has never been anything general, nothing said positively about it but I think the whole and sole object was to frighten.

Question: To frighten whom?

Answer: To frighten the colored people into a kind of obedience to them, so that they could be subverted to the interests of the democratic party.... They would say, "Next election we'll be certain to gain it, for the negroes know their own interests, and will not vote against us."...

Question: Is there any understanding in that order that binds its members to deny their membership?

Answer: Yes, sir.... You are bound to deny it under penalty of death.

Question: Suppose they become witnesses in court?

Answer: They do it, then, at the penalty of life. Of course it wouldn't be profitable or safe. It is not profitable for me now. I am in danger every night of my life, and every day too....

Question: Suppose a member of that organization is called as a witness for the organization to defend it, how far does his obligation go?

Answer: He is bound to do all he can. Suppose a case was got up—a murder case. I belonged to the party. Well, if they were to arrest a man, and he was charged with this murder, and I was to be called on as a witness to prove that he was with me that night, although I had not seen him at all, I would have to go and swear that he was there that night with me.... Several cases have been got up here on suspicion of Ku-Klux Klanism, but they are always proved out, because they can produce abundant proof.... They are bound to clear each other at the risk of their lives....

Question: How does it affect the obligation of a juror, if he goes on a jury to try a member?

Answer: He has to do all he can for the prisoner; it makes no difference what capacity he is in, he is bound to do all he can for him....

Question: Have any of these men in town said anything to you on the subject of your testifying here?

Answer: Yes, sir.

Question: Who?

Answer: I have been spoken to by Bloodworth, and Wallace.... He says it's reported ... that I had received a certain amount of money, &c., and transportation into Canada, &c....

Question: Did they do anything to prevent your testifying?

Answer: Yes, sir; they told me I had better not, if I had any intention of doing it ... because they would have went for me.... I would have been killed. Death would have been my portion. That's the inference.

By Mr. STEVENSON:...

Question: Where did you get your disguises?

Answer: My disguise I got at the shop—it was just a piece of oil-cloth—at the shop I worked at....

Question: Do you know the two constables in this town?...Do you know whether either of them belongs to this organization?

Answer: Yes, sir; they both belong to it....

By Mr. VAN TRUMP:

Question: You say you are living here now?

Answer: Yes, sir.

Question: What are you doing, what is your business?

Answer: Carriage-maker.

Question: What are you employed at just now?

Answer: Right now?

Question: Yes.

Answer: I am employed in giving in evidence, I suppose.

Question: You know what I mean. Is that the sharp way you intend to answer my questions?

Answer: You asked me what I am doing. I am simply answering questions put to me.

Question: Is that the way you intend to answer?

Answer: I don't know any other way.

Question: Do you not know that I meant what business are you engaged at in town just now outside of being a witness?

Answer: Nothing at all, only my work....

Question: About three months ago you went to Hall for what purpose?

Answer: I have told you.

Question: For what purpose?

Answer: I never say anything twice.

Question: You will say it twice or half a dozen times if I want it.

Answer: I have told you; don't try to intimidate me.

Question: I do not think a man that has belonged to the Ku-Klux is easily intimidated.

Answer: But I think that is your purpose.

Question: Not a bit of it.

Answer: I am mightily fooled in manner if it is not.

Question: What purpose did you go there for?

Answer: To tell him about the Ku-Klux business, and that I wanted to get out.... I thought he might put me on a plan to get out of it—that's what I thought....

Question: What plan did he put you upon?

Answer: The plan of State's evidence.... I told him I was willing to do almost anything to get out; that I didn't consider that there was any honor attached to the party....

Question: How do you know Dr. Bratton is a Ku-Klux?

Answer: By ... signs and by other conversations, by evidence....

Question: What evidence?

Answer: I have evidence from Rufe McLain's own lips.

Question: What signs have you?

Answer: I have the signs to recognize every one.

Question: You swear to that?

Answer: Yes, sir.

Question: Right here, this afternoon?

Answer: Yes, right here, this afternoon.

Question: Dr. Bratton?

Answer: Yes, sir.

Question: Is there more than one Dr. Bratton here?

Answer: Only one.

Question: You swear here, this sunshiny afternoon?

Answer: I would swear it if was winter-time and the snow forty feet deep on the ground....

Question: Have you never talked to each other?

Answer: Yes, sir.

Question: Since or before that [exchange of signs]?

Answer: Before that.

Question: Why not since?...

Answer: Because him and others of his same stamp hate me.

Question: When did that hatred begin?

Answer: About three months ago.

Question: Why was it commenced three months ago?

Answer: A suspicion was gotten up.

Question: How did it come up?

Answer: I got on a breeze [rowdy, possibly drunk] one day—I am a pretty wild chap—so you have been informed.

Question: What do you say about it?

Answer: I am; I don't deny it. I got on a breeze one day in the street, and a man came to me and ordered me in a prompt manner to go to jail, and threatened to lay his hands on me, and I told him if he did I would ruin him. I only meant I would ruin him physically, give him a decent, genteel punching....So they got up a report then...that I had made a report of the Ku-Klux business. Then reports were circulated that I was to get a large amount of money from Major Merrill and had a promise of a certain amount of money and transportation into Canada, and that I had got some from...Mr. Hall....I had then never said a word to either Mr. Hall or Major Merrill....

Question: How intimate is he [Dr. Bratton] with you?

Answer: Not intimate at all....I never was intimate with an aristocrat like him....

Question: Do you say that the purpose you had... was the honest purpose brought about by the working of your conscience, that you wanted to get clear of this organization, and expose it as an honest man?

Answer: I do say so—unreservedly say so.

Question: For no other purpose?

Answer: No other purpose.

Question: No other reward?

Answer: No other reward.

Question: You swear that?

Answer: I swear that.

Question: Have you had the promise of any kind of property, or money, or valuable thing of any kind, for divulging the secrets of the Ku-Klux?

Answer: No, sir.

Question: By no person?

Answer: By no person.

Question: At no time?

Answer: At no time.

Question: And nowhere?

Answer: And nowhere....

By the CHAIRMAN:

Question: You have spoken of a penalty, which was communicated after the handkerchief was taken off and the oath was administered?

Answer: Yes, sir.

Question: In what form was it put?

Answer: With the pistols right at my heart and head; and the penalty was death.

Question: How was it expressed?

Answer: The penalty was that if I divulged these things, may I meet a traitor's doom—death, death, death....

****

YORKVILLE, SOUTH CAROLINA, July 25, 1871.
ELIAS HILL (colored) sworn and examined.
By the CHAIRMAN:

Question: Where do you live?

Answer: In Clay Hill precinct in this county, (York.)

Question: How long have you lived there?

Answer: I was born and raised there....

Question: How old are you?

Answer: Fifty years. I was born in May, 1819.

Question: How long have you been in your present crippled condition?

Answer: I was afflicted and became disabled from walking when I was seven years of age....

Question: Since that time have you been as badly afflicted as you are now?

Answer: I continued to get gradually worse from that time until the present....

Question: What disease was the cause of that?

Answer: The doctor said it was rheumatism.

Question: How were you maintained?

Answer: My father bought himself some thirty-odd years ago..., and that made him free; and when my people were sold, he bought my mother, but he could not get her without taking me; as I was a cripple, they compelled him in the contract to take me....

Question: Then you were not a slave?

Answer: I was born a slave, but never served.

Question: Can you read and write?

Answer: Yes, sir.

Question: When and how did you learn that?

Answer: I learned that gradually, between the years 1830 and 1845, from the school children, and catching it up as I could....

Question: State whether at any time men in disguise have come to the place where you live, and, if so, what they did and said. First, state when it was.

Answer: On the night of the 5th of last May, after I had heard a great deal of what they had done in that neighborhood, they came. It was between 12 and 1 o'clock at night, when I was awakened and heard the dogs barking, and something walking, very much like horses. As I had often laid awake listening for such persons, for they had been all through the neighborhood, and disturbed all men and many women, I supposed that it was them. They came in a very rapid manner, and I could hardly tell whether it was the sound of horses or men. At last they came to my brothers door, which is in the same yard, and broke open the door and attacked his wife, and I heard her screaming and mourning. I could not understand what they said, for they were talking in an outlandish and unnatural tone, which I had heard they generally used at a negro's house. I heard them knocking around in her house. I was lying in my little cabin in the yard. At last I heard them have her in the yard. She was crying, and the Ku-Klux were whipping her to make her tell where I lived. I heard her say, "Yon is his house."...Some one then hit my door. It flew open. One ran in the house, and stopping about the middle of the house, which is a small cabin, he turned around...and said "Who's here?" Then I knew they would take me, and I answered, "I am here." He shouted for joy, as it seemed, "Here he is! Here he is! We have found him!" and he threw the bed clothes off of me and caught me by one arm, while another man took me by the other and they carried me into the yard between the houses, my brother's and mine, and put me on the ground beside a boy. The first thing they asked me was, "Who did that burning? Who burned our houses?" gin-houses, dwelling-houses and such. Some had been burned in the neighborhood. I told them it was not me; I could not burn houses; it was unreasonable to ask me. Then they hit me with their fists, and said I did it, I ordered it. They went on asking me didn't I tell the black men to ravish all the white women. No, I answered them. They struck me again with their fists on my breast, and then they went on, "When did you hold a night-meeting of the Union League, and who were the officers? Who was the president?" I told them I had been the president, but that there had been no Union League meeting held...since away in the fall. This was the 5th of May. They said that Jim Raney, that was hung, had been at my house since the time I had said the League was last held, and that he had made a speech. I told them he had not, because I did not know the man. I said, "Upon honor." They said I had no honor and hit me again. They went on asking me hadn't I been writing to Mr. A. S. Wallace, in Congress, to get letters from him. I told them I had. They asked what I had been writing about? I told them "Only tidings." They said, with an oath, "I know the tidings were d—d good, and you were writing something about the Ku-Klux, and haven't you been preaching and praying about the Ku-Klux?" One asked, "Haven't you been preaching political sermons?" Generally, one asked me all the questions, but the rest were squatting over me—some six men I counted as I lay there. Said one, "Didn't you preach against the Ku-Klux," and wasn't that what Mr. Wallace was writing to me about. "Not at all." I said. "Let me see the letter," said he; "What was it about?" I said it was on the times. They wanted the letter. I told them if they would take me back into the house, and lay me in the bed, which was close adjoining my books and papers, I would try and get it. They said I would never go back to that bed, for they were going to kill me—"Never expect to go back; tell us where the letters are." I told them they were on the shelf somewhere, and I hoped they would not kill me. Two of them went into the house. My sister says that as quick as they went into the house they struck the clock at the foot of the bed. I heard it shatter. One of the four around me called out, "Don't break any private property, gentlemen, if you please; we have got him we came for, and that's all we want." I did not hear them break anything else. They staid in there a good while hunting about and then came out and asked me for a lamp. I told them there was a lamp somewhere. They said "Where?" I was so confused I said I could not tell exactly. They caught my leg—you see what it is—and pulled me over the yard and then left me there, knowing I could not walk nor crawl, and all six went into the house. I was chilled with the cold lying in the yard at that time of night, for it was near 1 o'clock, and they had talked and beaten me and so on until half an hour had

passed since they first approached. After they had staid in the house for a considerable time, they came back to where I lay and asked if I wasn't afraid at all. They pointed pistols at me all around my head once or twice, as if they were going to shoot me, telling me they were going to kill me, wasn't I ready to die? and willing to die? didn't I preach? that they came to kill me—all the time pointing pistols at me....I told them that I was not exactly ready; that I would rather live; that I hoped they would not kill me that time. They said they would; I had better prepare. One caught me by the leg and hurt me, for my leg for forty years has been drawn each year, more and more year by year, and I made moan when it hurt so. One said "G-d d—n it, hush!" He had a horsewhip, and he told me to pull up my shirt and he hit me. He told me at every lick "Hold up your shirt." I made a moan every time he cut with the horsewhip. I reckon he struck me eight cuts right on the hip bone; it was almost the only place he could hit my body, my legs are so short—all my limbs drawn up and withered away with pain. I saw one of them standing over me or by me motion to them to quit. They all had disguises on. I then thought they would not kill me. One of them then took a strap and buckled it around my neck and said, "Let's take him to the river and drown him." "What course [which way] is the river?" they asked me. I told them, east. Then one of them went feeling about, as if he was looking for something, and said, "I don't see no east! Where is the d—d thing?" as if he did not understand what I meant. After pulling the strap around my neck, he took it off and gave me a lick on my hip where he had struck me with the horsewhip. One of them said, "Now you see I've burned up the d—d letter of Wallace's and all," and he brought out a little book and says, "What's this for?" I told him I did not know; to let me see with a light and I could read it. They brought a lamp and I read it. It was a book in which I had kept an account of the school. I had been licensed to keep a school. I read them some of the names. He said that would do, and asked if I had been paid for those scholars I had put down? I said no. He said I would now have to die. I was somewhat afraid, but one said not to kill me. They said "Look here! Will you put a card in the paper next week like June Moore and Sol Hill?" They had been prevailed on to put a card in the paper to renounce all republicanism and never vote. I said, "If I had the money to pay the expense, I could." They said I could borrow, and gave me another lick. They asked me, "Will you quit preaching?" I told them I did not know. I said that to save my life. They said I must stop that republican paper that was coming...to me from Charleston....They said I must stop it, quit preaching, and put a card in the newspaper renouncing republicanism, and they would not kill me; but if I did not they would come back the next week and kill me. With that one of them went into the house where my brother and my sister-in-law lived, and brought her to pick me up. As she stooped down to pick me up one of them struck her, and as she was carrying me into the house another struck her with a strap. She carried me into the house and laid me on the bed. Then they gathered around and told me to pray for them. I tried to pray. They said "Don't you pray against Ku-Klux, but pray that God may forgive Ku-Klux. Don't pray against us.. Pray that God may bless and save us." I was so chilled with cold lying out of doors so long and in such pain I could not speak to pray, but I tried to, and they said that would do very well, and all went out of the house except one. He handed me back a little book, that schoolbook, saying, "Here's that little book;" but it seemed that he forgot to speak in that outlandish tone that they use to disguise their voices. He spoke in his common, plain voice, and then he went out....

Question: How were they disguised?

Answer: With coverings over their faces. Some had a kind of check disguise on their heads. One had black oil-cloth over his head, and something like gloves covering his hands and wrists....

Question: Had you been president of the Union League?

Answer: Yes, sir. They charged that, and I owned it.

Question: Had there been political meetings held at your house.

Answer: Yes, sir, and I owned that; but they were not this year.

Question: Had you been preaching?

Answer: Yes, sir, regularly.

Question: For how long?

Answer: Every month. I have been preaching regularly for some ten years or more, with a license to preach.

Question: To what church do you belong?

Answer: To the Baptist church....

Question: Had you anything to do with anybody who was connected with the burning of property—gin-houses and barns?

Answer: No, sir....I only heard of the burnings as everybody else did.

Question: You spoke of others who were visited in your neighborhood by the Ku-Klux?

Answer: Yes, sir....

Question: State how many have been whipped, according to information which you believe to be true?

Answer: They went on and whipped J. P. Hill's wife the same night they were at my house.

Question: Who else?

Answer: Julia, Miles Barron's wife. Rumor says they committed a rape on her....Samuel Simrell's house was burned down that night....

Question: What effect did this have on the colored people up there—were they alarmed?

Answer: Yes, sir; so alarmed that they did not sleep in their houses at night.

Question: How many slept out?

Answer: I did not hear of any who did not sleep out...; during last winter and spring all slept out from the effect of this excitement and fear....

By Mr. STEVENSON:...

Question: I see the following article in the *Yorkville Inquirer* of July 20, 1871:

"GOING TO LIBERIA.—We learn that a large number of negroes—comprising sixty or eighty families—in...this county, have determined to emigrate to Liberia [a nation in West Africa founded by former slaves], and are now making their arrangements to embark in the vessel of the Colonization Society which will sail from Charleston or Baltimore early in November next. Rev. Elias Hill and June Moore (two colored men of this county) are at the head of the movement....We understand that several hundred other negroes in this county are making preparations to follow in the vessel which sails next May."

Answer: That did come out in last week's paper, but it surprised me very much when I saw that after I had made preparation, and had been writing and inquiring in this matter merely for myself personally, it should be taken up in a public print in such a manner calling me a leader. It was because of the outrages of the Ku-Klux that I took the resolution and made and am making preparations, and others are doing the like;...we do not believe it possible...for our people to live in this country peaceably, and educate and elevate their children to that degree which they desire....I think so from reading history and from the present state of things around us....

Question: Do you not believe that, now that the white people have pledged themselves in a public meeting to be quiet and protect you, they will do it?

Answer: They pledged themselves at that meeting in February...to protect the colored people in case of outrage....I will tell you how we proved them. When the Ku-Klux...came to my house and beat my sister-in-law and me, a young man, her son, rushed off to Mr. James L. Bigger, telling him to wake up, that there was distress at our house..., and asking him to come to our relief; but he refused to come, and the next day he was heard to say that he...knew they were coming; he knew well what they came for; and that

we might never expect anything else. All my white neighbors, after pledging themselves...to give us aid in time of trouble, every one of them was heard to rejoice...that so many were whipped, and telling all the causes and reasons—all this they did, their pledge to the contrary....

By Mr. STEVENSON:...

Question: What is the feeling out there now among the colored people?

Answer: Those that are not arranging to go to Liberia have some hope, through the operation of this sub-committee here and elsewhere, and...through the punishment of the Ku-Klux, who are the neighbors generally, so that the times will eventually come that those who want to go away now may stay, finding that they can live in peace. But for certain of us, we have lost hope entirely....

Question: What is the temper of the white people...?

Answer: ...I will tell you the impression: They are so afraid just now....The other day, when the summons came for me to come here, a young man that I had thought was innocent was seen to jump out of his father's house and run, without coat or hat, as if for his life. Hearing of so many Ku-Klux having been taken up in other counties, and expecting that these men were after him, he...ran. Not one in fifty of them now but is uneasy and trembling at the sight of an officer or a blue-coat, and staying out in the woods by day, and some by night, like we used to....Now the white men, the young men and boys, from fifteen to the gray-headed, are out, some by night and hunting by day, an excuse that if a summons should come for them they would be absent. Some in my neighborhood have fled the State, and others are ready to go.

Question: What, in your judgment, would be the condition of affairs if the United States troops were not here?

Answer: I would not then have come up here to report for anything in the world, for I would have expected to have been killed to-night if I had. Men have been run out of the State for reporting outrages....

By Mr. VAN TRUMP:...

Question: When you get to preaching, do you not show up the wrongs and oppressions suffered from these white people?...

Answer: No, sir; not at all. I was accused of that on the night when they beat me; but that is not the subject on which I preach; it is Scriptural salvation.

Question: You have the idea that these white people are determined to put you black people down?

Answer: Yes, sir; I have that idea very strongly. They are determined to keep us from using any influence for republicanism, which we believe is God's will. I do believe it comes nearer to God's will and universal love and friendship in this world than any other.

Question: You mean republican government?

Answer: Yes, sir.

Question: Do you also mean the republican party?

Answer: Yes, sir. I believe the republican party advocates what is nearer the laws of God than any other party, and therefore I feel that it is right.

Question: When you are preaching, do you preach republicanism in your sermons?

Answer: No, sir; I preach the Gospel....

Question: You say that, instead of the white people coming to your rescue on the night of the 5th of May, as they had pledged themselves to, the next day when they heard of it they rejoiced?

Answer: That is the report, sir....

Question: Who rejoiced?...

Answer: My near neighbors. Do you want their names?

Question: Yes.

Answer: James L. Bigger.... J. L. Barry—[The witness had several times in the foregoing examination suddenly changed his voice for a moment to a hoarse whisper.]

Question: Why do you whisper when you mention persons? Can others hear you outside of this room?

Answer: No, I suppose not, but I feel afraid of others hearing. We are always afraid now and careful....

Question: You need not whisper the names here.

Answer: But I am always so suspicious in speaking of these things, always watching, so that I do it even in answering you....
By Mr. STEVENSON:

Question: Did you ever give to your congregations of colored people, whether in sermons or otherwise, advice to commit any kind of violence on any person or on anybody's property?

Answer: Never.

****

YORKVILLE, SOUTH CAROLINA, July 27, 1871.
HAMPTON HICKLIN (colored) sworn and examined.
By the CHAIRMAN:

Question: Where do you live?

Answer: I live about seven miles from here....

Question: What did you do there?

Answer: I was working a farm. I started a farm there, but then I had to leave that, and I went over into North Carolina....

Question: Were you visited at any time by the Ku-Klux?

Answer: Yes, sir; I was visited here seven times by them before I went away....

Question: Do you know young Langdon Cheve McCallum?

Answer: I know Cheve McCallum.

Question: How long have you known him?

Answer: I can't tell you how long. I have been living here fifteen or sixteen years; ever since anybody.

Question: Does he know you?

Answer: He ought to know me. I have seen him enough at Elison Creek church.

Question: Did you ever talk to him?

Answer: Yes, sir. Me and Cheve and Tom and Gus McCallum—all three of the boys I know, and the father.

Question: Tell us when the McCallums came to your house, and what they did....

Answer: The first time they came to my house they came on a Tuesday night about 10 o'clock. I got away that night. They came back again on a Friday night. I got away that night, and I came to York and told the sheriff, and he says, "Do you know who they are?" I said, "I have an idea." He says, "If you know tell me, and I will go out and take them up." And I says, "All right. If they come again I will tell you...." They came back to me again..., but they didn't get me. I got away, and saw them, and I came in and told the sheriff....

Question: What did they say?

Answer: They tore down my chimney and shot the turkeys, and took all the things and mashed them up, and whipped my wife. She would not tell where I was....I laid in the corner of the fence. I was as close to them as that, [two yards,] in the briers....There was Andrew Hoge. He was captain. And Thomas Nichols says to Andrew, "I told you you could not catch Hamp." And Johnny says—

Question: Johnny who?

Answer: Johnny Nichols. The next was William Jackson, Sam Jackson's son. That is three; there was four. The next one was Matthew Parrot, a one-armed fellow. A sugar-cane mill caught his hand, and they cut it off....Then I came on to the sheriff, and...I told him, "You said for me, if I knew, to come and tell you, and now I will tell you." He said, "All right, Hamp. Come into this room;" and...then I told him; and he says, "I will give you good advice, Hamp." He says, "You go right home, and leave here and go to North Carolina."...On Sunday I had been at Charlotte [North Carolina], and I came back about half past 10 o'clock on Sunday night. About half after 11, after I laid down, they got me; then they whipped me. They had my hands tied, and they whipped me and whipped me until they cut me all to pieces....They said, "Sheriff Glenn told us to kill you."...They had me then and they whipped me, and whipped me, and whipped me, and whipped me, and whipped me....They told me over everything I had told the sheriff. I had told to the sheriff all that in this very room, at this very table where we are sitting....

By Mr. VAN TRUMP:...

Question: You recognized William Jackson and the Nichols boys and Matthew Parrot, you said?

Answer: Yes, sir.

Question: Did anybody speak to William Jackson and Matthew Parrot?

Answer: No, sir.

Question: How did you know them?

Answer: I knew them.

Question: In the first place, you said the only way you knew these men was by their talking—calling names?

Answer: Yes, sir; the way I came to know Matthew Parrot to be qualified, he was there, was this fellow Jones, my cousin, that they had tied around the neck to take him out to make him tell. He told me it was Matthew Parrot....He [Parrot] held Jones, and he didn't have but one arm and held him, and he knew him. He took him by one hand. He had just one hand; his hand was off up to here....

Question: Are there not a great many men in South Carolina with one arm?

Answer: No, sir.

Question: There are not?

Answer: No, not right about here....I have been here a good while, and I knows; I am certain I knows them. I knows our citizen too well, [laughing.]

Question: What is tickling you?

Answer: Because you want to sort o' trap me up to think I don't know the man.

Question: Do you mean to say that you don't know anybody in this county who is a white man, and has but one arm, because of the war?

Answer: No, sir, not where I live....I can tell you the whole part about this thing. I would not have put myself to no great trouble, but I was depending upon the sheriff to take them up, and I followed these men to the houses, and I found out when I came to the sheriff to protect me that he was doing all he could for them.

Question: Was he a Ku-Klux too?

Answer: I don't know what else, or he wouldn't have told me to go away when I wanted him to take them.

Question: You have changed your opinion of Sheriff Glenn?

Answer: Yes, sir; I had to tell him so.

Question: When Major Merrill has so much confidence in the sheriff, why do you doubt him?

Answer: I told the major...that I doubted him [Sheriff Glenn], and he had deceived me, and he has deceived more than me....

Question: He must be a terrible sheriff. Who got that into your head?

Answer: Nobody but my own knowledge. A man deceives me in one case, and I don't allow him to deceive me any more, [laughing.]

Question: What amuses you so?

Answer: I don't know as I can tell you. I just consider that you thought I didn't know these men, and want to trap me up on that. I know them as well as you can make figures on that paper, [laughing.]...

Question: Nobody has been talking to you about the sheriff?

Answer: No, sir; I am telling you the fact. I am telling the truth. It is just my opinion.

Question: May be you have a wrong opinion about him. Suppose I told you that it has been sworn to by a highly respectable witness that this Sheriff Glenn has been helping Major Merrill to get up a full list of all those black people who have been whipped by the Ku-Klux, would that change your opinion? If Major Merrill has such confidence in Sheriff Glenn that he...gets him to assist in keeping an account, so that the Government of the United States shall know exactly...how you black people have been wronged, would that change your opinion?

Answer: It is as I tell you about the sheriff....I respect him for what he has done, and am willing to give him his own, but...if I were to tell you...what I know, and...we could bring in fifteen men to say against the sheriff, in spite of all he could do against it.

Question: What can you bring against him?

Answer: We can bring a right smart against the sheriff.

Question: What is it?

(No answer.)

Question: I will give you reasonable time for you to say whether you will give it to us or not.

Answer: I don't suppose I am obliged to. The other fellows will state their evidence....
The CHAIRMAN....[G]o on and answer the Question.

Answer: I was telling him about this committee, because he has fooled so many—all we colored people—about this Ku-Kluxing. He has sunk us in the dark. I told you, Mister, we put our dependence in the sheriff a good deal more than our Maker. We thought the sun rose and set in the sheriff until we found this out....

By Mr. VAN TRUMP:

Question: Did you tell him who beat you?

Answer: Yes; and...he replied, "You fellows go home and behave yourselves; go to work and vote the right ticket, and there will be no more Ku-Kluxing."

Question: Did that satisfy you?

Answer: That satisfied me; but I spoke to Mr. Glenn, and said, "You ought not to fool any man about his principles. Let every man have his principles."

Question: I don't want all the conversation.
By MR. STEVENSON:

Question: I want that conversation. Go on and tell what you said to the sheriff.

Answer: I says to him, "Mr. Glenn, you ought not to fool no man in his principles. Let a man just vote as he pleases; but when the colored man is away working hard, and trying to make something, we get beaten and abused, and come to you as a friend, when we are bothered, and all you say is, 'You fellows go home and go to work,' and at this very time these fellows were shooting at us, and chasing us, and beating us, and we could not sleep in our houses all the winter." For three months I slept in the woods, and every time I would come to him he would say, "Go home and go to work."

****

YORKVILLE, SOUTH CAROLINA, July 27, 1871.
MARTHA GARRISON (colored) sworn and examined.
By the CHAIRMAN:

Question: Are you married now?

Answer: Yes, sir.

Question: Was your name Martha Woods?

Answer: Yes, sir....

Question: Do you know young Cheves McCallum?

Answer: Yes, sir; I know him well.

Question: How long have you known him?

Answer: All my life.... [W]e used to play together....

Question: Go on and say whether the Ku-Klux ever came to your house at night, and, if so, what they did?...

Answer: [A]bout three months ago... [t]hey came there. The first time was Sunday night. They hallooed and cursed, and told me to open the doors; and when I got up they were in the house, and had broken the door down. They hallooed, "Go and get the old man." I said, "There is no man in here." Then they hallooed, "Kindle a light," and as it lighted they saw pap.

Question: What was his name?

Answer: Addison Woods; and they grabbed him and carried him out to the kitchen, all of them but three, and they staid in there, and run to the bed to see if there was anybody else. Three of them staid in there; one kindled up a light, and the other went back to the bed to see if there was anybody else in bed. As they jerked the cover off he jumped up.

Question: Who?

Answer: Jack Garrison, my husband; and he run out. The captain was standing in the middle of the floor; as he ran out of the door the captain shot at him, and two of them out of doors shot at him. But he got loose, and pap got loose too. They came to the house and broke the things, and asked me if he hadn't a militia gun. I said, "No." He said I was a d—d liar. I said he hadn't. They said, "Can you swear he had not?" I said, "Yes." The captain said to let me off then; I was telling the truth. Then they went on and said they would not trouble me; they believed I was telling the truth. The next night they came back; when they left they told us if we told what they broke and did they would come back and kill us. Our folks told. I didn't say a word. I told pappy about it, and he told some other black one, and he told it; and Saturday night they came back and

hallooed, "Open the door, G—d d—n you," and came in, and every one run in the room, and they lit the matches, and three of them held me, and four of them took me and whipped me.

Question: With what?

Answer: With hickories. They hit me in the head with a gun. There was a bundle of hickories as big as my wrist.

Question: Was that mark, which is on your face, caused by that?

Answer: Yes, sir.

Question: What is that from?

Answer: From the whipping. I couldn't see out of my eye for a long time. They whipped me for telling. They said I had reported them.

Question: Did you tell who they were?

Answer: No, sir; I didn't tell nobody who they were.

By Mr. VAN TRUMP:

Question: You told your papa?

Answer: Yes, sir; nobody else.

By the CHAIRMAN:

Question: Who where they? Did you know?

Answer: Yes, sir. I knew four good: Tom McCallum, and Cheve McCallum, and Gus McCallum, and Lee Williams.... [A]ll four of them... were there both times....

Question: How many were there?

Answer: The first night there was nine; the last, twenty-seven.

Question: They were disguised?

Answer: Yes, sir....

Question: What did they want with Garrison? Did they say?

Answer: They said they wanted to kill him.

Question: Did they say what for?

Answer: Yes, sir. They said he was captain of Clay Hill [militia] company, and they 'low'd to kill him.

Question: Was he captain of Clay Hill company?

Answer: He was captain once.

Question: Where is he now?

Answer: He is out here.

Question: Is he here in attendance?

Answer: Yes, sir.

Question: How old are you?

Answer: Just twenty.

By Mr. VAN TRUMP:

Question: I only want to see whether you are right in regard to knowing these men. How did you know Thomas McCallum?

Answer: By his talk; and he was standing at the foot of my bed, with the disguise half off his face. It was to one side, so he could see me.

Question: Was it because it was too small?

Answer: No, sir; he shoved it off to one side.

Question: How far did the McCallums then live from you?

Answer: Two miles.

Question: How did you know Cheves McCallum?

Answer: He was the one that struck me the first lick, and his disguise fell in the bed, right on me.

Question: Was there a light in the house?

Answer: Yes, sir.

Question: Did you speak to him then when you saw who it was?

Answer: No, sir; I never said a word.

Question: How did you know Gus?

Answer: His fell off, too, when they were fighting.

Question: Who were fighting?

Answer: When they were whipping me....

Question: How did you know Lee Williams?

Answer: When Gus went to pick up his [disguise] on the floor, he had his gun on the floor, and as he rose up he knocked off Lee Williams's [disguise]....I knew them anyhow before I saw the faces.

Question: It is singular that the disguises were knocked off, or fell off, of everybody in the room.

Answer: These four were whipping me....

Question: Did they threaten you?

Answer: Yes, sir. They said they would kill me if I told....

****

YORKVILLE, SOUTH CAROLINA, July 27, 1871.
ANDREW CATHCART (colored) sworn and examined.
By the CHAIRMAN:

Question: How old are you?

Answer: I am about seventy-seven years old....

Question: Where do you live?

Answer: ...[O]n a plantation that I bought in slavery times. I bought myself about twenty years ago, and then worked and bought myself a little plantation....

Question: How many acres do you own down there?

Answer: ...[T]ogether it makes ninety-eight acres....

Question: Have you got it all paid for?

Answer: Yes, sir; all.

Question: Go on and tell us what you know of the operations of the Ku-Klux in your neighborhood—what they did to you.

Answer: When they first came in to me they said, "Ku-Klux, Ku-Klux, Ku-Klux," and catched hold of me, and says one, "Have you any arms?" I said I had a rifle up there. They said, "Take it down and break it all to peices [sic]." I got it and went to my hearth and broke it all to pieces there on the rocks of my fire-place, and then bent the muzzle, and they struck me a few licks while I was at it. The men talked to me; I think it was one Henry Reeves spoke to me; and I looked at him, and every time I would go to look at him, he would slap me in the face....He was a man that had lived with me, and I knew his voice when I heard it....I knew the man's temper; I have seen him in good humor and in ill humor. He is a fractious sort of a man. The next thing they said was, "Where is your money?" I told them I had no money. Says he, "Open the chest, or I will break it open, and open it damned quick." My wife handed him the keys and they opened the chest....."Come," says he, "damn him, take him out and hang him, kill him, shoot him, take him out and shoot him." As they marched me out of the door one stood inside of the door and turned back as they marched me out. I took him to be one Jimmy Jones, that I had worked with for five years. His father is an old man. I farmed for him, and made him corn and cotton, and took care of it until he died. He came back and sat down and commenced plundering the chest. The old woman sat right by him; her knees were right against it, and his gown fell off he was so busy plundering, and then she looked and saw his pantaloons, and knew the pantaloons; she knew the coat and the pockets of his coat; she knew them well....Then after he had plundered and taken out several things, such things as would be useful to him, they marched me out, and he went on with Henry Reeves....He took the butt of an Army gun and struck me on the head, and dropped me to my knees. I scrambled a while and got up....I spit blood after that for two months from that blow....[T]hey presented their guns at me. I turned around and said, "O Lord, have mercy upon me! Lord have mercy on my soul!" I said, "You can kill me if you see cause." I expected that was to be my last word....Then they marched down to the house where my daughter and another woman taught school. They had authority to teach...agreeable to the law. They went down there and tore the school-house all to pieces; they worked on it half to quarter of an hour....One hallooed, "Burn it up;"...they raised a fire..., but after they went off I crawled under there, and put the fire out, and saved it.

Question: Had that building been used as a school?

Answer: Yes, sir; for two years.

Question: For white or colored children?

Answer: For colored children....

Question: How many were there of them?

Answer: I saw there were fifteen or twenty of them....

Question: Did you see the kind of disguises they wore?

Answer: Yes, sir; they had on some sort of caps—one thing and another—and sort of horns one had....

Question: Did you recognize any others than the two you have mentioned?

Answer: I can mention this Ben Presley; Ben Presley is my nigh neighbor; I know him by his walk and by his looks and by his motion; and when he first began to talk he said that I was a ruler—"You think you will rule; but, God damn you, you shall not rule." I told him I always kept myself as humble since my freedom as before, and I did not want to rule anything. He says, "You have got a bald-faced horse that you ride up and down the road."

I told him I did not ever ride him. He said, "Well, your son does." I told him "He didn't ride often." He talked in his plain, natural voice then, and I knew him. He is a man I am used to....

Question: Is he a drinking man?

Answer: Yes, sir; he drinks pretty smart, at times. The same night they came on Charlie Bryant's...; they could hear them two miles off shooting and knocking and hallooing.

Question: What did they do with Charlie Bryant?

Answer: He was...not at his place, but they abused his wife pretty bad; they liked to have killed her. They knocked her down, I think, with a pistol..., and beat her, so her child said, after she was down. She did not know much about it, for she was as bloody as a hog that had been stuck....

Question: Have you taken any part in the public affairs of that township except in getting up this school-house?

Answer: No, sir....
By Mr. STEVENSON:

Question: Had you been a republican leader?

Answer: I had never been leader of nothing, but I voted the republican ticket....

Question: You spoke of an Army gun; what did you mean by that?

Answer: I mean by an Army gun, one of those rifles such as the blacks had mustering with—the colored militia. They had bayonets on the guns that night that they beat me.

Question: They had one of those guns?

Answer: Yes, sir, more than one. I saw two or three, maybe.
By Mr. VAN TRUMP:

Question: When did you get your gun?

Answer: It was an old rifle I had got long before;... I made no use of it....

Question: ...Who is Henry Reeves?

Answer: He is Henry Reeves; he lives down here not far from Nely Miller's.

Question: What is his business?

Answer: Only a farmer....[A]fter he spoke I knew his voice, and I looked at him and he would put his face right up in mine and slap me.

Question: You did not have much chance to see?

Answer: Yes, sir. After he did that I would keep looking. I looked at his body and shoulders, and I knew the make of the whole man, and knew his voice and everything....

Question: Is not that a very dangerous way to prove a man guilty, because he is made like somebody else?

Answer: Yes, sir; but did you never see a man you were so used to that you could tell him by looking at the build of the man and the voice.... And this man was like one of my home folks to me. He had not talked to me for a year, but when he spoke I looked up like it was one of my home folks....

Question: Let me ask you now—as an old man of seventy-seven years, who cannot expect to live very long—

Answer: No, sir, of course not.

Question: Let me ask you, if Henry Reeves's life depended on the fact would you swear that he was there?

Answer: I would swear that it was a man made just like him, and talking like him, and acting like him in passion and temper....

Question: Who is Jimmy Jones?

Answer: He has just got to be a man. I worked for his uncle for about five years when he was a boy and unable to work for one or two years; then he came up and worked with me.

Question: What is his business?

Answer: Farming. As I went to come out of the door when they marched me out, he stood in the door and turned and came right back and commanded the chest to be unlocked, and called for my money—my cotton money.... [H]e went right to the chest; he had often seen me put it there. He sometimes worked with me, working a little farm. He went at it just as orderly as if he knew all about it.

Question: But how did you know it was Jones?

Answer: He had on a pair of pantaloons...that I knew, and I am particularly confident that I knew his walk;...sort of a teetering walk, a sort of swing that made me look at him.

Question: Is James Jones the only man you ever saw who had a swinging walk?

Answer: No, sir; but if it is a person you have been working with a long time and have noticed particular you can tell the walk. There may be a walk like his, but to the best of my knowledge that was him.

Question: Would you swear it was him?

Answer: I will tell you more. My wife looked at him, and his gown that he had on fell off while he was there. He had been to our house several times before that, and she had looked at his clothes. He is like one of our home folks, and she knew them. There was the same pantaloons and the same coat pockets, all agreed just for him, and he stammered a sort of talk like this. [The witness assuming an unnatural bass tone.] He tried to talk a sort of Irish, outlandish like that—to keep us from understanding him, or that it was him, until they got mad, and then they talked naturally.... Sometimes he would talk pretty naturally in his own voice again, and we knew his foolish ways; he is a mighty brickety [conceited or headstrong] fellow....

Question: You are satisfied that these three men were there that night and Ku-Kluxed you?

Answer: I believe it with the bottom of my heart....

Question: Did you tell anybody that you found or discovered Reeves, or Jones, or Presley?

Answer: No, sir; I never told that to anybody.

Question: Who did you first tell it to?

Answer: Here is the first place I ever made the discovery to anybody, when I told it here to day.... I gave little scattering hints [before], but I never made it plain.

Question: Who did you give scattering hints to?

Answer: Dr. Barron was talking to me, and I told him I knew the men, and he told me it was a very difficult thing without I was confident. I would not positively say....
By Mr. STEVENSON:

Question: Why did you not tell these names before to-day?

Answer: Because they would have killed me. I began to talk a little about it, and I heard something. They laid a trap. There was a paper that they would be on me again....Mark you, I am a negro and cannot read or write, but I know some few things....

AFTERWORD

"Fellow-citizens, we cannot escape history"

—ABRAHAM LINCOLN

Unlike fairy tales and bedtime stories, history books do not always have happy endings. Perhaps if this volume of *American Conversations* stopped in 1776 with the Declaration's ringing words, in 1789 with the new nation launched, or even in 1865 with the rebellion crushed, one could fashion a conclusion that, while not as sunny as "they all lived happily ever after," at least would have sunshine amid the shadows.

It is hard to find many bright spots when a book closes in the 1870s, a dark and bloody era indeed. That African Americans found their dreams dashed was only part of a national retreat from the "new birth of freedom" that Abraham Lincoln had hoped for at Gettysburg. President Ulysses S. Grant's administration (1869–1877) was flooded by a tide of tawdry scandals. A terrible depression stalked the land, driving untold numbers into destitution. In 1877, desperate workers launched massive strikes that took over some cities before being brutally crushed by state and federal troops. In 1877, too, the presidential election between the Republican Rutherford B. Hayes and the Democrat Samuel J. Tilden was only resolved in favor of Hayes by a backroom deal that, among other things, made the new president drive the last nail in Reconstruction's coffin.

Not even the nation's Centennial Exposition, held in Philadelphia during the summer of 1876, can hide the hard fact that this was not exactly America's finest hour. The millions who flocked to the fair—its theme was "Progress of the Age"—came to celebrate the country's success and to gawk at electric lights, telephones, typewriters, and other wondrous inventions that promised more success to come. Celebration, of course, required forgetting not only Reconstruction's collapse and the first "Great Depression" but also the ongoing conquest of Native Americans and the continuing relegation of white women to second-class status. In 1876 as in 1776, Americans born the "wrong" gender or color were largely confined to the nation's margins.

Amnesia also included forgetting the horrors and lessons of the Civil War. Though Memorial Day became a holiday soon after 1865, it was devoted to mourning lost loved ones, not pondering the fate of the "national regeneration" that was, Frederick Douglass had said in 1863, the conflict's "sacred significance." By 1876, some Union and Confederate veterans were even observing Memorial Day together in a spirit of reconciliation. Just as Mathew Brady and Alexander Gardner found that no one would buy their war photographs anymore (Chapter 19), so Douglass railed against "national forgetfulness."[1]

Ending *American Conversations* in the 1870s, then, would be reason enough for melancholy as this expedition through America's past nears an end. But there are other reasons, too, among them the lingering, nagging sense that this book, long as it is, still leaves out so many fascinating Americans who belong in the company of Private Martin and Dr. Hamilton, of Mrs. Rowlandson and Reverend Apess. Thinking about all of those people, I feel like the historian Barbara Tuchman, who finished her classic work, *The Proud Tower*, with "an acute awareness of what I have not included. The faces and voices of all that I have left out crowd around me as I reach the end."[2]

Besides being haunted by faces and voices, another reason melancholy settles over the book's final pages is the realization that, whatever any historical work's merits, it remains a long way from getting at what every student of history seeks to recover: the color, the texture, the very *feel* of past times. Just as no obituary can truly capture a person—What did her voice sound like? What made him laugh? What books did she cherish? What friends sustained him? What did she think about in the middle of a long night or at the dawn of a new day?—so the past remains elusive. This sense of falling short comes with the scholarly territory. Louis Menand, at the end of his prizewinning book *The Metaphysical Club*, confessed that "I have not begun to do justice to the people and the events I have tried to bring to life in these pages."[3] A healthy humility is one thing historical study instills: How much there is to learn, and how, the more you learn, the more you realize the limits to your knowledge.

Depressing? Dispiriting? Not to worry: Sources of solace help keep melancholy at bay. For one thing, the journey that is this book should be part of a much longer sojourn. Perhaps *American Conversations* leaves you wanting to read more of what Thomas Paine wrote or see more of what Thomas Cole drew; go beyond the excerpts and examples here. Perhaps you wish to explore more thoroughly the context of Mary Rowlandson's work, or George Fitzhugh's; use the Further Reading to light your way. Perhaps you have a hankering to head off in new directions, to visit Westerners or workers or other Americans absent here; then this book is not an ending but a beginning, the start of a longer trek through the "foreign country" of the past.

As with your own journey, so with the 1870s. For all the grim news coming out of the United States—scandals and strikes, terror and amnesia—there was, as Frederick Douglass kept saying, reason for hope. The amazing thing about Reconstruction, Douglass wrote in 1880, is "not that freedmen have made so little progress, but, rather, that they have made so much; not that they have been standing still, but that they have been able to stand at all." "The situation...is discouraging," he admitted three years later, "but with all its hardships and horrors, I am neither desperate nor despairing as to the future." Why? Because "the discussion concerning the Negro still goes on....All talk of its being a dead issue is a mistake," Douglass continued. "It may for a time be buried, but it is not dead....[I]t will rise again, and again, and again, with increased life and vigor."[4]

Douglass was not alone in refusing to lose hope. Many other African Americans during those dark years held onto bright memories of Reconstruction's promise. During the 1930s, interviewers of aged former slaves found tales still fresh about the "good times in the country" after the Civil War, when "the colored used to hold office." Occasionally pulling out scrapbooks of newspaper clippings saved for decades, these elderly African Americans taught their children and grandchildren "about the old times, mostly about the Reconstruction, and the Ku Klux."[5]

Along with powerful memories, Reconstruction also bequeathed to the nation two constitutional amendments, along with the deployment of federal power (such as the one you visited in the last chapter) that might be summoned again someday. The late Peter J. Parish called the two amendments "time-bombs which ticked away at the heart of the American constitutional system for a century. Like other measures, including...the Force Acts [against the Klan], they set precedents and taught lessons which could be invoked and applied a century later." In 1867, a congressman had insisted that "justice and equality" for African Americans required "the strong arm of *power*, outstretched from the central authority here in Washington."[6] It would be a century before that arm stretched out again, but when it did, it wielded weapons forged during Reconstruction.

Parish also calls our attention to truths so basic that they often get overlooked. "It is stating the obvious to say simply that the war preserved the Union and destroyed slavery, but it still needs to be said, for the obvious is too easily taken for granted. Neither of these major achievements was obvious—or even likely—when the war began in 1861." Yet in just four years, "[a]n institution with two hundred years' history in North America…was swept away."[7]

The other achievement, saving the Union, was perhaps even more important. Hard as it is to appreciate today, for three generations after the American nation's founding many people considered the United States an awkward, sickly creature unlikely to live long. Just a week after Abraham Lincoln took office in March 1861, a sardonic New Yorker named George Templeton Strong confided to his diary that "The political entity known as the United States of America is found out at last.…The bird of our country is a debilitated chicken, disguised in eagle feathers. We have never been a nation; we are only an aggregate of communities." Yet four years later even the skeptical Strong had to admit that "The people has (I think) just been bringing forth a new American republic—an amazingly large baby—after a terribly protracted and severe labor, without chloroform [an anesthetic]."[8] Never again would disunion, much talked about from 1776 to 1865, be a serious topic in the American conversation.

As Parish put it,[9]

> The Civil War was above all the supreme test of the strength, meaning and purpose of the American experiment—a test on the one hand of its stability, resilience and capacity for survival and, on the other, of its democracy, freedom, justice and equality. The obvious fact that it failed parts of that test, and passed others with less than distinction, should not obscure the importance of its success in passing the crucial test of survival. If the Union survived its promise survived, and the enduring promise was at least as important as specific and repeated failures to live up to it.

Just what *was* the nation's promise? As Lincoln knew, it lay in the words "All Men are Created Equal." He knew, too, that these words were no more a reality in 1865 than they had been in 1776. But, as you read in Chapter 18, he advised against giving up. The nation's founders "meant to set up a standard maxim for free society, which should be…constantly looked to, constantly labored for, and even though never perfectly attained, constantly approximated, and thereby constantly spreading and deepening its influence, and augmenting the happiness and value of life to all people of all colors everywhere." *All* people, *all* colors, *everywhere*: like Thomas Paine and Thomas Jefferson before him, Lincoln believed that America's experiment would shape the very future of the globe, that "the Declaration…gave liberty, not alone to the people of this country, but hope to the world for all future time."[10]

Nor would expounding on the Declaration's meaning be confined to the likes of Lincoln. The ink on the parchment was barely dry in 1776 before Americans of all sorts set about making it their own. Within months, an African American named Lemuel Haynes launched his antislavery work, "Liberty Further Extended," with passages from the Declaration. A generation later, Reverend William Apess had the wrong document but the right idea when, demanding that Indians be treated better, he pointed out that "all men are born free and equal, says the Constitution of the country." And a generation after that, at Philadelphia's 1876 Centennial Exposition, a party of women crashed the July 4 ceremonies to read "Woman's Declaration of Independence." From Lemuel Haynes on, blacks were among the leaders in this campaign—still being waged today—both *for* the Declaration and *against* defining it narrowly. "The colored people had read the Declaration until it had become part of their natures," wrote a North Carolina African American in 1868. Certainly eleven freedmen in Alabama at the time knew it cold. Petitioning against injustice by local courts, fraudulent labor contracts, and other assaults on their newfound liberty, they concluded by pointing out the obvious: "This is not the persuit of happiness."[11]

America's promise, then, lay in the *pursuit* of happiness, not in happiness itself. If the nation, then and since, has kept women, workers, and people of color from fully joining the pell-mell chase after that elusive (and personal) goal, folks like the Grimké sisters and Frederick Douglass (among countless others) have called it to account, often by using the very words written in 1776. That those words still have life and power, still inspire and nag at the conscience, proves Lincoln right when he said: "Fellow-citizens, *we* cannot escape history."[12]

Endnotes

1. David W. Blight, *Race and Reunion: The Civil War in American Memory* (Cambridge, MA, 2001), 1 ("sacred"); David W. Blight, *Frederick Douglass' Civil War: Keeping Faith in Jubilee* (Baton Rouge, LA, 1989), 231 ("forgetfulness").

2. Barbara W. Tuchman, *The Proud Tower: A Portrait of the World Before the War, 1890–1914* (New York, 1966), xv.

3. Louis Menand, *The Metaphysical Club* (New York, 2001), 445.

4. Gary B. Nash et al., *The American People: Creating a Nation and a Society*, v. I (New York, 1986), 559; Philip S. Foner, ed., *The Life and Writings of Frederick Douglass*, v. IV (New York, 1955), 358–59.

5. Eric Foner, *Reconstruction: America's Unfinished Revolution, 1863–1877* (New York, 1988), 610–11.

6. Peter J. Parish, *The American Civil War* (New York, 1975), 623–24; James M. McPherson, " 'For A Vast Future Also': Lincoln and the Millennium," in Susan-Mary Grant and Peter J. Parish, eds., *Legacy of Disunion: The Enduring Significance of the American Civil War* (Baton Rouge, LA, 2003), 146.

7. Parish, *American Civil War*, 630.

8. Parish, "Abraham Lincoln and American Nationhood," in Grant and Parish, eds., *Legacy of Disunion*, 129.

9. Parish, *American Civil War*, 651–52.

10. McPherson, "Lincoln and the Millennium," in Grant and Parish, eds., *Legacy of Disunion*, 136.

11. Ruth Bogin, " 'Liberty Further Extended': A 1776 Antislavery Manuscript by Lemuel Haynes," *William and Mary Quarterly*, 3d ser., 40 (1983), 85–105; James H. Merrell, "Declarations of Independence: Indian-White Relations in the New Nation," in Jack P. Greene, ed., *The American Revolution: Its Character and Limits* (New York, 1987), 217 (Apess); Foner, *Reconstruction*, 114 (African Americans), 565 (women).

12. Annual Message to Congress, December 1, 1862, in Michael P. Johnson, ed., *Abraham Lincoln, Slavery, and the Civil War: Selected Writings and Speeches* (Boston, 2001), 217. I use this phrase in a different sense than Lincoln did in this message. Here he meant that he and Congress could not escape the judgment of historians in the future, not that no one can escape the weight of the past. Nonetheless, elsewhere Lincoln made clear that he felt, for good or ill, the power of the past to shape the present and future.

FURTHER READING

CHAPTER 1

AFRICANS, AMERICANS, AND EUROPEANS
IMAGINE THEIR ORIGINS

"In the beginning"

Africa

Ajayi, J. F. A., and Michael Crowder, eds. *History of West Africa*. Volume One. 3rd edition. New York: Longman, 1985.

Awolalu, J. Omosade, and P. Adelumo Dopamu. *West African Traditional Religion*. Ibadan, Nigeria: Onibonoje Press and Book Industries Limited, 1979.

Beier, Ulli, ed. *The Origin of Life and Death: African Creation Myths*. London: Heineman, 1966.

Davidson, Basil. *A History of West Africa, 1000–1800*. The Growth of African Civilisation Series. Revised edition. London: Longman Group Limited, 1977.

Fage, J. D. *A History of West Africa: An Introductory Survey*. 4th edition. Cambridge, England: Cambridge University Press, 1969.

Mbiti, John S. *Introduction to African Religion*. Second revised edition. London: Heinemann, 1991.

Stride, G. T., and Caroline Ifeka. *Peoples and Empires of West Africa: West Africa in History, 1000–1800*. New York: Africana Publishing Corporation, 1971.

Thornton, John. *Africa and Africans in the Making of the Atlantic World, 1400–1800*. 2nd edition. New York: Cambridge University Press, 1998.

Vansina, Jan. *Oral Tradition as History*. Madison: University of Wisconsin Press, 1985.

Zahan, Dominique. *The Religion, Spirituality, and Thought of Traditional Africa*. Trans. Kate Ezra Martin and Lawrence M. Martin. Chicago: The University of Chicago Press, 1979 (orig. pub. 1970).

America/Iroquoia

Axtell, James, ed. *The Indian Peoples of Eastern America: A Documentary History of the Sexes*. New York: Oxford University Press, 1981.

Cornplanter, Jesse J. *Legends of the Longhouse…Told to Sah-Nee-Weh, The White Sister*. Philadelphia: J. B. Lippincott, 1938.

Engelbrecht, William. *Iroquoia: The Development of a Native World*. Syracuse: Syracuse University Press, 2003.

Fenton, William N. *The Great Law and the Longhouse: A Political History of the Iroquois Confederacy*. Norman: University of Oklahoma Press, 1998.

Hudson, Charles M. *The Southeastern Indians*. Knoxville: The University of Tennessee Press, 1976.

Mann, Barbara Alice. *Iroquoian Women: The Gantowisas*. American Indian Studies, vol. 4. New York: Peter Lang, 2000.

Salisbury, Neal. "The Indians' Old World: Native Americans and the Coming of Europeans." *William and Mary Quarterly*, 3rd Series, vol. 53, no. 3 (July 1996), pp. 435–58.

Snow, Dean R. *The Iroquois*. Cambridge, MA: Blackwell, 1994.

Wallace, Anthony F. C. *The Death and Rebirth of the Seneca*. New York: Alfred A. Knopf, Inc., 1970.

England/Europe

Bobrick, Benson. *Wide as the Waters: The Story of the English Bible and the Revolution It Inspired*. New York: Simon and Schuster, 2001.

Bruce, F. F. *History of the Bible in English: From the Earliest Versions*. 3rd edition. New York: Oxford University Press, 1978.

Meinig, D. W. *The Shaping of America: A Geographical Perspective on 500 Years of History. Volume I: Atlantic America, 1492–1800*. New Haven: Yale University Press, 1986.

Nicolson, Adam. *God's Secretaries: The Making of the King James Bible*. New York: HarperCollins, 2003.

CHAPTER 2

CABEZA DE VACA SURVIVES AMERICA

"I walked lost and naked through many and very strange lands"

Adorno, Rolena, and Patrick Charles Pautz, ed. *Alvar Núñez Cabeza de Vaca: His Account, His Life, and the Expedition of Pánfilo de Narváez*. 3 vols. Lincoln: University of Nebraska Press, 1999.

Ahern, Maureen. "The Cross and the Gourd: The Appropriation of Ritual Signs in the *Relaciones* of Alvar Núñez Cabeza de Vaca and Fray Marcos de Niza." In *Early Images of the Americas: Transfer and Invention*. Ed. Jerry M. Williams and Robert E. Lewis. Tucson: University of Arizona Press, 1993, pp. 215–44.

Bauer, Ralph. *The Cultural Geography of Colonial American Literatures: Empire, Travel, Modernity.* Cambridge Studies in American Literature and Culture. Cambridge, England: Cambridge University Press, 2003.

Bishop, Morris. *The Odyssey of Cabeza de Vaca.* Westport, CT: Greenwood Press, 1971 (orig. pub. 1933).

Bolton, Herbert E. *The Spanish Borderlands: A Chronicle of Old Florida and the Southwest.* New Haven: Yale University Press, 1921.

Elliott, J. H. *Empires of the Atlantic World: Britain and Spain in America, 1492–1830.* New Haven: Yale University Press, 2006.

Fernández, José B. *Alvar Núñez Cabeza de Vaca: The Forgotten Chronicler.* Miami: Ediciones Universal, 1975.

Hoffman, Paul E. *A New Andalucia and a Way to the Orient: The American Southeast During the Sixteenth Century.* Baton Rouge: Louisiana State University Press, 1990.

Howard, David A. *Conquistador in Chains: Cabeza de Vaca and the Indians of the Americas.* Tuscaloosa: The University of Alabama Press, 1997.

Hudson, Charles, and Carmen Chaves Tesser, eds. *The Forgotten Centuries: Indians and Europeans in the American South, 1521–1704.* Athens: University of Georgia Press, 1994.

Lockhart, James, and Stuart B. Schwartz. *Early Latin America: A History of Colonial Spanish America and Brazil.* Cambridge Latin American Studies, no. 46. Cambridge, England: Cambridge University Press, 1983.

Milanich, Jerald T., and Susan Milbrath, eds. *First Encounters: Spanish Explorations in the Caribbean and the United States, 1492–1570.* Ripley P. Bullen Monographs in Anthropology and History, no. 9. Gainesville: University of Florida Press and the Florida Museum of Natural History, 1989.

Quinn, David B. *North American from Earliest Discovery to First Settlements: The Norse Voyages to 1612.* New York: Harper and Row, Publishers, 1977.

Rabasa, José. *Writing Violence on the Northern Frontier: The Historiography of Sixteenth-Century New Mexico and Florida and the Legacy of Conquest.* Latin America Otherwise: Languages, Empires, Nations. Durham: Duke University Press, 2000.

Reséndez, Andrés. *A Land So Strange: The Epic Journey of Cabeza de Vaca. The Extraordinary Tale of a Shipwrecked Spaniard Who Walked Across America in the Sixteenth Century.* New York: Basic Books, 2007.

Sauer, Carl Ortwin. *Sixteenth Century North America: The Land and the People as Seen by the Europeans.* Berkeley: University of California Press, 1971.

Schneider, Paul. *Brutal Journey: The Epic Story of the First Crossing of North America.* New York: Henry Holt and Company, 2006.

Thomas, David Hurst, ed. *Columbian Consequences,* vol. 2: *Archaeological and Historical Perspectives on the Spanish Borderlands East.* Washington, DC: Smithsonian Institution, 1990.

Weber, David J. *The Spanish Frontier in North America.* New Haven: Yale University Press, 1992.

CHAPTER 3

JOHN WHITE AND THEODOR DE BRY EYE
THE INDIANS

"The True Pictures of those People"

Alexander, Michael, ed. *Discovering the New World: Based on the Works of Theodore De Bry.* New York: Harper and Row, Publishers, 1976.

Bucher, Bernadette. *Icon and Conquest: A Structural Analysis of the Illustrations of de Bry's Great Voyages.* Trans. Basia Miller Gulati. Chicago: The University of Chicago Press, 1981.

Chiappelli, Fredi, ed. *First Images of America: The Impact of the New World on the Old.* Berkeley: University of California Press, 1976.

Harriot, Thomas. *A Briefe and True Report of the New Found Land of Virginia. The Complete 1590 Theodor de Bry Edition.* New York: Dover Publications, Inc., 1972.

Horn, James. *A Kingdom Strange: The Brief and Tragic History of the Lost Colony of Roanoke.* New York: Basic Books, 2010.

Hulton, Paul. *America 1585: The Complete Drawings of John White.* Chapel Hill: The University of North Carolina Press, 1984.

Hulton, Paul, and D. B. Quinn, eds. *The American Drawings of John White, 1577–1590.* Chapel Hill: The University of North Carolina Press, 1964.

Kupperman, Karen Ordahl. *Roanoke: The Abandoned Colony.* Totowa, NJ: Rowman and Allanheld, 1984.

Kupperman, Karen Ordahl, ed. *America in European Consciousness, 1493–1750.* Chapel Hill: The University of North Carolina Press, 1995.

Lorant, Stefan, ed. *The New World: The First Pictures of America. Made by John White and Jacques Le Moyne and Engraved by Theodore De Bry. With Contemporary Narratives of the Huguenot Settlement in Florida, 1562–1565, and the Virginia Colony, 1585–1590.* New York: Duell, Sloan and Pearce, 1946.

Mancall, Peter C. *Hakluyt's Promise: An Elizabethan's Obsession for an English America*. New Haven: Yale University Press, 2007.

Milton, Giles. *Big Chief Elizabeth: The Adventures and Fate of the First English Colonists in America*. New York: Picador, 2000.

Oberg, Michael Leroy. *The Head in Edward Nugent's Hand: Roanoke's Forgotten Indians*. Philadelphia: University of Pennsylvania Press, 2008.

Quinn, David Beers, ed. *New American World: A Documentary History of North American to 1612*. Volume III: *English Plans for North America. The Roanoke Voyages. New England Ventures*. New York: The Arno Press and Hector Bye, Inc., 1979.

Quinn, David Beers, ed. *Set Fair for Roanoke: Voyages and Colonies, 1584–1606*. Chapel Hill: The University of North Carolina Press, 1985.

Sloan, Kim. *A New World: England's First View of America*. Chapel Hill: The University of North Carolina Press, 2007.

CHAPTER 4

MRS. ROWLANDSON ENDURES TRAVELS AND TRAVAILS

"Come, go along with us"

Arnold, Laura. "'Now…Didn't Our People Laugh?': Female Misbehavior and Algonquian Culture in Mary Rowlandson's *Captivity and Restauration*." *American Indian Culture and Research Journal*, vol. 21, no. 4 (1997), pp. 1–28.

Axtell, James. "The White Indians of Colonial America." In Axtell, *The European and the Indian: Essays in the Ethnohistory of Colonial North America*. New York: Oxford University Press, 1981.

Castiglia, Christopher. *Bound and Determined: Captivity, Culture-Crossing, and White Womanhood from Mary Rowlandson to Patty Hearst*. Chicago: The University of Chicago Press, 1996.

Davis, Margaret H. "Mary White Rowlandson's Self-Fashioning as Puritan Goodwife." *Early American Literature*, vol. 27, no. 1 (1992), pp. 49–60.

Demos, John. *The Unredeemed Captive: A Family Story from Early America*. New York: Alfred A. Knopf, Inc., 1995.

Derounian-Stodola, Kathryn Zabelle, ed. *Women's Indian Captivity Narratives*. New York: Penguin Books, 1998.

Derounian-Stodola, Kathryn Zabelle, and James Arthur Levernier. *The Indian Captivity Narrative, 1550–1900*. New York: Twayne Publishers, 1993.

Drake, James D. *King Philip's War: Civil War in New England, 1675–1676*. Amherst: University of Massachusetts Press, 1999.

Faery, Rebecca Blevins. *Cartographies of Desire: Captivity, Race, and Sex in the Shaping of an American Nation*. Norman: University of Oklahoma Press, 1999. Chapter 1.

Lepore, Jill. *The Name of War: King Philip's War and the Origins of American Identity*. New York: Alfred A. Knopf, Inc., 1998.

Namias, June. *White Captives: Gender and Ethnicity on the American Frontier*. Chapel Hill: The University of North Carolina Press, 1993.

Neuwirth, Steven. "Her Master's Voice: Gender, Speech, and Gendered Speech in the Narrative of the Captivity of Mary White Rowlandson." In Merril D. Smith, ed. *Sex and Sexuality in Early America*. New York: New York University Press, 1998, pp. 55–86.

Pearce, Roy Harvey. *Savagism and Civilization: A Study of the Indian and the American Mind*. 1953; revised edition, Baltimore: Johns Hopkins University Press, 1965.

Puglisi, Michael J. *Puritans Besieged: The Legacies of King Philip's War in the Massachusetts Bay Colony*. Lanham, MD: University Press of America, 1991.

Salisbury, Neal, ed. *The Sovereignty and Goodness of God, Together with the Faithfulness of His Promises Displayed. Being a Narrative of the Captivity and Restoration of Mrs. Mary Rowlandson and Related Documents*. The Bedford Series in History and Culture. Boston: Bedford Books, 1997 (orig. pub. 1682).

Slotkin, Richard. *Regeneration Through Violence: The Mythology of the American Frontier, 1600–1800*. Middletown, CT: Wesleyan University Press, 1973.

Slotkin, Richard, and James K. Folsom, eds. *So Dreadfull a Judgment: Puritan Responses to King Philip's War, 1676–1677*. Hanover: University Press of New England for Wesleyan University Press, 1978.

Toulouse, Teresa. *The Captive's Position: Female Narrative, Male Identity, and Royal Authority in Colonial New England*. Philadelphia: University of Pennsylvania Press, 2007.

Ulrich, Laurel Thatcher. *Good Wives: Image and Reality in the Lives of Women in Northern New England, 1650–1750*. New York: Alfred A. Knopf, Inc., 1982.

VanDerBeets, Richard. *Held Captive by Indians: Selected Narratives, 1642–1836*. Revised edition. Knoxville: The University of Tennessee Press, 1994.

VanDerBeets, Richard. *The Indian Captivity Narrative: An American Genre*. Lanham, MD: University Press of America, 1984.

Vaughan, Alden T., and Edward W. Clark, eds. *Puritans Among the Indians: Accounts of Captivity and Redemption, 1676–1724*. Cambridge, MA: The Belknap Press of Harvard University Press, 1981.

CHAPTER 5

DR. HAMILTON REPORTS ON HIS SUMMER VACATION

"These infant countrys of America"

Breslaw, Elaine G. *Dr. Alexander Hamilton and Provincial America: Expanding the Orbit of Scottish Culture*. Baton Rouge: Louisiana State University Press, 2008.

Bridenbaugh, Carl, ed. *Gentleman's Progress. The Itinerarium of Dr. Hamilton, 1744*. Chapel Hill: The University of North Carolina Press, 1948.

Bushman, Richard. *The Refinement of America: Persons, Houses, Cities*. New York: Alfred A. Knopf, Inc., 1992.

Martin, Wendy, ed. *Colonial American Travel Narratives*. New York: Penguin Books, 1994.

Micklus, Robert. *The Comic Genius of Dr. Alexander Hamilton*. Knoxville: The University of Tennessee Press, 1990.

Shields, David S. *Civil Tongues and Polite Letters in British America*. Chapel Hill: The University of North Carolina Press, 1997.

Wood, Gordon S. *The Radicalism of the American Revolution*. New York: Alfred A. Knopf, Inc., 1992. Part I, "Monarchy."

CHAPTER 6

BEN FRANKLIN COMPOSES HIS LIFE

"A young man of promising parts"

Brands, H. W. *The First American: The Life and Times of Benjamin Franklin*. New York: Doubleday, 2000.

Franklin, Benjamin. *The Autobiography of Benjamin Franklin*. Ed. Louis P. Masur. The Bedford Series in History and Culture. Boston: Bedford Books of St. Martin's Press, 1993.

Isaacson, Walter. *Benjamin Franklin: An American Life*. New York: Simon and Schuster, 2003.

Jennings, Francis. *Benjamin Franklin, Politician: The Mask and the Man*. New York: W. W. Norton and Company, 1996.

Lopez, Claude-Anne, and Eugenia W. Herbert. *The Private Franklin: The Man and His Family*. New York: W. W. Norton and Company, 1975.

Middlekauff, Robert. *Benjamin Franklin and His Enemies*. Berkeley: University of California Press, 1996.

Morgan, Edmund S. *Benjamin Franklin*. New Haven: Yale University Press, 2002.

Seavey, Ormond. *Becoming Benjamin Franklin: The Autobiography and the Life*. University Park: The Pennsylvania State University Press, 1988.

CHAPTER 7

COLONISTS DECLARE INDEPENDENCE

"The last cord now is broken"

Armitage, David. *The Declaration of Independence: A Global History*. Cambridge, MA: Harvard University Press, 2007.

Becker, Carl L. *The Declaration of Independence: A Study in the History of Political Ideas*. 2nd edition. New York: Alfred A. Knopf, Inc., 1942.

Boyd, Julian P. *The Declaration of Independence. The Evolution of the Text as Shown in Facsimiles of Various Drafts by Its Author, Thomas Jefferson*. Princeton: Princeton University Press, 1945.

Breen, T. H. *American Insurgents, American Patriots: The Revolution of the People*. New York: Hill and Wang, 2010.

Ellis, Joseph J. *American Sphinx: The Character of Thomas Jefferson*. New York: Alfred A. Knopf, Inc., 1997.

Ellis, Joseph J., ed. *What Did the Declaration Declare?* Historians at Work. Boston: Bedford/St. Martin's, 1999.

Fliegelman, Jay. *Declaring Independence: Jefferson, Natural Language, and the Culture of Performance*. Stanford, CA: Stanford University Press, 1993.

Foner, Eric. *Tom Paine and Revolutionary America*. New York: Oxford University Press, 1976.

Fruchtman, Jack, Jr. *Thomas Paine: Apostle of Freedom*. New York: Four Walls Eight Windows, 1994.

Greene, Jack P. "Paine, America, and the 'Modernization' of Political Consciousness." *Political Science Quarterly*, vol. 93 (1978/79), pp. 73–92.

Greene, Jack P. "Search for Identity: An Interpretation of the Meaning of Selected Patterns of Social Response in Eighteenth-Century America." In Greene, *Imperatives, Behaviors, and Identities: Essays in Early American Cultural History*. Charlottesville: The University Press of Virginia, 1992, pp. 143–73.

Hawke, David Freeman. *Paine*. New York: Harper and Row, Publishers, 1974.

Hawke, David Freeman. *A Transaction of Free Men: The Birth and Course of the Declaration of Independence*. 2nd edition. New York: Da Capo Press, 1989 (orig. pub. 1964).

Keane, John. *Tom Paine: A Political Life*. Boston: Little, Brown and Company, 1995.

Maier, Pauline. *American Scripture: Making the Declaration of Independence*. New York: Alfred A. Knopf, Inc., 1997.

Paine, Thomas. *Common Sense*. Ed. Isaac Kramnick. New York: Penguin Books, 1982.

Paine, Thomas. *Common Sense and Related Writings*. Ed. Thomas P. Slaughter. The Bedford Series in History and Culture. Boston: Bedford/St. Martin's Press, 2001.

Raphael, Ray. *Founders: The People Who Brought You a Nation*. New York: New Press, 2009.

Wills, Garry. *Inventing America: Jefferson's Declaration of Independence*. New York: Random House, 1978.

CHAPTER 8

REBELS MAKE UP NEW STATES

"Constitutions employ every Pen"

Adams, Willi Paul. *The First American Constitutions: Republican Ideology and the Making of the State Constitutions in the Revolutionary Era*. Chapel Hill: The University of North Carolina Press, 1980.

Crowl, Philip A. *Maryland During and After the Revolution: A Political and Economic Study*. Baltimore: The Johns Hopkins University Press, 1943.

Hoffman, Ronald. *A Spirit of Dissension: Economics, Politics, and the Revolution in Maryland*. Baltimore: The Johns Hopkins University Press, 1973.

Holton, Woody. *Forced Founders: Indians, Debtors, Slaves, and the Making of the American Revolution in Virginia*. Chapel Hill: The University of North Carolina Press, 1999.

Kruman, Marc W. *Between Authority and Liberty: State Constitution Making in Revolutionary America*. Chapel Hill: The University of North Carolina Press, 1997.

Rosswurm, Steven. *Arms, Country, and Class: The Philadelphia Militia and the "Lower Sort" During the American Revolution, 1775–1783*. New Brunswick: Rutgers University Press, 1987.

Ryerson, Richard Alan. *The Revolution Is Now Begun: The Radical Committees of Philadelphia, 1765–1776*. Philadelphia: University of Pennsylvania Press, 1978.

Selby, John E. *The Revolution in Virginia, 1775–1783*. Williamsburg: The Colonial Williamsburg Foundation, 1988.

Wood, Gordon S. *The Creation of the American Republic, 1776–1787*. Chapel Hill: The University of North Carolina Press, 1969.

CHAPTER 9

PRIVATE MARTIN TELLS WAR STORIES

"Great men get great praise, little men, nothing"

Bodle, Wayne, *The Valley Forge Winter: Civilians and Soldiers in War*. University Park: The Pennsylvania State University Press, 2002.

Buel, Richard, Jr. *Dear Liberty: Connecticut's Mobilization for the Revolutionary War*. Middletown, CT: Wesleyan University Press, 1980.

Carp, E. Wayne. *To Starve the Army at Pleasure: Continental Army Administration and American Political Culture, 1775–1783*. Chapel Hill: The University of North Carolina Press, 1984.

Dann, John C., ed. *The Revolution Remembered: Eyewitness Accounts of the War for Independence*. Chicago: The University of Chicago Press, 1980.

Fischer, David Hackett. *Washington's Crossing*. New York: Oxford University Press, 2004.

Higginbotham, Don. *War and Society in Revolutionary America: The Wider Dimensions of Conflict*. Columbia: University of South Carolina Press, 1988.

Hoffman, Ronald, and Peter J. Albert, eds. *Arms and Independence: The Military Character of the American Revolution*. Charlottesville: The University Press of Virginia, 1984.

Kammen, Michael. *A Season of Youth: The American Revolution and the Historical Imaginative*. New York: Alfred A. Knopf, Inc., 1978.

Martin, James Kirby, and Mark Edward Lender. *A Respectable Army: The Military Origins of the Republic, 1763–1789*. Arlington Heights, IL: Harlan Davidson, Inc., 1982.

Martin, Joseph Plumb. *A Narrative of a Revolutionary Soldier: Some of the Adventures, Dangers, and Sufferings of Joseph Plumb Martin*. New York: Signet Classic, New American Library, Penguin Putnam, Inc., 2001 (orig. pub. 1830).

Martin, Joseph Plumb. *Ordinary Courage: The Revolutionary War Adventures of Joseph Plumb Martin*. Ed. James Kirby Martin. St. James, NY: Brandywine Press, 1993.

McCullough, David. *1776*. New York: Simon and Schuster, 2005.

Middlekauff, Robert. *The Glorious Cause: The American Revolution, 1763–1789*. 2nd edition. New York: Oxford University Press, 2005.

Nash, Gary B. *The Unknown American Revolution: The Unruly Birth of Democracy and the Struggle to Create America*. New York: Penguin Books, 2006.

Neimeyer, Charles Patrick. *America Goes to War: A Social History of the Continental Army*. The American Social Experience Series. New York: New York University Press, 1996.

Purcell, Sarah J. *Sealed with Blood: War, Sacrifice, and Memory in Revolutionary America*. Philadelphia: University of Pennsylvania Press, 2002.

Raphael, Ray. *A People's History of the American Revolution: How Common People Shaped the Fight for Independence*. New York: New Press, 2001.

Resch, John. *Suffering Soldiers: Revolutionary War Veterans, Moral Sentiment, and Political Culture in the Early Republic*. Amherst: University of Massachusetts Press, 1999.

Resch, John, and Walter Sargent, eds. *War and Society in the American Revolution: Mobilization and Home Fronts*. Dekalb: Northern Illinois University Press, 2007.

Royster, Charles. *A Revolutionary People at War: The Continental Army and American Character, 1775–1783*. Chapel Hill: The University of North Carolina Press, 1979.

Shy, John. *A People Numerous and Armed: Reflections on the Military Struggle for American Independence*. Revised edition. Ann Arbor: University of Michigan Press, 1990 (orig. pub. 1976).

Waldstreicher, David. *In the Midst of Perpetual Fetes: The Making of American Nationalism, 1776–1820*. Chapel Hill: The University of North Carolina Press, 1997.

Young, Alfred F. *The Shoemaker and the Tea Party: Memory and the American Revolution*. Boston: Beacon Press, 1999.

CHAPTER 10

Parson Weems Invents George Washington

"I can't tell a lie, Pa"

Albanese, Catherine L. "Our Father, Our Washington." Chapter 5 in Albanese, *Sons of the Fathers: The Civil Religion of the American Revolution*. Philadelphia: Temple University Press, 1976, pp. 143–81.

Boorstin, Daniel J. *The Americans: The National Experience*. New York: Random House, 1965.

Brookhiser, Richard. *Founding Father: Rediscovering George Washington*. New York: The Free Press, 1996.

Casper, Scott E. *Constructing American Lives: Biography and Culture in Nineteenth-Century America*. Chapel Hill: The University of North Carolina Press, 1999.

Chernow, Ron. *Washington: A Life*. New York: Penguin Press, 2010.

Cunliffe, Marcus. *George Washington: Man and Monument*. Revised edition. New York: New American Library, 1982.

Fliegelman, Jay. "George Washington and the Reconstituted Family." In Fliegelman, *Prodigals and Pilgrims: The American Revolution Against Patriarchal Authority, 1750–1800*. Cambridge, England: Cambridge University Press, 1982, pp. 197–226.

Freeman, Douglas Southall. *George Washington. A Biography*. Vol. I: Young Washington. New York: Charles Scribner's Sons, 1948.

Furstenberg, François. *In the Name of the Father: Washington's Legacy, Slavery, and the Making of a Nation*. New York: Penguin Book, 2006.

Harris, Christopher. *Public Lives, Private Virtues: Images of American Revolutionary War Heroes, 1782–1832*. New York: Garland Publishing, Inc., 2000.

Higginbotham, Don, ed. *George Washington Reconsidered*. Charlottesville: The University Press of Virginia, 2001.

Kammen, Michael. *A Season of Youth: The American Revolution and the Historical Imaginative*. New York: Alfred A. Knopf, Inc., 1978.

Robertson, James Harvey. *American Myth, American Reality*. New York: Hill and Wang, 1980.

Schwartz, Barry. *George Washington: The Making of an American Symbol*. New York: The Free Press, 1987.

Weems, Mason L. *The Life of Washington*. Ed. Marcus Cunliffe. Cambridge, MA: The Belknap Press of Harvard University Press, 1962 (ninth edition, orig. pub. 1809).

Wills, Garry. *Cincinnatus: George Washington and the Enlightenment*. Garden City, NY: Doubleday and Company, Inc., 1984.

Wood, Gordon S. "The Greatness of George Washington," in Higginbotham, ed., *George Washington Reconsidered*, pp. 309–30.

CHAPTER 11

Monsieur Tocqueville Visits America

"The general equality of condition among the people"

Bentzel, Anne. *Traveling Tocqueville's America: Retracing the 17-State Tour that Inspired Alexis de Tocqueville's Political Classic* Democracy in America. Baltimore: The Johns Hopkins University Press for C-SPAN, 1998.

Brogan, Hugh. *Alexis de Tocqueville: A Life*. New Haven: Yale University Press, 2007.

Brogan, Hugh. *Tocqueville*. Bungay, England: Fontana, 1973.

Cohen, David. *Chasing the Red, White, and Blue: A Journey in Tocqueville's Footsteps Through Contemporary America*. New York: Picador USA, 2001.

Damrosch, Leopold. *Tocqueville's Discovery of America*. New York: Farrar, Straus and Giroux, 2010.

Eisenstadt, Abraham S., ed. *Reconsidering Tocqueville's* Democracy in America. New Brunswick: Rutgers University Press, 1988.

Ledeen, Michael Arthur. *Tocqueville on American Character: Why Tocqueville's Brilliant Exploration of the American Spirit Is as Vital and Important Today as It Was Two Hundred Years Ago*. New York: St. Martin's Press, Truman Talley Books, 2000.

Masugi, Ken, ed. *Interpreting Tocqueville's* Democracy in America. New York: Rowman and Littlefield Publishers, Inc., 1991.

Masur, Louis P. *1831: Year of Eclipse*. New York: Hill and Wang, 2001.

McCarthy, Eugene J. *America Revisited: 150 Years after Tocqueville*. Garden City, NY: Doubleday and Company, Inc., 1978.

Pierson, George Wilson. *Tocqueville in America*. Baltimore: The Johns Hopkins University Press, 1996 (orig. pub. as *Tocqueville and Beaumont in America* [1938]).

Reeves, Richard. *American Journey: Traveling with Tocqueville in Search of* Democracy in America. New York: Simon and Schuster, 1982.

Schleifer, James T. *The Making of Tocqueville's* Democracy in America. Chapel Hill: The University of North Carolina Press, 1980.

Siedentop, Larry. *Tocqueville*. Pastmasters. New York: Oxford University Press, 1994.

Tocqueville, Alexis de. *Democracy in America*. Trans. and ed. Harvey C. Mansfield and Delba Winthrop. Chicago: The University of Chicago Press, 2000.

Tocqueville, Alexis de. *Journey to America*. Trans. George Lawrence. Ed. J. P. Mayer. Garden City, NY: Anchor Books of Doubleday and Company, Inc., 1971.

Wilentz, Sean. "Many Democracies: On Tocqueville and Jacksonian America." In Eisenstadt, ed., *Reconsidering Tocqueville's* Democracy in America, pp. 207–28.

Wolin, Sheldon S. *Tocqueville Between Two Worlds: The Making of a Political and Theoretical Life*. Princeton: Princeton University Press, 2001.

CHAPTER 12

COLE AND COMPANY PAINT NATURE'S NATION

"The thoroughly American branch of painting"

Baigell, Matthew. *Albert Bierstadt*. New York: Watson-Guptill Publications, 1981.

Boime, Albert. *The Magisterial Gaze: Manifest Destiny and American Landscape Painting* c. *1830–1865*. New Directions in American Art. Washington, DC: Smithsonian Institution Press, 1991.

Carr, Gerald L. *In Search of the Promised Land: Paintings by Frederic Edwin Church*. New York: Berry-Hill Galleries, Inc., 2000.

Cole, Thomas. *The Collected Essays and Prose Sketches*. Ed. Marshall Tymn. The John Colet Archive of American Literature, 1620–1920. Number 7. St. Paul, MN: The John Colet Press, 1980.

Czestochowski, Joseph S. *The American Landscape Tradition: A Study and Gallery of Paintings*. New York: E. P. Dutton, Inc., 1982.

Harris, Neil. *The Artist in American Society: The Formative Years, 1790–1860*. Chicago: The University of Chicago Press, 1966.

Howat, John K. *American Paradise: The World of the Hudson River School*. New York: The Metropolitan Museum of Art Distributed by Harry N. Abrams, Inc., 1987.

Howat, John K. *The Hudson River and Its Painters*. New York: The Viking Press, 1972.

Kelly, Franklin. *Frederic Edwin Church and the National Landscape*. New Directions in American Art. Washington, DC: Smithsonian Institution Press, 1988.

Kelly, Franklin, and Gerald L. Carr. *The Early Landscapes of Frederic Edwin Church, 1845–1854*. Fort Worth: University of Texas Press, 1987.

Miller, Angela. *The Empire of the Eye: Landscape Representation and American Cultural Politics, 1825–1875*. Ithaca: Cornell University Press, 1993.

Miller, David C., ed. *American Iconology: New Approaches to Nineteenth-Century Art and Literature*. New Haven: Yale University Press, 1993.

Miller, Perry. "Nature and the National Ego." In Miller, *Errand into the Wilderness*. Cambridge, MA: The Belknap Press of Harvard University Press, 1956, pp. 204–16.

Minks, Louise. *The Hudson River School*. New York: Crescent Books, 1989.

Noble, Louis Legrand. *The Life and Works of Thomas Cole*. Ed. Elliot S. Vesell. The John Harvard Library. Cambridge, MA: The Belknap Press of Harvard University Press, 1964.

Novak, Barbara. *Nature and Culture: American Landscape Painting, 1825–1875*. Revised edition. New York: Oxford University Press, 1995.

Powell, Earl A. *Thomas Cole*. New York: Harry N. Abrams, Inc., Publishers, 1990.

Truettner, William H., ed. *The West as America: Reinterpreting Images of the Frontier, 1820–1920*. Washington, DC: Smithsonian Institution Press for the National Museum of American Art, 1991.

Truettner, William H., and Allan Wallach, eds. *Thomas Cole: Landscape into History*. New Haven and Washington, DC: Yale University Press and National Museum of American Art, 1994.

CHAPTER 13

Rev. Apess Rewrites American History

> *"Let every man of color wrap himself in mourning, for the 22nd of December and the 4th of July are days of mourning and not of joy"*

Apess, William. *On Our Own Ground: The Complete Writings of William Apess, A Pequot*. Ed. Barry O'Connell. Amherst: University of Massachusetts Press, 1992.

Apess, William. *A Son of the Forest and Other Writings*. Ed. Barry O'Connell. Amherst: University of Massachusetts Press, 1997.

Calloway, Colin G., ed. *After King Philip's War: Presence and Persistence in Indian New England*. Hanover: University Press of New England, 1997.

Hauptman, Laurence M., and James D. Wherry, eds. *The Pequots in Southern New England: The Fall and Rise of an American Indian Nation*. Norman: University of Oklahoma Press, 1990.

Herndon, Ruth Wallis. *Unwelcome Americans: Living on the Margin in Early New England*. Philadelphia: University of Pennsylvania Press, 2001.

Jaskoski, Helen, ed. *Early Native American Writing: New Critical Essays*. New York: Cambridge University Press, 1996.

Krupat, Arnold. *For Those Who Came After: A Study of Native American Autobiography*. Berkeley: University of California Press, 1985.

Krupat, Arnold. *The Voice in the Margin: Native American Literature and the Canon*. Berkeley: University of California Press, 1989.

Lepore, Jill. *The Name of War: King Philip's War and the Origins of American Identity*. New York: Alfred A. Knopf, Inc., 1998.

Mandell, Daniel R. *Tribe, Race, History: Native Americans in Southern New England, 1780–1880*. Baltimore: The Johns Hopkins University Press, 2008.

Melish, Joanne Pope. *Disowning Slavery: Gradual Emancipation and "Race" in New England, 1780–1860*. Ithaca: Cornell University Press, 1998.

Murray, David. *Forked Tongues: Speech, Writing, and Representation in North American Indian Texts*. Bloomington: Indiana University Press, 1991.

Simmons, William S. *Spirit of the New England Tribes: Indian History and Folklore, 1620–1984*. Hanover: University Press of New England, 1986.

Wyss, Hilary E. *Writing Indians: Literacy, Christianity, and Native Community in Early America*. Amherst: University of Massachusetts Press, 2000.

CHAPTER 14

The Grimké Sisters Upset America

> *"We Abolition women are turning the world upside down"*

Barnes, Gilbert H., and Dwight L. Dumond, eds. *Letters of Theodore Dwight Weld, Angelina Grimké Weld, and Sarah Grimké, 1822–1844*. 2 vols. New York: D. Appleton-Century Company, Inc., 1934.

Bartlett, Elizabeth Ann. *Liberty, Equality, Sorority: The Origins and Interpretation of American Feminist Thought: Frances Wright, Sarah Grimké, and Margaret Fuller*. Brooklyn, NY: Carlson Publishing, Inc., 1994.

Berg, Barbara J. *The Remembered Gate: Origins of American Feminism: The Woman and the City, 1800–1860*. New York: Oxford University Press, 1978.

Browne, Stephen Howard. *Angelina Grimké: Rhetoric, Identity, and the Radical Imagination*. Rhetoric and Public Affairs Series. East Lansing: Michigan State University Press, 1999.

Ceplair, Larry, ed. *The Public Years of Sarah and Angelina Grimké: Selected Writings, 1835–1839*. New York: Columbia University Press, 1989.

Grimké, Angelina. *An Appeal to the Women of the Nominally Free States, Issued by an Anti-Slavery Convention of American Women Held…May 1837*. Second edition. Boston: Isaac Knapp, 1838.

Grimké, Sarah. *Letters on the Equality of the Sexes and Other Essays*. Ed. Elizabeth Ann Bartlett. New Haven: Yale University Press, 1988 (orig. pub. Boston, 1838).

Hersh, Blanche Glassman. *The Slavery of Sex: Feminist-Abolitionists in America*. Urbana: University of Illinois Press, 1978.

Hoffert, Sylvia D. *When Hens Crow: The Woman's Rights Movement in Antebellum America*. Bloomington: Indiana University Press, 1995.

Isenberg, Nancy. *Sex and Citizenship in Antebellum America*. Chapel Hill: The University of North Carolina Press, 1998.

Jeffrey, Julie Roy. *The Great Silent Army of Abolitionism: Ordinary Women in the Antislavery Movement*. Chapel Hill: The University of North Carolina Press, 1998.

Lerner, Gerda. *The Feminist Thought of Sarah Grimké*. New York: Oxford University Press, 1998.

Lerner, Gerda. *The Grimké Sisters from South Carolina: Rebels Against Slavery*. Boston: Houghton Mifflin Company, 1967.

Lumpkin, Katharine Du Pre. *The Emancipation of Angelina Grimké*. Chapel Hill: The University of North Carolina Press, 1974.

McCarthy, Timothy Patrick, and John Stauffer, eds. *Prophets of Protest: Reconsidering the History of American Abolitionism*. New York: The New Press, 2006.

Newman, Richard S. *The Transformation of American Abolitionism: Fighting Slavery in the Early Republic*. Chapel Hill: The University of North Carolina Press, 2002.

Pierson, Michael D. *Free Hearts and Free Homes: Gender and American Antislavery Politics*. Gender and American Culture. Chapel Hill: The University of North Carolina Press, 2003.

Sklar, Kathryn Kish, ed. *Women's Rights Emerges within the Antislavery Movement, 1830–1870: A Brief History with Documents*. The Bedford Series in History and Culture. Boston: Bedford/St. Martin's, 2000.

Smith-Rosenberg, Carroll. *Disorderly Conduct: Visions of Gender in Victorian America*. New York: Alfred A. Knopf, Inc., 1985.

Yellin, Jean Fagan. *Women and Sisters: The Antislavery Feminists in American Culture*. New Haven: Yale University Press, 1989.

Yellin, Jean Fagan, and John C. Van Horne, eds. *The Abolitionist Sisterhood: Women's Political Culture in Antebellum America*. Ithaca: Cornell University Press, 1994.

CHAPTER 15

José Enrique de la Peña Remembers the Alamo

"A series of unfortunate incidents"

Anderson, Gary Clayton. *The Conquest of Texas: Ethnic Cleansing and the Promised Land, 1820–1875*. Norman: University of Oklahoma Press, 2005.

Brear, Holly Beachley. *Inherit the Alamo: Myth and Ritual at an American Shrine*. Austin: University of Texas Press, 1995.

Burke, James Wakefield. *Davy Crockett: The Man Behind the Myth*. Austin: Eakin Press, 1987.

Campbell, Randolph B. *Gone to Texas: A History of the Lone Star State*. New York: Oxford University Press, 2003.

Crisp, James E. *Sleuthing the Alamo: Davy Crockett's Last Stand and Other Mysteries of the Texas Revolution*. New York: Oxford University Press, 2005.

Davis, William C. *Lone Star Rising: The Revolutionary Birth of the Texas Republic*. New York: Free Press, 2004.

De La Peña, José Enrique. *With Santa Anna in Texas: A Personal Narrative of the Revolution*. Trans. and ed. Carmen Perry. Expanded edition. College Station: Texas A & M University Press, 1997.

Flores, Richard R. *Remembering the Alamo: Memory, Modernity, and the Master Symbol*. Austin: University of Texas Press, 2002.

Groneman, William. *Defense of a Legend: Crockett and the de la Peña Diary*. Plano: Republic of Texas Press, 1994.

Groneman, William. *Eyewitness to the Alamo*. Revised edition. Plano: Republic of Texas Press, 2001.

Lack, Paul D. *The Texas Revolutionary Experience: A Political and Social History, 1835–1836*. College Station: Texas A & M University Press, 1992.

Lindley, Thomas Ricks. *Alamo Traces: New Evidence and New Conclusions*. Plano: Republic of Texas Press, 2003.

Lofaro, Michael A., and Joe Cummings, eds. *Crockett at Two Hundred*. Knoxville: The University of Tennessee Press, 1989.

Long, Jeff. *Duel of Eagles: The Mexican and U.S. Fight for the Alamo*. New York: William Morrow and Company, Inc., 1990.

Matovina, Timothy M., ed. *The Alamo Remembered: Tejano Accounts and Perspectives*. Austin: University of Texas Press, 1995.

Montejano, David. *Anglos and Mexicans in the Making of Texas, 1836–1986*. Austin: University of Texas Press, 1987.

Poyo, Gerald E., ed. *Tejano Journey, 1770–1850*. Austin: University of Texas Press, 1996.

Ramos, Raúl A. *Beyond the Alamo: Forging Mexican Ethnicity in San Antonio, 1821–1861*. Chapel Hill: The University of North Carolina Press, 2008.

Roberts, Randy, and James S. Olson. *A Line in the Sand: The Alamo in Blood and Memory*. New York: Simon and Schuster, 2001.

Tijerina, Andrés. *Tejanos and Texas Under the Mexican Flag, 1821–1836*. College Station: Texas A & M University Press, 1994.

Trouillot, Michel-Rolph. *Silencing the Past: Power and the Production of History*. Boston: Beacon Press, 1995.

Weber, David J. *The Mexican Frontier, 1821–1846: The American Southwest Under Mexico*. Albuquerque: University of New Mexico Press, 1982.

CHAPTER 16

FREDERICK DOUGLASS CONSTRUCTS A LIFE

"I felt a degree of freedom"

Andrews, William L. *To Tell a Free Story: The First Century of Afro-American Autobiography, 1760–1865*. Urbana: University of Illinois Press, 1986.

Andrews, William L, ed. *African American Autobiography: A Collection of Critical Essays*. Englewood Cliffs, NJ: Prentice Hall, 1993.

Andrews, William L., ed. *Critical Essays on Frederick Douglass*. Boston: G. K. Hall and Company, 1991.

Blassingame, John W., ed. *The Frederick Douglass Papers. Series One: Speeches, Debates, and Interviews. Volume 1: 1841–1846*. New Haven: Yale University Press, 1979.

Blassingame, John W., John R. McKivigan, and Peter P. Hinks, eds. *The Frederick Douglass Papers. Series Two: Autobiographical Writings. Volume 1: Narrative*. New Haven: Yale University Press, 1999.

Blight, David W. *Frederick Douglass' Civil War: Keeping Faith in Jubilee*. Baton Rouge: Louisiana State University Press, 1989.

Douglass, Frederick. *Narrative of the Life of Frederick Douglass, An American Slave, Written by Himself*. Ed. David W. Blight. The Bedford Series in History and Culture. Boston: Bedford Books of St. Martin's Press, 1993.

Fisher, Dexter, and Robert B. Stepto, eds. *Afro-American Literature: The Reconstruction of Instruction*. New York: The Modern Language Association of America, 1979.

Gates, Henry Louis, Jr. *Figures in Black: Words, Signs, and the "Racial" Self*. New York: Oxford University Press, 1987.

Lampe, Gregory P. *Frederick Douglass: Freedom's Voice, 1818–1845*. East Lansing: Michigan State University Press, 1998.

Martin, Waldo E., Jr. *The Mind of Frederick Douglass*. Chapel Hill: The University of North Carolina Press, 1984.

McCarthy, Timothy Patrick, and John Stauffer, eds. *Prophets of Protest: Reconsidering the History of American Abolitionism*. New York: The New Press, 2006.

McFeely, William S. *Frederick Douglass*. New York: W. W. Norton and Company, 1990.

Newman, Richard S. *The Transformation of American Abolitionism: Fighting Slavery in the Early Republic*. Chapel Hill: The University of North Carolina Press, 2002.

Preston, Dickson J. *Young Frederick Douglass: The Maryland Years*. Baltimore: The Johns Hopkins University Press, 1980.

Quarles, Benjamin. *Black Abolitionists*. New York: Oxford University Press, 1969.

Rael, Patrick. *Black Identity and Black Protest in the Antebellum North*. Chapel Hill: The University of North Carolina Press, 2002.

Stewart, James Brewer. *Holy Warriors: The Abolitionists and American Slavery*. New York: Hill and Wang, 1976.

Sundquist, Eric J., ed. *Frederick Douglass: New Literary and Historical Essays*. Cambridge, England: Cambridge University Press, 1990.

CHAPTER 17

GEORGE FITZHUGH DEFENDS SLAVERY

"Negro slaves are the happiest people in the world"

Faust, Drew Gilpin. *A Sacred Circle: The Dilemma of the Intellectual in the Old South, 1840–1860*. Baltimore: The Johns Hopkins University Press, 1977.

Faust, Drew Gilpin, ed. *The Ideology of Slavery: Proslavery Thought in the Antebellum South, 1830–1860*. Baton Rouge: Louisiana State University Press, 1981.

Finkelman, Paul, ed. *Defending Slavery: Proslavery Thought in the Old South. A Brief History with Documents*. Boston: Bedford/St. Martin's, 2003.

Fitzhugh, George. *Cannibals All! Or, Slaves Without Masters*. Ed. C. Vann Woodward. Cambridge, MA: The Belknap Press of Harvard University Press, 1960 (orig. pub. 1857).

Fitzhugh, George. *Sociology for the South, Or the Failure of Free Society*. Richmond, VA: A. Morris, 1854.

Frederickson, George M. *The Black Image in the White Mind: The Debate on Afro-American Character and Destiny, 1817–1914*. New York: Harper Torchbook, 1972.

Genovese, Eugene D. *The World the Slaveholders Made: Two Essays in Interpretation*. New York: Pantheon Books, 1969.

Tise, Larry E. *Proslavery: A History of the Defense of Slavery in America, 1701–1840*. Athens: University of Georgia Press, 1987.

Wish, Harvey. *George Fitzhugh: Propagandist of the Old South*. Baton Rouge: Louisiana State University Press, 1943.

CHAPTER 18

Presidnt Lincoln Articulates America

"Let us strive on to finish the work we are in"

Bennett, Lerone, Jr. *Forced into Glory: Abraham Lincoln's White Dream*. Chicago: Johnson Publishing Company, 2000.

Blight, David. *Frederick Douglass' Civil War: Keeping Faith in Jubilee*. Baton Rouge: Louisiana State University Press, 1989.

Braden, Waldo W. *Abraham Lincoln, Public Speaker*. Baton Rouge: Louisiana State University Press, 1988.

Briggs, John Channing. *Lincoln's Speeches Reconsidered*. Baltimore: The Johns Hopkins University Press, 2005.

Bruce, Robert B., ed. *Abraham Lincoln's Changing Views on Slavery*. St. James, NY: Brandywine Press, 2001.

Burlingame, Michael. *The Inner World of Abraham Lincoln*. Urbana: University of Illinois Press, 1994.

Burton, Orville Vernon. *The Age of Lincoln*. New York: Hill and Wang, 2007.

Current, Richard N. *The Lincoln Nobody Knows*. New York: Hill and Wang, 1958.

Donald, David Herbert. *Lincoln*. New York: Simon and Schuster, 1995.

Donald, David Herbert. *Lincoln Reconsidered: Essays on the Civil War Era*. 3rd edition. New York: Vintage Books, 2001.

Fehrenbacher, Don E. *Lincoln in Text and Context: Selected Essays*. Stanford, CA: Stanford University Press, 1987.

Ferguson, Andrew. *Land of Lincoln: Adventures in Abe's America*. New York: Atlantic Monthly Press, 2007.

Foner, Eric. *The Fiery Trial: Abraham Lincoln and American Slavery*. New York: W. W. Norton and Company, 2010.

Gienapp, William E. *Abraham Lincoln and Civil War America: A Biography*. New York: Oxford University Press, 2002.

Jaffa, Harry V. *Crisis of the House Divided: An Interpretation of the Issues in the Lincoln-Douglas Debates*. Chicago: The University of Chicago Press, 1982 (orig. pub. 1959).

Johnson, Michael P., ed. *Abraham Lincoln, Slavery, and the Civil War: Selected Writings and Speeches*. The Bedford Series in American History and Culture. Boston: Bedford/St. Martin's, 2001.

McPherson, James M. *Abraham Lincoln and the Second American Revolution*. New York: Oxford University Press, 1990.

McPherson, James M. *Drawn with the Sword: Reflections on the American Civil War*. New York: Oxford University Press, 1996.

McPherson, James M., ed. *"We Cannot Escape History": Lincoln and the Last Best Hope of Earth*. Urbana: University of Illinois Press, 1995.

Oakes, James. *The Radical and the Republican: Frederick Douglass, Abraham Lincoln, and the Triumph of Antislavery Politics*. New York: W. W. Norton and Company, 2007.

Stauffer, John. *Giants: The Parallel Lives of Frederick Douglass and Abraham Lincoln*. New York: Twelve, 2008.

White, Ronald C., Jr. *Lincoln's Greatest Speech: The Second Inaugural*. New York: Simon and Schuster, 2002.

Wills, Garry. *Lincoln at Gettysburg: The Words that Remade America*. New York: Simon and Schuster, 1992.

Wilson, Douglas L. *Honor's Voice: The Transformation of Abraham Lincoln*. New York: Alfred A. Knopf, Inc., 1998.

Wilson, Douglas L. *Lincoln's Sword: The Presidency and the Power of Words*. New York: Alfred A. Knopf, Inc., 2007.

CHAPTER 19

Cameramen and Other Artists Picture Gettysburg

"Photographic presentments will be accepted by posterity with an undoubting faith"

[Campbell, William P.] *The Civil War: A Centennial Exhibition of Eyewitness Drawings*. Washington, DC: National Gallery of Art, Smithsonian Institution, 1961.

Cullen, Jim. *The Civil War in Popular Culture: A Reusable Past*. Washington, DC: Smithsonian Institution Press, 1995.

Davis, William C., ed. *The Image of War, 1861–1865*. Six Volumes. New York: Doubleday and Company, Inc., 1981–1984.

Donald, David, general ed. *Divided We Fought: A Pictorial History of the War, 1861–1865*. New York: The Macmillan Company, 1952.

Faust, Drew Gilpin. *This Republic of Suffering: Death and the American Civil War*. New York: Alfred A. Knopf, Inc., 2008.

Frassanito, William A. *Early Photography at Gettysburg*. Gettysburg, PA: Thomas Publications, 1995.

Frassanito, William A. *Gettysburg: A Journey in Time*. New York: Charles Scribner's Sons, 1975.

Gardner, Alexander. *Gardner's Photographic Sketch Book of the Civil War*. New York: Dover Publications, Inc., 1959 (orig. pub. 1866).

Holzer, Harold, and Mark E. Neely, Jr. *Mine Eyes Have Seen the Glory: The Civil War in Art*. New York: Orion Books, 1993.

Horan, James D. *Mathew Brady: Historian with a Camera*. New York: Crown Publishers, Inc., 1955.

Huddleston, John. *Killing Ground: Photographs of the Civil War and the Changing American Landscape*. Creating the North American Landscape. Baltimore, MD: The Johns Hopkins University Press, 2002.

Johnson, Brooks. *An Enduring Interest: The Photographs of Alexander Gardner*. Norfolk, VA: The Chrysler Museum, 1991.

Le Beau, Bryan F. *Currier & Ives: America Imagined*. Washington, DC: Smithsonian Institution Press, 2001.

Meredith, Roy. *Mr. Lincoln's Camera Man*. New York: Charles Scribner's Sons, 1946.

Miller, Francis Trevelyan, ed. *The Photographic History of The Civil War, in Ten Volumes*. New York: The Review of Reviews, Inc., 1911.

Neely, Mark E., Jr. *The Civil War and the Limits of Destruction*. Cambridge, MA: Harvard University Press, 2007.

Neely, Mark E., Jr., and Harold Holzer. *The Union Image: Popular Prints of the Civil War North*. Chapel Hill: The University of North Carolina Press, 2000.

Panzer, Mary. *Mathew Brady and the Image of History*. Washington, DC: Smithsonian Institution Press for the National Portrait Gallery, 1997.

Schantz, Mark S. *Awaiting the Heavenly Country: The Civil War and America's Culture of Death*. Ithaca: Cornell University Press, 2008.

Snyder, Joel. *American Frontiers: The Photographs of Timothy H. O'Sullivan, 1867–1874*. New York: Aperture, 1981.

Sontag, Susan. *Regarding the Pain of Others*. New York: Farrar, Straus and Giroux, 2003.

Sweet, Timothy. *Traces of War: Poetry, Photography, and the Crisis of the Union*. Baltimore: The Johns Hopkins University Press, 1990.

Trachtenberg, Alan. *Reading American Photographs: Images as History, Mathew Brady to Walker Evans*. New York: Hill and Wang, 1989.

Thompson, W. Fletcher, Jr. *The Image of War: The Pictorial Reporting of the American Civil War*. New York: Thomas Yoseloff, 1959.

Williams, Hermann Warner, Jr. *The Civil War: The Artists' Record*. Boston: Beacon Press, 1961.

CHAPTER 20

CONGRESSMEN INVESTIGATE THE KU KLUX KLAN

"The terrorism was so great"

Berlin, Ira, et al., eds. *Remembering Slavery: African Americans Talk About Their Personal Experiences of Slavery and Freedom*. New York: The New Press, 1998.

Blight, David G. *Frederick Douglass' Civil War: Keeping Faith in Jubilee*. Baton Rouge: Louisiana State University Press, 1989.

Botkin, B. A., ed. *Lay My Burden Down: A Folk History of Slavery*. Federal Writers' Project. Chicago: The University of Chicago Press, 1945.

Carter, Dan T. *When the War Was Over: The Failure of Self-Reconstruction in the South, 1865–1867*. Baton Rouge: Louisiana State University Press, 1985.

Dailey, Jane, Glenda Elizabeth Gilmore, and Bryant Simon, eds. *Jumpin' Jim Crow: Southern Politics from Civil War to Civil Rights*. Princeton: Princeton University Press, 2000.

Du Bois, W. E. B. *Black Reconstruction in America: An Essay Toward a History of the Part Which Black Folk Played in the Attempt to Reconstruct Democracy in America, 1860–1880*. New York: Atheneum, 1969.

Foner, Eric, and Olivia Mahoney. *America's Reconstruction: People and Politics after the Civil War*. New York: Harper/Collins Publishers, 1995.

Foner, Eric. *Nothing But Freedom: Emancipation and Its Legacy*. Baton Rouge: Louisiana State University Press, 1983.

Foner, Eric. *Reconstruction: America's Unfinished Revolution, 1863–1877*. New York: Harper and Row, Publishers, 1988.

Foner, Eric. *A Short History of Reconstruction, 1863–1877*. New York: Harper and Row, Publishers, 1990.

Franklin, John Hope. *Reconstruction After the Civil War*. 2nd edition. Chicago: The University of Chicago Press, 1994.

Gillette, William. *Retreat from Reconstruction, 1869–1879*. Baton Rouge: Louisiana State University Press, 1979.

Holt, Thomas. *Black Over White: Negro Political Leadership in South Carolina During Reconstruction*. Urbana: University of Illinois Press, 1977.

Horn, Stanley F. *Invisible Empire: The Story of the Ku Klux Klan, 1866–1871*. Boston: Houghton Mifflin Company, 1939.

Jenkins, Wilbert L. *Climbing up to Glory: A Short History of African Americans During the Civil War and Reconstruction*. Wilmington, DE: Scholarly Resources, Inc., 2002.

Kaczorowski, Robert J. *The Politics of Judicial Interpretation: The Federal Courts, the Department of Justice, and Civil Rights, 1866–1876.* New York: Oceana Press, 1985.

Rable, George C. *But There Was No Peace: The Role of Violence in the Politics of Reconstruction.* Athens: University of Georgia Press, 1984.

Regosin, Elizabeth. *Freedom's Promise: Ex-Slave Families and Citizenship in the Age of Emancipation.* Charlottesville: The University Press of Virginia, 2002.

Richardson, Heather Cox. *The Death of Reconstruction: Race, Labor, and Politics in the Post-Civil War North, 1865–1901.* Cambridge, MA: Harvard University Press, 2001.

Rozwenc, Edwin C., ed. *Reconstruction in the South.* 2nd edition. Lexington, MA: D.C. Heath and Company, 1972 (orig. pub. 1952).

Shenton, James P., ed. *The Reconstruction: A Documentary History of the South after the War: 1865–1877.* New York: G. P. Putnam's Sons, 1963.

Sterling, Dorothy. *The Trouble They Seen: The Story of Reconstruction in the Words of African Americans.* New York: Da Capo Press, 1994 (orig. pub. 1976).

Swinney, Everette. *Suppressing the Ku Klux Klan: The Enforcement of the Reconstruction Amendments.* New York: Garland, 1987.

Tourgée, Albion W. *A Fool's Errand. By One of the Fools. A Novel. Together with Part II, The Invisible Empire. An Historical Review of the Epoch on Which This Tale Is Based.* New York: Fords, Howard, and Hulbert, 1880.

Trelease, Allen W. *White Terror: The Ku Klux Klan Conspiracy and Southern Reconstruction.* New York: Harper and Row, Publishers, 1971.

U.S. 42D Congress, 2nd Session. *Report of the Joint Select Committee to Inquire Into the Condition of Affairs in the Late Insurrectionary States.* 13 vols. Washington, DC: Government Printing Office, 1872.

Williams, Lou Falkner. *The Great South Carolina Ku Klux Klan Trials, 1871–1872.* Athens: University of Georgia Press, 1996.

Witt, John Fabian. *Patriots and Cosmopolitans: Hidden Histories of American Law.* Cambridge, MA: Harvard University Press, 2007. Chapter Two: Exits.

Zuczek, Richard. *State of Rebellion: Reconstruction in South Carolina.* Columbia: University of South Carolina Press, 1996.